THIRD EDITION

Comparative
Health Information
Management

THIRD EDITION

Comparative Health Information Management

Ann H. Peden, PhD, RHIA, CCS

DELMAR
CENGAGE Learning

Australia • Brazil • Japan • Korea • Mexico • Singapore • Spain • United Kingdom • United States

DELMAR
CENGAGE Learning™

Comparative Health Information Management, Third Edition

Peden, Ann H.

Vice President, Editorial: Dave Garza

Director of Learning Solutions:
Matthew Kane

Executive Editor: Rhonda Dearborn

Managing Editor: Marah Bellegarde

Senior Product Manager: Jadin
Babin-Kavanaugh

Editorial Assistant: LaurenWhalen

Vice President, Marketing: Jennifer Baker

Marketing Director: Wendy Mapstone

Senior Marketing Manager: Nancy Bradshaw

Marketing Coordinator: Erica Ropitzky

Production Director: Wendy Troeger

Production Manager: Andrew Crouth

Content Project Manager: Anne Sherman

Senior Art Director: Jack Pendleton

Technology Project Manager: Chris Catalina

For product information and technology assistance, contact us at
Cengage Learning Customer & Sales Support, 1-800-354-9706

For permission to use material from this text or product,
submit all requests online at **www.cengage.com/permissions.**
Further permissions questions can be emailed to
permissionrequest@cengage.com

Library of Congress Control Number: 2010941266

ISBN-13: 978-1-111-12562-2

ISBN-10: 1-111-12562-7

Delmar
5 Maxwell Drive
Clifton Park, NY 12065-2919
USA

Cengage Learning is a leading provider of customized learning solutions with office locations around the globe, including Singapore, the United Kingdom, Australia, Mexico, Brazil, and Japan. Locate your local office at:
international.cengage.com/region

Cengage Learning products are represented in Canada by Nelson Education, Ltd.

To learn more about Delmar, visit **www.cengage.com/delmar**

Purchase any of our products at your local college store or at our preferred online store **www.cengagebrain.com**

Notice to the Reader

Printed in the United States of America
2 3 4 5 6 7 14 13 12

CONTENTS

PREFACE   xi

ACKNOWLEDGMENTS   xvii

ABOUT THE AUTHOR   xxi

Chapter 1 **Introduction**   1

Mary E. Morton, PhD, RHIA
Ann H. Peden, PhD, RHIA, CCS

The Changing Face of Health Care in America   2
Impact on the Role of the Health Information Manager   18

Chapter 2 **Hospital-Based Care**   29

Angela L. Morey, MSM, RHIA
Ann H. Peden, PhD, RHIA, CCS
Sonya D. Beard, MSEd, RHIA

Introduction to Setting   30
Regulatory Issues   34
Documentation   35
Reimbursement   42
Information Management   51
Quality and Utilization Management   56
Risk Management and Legal Issues   58
Role of the Health Information Management Professional   59
Trends   62

Chapter 3 **Freestanding Ambulatory Care**   69

Elizabeth D. Bowman, MPA, RHIA

Introduction to Setting   70
Regulatory Issues   73

Documentation	77
Reimbursement	91
Information Management	94
Quality Improvement and Utilization Management	101
Risk Management and Legal Issues	103
Role of the Health Information Management Professional	104
Trends	105

Chapter 4 Managed Care

113

Cecile Favreau, MBA, CPC
Lynn Kuehn, MS, RHIA, CCS-P, FAHIMA

Introduction to Settings and Plans	114
Regulatory Issues	120
Documentation	123
Revenue Generation	124
Information Management	128
Quality Improvement and Utilization Management	134
Risk Management and Legal Issues	137
Role of the Health Information Management Professional	139
Trends	140

Chapter 5 Dialysis

147

Ann H. Peden, PhD, RHIA, CCS

Introduction to Setting	148
Regulatory Issues	151
Documentation	152
Reimbursement	159
Information Management	160
Quality Assessment, Performance Improvement, and Utilization Management	167
Risk Management, Legal, and Ethical Issues	171
Role of the Health Information Management Professional	172

Chapter 6 Correctional Facilities

177

Nina Dozoretz, MA, RHIA, CCHP
Barbara Manny, MS, RHIA
Brianna McCloe Rogers, RHIA

Introduction to Setting	178
Regulatory Issues	192
Documentation	194
Reimbursement and Funding	198
Information Management	199

Quality Management, Performance Improvement,
and Utilization Management 203
Risk Management and Legal Issues 204
Role of the Health Information Management Professional 205
Trends 206

Chapter 7   Mental Health: Long-Term and Acute Services   213

C. Harrell Weathersby, MSW, PhD

Introduction to Setting 214
Regulatory Issues 227
Documentation 228
Reimbursement and Funding 239
Information Management 240
Quality Improvement and Utilization Management 248
Risk Management and Legal Issues 249
Role of the Health Information Management Professional 252
Trends 253

Chapter 8   Substance Abuse   261

Melissa King, MPPA, RHIA
Frances Wickham Lee, MBA, RHIA
Kimberly D. Taylor, RHIA

Introduction to Setting 262
Regulatory Issues 273
Documentation 275
Reimbursement and Funding 285
Information Management 286
Quality Improvement and Utilization Management 291
Risk Management and Legal Issues 292
Role of the Health Information Management Professional 295
Trends 300

Chapter 9   Facilities for Individuals with Intellectual or Developmental Disabilities   309

Nan R. Christian, MEd
Judy S. Westerfield, MEd
Elaine C. Jouette, MA, RHIA

Introduction to Setting 310
Regulatory Issues 314
Documentation 315

Reimbursement and Funding   321
Information Management   322
Quality Improvement and Utilization Management   337
Risk Management and Legal Issues   338
Role of the Health Information Management Professional   341
Trends   342

Chapter 10   Long-Term Care   347

Barbara A. Gorenflo, RHIA
Kris King, MS, RHIA, CPHQ

Introduction to Setting   348
Regulatory Issues   354
Documentation   357
Reimbursement and Funding   364
Information Management   369
Quality Improvement and Utilization Management   377
Risk Management and Legal Issues   380
Role of the Health Information Management Professional   380
Trends   383

Chapter 11   Rehabilitation   389

Terry Winkler, MD
Ann H. Peden, PhD, RHIA, CCS

Introduction to Setting   390
Regulatory Issues   400
Documentation   410
Reimbursement and Funding   414
Information Management   420
Quality Improvement and Utilization Management   425
Risk Management and Legal Issues   426
Role of the Health Information Manager   427
Trends   427

Chapter 12   Home Health Care   435

Ida Blevins, RHIA
Gwen D. Smith, RHIA
Kim A. Boyles, MS, RHIA

Introduction to Setting   436
Regulatory Issues   439
Documentation   441
Reimbursement and Funding   445
Information Management   448
Quality Improvement and Utilization Management   453

Risk Management and Legal Issues 455
Role of the Health Information Management Professional 457
Trends 457

Chapter 13 Hospice 463

Teresa Sherfy, RHIT
Karen M. Staszel, RHIA

Introduction to Setting 464
Regulatory Issues 466
Documentation 471
Reimbursement and Funding 474
Information Management 479
Quality Assessment/Performance Improvement and Utilization Management 483
Risk Management and Legal Issues 486
Role of the Health Information Management Professional 486
Trends 487

Chapter 14 Dental Care Settings 491

Francis G. Serio, DMD, MS, MBA
Denise D. Krause, PhD
Cheryl L. Berthelsen, PhD, RHIA

Introduction to Care Settings 492
Regulatory Issues 501
Documentation 503
Reimbursement 510
Information Management 512
Quality Improvement and Utilization Management 517
Risk Management and Legal Issues 518
Role of the Health Information Management Professional 520
Trends 521

Chapter 15 Veterinary Settings 527

Margaret L. Neterer, MM, RHIA

Introduction to Setting 528
Regulatory Issues 530
Documentation 533
Reimbursement 535
Information Management 538
Quality Improvement and Utilization Management 544
Risk Management and Legal Issues 544
Role of the Health Information Management Professional 548
Trends 549

Chapter 16 Consulting 555

Karen Wright, MHA, RHIA, RHIT
Scott Wright, MBA

Introduction to Setting 557
Regulatory Issues 559
Documentation 560
Reimbursement and Compliance 561
Role of the Health Information Management Professional 561
Trends 573

INDEX 579

PREFACE

Health care is provided in a wide variety of settings, with regulatory, reimbursement, and other information management issues that are unique to each. Today's health information managers are building challenging careers in what were once considered nontraditional sites. Managing the information flow within and among these sites, especially in light of the technologies making electronic health records possible, is a challenge for today's health information managers. *Comparative Health Information Management* was developed to assist health information students meet this challenge. This text includes 15 chapters on diverse settings ranging from hospital-based care to veterinary care in which students of health information management may find employment upon graduation. A sixteenth chapter on consulting, provides helpful information to any health information management professional who is considering a career as a consultant in any of the various settings described in the earlier chapters. The contributors come from both the educational and practice arenas and were chosen for their particular expertise in the different content areas.

ABOUT THE THIRD EDITION

The text opens with an introductory chapter that describes the recent history of health care in the United States and the changes taking place in the twenty-first century. The introduction covers such topics as the effect of changes in payment systems on health care, an overview of regulatory and accreditation issues affecting health care, including a section on the Health Insurance Portability and Accountability Act (HIPAA), and the evolution of the electronic health record. The third edition includes new federal initiatives in such areas as auditing, reimbursement, and quality reporting. This chapter also addresses incentive programs for electronic health record implementation and other changes affecting health information services that have been brought about by federal legislation. Chapter 1 explores how these changes affect the HIM professional and lays a foundation of resources that can assist in meeting the challenges of the twenty-first century.

The remaining setting-based chapters follow a consistent template, facilitating a comparison of the different sites by students. Each chapter includes discussions of the following: introduction to setting; regulatory issues; documentation; reimbursement and funding; information management, including data flow, coding and classification, electronic information systems, and data sets; quality improvement and utilization management; risk management and legal issues; role of the HIM professional; and trends. Although the chapters refer to and build on one another, they can stand alone and may be used out of sequence or as modules.

Chapter 2 discusses HIM issues unique to hospital-based care. This chapter has been expanded from previous editions to include acute care. A discussion of long-term acute care hospitals has also been relocated to this chapter and a new accrediting organization for hospitals is also introduced in Chapter 2. Chapter 3 details a wide variety of ambulatory health care settings and their information management issues. New information in this chapter includes issues related to meaningful use of electronic health records, patient portals, and the "medical home" concept, as well as updated information pertinent to various specialized ambulatory settings. Chapter 4 provides fundamental information on the spectrum of managed care models with which health information managers interact today, including a new section on consumer-directed health plans. Chapter 5 discusses both dialysis providers and the regional networks that monitor them. The new end-stage renal disease prospective payment system is explained along with recent changes in data collection and reporting. Recent changes in documentation and other requirements brought about by the 2008 revisions to the Conditions for Coverage are also detailed in Chapter 5. Chapter 6 explains terms and issues related to health care for incarcerated persons. Updates to this chapter reflect the progress that has been made in correctional health care in recent years. Chapter 7 discusses both community-based and inpatient mental health care issues. Updated information regarding the inpatient psychiatric facility prospective payment system is included along with new material on data collection and reporting initiatives of the federal government. Chapter 8 explains health information issues affecting facilities offering treatment and rehabilitation for chemical dependencies. New information on evidence-based treatment is provided along with updated information on data sets related to substance abuse. Issues related to confidentiality of substance abuse records in an era of health information exchange are also discussed. Chapter 9 describes the unique information maintained in facilities offering care and training for individuals with intellectual or developmental disabilities. The third edition provides updated terminology along with expanded detail regarding federal regulations affecting this setting. Chapter 10 explains the increasingly sophisticated data management needs of long-term-care settings, including updated information on quality reporting. Recent changes in federal regulations are also included as well as an introduction to the "culture change movement" in long-term care. Chapter 11 explains information management issues in programs designed to improve function for patients who have suffered a debilitating illness or injury. In addition to updated regulatory information, this chapter provides an introduction to recent proposals to bundle payments for various types of post-acute care. Chapter 12 discusses home care information management issues, including the home health prospective payment system and provides updated information on both federal regulations and voluntary accreditation for home health services. Chapter 13 outlines requirements for entities providing health care and support for persons who are terminally ill and their families. This chapter reflects the revised Conditions of Participation for hospice as well as current trends in hospice care. Chapter 14 provides insight into health information needs for maintaining and improving oral health. Dental terminology is highlighted in a new feature of this chapter that can help familiarize students with the specialized language of dentistry. Chapter 15 describes the health information services in the veterinary medicine setting. Reorganized content provides current information on health information management in settings providing care for animals. Chapter 16 provides practical advice to the health information practitioner considering working as a consultant in any of the health care settings described in this book, including information on the impact of recent federal legislation on the consultant's practice.

FEATURES OF THE TEXTBOOK

Each chapter of *Comparative Health Information Management* contains the following learning elements:

- **Learning Objectives.** The learning objectives are outcome-based and identify and organize learning expectations for more effective studying.

- **Introduction to Setting.** This feature at the beginning of each chapter gives learners a quick snapshot of the particular setting under discussion, including common names for the setting, a description, and synonyms.

- **Summary.** Each chapter includes a brief review of the chapter content, with a focus on key points the learner should retain.

- **Key Terms and Definitions.** Unfamiliar or critical vocabulary words are listed and defined alphabetically at the end of each chapter and appear in bold on their first use within that chapter.

- **Review Questions.** A series of knowledge-based and critical thinking review questions challenge learners to apply what they have learned. These may be used for self-study or assigned for class discussion. The answers to the review questions appear in the Instructor's Manual.

- **Web Activity.** Updated web activities in this edition challenge learners to explore information beyond the book for each setting.

- **Case Study.** Real-word case studies based on the chapter content are included to challenge learners to apply what they have learned. Each case includes a series of questions to guide learners through the problem-solving process. Cases may be used for in-class discussion or assigned for individual practice. Suggested answers to the cases are included in the Instructor's Manual.

- **References and Suggested Readings, Key Resources.** Each chapter includes a list of references for futher self-guided exploration as well as a list of key organizations and associations pertinent to the chapter that will lead the learner to additional information.

NEW TO THE THIRD EDITION

- **Changes to payment systems.** Since the publication of the second edition, Medicare has implemented changes to payment systems and to Conditions of Participation or Conditions for Coverage in several settings. Updated regulations in these areas are presented in the appropriate chapters.

- **American Recovery and Reinvestment and HITECH Acts.** The third edition includes information about these key changes and how they affect health information systems.

- **ICD-10-CM/PCS and DSM-V.** References to code sets have been re-worded to reflect the transition to ICD-10-CM/PCS, and DSM-V in 2013. Updated data collection systems and quality reporting requirements have been incorporated into several chapters along with updated material on electronic health records. Revisions to sections on accrediting organizations, such as the addition of newly recognized organizations with deeming authority, have been incorporated where appropriate. (See the Content section of this preface for examples of new information provided by chapter.)

- **Web Activities and Key Resources** have been updated to help students research the latest regulatory information in the ever-changing health care environment.

- Chapter 2 has been expanded to include all types of hospital care, allowing this edition to serve as an introductory text for all major health care settings.

- Instructor Resources have been fully updated, and the instructor package now includes a test bank and presentations in PowerPoint™.

INSTRUCTOR RESOURCES

The following resources are available with the third edition to provide instructors with the tools they need to teach and assess student progress:

Instructor's Manual, ISBN 978-1-1111-2564-6

The Instructor's Manual contains answer keys for all chapter reviews and case studies. It also includes a tool to help identify the competencies and knowledge clusters applicable for associate degree and baccalaureate programs.

Instructor Resources, ISBN-13: 978-1-1111-2563-9

Spend less time planning and more time teaching! The following instructor resources are available either on CD-ROM or online:

- The electronic **Instructor's Manual** contains course preparation materials, including sample syllabi, domain mapping, and complete answer keys for each textbook chapter.

- The **Computerized Test Bank** in **ExamView**® makes generating tests and quizzes a snap. With more than 600 questions to choose from, you can create customized assessments for your students with the click of a button.

- Customizable instructor support **slide presentations in PowerPoint**™ format focus in on key points in each chapter.

If you want to access these resources online, go to http://login.cengage.com/ cb/ and click on 'Create a New Faculty Account' to create your single-user sign-on (SSO) account. Contact your sales representative if you have any difficulty.

ACKNOWLEDGMENTS

This book is the result of the efforts of numerous persons. Shirley Anderson had the vision for Delmar's HIM (Health Information Management) series and first suggested this text to the Delmar editorial staff. In 1994, Delmar assembled a focus group of HIM practitioners and educators to plan the first edition. Accepting the role of editor for this text was much easier given the groundwork that had been laid by the thoughtful contributions of my HIM colleagues.

The author is very grateful for the work of the contributors to the first and second editions, who created a superb body of work that the current contributors were able to update, revise, and refine. The names of all contributors, both previous and current, are listed at each chapter heading, although some of the earlier contributors were not able to participate in the third edition. I would like to give these individuals special recognition for their groundbreaking work in the development of previous editions of this text: Lynn Kuehn for the chapter on managed care, Barbara Manny and Brianna McCloe Rogers for the correctional chapter, Frances Wickham Lee and Kimberly Taylor for the substance abuse chapter, Elaine C. Jouette and Judy S. Westerfield for the chapter on services for individuals with intellectual and developmental disabilities, Kris King for the long-term care chapter, Gwen D. Smith and Kim Boyles for the home health chapter, Karen Staszel for the hospice chapter, and Cheryl Berthelsen for the dental chapter. I owe a tremendous debt of gratitude to these contributors for developing the first and second editions, thereby providing an excellent foundation for the current edition.

The reviewers also played a major role in the development and refinement of this book. Their insights kept us focused on the needs of the readers, and their excellent suggestions have helped make the third edition "new and improved." The author and publisher would like to thank the following persons for their role in shaping this text by serving as reviewers during the preparation of the manuscript:

Patricia Buttner, RHIT, CCS, LPN
Instructor
Greenville Technical College
Greenville, SC

Mona Calhoun, MS, RHIA
Chairperson Health Information Management Program
Coppin State University
Baltimore, MD

Crystal A. Clack, MS, RHIA, CCS
Adjunct Faculty
Devry University

Marie T. Conde, MPA, RHIA, CCS, AHIMA Certified ICD-10-CM/PCS
  Trainer
HIT Program Director and Instructor
City College of San Francisco
San Francisco, CA

Melanie Endicott, MBA/HCM, RHIA, CCS, CCS-P
HIM Program Director
Spokane Community College
Spokane, WA

Nancy Entwistle
Instructor
Caritas Laboure College
Norton, MA

Betty Haar, BS, RHIA
Program Director
Kirkwood Community College
Cedar Rapids, IA

Gerald B. Harkless, MA, BS, RHIA
Adjunct Faculty Instructor
Alamo Colleges/St. Philip's College
San Antonio, TX

Lorraine Kane
Instructor
SUNYIT Ithaca
Utica, NY

Kelli Lewis, RHIA
Clinical Education Coordinator
Polk State College
Winter Haven, FL

Gloria Madison, MS, RHIA
HIT Program Director/Faculty
Moraine Park Technical College
West Bend, WI

LaShunda B. Smith MSM, RHIA
Instructor
Alabama State University
Montgomery, AL

Julie Wolter, MA RHIA
Assistant Professor
Saint Louis University
St. Louis, MO

The chapter authors are also grateful for expert assistance and advice provided to them by others. For Chapter 5: Brenda Dyson and the staff of Network 8 for sharing their knowledge of the ESRD networks and dialysis facilities. For Chapter 6: Stacey L. Goldstein for sharing her knowledge of correctional mental health systems. For Chapter 7: Tessie Smith, Ellen Crawford, Ted Lutterman, Barbara Carpenter, and Mary Crossman. For Chapter 11: Debbie Hill and the Staff of Cox Walnut Lawn Rehabilitation Program of Springfield, Missouri, for their assistance in making revisions. For Chapter 15: Various members of the American Veterinary Health Information Management Association (AVHIMA) for providing editorial support, especially Kathleen Ellis, RHIT, RN, BS, and Roberta Schmidt, RHIA, health information management professionals for the colleges of veterinary medicine at the University of Illinois and Ohio State University, respectively.

I would like to thank Michelle Green for her assistance with material for the test bank. I also want to thank the editorial staff of Delmar Learning for their work on the project and the many ways that they supported and enhanced my efforts, including thanks to Lauren Whalen and Rhonda Dearborn. In particular, I would like to thank Jadin Babin-Kavanaugh for her pleasant and encouraging communication, for her excellent organizational skills, and for a fantastic job of keeping this project on track from start to finish.

I am very grateful for the support and encouragement I have received from my colleagues at the University of Mississippi Medical Center. I want to thank the administration of the school and Dr. Clyde Deschamp, chair of the Department of General Health Professions, for creating an environment conducive to professional growth and the acceptance of professional challenges. I also thank my fellow faculty members for giving their best to our students and for their support and encouragement, including their service as contributors to this edition. I thank the many guest lecturers and field trip guides who have shared their knowledge of health information management in traditional and nontraditional settings with my students and with me. I want to thank Doris Austin for the many ways she helps me to "stay of top of things," especially when faced with time constraints. I also thank my daughter Hope Peden Vandersteen for her assistance and insights.

I thank my family, especially my husband, Sam, my children, Eric, Jericho, and Hope, and their spouses, my mother and father, my mother-in-law, and also my church family for their encouragement and their prayers. And I thank the One who hears and answers prayer, His Son, who "always lives to make intercession," and His Spirit, who "also helps in our weaknesses."

ABOUT THE AUTHOR

ANN H. PEDEN, PHD, RHIA, CCS, is professor of health informatics and information management in the School of Health Related Professions at the University of Mississippi Medical Center in Jackson, Mississippi. She has her PhD in Clinical Health Sciences from the University of Mississippi and her MBA from Louisiana Tech University, where she also previously taught. Before teaching, she served as director of medical records at St. Francis Medical Center in Monroe, Louisiana. She completed her undergraduate education at the University of Mississippi.

Dr. Peden's awards include the American Health Information Management Association's "Professional Achievement Award" and the Mississippi Health Information Management Association's "Distinguished Member Award" and "Legacy Award." She has been honored as "Teacher of the Year" for the University of Mississippi's School of Health Related Professions and was also named to the university's Nelson Order in recognition of teaching excellence. Her service to the profession of health information management includes serving as a member of the board of directors of the Commission on Accreditation of Health Informatics and Information Management Education and terms as president of the Louisiana Medical Record Association and the Mississippi Health Information Management Association. She has also served as a member of the nominating committee of the American Health Information Management Association (AHIMA), and as the chair of AHIMA's Coding Policy and Strategy Committee.

ABOUT THE CONTRIBUTORS

SONYA D. BEARD, MSED, RHIA, has been employed in the healthcare arena as a health information management professional for over 20 years, nine of which are associated with the educational sector. Throughout her career she has been involved with various professional and community organizations. She graduated from The University of Mississippi with a Bachelor of Science degree in Health Information Management. She has a Master of Science degree in Education with an emphasis on Workforce Leadership from Mississippi State University.

IDA BLEVINS, RHIA, is a supervisor in the Home Health Services Department at St. John's Hospital, Springfield Illinois. She is a graduate of Illinois State University, Normal, IL. Along with her extensive hospital, ambulatory care and private sector HIM and coding experience, she has been actively involved in the home care industry for over 14 years. She authored the *Home Health Compliance Manual,* co-authored *ICD-9-CM Diagnostic Coding for Long-Term Care and Home Care,* 2nd Edition, as well as authoring numerous journal articles related to HIM in home care. Additionally, she serves as the Facilitator for AHIMA's Home Health and Hospice Community of Practice. Ida served multiple terms on the Board of Directors of the Illinois Home Care Council and provides *ICD-9-CM* coding seminars and auditing/consulting for home health agencies across the country. She was an HIM representative panelist for the 3M/Fazzi OASIS Integrity Project and served on the Clinical Advisory Panel for the OASIS Certificate and Competency Board. She is currently also a consultant with OASIS Answers, Inc.

ELIZABETH D. BOWMAN, MPA, RHIA, is a professor in the Department of Health Informatics and Information Management at the University of Tennessee Health Science Center in Memphis, TN. She is a graduate of Millsaps College and has a Master of Public Administration degree with a concentration in Health Services Administration from the University of Memphis. She obtained a post-baccalaureate certificate in medical record administration from the School of Medical Record Administration at Baptist Memorial Hospital in Memphis. Mrs. Bowman has extensive experience in teaching health information practices in nonacute settings as well as medical terminology, ICD-9-CM and CPT coding, health information technology and systems, and statistics.

NAN R. CHRISTIAN, MS, LCIDDT, LCMHT, is Director of Education/Quality Service Manager at Hudspeth Regional Center and Adjunct Faculty at Belhaven University. She is a graduate of the University of Mississippi with a B.A. in Communicative Disorders and received her M.S. degree in Speech and Hearing Services from the University of Southern Mississippi. She obtained post-graduate work from the University of Southern Mississippi in School Supervision and Administration and School Psychometry. Ms. Chrisitian has over 39 years of professional experience in special education, administration, and speech pathology. She has been recognized by Cambridge Who's Who as "Professional of the Year" representing Special education administration for the 2009–2010 year.

NINA F. DOZORETZ, MA, RHIA, CCHP, is a senior health service official in the Department of Homeland Security, Immigration and Customs Enforcement Office of Detention Policy and Planning in Washington, DC. She received her

Bachelor of Science degree in Medical Records Administration from Daemen College in Buffalo, New York. She obtained her Master in Arts degree in Computers and Resource Management from Webster University in Albuquerque, New Mexico. Ms. Dozoretz is a retired Captain in the United States Public Health Service and is a Certified Correctional Healthcare Professional by the National Commission Correctional Health Care. She has extensive experience in administering and directing national detention health care programs, developing detention and correctional health care standards and conducting correctional and detention facility inspections and audits.

CECILE FAVREAU, MBA, CPC, has worked in health care for over twenty-five years with a large concentration of that time spent in the health insurance industry working for two large insurers. Currently employed as a Professional Relations Specialist for a very large multispecialty group practice of a teaching hospital, Cecile is responsible for training providers regarding accurate billing as well as the creation and revision of encounter forms (superbills) and researching payment issues. She also teaches in the Allied Health curriculum of a post-secondary school. Cecile is very committed to the concept of providing an environment of quality learning and enjoys celebrating the successes of her students.

BARBARA A. GORENFLO, RHIA, is the Assistant Administrator of Beechwood Continuing Care in Getzville, New York. Before her current position, she was the Director of Health Information Management. She has a BS degree in Medical Record Administration from Daemen College, Amherst, New York. She has served as Clinical Instructor for Health Information Technology students at Trocaire and Erie Community Colleges. Mrs. Gorenflo contracts with several long-term care facilities and renal dialysis centers for medical record consulting services. She is a presenter on medical record documentation issues as well as on HIPAA compliance.

MELISSA KING, MPPA, RHIA, is the Business Office Administrator at Community Counseling Services, a community mental health center in Mississippi. She obtained a bachelor's degree in Health Record Administration from the University of Mississippi Medical Center. She obtained her Master's Degree in Public Policy and Administration from Mississippi State University. She has extensive experience in all aspects of health information management in community mental health, including alcohol and drug treatment programs, reimbursement issues, and information systems planning, implementation, and maintenance.

DENISE D. KRAUSE, PHD, is an associate professor and director of research and education information technology at the University of Mississippi Medical Center. She is a graduate of the University of Kansas and has Masters' degrees in International Policy and Russian from the Monterey Institute of International Studies in California, and Master's and PhD degrees in Preventive Medicine with a concentration in epidemiology from the University of Mississippi Medical Center. She has completed professional technical training in networking and information technology. As director of research and education information technology, Dr. Krause is managing numerous technology projects to support research and education, investigating solutions to improve health systems, and is building IT infrastructure and capacity to support research at UMMC.

ANGELA MOREY, MSM, RHIA, is an assistant professor in the Health Informatics and Information Management Department at the University of Mississippi Medical Center. She is a graduate of the Health Information Management program at the Medical College of Georgia and has a Master of Science in Management degree with a concentration in Organizational Behavior and Development from Georgia State University. Ms. Morey has extensive experience in teaching health information practices in acute settings as well as medical terminology, performance improvement, organizational management, healthcare statistics and legal aspects of health information management.

MARY E. MORTON, PHD, RHIA, is an associate professor in the Health Informatics and Information Management program at the University of Mississippi Medical Center. She is a graduate of Louisiana Tech University, holds a Master of Library and Information Science from Louisiana State University, and a PhD in Information Science and Technology from Drexel University. Dr. Morton also served on the faculty at Temple University and previously worked in several positions at Baton Rouge General Medical Center in Louisiana. She has conducted electronic health record research and was recipient of the Mississippi Health Information Management Association's (MSHIMA) Research Award in 2010.

MARGARET L. NETERER, MM, RHIA, is currently interim manager of the Medical Records Service for the Michigan State University Veterinary Teaching Hospital in East Lansing, Michigan, having retired from the manager's positon in 2006. During her 25 years in this position, Ms. Neterer also held leadership responsibility at various levels in both veterinary and human health information management professional associations, as well as committee service with the American Veterinary Medical Association. Her areas of expertise include all aspects of management and supervision of veterinary health information services as well as standard-setting in veterinary medical informatics. She created and manages an online course in medical record maintenance for veterinarians.

FRANCIS G. SERIO, DMD, MS, MBA, FICD, FACD, FADI, is Associate Dean for Clinical Affairs and Professor at the East Carolina University School of Dental Medicine. He is also a Diplomate of the American Board of Periodontology. Dr. Serio completed his undergraduate studies at Johns Hopkins University and received his D.M.D. degree from the University of Pennsylvania. He earned his M.S. and certificate in Periodontics at the University of Maryland and his MBA from Millsaps College. He was inducted into the International College of Dentists in 2003, and the American College of Dentists in 2004. Dr. Serio previously taught at the University of Maryland and was Professor and Chairman of the Department of Periodontics and Preventive Sciences at the University of Mississippi School of Dentistry from 1993–2009. His professional interests include educating predoctoral dental students, the pathogenesis of aggressive periodontitis, periodontal plastic surgery, international volunteer dentistry, and the continuing dental education of general dentists and dental hygienists. He has presented over 120 lectures and continuing education courses in the United States and around the world. He is founder of the Dominican Dental Mission Project, which has received both The President's Volunteer Action Award and The Daily Points of Light Award. He has also been actively involved in Dentistry Overseas, a joint project between the American Dental Association and Health Volunteers Overseas, and many other international volunteer dental activities. Dr. Serio has written or co-authored over 40 scientific articles and four books.

TERESA SHERFY, RHIT, is the Information Services Manager at Hospice of Southern Illinois in Belleville, Illinois. She is a graduate of Southwestern Illinois College with an associate degree in Health Information Technology. Mrs. Sherfy has more than 15 years of experience working in hospice medical records, quality improvement, compliance, and information systems management.

C. HARRELL WEATHERSBY, MSW, PHD, holds a Master's degree in social work and a doctorate in English. He has served in the past as Executive Director of Region XIV Mental Health Center in Mississippi and Regional Manager for Mental Health Region IX in Louisiana. He has also been employed as Director of the Mississippi State Hospital Division of Community Services, which provides support services to people with severe mental illness who have been discharged from the hospital and as statewide Coordinator of the Community Support Program in the Mississippi Department of Mental Health. In 1991 he received a commendaton from the Mississippi Senate for his work with persons with mental illness and was honored with the C. Harrell Weathersby "Father of the Mississippi Alliance for the Mentally Ill" Award, for his assistance in establishing the Alliance for the Mentally Ill chapter in Mississippi. This award has since been given in his name to an outstanding mental health professional at the annual Mississippi AMI Conference for Mental Health Professionals. He has also worked in a variety of other human services areas, including developmental disability, juvenile justice, and protective services for children. As a result of his ongoing interest and work in the area of cultural diversity he was awarded a Fulbright travel grant to South African in 2004. He retired from Southeastern Louisiana University in 2006 and currently teaches part-time as an adjunct professor in the Tulane Universtity School of Social Work.

TERRY WINKLER, MD, CLCP, is in private practice in Springfield, Missouri, as a board-certified specialist in physical medicine and rehabilitation and as a subspecialist in spinal cord injury medicine. He is a past medical director of Cox hospital rehabilitation program and medical director of the Curative Rehabilitation Center, a freestanding outpatient rehabilitation program. His practice focused on spinal cord injury, acquired brain injury, amputations, and life care planning. Dr. Winkler has served on committees reviewing research grants concerning spinal cord injury, and peer reviews articles for publication in the *Archives of Physical Medicine and Rehabilitation*. Dr. Winkler has numerous publications regarding life care planning and has contributed to every major text in the field of life care planning, contributed to a college text on rehabilitation record systems, and has written on the effects of aging with spinal cord injury. Dr. Winkler holds an academic appointment as clinical associate faculty at the University of Florida—Gainesville, where he teaches life care planning. At Southern Missouri State University in Springfield, Missouri, he taught differential diagnosis to the doctoral-level physical therapy students. Dr. Winkler's undergraduate training at Louisiana Tech University included a double major in premedical studies and medical record administration. He attended the Louisiana State University School of Medicine and then completed residency training in rehabilitation medicine in Little Rock, Arkansas. Past honors include The Americas Award, Alumnus of the Year at Louisiana Tech University, "Who's Who among Young Americans," and the Jean Claude Belot Award from the Harvard University health sciences program. In addition to his active medical practice, Dr. Winkler is a certified life care planner, has served as a commissioner on the Commission for Health Care Certification. He continues to serve on the board of the Foundation of Life Care Planning and the editorial board of the *Journal of Life Care Planning*.

KAREN WRIGHT, MHSA, RHIA, RHIT, has a Master of Health Administration from Ohio University and a bachelor's degree in Health Information Administration from Ohio State University. She has been the coordinator and instructor of Health Information Technology at Hocking College for the over 20 years. In addition to being the transcription supervisor and then director of a medical record department in a 365-bed acute care hospital, Karen has been a consultant at acute care hospitals; nursing, chemical dependency, and behavioral health care facilities; as well as for physician's private practices.

SCOTT WRIGHT, MBA, has a Masters of Business Administration from Ohio University and has served as the Director of the Small Business Development Center at Ohio University. He is an instructor of Finance at Ohio University, where he has taught for the over 20 years. He has most recently traveled to Germany and Italy directing student consulting projects for various businesses. In addition, Scott has owned and operated many types of businesses.

CHAPTER 1

Introduction

MARY E. MORTON, PHD, RHIA

ANN H. PEDEN, PHD, RHIA, CCS

LEARNING OBJECTIVES

Upon successful completion of this chapter, you should be able to:

- Describe important changes affecting health care delivery in the United States.

- Explain the impact of health care changes on the health information manager.

- Identify expanding opportunities available to health information managers.

THE CHANGING FACE OF HEALTH CARE IN AMERICA

U.S. Hospitals and Twentieth-Century Health Care

The twentieth century saw numerous changes in the delivery of health care services. Before the twentieth century, hospitals were perceived as places where people went to die. Antibiotics had not yet been developed, and hospitals offered very little in the way of technology. There was no effective oversight of hospital operations by any outside regulatory authority. However, the twentieth century began a new era for hospitals. For example, in 1910, the **Flexner Report** examined the state of medical education in the United States. The authors of this report, who had been commissioned by the Carnegie Foundation, emphasized the importance of hospital-based training in preparing competent physicians (Litman & Robins, 1991). Shortly after publication of that report, the **American College of Surgeons (ACS)** was founded and began establishing standards for hospitals as part of its mission to improve the quality of care for surgical patients (ACS, 2010). The Flexner Report and the ACS's hospital standardization program inaugurated needed changes that improved the quality of hospital care and increased the American public's expectations of hospitals.

The first health information managers, or "medical record librarians" as they were then called, played an important role in efforts to improve patient care in hospitals. The American College of Surgeons' hospital standardization program emphasized the importance of maintaining medical records, and subsequent accrediting agencies, such as the Joint Commission, have continued to emphasize the role of accurate and complete health information in providing high-quality patient care.

In 1946, the **Hill-Burton Act** authorized an investigation to determine the need for more hospitals and provided money for their construction. Admissions to hospitals increased dramatically during the mid-twentieth century, as did hospital costs. This period of hospital expansion resulted in increased opportunities for health information practitioners, because at that time a large majority of health information managers practiced in hospital settings.

The latter part of the twentieth century was marked by continued changes in health care. New legislation, payment issues, technological advances, and changes in society are making a significant impact on the delivery of health care in the new millennium.

Payment Issues Affecting Health Care Delivery

Payment issues have had a tremendous impact on health care delivery in the United States during the late twentieth and early twenty-first centuries. With an increasing number of patients insured under federal and state health programs, changes in payment mechanisms for these programs have affected all types of health care settings.

Overview of Federal and Federal-State Health Programs

In 1965, Congress enacted, as amendments to the Social Security Act, Title XVIII and Title XIX, commonly known as Medicare and Medicaid. **Medicare**

(Title XVIII) provides health benefits for Social Security recipients and other qualified individuals and consists of four parts: Part A, Hospital Insurance; Part B, Medical Insurance; and—more recently—Part C, Medicare Advantage, and Part D, Prescription Drug Coverage. Part A helps pay for hospital inpatient care, some home health care, skilled nursing care, and hospice care. Part B provides coverage for physician services, hospital outpatient services, some home health care, medical equipment and supplies, and other health services (CMS, 2005). Part D, created by the **Medicare Prescription Drug, Improvement, and Modernization Act of 2003 (MMA)**, is optional insurance coverage available to all Medicare beneficiaries that is designed to lower prescription drug costs (Casto & Layman, 2009). Medicare beneficiaries pay a monthly premium for the Parts B and D benefits, but not for Part A (CMS, 2005, 2010f). Beneficiaries may opt to purchase a managed care plan to provide their health care services and prescription drugs. Under this option, known as Part C, or Medicare Advantage, the beneficiary purchases a health insurance plan offered by one of the private companies approved by Medicare. These plans may offer coverage for services excluded by Parts A and B, but the premiums, out-of-pocket expenses, and rules for coverage vary by plan. Under Part C, beneficiaries pay a monthly premium for the insurance plan, in addition to their Part B premium (DHHS, 2010).

Medicaid (Title XIX) provides medical assistance to lower-income individuals and families. Federal and state governments jointly fund the Medicaid program. Because each state establishes and administers its own program, Medicaid services and eligibility requirements vary from state to state (Klees, Wolfe, & Curtis, 2009). The Patient Protection and Affordable Care Act (Health Reform), passed in 2010, expanded Medicaid eligibility requirements (Pub. L. No. 111-148, 2010).

The **Centers for Medicare and Medicaid Services (CMS)** is a federal agency within the Department of Health and Human Services. It was created in 1977 to administer the Medicare and Medicaid programs. CMS maintains its headquarters in Baltimore, Maryland, and has 10 regional offices nationwide. The headquarters administers the national direction of the Medicare and Medicaid programs, while the regional offices provide CMS with the local presence necessary for quality customer service and oversight.

CMS mainly acts as a purchaser of health care services for the Medicare and Medicaid beneficiaries. Four key principles for Medicare/Medicaid standards are:

1. Assuring that Medicare and Medicaid are properly administered by their contractors and state agencies
2. Establishing policies for the reimbursement of health care providers
3. Conducting research on the effectiveness of various methods of health care management, treatment, and financing
4. Assessing the quality of health care facilities and services

Medicare/Medicaid manuals, interim manual instructions, and Medicare transmittals are distributed to Medicare administrative contractors, CMS regional offices, federal agencies, state agencies, and congressional offices.

Medicare providers may obtain copies of Medicare/Medicaid manuals and transmittals from the CMS Web site.

Congress created the **Children's Health Insurance Program (CHIP)** as part of the Balanced Budget Act of 1997. CHIP, also known as Title XXI, allows states to offer health insurance plans for children, up to age 19, who are not already insured.

CHIP affords families who earn too much to qualify for Medicaid an opportunity to obtain health insurance for their children (CMS, 2010e). The increase in federal and state health insurance programs has made governmental regulations and payment systems important factors in health care delivery.

Payment Changes Affected Hospitals First

When Medicare was implemented in 1966, it paid for health care benefits under a **fee-for-service** plan, which operated in a manner similar to that of most health insurance plans of the day. Health care providers received a fee for each service provided—each office visit, each day in the hospital, each treatment, and so on. As the costs of this program continued to escalate, the federal government began to look at ways to hold them down, initially by targeting hospital costs. In 1982, enactment of the Medicare inpatient **prospective payment system (PPS)** (a system based on payment amounts determined before services are rendered) forced hospitals into a new way of looking at the utilization of their services. This signaled a change in the locations and methods of delivery of health care for the future. Medicare payments to hospitals switched from a **per diem** (per day) basis to a per case basis. Before the prospective payment arrangement, hospitals received payment for each day that the patient stayed in the hospital (per diem). However, prospective payment based any reimbursement primarily on the patient's condition and surgical treatment, regardless of the number of days the patient stayed in the hospital. Under prospective payment, the hospital's cash flow improved if patients were discharged earlier, because costs for extra days in the hospital could not be adequately recovered from Medicare. Hospitals, particularly those with a high volume of Medicare patients, began to have an incentive to encourage shorter inpatient stays and to treat patients in the least costly setting possible. In some states, payers other than Medicare began to implement prospective payment. Increasingly, hospitals began to emphasize programs that shifted care from inpatient settings to alternate care settings, such as outpatient and home care.

Health information managers are crucial to a hospital's success under prospective payment, because the data provided by health information services are the basis for inpatient reimbursement under Medicare. Just as the American College of Surgeons' hospital standardization program first brought attention to the role that the then medical record librarians played in the provision of quality patient care in hospitals, Medicare's prospective payment system highlighted the role that health information managers play in the financial health of hospitals. Data transformed into information by health information services continues to be an important factor in numerous decisions hospitals must make in the twenty-first century, such as decisions regarding contracts with managed care organizations.

Managed care organizations (discussed more fully in Chapter 4) became a force during the 1990s, further lowering hospital utilization rates. The earliest so-called prepaid health care models, such as Kaiser Permanente in the western United States, have been in existence since the 1930s (Kaiser Permanente, n.d.). In the mid-1970s, the federal government stimulated the development of one type of managed care organization, the health maintenance organization (HMO). The name "health maintenance organization" relates to the financial incentive for the health care provider to keep patients healthy. A common method of paying providers in an HMO is the **capitation** model. Under capitation, providers are paid based on the number of patients they agree to treat, rather than on the number of services they provide. Therefore, it is more profitable to the provider if the patient requires fewer services. These types of plans emphasize prevention of disease (health maintenance). When disease occurs, however, treatment is provided in the least costly setting.

Increased Scrutiny of Improper Payments, Fraud, Abuse, and Waste

Federal legislation passed in the early twenty-first century created audit programs and compliance initiatives to prevent improper or fraudulent payments made under federal health programs. CMS's **Recovery Audit Contractor (RAC)** program was designed to recover improper Medicare payments (Dimick, 2010), while the **Medicaid Integrity Program (MIP)** focuses upon Medicaid overpayments (CMS, 2009a). **Zone Program Integrity Contractors (ZPICs)** identify and investigate malicious fraud within seven geographic zones (CMS, 2009b). Each state is also monitored by its federally designated **quality improvement organization (QIO)**. The QIOs work under contract with CMS to improve the quality of care delivered to Medicare beneficiaries (CMS, 2010b). These responsibilities include conducting focused coding and documentation audits at the direction of CMS (Gentul & Davis, 2007). Using specialized software, QIOs are able to identify hospitals with outliers and payment errors (Casto & Layman, 2009). These federal initiatives have also led to increased auditing by private payers (Dimick, 2010). To meet the demands of increasing external scrutiny, many providers have developed **clinical documentation improvement (CDI)** programs to facilitate accurate documentation, coding and reporting of quality data (AHIMA, 2010a).

Pay-for-Performance

Reimbursement is becoming more closely tied to quality outcomes with the emergence of **pay-for-performance (P4P)** systems. These incentive-based programs reward or penalize providers based upon their ability to meet preestablished targets for delivery of health care services. Growth of P4P programs is evident within Medicare and Medicaid, as well as private health insurance and managed care companies (Casto & Layman, 2009).

Hospitals are required by CMS to report quality information for established inpatient quality measures through the **Hospital Inpatient Quality**

Reporting (IQR) program. In addition, the **Hospital Outpatient Quality Data Reporting Program (HOP QDRP)** became effective in 2009. Data from IQR and HOP QDRP are made publically available to enable consumers to make more informed decisions about their health care. Hospitals that do not participate receive a reduced annual Medicare payment. The **Physician Quality Reporting Initiative (PQRI)** is CMS's voluntary reporting program for physician providers. Under the PQRI, participants receive an incentive for reporting quality measures for Medicare beneficiaries. Most state Medicaid programs have implemented P4P programs as well; however, the targeted providers, reimbursement methodologies, and quality measures vary by state (Casto & Layman, 2009; CMS QualityNet, 2010).

Incentive-Based Program for Adoption of Health Information Technology

The **American Recovery and Reinvestment Act (ARRA)**, also known as the "Stimulus Act" or the "Recovery Act", was passed in 2009. ARRA allocated $17 billion in incentives through Medicare and Medicaid reimbursement to assist providers and organizations in the early adoption of electronic health records (Dennis, 2010). Providers failing to demonstrate **meaningful use** of health information technology by 2016 will be financially penalized (AHIMA, 2010b). ARRA has significantly impacted the health care industry in other areas and is further discussed later in the chapter.

Effects of Payment and Financial Changes on Other Settings

Other settings, such as ambulatory care, home health, and long-term care, have been affected both directly and indirectly by payment and other financial changes.

The hospital inpatient prospective payment system (IPPS) obviously affected the delivery of care to hospital inpatients. The IPPS, along with a shift toward managed care, contributed to the increased utilization of ambulatory health care services (services provided in settings where patients generally do not stay overnight). With more patients receiving treatment in ambulatory settings, payers began monitoring ambulatory data and payment more carefully.

Starting with payments to physicians, Congress enacted a law in 1991 creating a professional fee schedule (PFS), which was implemented in 1992. Before the implementation of the fee schedule, Medicare payments to physicians were based on charges. If the physician's charge was in line with what other physicians in the same specialty usually charged for that service, Medicare would pay its share of the charge. When the fee schedule was implemented, it quantified the physician work, practice expense, and malpractice expense of each service to determine what that service was "worth" relative to other services. Implementation of a payment system based on the "relative value" of services removed from participating physicians the ability to establish their own charges for Medicare patients. Payments under the fee schedule are based on codes representing services performed by physicians and other qualified providers (CMS, 2010h). (More information on the relative value system can be found in Chapter 3.)

In 2000, Medicare began paying hospitals for ambulatory care under an outpatient prospective payment system (OPPS), which is based on codes submitted by the hospital. (See Chapter 2.) As with the hospital IPPS, adequate documentation and accurate coding are extremely important, along with an understanding of the complex regulations governing the PPS. For both physicians and hospitals, greater demands are being placed on the health information systems of ambulatory health care providers. Health information managers are knowledgeable in coding, billing, and clinical documentation—all crucial components in the increasingly complex health data environment facing all types of health care providers.

Medicare payment changes have also affected other health care settings. Skilled nursing facilities came under a prospective payment system in 1998. (See Chapter 10.) The home health prospective payment system became effective in the year 2000. (See Chapter 12.) A prospective payment system for inpatient rehabilitation hospital services (Chapter 11) was implemented in January 2002, followed by implementation of a PPS for long-term care hospitals (Chapter 2) in October of that year (CMS, 2010g). In January 2005, a PPS for inpatient psychiatric facilities (Chapter 7) became effective (CMS, 2010a). Although the hospital-oriented PPSs are based largely on diagnostic and procedural coding, other PPSs rely on additional types of clinical data that are captured on patient assessment instruments periodically throughout each episode of care. (See Table 1-1 for an overview of Medicare PPSs.) Health information managers with skills in systems analysis can be valuable team members in ensuring a smooth flow of accurate data for any prospective payment system.

TABLE **1-1**

Medicare Prospective Payment Systems

Setting	Basis for Payment	Key Data Collection Instruments	Year PPS First Implemented
Hospital Inpatient	Medicare Severity Diagnosis Related Groups (MS-DRGs)	Uniform Bill-04 (UB-04)	1982
Skilled Nursing Facilities	Resource Utilization Groups (RUGs)	Minimum Data Set (MDS)	1998
Hospital Outpatient	Ambulatory Payment Classifications (APCs)	Uniform Bill-04 (UB-04)	2000
Home Health	Home Health Resource Groups (HHRGs)	Outcomes and Assessment Information Set (OASIS)	2000
Inpatient Rehabilitation	Case Mix Groups (CMGs)	Inpatient Rehabilitation Facility Patient Assessment Instrument (IRF-PAI)	2002
Long-term Care Hospitals	Long-term Care Diagnosis Related Groups (MS-LTC-DRGs)	Uniform Bill-04 (UB-04)	2002
Inpatient Psychiatric Facilities	Per diem payment, adjusted for specific DRGs and comorbidities	Uniform Bill-04 (UB-04)	2005

Source: *Prospective Payment Systems—General Information*, Centers for Medicare and Medicaid Services. http://www.cms.gov/ProspMedicareFeeSvcPmtGen/ (CMS, 2010).

Other Regulatory and Accreditation Issues Affecting Health Care

Much attention has been focused on health care financing issues in recent years. However, many other challenges face today's health care organizations, ranging from standardization of electronic transactions to implementation of **electronic health records (EHRs)**.

The Health Insurance Portability and Accountability Act of 1996 (HIPAA)

The **Health Insurance Portability and Accountability Act of 1996 (HIPAA)** was enacted to achieve many purposes. As the name implies, one purpose of this legislation was to address the problem of the rising number of uninsured and underinsured Americans by making health insurance portable. For example, HIPAA allows a person with a preexisting medical condition to obtain insurance benefits related to that condition when changing jobs. Another aspect of HIPAA addresses problems of health care fraud and abuse. However, the provisions of HIPAA that have had the greatest impact on health care providers have been its **administrative simplification** provisions. (See Figure 1-1 for an overview of the HIPAA legislation.)

To whom do the administrative simplification provisions apply? In the original HIPAA legislation, **covered entities (CEs)** are health plans, health care clearinghouses, and health care providers who transmit health information in electronic form (Standards for privacy of individually identifiable health information, 2000; Security and Privacy, 2009). The **Health Information Technology for Economic and Clinical Health Act (HITECH)** was passed in 2009 as Title XIII of the American Recovery and Reinvestment Act (ARRA). HITECH

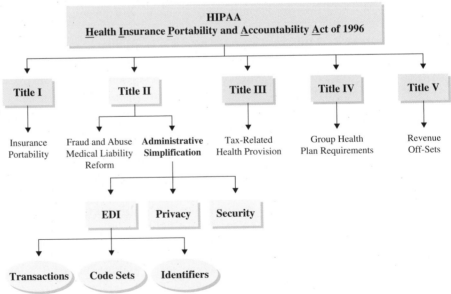

FIGURE **1-1** HIPAA Administrative Simplification Provisions.

amended the HIPAA privacy and security rules by introducing additional privacy regulations, breach notification rules, and stiffer penalties for security violations (AHIMA, 2010c). **Business associates (BAs)** (partners or contractors working for covered entities) are now also held accountable for complying with certain provisions in the privacy and security regulations. These requirements also extend to emerging entities not in existence when the HIPAA rule was initially released (such as health information exchanges, regional health information organizations, personal health record (PHR) operators and e-prescribing gateways) (Dennis, 2010; Rhodes & Rode, 2010). Health information managers play an important role in the implementation and oversight of HIPAA standards. For example, HIPAA's electronic data interchange (EDI) standards include standards for code sets, an arena in which health information managers possess expertise. The August 17, 2000, final rule regarding transactions and standardized code sets for EDI included the following code set standards:

a. *International Classification of Diseases, 9th Edition, Clinical Modification (ICD-9-CM), Volumes 1 and 2*
b. *International Classification of Diseases, 9th Edition, Clinical Modification, Volume 3, Procedures*
c. *National Drug Codes (NDC)*
d. *Code on Dental Procedures and Nomenclature (CDT)*
e. The combination of *Health Care Common Procedure Coding System (HCPCS)* and *Current Procedural Terminology© (CPT)*

(Standards for electronic transactions, 2000)

On January 16, 2009, the U.S. Department of Health and Human Services (HHS) published a Final Rule for the adoption of **ICD-10-CM** and **ICD-10-PCS** code sets to replace the ICD-9-CM code sets required by HIPAA (DHHS, 2009). The compliance date for adoption is October 1, 2013 (Moynihan, 2010). Both of these systems offer greater detail and more current terminology than does ICD-9-CM. ICD-10-CM and ICD-10-PCS also provide greater capacity for future expansion. Furthermore, ICD-10-CM is compatible with ICD-10, the World Health Organization's classification system, which is used by most other countries. In order to accommodate the transition to ICD-10-CM/PCS, DHHS also mandated plans and providers to upgrade transaction standards for processing electronic claims by January 2012 (Moynihan, 2010; Administrative requirements, 2009).

As long-standing advocates for confidentiality of patient information, health information managers also play a key role in the implementation and enforcement of the HIPAA privacy rule. The privacy rule established regulations for handling **protected health information (PHI)**, which is any individually identifiable health information.

The privacy rule is quite complex, and only a brief overview of HIPAA privacy is provided here. (The complete rule and other educational materials are available at the CMS Web site, http://www.cms.gov.) The privacy rule describes how PHI, whether in paper or electronic form, may be used or disclosed. In general, an authorization from the patient or legal representative is required for use or disclosure of PHI. The authorization must contain certain core elements, such as a description of the information to be used or disclosed, who is authorized to make the disclosure, to whom the covered entity may make the requested use or disclosure, the purpose of the requested use or disclosure, an expiration date or event, and the signature of the individual and date. The authorization must also contain certain required statements, such as the individual's right to revoke the authorization in writing. However, a covered entity is permitted to use or disclose PHI for treatment, payment, or health care operations (TPO), within the definitions of the regulation, without a specific authorization for each use or disclosure. HIPAA also requires that each covered entity provide its patients with a written notice of privacy practices (NPP) that explains how the covered entity might use or disclose the individual's health information. The NPP also must contain certain required elements and statements. Additionally, the privacy rule explains how the individual may restrict uses and disclosures of PHI as well as the individual's right to access or amend PHI. The HITECH Act extends a consumer's right to restrict disclosures under certain conditions (Rhodes & Rode, 2010). Furthermore, an individual has a right to receive an accounting of disclosures of PHI made by a covered entity in the six years before the date on which the accounting is requested, with exceptions for certain types of disclosures made for TPO. However, HITECH specifies that if a covered entity or business associate utilizes an electronic health record (EHR), patients have the right to receive a full account of all disclosures made (including those for TPO) during the three years prior to the date of request. In addition, HITECH obligates CEs maintaining EHRs to provide the requesting parties with an electronic copy of their PHI or, at the direction of the requestor, transmit an electronic copy to a designated party (Dennis, 2010).

Whereas the privacy rule protects PHI in both paper and electronic formats, the purpose of the security rule is to protect PHI that is maintained in electronic form. Each covered entity must analyze its systems for the electronic maintenance and transmission of PHI to identify and correct security risks. Security risks can be anything from unauthorized "hacking" of information systems to damage caused by natural disasters. There are some required elements in the security standards, but some of the implementation specifications are stated to be "addressable." For addressable implementation specifications, the covered entity must describe how it will implement the required standards in a manner that is appropriate for the environment of the facility (Amatayakul, 2003). To minimize security risks, system users need to be identified and properly authenticated, audit trails and logs should be maintained and reviewed, appropriate backup systems should be in place, the members of the workforce should be educated about system security, and so on. The American Health Information Management Association (AHIMA) and the Healthcare Information and Management Systems Society (HIMSS) are good sources of information for health information managers with regard to HIPAA security issues. (See the Key Resources section at the end of the chapter for AHIMA and HIMSS contact information and Web sites.) HITECH also requires business associates and certain noncovered entities to comply with certain administrative, physical, and technical safeguards described in the security regulations (Dennis, 2010). Figure 1-2 lists

TITLE 45–PUBLIC WELFARE

Subtitle A–Department of Health and Human Services
Part 164–Security and Privacy

164.306	Security standards: General rules.
164.308	Administrative safeguards.
164.310	Physical safeguards.
164.312	Technical safeguards.
164.314	Organizational requirements.
164.316	Policies and procedures and documentation requirements.
164.318	Compliance dates for the initial implementation of the security standards.
Appendix	Appendix A to Subpart C—Security Standards: Matrix
164.404	Notification to individuals.
164.406	Notification to the media.
164.408	Notification to the Secretary.
164.410	Notification by a business associate.
164.412	Law enforcement delay.
164.414	Administrative requirements and burden of proof.
164.502	Uses and disclosures of protected health information: General rules.
164.504	Uses and disclosures: Organizational requirements.
164.506	Uses and disclosures to carry out treatment, payment, or health care operations.
164.508	Uses and disclosures for which an authorization is required.
164.510	Uses and disclosures requiring an opportunity for the individual to agree or to object.
164.512	Uses and disclosures for which an authorization or opportunity to agree or object is not required.
164.514	Other requirements relating to uses and disclosures of protected health information.
164.520	Notice of privacy practices for protected health information.
164.522	Rights to request privacy protection for protected health information.
164.524	Access of individuals to protected health information.
164.526	Amendment of protected health information.
164.528	Accounting of disclosures of protected health information.

FIGURE **1-2** Selected section titles (not exhaustive) of regulations implementing the HIPAA security and privacy rules, including the breach notification requirements added by HITECH in 2009.

Source: Security and privacy. *Code of Federal Regulations*, Title 45, Subtitle A, Part 164, 2009 ed.

selected sections of the security and privacy rule, including sections amended by HITECH, such as the breach notification rules, which specify when individual patients, the media, and the Secretary of HHS must be notified of security breaches.

Accreditation Issues Affecting Health Care

Health care organizations generally must be licensed by the state. **Licensure** is a governmental process that requires that a facility meet certain regulations set by the state in order to provide care. Many health care organizations also choose to pursue **accreditation**, which is a voluntary process in which facilities agree to follow a set of standards and receive recognition for having met those standards. The health care settings described in this book may be accredited by a variety of organizations, whose accreditation standards are regularly updated and whose accreditation processes may also change. Health information managers play an important role in the accreditation process and should stay up to date regarding the latest information from the organizations that accredit their facilities. Table 1-2 provides an overview of the settings covered in this textbook and some of the accrediting organizations for each setting. Contact information for these organizations is listed in the Key Resources section of the appropriate chapters.

Other Regulatory Issues Affecting Health Care

Many health care settings are also affected by federal regulations known as Conditions of Participation or Conditions for Coverage. Health care organizations that want to "participate" in federal programs must be **Medicare certified**, which means they have demonstrated that they meet the standards set forth in the relevant Conditions of Participation/Coverage. Routine surveys to determine whether health care organizations meet these standards are conducted by the designated **state agency** for each state. In addition to administering the federal requirements for participation in Medicare and Medicaid programs, the state agency ordinarily administers applicable state licensure requirements as well. Because the state agency conducts its surveys in accordance with federal guidelines, CMS publishes detailed instructions for state surveyors in its *State Operations Manual (SOM)*. The appendices to the *SOM* contain survey forms and other instructions specific to each setting that health information managers may find helpful (see Figure 1-3).

The federal government has granted "deeming" authority to certain voluntary accrediting organizations for some of their programs. This means that a health care provider who is accredited by such an organization is "deemed" to meet the Conditions of Participation and does not have to undergo a separate survey process by the state agency. This concept is known as **deemed status**. However, for many of the health care settings described in this book, deemed status is not available, meaning that if these facilities choose voluntary accreditation, they are still required to undergo regular surveys by the state agency as well. (See the Web Activity section at the end of the chapter to locate one accrediting organization's list of deemed status options.)

TABLE **1-2**
Health Care Settings and Examples of Relevant Voluntary Accrediting Organizations
(Note: This list is not exhaustive.)

Chapters	Setting	Organizations
2	Hospital-Based Care	American Osteopathic Association
		DNV Healthcare (National Integrated Accreditation for Healthcare Organizations)
		The Joint Commission
3	Freestanding Ambulatory Care	Accreditation Association for Ambulatory Health Care
		Commission for the Accreditation of Birth Centers
		The Joint Commission
		American Association for Accreditation of Ambulatory Surgery Facilities
4	Managed Care	Accreditation Association for Ambulatory Health Care
		The Joint Commission
		National Committee for Quality Assurance
6	Correctional Facilities	American Correctional Association
		The Joint Commission
		National Commission on Correctional Health Care
7 and 8	Mental Health and Substance Abuse	Commission on Accreditation of Rehabilitation Facilities
		The Joint Commission
9	Facilities for Individuals with Intellectual or Developmental Disabilities	Commission on Accreditation of Rehabilitation Facilities
		Council on Quality and Leadership
		The Joint Commission
10	Long-Term Care	The Joint Commission
11	Rehabilitation Facilities	Commission on Accreditation of Rehabilitation Facilities
		The Joint Commission
12	Home Health Care	Community Health Accreditation Program
		The Joint Commission
		Accreditation Commission for Health Care, Inc.
13	Hospice	Community Health Accreditation Program
		The Joint Commission
		Accreditation Commission for Health Care, Inc.
15	Veterinary	American Animal Hospital Association

APPENDICES

Appendix	Description
A	Hospitals
AA	Psychiatric Hospitals
B	Home Health Agencies
C	Laboratories and Laboratory Services
D	Portable X-ray Service
E	Outpatient Physical Therapy or Speech Pathology Services–Interpretive Guidelines
G	Rural Health Clinics (RHCs)
H	End-Stage Renal Disease Facilities
I	Life Safety Code
J	Intermediate Care Facilities for Persons with Mental Retardation
K	Comprehensive Outpatient Rehabilitation Facilities
L	Ambulatory Surgical Services Interpretive Guidelines and Survey Procedures
M	Hospice
P	Survey Protocol for Long-term Care Facilities
PP	Interpretive Guidelines for Long-term Care Facilities
Q	Determining Immediate Jeopardy
R	Resident Assessment Instrument for Long-term Care Facilities
T	Swing-Beds
U	Responsibilities of Medicare Participating Religious Nonmedical Healthcare Institutions
V	Responsibilities of Medicare Participating Hospitals in Emergency Cases
W	Critical Access Hospitals (CAHs)

FIGURE **1-3** State Operations Manual.

The Impact of Quality on Health Care

A series of reports published by the **Institute of Medicine** in the early twenty-first century highlighted the prevalence of medical errors and the importance of improving patient safety (Institute of Medicine, 1999, 2001, 2003). This heightened awareness triggered a number of initiatives focused upon improving the quality of care delivered in the United States. In 2002, the Joint Commission created a **National Patient Safety Goals (NPSG)** program to help accredited health care institutions focus upon specific patient safety concerns (Joint Commission, 2009). In 2005, Congress enacted the Patient Safety and

Quality Improvement Act. The final rule was subsequently passed in 2008 and became effective in January 2009. The Act created a voluntary program to promote the sharing of patient safety event information with **patient safety organizations (PSOs)**. Health and Human Services will aggregate and de-identify the data in order to uncover trends and patterns in patient safety (Viola, Kallem, & Bronnert, 2009).

The **National Quality Forum (NQF)**, a private, not-for-profit organization focused on improving quality through development and endorsement of performance measurement, collaborated with CMS to develop measures for the Physician Quality Reporting Initiative (PQRI). Through a contract with the U.S. Department of Health and Human Services, NQF continues to provide support for improved quality of health care services (Zeman, 2010). Several additional pieces of legislation were subsequently passed that stress the urgency of reducing medical errors, as well as improving the efficiency and efficacy of care. The Medicare Prescription Drug, Improvement, and Modernization Act of 2003 (MMA), the American Recovery and Reinvestment Act of 2009 (ARRA), and the **Patient Protection and Affordable Care Act (PPACA or Health Reform)** call for increased reporting of quality measures by health care providers. Furthermore, each emphasizes the potential role that health information technology and electronic health records may play in reducing preventable medical errors.

Technological Changes Affecting Health Care

Fragmented health records can lead to medical errors, duplicate testing, and increased costs. It is estimated that **electronic health records (EHRs)** can improve patient care, reduce medical errors, and provide simultaneous access to patient data, greater security, improved legibility, better communication, and more complete documentation (Shekelle, Morton, & Keeler, 2006; Institute of Medicine, 1991, 1997). Because patients are treated in a variety of settings, health care professionals have recognized the need for a **longitudinal patient record** that would maintain health care information throughout the patient's life. Within a given enterprise (which can range from a single facility to a complex integrated health care delivery system), electronic data can be stored in a clinical data repository (CDR). Access to the data in the CDR can be structured to provide clinicians with a view of the patient's data over time through a single point of entry (Soule, 2001). Although this technology produces a longitudinal view of data within the enterprise, lack of data from providers outside the enterprise prevents such a system from maintaining a complete lifetime view of patient data. Groups ranging from the Institute of Medicine to the U.S. General Accounting Office have emphasized improvements in the quality of patient care, patient safety, and cost savings that could be achieved through the implementation of information technology. The ultimate information technology goal for many health care organizations is to achieve an electronic health record (EHR) that goes beyond merely storing and retrieving data in a repository. EHRs that include capabilities such as generating clinical alerts and reminders and furnishing readily available decision support can provide patient care benefits in all health care settings.

The IOM first called for adoption of electronic health records in 1991 in its landmark publication, *The Computer-Based Patient Record: An Essential Technology for Health Care* (Institute of Medicine, 1991). The Institute's subsequent reports (1999, 2001, 2003) addressing patient safety concerns prompted the federal government to launch a **health information technology (HIT)** adoption initiative in 2004 that envisioned electronic health records (EHRs) for all Americans by the year 2014. The **Office of the National Coordinator for Health Information Technology (ONC)** was subsequently established in 2005 to promote HIT adoption and guide the development of a **Nationwide Health Information Network (NHIN)**. Using a shared architecture, the network will facilitate interoperable standards for health information exchange (HIE) of data and communication among health care providers, payers, government, and consumers (Amatayakul, 2009).

In 2009, the American Recovery and Reinvestment Act (ARRA) was passed, which included numerous programs and incentives promoting HIT adoption. Title XII of ARRA, subtitled *Health Information Technology for Economic and Clinical Health Act (HITECH)*, contains many of the provisions required to advance development of the NHIN and health information exchange. In addition to the HIT adoption incentive program mentioned previously, ARRA provided billions of dollars to fund health IT, standards development initiatives, training and workforce development, broadband expansion, and additional requirements for health information exchange (Blumenthal, 2010).

Health information exchange (HIE) is a process that has been defined as "the electronic movement of health-related information among organizations according to nationally recognized standards" (NAHIT, 2008, p. 6). An **HIE organization** "oversees and governs the exchange of health-related information among organizations according to nationally recognized standards" (p. 6). This term has often been used synonymously with **regional health information organization (RHIO)**, which is a "health information organization that brings together health care stakeholders within a defined geographic area and governs health information exchange among them for the purpose of improving health and care in that community" (p. 6). ARRA allocated $564 million to support state programs in the development of HIE within their geographic regions. Furthermore, ARRA directed the ONC to establish up to 70 Health IT **Regional Extension Centers (RECs)** to provide technology assistance to health care providers in the adoption and meaningful use of HIT (Blumenthal, 2010; Dennis, 2010).

A key component of the NHIN is a focus on consumers, as patients today are more empowered and actively involved in their health care than ever before. Two technologies that enable consumers to track data related to their own health are personal health records (PHRs) and health record banks. According to the Markle Foundation, a **personal health record (PHR)** is "an Internet-based set of tools that allows people to access and coordinate their lifelong health information and make appropriate parts of it available to those who need it" (2003, p. 2). The Markle Foundation goes on to describe the following attributes of a PHR:

- Each person controls his or her own PHR. Individuals decide which parts of their PHR can be accessed, by whom, and for how long.
- PHRs contain information from one's entire lifetime.
- PHRs contain information from all health care providers.
- PHRs are accessible from any place at any time.
- PHRs are private and secure.
- PHRs are "transparent." Individuals can see who entered each piece of data, where it was transferred from, and who has viewed it.
- PHRs permit easy exchange of information with other health information systems and health professionals (2003, pp. 2–3).

Is there any relationship between an EHR and a PHR? An EHR can contribute toward a PHR in that some EHRs provide personal health record capabilities that allow patients to view their own information and to communicate with their health care providers (Soule, 2001).

The concept of **health record banking**, or health data banking, is relatively new to health care. It has been compared to financial banking, where the consumer has control over deposits and withdrawals (Wolter, 2007). Under this model, the patient may allow certain entities, such as hospitals or other providers, to access or deposit data in the account; therefore, multiple entities, in addition to the patient, would contribute to the contents of the bank account (Dolan & Wolter, 2008).

These technological advances offer expanded career opportunities to the health information management professional. Expertise in the areas of privacy, security, health care standards, and management of electronic health information will be required to achieve health information exchange.

Other Issues Affecting the Delivery of Health Care

Several other factors have contributed to the changes in health care delivery. For example, another change that is occurring in health care is a shift from independent institutions and practitioners to networks of health care providers. Hospitals, physicians, and other health care providers have joined together to provide the broad range of services necessary to meet the expectations of the various types of health care plans currently available.

Technological advances in care delivery have also had an important impact on health care services. As technology has improved, it has become possible to provide in other settings treatment that once required days or weeks of hospital inpatient care. Patients undergo procedures in ambulatory surgery centers and go home after a short (four- to six-hour) waiting period, thus avoiding costs associated with an overnight stay in a hospital. Other treatments once provided only in hospitals are now provided to patients at home, bringing health care practitioners and equipment to the patient's residence. With the advent of **telemedicine**, patients and clinicians separated by hundreds of miles can interact with one another by electronic means. In a telemedicine session, the patient is generally in a remote location from the physician, and medical information, which may include images and video, is transmitted back and forth between the two locations electronically (American Health Information Management Association, 1997). Use of technologies and devices to remotely monitor a patient's condition is referred to as **telehealth** (CMS, 2010c). **Telesurgery** involves use of robotic technology to assist with or perform procedures remotely (Sterbis et al., 2008). The advantages of using these technologies include "reduced costs, increased patient access to providers, improved quality and continuity of care, and more convenience to the patient" (Majerowicz & Tracy, 2010, p. 53). However, this technology presents new challenges in health information management with regard to confidentiality and security of information, maintenance of appropriate licensure and regulatory requirements, and reimbursement.

The **patient-centered medical home model** was developed in an effort to better coordinate care across the continuum. Under this model, the primary care physician acts as a "gatekeeper" to coordinate the patient's care across providers. It addresses preventive, acute, and chronic care needs (Dimick, 2008). The Patient Protection and Affordable Care Act (PPACA or Health Reform) calls for use of the medical home model and extension of telehealth services to improve health outcomes (Patient Protection and Affordable Care Act, 2010). The Health Reform Act also requires increased quality reporting requirements for health care providers, which will impact the health information manager's role.

In addition to technological trends, changes in society are affecting health care providers. The average age of the U.S. population is increasing, and a growing number of Americans are suffering from chronic diseases and illnesses associated with advancing age. Long-term care facilities, home health agencies, hospices, and dialysis facilities are important in caring for patients with chronic and sometimes terminal diseases. Both elderly and younger patients benefit from services provided by rehabilitation facilities and mental health services. Individuals with addictive behaviors can find help in substance abuse treatment facilities. The United States' large prison population creates a demand for health care services in correctional institutions. Good health information management practices are important in the care of all of these special populations.

IMPACT ON THE ROLE OF THE HEALTH INFORMATION MANAGER

Regulatory, technological, and social changes have affected the role of the health information manager. Although the profession of health information management (HIM) originated in the acute care hospital setting, the shift from inpatient to other care settings has expanded opportunities for health information managers beyond this traditional role. In the acute care setting, the skills of the health information manager are vital, because quality information is more important than ever to the hospital. In today's hospital, a health information manager is as likely to be found working in the emergency department coordinating the collection of trauma data as in the traditional

HIM departmental setting supervising records management processes. Responsibilities in the more traditional roles are also transitioning to management of a "virtual department." The electronic health record has removed the physical boundaries from the HIM department, allowing many employees to work from home or remote sites. Although many acute care facilities have reduced the ranks of middle managers, many excellent opportunities are still available in the acute care setting for those who possess the data analysis and information management skills to help a hospital thrive in this increasingly data-driven health care environment. However, the greatest growth in employment opportunities for health information managers is occurring outside the purely acute care setting.

As stated earlier, other issues affecting health care delivery, such as changing patient demographics and societal factors, have increased the number of persons needing certain types of health care services (e.g., long-term care, care in correctional facilities). Health information managers are currently being employed in an ever-widening array of health care facilities. Ambulatory care facilities, health maintenance organizations, home health care agencies, hospices, dialysis facilities, long-term care facilities, rehabilitation organizations, facilities for the intellectually or developmentally disabled, mental health facilities, treatment centers for substance abuse, correctional facilities, dental clinics, and veterinary clinics recognize the importance of the skills possessed by the health information manager. Health care providers in a wide variety of settings look to health information managers for expertise, as employees or as consultants. Resources for HIM professionals interested in developing and maintaining skills in diverse practice arenas may be found in the communities of practice (CoPs) sponsored by AHIMA. The CoPs provide a forum for information sharing among health information professionals with specialized interests. The communities are dynamic—new communities may be created and inactive communities may be dissolved in response to the needs of the participants. AHIMA members can access the CoPs at AHIMA's Web site. (See the Key Resources section at the end of the chapter.)

The knowledge and talents of health information managers will continue to be important in the vast assortment of individual provider settings and to the health care system as a whole in light of the growing need for high-quality patient information that is accessible in a secure and confidential manner within and across settings.

SUMMARY

Health care in the United States underwent drastic changes in the twentieth century that have continued into the new millennium. The hospital industry flourished as medical science and technology made strides in the improvement of patient care. As health care costs increasingly became a public concern, the health care field became more diverse, with a much broader range of care settings available to the patient.

Changes in the health care field have affected the profession of health information management, adding more opportunities. The health information manager's skills in data collection, retrieval, analysis, and reporting, as well as technical skills in information technology, which have long been appreciated in the inpatient setting, are now needed and valued in other settings. Changes in reimbursement methodologies, the regulatory environment, patient care delivery, information technology, relationships among health care providers, and in society in general have affected health care and the role of the health information manager. The result has been that additional employment and consulting opportunities are available to health information managers today that did not exist in the past.

KEY TERMS

accreditation a voluntary process in which facilities agree to follow a set of standards and receive recognition for having met those standards.

administrative simplification provisions of the Health Insurance Portability and Accountability Act (HIPAA) that address standardization of electronic data interchange, privacy of health information, and security of health data.

American College of Surgeons (ACS) a professional organization founded in 1913 to "improve the quality of care for the surgical patient by setting high standards for surgical education and practice" (ACS, 2003, p. 1). In the early twentieth century, the ACS established a hospital standardization program that was the forerunner of today's accreditation organizations.

American Recovery and Reinvestment Act (ARRA) Also known as the "Stimulus Act" or the "Recovery Act," ARRA (Public Law 111-5) was enacted in 2009. Its main purpose was to create jobs and stimulate economic growth; however, it contains many provisions for health care, including billions of dollars for health information technology. Title XIII of ARRA was given a subtitle—Health Information Technology for Economic and Clinical Health Act (HITECH)—which addresses many of the health information and technology requirements, including Subpart D–Privacy.

business associate (BA) partner or contractor performing a job or service on behalf of a covered entity. The original HIPAA legislation required covered entities to have a business associate agreement with any organization that handled or encountered its PHI in order to perform the contracted work. BAs are also accountable for complying with certain provisions in the privacy and security regulations, as required by ARRA.

capitation a method of payment for health care in which the health care provider receives a monthly payment based on the number of persons the provider has agreed to treat, regardless of the number of persons actually treated or the amount of service rendered.

Centers for Medicare & Medicaid Services (CMS) a federal agency within the Department of Health and Human Services. Its main focus is to administer the Medicare and Medicaid programs. Formerly known as the Health Care Financing Administration (HCFA).

Children's Health Insurance Program (CHIP) Also known as Title XXI of the Balanced Budget Act of 1997, CHIP allows states to offer health insurance plans for children, up to age 19, who are not already insured. CHIP affords families who earn too much to qualify for Medicaid an opportunity to obtain health insurance for their children.

clinical documentation improvement (CDI) program a locally implemented program focused upon improving the quality of clinical documentation to "facilitate an accurate representation of health care services through complete and accurate reporting of diagnoses and procedures" (AHIMA, 2010a, ¶4). Accurate clinical documentation can positively affect reimbursement, severity of illness and mortality risk assessment, and reporting of quality and pay-for-performance measures.

covered entity (CE) under HIPAA, a health plan, a health care clearinghouse, or any health care provider that transmits health information in electronic form.

deemed status the status of a health care provider that is deemed to meet federal *Conditions of Participation* by virtue of accreditation by a federally approved voluntary accrediting organization. With deemed status, the health care provider's accreditation satisfies the *Conditions of Participation*; routine surveys by the state agency are unnecessary.

electronic health record (EHR) a system in which a health care provider maintains individual patient health records electronically. Fully developed EHRs include capabilities such as generating clinical alerts and reminders and providing readily available decision support.

fee-for-service a method of payment for health care in which the health care provider charges and is paid for each item of service provided.

Flexner Report a report published in 1910, examining the state of medical education in the United States and Canada. The Flexner Report resulted in sweeping changes in the way North American physicians were educated.

health information exchange (HIE) a process defined as "the electronic movement of health-related information among organizations according to nationally recognized standards" (NAHIT, 2008, p. 6). Contrast with HIE organization.

health information technology (HIT) electronic health records and related information systems to manage health care processes. The major focus of the HITECH Act of 2009 is to promote adoption of HIT in an effort to improve the quality, efficiency, and safety of health care delivery while reducing costs and minimizing medical errors.

Health Information Technology for Economic and Clinical Health Act (HITECH) The Health Information Technology for Economic and Clinical Health (HITECH) Act was enacted as part of the American Recovery and Reinvestment Act of 2009 to promote the adoption and meaningful use of health information technology. Subpart D amends the HIPAA privacy and security rules by introducing additional privacy regulations, breach notification rules, and stiffer civil and criminal penalties for security violations.

Health Insurance Portability and Accountability Act of 1996 (HIPAA) Also known as the Kassebaum-Kennedy Act, HIPAA provisions include the portability of health care benefits (for example, upon an individual change of employment), prevention of fraud and abuse in health care, and simplification of the electronic interchange of health care data, while improving the privacy and security of health information.

health record banking a concept analogous to online financial banking, where the patient controls access to the health record "account." Deposits and withdrawals may be made by authorized individuals. An alternative to a personal health record (PHR), while achieving similar goals.

HIE organization an entity that "oversees and governs the exchange of health-related information among organizations according to nationally recognized standards" (NAHIT, 2008, p. 6). Often used synonymously with regional health information organization

(RHIO), which focuses more on HIE within a specific region. Contrast with health information exchange, which is a process rather than an entity.

Hill-Burton Act the "Hospital Survey and Construction Act" enacted by Congress in 1946. This legislation provided federal money to determine the need for more hospitals and to pay for their construction. (Note: Facilities receiving Hill-Burton funds agreed to provide a reasonable volume of service to patients who are unable to pay, an obligation that is still monitored by the federal government today.)

Hospital Inpatient Quality Reporting (IQR) a national quality initiative implemented by CMS as required by the Medicare Prescription Drug, Improvement, and Modernization Act (MMA) of 2003. IQR requires hospitals to submit data for certain quality measures, which are made publically available to consumers via the Hospital Compare Web site. While program participation is voluntary, hospitals that do not participate receive a reduced Medicare Annual Payment Update.

Hospital Outpatient Quality Data Reporting Program (HOP QDRP) a national quality program implemented by CMS that is modeled after the Hospital Inpatient Quality Reporting (IQR) initiative. Hospitals must report data for standardized quality measures for outpatient hospital services, which are made publically available to consumers via the Hospital Compare Web site. Participation is required in order to receive the full annual update to the Outpatient Prospective Payment System (OPPS) payment rate.

ICD-10-CM the United States' clinical modification of the World Health Organization's diagnostic disease classification (International Classification of Diseases, 10th Revision, Clinical Modification). Effective October 1, 2013, ICD-10-CM is the diagnosis code set required by HIPAA.

ICD-10-PCS the United States' procedural coding system for inpatient, acute care settings (International Classification of Diseases, 10th Revision, Procedural Coding System). Effective October 1, 2013, ICD-10-PCS is the replacement for ICD-9-CM, volume 3, one of the original code sets required by HIPAA.

Institute of Medicine Health division of the National Academy of Sciences. It is an independent, nonprofit organization that serves as a national advisor on matters related to health improvement.

licensure a governmental process in which a facility must meet certain regulations, set by the state, in order to provide care.

longitudinal patient record a record documenting a patient's health status, conditions, and treatments throughout his or her life and across multiple facilities, providers, and health care encounters.

meaningful use a concept called for by ARRA. In order for health care providers to become eligible for reimbursement incentives and eventually avoid financial penalties through Medicare and Medicaid, they must demonstrate meaningful use of certified electronic health record (EHR) technology. On January 13, 2010, an interim final rule was published that specified an initial set of standards, implementation specifications, and certification criteria for electronic health record (EHR) technology. The concept refers to a set of criteria and measures, rather than a single definition, and is being implemented in three phases though a series of published rules.

Medicaid Title XIX of the 1965 Amendments to the Social Security Act, Medicaid is jointly funded by federal and state governments and provides medical assistance to lower-income individuals and families.

Medicaid Integrity Program (MIP) a national strategy created as a result of the Deficit Reduction Act of 2005 (Section 1936 of the

Social Security Act) to detect and prevent Medicaid fraud, waste, and abuse. It uses contracted reviewers to audit the accuracy of Medicaid payments made to health care providers.

Medicare Title XVIII of the 1965 Amendments to the Social Security Act, Medicare provides health benefits for Social Security recipients and other qualified individuals.

Medicare certification process in which a state agency determines that a health care organization meets the standards set forth in the relevant Conditions of Participation or Conditions of Coverage and is therefore eligible for participation in the Medicare program.

Medicare Prescription Drug, Improvement, and Modernization Act of 2003 (MMA) Also known as the Medicare Modernization Act, MMA made significant revisions to the Medicare program by calling for the creation of Part D, e-prescribing for prescription drug plans, revision of claims processing, and a Medicare payment recovery demonstration project that ultimately resulted in the Recovery Audit Contractor (RAC) initiative.

National Patient Safety Goals (NPSG) program created by the Joint Commission in 2002 to help accredited health care institutions focus upon specific patient safety concerns. In an effort to focus on the most critical patient safety issues, NPSGs are updated annually based upon review of literature and available databases.

National Quality Forum (NQF) a private, nonprofit, membership organization focused upon improving the quality of care through national goal setting, development and endorsement of performance measurement standards, and educational initiatives. NQF collaborated with CMS to develop measures for the Physician Quality Reporting Initiative (PQRI). Through a contract with the U.S. Department of Health and Human Services, NQF continues to provide support for improved quality of health care services.

Nationwide Health Information Network (NHIN) "a set of standards, services and policies that enable secure health information exchange over the Internet. The NHIN will provide a foundation for the exchange of health IT across diverse entities, within communities and across the country, helping to achieve the goals of the HITECH Act. This critical part of the national health IT agenda will enable health information to follow the consumer, be available for clinical decision making, and support appropriate use of health care information beyond direct patient care so as to improve population health." (DHHS, Health IT Web Site)

Office of the National Coordinator for Health Information Technology (ONC) "the principal Federal entity charged with coordination of nationwide efforts to implement and use the most advanced health information technology and the electronic exchange of health information. The position of National Coordinator was created in 2004, through an Executive Order, and legislatively mandated in the Health Information Technology for Economic and Clinical Health Act (HITECH Act) of 2009" (DHHS, Health IT Web Site).

patient-centered medical home model a care model in which the primary care physician acts as a "gatekeeper" to coordinate the patient's care across providers. It addresses preventive, acute, and chronic care needs and also provides patients with access to electronic tools such as provider-patient e-mail, online appointment scheduling applications, and electronic health record data. The Patient Protection and Affordable Care Act (PPACA or Health Reform) calls for use of the medical home model to improve health outcomes.

Patient Protection and Affordable Care Act (PPACA or Health Reform) A federal statute signed into law on March 23, 2010, as Public Law 111-148. PPACA contains a number of health care provisions, most notably an expansion of Medicaid eligibility requirements. The Health Reform Act also increases quality reporting requirements for health care providers.

patient safety organizations (PSOs) "organizations that can work with clinicians and health care organizations to identify, analyze, and reduce the risks and hazards associated with patient care" (AHRQ, Online). The Patient Safety and Quality Improvement Act of 2005 called for development of PSOs to help determine the root causes, risks, and harms of health care safety issues.

pay-for-performance (P4P) emerging incentive-based reimbursement programs that reward or penalize providers based upon their ability to meet preestablished quality and performance targets for delivery of health care services.

per diem per day. A per diem payment is a payment rendered to an institution based on the number of days of service provided.

personal health record (PHR) "an Internet-based set of tools that allows people to access and coordinate their lifelong health information and make appropriate parts of it available to those who need it" (Markle Foundation, 2003, p. 2).

Physician Quality Reporting Initiative (PQRI) voluntary, incentive-based quality reporting system for eligible professionals who report data on quality measures for covered professional services provided to Medicare beneficiaries. It was established as a requirement by the 2006 Tax Relief and Health Care Act (TRHCA) (P.L. 109-432) and is implemented yearly by CMS through an annual rule-making process; therefore, program requirements and measures may vary from year to year.

prospective payment system (PPS) a payment system in which payment levels for health care services are determined before the services are rendered. In a prospective payment system, the unit of payment is not based solely on the individual services provided, but on payment units that represent general groupings of patient encounters, hospital stays, or episodes of care.

protected health information (PHI) individually identifiable health information.

quality improvement organization (QIO) "private, mostly not-for-profit organizations, which are staffed by professionals, mostly doctors and other health care professionals, who are trained to review medical care and help beneficiaries with complaints about the quality of care and to implement improvements in the quality of care available throughout the spectrum of care. QIO contracts are three years in length, with each 3-year cycle referenced as an ordinal scope of work (SOW)." (CMS, 2010d)

Recovery Audit Contractor (RAC) a third-party entity working under the direction of CMS to detect improper Medicare payments through review of providers' medical records and Medicare claims data.

Regional Extension Center (RECs) Nonprofit organizations called for by ARRA and initially funded by federal grants to provide health information technology support to providers. RECs offer technical assistance, guidance, and support to help providers become meaningful users of certified electronic health record technology. An additional goal of the REC program is to create HIT jobs.

regional health information organization (RHIO) a "health information organization that brings together health care stakeholders within a defined geographic area and governs health information exchange among them for the purpose of improving health and care in that community" (NAHIT, 2008, p. 6). Often used synonymously with HIE organization, which is a broader term that encompasses the use of nationally recognized standards and is not limited by geographic boundaries.

state agency   the agency of the state government responsible for administering the federal requirements for participation in Medicare and Medicaid programs. The state agency is ordinarily also charged with administering applicable licensure requirements for the state.

telehealth   "such technologies as telephones, facsimile machines, electronic mail systems, and remote patient monitoring devices which are used to collect and transmit patient data for monitoring and interpretation" (CMS, 2010c).

telemedicine   the practice of medicine in which electronic signals are utilized to transmit clinical information from one site to another. Generally, the patient is in a remote location from the physician, and medical information, which may include images and video, is transmitted back and forth between the two locations electronically.

telesurgery   the use of robotic technology to assist with or perform procedures remotely.

Zone Program Integrity Contractor (ZPIC) program   program implemented by CMS to identify and investigate malicious fraudulent claims activity within Medicare's seven geographic regions (zones).

REVIEW QUESTIONS

Knowledge-Based Questions

1. What are some of the changes that have affected hospitals during the twentieth and twenty-first centuries?
2. How have payment issues affected health care delivery?
3. What is fee-for-service payment?
4. What is a per diem payment?
5. What is pay-for-performance?
6. As a general rule, what is the basis for payment in a health maintenance organization?
7. Explain the administrative simplification provisions of HIPAA.
8. What is the patient-centered medical home model?
9. What impact have the changes in health care had on the health information manager?
10. Into what health care settings other than hospitals have health information managers moved?

Critical Thinking Questions

1. How can the health information manager contribute to improved data quality in a variety of settings?
2. Describe common concerns with regard to health information management in health information exchange, telemedicine, and the longitudinal patient record.
3. Select a health care setting other than a hospital. What would you expect the similarities to be between the role of the health information manager in a hospital and in one of the other health care settings? What would you expect the differences to be?

WEB ACTIVITY

Visit the Joint Commission's Web site at http://www.jointcommission.org.

1. Search for a fact sheet on the "tracer methodology" used by surveyors in the Joint Commission site visit process. Describe how the tracer methodology works and what its impact might be on health information management.
2. Search for information on *deemed status*. Which Joint Commission programs offer federal deemed status options?

CASE STUDY

Kerry Kaiser, RHIA, is Getwell Hospital's HIPAA privacy officer and the chair of its HIPAA Compliance Committee. The committee is concerned with all aspects of HIPAA compliance, including transactions, privacy, and security.

1. What items might the committee's agenda include in each of these three areas?
2. Where might Kerry find resources to assist the committee in carrying out its duties?

REFERENCES AND SUGGESTED READINGS

Administrative Requirements, 45 C.F.R. pt. 162 (2009).

[AHRQ] Agency for Healthcare Research and Quality. *Patient Safety and Quality Improvement Act of 2005 (Patient Safety Act): An Overview.* [Online]. http://www.pso.ahrq.gov/regulations/regulations.htm [2010, May 31].

Amatayakul, M. (2003). Translating the language of security (HIPAA on the Job series). *Journal of the American Health Information Management Association, 74*(6), 16A–16D.

Amatayakul, M. K. (2009). *Electronic health records: A practical guide for professionals and organizations* (4th ed.). Chicago: American Health Information Management Association.

[ACS] American College of Surgeons. (2010, January 12). What is the American College of Surgeons? [Online]. http://www.facs.org/about/corppro.html [2010, June 3].

[AHIMA] American Health Information Management Association. (1997). *Issue: Telemedical Records.* [practice brief]. D. M. Fletcher (author). [From *Journal of the American Health Information Management Association, 68*(4).]

[AHIMA] American Health Information Management Association. (2010a). Practice brief: Guidance for clinical documentation improvement programs. *Journal of AHIMA, 81*(5), 45–50.

[AHIMA] American Health Information Management Association. (2010b). Meaningful use: Provider requirements. *Meaningful Use White Paper Series,* http://www.ahima.org/arra/documents/Paperno2-MeaningfulUse-ProviderRequirements.pdf [2010, May 12].

[AHIMA] American Health Information Management Association. (2010c). *Health Care Reform and Health IT Stimulus: ARRA and HITECH* [Online]. http://www.ahima.org/arra/ [2010, May 12].

Asmonga, D. (2009). ARRA opportunities and omissions: New legislation seeks to jumpstart health IT, but issues remain. *Journal of the American Health Information Management Association, 80*(5), 16–18.

Blumenthal, D. (2010). Launching HITECH. *New England Journal of Medicine, 362*(5), 382–385.

Casto, A. B., & Layman, E. (2009). *Principles of healthcare reimbursement* (2nd ed.). Chicago: AHIMA.

[CMS] Centers for Medicare & Medicaid Services. (2005). *Medicare program: General information* [Online]. http://www.cms.gov/MedicareGenInfo/ [2010, May 11].

[CMS] Centers for Medicare & Medicaid Services. (2006). *Comprehensive Medicaid integrity plan of the Medicaid Integrity Program* [Online]. http://www.cms.gov/DeficitReductionAct/Downloads/CMIP%20Initial%20July%202006.pdf [2010, May 11].

[CMS] Centers for Medicare & Medicaid Services. (2009a). Medicaid Integrity Program: General information [Online]. http://www.cms.gov/MedicaidIntegrityProgram/ [2010, May 11]

[CMS] Centers for Medicare & Medicaid Services. (2009b). Benefit integrity (Chapter 4). *Medicare Program Integrity Manual.* http://www.cms.gov/manuals/downloads/pim83c04.pdf [2010, May 29].

[CMS] Centers for Medicare & Medicaid Services. (2010a). *Inpatient psychiatric PPS, overview* [Online]. http://www.cms.gov/InpatientPsychFacilPPS/ [2010, May 25].

[CMS] Centers for Medicare & Medicaid Services. (2010b). *Quality improvement organizations* [Online]. http://www.cms.gov/QualityImprovementOrgs/ [2010, May 11].

[CMS] Centers for Medicare & Medicaid Services. (2010c). *Telemedicine and telehealth.* http://www.cms.gov/telemedicine/ [2010, May 25].

[CMS] Centers for Medicare & Medicaid Services. (2010d). *Quality improvement organizations.*

http://www.cms.gov/QualityImprovementOrgs/ [2010, May 29].

[CMS] Centers for Medicare & Medicaid Services. (2010e). *Children's Health Insurance Program (CHIP)* [Online]. http://www.cms.gov/ NationalCHIPPolicy/ [2010, June 2].

[CMS] Centers for Medicare & Medicaid Services. (2010f). *Medicare and you: 2010* [Online]. http://www.medicare.gov/publications/pubs/pdf/10050.pdf [2010, May 3].

[CMS] Centers for Medicare & Medicaid Services. (2010g). *Overview. Prospective payment systems–General information.* [Online]. http://www.cms.gov/ProspMedicareFeeSvcPmtGen [2010, June 3].

[CMS] Centers for Medicare & Medicaid Services. (2010h). *Physician fee schedule.* [Online]. http://www.cms.gov/PhysicianFeeSched/ [2010, June 3].

[CMS] Centers for Medicare & Medicaid Services. QualityNet. [Online]. http://www.qualitynet.org [2010, May 12].

Dennis, J. C. (2010). *Privacy: The impact of ARRA, HITECH, and other policy initiatives.* Chicago: AHIMA.

Dimick, C. (2008). Home sweet home: Can a new care model save family medicine? *Journal of the American Health Information Management Association, 79*(8), 24–8.

Dimick, C. (2010). The year of the audit. *Journal of the American Health Information Management Association, 81*(3), 22–25, 64.

Dolan, M., & Wolter, J. (2008, October). *Identification of different personal health record products and models for use in educating the consumer and HIM professional.* Paper presented at the AHIMA Convention, Seattle, WA.

Gentul, M. K., & Davis, N. A. (2007). Structure and organization of the coding function. In L. A. Schraffenberger & L. Kuehn (Eds.), *Effective management of coding services: The clinical coding manager's handbook* (pp. 3–47). Chicago: AHIMA.

Institute of Medicine. (1991). R. S. Dick & E. B. Steen (Eds.). *The computer-based patient record: An essential technology for health care.* Washington, DC: National Academy Press.

Institute of Medicine. (1997). R. S. Dick, E. B. Steen, & D. E. Detmer (Eds.). *The computer-based patient record: An essential technology for health care* (Rev. ed.). Washington, DC: National Academy Press.

Institute of Medicine. (1999). *To err is human: Building a safer health system.* Washington, DC: National Academy Press.

Institute of Medicine. (2001). *Crossing the quality chasm: A new health system for the 21st century.* Washington, DC: National Academy Press.

Institute of Medicine. (2003). *Patient safety: Achieving a new standard for care.* Washington, DC: National Academies Press.

Joint Commission. (2009). *Facts about the National Patient Safety Goals* [Online]. http://www.jointcommission.org/PatientSafety/NationalPatientSafetyGoals/npsg_facts.htm [2010, May 12].

Kaiser Permanente. (n.d.). *Kaiser Permanente: More than 60 years of quality* [Online]. http://xnet.kp.org/newscenter/aboutkp/historyofkp.html [2010, June 3].

Klees, B. S., Wolfe, C. J., & Curtis, C. A. (2009). *Brief summaries of Medicare & Medicaid: Title XVIII and Title XIX of the Social Security Act.* Baltimore: Centers for Medicare & Medicaid Services. [Online]. http://www.cms.gov/MedicareProgramRatesStats/Downloads/MedicareMedicaidSumMedica2009.pdf [2010, June 3].

Litman, T., & Robins, L. (1991). *Health politics and policy* (2nd ed.). Clifton Park, NY: Delmar Cengage Learning.

Majerowicz, A. & Tracy, S. (2010). Telemedicine: Bridging gaps in healthcare delivery. *Journal of the American Health Information Management Association, 81*(5): 52–53, 56.

Markle Foundation. (2003, July 1). *The personal health working group: Final report* [Online]. http://www.connectingforhealth.org/resources/final_phwg_report1.pdf [2010, June 3].

Moynihan, J. (2010). Preparing for 5010: Internal testing of HIPAA transaction upgrades recommended by December 31. *Journal of the American Health Information Management Association, 81*(1), 23–26.

[NAHIT] National Alliance for Health Information Technology. (2008, April 28). *Report to the Office of the National Coordinator on defining key health information technology terms* [Online]. http://healthit.hhs.gov/portal/server.pt/gateway/PTARGS_0_10741_848133_0_0_18/10_2_hit_terms.pdf [2010, May 14].

Patient Protection and Affordable Care Act of 2010, Pub. L. No. 111-148 (March 23, 2010).

Rhodes, H., & Rode, D. (2010). ARRA on the job: HIPAA too. *Journal of the American Health Information Management Association, 81*(1), 38–39.

Security and Privacy, 45 C.F.R. pt. 164 (2009).

Shekelle, P. G., Morton, S. C., & Keeler, E. B. (2006, April). *Costs and benefits of health information technology* (AHRQ Publication No. 06-E006). Rockville, MD: Agency for Healthcare Research and Quality.

Soule, D. (2001). What's new in clinical data repositories? *Journal of the American Health Information Management Association, 72*(10), 35–39.

Standards for Electronic Transactions. (2000, August 17). *Federal Register*, pp. 50311–50373.

Standards for Privacy of Individually Identifiable Health Information; Final Rule. (2000, December 28). *Federal Register*, pp. 82461–82829.

Sterbis, J. R., Hanly, E. J., Herman, B. C., Marohn, M. R., Broderick, T. J., Shih, S. P., Harnett, B., Doarn, C., & Schenkman, N. S. (2008). Transcontinental telesurgical nephrectomy using the da Vinci Robot in a porcine model. *Urology, 71*(5), 971–973.

[DHHS] U.S. Department of Health and Human Services. *Federal Register*. Vol. 74, No. 11. (January 16, 2009). 45 CFR pt. 162. HIPAA Administrative Simplification: Modifications to Medical Data Code Set Standards to Adopt ICD–10–CM and ICD–10–PCS Final rule [Online]. http://edocket.access.gpo.gov/2009/pdf/E9-743.pdf [2010, May 12].

[DHHS] U.S. Department of Health and Human Services. Health IT Web Site. [Online]. http://www.healthit.hhs.gov [2010, May 31].

[DHHS] U.S. Department of Health and Human Services. The official U.S. government site for Medicare. *Medicare Advantage (Part C)*. [Online]. http://www.medicare.gov/navigation/medicare-basics/medicare-benefits/part-c.aspx [2010, May 11].

Viola, A. F., Kallem, C., & Bronnert, J. (2009). A next act for patient safety: Previewing the Patient Safety and Quality Improvement Final Rule. *Journal of the American Health Information Management Association, 80*(4), 30–35.

Wolter, J. (2007). Health record banking: An emerging PHR model. *Journal of the American Health Information Management Association, 78*(9), 2–83.

Zeman, V. L. (2010). Clinical quality management. In K. M. LaTour & S. E. Maki (Eds.), *Health information management: Concepts, principles, and practice* (3rd ed., pp. 517–558). Chicago: AHIMA.

KEY RESOURCES

American College of Surgeons
http://www.facs.org

American Health Information Management Association
http://www.ahima.org

The Carnegie Foundation for the Advancement of Teaching
http://www.carnegiefoundation.org

Centers for Medicare & Medicaid Services (CMS)
http://www.cms.gov
For beneficiary questions about Medicare
http://www.medicare.gov

Code of Federal Regulations
http://www.gpoaccess.gov/cfr

Commission on Accreditation of Rehabilitation Facilities
http://www.carf.org

DNV Healthcare, Inc.
http://www.dnvaccreditation.com

Federal Register
http://www.gpoaccess.gov/fr

Healthcare Information and Management Systems Society (HIMSS)
http://www.himss.org

The Joint Commission
http://www.jointcommission.org

National Quality Forum
http://www.qualityforum.org

Office of the National Coordinator for Health Information Technology (ONC)

U.S. Department of Health and Human Services
http://healthit.hhs.gov

CHAPTER 2

Hospital-Based Care

ANGELA L. MOREY, MSM, RHIA

ANN H. PEDEN, PHD, RHIA, CCS

SONYA D. BEARD, MSED, RHIA

LEARNING OBJECTIVES

Upon successful completion of this chapter, you should be able to:

- Describe types of care provided by hospitals.

- Explain regulatory and accreditation standards that apply to hospital-based care.

- Discuss documentation issues in hospital-based care.

- Describe reimbursement methods for hospital-based care.

- Identify coding and classification systems used in hospital-based care.

- Describe data sets utilized for hospital-based care.

- Cite factors in avoiding legal risk in hospital-based care.

- Define roles of the health information management professional in hospital-based care.

Setting	Description	Synonyms
	Examples of Hospital Inpatient Settings	
Hospital Inpatient Unit	An organizational unit of a hospital providing room, board, and continuous general nursing service in an area of the hospital where patients generally stay overnight (Glondys, 2000)	Ward; Nursing Unit
Intensive Care Unit	"A hospital patient care unit for patients with life-threatening conditions who require intensive treatment and continuous monitoring" (Slee, Slee, & Schmidt, 2008, p. 305)	ICU
	Examples of Hospital Outpatient Settings	
Hospital Outpatient Unit	An organizational unit of a hospital providing health services to patients who are generally ambulatory and who are not currently inpatients (Glondys, 2000)	Outpatient Department
Hospital Outpatient Clinic	A type of hospital outpatient unit generally organized based on the clinical specialty of the care providers or the types of services needed by the patients (Glondys, 2000)	Clinic
Hospital Emergency Unit	An organizational unit providing medical services needed on an urgent or emergency basis (Glondys, 2000)	Emergency Department
Hospital Observation Unit	An organizational unit for monitoring unstable patients and assessing whether or not they require inpatient admission	Observation Services
Hospital Ambulatory Surgery Unit	An organizational unit for performing elective surgical procedures on patients who generally do not stay at the hospital overnight	Ambulatory Surgery Department
Partial Hospitalization Unit	An organizational unit providing services to behavioral health patients who spend part of the day or night in the hospital setting	Partial Hospitalization Services
	Hospital-Based Long-Term Acute Care	
Long-Term Acute Care Hospital	A facility providing specialized acute care for patients averaging a length of stay of 25 days or more	Long-Term Care Hospital LTAC, LTCH, or LTACH

INTRODUCTION TO SETTING

Hospitals provide a wide array of services in the twenty-first century. The role of the hospital has expanded from providing short-term acute care to providing many different types of care ranging from ambulatory services to long-term acute care. To discuss every possible type of hospital care could fill several volumes, so this chapter will focus on three basic types of care: hospital-based ambulatory care, hospital inpatient care, and long-term acute care.

Types of Settings

A hospital is a "healthcare institution that has an organized professional staff and medical staff, and inpatient facilities, and which provides medical, nursing, and related services" (Slee, Slee, & Schmidt, 2008, p. 270). According to the American Hospital Association (2010), a hospital must maintain at least six inpatient beds and care must be readily available for the patients who stay an average of 24 hours or more per admission. Health care services provided to patients in a hospital can be categorized as either inpatient (acute care) or outpatient (ambulatory care). Inpatient care is comprised of health care services, room and board, and continuous nursing care provided to a patient in a hospital unit. Outpatient care includes health care services provided in a hospital-based clinic or department that is not dedicated as an acute care unit (Odom-Wesley, 2009). Long-term acute care is provided in a hospital setting where the patient length of stay is 25 days or longer, on average.

Inpatient Short-term, Acute Care

Inpatient short-term acute care is the type of care generally associated with hospitals. Patients who are in need of around-the-clock acute care are admitted as hospital inpatients upon the order of a physician. Hospitals may be general hospitals or specialty hospitals that focus on certain types of services, illnesses, or specific types of patients (e.g., pediatric hospitals). Hospitals provide a comprehensive range of services to patients who are acutely ill. Patients are discharged when their conditions are stable and further recuperation can continue in a less acute setting. In U.S. hospitals in 2008, the average length of stay was 5.0 days (AHA, 2009).

Hospital-Based Ambulatory Care

Hospital-based **ambulatory surgery** began developing in hospitals during the 1970s and grew rapidly in subsequent years as advances in technology enabled health care providers to perform many types of surgery on an ambulatory basis that once could be performed only on an inpatient basis. In fact, certain surgical procedures are reimbursed by third-party payers only when performed in the ambulatory setting (unless a particular patient's condition makes ambulatory surgery unsafe) (Lawrence and Jonas, 1990).

Another type of ambulatory care that has existed in hospitals since the late 1800s is the hospital clinic. Early hospital clinics provided care for the poor and an educational experience for physicians-in-training. With the advent of Medicare and Medicaid, most clinic visits are now reimbursed, which was not always the case before the implementation of these federal programs (Lawrence & Jonas, 1990). Many hospitals still facilitate the teaching function of the clinics by organizing their clinics by medical specialty.

Emergency care is yet another type of ambulatory service provided by hospitals. Most hospitals have an organized emergency department providing a wide range of services. The emergency department may be staffed as a trauma center and be the first area in which an acutely ill patient is treated before hospitalization. However, most patients use the emergency department as an ambulatory care service. For example, a physician may see his or her private patients in the emergency department to evaluate an acute condition or trauma that occurs outside normal office hours. Other patients present themselves in the emergency department for treatment as outpatients when a primary care physician is not available to them (Lawrence & Jonas, 1990). Emergency department visits in the United States increased 32 percent between 1996 and 2006—from 90.3 million to 119.2 million (ACEP, n.d.).

One type of outpatient setting that very much resembles the inpatient setting is that of hospital **observation services**. Observation services may be provided in a regular inpatient unit or in a designated observation unit. According to Medicare, observation services are "furnished by a hospital on the hospital's premises, including use of a bed and periodic monitoring by a hospital's nursing or other staff, which are reasonable and necessary to evaluate an outpatient's condition or determine the need for a possible admission to the hospital as an inpatient" (CMS, 2003a, §230.6A). The physician should make a determination whether the patient meets criteria for admission as an inpatient within a 24-hour time frame. Some payers have strict rules limiting observation care to 23 hours and 59 minutes, whereas other payers have no strictly enforced limits on observation care. If an observation patient is not admitted to inpatient status, arrangements are made for care in another setting, the patient is discharged or transferred, and the stay is counted and billed as an outpatient encounter.

A **partial hospitalization program (PHP)** is also considered to be a type of hospital outpatient program. Medicare defines partial hospitalization as "a distinct and organized intensive treatment program for patients who would otherwise require inpatient psychiatric care" (CMS, 2003a, §230.5C). In a partial hospitalization program, the patient may receive a variety of services such as individual or group therapy; occupational therapy; diagnostic services; services of social workers, psychiatric nurses, and other staff; along with other types of services (CMS, 2003a). The patient receives services for a substantial number of hours each day but is not present at the hospital on a 24-hour basis.

Finally, many settings in the hospital that provide services to inpatients also provide services to outpatients. For example, hospital ancillary services, such as the hospital laboratory or the radiology department, may perform tests on hospital outpatients as well as inpatients.

Long-term Acute Care

Long-term acute care represents another type of hospital setting. A long-term care hospital (LTCH) can be either a freestanding facility or a "hospital within a hospital." In the 1980s, the Medicare program defined the characteristics of LTCH facilities and exempted them from the original hospital inpatient PPS. By the year 1997, there were 195 LTCHs in the United States, and by 2007 the number had grown to 396—more than doubling in a 10-year period (MedPAC, 2009). A specialized PPS for LTCHs has been in place since the year 2002 (CMS, 2002f). The LTCH PPS will be discussed later in this chapter.

Types of Patients

Hospital patients come from every walk of life and are treated for a wide range of conditions, whether as inpatients, outpatients, or long-term acute care patients.

Hospital Inpatients

Hospital inpatients are acutely ill individuals who are treated in an area of the hospital where patients generally stay overnight (Glondys, 2000). A patient may be admitted for a medical condition that can be managed without surgical intervention, or the patient's condition may require surgery. Depending on the size and complexity of the hospital, different types of inpatients may be cared for in designated units (cardiology, orthopedics, and so on.) Critically ill inpatients may be cared for in an intensive care unit.

Hospital Outpatients

Both acute and chronic illnesses can be treated on an ambulatory basis. The following classification of patients is based on the types of services the patients receive rather than on characteristics of the patients themselves (Hanken & Waters, 1994). In general, a **hospital outpatient** is a patient who is evaluated or treated at a hospital facility but is not admitted as an inpatient. Examples of various categories of hospital outpatients:

- **Clinic outpatient:** an outpatient treated in an organized clinic of the hospital in which hospital staff evaluate the patient and manage the patient's care
- **Referred hospital outpatient:** an outpatient who is referred to the hospital for specific services, such as laboratory or radiology examinations. The hospital is responsible only for providing the diagnostic or therapeutic services requested, while the referring physician is responsible for evaluating and managing the patient's care. A related term is *reference laboratory services*, which is used to describe laboratory services performed for other providers. (Note that the term *referral* carries a different meaning when one physician "refers" a patient to another physician. In a physician-to-physician referral, responsibility for evaluating and managing the patient's care is often transferred from the referring to the receiving physician.)
- **Emergency outpatient:** an outpatient evaluated and treated in the emergency department of the hospital

Long-Term Acute Care Hospital Patients

Patients admitted to a long-term care hospital (LTCH) are generally more acutely ill than patients in other long-term care settings. In fact, patients are often admitted to the LTCH directly from a short-stay hospital intensive care unit. Their medical conditions are complex (e.g., respiratory conditions with ventilator dependence), and they require more acute-type services such as cancer treatment, head trauma treatment, and pain management. Comprehensive rehabilitation is also a common service provided to LTCH patients. As opposed to that of a short-stay acute care hospital, the average length of stay in an LTCH is 25 days or more (Liu et al., 2001; ALTHA, n.d.).

Types of Caregivers

Just as there are many different types of hospital patients, there are many different types of caregivers who participate in hospital care. Physicians from every specialty see hospital patients on both an inpatient and an outpatient basis. Nurses provide nursing care to both inpatients and outpatients. Other health professionals, such as physical therapists, occupational therapists, clinical laboratory scientists, and pharmacists—to name only a few—may provide diagnostic or therapeutic services to hospital patients.

In the typical inpatient acute care area of the hospital, physicians visit their patients daily to manage their care. This daily physician visit pattern is also generally found in LTCHs. In other areas of the hospital, such as the hospital emergency department, physicians are generally on duty 24 hours a day. Often, specialty certifications are necessary for physicians and other caregivers in specialized hospital areas. For example, caregivers in the emergency department have usually received specialized training and certification in basic and advanced life support.

One type of caregiver that is unique to the hospital setting is the **hospitalist**. A hospitalist is a physician who provides comprehensive care to hospitalized patients but who does not ordinarily see patients outside of the hospital setting. The hospitalist communicates with the patient's primary care physician during the hospital stay and returns the patient to the primary physician's care after the patient is discharged. The advantage to the patient is that the hospitalist is a specialist in dealing with conditions that require hospitalization and is not distracted by the duties of seeing patients in the clinic setting. The number of hospitalists in the U.S. was estimated to be about 1,000 in 1996, but that number had grown to over 23,000 by 2007. This number is expected to increase as more hospitals continue to add hospitalist programs (New study finds over half of U.S. hospitals utilize hospitalists, 2009).

REGULATORY ISSUES

Licensure

Hospitals must be licensed by the state in which they are located. Licensure requirements vary from state to state. In some states, meeting federal standards or the standards of a voluntary accrediting agency largely fulfills licensing requirements. To obtain the licensure requirements for hospitals in a given state, a health information manager would contact the agency in that state responsible for licensure of hospitals. Often, licensure requirements are available at the state agency's Web site.

Federal Regulations

To be eligible to receive payment from Medicare, hospitals must meet the federal requirements contained in the Conditions of Participation for Hospitals (2009) or be "deemed" to meet these requirements by virtue of voluntary accreditation by an approved agency. Accreditation by the Joint Commission (TJC), the Healthcare Facilities Accreditation Program (HFAP) of the American Osteopathic Association (AOA), or the National Integrated Accreditation of Healthcare Organizations (NIAHO) program of DNV Healthcare, Inc. provides "deemed" status for hospitals with regard to the Conditions of Participation.

To meet federal program requirements, each state's own certifying agency surveys nonaccredited hospitals, comparing their practices to standards in the Conditions of Participation for Hospitals. In addition, both state-surveyed and voluntarily accredited hospitals may be randomly selected for validation surveys conducted by the Centers for Medicare & Medicaid Services (CMS).

Accreditation

Hospitals voluntarily seek accreditation to demonstrate to their patients, to their communities, to insurers, to managed care organizations, and to others that their organizations are providing quality care. As previously mentioned, the Joint Commission, the AOA's Healthcare Facilities Accreditation Program (HFAP), and DNV Healthcare's NIAHO program offer voluntary accrediting programs whose standards and survey processes are "deemed" to be in compliance with the federal Conditions of Participation. The majority of U.S. hospitals are accredited by the Joint Commission. Of the three accrediting programs with deeming authority (TJC, HFAP, and NIAHO), the most recent addition is the NIAHO, a program of DNV Healthcare, Inc., an international organization originating in Norway. CMS granted DNV deeming authority in 2008 (DNV, 2010). The DNV approach is based on a combination of the ISO 9001 quality management protocols and the Conditions of Participation for Hospitals (Dowling, 2008). Both the Joint Commission and HFAP perform on-site surveys every three years, whereas DNV performs an annual on-site survey.

DOCUMENTATION

The fundamentals of good patient documentation are essential in the hospital setting. Good documentation is important not only to meet accrediting and regulatory guidelines, but also to provide high-quality care and to demonstrate the appropriateness of payments to the hospital. The extent of documentation in a hospital record will depend in part on the type of services received. For example, the records of a surgery patient, whether ambulatory surgery or inpatient surgery, typically include the following documents:

- a history and physical examination report
- an operation report
- anesthesia records
- postoperative recovery notes
- pathology reports (when appropriate)

Another example of how the nature of the service affects the documentation is the extensive and detailed documentation that is needed for patients treated in critical care units. On the other hand, some hospital records, such as those of referred outpatients, contain minimal information that sometimes consists of a set of orders and test results. However, because there must be a physician order documented for every test the hospital performs, even these records are frequently audited by third-party payers. Another important documentation element that must be obtained from the physician when a test is ordered is clinical information that describes the reason for the test. Without information on the diagnoses or symptoms that prompted the physician to order the test, the hospital lacks the information needed to demonstrate that the test was medically necessary and risks losing reimbursement.

Joint Commission Documentation Requirements

As the body that surveys most hospitals, the Joint Commission's standards regarding documentation merit attention. The Joint Commission has transitioned itself to accommodate the changes in health care that have taken place since the turn of the century. The Information Management (IM) standards for hospitals have been updated to reflect those changes and are outlined below (Joint Commission, 2010).

- Management of information
- Continuity of information management processes
- Privacy of health information
- Security and integrity of health information
- Management of the collection of health information (i.e., data sets)
- Retrieval, dissemination, and transmission of health information in usable formats

Although many of the standards that have a direct impact on health information and health information services are found in the Information Management (IM) section, several other relevant Joint Commission standards are found in the Record of Care, Treatment, and Services (RC) and the Provision of Care, Treatment, and Services (PC) sections. To outline all of the Joint Commission's documentation standards is beyond the scope of this chapter. Instead, the chapter will demonstrate how a health information manager could review the standards to locate those relevant to a particular purpose. For example, standard RC.02.01.03, "The patient's medical record documents operative or other high-risk procedures and the use of moderate or deep sedation or anesthesia" (Joint Commission, 2010, p. 411), would be relevant in assessing documentation for surgical cases. Elements of performance (EPs) for this standard deal with the following issues, to name a few:

- Documentation of a preoperative or provisional diagnosis before surgery by the licensed independent practitioner responsible for the patient
- Medical history and physical examination recorded in the medical record before a procedure is performed
- Operative reports dictated or written upon completion of the procedure and before the patient is transferred to the next level of care

- Operative reports include the name of the practitioner performing the procedure and assistants, the name and description of procedure, findings, estimated blood loss, specimens removed, and the postoperative diagnosis
- When the operative report is not placed in the medical record immediately after surgery, a progress note is entered before the patient is transferred to the next level of care

A second example may be found in the standards that the Joint Commission has established for documentation in the records of patients receiving "continuing ambulatory care services," such as clinic outpatients. As required by standard RC.02.01.07, "The medical record contains a summary list for each patient who receives continuing ambulatory care services" (Joint Commission, 2010, p. 417). This summary list must be initiated for the patient by the third visit and should include lists of

- Significant medical diagnoses and conditions
- Significant operative and invasive procedures
- Adverse and allergic drug reactions
- Current medications, over-the-counter medications, and herbal preparations

The summary list should also be updated when there are changes in diagnoses, medications, or allergies to medications and whenever a procedure is performed. The summary list must also be "readily available to practitioners who need access to the information of patients who receive continuing ambulatory care services in order to provide care, treatment, and services" (Joint Commission, 2010, p. 418). Although the description of the summary list brings to mind a form bound in the front of a paper record, this information is often maintained in electronic format. Figure 2-1 depicts how the data required to meet this standard might be collected. Other information that the hospital clinic needs to make readily available may also be collected and displayed, such as immunization records for pediatric patients.

A third example of service-specific documentation requirements comes from the Joint Commission standards that pertain to records of emergency patients. Some of the documentation requirements specific to patients receiving urgent or immediate care are found under standard RC.02.01.01 as follows (Joint Commission, 2010):

- When emergency, urgent, or immediate care is provided, the time and means of arrival are also documented in the medical record.
- The medical record notes when a patient receiving emergency, urgent, or immediate care left against medical advice.
- The medical record of a patient receiving emergency, urgent, or immediate care notes the conclusions at termination of treatment, including final disposition, condition at discharge, and instructions for follow-up care.
- The medical record contains a copy of the information made available to practitioners or organizations providing follow-up care.

YOURTOWN HOSPITAL
YOURTOWN, USA
AMBULATORY SUMMARY LIST

<Patient Identification>

SIGNIFICANT MEDICAL DIAGNOSES AND CONDITIONS

SIGNIFICANT OPERATIVE/INVASIVE PROCEDURES

DATE	DIAGNOSES/CONDITIONS	DATE	PROCEDURES

ALLERGIES AND ADVERSE DRUG REACTIONS

DATE	ALLERGY	DATE	ALLERGY	DATE	ALLERGY

MEDICATIONS, INCLUDING OVER-THE-COUNTER AND HERBAL PREPARATIONS

DATE	MEDICATION	DATE	MEDICATION

FIGURE **2-1** Sample summary list form for ambulatory care patient records.

DATE	MEDICATION	DATE	MEDICATION

FIGURE **2-1** (*Continued*)

Other Factors in Hospital Documentation

Documentation in the hospital setting is also important because of the role it plays in determining the level of physician service provided. The level of service determines the appropriate code, which determines the physician's reimbursement. (Reimbursement to the *hospital* is discussed in the Reimbursement section of this chapter.) This issue is particularly important in teaching hospitals in which **residents**, as part of their graduate medical education, participate with teaching physicians in caring for patients. The *Code of Federal Regulations* contains the basic rules that regulate Medicare payments to teaching physicians (Physician services in teaching settings, 2009). How these rules are applied is explained in the *Medicare Claims Processing Manual*, along with specific examples of acceptable and unacceptable documentation (CMS, 2009).

Most teaching hospitals pay residents a salary, to which Medicare contributes through indirect medical education allowances. In this situation, a professional service performed by a resident is not paid on a fee-for-service basis, but a teaching physician who is present during the service may bill Medicare. For evaluation and management services, the teaching physician's documentation must make it clear that the teaching physician was present during the key portion of the service and that the teaching physician evaluated and participated in the management of the patient. Merely countersigning the resident's note is insufficient documentation to justify payment (CMS, 2009a).

Figure 2-2 provides examples of Medicare's rules regarding fee payments for services of teaching physicians. These rules are excerpted from the *Code of Federal Regulations* and are relevant to a discussion of hospital-based care, because teaching physicians practice in teaching hospitals. They apply to documentation in Medicare records in all states, and in some states to Medicaid records also.

There is an "outpatient exception" to the rules provided in Figure 2-2. However, not all outpatient care falls under the outpatient exception, so the "general" rules will apply in those instances. Figure 2-3 provides another excerpt from the *Code of Federal Regulations* that explains the outpatient exception.

Section 415.172 Physician fee schedule payment for services of teaching physicians.

(a) General rule. If a resident participates in a service furnished in a teaching setting, physician fee schedule payment is made only if a teaching physician is present during the key portion of any service or procedure for which payment is sought.

(1) In the case of surgical, high-risk, or other complex procedures, the teaching physician must be present during all critical portions of the procedure and immediately available to furnish services during the entire service or procedure.

(i) In the case of surgery, the teaching physician's presence is not required during opening and closing of the surgical field.

(ii) In the case of procedures performed through an endoscope, the teaching physician must be present during the entire viewing.

(2) In the case of evaluation and management services, the teaching physician must be present during the portion of the service that determines the level of service billed. (However, in the case of evaluation and management services furnished in hospital outpatient departments and certain other ambulatory settings, the requirements of Section 415.174 apply.)

(b) Documentation. Except for services furnished as set forth in (the exceptions). . ., the medical records must document the teaching physician was present at the time the service is furnished. The presence of the teaching physician during procedures may be demonstrated by the notes in the medical records made by a physician, resident, or nurse. In the case of evaluation and management procedures, the teaching physician must personally document his or her participation in the service in the medical records. . . .

FIGURE **2-2** Examples of Medicare rules regarding fee payments for services of teaching physicians. (Excerpted from 42 CFR 415.172)

Section 415.174 Exception: Evaluation and management services furnished in certain centers.

(a) In the case of certain evaluation and management codes of lower and mid-level complexity . . . carriers may make physician fee schedule payment for a service furnished by a resident without the presence of a teaching physician. For the exception to apply, all of the following conditions must be met:

(1) The services must be furnished in a center that is located in an outpatient department of a hospital or another ambulatory care entity in which the time spent by residents in patient care activities is included in determining intermediary payments to a hospital. . . .

(2) Any resident furnishing the service without the presence of a teaching physician must have completed more than 6 months of an approved residency program.

(3) The teaching physician must not direct the care of more than four residents at any given time and must direct the care from such proximity as to constitute immediate availability. The teaching physician must—

(i) Have no other responsibilities at the time;

(ii) Assume management responsibility for those beneficiaries seen by the residents;

(iii) Ensure that the services furnished are appropriate;

(iv) Review with each resident during or immediately after each visit, the beneficiary's medical history, physical examination, diagnosis, and record of tests and therapies; and

(v) Document the extent of the teaching physician's participation in the review and direction of the services furnished to each beneficiary.

(4) The range of services furnished by residents in the center includes all of the following:

(i) Acute care for undifferentiated problems or chronic care for ongoing conditions.

(ii) Coordination of care furnished by other physicians and providers.

(iii) Comprehensive care not limited by organ system, or diagnosis.

(5) The patients seen must be an identifiable group of individuals who consider the center to be the continuing source of their health care and in which services are furnished by residents under the medical direction of teaching physicians. . . .

FIGURE **2-3** Explanation of Medicare's outpatient exception. (Excerpted from 42 CFR 415.174)

An early audit initiative of the Office of the Inspector General (OIG) of the U.S. Department of Health and Human Services was known as PATH (Physicians at Teaching Hospitals). As a result of the PATH audits, teaching hospitals that lacked documentation to substantiate Medicare payments to faculty physicians who supervised residents repaid millions of dollars to the

Medicare program. Although the PATH initiative is no longer a part of the OIG work plan, documentation in teaching hospitals is monitored in other ways, including by the hospital's own internal compliance program.

REIMBURSEMENT

There are various mechanisms for reimbursing hospital care. Reimbursement concepts related to managed care are discussed in Chapter 4, but other reimbursement mechanisms, including diagnosis related groups (DRGs) and ambulatory payment classifications (APCs), are discussed here.

Hospital Chargemaster or Charge Description Master (CDM)

For most ancillary services such as laboratory and radiology, the hospital usually maintains a computerized data file called the **chargemaster** or **charge description master (CDM)**, which lists appropriate codes for the service and the hospital's charge for that service. Unlike surgery and other more complex procedures that require human intervention to assign a code based on documentation in the patient record, chargemaster procedures are automatically coded by a computer program when the charge for the service is entered. Therefore, it is important to properly maintain the chargemaster file, making sure that it reflects current codes and reasonable charges.

Medicare

Medicare is a federal program that pays for health care for older Americans and disabled persons. Payments to hospitals fall under Part A of Medicare, whereas payments for physician's services fall under Part B. CMS contracts with private organizations that handle the claims processing and payments for the Medicare program in a given region. In the past, the claims processing organization for Medicare Part A was called the **fiscal intermediary (FI)**, and the organization that processed Medicare Part B claims was known as the **Medicare carrier**. However, due to the Medicare Prescription Drug, Improvement, and Modernization Act of 2003, CMS has replaced these contractors with entities called **Medicare Administrative Contractors (MACs)**. A total of 19 MAC contracts were awarded by CMS, with the last one being completed in January 2009. The majority of these contracts are with entities that cover both Part A and Part B services and are considered A/B MACs. These entities are required to develop payment policies called Local Coverage Determinations (LCDs) or Local Medical Review Policies (LMRPs). These policies educate health care providers on how to submit accurate claims for reimbursement. Although the issues related to documentation by teaching physicians discussed earlier in this chapter are Part B issues, the information provided in this section relates to hospital reimbursement, or Part A of Medicare.

The Hospital Inpatient Prospective Payment System (IPPS) and Diagnosis Related Group (DRG) Payment Window

As described in Chapter 1, Medicare reimburses hospitals for inpatient care under the **Hospital Inpatient Prospective Payment System (IPPS)**, which pays the hospital on a "per case" basis according to the **diagnosis related group**

(DRG) assigned to each patient's stay. Prior to 2007, there were 538 DRGs that grouped patients according to diagnosis, expected resource consumption, and other characteristics. In 2007, CMS replaced these DRGs with 745 **Medicare-Severity DRGs (MS-DRGs)**, which take into account various levels of patient illness, using secondary diagnoses. Some secondary diagnoses are classified as complications or comorbidities (CCs), and others are classified as major complications or comorbidities (MCCs), depending on the impact that the condition has in combination with the patient's principal diagnosis. Surgical and certain other procedures also influence the MS-DRG assignment, as do the patient's discharge status and other factors, in some instances. Codes for diagnoses and procedures, along with other data elements, are submitted as part of the bill to the contractor who processes Medicare claims. A software program known as a "grouper" uses these data elements to assign the case to the appropriate DRG. Each DRG is associated with a relative weight that serves as a multiplier to determine the payment that the hospital receives. The relative weight is multiplied times the hospital's PPS rate or blended rate to arrive at a payment. For example, if the relative weight of a certain DRG is 1.5000 and the hospital's PPS rate is $6,500, the payment for that DRG would be calculated as follows: $1.5000 \times 6,500 = \$9,750$. An excerpt from the MS-DRG Table for 2010, presented in Figure 2-4, illustrates the impact of MCCs and CCs on the relative weights of the DRGs and thus on the payments to the hospital. Note the three DRGs for "Tracheostomy for Face, Neck, and Mouth Diagnoses" (011, 012, and 013), and observe the difference in their relative weights, depending on whether the case involved an MCC, CC, or neither.

DRG payments are reduced when the patient's length of stay (LOS) is less than the geometric mean LOS for the DRG and the patient is transferred to another hospital covered by the acute IPPS or, for certain MS-DRGs, discharged to a post-acute setting such as a long-term care hospital, rehabilitation or psychiatric facility, skilled nursing facility, or certain other settings (CMS, 2009c). The second and third columns in Figure 2-4 specify whether and how the DRG is subject to the post-acute transfer policy. Payment is reduced even further for qualifying transfers in DRGs that are subject to the "special pay" rule.

When a hospital provides services to a Medicare patient as an outpatient within 72 hours before a related inpatient admission, charges for those outpatient services must not be billed separately. Instead, the outpatient diagnoses and procedures must be coded and submitted with the inpatient bill. Because some hospital admissions occur unexpectedly within 72 hours after outpatient treatment, hospitals have inadvertently submitted both inpatient and outpatient bills to Medicare in these cases, in violation of the 72-hour rule. Medicare requires hospitals to implement systems to avoid submitting separate bills for outpatients admitted to inpatient status within the 72-hour window. Failure to comply with the 72-hour rule may result in financial penalties to the hospital. The Office of the Inspector General's (OIG's) work plan for 2010 included a commitment to review the appropriateness of outpatient payments for patients seen immediately before or after acute care stays (OIG, 2010).

MS-DRG	FY 2010 Final Rule Post-Acute DRG	FY 2010 Final Rule Special Pay DRG	MDC	TYPE	MS-DRG Title	Weights	Geometric Mean LOS	Arithmetic Mean LOS
001	No	No	PRE	SURG	HEART TRANSPLANT OR IMPLANT OF HEART ASSIST SYSTEM W MCC	24.8548	31.5	43.9
002	No	No	PRE	SURG	HEART TRANSPLANT OR IMPLANT OF HEART ASSIST SYSTEM W/O MCC	11.7540	16.4	21.2
011	No	No	PRE	SURG	TRACHEOSTOMY FOR FACE, MOUTH & NECK DIAGNOSES W MCC	4.7341	12.7	16.3
012	No	No	PRE	SURG	TRACHEOSTOMY FOR FACE, MOUTH & NECK DIAGNOSES W CC	3.0306	8.8	10.5
013	No	No	PRE	SURG	TRACHEOSTOMY FOR FACE, MOUTH & NECK DIAGNOSES W/O CC/MCC	1.8643	5.7	6.9
052	No	No	01	MED	SPINAL DISORDERS & INJURIES W CC/MCC	1.4836	4.5	6.3
053	No	No	01	MED	SPINAL DISORDERS & INJURIES W/O CC/MCC	0.8382	3.1	4.0

FIGURE 2-4 Selected MS-DRGs excerpted from the 2010 MS-DRG Table.

The Hospital Outpatient Prospective Payment System (OPPS) and Ambulatory Payment Classifications (APCs)

The basic units of payment in Medicare's **Hospital Outpatient Prospective Payment System (HOPPS or OPPS)** are known as **ambulatory payment classifications (APCs)**. The APC system, implemented in the year 2000, established groups of outpatient procedures and services that have similar clinical characteristics and similar costs. One major difference between the APC and DRG systems is that an outpatient may be assigned more than one APC per encounter, whereas an inpatient is assigned only one DRG per hospital admission. Consider the case of an emergency department patient whose visit includes evaluation and management, X-rays, and a procedure. In such a case, as many as three APCs may be generated—one APC for the evaluation and management services, a second APC for the X-rays, and a third APC for the procedure. APCs are based on Healthcare Common Procedural Coding System (HCPCS) codes assigned by the hospital. The hospital's reimbursement from Medicare is the dollar amount associated with each APC as updated by CMS on an annual basis. See Figure 2-5 for excerpts from the APC table for the calendar year 2010.

Notice that in Figure 2-5 each APC is assigned a **status indicator**, which is an alphabetic character that indicates the APC type and whether or how that APC is paid under the OPPS. The four status indicators that appear in the excerpt in Figure 2-5 are S, T, P, and V. A status indicator of T means that the associated APC represents a significant procedure that is **discounted** (paid at less than the full amount) when other procedures are performed with it. The S status indicator represents a significant service that is *not* discounted when more than one APC is present on a claim. The P status indicator means that the associated APC is a partial hospitalization service. The V status indicator represents a medical visit with its associated evaluation and management services. All four of the status indicators in Figure 2-5 are paid under the OPPS. Status indicators S, T, and V are paid as separate APCs, and status indicator P is paid on a per diem APC basis. In 2010, there were 23 different status indicators (Changes to the Hospital Outpatient Prospective Payment System and CY 2010 Payment Rates, 2009).

Medical visits in a hospital clinic or emergency department (ED) are classified and paid according to level of service based on evaluation and management (E&M) coding. In determining the level of service of an encounter, hospitals have developed their own criteria for assigning the E&M codes and have not followed the same guidelines that physicians follow. Although CMS at one time expressed the intent to develop standard guidelines for hospital evaluation and management services, in 2009 they announced that no such guidelines appeared to be necessary. CMS studies have shown that the current system of permitting hospitals to use their own guidelines based on the use of hospital resources has produced acceptable results (CMS 2009b).

In 2008, CMS implemented "Composite APCs" for certain categories of encounter-based hospital outpatient services. These composite APCs allow

Addendum A - OPPS APCs for Calendar Year 2010

APC	Group Title	SI	Relative Weight	Payment Rate	National Unadjusted Copayment	Minimum Unadjusted Copayment
1	Level I Photochemotherapy	S	0.5302	$35.72		$7.15
2	Fine Needle Biopsy/Aspiration	T	1.5111	$101.79		$20.36
3	Bone Marrow Biopsy/Aspiration	T	3.0998	$208.81		$41.77
4	Level I Needle Biopsy/Aspiration Except Bone Marrow	T	4.5991	$309.80		$61.96
5	Level II Needle Biopsy/Aspiration Except Bone Marrow	T	7.8145	$526.40		$105.28
6	Level I Incision & Drainage	T	1.4557	$98.06		$19.62
7	Level II Incision & Drainage	T	12.6217	$850.22		$170.05
8	Level III Incision and Drainage	T	19.4063	$1,307.25		$261.45
12	Level I Debridement & Destruction	T	0.4436	$29.88		$5.98
13	Level II Debridement & Destruction	T	0.8789	$59.20		$11.84
15	Level III Debridement & Destruction	T	1.5412	$103.82		$20.77
16	Level IV Debridement & Destruction	T	2.7982	$188.49		$37.70
17	Level VI Debridement & Destruction	T	21.2653	$1,432.47		$286.50
19	Level I Excision/Biopsy	T	4.3625	$293.87	$64.46	$58.78
20	Level II Excision/Biopsy	T	8.2028	$552.56		$110.52
21	Level III Excision/Biopsy	T	17.4975	$1,178.67		$235.74
22	Level IV Excision/Biopsy	T	23.388	$1,575.46	$354.45	$315.10
28	Level I Breast Surgery	T	24.7516	$1,667.32		$333.47
29	Level II Breast Surgery	T	34.1654	$2,301.45	$581.52	$460.29
30	Level III Breast Surgery	T	41.9997	$2,829.18	$747.07	$565.84
172	Level I Partial Hospitalization (3 services)	P	2.223	$149.75		$29.95
173	Level II Partial Hospitalization (4 or more services)	P	3.1286	$210.75		$42.15
604	Level 1 Hospital Clinic Visits	V	0.8593	$57.88		$11.58
605	Level 2 Hospital Clinic Visits	V	1.0337	$69.63		$13.93
606	Level 3 Hospital Clinic Visits	V	1.3222	$89.07		$17.82
607	Level 4 Hospital Clinic Visits	V	1.683	$113.37		$22.68
608	Level 5 Hospital Clinic Visits	V	2.4853	$167.41		$33.49

FIGURE **2-5** Selected APCs excerpted from the 2010 Addendum A.

only a single payment for certain common combination services provided on the same date of service. For example, an emergency department visit followed by observation services would be combined into an "Extended Assessment and Management Composite" APC. Composite APCs are meant to provide incentives to health care providers to efficiently utilize resources while conducting similar services. A list of 2009 CMS composite APCs include:

- APC 8000 Cardiac Electrophysiological Evaluation and Ablation
- APC 8001 LDR Prostate Brachytherapy
- APC 8002 Level 1 Extended Assessment and Management Composite
- APC 8003 Level 2 Extended Assessment and Management
- APC 8004 Ultrasound
- APC 8005 CT and CTA without Contrast
- APC 8006 CT and CTA with Contrast
- APC 8007 MRI and MRA without Contrast
- APC 8008 MRI and MRA with Contrast
- APC 0172 Level 1 Partial Hospitalization (3 services)
- APC 0173 Level 2 Partial Hospitalization (4 or more services)

Because of the potential savings to the Medicare program, this trend of bundling services will likely continue and expand to more APCs.

Another change related to observation services is that CMS no longer requires specific diagnosis criteria (chest pain, asthma, congestive heart failure) that were previously necessary for separate payment of observation. There is a separate code that must be used for billing observation services. All related services provided to the patient, including specified "visit" or evaluation and management codes, should be coded in addition to the observation code. A written order from a physician is required for admission to observation care. (If the physician determines during the observation stay that the patient needs a higher level of care, another order must be written to admit the patient as an inpatient.) The patient must be in observation care for at least 8 hours as documented in the medical record by timed admission notes, progress notes, and discharge instructions (notes) signed by the physician. Medical record documentation must also note that the physician explicitly assessed patient risk to determine that the patient would benefit from observation care (American College of Emergency Physicians, n.d.).

The OPPS allows additional payments to cover the costs of innovative medical devices, drugs, and biologicals. Called "pass-through payments," these categories provide separate payments in addition to regular APC payments. Payments for a given drug, device, or biological can be made on a pass-through basis for two to three years (CMS, 2002b). Hospital-based clinics are considered to be "provider-based clinics" under the OPPS. When a Medicare patient is seen in a hospital-based clinic, the clinic receives an APC payment and the physician receives a reduced payment for his or her services (because there is no practice expense—it has been shifted to the hospital). The total of the two payments is greater than the full fee schedule payment that a physician in a freestanding clinic would receive. Furthermore, hospitals with provider-based facilities "may receive higher reimbursement when they include the costs of a provider-based entity on their cost reports. (F)acilities may also benefit from enhanced disproportionate share hospital (DSH) payments, upper payment limit (UPL) payments, or graduate medical education payments for which they would not normally be eligible. In addition, provider-based status for outpatient clinics may increase coinsurance liability for Medicare beneficiaries" (OIG, 2009, p 3). For these reasons, CMS scrutinizes applications for provider-based status from clinics that had not claimed any hospital affiliation before the implementation of the OPPS. Also, the provider-based status of existing facilities may be reviewed by the Office of the Inspector General for appropriateness (OIG, 2009).

It is important to remember that details of the OPPS change annually. To obtain the most current information, the health information manager should consult the latest regulations at the CMS or *Federal Register* Web sites.

Long-Term Care Hospital Prospective Payment System (LTCH PPS)

Since October 1, 2002, Medicare payments to long-term care hospitals have been determined by a diagnosis related group (DRG)–based prospective payment system (PPS). Although the numbers and titles of most of the Medicare severity long-term care diagnosis related groups (MS-LTC-DRGs) are similar to those of inpatient MS-DRGs, the LTC-DRGs differ from inpatient DRGs in relative weights and in their associated lengths of stay. LTC-DRGs are also similar to inpatient DRGs in that they are based on the patient's principal diagnosis, additional diagnoses, procedures performed during the stay, age, sex, and discharge status. The LTCH PPS calculates a per-discharge payment to the facility, based on the product of the LTC-DRG relative weight multiplied times a federally determined payment rate. For MS-DRGs unlikely to be used in the LTCH setting, the relative weight is zero. A listing of the top 20 MS-LTC-DRGs for 2008 in Table 2-1 provides an overview of the types of cases commonly treated in a long-term acute care hospital.

Medicare has developed specific rules to discourage the transfer of patients between the LTCH and other facilities for financial rather than clinical reasons. There are three payment mechanisms that address this issue. One is the concept of the "interrupted stay," which applies to transfers to and from an acute care hospital, inpatient rehabilitation facility, or skilled nursing facility. In the case of a patient who is discharged to one of these facilities and is readmitted to the same LTCH within a certain number of days (the number of days varies according to the type of facility), the LTCH episode is considered one interrupted stay and the LTCH receives only one MS-LTC-DRG payment rather than two. Another mechanism is the 5 percent rule, which applies only to transfers to and from a colocated facility, such as a hospital-within-a-hospital or a satellite facility. Once 5 percent of all discharges for the fiscal year are made up of transfers from the LTCH to the colocated facility and back, these cases are paid as one LTCH admission rather than two, regardless of the number of days in the intervening stay. The third rule applies to the initial admission from any given hospital to the LTCH. The rule allows the LTCH to be paid MS-LTC-DRG rates for patients admitted from a particular acute

TABLE **2-1**
Top 20 MS-LTC-DRGs in 2008

MS-LTC-DRG	Description	Discharges	Percent
207	Respiratory system diagnosis with ventilator support 96+ hours	14,986	11.5
189	Pulmonary edema and respiratory failure	8,745	6.7
871	Septicemia or severe sepsis without ventilator support 96+ hours with MCC	6,482	5.0
177	Respiratory infections and inflammations with MCC	4,340	3.3
592	Skin ulcers with MCC	4,004	3.1
949	Aftercare with CC/MCC	3,752	2.9
193	Simple pneumonia and pleurisy with MCC	2,696	2.1
593	Skin ulcers with CC	2,590	2.0
190	Chronic obstructive pulmonary disease with MCC	2,558	2.0
208	Respiratory system diagnosis with ventilator support <96 hours	2,486	1.9
945	Rehabilitation with CC/MCC	2,275	1.7
178	Respiratory infections and inflammations with CC	1,964	1.5
559	Aftercare, musculoskeletal system, and connective tissue with MCC	1,944	1.5
573	Skin graft and/or debridement for skin ulcer or cellulitis with MCC	1,912	1.5
539	Osteomyelitis with MCC	1,903	1.5
682	Renal failure with MCC	1,738	1.3
166	Other respiratory system OR procedures with MCC	1,693	1.3
291	Heart failure and shock with MCC	1,688	1.3
862	Postoperative and post-traumatic infections with MCC	1,672	1.3
919	Complications of treatment with MCC	1,659	1.3
	Top 20 MS-LTC-DRGs	71,087	54.3
	Total	130,869	100.0

Source: MedPAC, 2010

care hospital until the number of patients admitted from that facility exceeds 25 percent of the total admissions to the LTCH. After the 25 percent threshold is reached, the LTCH is paid the lesser of the LTCH PPS rate or the acute hospital PPS rate for admissions from that hospital. There are some exceptions to the 25 percent rule to accommodate rural LTCHs and those in metropolitan areas with dominant or single acute care hospitals. Other factors beyond the scope of this discussion such as short-stay and high-cost outliers can also affect Medicare payment to the LTCH (MedPAC, 2008).

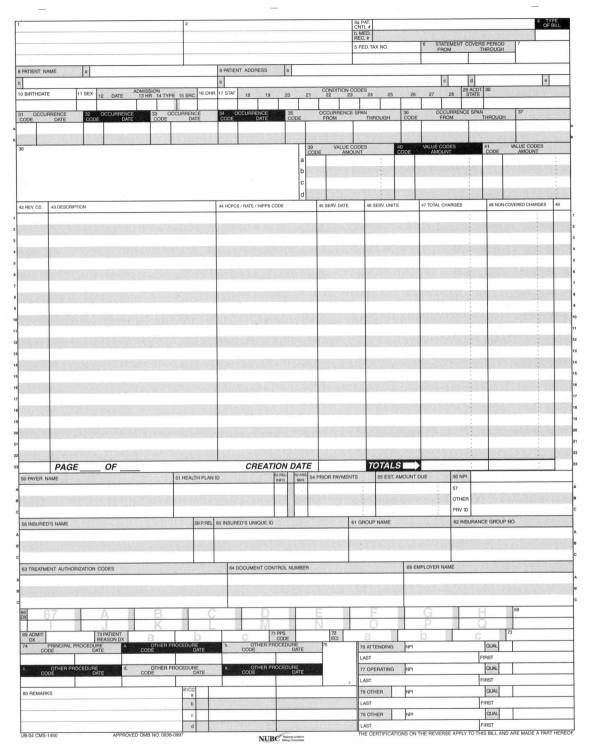

FIGURE 2-6 The UB-04 (CMS 1450) Uniform Bill.

Other Payers

Other payers may pay for hospital outpatient care under a variety of systems. Traditional indemnity insurance plans pay the usual, customary, and reasonable charges of the hospital. However, fewer patients are enrolled in a pure indemnity type of plan. Generally, there are incentives for patients to use the services of a provider who has agreed not to exceed certain limits on charges. For more information on the wide range of payment mechanisms for health care, see Chapter 4.

Billing

The Uniform Bill (UB-04 or CMS 1450) is the standard form for submitting information to third-party payers when filing claims for hospital services (see Figure 2-6). In 2007, The National Uniform Billing Committee (NUBC) updated the form in order to accommodate more diagnosis and procedure codes in anticipation of the implementation of ICD-10-CM and ICD-10-PCS. The revised form also meets electronic data standards and allows for Present on Admission indicators as well as National Provider Identifiers. Under HIPAA, physicians use the CMS 1500 (08-05) form for submitting claims. This revised form allows for National Provider Identifier reporting. However, the use of paper bills and claim forms is diminishing. Electronic transmission of claims is the norm for both hospital and physician claim submission.

INFORMATION MANAGEMENT

Coding and Classification

Coding of diseases and procedures serves several purposes in hospital-based care. Hospitals can use coded data to study patterns in the services they render or to assist in the evaluation of the outcomes of care. Accurate coding is also crucial to receiving appropriate reimbursement for hospital-based care.

International Classification of Diseases

The clinical modification of the *International Classification of Diseases,* developed by the National Center for Health Statistics, is the classification system used for coding the patient's condition, diagnosis, or reason for encounter for both inpatients and outpatients. Federal regulations have scheduled *ICD-10-CM* to replace the disease classification of *ICD-9-CM* in 2013. Likewise, *ICD-10-PCS* (procedure classification system developed by CMS) replaces the procedure section (Volume 3) of *ICD-9-CM*. Hospitals are required to use the *ICD* procedure classification for reporting operations and other procedures only for inpatients.

Healthcare Common Procedural Coding System (HCPCS)

The Healthcare Common Procedural Coding System (HCPCS) is the system required by CMS for coding services provided to Medicare patients. CMS adopted the American Medical Association's *Current Procedural Terminology*© as the coding system comprising the bulk of HCPCS. The *CPT* codes are designated by CMS as "Level I" codes. The codes that CMS developed are known as HCPCS "Level II" or national codes. These are alphanumeric codes, consisting of a letter (A–V) and four numerical digits. (Note: HCPCS Level III or local codes were discontinued in 2003.)

Revenue Codes

Revenue codes are reported on the UB-04 to indicate the general nature of the service provided. To file a valid claim, the revenue code must be appropriate to the HCPCS code listed with it. Therefore, to avoid rejection of claims, the appropriate revenue codes are usually included in the chargemaster file along with the HCPCS code for the service being billed.

Coding Edits

Medicare Administrative Contractors process hospital inpatient bills using the Medicare Code Editor (MCE) and hospital outpatient claims using the Outpatient Code Editor (OCE). These code editors identify coding errors on hospital bills that can cause the claim to be rejected. National Correct Coding Initiative (NCCI or CCI) edits also apply to the APC system. The purpose of the CCI edits is to prohibit unbundling of procedures, a practice that results in excessive payment to the provider when multiple codes are reported instead of a combination code. The CCI edits are voluminous and are updated quarterly, making it difficult to keep abreast of them using manual methods. Most hospitals use code-editing software to flag codes that contain possible code editor or CCI errors. Identifying and correcting errors before the bill is submitted results in more efficient claims processing and a better cash flow for the hospital.

Data and Information Flow

Most hospitals begin the patient's record with the registration process. Information necessary to identify the patient is gathered and recorded. Generally, this identifying information is entered into an electronic database, or master patient index system, and may also be printed out or manually recorded for immediate reference. As various assessments, diagnostic procedures, and treatments are completed, the results are incorporated into the patient's record, along with diagnostic impressions or conclusions and plans for future care.

The patient's record must be readily available when a patient is seen in any hospital setting. When a hospital uses an electronic health record (EHR), the patient record can be accessed by diverse providers throughout the hospital as the patient arrives at various departments for different services. A hospital using a paper record or a hybrid (part electronic, part paper) record could achieve this goal by maintaining all components of the paper record together and delivering the record to the hospital locations where the patient is being seen. When a complete paper record is maintained in one location, this is called a unit record. In this scenario, all records of inpatient, clinic, emergency, or any other type of hospital encounter would be maintained in a single record, centralized in the health information services area of the hospital. However, in a large facility with numerous clinics that may not be physically close to one another, maintaining a single paper record is much more challenging. In this situation, certain clinics may maintain their own records. When a patient has more than one record in various hospital locations, the Joint Commission requires that "the hospital either assemble or make available in a summary in the medical record all information required to provide patient care, treatment, and services" (Joint Commission, 2010, p. 405).

Because of ARRA incentives, more hospitals are expected to adopt electronic health records, meaning that more components of the patient's clinical record will be accessible electronically. The move toward EHRs will help solve the problem of making the record quickly available in any setting.

Electronic Health Records and Computer Systems

As with many areas of health care, the first computer applications in hospitals were related to billing functions. However, the importance of maintaining clinical information electronically began to receive attention in the 1990s, receiving impetus from the Institute of Medicine (IOM) 1991 publication, *The Computer-Based Patient Record: An Essential Technology for Health Care*. Although decades have passed since this seminal work was released, hospitals have lagged in the adoption of electronic health records.

In 2009, Congress passed the **American Recovery and Reinvestment Act (ARRA)**, which included a Medicare and Medicaid incentive program for health care providers who demonstrate the ability to "meaningfully use" EHRs. In order to meet the definition of "meaningful use," providers must utilize a certified EHR product in such a way that the electronic exchange of information improves the quality of care provided to patients, including the capability of submitting clinical quality measures data (AHIMA, 2010). While this program initially provides incentive payments to hospitals and clinicians, Medicare providers will start to be penalized in 2016 if they are not meeting meaningful use requirements.

Proposed rules for meaningful use for hospitals were published in the *Federal Register* in 2010. The proposed "Stage 1" criteria for meaningful use of electronic health records by hospitals were as follows (Electronic Health Record Incentive Program, Proposed Rule, 2010, pp. 1867–1870):

- Use of CPOE (computerized provider order entry) for orders (any type) directly entered by authorizing provider....
- Implement drug-drug, drug-allergy, drug-formulary checks.
- Maintain an up-to-date problem list of current and active diagnoses based on ICD–9–CM or SNOMED CT®.
- Maintain active medication list.
- Maintain active medication allergy list.
- Record demographics (including) preferred language, insurance type, gender, race, ethnicity, date of birth, date and cause of death in the event of mortality.

- Record and chart changes in vital signs (including) height, weight, blood pressure, (c)alculate and display BMI, (p)lot and display growth charts for children 2–20 years, including BMI.
- Record smoking status for patients 13 years old or older.
- Incorporate clinical lab test results into EHR as structured data.
- Generate lists of patients by specific conditions to use for quality improvement, reduction of disparities, and outreach.
- Report hospital quality measures to CMS or the States.
- Implement 5 clinical decision support rules related to a high priority hospital condition, including diagnostic test ordering, along with the ability to track compliance with those rules.
- Check insurance eligibility electronically from public and private payers.
- Submit claims electronically to public and private payers.
- Provide patients with an electronic copy of their health information (including diagnostic test results, problem list, medication lists, allergies, discharge summary, procedures), upon request.
- Provide patients with an electronic copy of their discharge instructions and procedures at time of discharge, upon request.
- Capability to exchange key clinical information (for example, discharge summary, procedures, problem list, medication list, allergies, diagnostic test results) among providers of care and patient authorized entities electronically.
- Perform medication reconciliation at relevant encounters and each transition of care.
- Provide summary care record for each transition of care and referral.
- Capability to submit electronic data to immunization registries and actual submission where required and accepted.
- Capability to provide electronic submission of reportable lab results (as required by state or local law) to public health agencies and actual submission where it can be received.
- Capability to provide electronic syndromic surveillance data to public health agencies and actual transmission according to applicable law and practice.
- Protect electronic health information created or maintained by the certified EHR technology through the implementation of appropriate technical capabilities.

Although many hospitals anticipated challenges in meeting the "meaningful use" requirements, an EHR with the capabilities described in the proposed regulation offers numerous advantages both to the patient and to the clinicians who care for the patients. Because in a given day a patient may receive evaluation and treatment in several different hospital departments, an EHR that is readily available to all who see the patient can improve patient care. Patient safety can be enhanced through the use of computerized provider order entry (CPOE) by linking to decision support systems that warn of possible drug interactions or wrong dosages and by alerting prescribing clinicians to patient allergies. An EHR can also generate reminders of services that are needed by a patient. These are just a few of the ways in which an EHR can benefit patient care in a hospital setting.

Although the "Stage 1" meaningful use criteria do not specify that all physician documentation be maintained electronically, this is likely to be an ultimate goal in many hospitals. In hospitals that have electronic physician documentation systems, the physician may enter progress notes and other health information using a keyboard. However, another method of capturing physician documentation for use in an EHR is already in use in some hospital departments—voice recognition technology. With a voice recognition system, the physician can dictate reports directly to an electronic system. The computer converts the spoken word into a report without the labor of a transcriptionist typing the report, although a transcriptionist or the physician may edit the report for accuracy before it becomes part of the record. The report can also be electronically signed by the physician who generated the report. Voice recognition systems have been found particularly useful in emergency and radiology departments.

Data Sets
Standardization Efforts

The two basic data sets that apply to hospital-based care are the **Uniform Hospital Discharge Data Set (UHDDS)** and the **Uniform Ambulatory Care Data Set (UACDS)**. The UHDDS is very important for inpatient coding and reporting, as it specifies definitions and rules for selecting the principal diagnosis, other diagnoses, the principal procedure, and several other elements that are critical in DRG assignment and payment. The UACDS is a 16-item data set that differs from the UHDDS. For example, the UHDDS definition and rules for principal diagnosis do not apply in the outpatient setting. In 1996, the NCVHS developed a set of 42 core health data elements that could be used in either the inpatient or outpatient setting, which has been under review but has never been rejected or adopted (NCVHS, 1996).

Data Elements for Emergency Department Systems (DEEDS) is a data set that is specific to the emergency department setting. Version 1.0 of DEEDS included more than 150 data elements in the following eight categories:

- Patient identification data
- Facility and practitioner identification data
- ED payment data
- ED arrival and first assessment data
- ED history and physical examination data
- ED procedure and result data
- ED medication data
- ED disposition and diagnosis data (NCIPC, 1997)

DEEDS also includes standards for electronic data interchange (EDI) and can therefore facilitate exchange of information with other health care information systems.

The greatest impetus toward collection of standardized data in ambulatory and all other health care settings has been provided by the Health Insurance Portability and Accountability Act (HIPAA). The HIPAA electronic data interchange (EDI) provisions require the adoption of standards for transactions, code sets, and identifiers. The Health Care Financing Administration (HCFA, the predecessor of CMS) delegated development and maintenance of the EDI standards to the following designated standards maintenance organizations (DSMOs):

- Accredited Standards Committee X12
- Dental Content Committee of the American Dental Association
- Health Level Seven
- National Council for Prescription Drug Programs
- National Uniform Billing Committee
- National Uniform Claim Committee (HCFA, 2000)

Common Working Files

For Medicare beneficiaries, CMS contracts for the maintenance of nine regional databases throughout the United States. A file, called the **common working file (CWF)**, is maintained for each beneficiary. Information from both Part A and Part B claims are maintained in these files, which are used by Medicare administrative contractors (MACs) for coordination of benefits, claims validation, and for tracking utilization patterns.

QUALITY AND UTILIZATION MANAGEMENT

Quality Assessment and Performance Improvement (QAPI)

Hospital accrediting agencies require that accredited hospitals implement hospital-wide performance improvement programs. For example, the Joint Commission's approach to performance improvement emphasizes designing processes, collecting data related to performance, analyzing the data collected (including comparing the hospital's performance to a standard or to that of peer hospitals), establishing priorities for processes to be improved, developing improvements for the priorities identified, and evaluating the degree of improvement achieved and sustained (Joint Commission, 2010). DNV Healthcare utilizes performance improvement standards from the International Standards Organization's ISO 9001 quality management system requirements.

CMS has implemented both a Hospital Inpatient Quality Reporting (IQR) initiative and a Hospital Outpatient Quality Data Reporting Program (HOP QDRP) in order to enhance public awareness of quality-of-care issues. The IQR requires participating hospitals to submit patient-level data on discharges involving: 1) Acute Myocardial Infarction (AMI) Care, 2) Heart Failure (HF) Care, 3) Pneumonia (PN) Care, and 4) Surgical Care Infection Prevention

(SCIP). This information is displayed on the Hospital Compare (www.hospitalcompare.hhs.gov) Web site for public viewing. In order for hospitals to receive their full Medicare annual payment update for the IPPS, they must fulfill all requirements for this program. The HOP QDRP includes outpatient department measures that focus on four topic areas: 1) Emergency Department (ED) Acute Myocardial Infarction (AMI) Care, 2) Chest Pain (CP), 3) Surgery, and 4) Imaging Efficiency (CMS, 2010). These results are made available to the public, and fulfilling HOP QDRP requirements is also necessary to receive the full payment update for the OPPS.

Another way in which quality affects reimbursement is the identification of hospital-acquired conditions (HACs) through the Present on Admission (POA) indicator associated with additional diagnoses coded on the hospital bill for inpatient services. Conditions that might otherwise increase reimbursement as CCs or MCCs do not increase reimbursement if they were acquired in the hospital—i.e., not present on admission.

In addition to and in alignment with CMS performance standards, the Joint Commission also reviews 1) Pregnancy and Related Conditions (PR) and 2) Children's Asthma Care (CAC). The results for all of these hospital core quality measures are reported on the Joint Commission's Quality Check (www.qualitycheck.org) Web site.

Utilization Management (UM)

Utilization management focuses on the appropriateness, efficiency, and cost-effectiveness of health care. In the current climate of managed care and with prospective payment systems for Medicare in place, it is more important than ever for hospitals to be sure they are rendering services efficiently. In the past, hospitals were reimbursed based either on their costs or their charges. Now both Medicare and private payers limit the charges and costs they will pay. To operate efficiently in such an environment requires a team effort from physicians, hospital staff, and administration.

In many hospitals, the staff members most directly responsible for monitoring utilization management are known as case managers. In earlier days, case managers often focused on working as liaisons between the medical staff and the patient and patient's family to make sure that necessary arrangements were made for a timely discharge. However, in recent years, the case management team's responsibilities have expanded to include working with the managed care contracting office, decision support personnel, and health information services, in addition to their traditional role with clinicians, patients, and patients' families. In some instances, the case management team may work with health information services in clinical documentation improvement programs to help assure that all of the documentation necessary for correct coding is present. In some hospitals, health information management professionals have administrative authority over case management services. Regardless of reporting relationships, the case management team can be an important ally to health information services.

RISK MANAGEMENT AND LEGAL ISSUES

Many hospitals have risk management departments, whose role is to protect the organization from financial loss that could occur as a result of **potentially compensable events (PCEs)**, which are occurrences that may result in litigation against the health care provider or that may require the health care provider to compensate an injured party. Almost all hospitals have occurrence (or incident) reporting systems that allow risk managers to track PCEs and to identify risk areas within the organization that can be targeted for improvement. Policies and procedures should be instituted to identify errors to be reported. Documentation of errors should be to the point and impartial (Roth, 2009). Some hospitals have moved from paper-based occurrence reporting to electronic systems that allow risk managers to receive, review, and analyze occurrence reports online. The specific challenges for risk management in hospitals are described in the following paragraphs.

Providing high-quality documentation of all patient encounters and services is a vital component of any risk management program. Health care providers must understand that only information documented in a manner that can be clearly interpreted will be used to judge whether or not appropriate patient care was given. Therefore, providers must ensure that all documentation is both legible and complete. All record entries should thoroughly describe the given situation and meet all regulatory requirements for content and authentication. Making sure that providers have properly timed/dated/signed an order or entry is an important step in following appropriate documentation guidelines.

Hospital outpatient services present unique challenges for hospital risk managers. Financial incentives to treat patients on an outpatient rather than an inpatient basis should be balanced with policies that encourage inpatient admission when appropriate in a given situation. Also, the limited duration of face-to-face contact between caregivers and patients in the outpatient setting requires extra attention to patient relations and documentation (Eubanks, 1990). Because telephone contact often precedes or follows an outpatient visit, documentation of these calls is important. Both what the patient tells the caregiver and what the caregiver tells the patient should be recorded. A follow-up telephone call is routine after many ambulatory surgery procedures. Proper documentation verifies that the patient was given correct instructions and provides evidence of the patient's condition after surgery. A follow-up phone call can be a good public relations tool as well, which is also an important element in risk management (Eubanks, 1990). Phone calls should be HIPAA compliant. When the patient is not available, a message containing clinical information (e.g., test results) should not be left on an answering machine or with a person other than the patient. A solid policy regarding which provider should contact the patient about an abnormal test result, what time frame is acceptable for test results notification, and the preferred mechanism for patient notification is critical to reducing liability. For noncompliant patients or for patients who cannot be reached directly, health care providers should consider sending test results via certified mail so that documentation can be maintained that attempts at notification were made.

The emergency department is an area in which the hospital is particularly at legal risk. Patients and family members being treated in the emergency room are often under extreme stress and are sometimes unlikely to be understanding of the stresses that the emergency department staff may be facing. Emergency department staff must be well versed not only in clinical assessment and treatment, but also in customer service and in legal aspects of emergency care. An example of a law with which the emergency department staff should be familiar is the **Emergency Medical Treatment and Active Labor Act (EMTALA)**, which imposes a legal duty on hospitals to screen and stabilize, if necessary, any patient who arrives in the emergency department (Curran, Hall, Bobinski, & Orentlicher, 1998). The purpose of EMTALA is to prevent the "dumping" of patients who may not be able to pay for emergency department services. Therefore, an appropriate screening cannot be delayed to inquire about insurance status or method of payment. If the patient is found to have an emergency medical condition, the hospital is required to stabilize the patient before attempting to transfer the patient elsewhere. In the case of a woman in active labor, stabilization generally means that delivery is completed before transfer (Special responsibilities of Medicare hospitals in emergency cases, 2009).

ROLE OF THE HEALTH INFORMATION MANAGEMENT PROFESSIONAL

The health information management (HIM) professional can play a variety of roles in hospital-based care. A health information manager may take a traditional type of role in health information services or may work in one of many other available positions. Most hospitals now have compliance departments, and the skills of health information managers are vital in promoting compliance with both billing and HIPAA regulations. Many hospitals are also employing health information managers in positions related to coding, such as chargemaster coordinators. There are many other possible roles for HIM in performance improvement, cancer registry, trauma registry, information systems, and financial services. The specifics of each of these positions will vary from institution to institution, but a general idea of what could be expected in selected positions is provided in the following sections.

Health Information Services

The health information services department deals with both inpatient and outpatient issues. Those in leadership positions in health information services must be familiar with accrediting and regulatory requirements that affect the patient record and must provide training for others in the department as appropriate.

Coding specialists generally work in health information services, although sometimes they report to patient financial services or the chief financial officer.

In some instances coders may specialize in coding specific types of cases. For example, some may specialize in outpatient coding. Because HCPCS/CPT codes are not required on inpatient bills, health information services will often assign certain coders to code all outpatient services. This arrangement allows coders to develop a specialization in outpatient coding rules, which are different from inpatient coding rules. Such specialization can lead to greater accuracy in outpatient coding. On the inpatient side, coders may specialize by service line, for example coding for cardiovascular services.

In hospitals still dealing with paper records, some hospitals may have supervisory-level positions designated to handle issues arising from the challenges of filing and retrieving a large number of records that may be requested at very short intervals. As more hospitals implement electronic health records, positions in health information services will deal less with storage and retrieval of records but will still be vital to assuring the accuracy, completeness, and legal acceptability of the electronic record. Activities such as release of information or data collection and analysis are still within the purview of the health information manager, whether the record is paper or electronic.

Compliance Officer

Most hospitals appoint full-time compliance officers who manage the compliance program. A health information manager possesses skills ideally suited for this position. In a large hospital or academic medical center, there are many activities for which compliance may be monitored, and a number of health information professionals may serve on the compliance staff. In many hospitals, the compliance program has developed into a distinct department. Health information managers may lead the compliance department and/or work in specialized compliance areas within the department. For example, some members of the compliance staff may focus on coding and billing issues, which would require expert knowledge of documentation and coding guidelines. HIPAA compliance is another area in which a health information manager can provide expertise. To meet HIPAA requirements, hospitals should have a privacy officer and a security officer. In some hospitals, these positions are combined, and in others they are separate. In some hospitals, these responsibilities may fall under the compliance department, and in others these duties are delegated to a member of the information systems or health information services staff. A HIPAA compliance officer and his or her staff can provide HIPAA training; develop policies, procedures, and forms; or monitor the hospital's ongoing compliance with the HIPAA privacy, security, and/or EDI regulations. Auditing is also an important activity of the compliance program, whether auditing records against codes submitted, auditing release of information for appropriate authorization, or auditing the appropriateness of employee access to electronic health information, to name a few areas that may be addressed in the compliance plan. Whenever an audit identifies a problem area, plans for corrective action are developed in conjunction with the hospital service involved. Because developing an effective compliance program is a team effort involving many departments and health care professionals, good leadership skills are vital.

Revenue Cycle

In a typical business, the revenue cycle involves all of the activities from pricing to selling and then collecting what is owed from the purchaser. In health care in general and in hospitals in particular, the revenue cycle is quite complex for many reasons, not the least of which is the involvement of third-party payers. To present an extreme oversimplification of a hospital revenue cycle, the revenue cycle begins before any services are rendered, when patient identification and insurance information are collected. Then, as the patient begins to receive services, there are charges to capture and clinician documentation to be recorded in the patient record. At the conclusion of services, information from the record must be abstracted and coded for the bill. Specialized software "scrubs" the bill and errors are corrected before the bill goes to the payer. Electronic systems are generally used to submit bills to payers, and paper processes are the norm for submitting bills to patients for the amounts that are the patient's responsibility. Accounts receivable are maintained, denials from third parties are investigated, and collection processes are initiated as appropriate until the hospital has determined that it has received the appropriate payment. Because many of the activities in the revenue cycle involve matters in which the health information manager possesses expertise, there are a variety of roles that an HIM professional can play in this arena. One obvious role is that of coding specialist, which has already been mentioned. Clinical documentation improvement programs are also important to the revenue cycle, and HIM professionals are knowledgeable of the type of documentation that is needed for accurate coding. Because much of the coding for an ambulatory patient's bill is generated automatically by the hospital's chargemaster, it is important that someone with knowledge of coding be involved in chargemaster maintenance. Some hospitals bring in health information managers as consultants to review their chargemasters. Sometimes health information managers are employed full-time in the patient financial services office and have supervision of the chargemaster among their duties. This is to make sure that HCPCS codes are added, changed, or deleted as appropriate and that they accurately reflect the procedures that are being performed. Duties may also involve working with the leaders of various departments to help set appropriate prices for services included in the chargemaster. A health information manager may also work in or with patient financial services to investigate rejected claims. Another role in the financial area is that of charge capture analyst, whose responsibilities include reviewing outpatient charges to ensure all charges are accurate and complete. Health information managers have also found employment in information systems, working with various electronic applications that move the revenue cycle along.

Other Roles

There are many other roles that a health information manager can play in the hospital setting. For example, performance improvement is an important area where the skills of health information managers are well utilized. An HIM professional can serve as a performance improvement specialist, collecting, analyzing, and reporting data. In some hospitals, a health information management professional serves as the director of the performance improvement department. Health information professionals also sometimes play a role in utilization management, medical staff services, and many other areas of the hospital.

TRENDS

Hospitals continue to merge with other health care facilities and to incorporate a wide variety of ambulatory and other services into their systems, increasing the complexity of hospital-based care. The role of hospitalists in caring for inpatients has expanded greatly since the mid-1990s, with more growth in the number of hospitalists expected in the future. The number of long-term acute care hospitals rose dramatically in the three decades following the 1980s, but the growth rate in this sector appears to have stabilized in recent years. Federal regulators and private accrediting organizations have placed a renewed focus on quality improvement initiatives within health care organizations. Reimbursement rates are often tied to these initiatives, and reported data is made available to the public via the Internet. Implementation of electronic health records is accelerating rapidly in light of the incentives and penalties promulgated by ARRA. One trend that cuts across several areas—documentation, coding, reimbursement, and revenue cycle management—is the increasing scrutiny given to coding and payment issues by auditing initiatives such as the Recovery Audit Contractor (RAC) and Medicaid Integrity Program (MIP) programs described in Chapter 1. Health information managers will experience increasing opportunities and challenges as they address the information needs and reimbursement challenges of more-complex hospital and health care networks.

SUMMARY

Hospitals offer a broad range of services. These include services performed in acute care units, ambulatory surgery units, hospital clinics, emergency services, observation services, partial hospitalization, and ancillary services.

Many different types of health care professionals participate in hospital patient care. Physicians, nurses, physical therapists, occupational therapists, clinical laboratory scientists, pharmacists, and others may provide diagnostic or therapeutic services to hospital patients. One type of provider unique to hospital care is the hospitalist—a physician who provides comprehensive hospital inpatient care to patients.

Hospital regulations require that all hospitals be licensed by the state in which they are located. Other regulations to which hospital services may be subject are found in the federal Conditions of Participation for Hospitals and in the accreditation standards of voluntary groups such as the Joint Commission, DNV Healthcare, and the American Osteopathic Association's Healthcare Facilities Accreditation Program (HFAP).

Documentation requirements for hospital inpatients and outpatients depend on the type of services received. Requirements for documentation in patient records can be found in the regulations and standards of governmental and voluntary accreditation agencies. Factors other than regulatory and accreditation requirements play a role in hospital documentation. Documentation audits to determine whether services billed are appropriately documented in the patient record are increasingly common. Health care providers lose reimbursement for services not properly documented. Rules have been promulgated to clarify what documentation is necessary to justify services billed by teaching physicians.

Reimbursement methodologies for inpatient and outpatient hospital care include managed care contracts, fee schedule payments, and prospective payment systems. A renewed focus on efficient use of health care resources will be a continuing trend as providers and payers seek ways to improve quality of care while reducing overall costs.

The major coding and classification systems used in the hospital inpatient and outpatient settings are the current modifications of *ICD* and HCPCS (whose major component is *CPT*). Medicare requires that diagnoses be reported on the UB-04, using the current clinical modification of *ICD* for both inpatients and outpatients. Inpatient procedures are coded with the most current version of the *ICD* procedure classification, whereas outpatient procedures must be reported with HCPCS. Revenue codes are used on both inpatient and outpatient bills to explain the general nature of the service performed.

Data and information flow into the patient record from each significant contact the patient has with a member of the health care team. The hospital must be able to provide access to all components of the patient's record when a patient is seen in any hospital setting. When using paper records, maintaining a comprehensive yet readily accessible record is a challenge. Electronic health record systems can help solve the problem of making the record quickly available to any patient unit. An electronic health record can be accessed by diverse providers throughout the hospital as the patient presents to various departments for different services.

HIPAA is one of the driving forces determining the standards for the data elements that should be maintained for every patient. UHDDS is a data set for hospital inpatients, and UACDS is an outpatient data set. DEEDS is a standard data set for emergency department services. A data set for each Medicare beneficiary is also found in the common working file maintained by Medicare Administrative Contractors.

Measuring and improving the quality of care is vital to providing quality services, meeting accreditation standards, and achieving optimum payment for services. Utilization management programs analyze the appropriateness, efficiency, and cost-effectiveness of patient care. Risk management focuses on improving care, documentation, and patient satisfaction to reduce the possibility of legal liability.

The HIM professional can play a variety of roles in the hospital setting. A health information manager may take a traditional type of role in health information services or may work in one of many other hospital departments.

The position of compliance officer is a position for which health information managers are particularly well suited. Many hospitals are also employing health information managers in various positions to help manage the revenue cycle. Health information managers also work in performance improvement roles and sometimes in other areas, such as utilization management.

KEY TERMS

ambulatory payment classifications (APCs) groupings of outpatient services (based on the HCPCS code assigned) that determine the payment the hospital receives under the Hospital Outpatient Prospective Payment System (HOPPS).

ambulatory surgery (also called "same-day" surgery) surgery in which it is planned that the patient will arrive at the facility, have surgery, recover from any anesthesia, and be ready for discharge in a single day, thus avoiding an overnight stay in the health care facility.

American Recovery and Reinvestment Act (ARRA) a federal law that, among other things, created an incentive program for health care providers to utilize EHRs for improved patient care.

chargemaster or **charge description master (CDM)** a computer file that contains a list of the Healthcare Common Procedural Coding System codes and associated charges for services provided to hospital patients.

clinic outpatient an outpatient treated in an organized clinic of the hospital, in which hospital staff evaluate the patient and manage the patient's care.

common working file a file maintained on each Medicare beneficiary in one of nine regional databases. This file contains claims history information from both Part A and Part B claims and data on utilization patterns of Medicare beneficiaries.

discounting reducing the payment for additional procedures or ambulatory patient groups so that these other items are not paid at the full rate, as they would be if they had been the only services performed in a given encounter.

Emergency Medical Treatment and Active Labor Act (EMTALA) a federal law that imposes a legal duty on hospitals to screen and stabilize, if necessary, any patient who arrives in the emergency department. The purpose of EMTALA is to prevent the "dumping" of patients who may not be able to pay for emergency department services.

emergency outpatient an outpatient evaluated and treated in the emergency department of the hospital.

fiscal intermediary (FI) before the implementation of MACs, an organization with a contract with CMS to process and pay Part A Medicare claims.

hospital inpatient an individual receiving health care services as well as room and board and continuous nursing care in a hospital unit where patients generally stay overnight.

hospital outpatient a hospital patient who receives care at the hospital but who is not admitted as an inpatient.

Hospital Inpatient Prospective Payment System (HIPPS or IPPS) Medicare's payment system for hospital inpatient services. The basic unit of payment in the IPPS is the Medicare Severity Diagnosis Related Group (MS-DRG).

Hospital Outpatient Prospective Payment System (HOPPS or OPPS) Medicare's payment system for hospital outpatient services. The basic unit of payment in the OPPS is the ambulatory payment classification (APC) of each service provided.

hospitalist "a physician who specializes in inpatient medicine" (Slee, Slee, & Schmidt, 2008, 275).

Medicare Administrative Contractor (MAC) an organization that has contracted with CMS to process Medicare claims. MACs have replaced fiscal intermediaries and Medicare carriers.

Medicare carrier before the implementation of MACs, an organization having a contract with the CMS to process and pay Part B Medicare claims.

Medicare-Severity diagnosis related groups (MS-DRGs) groupings of inpatient services (based on the diagnosis, expected resource consumption, and other characteristics) that determine the payment the hospital receives under the Hospital Inpatient Prospective Payment System (HIPPS).

observation services "services furnished by a hospital on the hospital's premises, including use of a bed and periodic monitoring by a hospital's nursing or other staff, which are reasonable and necessary to evaluate an outpatient's condition or determine the need for a possible admission to the hospital as an inpatient" (CMS, 2003a, §230.6A).

partial hospitalization program (PHP) an intensive treatment program in which patients receive services for part of each day. These patients would otherwise require inpatient psychiatric care (CMS, 2003a).

potentially compensable event (PCE) an occurrence that may result in litigation against the health care provider or that may require the health care provider to financially compensate an injured party.

referred hospital outpatient an outpatient who is referred to the hospital for specific services, such as laboratory or radiology examinations. The hospital is responsible only for providing the diagnostic or therapeutic services requested, while the referring physician is responsible for evaluating and managing the patient's care.

resident primarily, a licensed physician, dentist, or podiatrist who participates in an approved graduate medical education (GME) program. The term *resident* may also be applied to physicians with temporary or restricted licenses, or to unlicensed graduates of foreign medical schools who are authorized to practice only in a hospital (Physician services in teaching settings, 2009).

revenue codes used on the UB-04 to indicate the general nature of the services provided.

status indicator an alphabetic character that indicates the type of each APC and whether or how that APC is paid under the Hospital Outpatient Prospective Payment System (OPPS).

Uniform Ambulatory Care Data Set (UACDS) a 16-item data set approved by the National Committee on Vital and Health Statistics (NCVHS); one of the first attempts to standardize ambulatory data collection efforts.

Uniform Hospital Discharge Data Set (UHDDS) standard data elements to be collected from individual inpatient records. The UHDDS data definitions are important for correct reporting of inpatient data, for example on the UB-04.

REVIEW QUESTIONS

Knowledge-Based Questions

1. What has been the trend in the utilization of hospital-based services? What factors help account for this trend?
2. List and describe five different types of outpatient services.
3. List and describe three different types of hospital outpatients.
4. What organization accredits the majority of hospitals in the United States? Which accrediting organization most recently received "deeming authority" for its hospital accreditation program from CMS?
5. What are the key components that both inpatient and outpatient records must contain in the documentation of surgery?

6. What are the key issues with regard to documentation of services rendered by teaching physicians?
7. What is the hospital chargemaster or charge description master?
8. What are DRGs/APCs, and what is their impact on hospital reimbursement?
9. What coding systems are used in hospital-based care?
10. What is EMTALA?
11. What is ARRA?
12. What factors should be considered to avoid legal risk in hospital-based care?
13. Describe various roles of the HIM professional in hospital-based care.

Critical Thinking Questions

1. If the Joint Commission requires that "the hospital initiates and maintains a medical record for every individual assessed or treated," what factors allow a hospital to maintain minimal data, such as test results in the case of some referred outpatients?
2. Select two of the three hospital accrediting organizations mentioned in this chapter, and write a brief essay comparing and contrasting the two organizations that you selected. Use outside resources, if necessary, but remember to think critically and avoid relying heavily on marketing or promotional information.

WEB ACTIVITY

Visit the Web site of the Health Care Compliance Association at http://www.hcca-info.org. Locate information about the "CHC" certification offered by this group. Find the Healthcare Compliance Certification Board (HCCB) handbook, and look at the detailed content outline for HCCB's certification examination.

1. In which content areas do you feel you could demonstrate skill as a result of your health information management training?
2. Which content areas would require more training on your part?

CASE STUDY

Grace Greene, RHIA, has been offered a leadership position at Greater Good Hospital to assist in improving the hospital's revenues. The hospital recognized that her knowledge and experience in coding and clinical documentation would be valuable in this effort, but these are not the only skills that will be needed to fine-tune the hospital's revenue cycle. Recognizing that there are many components of the revenue cycle and many hospital departments that have a role to play, what are some of the processes that Grace and her team should examine in assessing where the hospital currently stands and in looking for possible areas of improvement?

REFERENCES AND SUGGESTED READINGS

[ALTHA] Acute Long Term Hospital Association. (n.d.). [Online]. http://www.altha.org [2010, June 3].

[ACEP] American College of Emergency Physicians. (n.d.). *Costs of Emergency Care* [Online]. http://www3.acep.org/patients.aspx?id=25902 [2010, May 24].

[ACEP] American College of Emergency Physicians. (n.d.). *Observation Care Payments to Hospitals* FAQ [Online]. http://www.acep.org/practres.aspx?id=30486 [2010, May 17].

[AHA] American Hospital Association. (2009). *Hospital statistics.* Chicago: Health Forum LLC.

Brodnik, M., McCain, M. C., Rinehart-Thompson, L. A., & Reynolds, R. B. (2009). *Fundamentals of Law for Health Informatics and Information Management.* Chicago: American Health Information Management Association.

[CMS] Centers for Medicare & Medicaid Services. (2002). Prospective Payment System for Long-Term Care Hospitals: Implementation and FY 2003 Rates. *Federal Register, 67* (169), pp. 55954–56090.

[CMS] Centers for Medicare & Medicaid Services. (2003a). Chapter II: Coverage of hospital services. *Hospital Manual* [Online]. http://www.cms.gov/Manuals/PBM/list.asp [2010, June 3].

[CMS] Centers for Medicare & Medicaid Services. (2009a). Section 100 - Teaching physician services. *Medicare Claims Processing Manual, Chapter 12 - Physicians/Nonphysician Practitioners* [Online]. https://www.cms.gov/manuals/downloads/clm104c12.pdf.

[CMS] Centers for Medicare & Medicaid Services. (2009b.) Medicare Program: Proposed Changes to the Hospital Outpatient Prospective Payment System and CY 2010 Payment Rates; Proposed Changes to the Ambulatory Surgical Center Payment System and CY 2010 Payment Rates; Proposed Rule. [Online]. http://edocket.access.gpo.gov/2009/E9-15882.htm [2010, May 29].

[CMS] Centers for Medicare & Medicaid Services. (2009c, September). Acute care hospital inpatient prospective payment system. *Medicare Learning Network Payment System Fact Sheet Series*. [Online]. http://www.cms.gov/MLNProducts/downloads/AcutePaymtSysfctsht.pdf [2010, May 30].

[CMS] Centers for Medicare & Medicaid Services. (2010, January). Hospital Outpatient prospective payment system. *Medicare Learning Network Payment System Fact Sheet Series*. [Online]. http://www.cms.gov/MLNProducts/downloads/HospitalOutpaysysfctsht.pdf [2010, May 30].

Changes to the Hospital Outpatient Prospective Payment System and CY 2010 Payment Rates, 74 Fed. Reg. 60316–60983 (2009) (to be codified at 42 C.F.R. pts. 410, 416, & 419).

Conditions of Participation for Hospitals, *Code of Federal Regulations*, Title 42, pt. 482, 2009 ed.

Curran, W. J., Hall, M. A., Bobinski, M. A., & Orentlicher, D. (1998). *Health Care Law and Ethics*. New York: Aspen Law & Business.

DNV. (2010, January 11). DNV Accreditation Program: Frequently asked questions [Online]. http://www.dnvaccreditation.com [2010, May 26].

Dowling, D. A. (2008). Industry trends. *Journal for Healthcare Quality Web Exclusive, 30*(6), W6–W13. [Online]. www.nahq.org/journal/online [2010, May 26].

Electronic Health Record Incentive Program; Proposed Rule, 75 Fed. Reg. 1844–2011 (2010) (to be codified at 42 C.F.R. pts. 412, et al.).

Eubanks, P. (1990). Outpatient care: A nationwide revolution. *Hospitals*, August 5, pp. 28–35.

Glondys, B. (2000). Glossary of healthcare services and statistical terms. In K. G. Youmans, *Basic Healthcare Statistics for Health Information Management Professionals* (pp. 139–175). Chicago: American Health Information Management Association.

Hanken, M. A., and Waters, K. A. (1994). *Glossary of Healthcare Terms*. Chicago: American Health Information Management Association.

[HCFA] Health Care Financing Administration. (2000, August 17). Announcement of Designated Standard Maintenance Organizations. 65 *Federal Register* 50373.

Institute of Medicine. (1991). *The Computer-based Patient Record: An Essential Technology for Health Care*. Washington, DC: National Academy Press.

Joint Commission. (2010). *Accreditation Process Guide for Hospitals*. Oakbrook Terrace, IL: Author.

Lawrence, R. S., & Jonas, S. (1990). Ambulatory care. In A. R. Kovner (Ed.), *Health Care Delivery in the United States* (4th ed., pp. 106–140). New York: Springer Publishing Company.

Liu, K., Baseggio, C., Wissoker, D., Maxwell, S., Haley, J., and Long, S. (2001). Long-term care hospitals under Medicare: Facility-level characteristics. *Health Care Financing Review, 23* (2), 1–18.

MedPAC. (2008, October). Long-term care hospitals payment system. *Payment Basics*. [Online]. http://www.medpac.gov [2010, May 29].

MedPAC. (2010, March). Long-term care hospital services. *Report to the Congress: Medicare Payment Policy* [Online]. http://www.medpac.gov [2010, May 29].

[NCIPC] National Center for Injury Prevention and Control. (1997). Data elements for emergency department systems, release 1.0. Atlanta, GA: Centers for Disease Control and Prevention. [Online]. http://www.cdc.gov/ncipc/pub-res/pdf/deeds.pdf [2003, August 4].

[NCVHS] National Committee on Vital and Health Statistics. (1996). Core health data elements: Report of the National Committee on Vital and Health Statistics [Online]. http://www.ncvhs.hhs.gov/ncvhsr1.htm#Future [2003, August 4].

New study finds over half of U.S. hospitals utilize hospitalists. (2009, January 9). *Medical News Today*. [Online]. http://www.medicalnewstoday.com/articles/134949.php [2010, May 31].

Odom-Wesley, B. (2009) *Documentation for Medical Records*. Chicago: American Health Information Management Association.

[OIG] Office of the Inspector General, U.S. Department of Health and Human Services. (2009). Centers for Medicare & Medicaid Services work plan for fiscal year 2010 [Online]. http://oig.hhs.gov/publications/docs/work-plan/2010/Work_Plan_FY_2010.pdf [2010, June 4].

Physician Services in Teaching Settings. 42 C.F.R. pt. 415, subpt. D, 2009 ed.

Roth, J. A. (2002). Risk management and quality improvement. In M. Brodnik, M. C. McCain, L. A. Rinehart-Thompson, & R. B. Reynolds (Eds.), *Fundamentals of Law for Health Informatics and Information Management* (pp. 289–314). Chicago: American Health Information Management Association.

Slee, D. A., Slee, V. N., & Schmidt, H. J. (2008). *Slee's Healthcare Terms* (5th ed.). Sudbury, MA: Jones and Bartlett.

Special Responsibilities of Medicare Hospitals in Emergency Cases. 42 C.F.R pt. 489, Sect. 24, 2009 ed.

KEY RESOURCES

Acute Long Term Hospital Association
http://www.altha.org

American College of Emergency Physicians
http://www.acep.org

American Health Information Management Association
http://www.ahima.org

American Hospital Association
http://www.aha.org

American Society for Healthcare Risk Management (ASHRM)
http://www.ashrm.org

Association of American Medical Colleges
http://www.aamc.org

Centers for Medicare & Medicaid Services
http://www.cms.gov

DNV Healthcare, Inc.
National Integrated Accreditation of Healthcare Organizations (NIAHO)
http://www.dnvaccreditation.com or
http://www.dnv.com

Health Care Compliance Association
http://www.hcca-info.org

Healthcare Facilities Accreditation Program (American Osteopathic Association)
http://www.hfap.org

Healthcare Financial Management Association
http://www.hfma.org

The Joint Commission
http://www.jointcommission.org

National Association of Long Term Hospitals
http://www.nalth.org

Office of the Inspector General
http://oig.hhs.gov

Society of Hospital Medicine
http://www.hospitalmedicine.org

CHAPTER 3

Freestanding Ambulatory Care

ELIZABETH D. BOWMAN, MPA, RHIA

LEARNING OBJECTIVES

Upon successful completion of this chapter, you should be able to:

- List the types of freestanding ambulatory centers and differentiate among them regarding the kinds of programs and services they offer.

- Define basic terms related to freestanding ambulatory care facilities.

- List the major agencies or organizations that set standards for the facility and interpret their standards.

- Discuss pertinent record completion, filing, quality assessment, coding, and indexing, and computer systems for freestanding ambulatory care facilities.

- Discuss payment systems for freestanding ambulatory care.

Setting	Description	Synonyms/Examples
Public Health Department	Organization that provides services to promote the health of the community as a whole, such as immunizations and disease screenings	Community Health
Community Health Center	Ambulatory setting originating in the 1960s to provide ambulatory care to the indigent of a particular neighborhood; subsequent legislation expanded scope to any medically underserved area or population	Federally Qualified Health Center (FQHC) Neighborhood Health Center
Rural Health Clinic	A health care clinic located in an underserved rural area and offering physician services as well as services of mid-level providers	RHC
Industrial Health Centers	Ambulatory setting in which care is provided to employees at their place of work or at an employer-contracted site	Industrial Clinic Occupational Health Center
Ambulatory Surgery Centers	Setting provided for surgery on an ambulatory basis	Surgicenter
Urgent Care Centers	Ambulatory care setting in which patients are seen on a walk-in basis without appointments	Minor Emergency Center Walk-in Clinic
Physician Private Practices	Setting in which physicians practice independently rather than being employed by an organization such as an urgent care center or clinic	Doctor's Office Solo Practice Group Practice
University Health Centers	Ambulatory setting in which care is provided to students while they are in college, as well as faculty and staff in some cases	Student Health University Health Employee Health
Birth Centers	Ambulatory setting that provides labor and delivery services for uncomplicated deliveries	Birthing Centers

INTRODUCTION TO SETTING

Care Settings

How is **freestanding ambulatory care** different from hospital-based ambulatory care? The obvious difference is that freestanding sites are not located within the hospital. There are a variety of types of freestanding settings, and freestanding ambulatory care is the one in which most people receive care. The type of ambulatory care facility determines the types of patients seen, the types of caregivers, and, therefore, the types of information collected.

A large portion of freestanding ambulatory care is provided by **physician private practices** in offices where physicians see ambulatory patients. Physicians may practice alone, called solo practice, or in a group. A group practice usually involves three or more physicians, either all of the same specialty or of different specialties. Physicians practicing together usually share records, equipment, and offices and have an arrangement to divide the profits of the practice. Historically, such practices have been the most common setting in which ambulatory care is provided.

Other types of ambulatory care have been developed to meet the needs of patients. **Public health departments**, for example, provide a variety of services to improve the health of the community as a whole, in addition to health care for individuals. An emphasis is placed on preventive services such as immunizations, screenings, and notifying contacts of patients with infectious conditions such as tuberculosis and syphilis, to prevent further spread of the condition throughout the community.

Community health centers were a result of federal social legislation in the 1960s. Their purpose is to meet the medical needs of people who, because of their location and their inability to pay, may not receive the care they need in the traditional physician's office or clinic. These clinics typically serve a defined neighborhood area (Geiger, 2005). In 1989, Congress passed legislation that allowed community health centers (and also migrant health centers) to receive special Medicare and Medicaid payments as **federally qualified health centers (FQHCs)**. FQHCs are nonprofit or public organizations that provide or arrange for comprehensive health care services to medically underserved areas or populations (HRSA, 2006).

Rural Health Clinics (RHCs) are health care clinics that utilize mid-level providers such as physician assistants and nurse practitioners in addition to physician services and are located in underserved rural areas (HRSA, 2006).

Urgent care centers arose to meet the need for care outside regular physicians' office hours, traditionally provided in expensive hospital emergency departments. Urgent care centers usually see patients on a walk-in basis without appointments and provide basically the same services as physicians' offices.

Ambulatory surgery centers (ASCs) arose to meet the need for a less-expensive setting than the hospital for low-risk surgical procedures. Their growth was fed by the Omnibus Reconciliation Act of 1980 that set up a Medicare payment system specifically for ASCs (ASSA, 2010). Although some physicians perform minor surgical procedures in their offices, the main difference in a freestanding ASC is that it usually has at least one full, dedicated operating room (Encyclopedia, n.d.); is often licensed by the state; and provides surgical privileges to doctors in the community, not just in one practice.

Industrial or **occupational health centers** provide care to employees at their place of work or at an employer-contracted site. Services range from providing care for minor injuries sustained on the job to providing physical examinations when employees are hired or when they are returning to work following an accident. They often provide screenings such as auditory tests for employees at risk of hearing loss or exposure-level tests for employees working with hazardous substances.

University health centers provide care to students while they are enrolled in college, as well as to faculty and staff in some cases. Some centers provide only minor services, whereas others provide the full scope of care. The extent of their services often depends on the size of the university and the range of services available to students outside the university community.

Birth centers and **family planning centers** arose to counteract what was felt to be rigidity by hospitals in providing birthing and family planning options. They provide a homelike atmosphere for deliveries and provide contraceptive and other family planning services. Hospitals historically would not allow family or other support persons within the labor and delivery suites. Alternative caregivers such as midwives were also not allowed to perform deliveries. Freestanding birth centers and family planning centers were developed to provide the homelike environment requested by patients along with a variety of caregivers providing support.

Types of Patients

The type of freestanding ambulatory facility is the first factor to consider in developing health information management services. The second important factor is the type of patients seen in the setting. As can be seen from the types of settings providing ambulatory care, a variety of patients are included. Patients seen in the ambulatory setting are not critically ill. Care may be provided to well patients, as in the case of well-baby care and the health screenings provided in industrial health settings. Most of the patients, however, are the ambulatory sick who may have minor acute problems, such as sore throats and earaches, or chronic conditions, such as heart disease and diabetes. All ages of patients are included. Some facilities see only a certain type of patient. Birth centers, for example, see pregnant women. Ambulatory surgery centers see patients with surgically treatable diseases. The types of patients seen by a facility affect the information that must be maintained. In a pediatric clinic, for example, information on immunizations and growth and development is necessary. Birth centers need to provide information on labor and delivery.

Types of Caregivers

The next information to find out in planning HIM services is what types of caregivers are seeing patients in the facility. Different types of caregivers provide different types of documentation, which affect the information available (see Figure 3-1). Because physician practices provide most ambulatory care services, physicians are the main caregivers. They may be in private practice, or they may be employees of settings such as university health or urgent care centers.

Other professionals such as **nurse practitioners** (**NPs**) also provide care in the ambulatory setting. A nurse practitioner is a registered nurse who has had additional training in areas such as family or pediatric care. NPs are often the primary caregivers in settings such as industrial clinics and neighborhood health centers. **Certified nurse midwives** (**CNMs**) often practice in birth and family planning centers. **Physician assistants** (**PAs**) may be seen in settings similar to those employing nurse practitioners. PAs are not nurses but have received training to use independent judgment in treating patients. Nonphysicians such as NPs, CNMs, and PAs, whose licenses allow them to exercise a degree of independent judgment under the supervision of a physician, are called **mid-level providers** (**MLPs**). Other practitioners that may be seen include dentists, nutritionists, and counselors.

Ambulatory Caregivers	Type of Service Provided
Physician	MD or DO providing complete medical care
Nurse Practitioner (NP)	Advanced practice RN providing care independently within a certain area of practice such as family care or pediatrics
Certified Nurse Midwife (CNM)	Advanced practice RN providing care during pregnancy, labor, and delivery in uncomplicated cases
Physician Assistant (PA)	Non-RN using independent judgment in providing care
Dentist	DDS or DMD specializing in care of the teeth and gums
Nutritionist	Practitioner providing advice and planning for patients' nutritional needs
Counselor/Therapist	Practitioner providing care for behavioral and mental problems
Psychologist	PhD providing care for behavioral and mental problems
Social Worker	Practitioner assisting patients with social and environmental problems
Chiropractor	Practitioner providing manipulation, usually of the spine, to improve health
Podiatrist	Practitioner providing care of the feet

FIGURE **3-1** Caregivers in freestanding ambulatory care.

REGULATORY ISSUES

Determining types of caregivers in a facility identifies both who is entering information into the health information system and who are the internal users of information. The regulations that a facility must follow determine the external users of information and standards for what information should be maintained. Regulations and standards are usually determined by accreditation, certification, and licensure bodies.

Licensure

The requirements for licensure vary by the type of facility. Because licensure standards are set by the state, often through the state department of health, they are different in every state. Laws governing which facilities must be licensed also differ from state to state. In most states, physicians' offices do not require licensure. Ambulatory surgery centers and birth centers, however, usually have to meet licensure standards. Most licensure standards include rules for what information must be maintained by the facility in its health records. They are, therefore, an excellent source of information on what must be included in the information system.

Medicare Certification

As noted in Chapter 1, certain types of health care facilities must be Medicare certified according to Medicare Conditions of Participation or Conditions of Coverage before they can participate in the Medicare program. Conditions of

Participation/Coverage exist for ambulatory surgical services, for rural health clinics, and for federally qualified health centers. In the case of rural health clinics (RHCs), Medicare certification confers a special status that permits reimbursement from both Medicare and Medicaid. The goal of the rural health clinic program is to increase access to primary care in medically underserved rural areas by using PAs, NPs, and CNMs in physician shortage areas (Rural Assistance Center, n.d.). Similarly, federally qualified health centers (FQHCs), which may provide health care to any medically underserved area or population, must meet the requirements in the FQHCs Conditions for Coverage to be eligible to receive special Medicare and Medicaid payments (42CFR491.1).

The Conditions of Coverage require ambulatory surgery centers to "maintain a medical record for each patient," including documentation of ...

1. Patient identification
2. Significant medical history and results of physical examination
3. Preoperative diagnostic studies (entered before surgery), if performed
4. Findings and techniques of the operation, including a pathologist's report on tissue removed during surgery, except those exempted by the governing body
5. Any allergies and abnormal drug reactions
6. Entries related to anesthesia administration
7. Properly executed informed patient consent
8. Discharge diagnosis (42CFR416.47)

Medicare standards for rural health clinics and FQHCs include a requirement that records be maintained for each patient and that a designated professional staff member be assigned the responsibility for maintenance of the records. Included in the requirements for record content are identification and social data, consent forms, pertinent medical history, assessment of the health status and health care needs of the patient, a brief summary of the visit, disposition and instructions to the patient, physical examinations, laboratory and other diagnostic results, consultant's findings, physician's orders, reports of treatment, and medications. In addition, the standards require that medical records be retained for at least six years from the date of the last entry in the record unless a longer retention period is required by state law (42CFR491.10).

Accreditation

Unlike licensure, which must be undertaken if required by the state, accreditation is a voluntary process. There are a variety of organizations that accredit ambulatory care facilities. Some of the organizations, like the Accreditation Association for Ambulatory Health Care Inc. and the Joint Commission accredit a wide variety of ambulatory settings. Other accrediting organizations, like the American Association for Accreditation of Ambulatory Surgery Facilities, Inc., only focus on a narrow segment of ambulatory care. (See Figure 3-2 for the accreditation organizations commonly found in ambulatory care.)

The Joint Commission is the best-known health care accreditation agency. It has developed the *Comprehensive Accreditation Manual for Ambulatory Health Care*, which includes standards for freestanding ambulatory care settings. When

Accreditation Organization	Standards
The Joint Commission	*Comprehensive Accreditation Manual for Ambulatory Health Care Accreditation Manual for Office-Based Surgery*
Accreditation Association for Ambulatory Health Care Inc.	*Accreditation Handbook for Ambulatory Health Care*
Commission for the Accreditation of Birth Centers	*CABC Birth Center Standards*
American Association for Accreditation of Ambulatory Surgery Facilities, Inc.	*Standards and Checklist Booklet Resource Manual*

FIGURE **3-2** Accreditation organizations in freestanding ambulatory care.

freestanding ambulatory facilities are accredited, it is also common for them to be accredited by the Accreditation Association for Ambulatory Health Care Inc. Its standards are published in the *Accreditation Handbook for Ambulatory Health Care.* Other accreditation agencies accredit only a particular type of ambulatory care. One example is the American Association for Accreditation of Ambulatory Surgery Facilities, Inc., which accredits only single or multispecialty surgical facilities owned or operated by American Board of Medical Specialties surgeons as well as American Osteopathic Association Bureau of Osteopathic Specialists surgeons. Another specialty accreditation organization is the Commission for the Accreditation of Birth Centers, with its *CABC Birth Center Standards.*

Although many facilities do not choose to be accredited, accreditation standards can still provide health information managers with a set of benchmarks for the information system within their facility. HIM professionals should be aware of accreditation standards in setting up new systems and evaluating existing ones to establish that the best practices are followed.

Other Regulations: Compliance

The **Office of the Inspector General (OIG)** in the Department of Health and Human Services is charged with checking the compliance of providers with the laws and regulations covering reimbursement for federal programs such as Medicare. This office has identified large sums of money that were received by providers through error or fraud. The Department of Justice has recouped billions of dollars under laws such as the Federal False Claims Act and the Health Insurance Portability and Accountability Act (HIPAA).

To avoid such penalties, providers are encouraged to develop a compliance plan that ensures conformity to federal requirements. The OIG has published model **compliance plans** to provide guidance for a variety of health settings, including individual and small group physician practices in developing internal controls. These plans include seven components as follows:

- Conducting internal monitoring and auditing
- Implementing compliance and practice standards
- Designating a compliance officer or contact

- Conducting appropriate training and education
- Responding appropriately to detected offenses and developing corrective action
- Developing open lines of communication
- Enforcing disciplinary standards through well-publicized guidelines

When conducting internal monitoring and auditing, practices are urged to audit both standards and procedures as well as claims submission. The claims audit may be retrospective (looking at previous claims) or prospective (looking at claims before submission). When a Medicare overpayment is discovered in a retrospective audit, the health care provider is required to disclose and refund the overpayment. One advantage of conducting a prospective audit is that errors can be caught before claim submission, allowing the practice to avoid the additional paperwork resulting from overpayment refunds. From a baseline audit, problem areas can be identified, and periodic audits must then be carried out at least once a year. Monitoring should be an ongoing process.

Once the risk areas have been identified, practice standards and procedures must be developed to deal with those risks. Suggestions from the OIG include "(1) Developing a written standards and procedures manual; and (2) updating clinical forms periodically to make sure they facilitate and encourage clear and complete documentation of patient care" (OIG, 2000, p. 59438). The main risk areas to be addressed include coding, billing, reasonable and necessary services, documentation, improper inducements, kickbacks, and self-referrals.

Ideally, one person should be designated as a compliance officer or contact. The role of this person would be to oversee the adherence of the practice/facility to the compliance plan that it has developed.

Targeted training and education programs should emphasize providing training for staff members most in need of training and for the areas of most risk. However, general training should cover all risk areas and include all staff members who could participate in or identify an error or a violation of the compliance program. Training must be ongoing and must address any changes in the laws, regulations, and coding systems that affect compliance.

When offenses are detected, a corrective action plan must be developed. There is a Provider Self-Disclosure Protocol, developed by the OIG, which should be followed in such cases. Open lines of communication are necessary to ensure that everyone is aware of how to report what they believe to be fraudulent or in error. Finally, disciplinary procedures must be in place to deal with violations of the compliance plan.

Another program that targets fraud and abuse is the **Medicaid Integrity Program** (MIP). This is a state and federal government initiative to identify fraud and abuse in the Medicaid program. (CMS State Program Integrity, n.d.) Under this program, Audit Medicaid Integrity Contractors (MICs) audit Medicaid providers to identify overpayments and to decrease inappropriate Medicaid claims (Medicaid Integrity Program Provider Audits, (2009).

DOCUMENTATION

Documentation involves the process of recording information about the care being provided in the ambulatory care center. Many factors influence what must be documented, including those factors already discussed: type of facility, types of patients, types of caregivers, and internal and external users of information. It is easiest to think about documentation by going through the care process with the patient to see what items of data must be maintained (see Figure 3-3). The documentation may be entered and maintained in a paper or an electronic medical record format.

Registration/Demographic Information

The first contact the patient usually has with any ambulatory care setting is the **registration** process. During this step, demographic information, such as the patient's name and address, and financial information, such as responsible party and insurance coverage, are collected. Often this information is first documented by having the patient complete a form upon arrival at the facility (see Figure 3-4). This information is then entered into the patient's record by clerical personnel either on an information form or in the demographics/finance section of an electronic information system or electronic medical record. Usually the original form completed by the patient does not become a part of the official record.

History and Physical

Once basic information has been received from the patient, the actual care process begins. The first step is finding out why the patient is being seen, or the **reason for visit**, and obtaining a history of the illness. The nurse often begins this process by asking the patient for the reason for visit and a brief history.

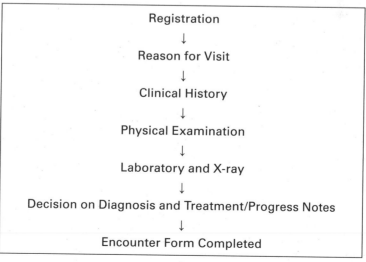

Registration
↓
Reason for Visit
↓
Clinical History
↓
Physical Examination
↓
Laboratory and X-ray
↓
Decision on Diagnosis and Treatment/Progress Notes
↓
Encounter Form Completed

FIGURE **3-3 Flow of care and documentation.**

Patient Data

MEDICAL RECORD NO _____

THIS IMPORTANT INFORMATION IS CONFIDENTIAL. PLEASE BE HONEST. ANSWER THE QUESTIONS AS BEST YOU CAN. IF YOU NEED ASSISTANCE, ASK YOUR PROVIDER.

Patient's Name:_____ ____/____/____
(last)   (first)   (middle)   **Social Security Number**

Previous Names Used:_____

Address:_____ ____/____/____/____
(street)   (city)   (state) (zip) (county)

Home Phone: (   )_____ **Sex:**___ **Race:**___ **Marital Status:** M__ S__ Sep__ D __ W __

Birth Date:_____ **Age:**____ **City:**_____ **State/Country of Birth:**_____ _____

Mother's Maiden Name:_____
(last)   (first)

Father's Name:_____ _____
(last)   (first)

No. in Family:_____ **Head of Household:**_____ **Guardian:**_____

Other Family   LAST   FIRST   DATE OF BIRTH   SEX   RELATIONSHIP

     Members: _____

_____

_____

_____

_____

Person to Contact in Case of Emergency:_____
(last)   (first)

     Relationship: _____ **Phone No: (   )**_____

     Address:_____
(street)   (city)   (state)   (zip)

Nearest Relative: _____
(last)   (first)

     Relationship: _____ **Phone No: (   )**_____

     Address:_____
(street)   (city)   (state)   (zip)

Previous Visits to The Regional Medical Center of Memphis (The Med)? No__ Yes__ Please Explain:

_____

Patient's Occupation:_____

Employment Status: Full-Time__ Part-Time__ Unemployed__ Retired__ Student__ Military__ Other__

Employer: _____ **Business Phone: (   )** _____ **Ext:**_____

Address:_____
(street)   (city)   (state)   (zip)

Religion: _____

Do you have any communication barriers for which you might require additional assistance?
     No__ Yes__: Language__ Please identify_____   Unable To Read__ Deaf___
     Blind_____   Other _____

Printed in **THE MED** Print Shop

FIGURE **3-4** Registration form. (Courtesy of Memphis FamilyCare Center.)

Sometimes the patient may complete a history form, either manually or on the computer. The comprehensiveness of the history depends on the patient's reason for visit. A visit for a sore throat, for example, would require only minimal information. A visit for shortness of breath would require a more exhaustive inquiry into the patient's past history and family and social history. The caregiver—either the physician, nurse practitioner, or physician assistant—then completes the physical. Like the history, the physical varies in completeness depending on the patient's reason for visit.

Laboratory and X-ray Reports

The history and the physical examination begin the fact-finding process to gain the information needed to make a diagnosis and to determine a plan of treatment. Sometimes additional information is needed, such as clinical laboratory tests and X-rays. Simple tests may often be provided in the office or clinic, but more-complicated procedures may require that the patient be referred elsewhere. In a paper system, results of the tests may be kept in a computer printout or may be recorded on a reporting slip. Providers striving for meaningful use of an electronic health record (EHR) should enter or import clinical lab test results into the EHR as structured data.

Progress Notes

Once all the needed information has been collected, the caregiver usually records diagnoses or major problems in narrative form, along with plans for treatment such as medications prescribed. In some settings, the documentation for the entire encounter may take the format of a long note, which may be handwritten or typed. In electronic health records, structured progress notes that may or may not utilize templates are common.

Encounter Form

At the end of the visit, an **encounter form** or **superbill** is usually generated (Figure 3-5). This form includes information on the patient's diagnoses and treatments, along with disease and procedure codes and charges. Usually completed, at least in part, by the caregiver, the encounter form may become a part of the patient's record. It may, however, be stored separately, because its main purpose is to provide information for billing and insurance processing rather than documenting the care process.

Copies of Hospital Records

If the patient has been hospitalized, copies of forms from the hospital, such as the operative report and discharge summary, are often sent to the facility. These are usually filed in the patient's record. As health information exchange becomes available in more communities, it is becoming possible to transmit information electronically between the hospital and the ambulatory setting.

Problem List

In facilities that see patients on an ongoing basis, a **problem list** is often used (Figure 3-6). The problem list is a numbered list of the patient's diagnoses or

Memphis FamilyCare Center Encounter Form

		Diagnoses: (List Primary Dx as #1)
Patient's Name	**Chart #**	1
		2
Patient's SSN	**Encounter #**	3
Date	**Age**	4
	Insurance Type (circle below)	5
New Patient Yes No	**TennCare Com Self Pay Other**	6

DX #	DESCRIPTION	KEY 1	DX #	DESCRIPTION	KEY 1	DX #	DESCRIPTION	KEY 1
	OFFICE VISITS			**MEDICATIONS con't.**			**LAB: OUTSIDE (con't.)**	
	New Pt. Problem (10)	99201		MMR	90707		Bilirubin: Direct	82251
	New Pt. Expanded (20)	99202		Phenergan	J2550		Blood Count (Reticulocyte)	85044
	New Pt. Detailed (30)	99203		Pneumovac	90732		Calcium	82310
	New Pt. Comprehensive (45)	99204		Polio (OPV)	90712		Carbon Dioxide (Bicarb.)	82374
	New Pt. Comprehensive (60)	99205		PPD (Intradermal)	86580		CPK	82550
	Est. Pt. Simple (5)	99211		Procardia	J9999		Culture: Bacterial-Routine	87070
	Est. Pt. Problem (10)	99212		Rocephin (250 mg.)	J0696		Culture: Blood	87040
	Est. Pt. Expanded (15)	99213		Tetanus	90703		Culture: Chlamydia	87110
	Est. Pt. Detailed (25)	99214		Tetramune	90720		Culture: GC	87081
	Est. Pt. Comprehensive (40)	99215		Toradol	J3490		Culture: Herpes	87252
	New Pt.-Well Child; 0-1 yr	99381		Other			Culture: Throat	87060
	New Pt.-Well Child; 1-4 yr	99382		Other			Culture: Urine (Quantat)	87086
	New Pt.-Well Child; 5-11 yr	99383					Culture/Sens. - Urine	87088
	New Pt.-Well Child; 12-17 yr	99384					Dilantin	80185
	New Pt.-Well Pt.; 18-39 yrs	99385		**LAB: IN-HOUSE**			Drug Screen (Indicate Drug)	80100
	New Pt.-Well Pt.; 40-64 yrs	99386		Accu - Check (Glucometer)	82948		Estrogen: Total	82672
	New Pt.-Well Pt.; over 65 yrs	99387		Albumin	82040		FANA	86255
	Est. Pt.-Well Child; 0-1 yr	99391		Alk. Phos.	84075		Folic Acid	82746
	Est. Pt.-Well Child; 1-4 yr	99392		ALT (SGPT)	84460		GC Probe	87178
	Est. Pt.-Well Child; 5-11 yr	99393		AST (SGOT)	84450		GGTP	82977
	Est. Pt.-Well Child; 12-17 yr	99394		Bilirubin - TOTAL	82250		Hemoglobin: Glycosylated	83036
	Est. Pt.-Well Pt.; 18-39 yrs	99395		BUN	84520		Hepatitis A Antibody	86296
	Est. Pt.-Well Pt.; 40-64 yrs	99396		CBC/Diff. (Automated)	85025		Hepatitis B Surface Anti.	86291
	Est. Pt.-Well Pt.; over 65 yrs	99397		Chlamydia	86631		Hepatitis C Antibody	86302
	Consultation	99243		Cholesterol	82465		Hepatitis Panel	80059
	Development Assessment	99178		Creatinine	82565		HGB	85018
	Other			Glucose	82947		HIV Antigen	86311
	Other			GTT	82951		Iron	83540
				HCG - Serum (Pregnancy)	84703		Isoenzymes	82552
				HCG - Urine (Pregnancy)	84702		Lead Level	83655
				HDL	83718		Lipase	83690
	PROCEDURES			Hematocrit	85014		Lithium (Quantitative)	80178
	Administering Vaccine	Q0124		Hemoccult	82270		Magnesium	83735
	Aerosol Trtmt: Initial	94664		KOH	87220		Pap Smear	88150
	Aerosol Trtmt: F/U	94665		Mono Spot	86308		Phenobarb Level	82205
	Chem. Destruct. Lesion: Female	56501		Panels:			PKU	84030
	Chem. Destruct. Lesion: Male	54050		Arthritis	80072		Prostate Specific Antigen	84153
	EKG	93000		Exec (General Health)	80050		Protime	85610
	Hearing Screening	V5008		Lipid	80061		Sensitivity, Antibiotic	87181
	Insert Implant Contracept. Cap.	11975		Liver	80058		Thyroid Panel w/TSH	80092
	Remove Foreign Body Ear(s)	69200		Potassium	84132		Thyroid Panel w/o TSH	80091
	Rem Impact. Cerumen One or Both	69210		Protein - Total	84155		TIBC	83550
	Remove Implant Contracept. Cap.	11976		Rheumatoid (RA)	86430		T-3 (Triiodothyronine)	84480
	Skin Biopsy	11100		Sed Rate - Automat.	85651		T-4 (Thyroxine): Total	84336
	Suture (specify length & site)			Serum Ketone	82009		Vol. Measure/Timed Coll. each	81050
	Other			Sickle Screen	85660		Other	
	Other			Sodium	84295		Other	
				Strep Screen	86403			
	MEDICATIONS			Triglyceride	84478			
	Bicillin up to 600,000	J0530		Uric Acid	84550		LAB Handling Fee	99000
	Bicillin up to 1,200,000	J0540		Urinalysis	81000		ACE Bandage	A4460
	Bicillin up to 2,400,000	J0580		VDRL/RPR/ART	86592		Other	
	B12	J3420		WBC	85048		Other	
	Demerol/Meperdine up to 50 mg.	J2175		Wet Mount	87210			
	Depo - Medrol 20mg	J1020		Other				
	Depo - Medrol 40mg	J1030		Other			**REFERRALS**	
	Depo - Medrol 80mg	J1100					Dental	
	Depo - Provera 150 mg	J1055					Dermatology	
	Depo - Testosterone	J1090					OB/GYN	
	DPT	90701					Other	
	HBV (Hepatitis B Vac.)	90731		**LAB: OUTSIDE**			Other	
	HIB (H Influenza B Vac.)	90737		Amylase	82150			
	Influenza	90724		B12	82607			

Comments:

Provider's Signature	Appt. Date

FIGURE **3-5** Encounter form. (Courtesy of Memphis FamilyCare Center.)

PROBLEM LIST

NO.	DIAGNOSED	PROBLEM DESCRIPTION / COMMENTS	TYPE	RESOLVED

FIGURE **3-6** Problem list. (Courtesy of Memphis FamilyCare Center.)

problems, often including allergies and medications taken. It should appear in a conspicuous place in the record, usually at the front, and must be updated regularly. The problem list, therefore, serves as a table of contents for the record by summarizing the patient's care over time. In electronic health record systems, maintaining an up-to-date problem list of current diagnoses as discrete data based on a standard coding system can demonstrate meaningful use (Electronic Health Record Incentive Program; Proposed Rule, 2010).

Special Requirements

The process just outlined is universal for most ambulatory care encounters. Some types of facilities or encounters may have more specialized documentation requirements because of the specialized care provided, as shown in Figure 3-7. In designing documentation methods for a facility, the type of facility and the care provided must be carefully considered.

Ambulatory Surgery Centers

Ambulatory surgery centers add surgical documentation to the basic documentation just discussed. Necessary testing is often done before the day of surgery and must be present in the record before the surgery is done. Another important item of documentation is the consent for treatment. The surgeon is responsible for explaining the risks and alternatives associated with the surgery and for obtaining the patient's consent to the procedure. This consent process is often documented on a consent for surgery form that includes

Type of Setting	Special Documentation Requirements
Ambulatory Surgery Center	Surgical Consent Operative Report Anesthesia Report Recovery Room Report Pathology Report Discharge instructions
Birth Centers	Prenatal Record Labor and Delivery Record Physical Assessment of Newborn Follow-Up Plan
Pediatric Care	Growth and Development Charts Immunization Record
Industrial Health	New-Hire Physical Return-to-Work Physical Transfer/Promotion and Annual Physical Health Monitoring Auditory and Vision Records

FIGURE 3-7 Special documentation requirements.

the name of the surgery, the name of the surgeon, the alternatives to the surgery, and the risks involved. The record should be checked to see that preoperative documentation is available, such as history and physical and pertinent laboratory findings. Intraoperative documentation includes data about the surgery. Each caregiver has a role in documenting the care given. The anesthesiologist must document the anesthesia given, any fluids given, and the patient's pulse, respiration, and blood pressure throughout the procedure. The surgeon must document the preoperative and postoperative diagnoses, the findings of the surgery, and the methods used. When the patient leaves the surgical suite, the care given during the recovery period must also be documented, including vital signs and recovery from general anesthesia. If tissue was removed during the surgery, a pathology report describing the gross and microscopic findings is also included. Finally, instructions to the patient must be documented to ensure that the patient knows postoperative wound care, complications to watch for, and when to return for follow-up, if necessary.

Birth Centers

In birth centers, labor and delivery is the process that must be documented. Such documentation usually begins with the prenatal record, which starts when the woman comes for initial care during the pregnancy. Because this care usually occurs in the physician's or midwife's office throughout the pregnancy, a copy of the office prenatal record must be sent to the birth center at regular intervals late in the pregnancy so that it is available at the time of the delivery. Prenatal documentation includes prenatal history and physical, weight gain, prenatal testing, gestational stage of the pregnancy, and any pregnancy complications.

Labor and delivery records provide documentation of the labor process, including the onset of labor, length of labor, labor monitoring, pain management during the labor process, and the method of delivery.

Physical assessment of the newborn is also entered in the birthing center record, including the Apgar score (a rating based on certain physical functions at one minute and five minutes after birth), an overall scoring of the physical condition of the newborn, weight, and other physical assessments.

Finally, a follow-up plan must be included that documents follow-up instructions such as when the mother and baby should return to the caregiver for evaluation.

Pediatric Preventive Health Services

For children, immunizations must be documented on an **immunization record** so that the caregiver can tell at a glance whether an immunization is needed on a particular visit (see Figure 3-8). **Growth and development charts** are also included that record height and weight to monitor growth patterns (see Figure 3-9). Electronic plotting and display of growth charts for children ages 2 to 20 years, including body mass index (BMI), is a proposed requirement for meaningful use of an electronic health record.

MEMPHIS FAMILYCARE CENTER
IMMUNIZATION RECORD

PATIENT NAME: _____ BIRTH DATE: _____ CLINIC MR #: _____

I have read the information contained in the "Important Information" form(s) about the disease(s) and the vaccine.
I have had an opportunity to ask questions which were answered to my satisfaction.
I believe I understand the benefits and risks of the vaccine(s) and request that the vaccine(s) indicated below be given
  to me or to the person named in the identification space on the form for whom I am authorized to make this request.

VACCINE	DATE GIVEN M/D/Y	AGE	SITE	VACCINE MANUFACTURER	VACCINE LOT NUMBER	HANDOUT PUB. DATE	NURSE INITIALS	SIGNATURE OF PARENT/GUARDIAN
DTP1								
DTP2								
DTP3								
DTP/DTaP4								
DTP/DTaP5								
DT								
DTP/Hib1								
DTP/Hib2								
DTP/Hib3								
DTP/Hib4								
Td								
OPV/IPV1								
OPV/IPV2								
OPV/IPV3								
OPV/IPV4								
MMR1								
MMR2								
Hib1								
Hib2								
Hib3								
Hib4								
HepB1								
HepB2								
HepB3								

FIGURE 3-8 Immunization record. (Courtesy of Memphis FamilyCare Center.)

Industrial Health Services/Occupational Medicine

Many different types of documentation are included in industrial health records, depending on the type of service provided. The record frequently includes physical examinations. Examinations may be done after hiring but before placement on the job. They provide a basis for assessing the employee's health at the time of hire versus various times later during the employment

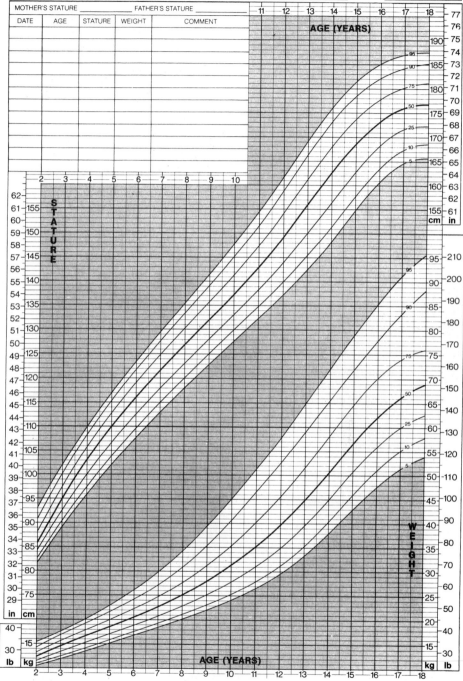

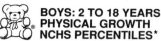

FIGURE 3-9 Height/weight record. (Courtesy of Memphis FamilyCare Center.)

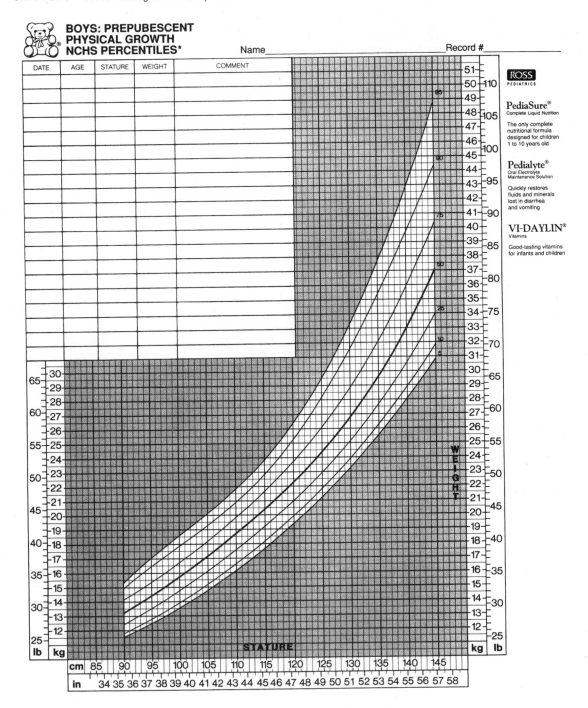

FIGURE **3-9** (Continued)

period. **Return-to-work physicals** are done for employees injured on the job who must be judged fit to work before returning to the workplace. Transfer or promotion and annual physicals are frequently provided for executive personnel. Health monitoring for exposure to hazardous or toxic substances or other health threats such as loud noise is also a common part of the industrial record. Vision records may be included for work settings where vision is an important factor in job performance, such as for pilots. Finally, if care is provided in the clinic for illness or accident treatment, the usual documentation of the care process must be included.

When selecting the documentation requirements for a particular facility, the HIM professional should begin with the universal components such as history and physical, progress notes, and laboratory and X-ray data. Then the particular needs of the site should be determined by looking at the specific type of care provided, which must be documented. Accreditation and licensure standards for the specific type of facility also help define the content of the documentation.

Record Format

The organization of data and information is defined as the record format (see Figure 3-10). There are three common formats for paper records: source oriented, integrated, and problem oriented. The traditional format is called **source oriented,** with the information presented according to its source, such as laboratory, X-ray, physician, nursing, and so forth. This format has the advantage of being familiar to caregivers, but it makes the process of reading the record and integrating data from the different sources more difficult.

In physicians' offices, the **integrated format** is frequently used. In this format, all information is entered in chronological order by visit. Other events such as telephone calls are listed chronologically between visits. Test results and copies of hospital records are entered as they are received. This method makes it easy to look at each episode of care. However, it is more difficult to look at the patient's care across time or, especially, to monitor a particular data element over time. For example, it is often desirable to look for trends in

Format	Characteristics
Source Oriented	Arranged according to source (e.g., laboratory, nursing, etc.)
Integrated	Chronological
Problem Oriented	Problem list Keyed to problem number
Electronic	Electronic format

FIGURE **3-10 Record formats.**

laboratory values. This is more difficult with the integrated format, because the laboratory results are scattered throughout the record rather than grouped into one location.

The **problem-oriented medical record (POMR)** is a third format that is occasionally used. The problem-oriented medical record was developed by Dr. Lawrence Weed to provide a more systematic method of record keeping. The key component of the POMR is the problem list. As was discussed previously, this is a list of the patient's problems and diagnoses and serves as a quick overview of the patient's health. In a true problem-oriented record, all parts of the record are indexed to the problem list. First, the clinical database consisting of the history, physical, and laboratory and X-ray findings is developed. Then a list of problems is developed and numbered. A plan indexed to the problem list is then generated, with a plan for each problem identified by problem number. Each order and progress note is also indexed to the problem number, so that it can be seen at a glance what problem is being addressed. Although the POMR is a systematic record-keeping process, it has not gained wide usage in ambulatory care. Generally, it is more likely seen in larger clinics with more caregivers and a greater need for coordination of care.

The choice of record format for paper records depends primarily on the preference of the caregivers. The main principle that must be followed, however, is that all caregivers within a facility must use the same format. Without this uniformity, it is very difficult to find data in records documented by different caregivers. When transitioning to an electronic medical record, paper records from previous encounters are often scanned into an electronic imaging system. An effective format is very important for efficient retrieval of these archived records. Committees are often formed to suggest a format and should consider the variety of users in making the decision.

The number of ambulatory care providers utilizing electronic record formats is increasing, at least in part because of the incentives in ARRA/HITECH for adopting electronic health record (EHR) systems and later the penalties for failing to adopt. Information in an EHR can be organized and entered in a variety of ways. The provider should select a certified EHR system with a format that will facilitate meeting the requirements of meaningful use. For example, some ambulatory providers previously adopted electronic systems that incorporated clinical lab results into their electronic medical record systems as scanned images, which would not meet the proposed meaningful use requirement to incorporate lab test results into the EHR as structured data.

One electronic format that is common in EHR systems is the use of templates for entering data. Some providers find that templates facilitate the record completion process. A number of EHR products include templates for different specialties and also permit customization of the templates by the provider. Figure 3-11 provides an example of a template for collecting information for a patient history.

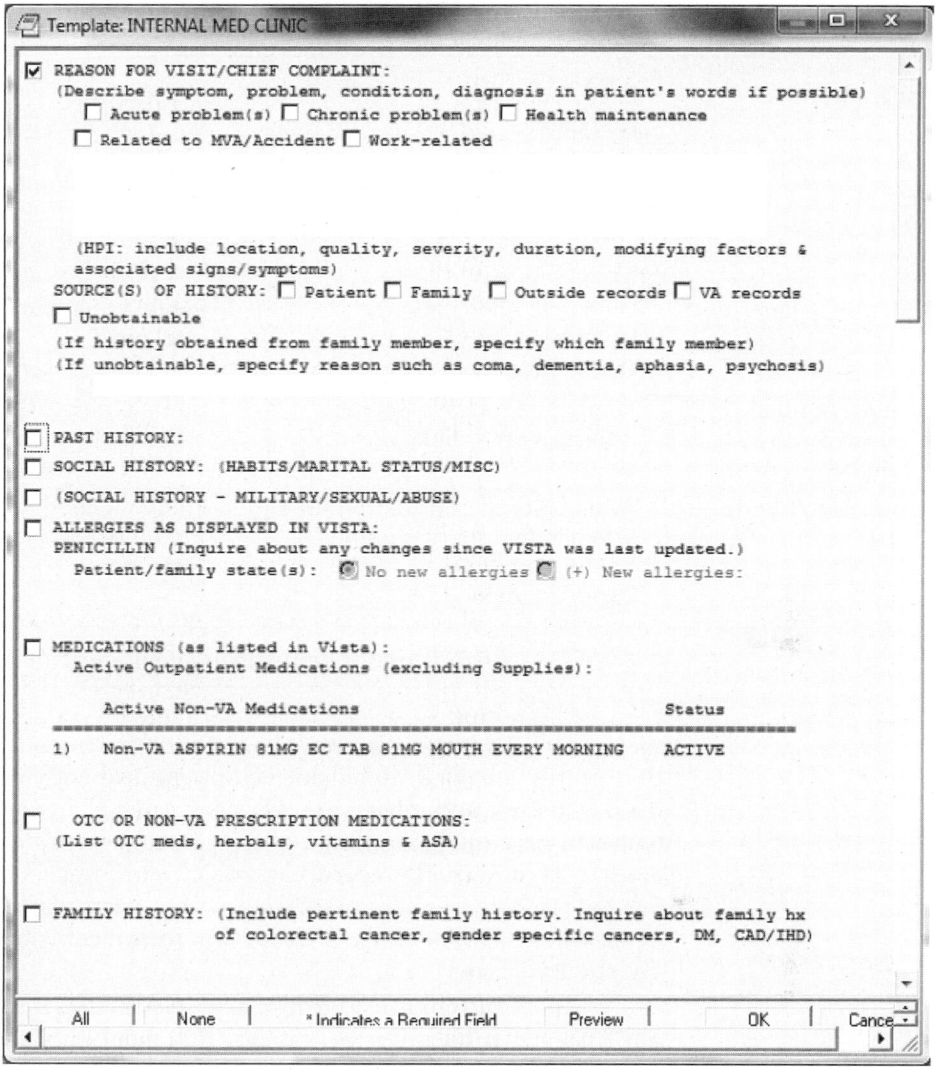
Template: INTERNAL MED CLINIC

REASON FOR VISIT/CHIEF COMPLAINT:
(Describe symptom, problem, condition, diagnosis in patient's words if possible)
Acute problem(s) Chronic problem(s) Health maintenance
Related to MVA/Accident Work-related

(HPI: include location, quality, severity, duration, modifying factors & associated signs/symptoms)
SOURCE(S) OF HISTORY: Patient Family Outside records VA records
Unobtainable
(If history obtained from family member, specify which family member)
(If unobtainable, specify reason such as coma, dementia, aphasia, psychosis)

PAST HISTORY:
SOCIAL HISTORY: (HABITS/MARITAL STATUS/MISC)
(SOCIAL HISTORY - MILITARY/SEXUAL/ABUSE)
ALLERGIES AS DISPLAYED IN VISTA:
PENICILLIN (Inquire about any changes since VISTA was last updated.)
Patient/family state(s): No new allergies (+) New allergies:

MEDICATIONS (as listed in Vista):
Active Outpatient Medications (excluding Supplies):

	Active Non-VA Medications	Status
1)	Non-VA ASPIRIN 81MG EC TAB 81MG MOUTH EVERY MORNING	ACTIVE

OTC OR NON-VA PRESCRIPTION MEDICATIONS:
(List OTC meds, herbals, vitamins & ASA)

FAMILY HISTORY: (Include pertinent family history. Inquire about family hx of colorectal cancer, gender specific cancers, DM, CAD/IHD)

All | None | * Indicates a Required Field | Preview | OK | Cancel

FIGURE 3-11 An example of a structured template in an electronic health record. In this particular system, when a checkbox in a section of the template is checked, that section expands for additional data entry. (Source: Department of Veterans Affairs. http://www.ehealth.va.gov/EHEALTH/CPRS_demo.asp/)

Patient Identifier/Filing Methods

Patient identifier refers to how the patient is identified in a health information system, whether paper based or electronic, and how information about that patient is found (see Figure 3-12). In small settings, the patient's name may be

Patient Identifier	Advantage	Disadvantage
Patient Name	Easily obtained No need for master patient index	Misspellings Many patients with same/similar names Need for secondary identifier to verify Cumbersome with a large number of records
Patient Number—unit or serial	Unique to each patient Uniform in length Confidentiality	Requires patient index to locate record
Patient Number—Social Security number	Most patients have Social Security number	Some patients do not have Social Security number Threat to privacy
Family Numbering	Availability of information for all family members together Useful for billing Useful in mailings	Frequent changes in family structure require changes in identification system

FIGURE **3-12** Patient identifiers used in ambulatory care.

the primary identifier. If a paper-based filing system is used in such a setting, the records are filed alphabetically by the patient's name. Such a system quickly becomes cumbersome, because patients frequently have the same name. In an electronic system, although the patient's name may be used to access that individual's record, electronic records must utilize a unique identifier for tracking the data associated with a particular patient. The patient's name is not suitable for use as the patient identifier in an EHR, because names are not unique.

When a system is too large to use an alphabetical system, a number is usually assigned to identify the patient. If a number is used, there must be a master patient index file by patient name to provide the patient's number. In an EHR, the patient's record could be found by searching the database using the patient's name or number. A secondary piece of information must frequently be used to verify that the correct patient has been found. Common secondary identifiers are the Social Security number, birth date, or mother's maiden name.

A variety of methods are used to assign these identifier numbers. One way is to first decide the number of digits to be used in the number and then to start at zero and assign the numbers. A six-digit number is frequently used to allow an adequate amount of numbers for the patient population. A decision would have to be made on whether the patient would keep the same number for all visits (a unit system) or would receive a new number for each visit to enable the facility to distinguish among visits by the number (serial system). Most ambulatory care facilities use the unit numbering system.

Some facilities have used the Social Security number to identify patients. Providers have found this method useful, because most Americans have a Social Security number. However, use of the Social Security number as the primary identifier is no longer considered a good practice for many reasons. Some patients, such as babies, do not have a number, and other patients may be using an incorrect one. In cases where the patient does not have a Social Security number, a pseudo number (false number) must be assigned. Using the Social Security number also raises issues of privacy, because the government maintains information about individuals using the Social Security number as an identifier. However, the primary reason for discontinuing the use of the Social Security number as the primary identifier is the increased risk of identity theft, which has become a serious problem in the United States.

A **family numbering system** is used in some facilities. With this numbering system, the family is assigned a number. All members of the family use the same number, with a suffix specifying their unique identifier within the family. The family number might be 425687, with the father being 425687-1, the mother 425687-2, and the child 425687-3. One advantage of this system is for settings in which the whole family is treated and when social and medical information about the entire family might be helpful in treating individuals. Family numbering can also be useful for billing purposes and mailings to family members. With the frequent changes in family structure through divorce and other family breakups, however, keeping up with the family unit and changing the record system to match it is a frustrating and frequently impossible task.

In selecting a patient identifier, the needs of the facility must be the primary consideration. In a facility where the patient may be seen once and never again, such as an ambulatory surgery center, it would be foolish to use a family numbering system. Industrial settings might use the employee number. A small facility using paper records may be well served by an alphabetical system. With an alphabetical system, a separate master patient index to identify the patient's number would not be needed. Again, the facts of facility type, caregivers, and patient type should determine the decision.

REIMBURSEMENT

Fee for Service

How is care paid for in freestanding ambulatory care settings? (See Figure 3-13.) The traditional method is called **fee for service**. In this system, the patient pays according to the type and amount of service provided. Usually, for example, there is a basic fee for the visit. Separate fees are assigned for laboratory tests, X-rays, or other services provided beyond the basic visit. In some facilities treating low-income patients, the fee for service may be charged based on a sliding scale, with the amount determined by the patient's income. The problem with fee for service has been that payers feel it offers an incentive to provide more service. A variety of systems have been devised to change the incentives from providing more service to providing only what is absolutely required by the patient's condition.

Payment System	Setting
Fee for Service	Any setting
Physician Fee Schedule	Physicians/Medicare Part B
ASC System	Ambulatory surgery/Medicare
Capitation	Any setting

FIGURE 3-13 Payment methods in freestanding ambulatory care.

Medicare Physician Fee Schedule

For physician reimbursement, Part B of Medicare now pays using the **Medicare Physician Fee Schedule (MPFS** or **PFS)**, which is based on the **resource-based relative value scale (RBRVS)**. Medicare Part B includes physician payment and payment for services for limited-license practitioners who treat only particular types of problems or parts of the body, such as dentists, oral and maxillofacial surgeons, optometrists, podiatrists, and chiropractors. Other services included are diagnostic tests other than clinical diagnostic lab tests, diagnostic and therapeutic radiology services, and physical and occupational therapy services (independent practice only) (*Medicare Physician Guide,* 2009). Nonphysician caregivers such as physician assistants, nurse practitioners, certified Registered Nurse Anesthetists, certified nurse midwives, clinical psychologists, and clinical social workers are also paid at a rate tied to the RBRVS (*Medicare Physician Guide,* 2009). Services provided to a patient by nurse practitioners or physician assistants when the physician is on site are termed *incident to* services and are fully reimbursed at the physician's rate provided by the fee schedule. **Locum tenens** physicians are those temporarily working in place of another physician. The regular physician bills for the services provided by the locum tenens physician. The fee schedule is based on the Healthcare Common Procedure Coding System (HCPCS). For each HCPCS code, there are three main components or relative value units (RVUs) influencing payment. These include an amount for physician work, an amount for overhead expenses, and an amount for malpractice expenses. These three amounts are specific for each HCPCS code. Each of these RVUs is adjusted by a geographic factor for the area in which the practice is located. The sum of the amounts from the three RVUs adjusted for geographic location is then multiplied by a uniform conversion factor, which is a fixed dollar amount, to determine the fee (*Medicare Physician Guide,* 2009). The fee schedule is revised to include new HCPCS codes and is published annually in the *Federal Register*.

Ambulatory Surgery Center Reimbursement

Freestanding ambulatory surgery centers are paid by Medicare based on a list of HCPCS/CPT codes for covered surgical procedures for Ambulatory Surgery Centers (ASCs), which is updated annually. Medicare's **ASC reimbursement system** was revised in 2008 and provides that ASCs receive a percentage of the outpatient prospective payment system rates (*CMS Medicare Claims Processing Manual*, 2009).

Capitation

RBRVS and ASC payments were efforts to prospectively set prices and to discourage excessive utilization of services. **Capitation** is a method of payment that carries this effort even further. Under capitation, caregivers receive a fixed amount of payment per month for everyone under their care enrolled in a particular health care plan. For this fixed amount of payment, all necessary health services must be provided. The incentive is, therefore, to provide only care that is absolutely necessary to avoid losing money.

Knowing the reimbursement methods affecting the facility is important for the HIM professional. Documentation of the patient's care must support the level of billing from the facility. For Medicare Physician Fee Schedule and ASC payments based on HCPCS codes, it is important that the documentation support the codes selected. More third-party payers are auditing ambulatory documentation to ensure that reimbursement matches the care documented.

Medicaid—Early and Periodic Screening, Diagnostic, and Treatment (EPSDT) Service

The **Early and Periodic Screening, Diagnostic, and Treatment (EPSDT) Service** is a program of Medicaid for children younger than 21. It ensures that these services are provided and paid for whether or not they are normally included under the state's Medicaid program. Screening services include history and physical, appropriate immunizations, health education, vision, hearing, and dental services. Problems identified under the screening provisions must then also be fully diagnosed and treated.

Reimbursement Resources

The Centers for Medicare & Medicaid Services (CMS) has a variety of manuals and materials that provide information about reimbursement under the Medicare and Medicaid programs. **Program manuals** provide the basic instructions for the two programs. **Program transmittals** are periodically issued to provide a revision for a specific manual. These manuals and transmittals must be reviewed to ensure that the facility is following the latest guidance. Claims for Medicare ambulatory care under Part B are filed with the Medicare administrative contractor (MAC-Part B) in a particular state or region. These Part B contractors (previously known as Medicare carriers) publish **Local Coverage Determinations (LCDs)**, which must be consistent with federal guidelines but provide further guidance for providers in the area served by a particular contractor. Most coverage determinations are local. However, Medicare has also developed **National Coverage Determinations (NCDs)** that apply to all contractors and providers nationwide. LCDs and NCDs are important references for coders, because they list diagnosis codes that indicate the medical necessity of certain procedures and services.

INFORMATION MANAGEMENT

Once the basic facts about the setting have been determined, the health information manager is able to evaluate or develop systems to meet the needs of the facility. All of the pieces of the puzzle come together in the HIM system.

Coding and Classification

Most facilities use some method to code diagnoses and procedures. This process involves assigning a string of characters (combination of numbers and/or letters) to each of the diagnoses and procedures according to an established classification method (see Figure 3-14). Coding is done in ambulatory care primarily to expedite the reimbursement process, because most third-party payers require codes for the diagnoses and procedures submitted on bills. Most computer systems can more easily use codes rather than verbal descriptions of the patient's diagnoses and procedures. The main factor usually considered in choosing coding systems for ambulatory care, therefore, is what systems are required by the third-party payers. Most ambulatory care settings do not want to code with one system for reimbursement and another for other classification purposes.

The current clinical modification of the *International Classification of Diseases* (*ICD-9-CM*, or *ICD-10-CM* after October 1, 2013) is the system most often used for coding diagnoses in ambulatory care. This system also includes procedure codes that are not used in ambulatory care settings. The disease classification for *ICD-9-CM* and *ICD-10-CM* is maintained by the National Center for Health Statistics of the U.S. government and is revised semiannually. These updates take effect in April and October of each year and require that ambulatory facilities update their coding, especially the pre-printed codes included on encounter forms or superbills. The **Healthcare Common Procedural Coding System (HCPCS)** is used in coding procedures and evaluation and management services in ambulatory care. Two levels of

Coding System	Use	Organization Responsible
International Classification of Diseases, Ninth Edition, Clinical Modification (Updated to *ICD-10-CM* in 2013)	Coding diagnoses	National Center for Health Statistics
Healthcare Common Procedure Coding System (HCPCS)	Coding procedures	
Level I *Current Procedural Terminology*		American Medical Association
Level II National Codes		Centers for Medicare & Medicaid Services (CMS)

FIGURE **3-14** Most common coding systems used in freestanding ambulatory care.

codes make up the HCPCS system. Level I consists of *Current Procedural Terminology (CPT)* codes developed by the American Medical Association (AMA). This coding system is revised by the AMA, and a new version of the codebooks is published each year. As with the revised diagnosis codes, changes in the *CPT* system must be included in encounter and superbill forms. Level I codes generally reflect physician services. Level II codes in HCPCS are called national codes and are developed by the Centers for Medicare & Medicaid Services (CMS) of the U.S. government. Level II codes usually classify nonphysician services such as dental care and ambulance services. Types of injections can also be specified using Level II codes. Most third-party payers require reporting of diagnoses using the current modification of *ICD*, and reporting of procedures and evaluation and management services using HCPCS.

Other coding systems may occasionally be seen in ambulatory settings. The **International Classification of Primary Care (ICPC)**, for example, is a coding system developed by the World Organization of National Colleges, Academies, and Academic Associations of General Practitioners/Family Physicians (WONCA). It includes chapters arranged by body systems, with components that describe the reason why the patient is being seen for care at the primary care level.

Data and Information Flow

Many health information professionals are most familiar with the work flow within the hospital HIM department. The work begins with the patient's discharge, and staffing requirements are often determined based on the number of discharges to be processed each day. In ambulatory care, on the other hand, the visit is the driving force in determining the work flow and staffing requirements (Figure 3-15). The visit creates the need for the patient's record to be located so that past care can be reviewed and the care process during the visit recorded.

The work flow begins when an **appointment** is scheduled for the patient. Standard scheduling and block appointment methods are typical appointment scheduling patterns. In **standard scheduling**, patients are scheduled continuously throughout the day, with appointment times at specific intervals (e.g., every 15 minutes). This method can sometimes result in wasted physician time when visit lengths are shorter than expected or when patients are "no-shows." Standard scheduling does not eliminate patient waiting time, because some visits run longer than the time allotted, putting all subsequent visits behind schedule. The block appointment methods help alleviate wasted physician time by scheduling multiple patients for the same time slot. The **block appointment method** assigns all patients in a large block at the same appointment time (e.g., 9:00 a.m. for all morning appointments), then patients are seen on a first-come, first-served basis. The disadvantage to the block appointment method is that patient satisfaction suffers when some patients have to wait several hours to see the physician. A modification of the standard and block appointment methods may sometimes be used, such as scheduling two patients at the top of each hour and two patients on the half hour, then seeing the patients in the order in which they arrive. The HIM department commonly

Patient Makes Appointment
↓
List of Appointments Is Generated
↓
Records Are Pulled
↓
Records Are Taken to Patient Care Area
↓
Patient Is Seen
↓
Care Is Documented
↓
Record Is Returned to HIM Department
↓
Record Is Checked for Completeness/Coded
↓
Completed Record Is Filed
↓
Later Reports Are Filed as Received

FIGURE 3-15 Work flow in a paper-based system.

receives a list of appointments several days before the patient's scheduled appointment. In a paper-based system, records for established patients are then pulled and made available on the day that the patient is to be seen. An electronic health record system provides the patient's information immediately at the time of encounter. For new patients, the record must be initiated at the time of the patient's appointment. Usually this process is begun by the receptionist or admissions clerk, who will see that identifying information is recorded, and basic record forms are provided in a new record for a paper-based system. Each encounter must then be documented during the patient's visit. **Walk-ins** present challenges in the flow of information. Walk-ins are patients who arrive without an appointment or who receive an appointment at the last minute. In paper-based systems, methods must be established for ensuring that medical records are available for these patients.

After the visit, the paper-based record must be returned to the HIM department and checked in to assure that it was received. In some facilities, the paper record is then filed. Other facilities, however, review the record to confirm that the documentation has been completed and that the sections of the record are placed in the correct order before the record is filed.

The work flow in a facility with an electronic health record is very different. The patient makes an appointment, which is entered in the registration/

```
┌─────────────────────────────────────────────────┐
│              Patient Makes Appointment            │
│                        ↓                          │
│                 Patient Is Seen                   │
│                        ↓                          │
│            Care Is Documented in EHR              │
│                        ↓                          │
│                 Record Is Coded                   │
│                        ↓                          │
│      Diagnostic Results Are Fed into the System   │
└─────────────────────────────────────────────────┘
```

FIGURE **3-16** Work flow in an Electronic Health Record system.

appointment system. When the patient arrives for the appointment, the demographic information is verified. When the care is given, the provider accesses the electronic health record and documents the care. Coding is then done from the EHR. Results of diagnostic tests may be automatically fed into the EHR as they are received after the appointment (Figure 3-16).

The patient identifier has an influence on how paper records are filed. When the patient's name is the primary identifier, the records are obviously placed in alphabetical order by patient last name. In systems using a number as a primary identifier, the record may be filed in straight numerical order. Large systems, however, are often set up in **terminal digit** order, in which the record is filed first by the last two digits of the number. For example, if the patient's number is 93-02-78, it would first be filed in the 78 section. Then it would be put in order by the middle digits, 02, and finally in numerical order by the first two digits, 93. This system allows for the files to expand evenly rather than having most of the activity at the end of the numbers assigned, as is found in a straight numerical system. If several clerical personnel perform the filing function, terminal digit has the additional advantage of spreading them throughout the filing area. In an electronic record system, patient records may be retrieved using their names, their patient numbers, or other pieces of information. Many ambulatory EHR systems begin the patient search with the patient's birth date and then identify the individual patient from the list generated.

Paper-based records are usually kept in file folders. These may be plain manila filing folders marked with the patient's identifier. Often, however, in either an alphabetical or a numerical system, a method of **color coding** is used on the folder. Each set of numbers or a group of letters is assigned a color on the folder. It is then easy to look at the files and to identify misfiles by the presence of a different color in a block of records of the same color. Paper records may be kept in a variety of equipment. File cabinets with file drawers are sometimes used, although these take up more space. Open-shelf filing is also commonly chosen. Sometimes motorized filing units are selected to house the records.

The addition of late reports is another function of the HIM department in a paper-based or image-based system. Laboratory and X-ray results are often sent to the HIM department after the visit and must be filed in the proper record.

Record Linkage to Other Sites/Facilities

Many freestanding ambulatory care centers have multiple sites and must find a way to provide patient information among the various sites. This task is easiest with an electronic health record that can be accessed from all sites. In such a system, any of the locations can access the patient's information through the computer.

In paper-based systems, the record can only be in one site at a time. Facilities use a variety of ways to maintain the location or home base of the record. In some sites, the patient designates a home facility where he or she is usually seen, and the record is routinely kept at that location. Other facilities keep the record in the last site where the patient was seen. In either case, if the patient is seen at a site other than the record's home base, a method must be chosen to have information available at another site when the patient is seen there. For scheduled visits, a courier is often used to transport the record to the site of the visit. For unscheduled visits, the pertinent parts of the record may be faxed to the other site from the home base. It is important, in either case, to have policies and procedures to ensure the safety of the record. If a courier is used, locked courier pouches may be needed to hold the record during transport and to avoid unauthorized viewing. Facilities that fax information between sites must ensure that the fax is being attended when the material is sent to avoid unauthorized access to the copies. Care must also be taken that the facsimile copies are properly disposed of. Electronic health records make access to a record available at any point of care.

Computer Systems

Ambulatory care centers often use computers to assist in the operation of the facility (see Figure 3-17). A **patient registration** or **appointment system**, for example, is often an important part of such a system for the HIM department. The patient's scheduled visit is entered into the computer, and a list of records needed for a particular day can then be automatically generated from the schedule.

A patient registration or appointment system is also vital for keeping up with basic identifying information about the patient. In such a system, basic information about the patient—including name, address, insurance, and responsible party—is collected when the patient is first seen. It is important that this information be updated at each visit to maintain an accurate file. The registration system may provide a master patient index for the HIM department, including the patient's record number, which is a vital identifier to enable the department to locate the patient's records.

Financial systems maintain information on services billed, insurance coverage determination, payment received from patients and insurance companies, and collections efforts. Some systems provide for electronic data

Computer Applications	Functions
Scheduling or Appointment System	System used to set up patient appointments
Patient Registration System	System used to enter demographic and financial information about the patient
Financial System	System used to maintain information on services billed, insurance coverage, and billing and collections
Electronic Health Record (EHR) System	System in which the patient record is kept in electronic form in a computer-based system
Decision Support System	System that aids the caregiver in making a diagnosis or treatment decision
Reminder System	System that reminds the caregiver of preventive services that should be scheduled on a regular basis, such as annual mammograms

FIGURE 3-17 Computer applications commonly seen in freestanding ambulatory care.

interchange (EDI) so that bills are sent electronically to third-party payers rather than using paper bills. Financial systems often tie in with the encounter form to show the services that the patient received during the visit. The HIM department may use data from the financial system to retrieve information for activities such as utilization management and quality assessment. In the financial system, there is also information on items billed, such as medications, diagnostic tests, and procedures.

Electronic health records (EHRs) are in use in some freestanding ambulatory care settings. Some physicians' offices and other ambulatory care settings are leading the way toward an electronic health record, because the ambulatory record is less complex and easier to maintain electronically than is the hospital record. EHR modules can be integrated with the current practice management system (Amayatakul, 2006). In other facilities, there is still a total dependence on the paper-based record. In most ambulatory care settings, the computer has primarily been used for administrative tasks. A study by DesRoches et al. showed that four percent of physicians reported that they had a full-functioning EHR, with 13 percent reporting a more basic system (DesRoches et al., 2008). However, ARRA incentives have resulted in an increased number of physicians adopting EHRs.

Some advantages of an electronic health record extend beyond just having the information on the computer where it can be accessed by multiple users across broad geographic areas. One of these functions is decision support. In **decision-support systems**, information about the patient's signs and symptoms as well as laboratory and other diagnostic tests may be used with an artificial intelligence system to help the physician in selecting a diagnosis. Automated online reminders can also be built into the system to remind physicians that patients need certain services such as immunizations for children, yearly mammograms, or routine monitoring.

Because of the potential of the EHR to improve patient safety and the quality of care, the federal government has created incentives for providers to move quickly to an EHR. Under the American Recovery and Reinvestment Act (ARRA), CMS was authorized to offer Medicare and Medicaid incentives to hospitals and providers to become "meaningful users" of electronic health records. For the first five years, providers are not required to participate in the program but receive incentive payments if they demonstrate "meaningful use." Starting in 2016, Medicare providers will be penalized if they do not comply with the meaningful use requirements. Professionals covered by the act include doctors of medicine or osteopathy, doctors of dental surgery or dental medicine, doctors of optometry, and chiropractors. The EHR technology used by these professionals must meet federal standards or be "certified."

CMS is also offering providers an incentive for adopting **e-prescribing**, which was defined in the *Federal Register* as:

> . . . the transmission using electronic media, of prescription or prescription-related information between a prescriber, dispenser, pharmacy benefit manager (PBM), or health plan, either directly or through an intermediary, including an e-prescribing network. E-prescribing includes, but is not limited to, two-way transmissions between the point of care and the dispenser. (Medicare Program Payment Policies, 2009)

Although e-prescribing is felt to improve the safety of the prescribing process, there has been limited adoption by providers. The incentive, it is hoped, will accelerate the adoption of this technology. The regulations require that a certain percentage of prescriptions must be submitted through an e-prescribing system for the professional to be eligible for the incentive. Other technologies are affecting ambulatory care. Handheld computers, smart phones, or personal digital assistants (PDAs) provide caregivers with a pocket-sized device that can be used to access information on topics, such as drugs. The device can also be connected to the ambulatory care center computer system through a cradle or wireless network to allow parts of the electronic medical record to be downloaded from or uploaded to the main system. Cell phones can also be used by patients to monitor and manage chronic conditions (Boland, 2007).

A main issue with PDAs and smart phones is security, because they are small enough to be lost or easily stolen. Input of large amounts of data is also difficult. Speech recognition technology will greatly enhance the functionality of PDAs when it is more reliable.

Another technology that is receiving some use by caregivers is electronic mail. Patients can query the caregiver about problems or ask for refills on medication. Once again, security can be an issue, because unauthorized persons may access the e-mail if appropriate safeguards are not in place. It is also important that e-mail communications be entered into the patient's medical record so that a record is kept (AHIMA, 2003).

The Internet can be used for remote accessing of information, too. Once again, security is the biggest issue, and means must be included in the system to ensure data security and integrity. Who may access information through the Internet must also be addressed. In some cases, patients wish to access their own records through the Internet, and policies must be devised to define what information they may access.

Patient portals are one answer to the confidentiality concerns regarding e-mail and patient access to the health record. According to Margret Amayatakul, Web portal technology provides patients with "a point of secure access to an organization's information system applications" (2009, p.503). Patients can use such secure portals to carry out activities such as scheduling visits and requesting medication refills. In some cases, patients are also allowed access to their medical records in this manner (Walters et. al., 2006). Because proposed rules for "meaningful use" of an EHR require that patients have electronic access to their health information, the use of patient portals is likely to become more common.

Data Sets

In many settings, minimum data sets have been developed to provide guidance on what information should be kept in patient records. A second function that these data sets serve is to provide standard definitions for the data set items collected. In ambulatory care, the Uniform Ambulatory Care Data Set (UACDS) has been developed to serve that purpose. This data set includes three main types of data: patient data, provider data, and encounter data. Patient data provides basic identifying information about the patient. Provider data includes information about the provider, such as a unique provider identifier and location. **Encounter** data includes the date, reason for encounter, services received, and disposition (Abdelhak et al., 2007). The minimum data set provides an excellent source for the HIM professional to determine the minimum data that must be kept for each encounter. In addition, definitions for terms such as *encounter* can help the HIM professional in developing statistical measures. It is important that the statistics measure the indicated items uniformly.

QUALITY IMPROVEMENT AND UTILIZATION MANAGEMENT

Quality Assessment and Performance Improvement

A major use of health information in ambulatory care is the assessment of the quality of care provided by the facility. The quality assessment and improvement process in ambulatory care follows the same methods used in other care settings. Problems or processes must be chosen for study, data must be collected to measure these processes, data must be assessed, and a method for improvement must be developed. The major difference in ambulatory care is that many factors affecting the quality of care are not within the sole control of the ambulatory facility. The patient's contact with the facility is usually brief, and the patient's outcome depends in large part on the patient's compliance with the care plan developed (Shalowitz, 2010). The patient's continuity of care may depend on factors in the patient's, not the facility's, control, such as missed appointments and consistent use of a primary provider to coordinate care. Methods to improve compliance must be included in the quality assessment process, because they affect the patient's outcome. Patient satisfaction is also an important part of the quality assessment process in ambulatory care, because the patient's compliance may be closely tied to satisfaction with the care received. The ability to determine the quality of care within a facility is highly dependent on the quality of data collected within the health record.

The Centers for Medicare & Medicaid Services have established a **physician quality reporting system** called PQRI, Physician Quality Reporting Initiative. Under this program, eligible providers such as physicians, podiatrists, physician assistants, nurse practitioners, and physical therapists report on a list of quality measures defined each year by CMS. According to CMS, "... a group practice may also potentially qualify to earn PQRI incentive payment equal to 2% of the group practice's total estimated Medicare Part B PFS allowed charges for covered professional services furnished during a 2010 PQRI reporting period based on the group practice meeting the criteria for satisfactory reporting specified by CMS." The measures to be collected may vary from year to year, and each year's requirements are published in the *Federal Register*. Measures include items such as the percentage of patients who received counseling on diet and exercise as well as a variety of screening tests such as mammograms and colonoscopies. For 2010, for example, there were 179 measures in 13 measures groups for patient with conditions such as diabetes mellitus, chronic kidney disease, and community-acquired pneumonia (CMS PQRI, 2010).

Utilization Management

Utilization management is the process of determining the appropriateness of services and treatment provided to the patient, based on the patient's needs (Abdelhak et. al., 2007). In the hospital setting, this process often focuses on whether the patient requires hospitalization. In ambulatory care, utilization management is more likely to focus on the necessity of a service such as referral to a specialist or the use of an expensive procedure such as a magnetic resonance imaging study or the appropriateness of referrals for hospitalization. Emphasis should be on services that are either high volume or high cost, because not all services can be examined. Standards or criteria that are credible and specific should be set.

There are two basic approaches to utilization management. One is **prospective review/precertification**, in which the service is examined before it is provided. Data is collected, usually by a nurse, from the patient and the physician. The facts of the individual case are compared to the appropriateness criteria. If the standards are met, the nurse can usually approve the service. If the standards are not met, a physician advisor may be asked to review the case and make a determination. Types of activities typically undergoing prospective review include authorization for referral, authorization for a procedure, preadmission review before hospitalization, and second surgical opinion.

The second major approach is **retrospective review**. In this methodology, care is looked at after it is given. Usually a sample of cases is selected. Data is then collected from medical records, and the information from the record is compared to the appropriateness standards. Feedback is then given to the appropriate caregiver regarding inappropriate care provided.

RISK MANAGEMENT AND LEGAL ISSUES

Many legal and risk management issues that arise in freestanding ambulatory care relate to the fact that much of the care is not provided by the caregiver but by the patient and the family (see Figure 3-18). Communication is a vital part of ensuring that the care is given as prescribed. Care recommendations, for example, are often provided through telephone calls. It is important that telephone calls be documented in the record so that some report exists of care recommendations. Prescribed medications must especially be documented, including the name of medication, dosages and amounts dispensed, dispensing instructions (with signature), prescription dates and discontinued dates, and problem identification numbers for which each medication was prescribed (Odom-Wesley et al., 2009). Failure to document such care can lead to a situation of the caregiver's word versus the patient's on whether needed advice was given and followed.

Documenting missed and canceled appointments is also vital, because patients can have adverse effects from not keeping an appointment as scheduled. Documenting that the appointment was missed or canceled provides additional information on the patient's responsibility in such a situation (Office Practice, n.d.). Freestanding ambulatory sites, particularly ambulatory surgery centers, often provide written instructions for patients to take home to help patient compliance and understanding (Odom-Wesley et al., 2009). Such instruction sheets should be included in the medical record. If they are not, a statement should be included in the record that a particular instruction sheet was given to the patient, and copies of the different instruction sheets should be kept on file in the facility.

Documentation of the physician's discussion regarding informed consent is especially important in ambulatory surgery settings but must be furnished

---

Risk Management Issues

Documenting Telephone Calls

Documenting Missed and Canceled Appointments

Documenting Written Discharge Instructions

Documenting Informed Consent Process

Documenting Changes since Last Visit

Documenting Noncompliance

Documenting Incidents

FIGURE **3-18** Risk management issues in freestanding ambulatory care.

for any invasive procedure, whatever the setting. A consent form signed by the patient should contain the substance of the items discussed, including alternatives to the procedure and any risks involved. Narrative progress notes should include further detail about the discussion regarding the procedure or service to be provided (Brodnik et al., 2009).

Caregivers should be advised to include documentation of changes since the patient's last visit and any evidence of noncompliance (What should be documented, n.d.). Such facts could be vitally important if a legal case should result.

Legibility is also a risk management issue. If prescriptions are illegible, for example, there is a risk that the medication will be dispensed incorrectly, potentially causing the patient harm. Some organizations have implemented systems in which providers use handheld devices to generate and print prescriptions to address this patient safety concern. An e-prescribing system also eliminates the problem of illegible prescriptions. Illegibility is also a problem in the area of compliance. If an auditor cannot read a provider's records, the documentation cannot be used to support the services billed, which could lead to legal issues with the OIG. Electronic health records solve the legibility issue, because all entries are present in an easily readable, digital format.

It is extremely important that abnormal test results be reviewed by the ordering physician. Each facility should develop a procedure to ensure that the physician sees the results and documents actions taken on the basis of the results. For example, in a paper record, physicians may be asked to initial the laboratory report and document in the progress notes section of the record that the patient was contacted and advised of what to do about abnormal results. An electronic health record system could place the laboratory result in the physician's queue for review and could prompt the physician for documentation on actions taken. Laboratory results that show a serious problem can send an automatic alert to the physician (Ferris et. al., 2009).

Many facilities use **incident** or **occurrence reports** as internal documentation of unusual events such as falls, incorrect medications given or taken, or other untoward occurrences. The purpose of the incident/occurrence report is to provide documentation of events so that facilities can take steps to avoid such events in the future. The report usually goes to the facility's attorney and is thus protected by attorney–client privilege. A copy of the incident report should not be placed in the record, but details about the event should be recorded there (Odom-Wesley et al., 2009).

ROLE OF THE HEALTH INFORMATION MANAGEMENT PROFESSIONAL

The role of the HIM professional in freestanding ambulatory care is to provide expertise concerning information, regulations, electronic information systems, and management. In a paper-based ambulatory care setting, the primary role of the HIM department is chart location and control, making information management and supervision of personnel the main functions of the HIM professional in this scenario. Information must be organized and stored in a way that makes it easy to retrieve, either through computerized or paper-based storage. With a paper-based system, personnel are needed to file and retrieve records and to make sure that loose sheets such as laboratory reports are placed in the correct record. These employees must be trained in filing methods and in confidentiality and security so that information is not released improperly. This training function may also include instruction of employees and caregivers outside the HIM department in proper documentation, use of the record, and confidentiality.

The role of the health information manager has been affected by the move to the EHR in freestanding ambulatory care. As facilities decide to implement EHRs, health information managers are involved in the implementation of these new systems and may serve as project managers. HIM professionals can also play a role in successfully helping physicians and other caregivers make workflow changes to more effectively utilize the functions of the EHR (*When the Doctor Calls*, 2005).

The implementation of an electronic record system changes the role of the HIM professional from one of managing the filing and retrieval of the paper record to one of managing the data contained in the record and the electronic record process. HIPAA also adds new roles for the HIM professional who may serve as the privacy and/or security officer for the facility.

In smaller ambulatory care settings, HIM professionals may often undertake roles outside those usually identified with health information management. In some settings, for example, HIM professionals have duties in areas such as purchasing or patient registration. Some HIM professionals have expanded their knowledge of the ambulatory setting and utilized their management and administrative skills to become medical group managers.

The HIM field is not as well known in ambulatory care as it has been in the hospital area. HIM professionals must also serve as marketers for their skills and have the flexibility to assume a variety of responsibilities.

TRENDS

Several trends are evident in freestanding ambulatory care. The first is the continuing shift of care to the ambulatory setting. As government programs such as diagnosis related groups (DRGs) have attempted to hold down hospital costs, a shift has taken place to the less-expensive ambulatory setting. This movement will continue, and the role of ambulatory care settings in the health care arena will be enhanced.

Another trend will be increased integration of freestanding ambulatory care sites with other health care facilities. Health care is increasingly provided by networks, including all facets of health care from primary care to specialized hospital care. Ambulatory care settings will increasingly find themselves part of this continuum of care and, therefore, part of bigger health care corporations. Such a shift will provide more support for individual ambulatory care settings but will also be expected to provide increased regulation and standardization of the health care process. An emphasis on holding down health care costs is resulting in additional scrutiny of ambulatory care documentation to determine whether it supports the reimbursement requested.

The concept of the **medical home** will provide innovations in health care that will impact the HIM professional. The medical home involves the primary care provider working with a team of health care professionals to provide care to patients using a whole-person concept. The primary care professional either provides all of the care to the patient or arranges for other care regardless of the site of care or the stage of life of the patient (Rosenthal, 2008). Without an EHR, the concept of a medical home for each patient would be difficult to carry out. The HIM professional will be involved in ensuring that the necessary health information is available at any point of care where the patient may be seen.

In health information management there will be an increased use of electronic health records in ambulatory care. The incentives provided through ARRA to move to the EHR will increase the momentum for its adoption. Because the ambulatory care process is less complex and less regulated than that in the hospital, ambulatory care centers have an excellent opportunity to become leaders in implementing EHR systems. HIM professionals should have excellent opportunities to participate in this trend.

SUMMARY

The HIM professional must be aware of many factors about a facility before providing information management services. The type of facility determines the types of caregivers and the types of patients seen, thus defining the documentation that must be provided. Accreditation and licensing standards as well as the reimbursement systems applicable to the setting also serve as benchmarks for documentation and storage and retrieval methods. HIM professionals looking at quality of care and utilization must be aware of the patient's role in following the plan of care and, thus, in the outcome achieved. Patients' participation in their care, or the lack of such participation, is also a risk management factor that affects documentation requirements. Knowledge of all these elements provides the HIM practitioner with the tools necessary to offer exceptional service to meet the needs of the ambulatory facility.

KEY TERMS

ambulatory surgery center (ASC)   a setting provided for surgery on an ambulatory basis. Centers usually have at least one full-time operating room and provide surgical privileges to physicians in the community.

appointment   scheduled time that a patient is to arrive at the health care facility.

appointment system   a system by which appointments are scheduled for patients.

ASC reimbursement system   a Medicare reimbursement system for ambulatory surgery in which the HCPCS codes are listed (ASC list) and reimbursed on a percentage of the outpatient prospective payment system rates.

birth center   ambulatory setting that provides labor and delivery services in uncomplicated deliveries.

block appointment method   an appointment scheduling method that assigns all patients in a large block for the same appointment time (e.g., 9:00 a.m. for all morning appointments), then patients are seen on a first-come, first-served basis.

capitation   a method of reimbursement in which the physician or facility receives a fixed amount each month for each patient enrolled in the plan, regardless of the amount of care that the patient receives.

certified nurse midwife (CNM)   a nurse practitioner who handles pregnancy, labor, and delivery.

color coding   a system that helps prevent the misfiling of records by assigning colors to numbers or letters and displaying those colors on the record folder so that misfiled records are easily spotted by their mismatched color patterns.

community health center   an ambulatory setting developed in the 1960s to provide ambulatory care to the indigent of a particular neighborhood. Subsequent legislation expanded the scope of these health centers to any medically underserved area or population.

compliance plan   a plan for ensuring that a facility/practice is complying with all laws and regulations, including those pertaining to reimbursement under Medicare and Medicaid.

Current Procedural Terminology (*CPT*)   a coding system for procedures that is used extensively in ambulatory care and that forms a part of HCPCS.

decision-support system   a computerized system that assists physicians in deciding on a diagnosis or treatment.

Early and Periodic Screening, Diagnostic, and Treatment (EPSDT) Service   a program of Medicaid for children younger than 21 that ensures that these services (screening, diagnostic, and treatment) are provided and paid for whether or not they are normally included under the state's Medicaid program.

encounter   face-to-face contact between the patient and the provider (Uniform Ambulatory Care Data Set).

encounter form   a form used for billing purposes that includes the services the patient received, the charges, and the diagnosis and procedure codes.

e-prescribing   a method of entering prescriptions into an electronic system that also transmits the prescription to the pharmacy to be filled.

family numbering system   a numbering system in which the family is given a number and each individual receives that number with a suffix indicating his or her position within the family.

family planning center   an ambulatory setting that provides family planning services.

federally qualified health center (FQHC)   a nonprofit or public organization that provides or arranges for comprehensive health care services to a medically underserved area or population.

fee for service   a reimbursement system in which the payment is based on the type and amount of service provided.

financial system   a computer system that maintains information on services billed, insurance determination, payment received, and collection efforts.

freestanding ambulatory care   care provided to patients who do not stay overnight in a setting not located within a hospital.

growth and development chart   a graphic recording of a child's height and weight over time.

Healthcare Common Procedural Coding System (HCPCS)   a system used by ambulatory care facilities to code procedures and services.

immunization record   record that maintains a list of immunizations that a child has received and often indicates when additional immunizations will be required.

incident report   internal documentation of an unusual event such as a fall, incorrect medications given or taken, or some other untoward occurrence. (See also *occurrence report*.)

incident to services provided to patients by mid-level providers, such as nurse practitioners or physician assistants, when the physician is on site.

industrial or **occupational health center** an ambulatory setting where care is provided to employees at their place of work.

integrated format a record format in which the information is entered in chronological order.

International Classification of Diseases, **9th Revision, Clinical Modification** (*ICD-9-CM*) a classification system used by ambulatory care facilities for coding diagnoses through September 30, 2013.

International Classification of Diseases, **10th Revision, Clinical Modification** (*ICD-10-CM*) a classification system used by ambulatory care facilities for coding diagnoses beginning October 1, 2013.

International Classification of Primary Care (**ICPC**) a coding system developed by the World Organization of National Colleges, Academies, and Academic Associations of General Practitioners/Family Physicians (WONCA). It includes chapters arranged by body systems, with components that describe the reason why the patient is being seen for care at the primary care level.

Local Coverage Determinations (**LCDs**) guidance documents published by Medicare Administrative Contractors (MACs) that include information on codes that indicate medical necessity of services. These policies apply to services covered under Medicare in the region served by the contractor. Local Coverage Determinations were formerly known as Local Medical Review Policies (LMRPs).

locum tenens an arrangement by which one physician temporarily works in place of another physician.

Medicaid Integrity Program a joint federal and state government initiative to identify fraud and abuse in the Medicaid system.

medical home a method of providing care in which the primary care provider works with a team of health care professionals to provide care to patients using a whole-person concept.

Medicare physician fee schedule (**MPFS** or **PFS**) a list of Medicare-covered services and their payment rates.

mid-level provider (**MLP**) a health care professional whose license permits a degree of independent judgment in treating patients, generally under the supervision of a physician. Examples of mid-level providers include nurse practitioners, physician assistants, and certified nurse midwives. Scope of practice and requirements for supervision vary by type of provider and by state.

National Coverage Determinations (**NCDs**) guidance documents published by Medicare that include information on codes that indicate medical necessity of services. These policies apply to services covered under Medicare throughout the nation.

nurse practitioner (**NP**) a registered nurse who has additional training and credentials that allow for limited independent practice.

occurrence report internal documentation of an unusual event such as a fall, incorrect medications given or taken, or some other untoward occurrence. (See also *incident report*.)

Office of the Inspector General (**OIG**) the office in the Department of Health and Human Services responsible for monitoring compliance with reimbursement laws and regulations.

patient identifier an item of data that identifies the patient in the health information management system, such as the patient's name or medical record number.

patient portal a secure method of patient access to his or her own information through a facility's electronic information system.

patient registration system a computer system that contains demographic and financial information for every patient.

physician assistant a professional who is not a nurse but has received training to use independent judgment in treating patients.

physician private practice a setting in which physicians practice in their own business rather than working for an organization such as a clinic or urgent care center owned or operated by others.

physician quality reporting system a system for physicians to report quality measures to CMS.

problem list a numbered list of the patient's problems over time that serves as a table of contents for the problem-oriented medical record.

problem-oriented medical record (POMR) format a record format in which the parts of the record are keyed to the problem number listed on the problem list.

program manuals for Medicare and Medicaid basic instructions for the two programs, developed by the Centers for Medicare & Medicaid Services.

program transmittals periodically issued by CMS to provide a revision for a specific program manual.

prospective review/precertification One of two basic approaches to utilization management, prospective review determines whether services are needed before they are provided.

public health department an organization that provides services to promote the health of the community as a whole, such as immunizations and disease screenings; usually an agency of state or local government.

reason for visit the reason provided by the patient for why care is requested.

registration the process by which basic demographic and financial information is obtained from the patient and entered into the health information system.

resource-based relative value scale (RBRVS) a reimbursement system used by Medicare Part B to reimburse physicians. It is based on the relative value of the services provided.

retrospective review One of two basic approaches to utilization management, retrospective review examines care after it has been given, to identify inappropriate care and provide feedback to the caregiver.

return-to-work physical a physical done before an employee may return to the job after an injury or illness.

rural health clinic (RHC) health care clinic that, in addition to physician services, utilizes mid-level providers such as physician assistants and nurse practitioners, and that is located in an underserved rural area.

source-oriented format a record format in which the information is organized according to the source of the information, such as laboratory, nursing, etc.

standard scheduling a method in which appointments are scheduled continuously throughout the day, with appointment times at specific intervals (e.g., every 15 minutes).

superbill a form used for billing purposes that includes the services the patient received, the charges, and diagnosis and procedure codes.

terminal digit filing a filing system in which records are filed first by the last two digits of their numbers, allowing files to expand evenly.

university health center an ambulatory setting in which care is provided to university staff and students.

urgent care center an ambulatory care setting in which patients are seen on a walk-in basis without appointments. These centers provide service for longer hours than do most private physician practices.

walk-ins patients who arrive without an appointment or who receive an appointment at the last minute.

REVIEW QUESTIONS

Knowledge-Based Questions

1. List and describe three types of freestanding ambulatory care settings.
2. Define the following terms used in ambulatory care: encounter, nurse practitioner, reason for visit, superbill.
3. Name the two main organizations that accredit ambulatory care.
4. List the major types of documentation that are basic to all ambulatory care encounters and settings.
5. What types of patient identifiers are used in ambulatory care?
6. What types of data are included in the uniform ambulatory care data set, and how does this affect the content of the ambulatory record?

7. What is the ASC reimbursement system, and how is it used in Medicare reimbursement?

Critical Thinking Questions

1. Compare and contrast the fee-for-service and PFS/RBRVS reimbursement systems.
2. How does documentation in an industrial health center differ from that in a physician's practice and why?
3. How is quality assessment in ambulatory care similar to and different from quality assessment in the acute inpatient setting?

WEB ACTIVITY

LCDs and NCDs can be reviewed at the Medicare Coverage Database at the CMS Web site. To begin, go to http://www.cms.gov. Select "Medicare," then under "Coverage" select "Medicare Coverage Determination Process." Review the information in the "Overview," then select "Coverage Center" under "Related Links inside CMS." At the Medicare Coverage Center, select "How to Use THE MEDICARE COVERAGE DATABASE" to access a booklet containing step-by-step instructions for searching the database. Follow instructions in the booklet to locate and review the LCD or NCD of your choice. What type of information does the LCD/NCD document contain? How might this information be useful to a freestanding ambulatory care provider?

CASE STUDY

Judy Jordan has just begun working as the health information manager in a very large physicians' group practice. The patient's name is the primary patient identifier used, and the records are filed alphabetically. Misfiles are a frequent problem, and in the large practice patients frequently have similar names. The records are not kept in a uniform format. Many of the doctors use an integrated format, but three of the physicians use the POMR. The practice wants to transition to an electronic health record. In reviewing the encounter forms, Judy finds codes that are no longer currently valid. Judy questions the staff and finds that no one can remember when the encounter form was updated. Bills are frequently returned for invalid codes. Electronic systems for patient registration and appointments have been implemented, but the staff also keeps a manual appointment log. A computer-generated list of appointments is given to the HIM clerk on the day prior to the appointments so that the records can be pulled and available when the patients arrive. Many appointments that are entered in the manual log are not also entered in the electronic appointment system. The HIM clerk, therefore, spends extensive time each day pulling records for those appointments that are not on the computer-generated list. Judy has been asked to make suggestions for making the office run more smoothly.

1. What are the main problems that she should identify?
2. Develop a plan to solve each of the problems identified above.

REFERENCES AND SUGGESTED READINGS

Abdelhak, M., Grostick, S., Hanken, M.A., Jacobs, E.B. (2007). *Health information: Management of a strategic resource* (3rd ed.). Philadelphia: Saunders Publishing.

Amatayakul, M. (2006). Ambulatory versus acute care EHRs. *Journal of AHIMA, 77*(6), 40–41.

Amatayakul, M. (2009). *Electronic health records: A practical guide for professionals and organizations* (4th ed.). Chicago: American Health Information Management Association.

Ambulatory Care Section. (2001). *Documentation for ambulatory care: Rev. ed.* Chicago: American Health Information Management Association.

Ambulatory Surgery Centers. *Encyclopedia of surgery.* Retrieved April 30, 2010, from http://www.surgeryencyclopedia.com/A-Ce/Ambulatory-Surgery-Centers.html.

[AHIMA] American Health Information Management Association. (2003). E-mail as a provider-patient communication medium and its impact on the electronic health record: Practice Brief. Retrieved May 3, 2010, from http://library.ahima.org/xpedio/groups/public/documents/ahima/bok1_021588.hcsp?dDocName=bok1_021588.

Boland, P. (2007). The emerging role of cell phone technology in ambulatory care. *Journal of Ambulatory Care Management, 30*(2), 126–133.

Brodnik, M. S., McCain, M. C., Rinehart-Thompson, L. A., & Reynolds, R. (2009). *Fundamentals of law for health informatics and information management.* Chicago: American Health Information Management Association.

[CMS] Centers for Medicare & Medicaid Services. (2009a). Chapter 14, Ambulatory Surgery Centers, in *Medicare Claims Processing Manual.* http://www.cms.gov/manuals/downloads/clm104c14.pdf.

[CMS] Centers for Medicare & Medicaid Services. (2009b). Medicaid integrity provider audits. (2009). Retrieved May 5, 2010, from http://www.cms.gov/ProviderAudits/Downloads/mipfactsheet.pdf.

[CMS] Centers for Medicare & Medicaid Services. (2010). Physician quality reporting initiative. Retrieved May 3, 2010, from http://www.cms.gov/PQRI/.

[CMS] Centers for Medicare & Medicaid Services. (n.d.). Overview, state program integrity support and assistance. Retrieved May 5, 2010, from http://www.cms.gov/FraudAbuseforProfs/.

Desroches, C. M., Campbell, E. G., Rao, S. R., Donelan, K., Ferris, T. G., Jha, A., Kaushal, R., Levy, D. E., Rosenbaum, S., Shields, A. E., & Blumenthal, D. (2008). Electronic health records in ambulatory care—a national survey of physicians. *New England Journal of Medicine, 359*(2), 50–60.

Electronic Health Record Incentive Program; Proposed Rule, 75 Fed. Reg. 1844–2011 (2010) (to be codified at 42 C.F.R. pts. 412, et al.).

Ferris, T. G., Johnson, S. A., Co, J. P. T., Backus, M., Perrin, J., Bates, D. W., & Poon, E. G. . (2009). Electronic results management in pediatric ambulatory care: Qualitative assessment, *Pediatrics, 123*(Suppl. 2), S85–S91.

Geiger, H. Jack. (2005). The first community health centers: A model of enduring value. *Journal of Ambulatory Care Management, 28*(4), 313–320.

[HRSA] Health Resources and Services Administration. (2006, June). *Comparison of the Rural Health Clinic and Federally Qualified Health Center Programs.* [Online]. http://www.ask.hrsa.gov/downloads/fqhc-rhccomparison.pdf [2010, June 5].

History of ASCs, The. (2010). National Surgery Center Association. Retrieved April, 30, 2010, from http://www.ascassociation.org/faqs/aschistory/.

Medicare Physician Guide: A Resource for Residents, Practicing Physicians, and Other Healthcare Professionals. (2009). Medicare Learning Network. Retrieved April 30, 2010, from http://www.cms.gov/MLNProducts/downloads/physicianguide.pdf.

Medicare Program; Payment Policies Under the Physician Fee Schedule. 74 Fed. Reg. 33593 (July 13, 2009).

Odom-Wesley, B., Brown, D., & Meyers, C. (2009). *Documentation for Medical Records.* Chicago: American Health Information Management Association.

Office practice: What works—Missed and cancelled appointments. (n.d.). CRICO/RMF. Retrieved May 3, 2010, from http://www.rmf.harvard.edu/patient-safety-strategies/office-practices/main/index2.aspx?id=14.

OIG Compliance Program for Individual and Small Group Physician Practices. (2000). *Federal Register, 65*(194), 59434–59452.

Rosenthal, T. C. (2008). The medical home: Growing evidence to support a new approach to primary care. *Journal of the American Board of Family Medicine, 21*(5), 427–440.

Rural Health Clinics, (n.d.). Rural assistance center. Retrieved April 30, 2010, from http://www.raconline.org/info_guides/clinics/rhc.php.

Shalowitz, Joel. (2010). Implementing successful quality outcome programs in ambulatory care: Key questions and recommendations. *Journal of Ambulatory Care Management, 33*(2), 117–125.

Walters, B., Barnard, D., & Paris, S. (2006). "Patient portals" and "e-visits." *Journal of Ambulatory Care Management, 29*(3), 222–224.

What should be documented. (n.d.). CRICO/RMF. Retrieved May 3, 2010, from http://www.rmf.harvard.edu/patient-safety-strategies/documentation/articles/index.aspx.

When the doctor calls: Opportunities in ambulatory care. (2005, August). *AHIMA Advantage, 9*(5).

KEY RESOURCES

Accreditation Association for Ambulatory Health Care, Inc. (AAAHC)
http://www.aaahc.org

Ambulatory Surgery Center Association
http://www.ascassociation.org

American Association for Accreditation of Ambulatory Surgery Facilities, Inc.
http://www.aaaasf.org

American Health Information Management Association
http://www.ahima.org

Commission for the Accreditation of Birth Centers
http://www.birthcenteraccreditation.org

Department of Health and Human Services Office of Inspector General Fraud Prevention and Detection
http://oig.hhs.gov/fraud.asp

The Joint Commission
http://www.jointcommission.org

Medical Group Management Association (MGMA)
http://www.mgma.com

National Association of Community Health Centers
www.nachc.com

Professional Association of Health Care Office Management
http://www.pahcom.com

Rural Assistance Center
http://www.raconline.org

CHAPTER 4

Managed Care

CECILE FAVREAU, MBA, CPC

LYNN KUEHN, MS, RHIA, CCS-P, FAHIMA

LEARNING OBJECTIVES

Upon successful completion of this chapter, you should be able to:

- Identify the various forms of managed care organizations and compare how they are structured.

- Explain why the term *member* is used to refer to individuals in this setting.

- Determine the accreditation organization most appropriate for each form of managed care organization.

- Describe the types of reimbursement that a managed care organization receives and the various methods of reimbursing providers of care.

- Describe the concept of coordination of benefits, and explain why it is important to a managed care organization.

- Explain why the structure of the managed care organization affects the way health care documentation is managed.

- Identify the basic requirements for electronic information systems in managed care.

- Explain why the Healthcare Effectiveness Data and Information Set (HEDIS) is helping to improve the quality of health care delivery in managed care.

- Identify the types of consumer-directed health plans and their characteristics.

- List and define the utilization management activities of a managed care organization.

Setting/Plan	Description	Synonyms/Examples
Health Maintenance Organization (HMO)	An insurance entity that provides or arranges for health services for a covered population after prepayment of a fixed premium.	Staff Model HMO Group Model HMO Network Model HMO IPA Model HMO Mixed Model HMO
Preferred Provider Organization (PPO)	An insurance entity that contracts with providers to create a preferred network. The insured population is allowed to use any provider, but using network providers results in a lesser cost to the patient.	Preferred Provider Network Preferred Provider Option
Point-of-Service (POS) Plan	An insurance plan that combines the health maintenance and preferred provider concepts, creating several levels of out-of-pocket cost options for the insured. The insured makes the choice at the time of service.	Point-of-Sale Plan Open-Ended HMO Open-Access HMO
Managed Indemnity Plan	An insurance plan that reimburses the insured for expenses incurred but incorporates some managed care principles to help control costs.	Modified Indemnity Insurance
Consumer-Directed Health Plans	Insurance plans that provide incentives to control costs of health benefits and health care. Individuals have greater freedom in health care spending up to a specific dollar amount and receive full coverage for in-network preventive care. Members incur higher out-of-pocket costs in the form of coinsurance and deductibles.	Customized Sub-Capitation Plan (CSCP) Flexible Spending Accounts (FSA) Health Savings Account (HSA) Health Savings Security Account (HSSA) Health Reimbursement Arrangement (HRA)
Integrated Delivery System (IDS)	A group of facilities contracted together to provide the comprehensive set of services that any patient may need. They are owned, leased, or grouped together by long-term contracts and are recognized by the public as a combined operating entity.	Integrated Delivery Network (IDN)

INTRODUCTION TO SETTINGS AND PLANS

Defining the managed care industry is like shooting at a moving target. Just when you think you have it figured out, someone thinks the market needs a different twist on a familiar theme. Managed care is the provision of comprehensive health care services coordinated through a primary care provider

(PCP), with emphasis on preventive care after the patient formally enrolls in a health care plan. Managed care is based on a preventive model and ensures convenient access by effective coordination of care, with a reduction in inappropriate utilization and costs. The PCP is a physician serving as a **gatekeeper** who coordinates all of the patient's health care and decides what, if any, additional care or testing is required.

Managed care began as an alternative delivery system in the mid-1970s but is now regarded more as the industry standard. The use of this type of health care has grown and will continue to grow as employers, the government, and other purchasers of health care want to provide higher-quality care at a lower cost.

The major types of **managed care organizations (MCOs)** are health maintenance organizations (HMOs), preferred provider organizations or networks (PPOs), and indemnity insurance plans that have incorporated some managed care features. Each of these is unique, and this dynamic industry also contains hybrid combinations of all of the major types of MCOs.

The terms *managed care* and *health maintenance organization* are not synonymous, although they are often misused interchangeably. HMOs use managed care techniques and are, therefore, MCOs. However, not all managed care organizations are HMOs—for example, PPOs and managed indemnity plans. The definitions, structure, operation, and information needs of all of these various types of organizations are the subject of this chapter.

Types of Managed Care Organizations

The types of managed care organizations found in the industry today are health maintenance organizations, preferred provider organizations, managed indemnity plans, and point-of-service plans.

Health Maintenance Organizations

Health maintenance organizations (HMOs) are business entities that either arrange for or provide health services to an enrolled population after prepayment of a fixed sum of money, called a premium. By receiving this premium, the HMO is paid to keep its patients healthy. Once the patient becomes ill, the prepayment serves as an incentive for the patient to seek early treatment and for the caregiver to provide care with the greatest efficiency and best possible outcome.

HMOs are found in a variety of different forms, each named by its organizational structure. Regardless of the structure, "the entity must have three characteristics to call itself an HMO:

1. An organized system for providing health care or otherwise assuring health care delivery in a geographic area
2. An agreed-upon set of basic and supplemental health maintenance and treatment services
3. A voluntarily enrolled group of people." (*A Glossary of Terms: The Language of Managed Care and Organized Health Care Systems*, 1994)

Staff Model   The **staff model HMO** is the most tightly organized HMO structure. The HMO entity owns the facilities and arranges for health care through employed physicians, who are allowed to see only the particular HMO's patients. All profits accrue to the HMO rather than to the physicians, and the physicians are paid salaries. Some staff model HMOs own only the clinic facilities and contract with local providers for the remainder of the services, such as hospital and ambulatory surgery services. Other staff model HMOs own a comprehensive group of facilities that provide all of the services under the same ownership. The staff model is the only model where the HMO actually owns the facilities where care is provided. Group Health Cooperative is an example of a staff model HMO. Most staff model HMOs changed their structures to another model during the 1990s.

Group Model   The **group model HMO** has an exclusive contract with a multispecialty medical group that provides all physician services. Other facilities necessary to provide the comprehensive health care package are contracted using the same methods used in other models. The contract with the multispecialty group may contain a year-end reconciliation clause, wherein the multispecialty group may receive a percentage of any unused premiums at year-end. This provides significant incentive for proper patient care and financial management. Physicians are employees of the group practice rather than employees of the HMO. A few group model HMOs are still active, including the well-known Kaiser Foundation Health Plan, in which the Permanente Medical Group provides physician services.

Network Model   The **network model HMO** contracts with more than one physician group, hospital, and other facilities to provide a comprehensive health care package. The physicians may share in some of the profit or loss of the HMO according to contract terms but are not required to provide care only to the patients of a particular HMO. The HMO portion of their business may vary from low to high participation.

Independent Practice Association Model   The **independent practice association (IPA) model** was developed primarily as a way for the solo practice physician to participate in the managed care market. This model has two varieties: the physician initiated and the insurance entity initiated. In the model initiated by physicians, the HMO is formed by the physicians who are placing their own resources as the start-up funds. The HMO contracts with each physician and the other facilities necessary to make up the HMO. In this variety of IPA, the physicians are highly at risk for the resources they use to back the HMO. They may also purchase large amounts of reinsurance, or stop-loss insurance, to provide insurance after expenses of a given amount have been paid per enrollee—such as after $50,000 or $100,000 per enrollee has been paid per year.

Insurance entities also develop IPA model HMOs because of their ease of development. A comprehensive group of providers and facilities, plus financial resources, are the only ingredients necessary to develop an IPA model—things readily available through most insurers. Either of these IPA models provides a wide choice of physicians from which enrollees may choose. However, financial viability has been difficult to achieve, as the independent physicians have little incentive to change their practice patterns, which is necessary to maintain profitability.

Mixed Model   The **mixed model HMO** operates within two or more different types of organizational structures to provide flexibility to members, diversity of income to the HMO, and attractive pricing to the employers. Mixed models can also be created during mergers and acquisitions.

Preferred Provider Organizations

In an effort to guide enrollees to more cost-effective providers, the **preferred provider organization (PPO)** was developed by the insurance industry. The providers that participate in the PPO agree to provide services to PPO patients at a discounted rate in return for the promise of a higher volume of patients. The patients who use the PPO providers pay little or no out-of-pocket expenses, whereas those who use other providers pay significantly higher portions of the providers' charges. Although the patient is not limited to a certain list of providers, there is a strong financial incentive to choose providers included in the PPO.

Managed Indemnity Plans

Indemnity insurance is the industry term for traditional health insurance, in which the insured patient is reimbursed for expenses after the care has been given. This traditional insurance often has **deductible** and **coinsurance** responsibilities for the insured. A deductible is the amount that the insureds must pay each year from their own pockets before the plan will make payments. Coinsurance is the portion of the cost for which the insured has financial responsibility, usually based on a fixed percentage. This coinsurance becomes effective on expenses above the deductible amount.

Traditional indemnity insurance places financial responsibility on the insureds but also gives them total freedom to use any provider of care they wish, at whatever price. Before the development of managed care, insurance companies thought that these deductible and coinsurance features would encourage insureds to purchase health care wisely. In reality, these features had little effect on purchasing decisions, while the costs of health care and health care premiums continued to rise out of control.

Managed indemnity plans were created to provide insureds with the freedom to choose their health care provider but also to control both premium levels and health care costs. The managed indemnity plans work the same as traditional insurance, with the addition of some cost-control measures. The most common cost-control measures included in these plans are preauthorization of expensive tests, surgical procedures, and inpatient hospitalizations, under the assumption that many of these may be unnecessary.

Critics say that managed indemnity plans are just an indemnity insurance company impersonating as managed care. This is said with good reason.

To truly qualify as an MCO, the plan needs to have direct involvement in how medicine is practiced. Simply preauthorizing certain services probably does not qualify. For the purposes of this discussion, however, managed care is left "to the eye of the beholder," and all types are included here.

Point-of-Service Plans

A point-of-service plan can incorporate any or all of the above managed care strategies. By enrolling in a point-of-service plan, insureds choose the type of provider to use and how much out-of-pocket expense they are willing to pay in return for that ability to choose. As an example, at the point of service (day of care), the patient can choose the HMO physician with no out-of-pocket cost, the PPO in-network provider at a 10 percent coinsurance cost, or a PPO out-of-network provider at a 20 percent coinsurance cost. Some point-of-service plans still require the PPO out-of-network provider to receive preauthorization for certain services, as in managed indemnity plans. With this point-of-service plan, the patient has a great freedom of choice.

With all of the managed care options included here, there are advantages and disadvantages to both providers and patients. The greater the freedom to choose a provider, the higher the out-of-pocket expense to the patient. The stricter the HMO control over practice patterns, the less at risk the provider income becomes. The individual patients and providers choose the amount of freedom or control with which they are willing to live and work.

Consumer-Directed Health Plans

Consumer-directed health plans arose out of employer need to curtail the double-digit premium increases they were experiencing every year. Another contributing factor to the increased interest in these types of plans is the frustration felt by physicians and consumers over the restrictions and complexity of managed care. These plans are appealing because consumers have flexibility in the management of their own care. Of course, there is a price associated with the flexibility—increased out-of-pocket costs. These types of plans are not managed care plans, because they contain no provisions to manage the patient's care. Rather, they give consumers control of routine health decisions and provide them with an additional method of reimbursing their health care expenses.

A **Flexible Spending Account (FSA)** is an account that is set up by the employee through his or her employer to cover health care costs. The employee cannot withdraw money from this account for anything other than health care. The amount deposited into the account is predetermined by the employee on a pay period basis, is pre-tax, and any amount left in the account at the end of the benefit year is retained by the employer, creating a "use it or lose it" incentive. This plan type is used to supplement generous benefit plans by paying low copayments and deductibles.

The **Health Reimbursement Arrangement (HRA)** is a mechanism by which an employer funds an account for its employees to pay for otherwise unreimbursed health care expenses. Contributions are made by the employer into the account and are tax deductible for the employer. Funds withdrawn by the employee to pay for health care are also tax exempt for the employee. Employees cannot cash out the balance of the account when they leave employment, but some employers may allow them to roll over the amount into retirement.

The **Health Savings Account (HSA)** was created as part of the Medicare Modernization Act and permits individuals and families who purchase high-deductible health insurance coverage to contribute to the account. These contributions can then be used to pay for costs associated with health care, including those that are applied to their deductible. Consumers who have coverage through an HSA cannot purchase supplemental insurance to cover costs incurred until the deductible is reached. Just as with the HRAs, the contributions to this account are not taxed and any withdrawals to pay for health care are also tax exempt. Withdrawals for nonmedical expenses can be made; however, the withdrawal will be subject to income taxation and an early withdrawal penalty of 10 percent for individuals under the age of 65. Balances roll over from year to year, and any balance in the account is retained by the employee when he or she changes jobs (CBO, 2006).

Types of Patients

Patients within a managed care organization are referred to as **members**. They have chosen a particular health plan, usually for a period of one year, and become members of the organization for that period of time. Some plans also refer to members as **subscribers** if they are the primary recipients of the insurance benefit, and as **dependents** if they are the spouse or child of the primary recipient. Families, or *insured units*, are also referred to as *contracts*, because the primary recipient makes the insurance decision for the entire family. If the subscriber of the insurance makes the decision to change managed care plans, the contract is lost to another managed care organization. Managed care organizations also refer to the number of individuals holding coverage with their company as the number of "covered lives."

All people eligible to receive care within the MCO are still referred to as "patients" while they are accessing the health care system. Because managed care organizations arrange for or provide care using a network of facilities, the patients are the same types of patients as seen in the individual facilities.

Types of Caregivers

The caregivers encountered in managed care are the traditional caregivers mentioned throughout this text. These caregivers provide illness-related care. In addition, managed care uses health educators to educate patients in preventive measures that can help them retain good health and case managers to administer disease management and chronic illness programs.

Illness

The primary care component of managed care uses physician extenders or mid-level providers to provide illness-related care more than do most other settings. Physician assistants (PAs) and nurse practitioners (NPs) both assist the primary care physicians by performing preventive services such as patient teaching and routine physical examinations, and by performing assessments of acute but non-life-threatening conditions for the physician. PAs and NPs are trained to perform tasks that might otherwise be completed by a physician but do not require the same level of education.

PAs must practice under the direction of a physician and have their documentation reviewed and countersigned by the physician. NPs are licensed registered nurses who have received master's-level training in areas of specialty such as adult, family, or pediatric practice. NPs can work independent of a physician but most frequently work as part of a team of primary care practitioners.

Wellness

Preventive care and wellness are a central focus of a health maintenance organization and most managed care organizations. Wellness coordinators or health educators are used in health plans to assist primary care providers in this portion of the mission.

No formal educational preparation is specifically required for the role of health educator. This role is filled by other health professionals who enjoy the teaching portion of health care. Nurses and dietitians function in a preventive role in managed care. Some organizations may also employ an exercise physiologist or physical therapist for cardiopulmonary rehabilitation and strengthening of members. A frequent role for the health educator is teaching chronic disease management for conditions such as asthma or diabetes. Specialized nurse educators extend the care provided by primary providers when they teach prenatal classes or write educational material for the members.

REGULATORY ISSUES

Managed care is concerned with two types of regulatory organizations: governmental agencies and voluntary accrediting associations.

Governmental Regulation

Governmental regulation takes place at the federal and state levels. The federal regulation is concerned with care provided to enrollees of government programs, and the state regulation is concerned with the managed care organization's insurance license.

The Centers for Medicare & Medicaid Services (CMS)

Medicare entered the managed care arena as a direct purchaser through the Balanced Budget Act of 1997, with a plan called Medicare+Choice (M+C) or Medicare Part C. The Medicare Modernization Act of 2003 increased payments to this program and renamed it **Medicare Advantage**. A beneficiary who enrolls in a Medicare Advantage plan is responsible for both the Medicare Part B premium, which is retained by the Medicare program, and any additional premium collected by the Medicare Advantage plan. Medicare Advantage plans may offer additional benefits, such as prescription drugs, eye exams, hearing aids, or routine physical exams, but at a minimum must provide the coverage that Medicare would provide.

Enrollment in M+C plans in 2002 was estimated at 5.6 million beneficiaries, or 11 percent of the Medicare population, but enrollment had started to decline. In 2004, after CMS implemented Medicare Advantage and increased payments to participating health plans, enrollment in the program began to rebound. In 2010, Medicare Advantage enrolled over 11 million beneficiaries, approaching almost one-quarter of the Medicare population.

The Medicare Managed Care Manual (found on the Internet at http://www.cms.gov/Manuals/IOM) provides information on participation, including information on the Quality Assessment and Performance Improvement requirements for Medicare managed care plans.

Clinical Laboratory Improvement Amendments of 1988

The **Clinical Laboratory Improvement Amendments of 1988 (CLIA)** were originally developed in response to concerns about potentially preventable deaths caused by poor Pap smear testing. This law was effective on September 1, 1992, and refers to all laboratories, including those operated in HMOs and physician practices within managed care networks.

The basic items that CLIA addresses are testing complexity, personnel standards, proficiency testing requirements, quality-control standards, patient test management, cytology testing, inspections, and fees. The regulations of CLIA require that every laboratory possess a certificate to operate and that sanctions are imposed on a laboratory that fails to meet the operational standards or proficiency testing guidelines. MCOs require proof of CLIA compliance during the laboratory contracting process. (Requirements are found online at http://www.cms.gov/clia/.)

State Regulation

Although many MCOs providing services to Medicare and Medicaid beneficiaries are regulated by CMS, many MCOs are not. MCOs with only commercial enrollees are regulated solely by their individual state insurance laws. These laws vary throughout the United States and are administered by the insurance commissioner's office or HMO regulatory agency in each state to ensure that the MCO is financially able to operate as an insurance company.

Voluntary Accreditation

There are several voluntary accreditation options for managed care. For example, the MCO could decide on any of these approaches:

- National Committee for Quality Assurance (NCQA) accreditation
- The Joint Commission (TJC) accreditation or Accreditation Association for Ambulatory Health Care (AAAHC) accreditation
- Both NCQA and TJC or AAAHC accreditation

An MCO could also select specific accrediting organizations for specific types of facilities within its network. For example, the MCO could choose among TJC, HFAP, or DNV (discussed in Chapter 2) for accreditation of its hospitals.

National Committee for Quality Assurance

The **National Committee for Quality Assurance** (**NCQA**, pronounced NIK-QWA) was formed in 1979 by the managed care industry. The Washington, DC-based organization originally did governmental reviews for federally qualified HMO status in the 1980s. In 1990, NCQA became an independent nonprofit organization, receiving a grant from the Robert Wood Johnson Foundation to develop a new set of standards separate from those of trade associations. In 2010, NCQA offered accreditation programs for health plan accreditation, wellness and health promotion, managed behavioral health care organizations, new health plans, and disease management.

The NCQA health plan accreditation standards include the following sections: quality management and improvement, utilization management, credentialing and recredentialing, members' rights and responsibilities, standards for member connections, and performance measures (NCQA, 2010). Other NCQA accreditation standards are organized differently. For example, there are seven sections in the disease management accreditation program standards: evidence-based programs, patient services, practitioner services, care coordination, measurement and quality improvement, program operations, and performance measurement. The accreditation process involves a two- to four-day site visit by three members of a survey team. Accreditation is granted for a provisional one year or a full three-year status, with any accreditation status being very difficult to obtain. While the survey is all-encompassing, the central focus is on the insurance aspects of the MCO.

NCQA manages the Healthcare Effectiveness Data and Information Set (HEDIS), the performance measurement tool used by more than 90 percent of the nation's health plans. (See Data Sets later in this chapter for additional information.) HEDIS performance measurement data are the basis for NCQA's Health Plan Report Card, a tool designed to help consumers learn more about their health plan options and the quality of care that the health plans provide. The Health Plan Report Card is available on the NCQA Web site and reports quality based on a star system, from one to four stars being assigned in five categories: Access and Service, Qualified Providers, Staying Healthy, Getting Better, and Living with Illness. Accredited HMOs and PPOs are rated against regional and national averages and benchmarks. Viewing this report card data allows consumers to make health plan enrollment choices based on both quality and cost.

The Joint Commission

The Joint Commission (TJC), formerly known as The Joint Commission on Accreditation of Healthcare Organizations (JCAHO), performs accreditation surveys for many types of facilities that are included in managed care networks, using the appropriate accreditation manual for each facility type.

Accreditation Association for Ambulatory Health Care

The Accreditation Association for Ambulatory Health Care (AAAHC) accredits the health care delivery portion of staff model, group model, and network model HMOs. AAAHC uses the Accreditation Handbook for Ambulatory

Accreditation Association	Applicability
National Committee for Quality Assurance (NCQA)	All HMO, PPO, and POS plans
Accreditation Association for Ambulatory Health Care (AAAHC)	Staff model HMOs at each clinic site, but not as an HMO; group model HMOs at the physician group, but not as an HMO; network model HMOs at the clinic site, but not as an HMO
The Joint Commission (TJC)	Each part of the entity may be individually accredited by the Joint Commission or another organization
URAC	Health Plan accreditation standards for HMOs and other integrated health plans; health network accreditation for PPOs

FIGURE **4-1** Voluntary accreditation associations.

Health Care to survey the physician office and clinic portions of these HMOs. The survey consists of an on-site visit by at least two surveyors for a minimum of two days and is aimed at the health care delivery rather than the insurance aspects of the HMO or MCO.

URAC

URAC (formerly the Utilization Review Accreditation Commission) began accrediting health plans and preferred provider organizations in 1996. URAC publishes both health plan and health network standards. The Health Plan accreditation program provides a comprehensive review of health plan operations in five areas: network management, quality improvement, credentialing, and member protection and utilization management. The Health Plan standards are appropriate for HMOs and other integrated health plans. On the other hand, Health Network accreditation does not include utilization management and is better suited for PPO accreditation. Figure 4-1 provides examples of voluntary accreditation associations and the organizations they accredit.

DOCUMENTATION

Documentation methods for different types of managed care organizations are determined by the structure of the organization, such as whether a clinic is owned by the MCO or contracts with the MCO.

Staff Model

Documentation requirements for staff model HMOs are set directly by the HMO. Documentation of services provided by all caregivers is found in the centralized record for the member, which is kept at the member's clinic. The primary care provider (PCP) functions as the gatekeeper and writes orders for all diagnostic and therapeutic procedures that the PCP cannot perform. Copies of the results of these procedures are sent to the PCP for review. Courtesy copies from inpatient admissions are also sent to the PCP for review and future reference.

The content of the clinic documentation is guided by appropriate accreditation association standards. The structure of the staff model HMO, with the physician as an employee, determines that the record is the property of the HMO.

Other models

The structure of other types of MCOs (group model, preferred provider organization, managed indemnity plan, and so on) places all documentation under the control of the physician group or physician serving as the primary care provider, rather than with the MCO. The MCO does not actually maintain any medical documentation, but ensures that the primary care providers will, by requiring it in their managed care contracts. Contract requirements are written to ensure that enough information is maintained to comply with the appropriate AAAHC, TJC, or NCQA standards.

REVENUE GENERATION

The MCO produces its revenue by selling an insurance product, which is the ability to provide quality health care to the member. In turn, the MCO must pay or reimburse the providers of care for the services they provide to the members on behalf of the MCO.

Managed Care Organization Revenue

Premium payments are received from multiple sources in MCOs. Employers pay the premiums for a large percentage of members, but some members pay their own premiums because of changes in employment or self-employment. Some MCOs also contract with the government to insure Medicare and Medicaid patients, and the MCO receives the premium directly from CMS or the individual states on behalf of these members.

The amount of premium payment can be determined in several ways. Community rating is a method of determining premiums that is based on actual or anticipated costs for members in a specific geographic location (city, metropolitan area, or state). Age/sex rating is a method of structuring premiums based on enrollee/membership statistics of age and sex. Composite rating is a method of determining premiums in which one uniform premium applies to all subscribers regardless of the number of claimed dependents. Experience rating determines premiums based on the actual utilization of individual subscriber groups. This method is not acceptable in a federally qualified HMO, but is the most frequently used method in traditional indemnity insurance. Patient conditions as identified by coded diagnoses can also be a factor in risk adjustment of premiums. (See the Coding and Classification section of this chapter for more information on diagnosis-based risk adjustment.)

Any premium rate can be structured to a lower amount by requiring a **copayment** from the member at the time of care. A copayment is usually a flat amount, such as $10 per visit.

Reimbursement to the Provider of Care

Salary

In a staff model HMO, providers of care are actual employees of the HMO. Providers work under contract but receive a monthly or bimonthly salary payment, regardless of whether their patient **panel** is full. A provider's panel is the group of patients who have chosen the provider as their primary care provider. The size of the panel is HMO-specific, either by raw numbers of members, such as 1,600 members, or stratified by age group, such as 400 children, 1,000 adults, and 200 seniors.

Capitation (Per Member Per Month)

Capitation is the payment of a fixed dollar amount for each covered person, for the provision of a predetermined set of health services for a specific period of time. Providers are responsible for providing all of the care needed to each of the patients for whom they receive capitation. With this capitation arrangement, the provider assumes the risk for the cost and the frequency of the services provided. As an example, the provider may receive $40 per month for each patient assigned to him or her, whether or not the patient receives care or makes multiple visits. This capitation payment is usually made monthly, based on the monthly patient panel, or assigned group of patients. This rate is known as "per member per month," or PMPM. Out of this capitation payment, providers must pay support staff and office expenses. Claims are sent to the MCO for information purposes only and not for payment processing. Providers who practice effectively can make money under this arrangement, whereas those who do not manage their resources well are financially at risk.

Per Diem

Per diem means "paid by the day or at a daily rate." These rates are negotiated with centers such as hospitals and skilled nursing facilities (SNFs). The per diem covers the nursing care plus room and board charges. Special procedures or surgical services are charged separately. This amount is the only payment the facility receives for the care.

Fee Schedule, Negotiated

The MCO and the provider can negotiate a fee schedule for a flat rate per procedure, visit, or service. This allows any provider willing to negotiate to be part of the MCO network, even those for which no historical data are available on use and cost. This method is normally used when services are needed on a less frequent basis, but the cost varies widely from case to case. Negotiating a fee schedule allows more consistent budgeting of payment dollars by the MCO.

Fee Schedule, Resource-Based Relative Value Scale

Another way to negotiate a fee schedule is to use the resource-based relative value scale (RBRVS) unit value as the base and negotiate the conversion factor (the dollar amount per unit) that provides appropriate reimbursement. As an example, if the RBRVS unit value for a procedure is 2.5 and the negotiated conversion factor is $45 for all procedures, the fee paid to the provider in this case would be $112.50.

Fee Schedule, Percentage of Medicare Physician Fee Schedule

Additionally, some payers will create their fee schedules based on a percentage of the Medicare fee schedule (e.g., 135% of Medicare Physician Fee Schedule). For example, if the Medicare allowable for a service is $85.60, the payer allowable would be $115.56.

Diagnosis Related Groups (DRGs)

Diagnosis Related Groups form the basis of the inpatient prospective payment system (IPPS) used by Medicare, some other payers, and some managed care organizations to reimburse acute care facilities. This payment system is a prospective payment system, meaning the rates are established before care is provided. Each patient's discharge is categorized into a diagnosis related group (DRG) based on the principal and secondary diagnoses including comorbidities and complications. Each DRG is assigned a payment weight based on the average resources to treat patients with that DRG. The goal of this payment system is to encourage facilities to manage their operations more efficiently by finding ways to deliver more cost-effective patient care without sacrificing the quality of the care.

Discounted Charges

In this method, the provider agrees to see MCO patients and charge the MCO the regular fee-for-service rate. The MCO discounts the rate by a certain amount, usually a percentage, before the payment is made. The negotiation of this payment method is the easiest to accomplish, offers the greatest financial risk to the MCO, and gives little financial incentive to the provider to practice more cost-effectively. The total charge may be limited by a maximum allowable threshold for a particular service.

Depending on the type of provider and the contract with the MCO, the provider receives payment from the MCO by means of one or more of these reimbursement mechanisms. Except when copayments are required as a provision of the health plan contract, any remaining balance cannot be billed to the member. Those balances become the "cost of doing business" for the provider and cannot be billed to any other party. Figure 4-2 summarizes the advantages and disadvantages of the different reimbursement methods.

Coordination of Benefits

Coordination of benefits (COB) means determining who the primary insurance payer is and ensuring that no more than 100 percent of the charges are paid to the provider and/or reimbursed to the patient.

Dual Insurance Coverage

Some patients have two insurers because both spouses receive coverage through their employer or because they have purchased an HMO policy to supplement the deficiencies of a basic policy such as Medicare. It is in the best interest of an MCO to determine and record who the primary insurance

Method	Provider	Advantage	Disadvantage
Salary	Physicians	Predictable revenue for the provider, regardless of number of patients in panel	Efficient providers cannot ask for a payment larger than the maximum panel size, limiting their total salary.
Capitation	Primarily physician services	Predictable expenses for the MCO and predictable revenue for providers	Works only when some patients do not seek care and a significant portion are not "sicker" than average.
Per Diem	Primarily inpatient facilities	Flat rate regardless of type of care given	Cood historical data is required to negotiate an appropriate rate.
Fee Schedule, Negotiated	Any noninpatient facility or physicians	Allows per-unit billing, but at a controlled and predetermined cost per unit	Can be negotiated without good historical data or for less frequently used providers.
Fee Schedule, RBRVS Based	Physician services	As above, but can be related to Medicare reimbursement	Not all procedures have an RBRVS value assigned to them.
Fee Schedule, Percentage of Medicare Physician Fee Schedule	Physician services	As above, and completely dependent on Medicare fee schedule	If the percentage is not significantly higher that Medicare, poor reimbursement is the result.
Diagnosis Related Groups (DRGs)	Acute inpatient facilities	Improved patient record documentation; incentive to improve quality of care	The hospital receives a flat amount regardless of the extent of care provided or the length of stay.
Discounted Charges	All providers	Easiest to establish, but provides no incentive for costeffectiveness by providers	Provides the greatest flexibility of charges for the provider and the greatest financial risk for the MCO.

FIGURE **4-2** Reimbursement to providers of care.

carrier is for each member so that the coordination of benefits rules can be applied correctly. In some cases, the MCO may be a secondary payer.

The method of determining the primary payer in dual-coverage cases is different from state to state. The most popular method used in determining the primary payer when both spouses carry insurance on the family is the "birthday rule." The spouse with the birthday earliest in the calendar year is the primary insurer for the children, with each spouse's insurance being primary for themselves. Determining whose insurance is primary for the family is important to the MCO, because, for a dual-covered family, the MCO may be the primary carrier for the subscriber only and not for the other family members.

If the subscriber's spouse carries the primary insurance for the family, the MCO is responsible for the full benefit level for the subscriber and only the unpaid balance—usually 20 percent or less—on the other family members. HMOs must follow the rules for determining when Medicare is the secondary payer.

The MCO that owns health care facilities can bill other primary payers for the care provided in its facilities or by its salaried or capitated providers, thus offsetting the expense of care. When paying claims, the MCO can direct claims to other payers if it is not the primary payer.

Workers' Compensation, Motor Vehicle Accidents, and Personal Injury Cases

Many MCO members are injured at work, in a motor vehicle accident, or by another individual. In these cases, the member may prefer to receive care from his or her PCP. It may, in fact, be better for the patient's overall health and wellness to see the PCP, who knows his or her medical history. In these situations, the MCO can submit a claim to the workers' compensation, motor vehicle, or personal injury carrier and receive reimbursement for the care provided. This diverts the expense to the appropriate insurance carrier, while the MCO's overhead and/or capitation remains the same.

INFORMATION MANAGEMENT

The information management system in a managed care organization is determined by the structure of the organization. If the managed care organization owns facilities that are part of the organization, the health information management system would be similar to the systems described in other chapters of this book.

The information gathered and maintained in the insurance portion of the organization is maintained using procedures and systems similar to those used in the medical insurance industry.

Coding and Classification Systems

The two basic coding and classification systems used to collect and manage data in managed care are the *ICD* diagnosis system and the HCPCS procedure system. Other systems may be used as the individual needs of an organization dictate.

International Classification of Disease, Clinical Modification

The current version of the *International Classification of Disease, Clinical Modification* (ICD-9-CM until October 1, 2013, and *ICD-10-CM* thereafter) is the classification system for diagnoses required by CMS on all health care claims received. This coding system is the only one used throughout the health care industry to describe diagnoses, and these codes are collected on all claims for all services in managed care.

HCPCS Codes and CPT Procedure Codes

Current Procedural Terminology (CPT), which is also known as Level 1 of the HCPCS coding system, is an American Medical Association (AMA) publication that describes physician diagnostic and therapeutic procedures and their codes. CMS incorporated the *CPT* codes into its Healthcare Common Procedural Coding System (HCPCS), used to describe physician services for reimbursement. *CPT* and the full HCPCS coding systems are the basis for the resource-based relative value scale (RBRVS) system. *CPT* codes are routinely collected on all claims except for facility charge claims for inpatients. Using *CPT* and HCPCS codes allows the MCO to compare services used and costs across delivery sites.

ICD-9-CM Volume 3 and ICD-10-PCS Procedure Codes

The Centers for Medicare & Medicaid Services (CMS) developed separate codes to describe medical procedures. *ICD-10-PCS* procedure codes were developed to replace *ICD-9-CM* Volume 3 procedure codes in 2013. These codes best describe procedures from a facility perspective and are mainly used to describe hospital inpatient services. MCOs collect these codes on UB-04 claims, the standard facility charge claim form.

Special Uses of Coded Data

Risk-Adjustment of Managed Care Premiums Diagnosis codes also have another use in Medicare Advantage plans—as a component of a system for adjusting premiums paid to health plans based on the patient's health status. Traditionally, Medicare adjusted its payments to health plans based on geographic and demographic factors associated with each enrollee (e.g., age, gender, Medicaid eligibility, and institutional status) (Tully & Rulon, 2000). Adding a diagnosis-based risk adjustment factor had the effect of increasing payments to a health plan for enrollees with conditions representing higher risk for more costly services. In 2000, the **Principal In-Patient Diagnostic Cost Group (PIP-DCG)** model was phased in as an initial mechanism for adjusting payments to Medicare managed care organizations based on patient diagnoses. When an enrollee was hospitalized, the principal diagnosis code determined the PIP-DCG, which in a limited way identified a certain amount of added risk based on the enrollee's health status. In 2004, CMS implemented a more comprehensive model that considered all sites of service, not just inpatient hospitalization, as well as other traditional risk adjustment factors such as sex and age. The new model uses selected diagnosis codes to place patients into groups known as **Hierarchical Condition Categories (HCCs)**. The numerical risk factor associated with each HCC is a component in determining the amount by which payment to the MCO is increased. Depending on the specific HCCs involved, if an enrollee falls into more than one HCC, additional risk may be calculated and the payment to the organization increased further. The risk adjustment factors are different for beneficiaries residing in the community and those in a long-term care institution. (See Figure 4-3 for an excerpt from the Medicare Advantage Ratebook, listing some of the HCCs and their risk adjustment factors.) In addition to the CMS-HCCs for Medicare Advantage health plans, there are also RxHCCs for adjusting Part D payments for beneficiaries enrolled in prescription drug plans. For both types of HCCs, diagnoses from one year are used to predict costs in the following year.

Variable	Disease Group	Community Factors	Institutional Factors
HCC1	HIV/AIDS	0.945	0.967
HCC2	Septicemia/Shock	0.759	0.764
HCC5	Opportunistic Infections	0.3	0.288
HCC7	Metastatic Cancer and Acute Leukemia	2.276	0.824
HCC8	Lung, Upper Digestive Tract, and Other Severe Cancers	1.053	0.47
HCC9	Lymphatic, Head and Neck, Brain, and Other Major Cancers	0.794	0.368
HCC10	Breast, Prostate, Colorectal, and Other Cancers and Tumors	0.208	0.182
HCC15	Diabetes with Renal or Peripheral Circulatory Manifestation	0.508	0.459
HCC16	Diabetes with Neurologic or Other Specified Manifestation	0.408	0.459
HCC17	Diabetes with Acute Complications	0.339	0.459
HCC18	Diabetes with Ophthalmologic or Unspecified Manifestation	0.259	0.459
HCC19	Diabetes without Complication	0.162	0.248
HCC21	Protein-Calorie Malnutrition	0.856	0.374
HCC25	End-Stage Liver Disease	0.978	0.654
HCC26	Cirrhosis of Liver	0.406	0.384
HCC27	Chronic Hepatitis	0.406	0.384
HCC31	Intestinal Obstruction/Perforation	0.311	0.345
HCC32	Pancreatic Disease	0.403	0.309
HCC33	Inflammatory Bowel Disease	0.241	0.205
HCC37	Bone/Joint/Muscle Infections/Necrosis	0.535	0.497
HCC38	Rheumatoid Arthritis & Inflammatory Connective Tissue Disease	0.346	0.215
HCC44	Severe Hematological Disorders	1.015	0.493
HCC45	Disorders of Immunity	0.912	0.427

FIGURE **4-3** Excerpt from Medicare Advantage HCC Coefficients Table.

Diagnosis Related Groups Diagnosis related groups (DRGs) were implemented in the early 1980s for use in describing inpatient services. The classification system groups inpatients who are medically related by diagnosis, treatment, and length of stay. Patients are grouped into major diagnostic categories (MDCs) and further subgrouped into a specific DRG. Only one DRG is assigned per stay.

Many MCOs collect the DRG number or determine the number by entering the ICD-9-CM diagnosis and procedure codes into a special computer program called a "grouper." Medicare pays a flat rate per inpatient stay, based on the DRG for that stay. This allows Medicare to more accurately predict the expenses for the insured population and forces the inpatient facility to share a large portion of the risk. The hospital receives a set payment, regardless of how many days the patient stays and how large the bill might actually be. This payment method is also used by some MCOs to pay inpatient claims, for similar reasons.

UB-04 Revenue Codes Revenue codes are collected on all claims submitted on a UB-04 claim form. Normally these forms contain facility and service charges from hospitals, skilled nursing facilities, and home care agencies. Revenue codes define a specific accommodation type, ancillary service, or billing calculation. They are four-digit numbers that are grouped into categories of numbers having similar meaning.

Data and Information Flow

Data Collection and Transfer

Data are collected differently depending on the structure of the MCO. Staff model and group model HMOs are able to collect encounter data on the patients they see in their clinics. All types of HMOs are able to collect referral data after a referral has been issued, and all types of MCOs are able to collect claims data from providers requesting payment.

Encounter Data An **encounter** is "a professional contact between a patient and a provider during which services are delivered" (Abdelhak, 2007, p. 133). Encounter data are collected at the time of the service and reported in its raw form, rather than in the form of claims (billing) data.

Referral Data A **referral** is an authorization to receive a specific health service from a specific health provider that will be paid for by the HMO. HMOs issue referrals before specialty care can be given. PPOs and managed indemnity plans do not issue referrals, because patients are allowed to see other providers if they are willing to pay the additional cost. Referral data are collected at the time the referral is given by all organizations that issue referrals.

Most MCOs process referrals by online request systems or telephone voice and data recognition systems to speed the processing. Authorization for care ahead of time in the form of a referral allows the MCO to direct patients to appropriate providers in the network and to record the estimated future expense that will be incurred for the care.

Claims Data Claims data are collected as a by-product of the claims payment process. IPA model HMOs, PPOs, and managed indemnity plans can access service data in the form of claims data. For facilities such as hospitals, the data available are from the UB-04 claim form. Data for physicians and similar providers are from their billing form, the CMS 1500.

Statistical Data

All available data, including encounter, referral, and claims data, are combined and organized to provide useful management statistics. The two major ways that statistics are divided in MCOs are by member and by contract. HMOs frequently work with statistical data by member, and PPOs and managed indemnity plans work with their data by contracts, although MCOs may use both methods.

By Per Member Per Month (PMPM) Frequency of service utilization and the cost of procedures is evaluated and displayed by employer purchasing group, by provider or facility site, and by provider panel, based on the number of members in the MCO for that month.

By Per Contract Per Month (PCPM) Frequency and cost are evaluated and displayed in the same way, based on the number of total contracts the MCO has for the month.

Electronic Information Systems

An electronic information system that is able to perform the functions necessary for managed care is vital to the profitability of the MCO. Some information system requirements for an MCO are much different than for either a hospital or physician office practice, even though MCOs may include these facilities in their networks. Many information system functions are designed to assist care providers and staff to appropriately utilize resources.

Basic System Requirements

Eligibility/Enrollment Enrollment is the process of placing a person into the database of covered individuals of the MCO. **Eligibility** refers to whether the person is allowed to receive care under the MCO contract and the dates of coverage. The enrollment database is similar to the master patient index found in health care facilities and includes dates of enrollment and disenrollment, demographic information, and the party responsible for paying the premium.

Benefit Levels The benefit level may not be the same for all members of an MCO. Most managed care organizations sell a variety of insurance packages, some that allow more services than do others or that allow certain benefits at a higher payment level than others. Benefit levels must be tracked for each individual member, because many members have dual insurance coverage or different benefit packages, even within the same family or contract. A system that only tracks this information for the subscriber may miss the detail necessary to divert claims to another, more appropriate payer.

Patient Registration and Scheduling Hospitals within an MCO require a patient registration system, and all service providers require some form of scheduling software to manage their health care environment.

Authorization and Referral Management   Managed care organizations provide preauthorization for admissions and procedures and issue referrals for care that cannot be provided by the PCP. This information must be maintained in the computer system and must be accessible to the PCP. The best systems include practice guidelines that are accessible and allow the PCP to review and document clinical decisions in real time within the information system.

Utilization Management/Case Management   Computer software should identify cases that are appropriate for case management through evaluation of encounter data, referral data, or claims data. This allows the utilization management staff to assist the PCP in managing the multiple resources needed to properly care for complicated cases. The best systems provide accessible information about clinical practice guidelines for both inpatient and outpatient management.

Billing/Claims Production   Staff model and group model HMOs require software to create claims for another primary insurer for patients with dual insurance coverage. In addition, this software should have the ability to post payments to these charges and maintain accounts receivable information for tracking purposes.

Payment/Claims Processing   The claims processing software allows the MCO to pay claims for authorized services and should verify the eligibility/enrollment files, benefit levels, and referral data before the payment is processed. Capitated visits should be recorded in the claims database even though no actual payment is processed. Without this capitated data, there is no information to manage the financial aspects of the MCO that are covered under capitation.

Cost Accounting   The cost accounting module of the information system should tie together the accounts payable portion of the business and the accounts receivable portion from premiums. In staff model HMOs, coordination of benefits (COB) income must also be tracked. COB income is received when the staff model HMO bills another primary insurer for services it provided in its clinics.

Advanced System Requirements

Electronic Health Record (EHR)   The answer to collecting patient health information and having it available throughout the network of facilities is ultimately the electronic health record. Without the EHR, the MCO is still a combination of different facilities that try their best to achieve effective communication in real time.

The HITECH Act is a component of the American Recovery and Reinvestment Act of 2009, signed into law to provide incentives to physician practices and other health care organizations for the implementation of EHR systems. This law provided incentive payments to both physicians and hospitals that demonstrate "meaningful use" of a "qualified EHR." The law also provided an additional $20,000 to physicians who utilize an electronic prescribing system and the Physician Quality Reporting Index (PQRI). The HITECH Act also specified that providers who had not adopted an EHR by 2015 would experience a decrease in Medicare reimbursement. The purpose of this legislation is to encourage providers to shift their medical documentation to an EHR to provide accurate, timely, and legible patient information and better continuity of patient care (CMS, 2009).

Executive Decision Making   Data from any or all of the information systems may be needed to determine where and when decisions are needed and to help in the decision-making process.

Data Sets

Healthcare Effectiveness Data and Information Set

The **Healthcare Effectiveness Data and Information Set (HEDIS)** is a core set of performance measures for managed care plans. HEDIS was designed in 1991 by NCQA to help employers compare health plans, understand the value of what their health care premium is purchasing, and hold the health plan accountable for performance against these measures. HEDIS provides a consistent measure of key performance areas, such as "Effectiveness of Care," "Access/Availability of Care," "Satisfaction with the Experience of Care," "Use of Services," "Cost of Care," and "Health Plan Stability." HEDIS contains more than 70 measures, such as the number of pregnant enrollees receiving prenatal care within the first trimester and childhood immunization status. A list of HEDIS measures is available at the NCQA Web site.

Employer-Specific Data Sets

Some national employers, such as IBM and Xerox, request data specifically on their enrollees, either using HEDIS indicators or by identifying their own issues for tracking. This information helps them determine whether the health plans they are contracted with are providing cost-effective, quality service to their employees and their families.

QUALITY IMPROVEMENT AND UTILIZATION MANAGEMENT

The accreditation associations, CMS, and many employer purchasing groups require an active quality improvement program within managed care organizations to ensure that care is delivered in a cost-effective manner, with consistently appropriate outcomes.

Quality Improvement

The components of a quality improvement program for a managed care organization are detailed as follows. They include an oversight committee that uses a comprehensive plan and the use of quality indicators to identify trends.

Oversight Committee Using a Comprehensive Plan

To ensure that quality improvement is a continuous process, MCOs use an oversight committee that is guided by a comprehensive quality plan. The quality plan is developed by the senior staff and approved by the board of directors at least annually. The oversight committee receives and reviews reports and project requests from subcommittees within the organization. The committee structure is designed to provide a place for each area of the business to report its quality issues and findings.

Quality Indicators

Quality indicators are a quantitative measuring tool for monitoring and evaluating performance. These indicators are important to an MCO, because it is very difficult to manage what has not been measured. Quality in an MCO has several aspects, including medical outcomes, operational effectiveness, patient satisfaction, and financial stability.

Operational Indicators The operational effectiveness indicators measure how well the MCO is performing in comparison to preset goals. These can also include patient satisfaction level goals about how well the "customer" or patient feels the MCO is performing. Examples include:

Telephone call turnaround time

Percentage of telephone calls answered in less than 30 seconds

Appointment availability—all service areas

Percentage of rescheduled appointments—administrative reasons

Pharmacy refill turnaround time

Lobby wait times

Claims processing turnaround time

Medical Indicators Medical indicators are also referred to as "outcome measures," because they express the MCO's ability to obtain a successful outcome from the care that is delivered. Some examples are:

Percentage of members receiving prenatal care in the first trimester

Percentage of babies born at or above an appropriate birth weight

Percentage of operative patients without wound infection

Unanticipated emergency room visits within 24 hours after surgery

Unplanned emergency department visits after primary care visit on same day

Rates of mammograms, Pap smears, immunizations, or physicals

Financial Indicators Financial stability can be measured using the following indicators:

Days in Claims Payable (calculated as the reverse of Days in Accounts Receivable) or

$$\frac{\text{Ending \$ in Claims Payable}}{\text{\$ in Claims Payable for the Period}} \div \text{Days in the Period}$$

Hospital bed days per 1,000 members

Number of avoidable hospital days

Hospital **bed days** are equivalent to the inpatient statistic known as inpatient service days. The measurement of bed days per 1,000 members is a standard MCO measurement that can be compared among MCOs nationwide. "Avoidable hospital days" is defined through the utilization management program and includes such items as performing an ambulatory diagnostic workup as an inpatient; delay in obtaining or failure to appropriately use home care services; and delay in receiving consultation, testing, or procedures. These types of indicators measure the MCO's overall ability to act as a unit for successful patient care and financial outcomes.

Tools from the Agency for Healthcare Research and Quality

The Agency for Healthcare Research and Quality (AHRQ) of the U.S. Department of Health and Human Services has developed several tools that can be of benefit to managed care organizations as well as other health care organizations (Stanton, 2003). A few of these tools include the following:

- National Guideline Clearinghouse™ (NGC)—a database of evidence-based clinical practice guidelines
- National Quality Measures Clearinghouse™ (NQMC)—a repository for evidence-based quality measures and measure sets
- Consumer Assessment of Healthcare Providers and Systems (CAHPS)—includes standardized survey instruments for assessing patients' experiences with ambulatory and facility care. CAHPS also provides access to comparative data through its benchmarking database.

Utilization Management

Utilization management is part of the quality improvement function of an MCO, as well as a method of cost control through prospective and retrospective review of services. These activities consist of:

- **preadmission certification,** which involves reviewing the necessity of an admission prior to its occurrence
- **preauthorization,** a review of elective procedures requiring prior approval for reimbursement
- **concurrent review,** reviewing services ordered for medical necessity during an inpatient hospitalization before they are provided
- **discharge planning,** arranging services that patients may require upon discharge

Preauthorization and/or Concurrent Review

Using clinical practice guidelines on potentially expensive or difficult cases can provide consistent quality of care and can save the MCO money by assuring the provision of the correct test or procedure at the correct time in the treatment plan. Preauthorization of expensive procedures can also perform the same function and can assist the MCO in locating the best-possible facility for performing the procedure.

Written Utilization Protocols and Coordination of Care

Written utilization protocols help providers deal with basically uncomplicated but common cases, and can help avoid unnecessary hospitalizations and provide quicker recovery for the patient. Coordination of care staff helps ensure that the patient receives care at the correct point from the correct providers. In addition, coordination of care staff helps the PCP manage chronic disease patients more effectively. Discharge planning is one form of coordination of care that helps inpatients by arranging a smooth transition to post-acute care.

RISK MANAGEMENT AND LEGAL ISSUES

Risk management in managed care is more comprehensive because of the wide variety of services provided under the managed care concept. Each of the facilities included in the managed care organization, both owned and contracted, monitors for potential risks that are particular to its own settings.

Documentation of care coordination between these settings is very important in managed care, because patients feel that "managed care" means that care happens, or should happen, seamlessly across many facilities. If this does not happen, patients may see their care as less than optimal and consider litigation.

Identifying Unusual Events

Unusual events are reported and tracked within the MCO. Unusual events represent a primary source of litigation for MCOs, similar to other health care providers. Unusual events can be the delay or denial of services that are later determined to have been necessary or emergent, failure to direct a patient to the proper source of care, or any medical incident normally tracked elsewhere, such as an incorrect medication administration.

Informed Consent for Procedures

The providers within the MCO use the same procedures as other providers when they obtain informed consent from patients or their legal representatives before performing procedures. In addition to individual liability on the part of the physician or facility, the MCO is also at risk for being a party to a malpractice suit.

Credentialing

Credentialing is "a process of review to approve a provider who applies to participate in a health plan. Specific criteria and prerequisites are applied in determining initial and ongoing participation in the health plan" (*A Glossary of Terms: The Language of Managed Care and Organized Health Care Systems,* 1994). The MCO performs its own investigation or contracts with an independent **credentials verification organization (CVO)** to conduct credentialing reviews. NCQA offers a certification program for credentials verification organizations. A CVO that achieves certification provides assurance to their MCO clients that the CVO is qualified and competent to conduct credentialing activities. The prerequisites that are evaluated include the credentialing elements verified traditionally by hospitals. These include:

1. Current competence in the field
2. Work history
3. Physical and mental health status
4. Challenges to licensure and registrations
5. Limitation or termination of clinical privileges
6. Pending professional liability actions
7. Felony convictions
8. Federal Drug Enforcement Administration registration
9. National Practitioner Data Bank information

Provider's Office Evaluation

In addition to personal credentialing of the provider, the provider's office is also evaluated to assess whether the office is organized and managed appropriately for inclusion in the MCO network.

Review of Structural Components The provider's office is evaluated, before the signing of a contract, for such items as acceptable facilities, available staff, accessibility of care, and systems for medical management including electronic information systems appropriate for the office or facility.

Record Review A health record review is completed to determine if the records are accessible, standardized in format, legible, properly secured to the folder, signed and dated, and contain the patient's name on each page. Other items may be evaluated based on the applicability of various accreditation standards, such as those of the Accreditation Association for Ambulatory Health Care (AAAHC), the Joint Commission (TJC), or the National Committee for Quality Assurance (NCQA).

Economic Credentialing

Economic credentialing is performed to ensure that the provider is not underutilizing services and compromising the health of the member or overutilizing services and creating unnecessary expense. The MCO uses statistical data such as the number of inpatient admissions per 1,000 members and charges per HCPCS code or DRG to evaluate financial performance. Economic credentialing results in the exclusion of a provider only in the rarest of situations and primarily for severe underutilization of services.

Recredentialing

Providers are recredentialed every two years to be sure that no new information is ignored. A tickler system is used to help reevaluate providers on time, checking such items as medical quality indicator results, malpractice claims experience, overall patient satisfaction rating, and the number of member complaints.

Contract Management

The MCO is built on contracted relationships. An index of contracts, including expiration dates and any proposed contract changes, is maintained to be sure all contracts remain valid and at an optimal level of reimbursement.

ROLE OF THE HEALTH INFORMATION MANAGEMENT PROFESSIONAL

Developing and Implementing Information Plan Based on Organizational Needs

The health information management (HIM) professional in managed care is found mainly in the staff model, group model, and network model HMO, performing the traditional role of health information manager. These HMO settings require the HIM professional to maintain security and confidentiality of records. In addition, the HIM professional performs data collection and coding of encounter data. The HIM professional is concerned with information storage and retrieval, appropriate information technology within the facilities, and personnel management. As in other facilities, this person normally participates extensively in, or leads, the preparation for an accreditation survey visit.

Specialized Functions

The HIM professional receives a unique mix of education and training that allows the individual to perform other functions that are less traditional within an MCO.

Enrollment Management

The enrollment database in an MCO is a highly detailed version of a master patient index, an index traditionally maintained by the HIM professional. The HIM professional's knowledge of data management and patient identification systems provides some of the best foundation possible for performing or supervising the enrollment management function.

Claims Processing/Management

One of the largest databases maintained in most MCOs is the claims database. In addition to management of the claims database, the claims processing supervisor helps determine whether claims are coded properly and are acceptable for payment. The HIM professional's medical knowledge, combined with financial experience or ability, can prepare him or her well for the role of claims processing supervisor.

Quality Management/Performance Improvement

Specialization in quality management/performance improvement by the HIM professional is likely in a managed care organization. Knowledge of all areas of health care provides an excellent foundation for a leadership role in performance improvement.

Risk Management and Credentialing

HIM professionals frequently fill the role of risk manager. The HIM professional's study of medicine, management, and the legal system provides an excellent background for performing the duties of risk manager, which include looking for ways to minimize the potential for injuries, responding promptly and appropriately when injuries occur, and planning for potential liability resulting from injuries (Abdelhak, 2007).

A related function is that of a credentialing specialist. An HIM professional may perform this function for the MCO directly or for a credentials verification organization (CVO). Some HIM professionals serve as chief executive officers or in other management positions in CVOs.

Chief Information Officer

The information technology expertise of the HIM professional can easily be used to perform the role of chief information officer (CIO) for a managed care organization.

TRENDS

Integrated Delivery Systems/Networks

Integrated delivery systems/networks (IDS/Ns) are groupings of facilities contracted together to provide the comprehensive set of services that a patient may need. These facilities and services are owned, leased, or grouped together through long-term contracts and are recognized by the public as being a combined operating entity.

Integrated delivery systems are not the same as managed care organizations, because they do not always contain an insurance provision. However, because an MCO requires a full network of providers, the IDS/N is a natural place to look when contemplating an MCO contract.

The Changing Role of the PCP

The primary care provider is playing less of a role in gatekeeping than ever before in many MCOs. Although most Medicare and Medicaid HMOs still retain the PCP gatekeeper function, other HMOs are abandoning the concept and reallocating the funds into stronger disease management and chronic care management programs. Evidence points toward this trend continuing as resources are funneled to the proper management of the sickest patients in the HMO.

In addition, the population will continue to transition to less restrictive MCO models, PPOs, and POS products without the gatekeeper function, if premiums remain comparable.

Possible Changes in Federal Programs

In 2009, the Medicare Payment Advisory Commission (MedPAC) noted that Medicare Advantage (MA) programs cost the Medicare program 14 percent more than traditional Medicare, on average. They recommended changes that would bring the costs of this program in line with the Medicare fee-for-service (FFS) program and also made recommendations to address the uneven quality of care across Medicare Advantage plans, including a mechanism to compare quality between MA plans and FFS providers.

Accountable Care Organizations (ACOs)

The Affordable Care Act established **Accountable Care Organizations (ACOs)** as one of the new pilot payment models for Medicare. Devers and Berenson provide the following description of ACOs:

> ACOs can generally be defined as a local entity and a related set of providers, including at least primary care physicians, specialists, and hospitals, that can be held accountable for the cost and quality of care delivered to a defined subset of traditional Medicare program beneficiaries or other defined populations, such as commercial health plan subscribers. The primary ways the entity would be held accountable for its performance are through changes in traditional Medicare provider payment featuring financial rewards for good performance based on comprehensive quality and spending measurement and monitoring. Public reporting of cost and quality information to affect public perception of an ACO's worth is another way of holding the ACO accountable for its performance. Proponents generally view three ACO characteristics as essential. These characteristics include: (1) the ability to provide, and manage with patients, the continuum of care across different institutional settings, including at least ambulatory and inpatient hospital care and possibly post acute care; (2) the capability of prospectively planning budgets and resource needs; and, (3) sufficient size to support comprehensive, valid, and reliable performance measurement" (2009, pp. 1–2).

The way in which ACOs combine payment mechanisms and care delivery is similar to the premise of an HMO (Cohen, 2010). However, there are several different organizational models that can utilize the ACO concept. The ACO model is one of several health care reform models with which health information managers may be involved in the twenty-first century.

SUMMARY

The structure of MCOs continues to change to meet market demand, with more MCOs changing to open network styles. Quality improvement and data management are two key areas within the managed care environment. These and many other areas hold excellent employment opportunities for HIM professionals. The managed care field will continue to change and grow, to meet the needs of purchasers and in an attempt to control health care expenses.

KEY TERMS

Accountable Care Organizations (ACOs)
"a local entity and a related set of providers, including at least primary care physicians, specialists, and hospitals, that can be held accountable for the cost and quality of care delivered to a defined subset of traditional Medicare program beneficiaries or other defined populations, such as commercial health plan subscribers. The primary ways the entity would be held accountable for its performance are through changes in traditional Medicare provider payment featuring financial rewards for good performance based on comprehensive quality and spending measurement and monitoring" (Devers and Berenson, 2009, pp. 1–2).

bed day an inpatient service received by one member for one 24-hour period.

capitation payment of a fixed dollar amount to a provider for each patient assigned to that provider, regardless of the amount of care the patient receives.

Clinical Laboratory Improvement Amendments of 1988 (CLIA) federal legislation that provides for regulation of all clinical laboratories, including those operated in HMOs and physician practices within managed care networks.

coinsurance the amount of expense that is the responsibility of the insured under an indemnity insurance policy, usually 20 percent.

concurrent review verifying medical necessity of tests and procedures ordered during an inpatient hospitalization.

coordination of benefits (COB) determining which insurance is the primary payer and ensuring that no more than 100 percent of the charges are paid to the provider and/or reimbursed to the patient.

copayment a flat-rate payment, such as $10 per visit, made by the covered individual for a specific service at the time of the service.

credentialing a process of review to approve a provider who applies to participate in a health plan.

credentials verification organization (CVO) an organization that contracts with a managed care organization or other health care organization to provide credential verification services for physicians and other clinicians seeking clinical privileges.

deductible the amount of expenses the insureds must pay each year from their own pockets before the plan will reimburse them.

dependent the spouse or child of the primary insurance recipient.

Diagnosis Related Groups (DRGs) basis of the inpatient prospective payment system used by Medicare to reimburse acute care facilities; also used in some MCO contracts.

discharge planning arranging post-discharge services for patients prior to discharge to provide continuity of care and aid in recuperation.

eligibility whether a person is able to receive benefits under an insurance policy.

encounter contact between a patient and a provider who is responsible for the assessment and evaluation of the patient at a specific contact, exercising independent judgment.

Flexible Spending Account (FSA) tax-free money an employee sets aside to use during a specified period for health care expenses.

gatekeeper the primary care provider who coordinates all of the patient's health care and decides what, if any, additional care is required.

group model HMO a model in which the HMO has an exclusive contract with a multispecialty medical group that provides all physician services and contracts with other facilities as necessary to provide comprehensive services. Kaiser Permanente is a successful example of this model. In general, the group model is uncommon.

health maintenance organization (HMO) a business entity that either provides or arranges for health services for a covered population after prepayment of a fixed premium.

Healthcare Effectiveness Data and Information Set (HEDIS) a core set of standard performance measures for managed care in the areas of effectiveness of care, access/availability of care, satisfaction with the experience of care, use of services, cost of care, health plan descriptive information, health plan stability, and informed health care choices.

Health Reimbursement Arrangement (HRA) is a mechanism by which an employer funds an account for its employees to pay for otherwise unreimbursed health care expenses.

Health Savings Account (HSA) an account set up by an employee with pretax income that is also not taxed when the employee withdraws from the account for medical expenses. Amounts left in the account at the end of the benefit year roll over to the next year. Withdrawals for nonmedical expenses are subject to income tax and a 10 percent penalty.

Hierarchical Condition Categories (HCCs) disease groupings based on *ICD* codes from both inpatient admissions and outpatient visits in Medicare Advantage organizations. HCCs are used to risk-adjust Medicare payments to MCOs.

indemnity insurance traditional health insurance in which the insured is reimbursed for expenses after the care has been given.

independent practice association (IPA) model an HMO model that was developed primarily as a way for the solo practice physician to participate in the managed care market.

integrated delivery systems/network (IDS/N) a group of facilities contracted together to provide the comprehensive set of services that any patient may need. They are owned, leased, or grouped together by long-term contracts and are recognized by the public as a combined operating entity.

managed care organization (MCO) an organization that provides comprehensive health services, coordinated through a primary care provider who acts as a gatekeeper, after the patient formally enrolls in the organization.

managed indemnity plans indemnity insurance plans that do not limit the insured's choice of health care providers but do include cost-control measures such as preauthorization of expensive tests, surgical procedures, and inpatient hospitalization.

Medicare Advantage a program by which eligible Medicare beneficiaries may choose to receive their health care through a qualified managed care plan, which in turn receives capitation payments from Medicare for each enrollee.

mixed model HMO an HMO that operates within two or more different types of organizational structures to provide flexibility to members.

member an individual who is enrolled in a managed care organization.

National Committee for Quality Assurance (NCQA) an accreditation association that accredits managed care organizations and related services. Their accreditation programs include health plan accreditation, wellness and health promotion, managed behavioral health care organizations, new health plans, and disease management.

network model HMO an HMO that contracts with multiple physician groups, hospitals, and other facilities to provide a comprehensive health care package.

panel the group of patients who have chosen a particular provider as their primary care provider.

per diem a reimbursement methodology where the payment is based on the number of days of care.

preadmission certification   review and approval of the medical necessity of inpatient care prior to the patient's admission.

preauthorization   review and prior approval for payment of a health care service.

preferred provider organization (PPO)   an insurance entity that contracts with providers to create a preferred network. The insured population is allowed to use any provider, but using network providers results in a lesser cost to the patient.

Principal In-Patient Diagnostic Cost Groups (PIP-DCGs)   the first risk adjustment model that Medicare used to adjust capitation payments made to Part C plans, based largely on the principal diagnoses of hospitalized enrollees. PIP-DCGs were replaced by HCCs in 2004.

referral   an authorization to receive from a specific health provider a specific health service that will be paid for by the HMO.

staff model HMO   the most tightly organized HMO structure. The HMO entity owns the facilities and arranges for health care through employed physicians, who are allowed to see only the particular HMO's patients.

subscriber   primary recipient of the insurance benefit.

URAC   an independent, nonprofit organization offering accreditation, education, and measurement programs. URAC's Health Plan standards are appropriate for HMOs and other integrated health plans. Its Health Network accreditation does not include utilization management and is better suited for PPO accreditation.

REVIEW QUESTIONS

Knowledge-Based Questions

1. What coding systems would be used to code a hospital claim submitted to an MCO for payment? What systems would be used for a physician claim?
2. What three characteristics are required for an organization to qualify as an HMO?
3. How does an MCO perform coordination of benefits?
4. What does the abbreviation PMPM mean, and why is it important in managed care?
5. What two benefits will the MCO realize from using online referral processing?
6. Explain the difference between coinsurance and copayment.
7. What contributed to the introduction of consumer-directed health plans?
8. Identify the types of consumer-directed health plans and their characteristics.

Critical Thinking Questions

1. Why wouldn't a managed indemnity plan collect referral data?
2. Why could the discounted charges reimbursement mechanism seem attractive to both the physician and the MCO?
3. Why would an MCO want to reimburse hospitals by a DRG payment?
4. An HMO with 50,000 members had 13,024 inpatient service days for last month. What formula would you use to determine bed days per 1,000, and what was this HMO's rate for last month?
5. Why is it crucial for an MCO to conduct utilization management activities?
6. What are the benefits of an EHR to a physician practice and its patients?

WEB ACTIVITY

Visit the NCQA Web site at http://www.ncqa.org and locate the latest list of HEDIS measures. If you were a health information manager in a pediatric clinic and were planning to present HEDIS results to your medical staff, which of the measures listed would you select for your report?

CASE STUDY

The senior management team of Efficient Network HMO is evaluating the year-end data related to emergency room (ER) expenses. One physician group within the network had ER expenses that were three times the rate of any other group within the network. Senior management has studied group operations and theorizes that three factors are influencing the high rate of expense. The group does not utilize triage nurses, does not have after-hours urgent care services, and has limited office hours from 8:30 to 11:30 a.m. and 1:30 to 5:00 p.m. An answering service, not staffed by nurses, relays calls during the remainder of the hours.

The physician group is willing to work on the problem but is asking for detailed, comparative information from the HMO's senior management team before it implements any changes. How would you, as the clinical data specialist for the HMO, answer the following questions:

1. What information would be useful to senior management of the HMO and the physician practice in evaluating the ER expenses?
2. What data sources would you use to obtain data?
3. How could the reports be structured to provide meaningful information?

REFERENCES AND SUGGESTED READINGS

Abdelhak, M., Hanken, M. A., Grostick, S., Jacobs, E. (Eds.). (2007). *Health information: Management of a Strategic Resource* (3rd ed.). St. Louis, MO: Saunders/Elsevier.

[CMS] Centers for Medicare & Medicaid Services. (2009, December 30). CMS proposes requirements for the electronic health records (EHR) Medicare incentive. http://www.cms.hhs.gov/apps/media/press/factsheet.asp?Counter=3563.

[CBO] Congressional Budget Office. (2006, December). *CBO Study: Consumer-Directed Health Plans: Potential Effects on Health Care Spending and Potential Outcomes.* Congress of the United States, Congressional Budget Office. http://www.cbo.gov/ftpdocs/77xx/doc7700/12-21-HealthPlans.pdf.

Cohen, J. T. (2010, March 11). A guide to accountable care organizations, and their role in the Senate's health reform bill. *Health Reform Watch.* [Online]. http://www.healthreformwatch.com/2010/03/11/a-guide-to-accountable-care-organizations-and-their-role-in-the-senates-health-reform-bill/ [2010, November 2].

Devers, K., & Berenson, R. (2009, October). Can accountable care organizations improve the value of health care by solving the cost and quality quandaries? *Robert Wood Johnson Foundation: Timely Analysis of Immediate Health Policy Issues.* [Online]. http://www.rwjf.org/files/research/acobrieffinal.pdf [2010, November 2].

A Glossary of Terms: The Language of Managed Care and Organized Health Care Systems (Rev. ed.). (1994). Minnetonka, MN: United HealthCare Corporation.

[NCQA] National Committee for Quality Assurance. (2010). *2010 NCQA Health Plan Accreditation Requirements.* [Online]. http://www.ncqa.org [2010, July 4].

Stanton, M. W. (2003). AHRQ Tools for Managed Care. *Research in Action 11.* AHRQ Pub. No. 03-0016. Rockville (MD): Agency for Healthcare Research and Quality.

Tully, L., & Rulon, V. (2000). Evolution of the uses of ICD-9-CM coding: Medicare risk adjustment methodology for managed care plans. *Topics in Health Information Management, 21*(2), 62–67.

KEY RESOURCES

Accreditation Association for Ambulatory
  Health Care, Inc. (AAAHC)
  http://www.aaahc.org

American Health Information Management
  Association (AHIMA)
  http://www.ahima.org

Clinical Laboratory Improvement Amendments
  of 1988
  http://www.cms.gov/clia/

The Joint Commission (TJC)
  www.jointcommission.org

Medicare Managed Care Manual
  Publication #100-16
  http://www.cms.gov/Manuals/IOM/

National Committee for Quality Assurance
  (NCQA)
  http://www.ncqa.org

URAC
  http://www.urac.org

CHAPTER 5

Dialysis

ANN H. PEDEN, PHD, RHIA, CCS

LEARNING OBJECTIVES

Upon successful completion of this chapter, you should be able to:

- Describe the care given to patients with end-stage renal disease (ESRD).

- Describe how and by whom dialysis facilities are surveyed for compliance with various regulations and standards.

- List key documentation requirements for dialysis patient records.

- State the source of payment for most dialysis treatment in the United States.

- Explain the role of the ESRD networks in the collection and aggregation of data on dialysis patients.

- Describe quality improvement activities in ESRD organizations.

- Describe the role of the health information management professional in organizations dealing with ESRD.

Setting	Description	Synonyms
Dialysis Facility	A facility where patients receive dialysis treatments, or home dialysis training and support services, or both.	End-Stage Renal Disease (ESRD) Facility
		Dialysis Unit
		Dialysis Center
		Dialysis Clinic
		Limited Care Unit
ESRD Network	One of 18 organizations with contracts with the Centers for Medicare & Medicaid Services (CMS), to assess the quality of care rendered to ESRD patients and to collect and analyze ESRD data	Network

INTRODUCTION TO SETTING

Dialysis is a procedure necessary to maintain the life of a person whose kidneys have failed. **Chronic kidney disease (CKD)** is a gradual loss of kidney function classified into five stages, with mild loss of kidney function in the early stages and severe or total loss in the later stages. In the final stage (Stage 5), the individual's kidneys are no longer able to perform the job of excreting the body's wastes or promoting homeostasis. At Stage 5 CKD, the patient requires some type of **renal replacement therapy (RRT)** (dialysis or a kidney transplant) to survive. The final stage of chronic kidney disease has also been known by the term **end-stage renal disease (ESRD)**. Although the term *chronic kidney disease* is preferred over the term *ESRD* in clinical usage, ESRD is still the term by which the U.S. national health insurance program for people with irreversible chronic kidney failure is known.

There are numerous organizations involved in caring for dialysis patients and in monitoring the quality of care rendered to dialysis patients. The two settings discussed in this chapter are ESRD facilities and ESRD networks. Of these two general types of settings, only the ESRD facility actually provides patient care. The **ESRD networks** process and analyze data provided by the ESRD facilities and provide other types of services, such as patient education.

There are several synonyms for facilities providing services to dialysis patients. The federal government uses the terms *ESRD facility* and *dialysis facility* for a facility offering dialysis services. The Joint Commission uses the terms *dialysis center* and *dialysis unit* for this type of facility. None of these terms is universally preferred over the others. This chapter uses the terms interchangeably. According to the Conditions for Coverage for End-Stage Renal Disease Facilities, a **dialysis facility** is "an entity that provides (1) outpatient maintenance dialysis services; or (2) home dialysis training and support services; or (3) both. A dialysis facility may be an independent or hospital-based unit ... or a self-care dialysis unit that furnishes only self-dialysis services"

(2008, 20476). In the U.S. in the year 2007, approximately 591 hospital-based and 4,330 freestanding ESRD facilities furnished dialysis services to patients on an outpatient basis (CMS, 2009).

Types of Patients

Patients requiring treatment in a dialysis unit generally are persons with stage 5 chronic kidney disease who have not yet undergone a kidney transplant or who for some reason are not candidates for a transplant. Because the kidneys of these patients are unable to filter out wastes, the end products of metabolism must be removed from their bodies by artificial means. Dialysis is a means of removing these wastes and maintaining the body's proper fluid, electrolyte, and acid-base balance by the process of diffusion.

There are two types of dialysis: hemodialysis and peritoneal dialysis. In **hemodialysis (HD)**, the patient's blood circulates outside the body (extracorporeally) through an artificial kidney (dialyzer) that removes metabolic wastes and helps maintain homeostasis. When a patient is expected to be on long-term hemodialysis, surgery is generally performed to create an easy means of vascular access, such as the creation of an arteriovenous fistula. To keep the body free of excessive waste products, the patient generally dialyzes three times per week for three to five hours per session. Patients may obtain hemodialysis treatment in freestanding dialysis facilities, in the dialysis unit of a hospital, or in their own homes. In 2007, over 90 percent of dialysis patients in the United States received hemodialysis on-site in an ESRD facility.

The most common type of dialysis facility is the freestanding dialysis facility. As noted previously, the ESRD facility provides dialysis care on-site for most of its patients. After training, some patients are able to perform their own hemodialysis at home with the aid of a friend or relative. However, these home hemodialysis patients and the peritoneal dialysis patients described as follows still present themselves at the dialysis facility at least monthly for evaluation. About 0.8 percent of dialysis patients perform home hemodialysis.

Peritoneal dialysis (PD) uses the patient's own abdominal cavity to filter out wastes. A tube is inserted through an incision into the patient's abdomen, and the dialysis solution (**dialysate**) is introduced into the peritoneal space. The dialysate draws the urea and other toxins out of the blood across the peritoneal membrane. Other products from the dialysate diffuse across the membrane into the blood.

In **continuous ambulatory peritoneal dialysis (CAPD)**, the patient is able to perform his or her own dialysis almost anywhere, because very little special equipment is required. The CAPD patient dialyzes three or four times a day, at home or at work. Approximately 3 percent of ESRD patients in the United States are on CAPD.

Continuous cycling peritoneal dialysis (CCPD) utilizes a machine to perform peritoneal dialysis once each day while the patient sleeps rather than three or four times throughout the day as in CAPD. Like the CAPD patients, CCPD patients generally come to the ESRD facility only for training and for monthly evaluations or when a complication arises. About 4 percent of dialysis patients in the United States use CCPD.

The type of dialysis treatment used is largely the patient's choice. CAPD patients generally choose this method because they can incorporate it into their routine and do not have to rely on others to assist with their dialysis. CCPD is a popular choice for children, because they can continue their daily routine and dialyze at night while sleeping. The disadvantage of both forms of peritoneal dialysis is the increased risk of infection. Also, any type of self-administered dialysis requires a patient who is motivated and capable of performing and documenting self-care. (See Table 5-1 for a summary of the prevalence of each modality.)

Types of Caregivers

A multidisciplinary team cares for patients in a dialysis unit. The caregivers who have the most contact with the patient on each visit are registered nurses and licensed practical nurses who are assisted by certified dialysis technicians. Nurses and technicians are employees of the dialysis facility and are present with the dialysis center patients on a daily basis.

Other professionals maintain a regular schedule of visits to the dialysis unit, although they do not ordinarily practice at the dialysis center on a daily basis. In a moderately large freestanding dialysis unit, these professionals are on-site several times a month to see patients. For example, physicians see patients on a regular basis and play a primary role in determining the patient's treatment regimen. Dietitians educate patients on the importance of following the prescribed diet and also monitor nutritional status. Social workers discuss psychosocial issues with patients and address problems that

TABLE 5-1

U.S. Prevalence of Various Dialysis Modalities, December 31, 2007

Modality	Count	Percentage
Center hemodialysis	338,109	91.7
Center self-hemodialysis	156	0.0
Home hemodialysis	2,999	0.8
CAPD	9,951	2.7
CCPD	16,389	4.4
Other PD	24	0.0
Uncertain dialysis	916	0.2
All	527,283	100.0

Source: 2009 USRDS Annual Data Report.

relate to family support, transportation, and other environmental factors that could affect the patient's compliance with the program of treatment. These other professionals usually see individual patients on a monthly basis and often more frequently.

ESRD personnel evaluate home hemodialysis and peritoneal dialysis patients' conditions on a regular basis, usually monthly. At one of these patients' regular visits to the dialysis unit, a nurse may examine the dialysis log sheets kept by the patient that contain information about each dialysis session. Health care workers check the patient's blood pressure, weight, and medications and also review the results of monthly lab tests. A nurse checks the patient's dialysis access sites for signs of infection. In addition, these monthly evaluations include visits with the social worker, dietitian, and physician.

One other caregiver, the transplantation surgeon, may see the dialysis patient only infrequently. The transplantation surgeon periodically evaluates dialysis patients to determine whether they are eligible for transplant. Usually, one transplantation surgeon sees many dialysis patients from numerous dialysis facilities in a given geographic area.

REGULATORY ISSUES

The most important regulations for dialysis providers are the federal regulations for ESRD facilities. Almost all dialysis facilities offer dialysis services to Medicare patients, so almost all dialysis facilities are subject to federal regulations. This is true whether the facility is freestanding or affiliated with a hospital or other organization.

A dialysis unit in a hospital accredited by the Joint Commission or another voluntary accrediting organization is also subject to that organization's standards in addition to federal standards. However, the federal regulations are generally more detailed with regard to dialysis operations than are voluntary standards, so a hospital dialysis facility that meets federal standards should have no problems meeting voluntary standards such as those of the Joint Commission.

Individual states may also have their own regulations for dialysis facilities. However, these are usually modeled on federal standards; so, again, the predominant regulatory issues in most states are found in the federal guidelines.

Surveys

Dialysis units are surveyed by each state's own surveying agency to determine if they are in compliance with both state and federal guidelines. For example, a survey team from the state department of health usually visits a dialysis facility annually and compares the facility's performance to federal regulations (and any state regulations that may apply). These surveys are usually unannounced, so the facility must be ready for a survey at any time.

In addition, federal surveyors from the CMS regional offices may conduct an unexpected **validation survey** to determine whether the state agencies to whom the regular surveys have been delegated are appropriately evaluating facilities according to federal regulations. Even though the primary purpose of the validation survey is to serve as a check on the state surveying agency, any deficiencies noted in the validation survey must still be corrected by the dialysis facility.

Federal Regulations

Federal regulations affecting ESRD facilities are found in the Conditions for Coverage for End-Stage Renal Disease Facilities (42 C.F.R. Part 405 Subpart U, 2008). These regulations are comprehensive and apply to every aspect of the facility's operation. Relevant information from federal regulations is interspersed throughout this chapter, under topics such as "Documentation" and "Data and Information Flow."

The Conditions for Coverage were extensively revised in 2008. Prior to the 2008 revision, dialysis facilities were required to obtain the services of a "medical record practitioner," such as a registered health information administrator (RHIA) or a registered health information technician (RHIT). The 2008 revisions dropped this requirement and also deleted the requirement that a member of the facility's staff must be designated to serve as supervisor of medical records. Although there is no longer a federal requirement to do so, it is still a good practice to designate an employee of the facility to monitor whether medical records are properly documented, completed, and preserved. In addition to designating an employee to oversee health record functions, many dialysis centers still contract with an RHIA or RHIT on a consulting basis to review their documentation systems.

ESRD Networks

ESRD networks were established by federal law to monitor quality and appropriateness of care provided to ESRD patients. The Omnibus Reconciliation Act (OBRA) of 1986 reorganized the ESRD program and set up 18 network areas across the United States to assess the quality of care given to ESRD patients (see Figure 5-1). Similarly to the Quality Improvement Organizations (QIOs) discussed in Chapter 1, the ESRD networks perform their work under contract with the Centers for Medicare & Medicaid Services (CMS). In addition to their quality assessment activities, the networks also collect and analyze data on ESRD patients in their regions. The networks monitor patient status changes and deal with patient grievances. They also publish an annual report of these and other activities. Some of these roles of the ESRD networks are discussed later in the chapter.

DOCUMENTATION

Dialysis facility records can be voluminous, because a patient can remain in dialysis treatment for decades and also because the treatments and evaluations are so frequent. Maintaining portions of the record electronically is a common practice in ESRD facilities because of the detailed information that must

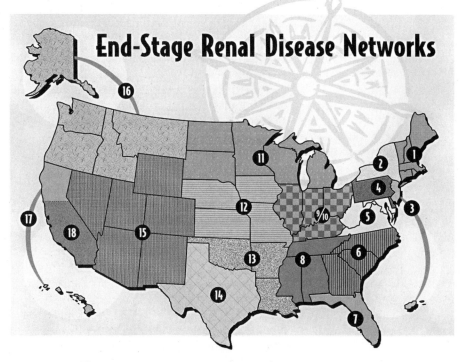

FIGURE **5-1** The 18 end-stage renal disease network organizations across the United States. (Courtesy of the Forum of ESRD Networks. Used with permission.) (http://www.esrdnetworks.org/)

be documented about the patient's condition, status, and treatment. Many dialysis facilities utilize hybrid records, maintaining a portion of the record electronically and the remainder of the record in paper format. Regardless of the method of maintaining patient records, the facility must be careful to document all required items.

According to the Conditions for Coverage, § 494.170, the dialysis facility "must maintain complete, accurate, and accessible records on all patients, including home patients...."

Patient Assessment and Plan of Care

Two important documentation requirements in the dialysis patient record are the patient assessment and the patient plan of care. The patient assessment is developed by an interdisciplinary team consisting of at least the following participants: the patient or the patient's designee, a registered nurse, a physician treating the patient for ESRD, a social worker, and a dietitian. According to federal regulations (42 C.F.R. 494.80), the comprehensive assessment must include evaluation in each of the thirteen areas below:

1. Current health status and medical condition, including comorbid conditions.
2. The appropriateness of the dialysis prescription, blood pressure, and fluid management needs.
3. Laboratory profile, immunization history, and medication history.
4. Factors associated with anemia, such as hematocrit, hemoglobin, iron stores, and potential treatment plans for anemia, including administration of erythropoiesis-stimulating agent(s).
5. Factors associated with renal bone disease.
6. Nutritional status (evaluated by a dietitian).
7. Psychosocial needs (evaluated by a social worker).
8. Dialysis access type and maintenance (for example, arteriovenous fistulas, arteriovenous grafts, and peritoneal catheters).
9. The patient's abilities, interests, preferences, and goals, including the desired level of participation in the dialysis care process; the preferred modality (hemodialysis or peritoneal dialysis) and setting (for example, home dialysis); and the patient's expectations for care outcomes.
10. Suitability for a transplantation referral, based on criteria developed by the prospective transplantation center and its surgeon(s). If the patient is not suitable for transplantation referral, the basis for nonreferral must be documented in the patient's medical record.
11. Family and other support systems.
12. Current patient physical activity level.
13. Evaluation for referral to vocational and physical rehabilitation services.

The following excerpt from the regulations (42 C.F.R. 494.80, p. 20479) outlines the required schedule for various assessment activities:

(b) Standard: Frequency of assessment for patients admitted to the dialysis facility.
   1. An initial comprehensive assessment must be conducted on all new patients (that is, all admissions to a dialysis facility), within the latter of 30 calendar days or 13 outpatient hemodialysis sessions beginning with the first outpatient dialysis session.
   2. A follow up comprehensive reassessment must occur within 3 months after the completion of the initial assessment to provide information to adjust the patient's plan of care specified in § 494.90.

(c) Standard: Assessment of treatment prescription. The adequacy of the patient's dialysis prescription, as described in § 494.90(a)(1), must be assessed on an ongoing basis as follows:
   1. Hemodialysis patients. At least monthly by calculating delivered **Kt/V**[1] or an equivalent measure.

---

[1]Kt/V is a means of measuring the adequacy of dialysis. In other words, Kt/V helps to determine whether the patient is dialyzing long enough or often enough to remove sufficient waste and excess fluid from the body. Adequate dialysis is important to patient survival.

2. Peritoneal dialysis patients. At least every 4 months by calculating delivered weekly Kt/V or an equivalent measure.

(d) Standard: Patient reassessment....(A) comprehensive reassessment of each patient and a revision of the plan of care must be conducted—

1. At least annually for stable patients; and
2. At least monthly for unstable patients including, but not limited to, patients with the following:
    (i) Extended or frequent hospitalizations;
    (ii) Marked deterioration in health status;
    (iii) Significant change in psychosocial needs; or
    (iv) Concurrent poor nutritional status, unmanaged anemia, and inadequate dialysis.

Federal regulations (42 C.F.R. 494.90) require the development of "a written, individualized comprehensive plan of care that specifies the services necessary to address the patient's needs, as identified by the comprehensive assessment and changes in the patient's condition," (Conditions for Coverage, 2008, p. 20479). Key elements of the plan of care are excerpted below (Conditions for Coverage, pp. 20479–20480):

(a) Standard: Development of patient plan of care. The interdisciplinary team must develop a plan of care for each patient. The plan of care must address, but not be limited to, the following:

1. Dose of dialysis. The interdisciplinary team must provide the necessary care and services to manage the patient's volume status; and achieve and sustain the prescribed dose of dialysis to meet a hemodialysis Kt/V of at least 1.2 and a peritoneal dialysis weekly Kt/V of at least 1.7 or meet an alternative equivalent professionally-accepted clinical practice standard for adequacy of dialysis.
2. Nutritional status. The interdisciplinary team must provide the necessary care and counseling services to achieve and sustain an effective nutritional status. A patient's albumin level and body weight must be measured at least monthly. Additional evidence-based professionally-accepted clinical nutrition indicators may be monitored, as appropriate.
3. Mineral metabolism. Provide the necessary care to manage mineral metabolism and prevent or treat renal bone disease.
4. Anemia. The interdisciplinary team must provide the necessary care and services to achieve and sustain the clinically appropriate hemoglobin/hematocrit level. The patient's hemoglobin/hematocrit must be measured at least monthly. The dialysis facility must conduct an evaluation of the patient's anemia management needs. For a home dialysis patient, the facility must evaluate whether the patient can safely, aseptically, and effectively administer erythropoiesis-stimulating agents and store this medication under refrigeration if necessary. The patient's response to erythropoiesis-stimulating agent(s), including blood pressure levels and utilization of iron stores, must be monitored on a routine basis.

5. Vascular access. The interdisciplinary team must provide vascular access monitoring and appropriate, timely referrals to achieve and sustain vascular access. The hemodialysis patient must be evaluated for the appropriate vascular access type, taking into consideration co-morbid conditions, other risk factors, and whether the patient is a potential candidate for arteriovenous fistula placement. The patient's vascular access must be monitored to prevent access failure, including monitoring of arteriovenous grafts and fistulae for symptoms of stenosis.

6. Psychosocial status. The interdisciplinary team must provide the necessary monitoring and social work interventions. These include counseling services and referrals for other social services, to assist the patient in achieving and sustaining an appropriate psychosocial status as measured by a standardized mental and physical assessment tool chosen by the social worker, at regular intervals, or more frequently on an as-needed basis.

7. Modality.
   (i) Home dialysis. The interdisciplinary team must identify a plan for the patient's home dialysis or explain why the patient is not a candidate for home dialysis.
   (ii) Transplantation status. When the patient is a transplant referral candidate, the interdisciplinary team must develop plans for pursuing transplantation. The patient's plan of care must include documentation of the—
       (A) Plan for transplantation, if the patient accepts the transplantation referral;
       (B) Patient's decision, if the patient is a transplantation referral candidate but declines the transplantation referral; or
       (C) Reason(s) for the patient's nonreferral as a transplantation candidate as documented in accordance with § 494.80(a)(10).

8. Rehabilitation status. The interdisciplinary team must assist the patient in achieving and sustaining an appropriate level of productive activity, as desired by the patient, including the educational needs of pediatric patients (patients under the age of 18 years), and make rehabilitation and vocational rehabilitation referrals as appropriate.

(b) Standard: Implementation of the patient plan of care.
   1. The patient's plan of care must—
      (i) Be completed by the interdisciplinary team, including the patient if the patient desires; and
      (ii) Be signed by team members, including the patient or the patient's designee; or, if the patient chooses not to sign the plan of care, this choice must be documented on the plan of care, along with the reason the signature was not provided.
   2. Implementation of the initial plan of care must begin within the latter of 30 calendar days after admission to the dialysis facility or

13 outpatient hemodialysis sessions beginning with the first outpatient dialysis session. Implementation of monthly or annual updates of the plan of care must be performed within 15 days of the completion of the additional patient assessments specified in § 494.80(d).

3. If the expected outcome is not achieved, the interdisciplinary team must adjust the patient's plan of care to achieve the specified goals. When a patient is unable to achieve the desired outcomes, the team must—

   (i) Adjust the plan of care to reflect the patient's current condition;

   (ii) Document in the record the reasons why the patient was unable to achieve the goals; and

   (iii) Implement plan of care changes to address the issues identified in paragraph (b)(3)(ii) of this section.

4. The dialysis facility must ensure that all dialysis patients are seen by a physician, nurse practitioner, clinical nurse specialist, or physician's assistant providing ESRD care at least monthly, as evidenced by a monthly progress note placed in the medical record, and periodically while the hemodialysis patient is receiving in-facility dialysis.

(c) Standard: Transplantation referral tracking. The interdisciplinary team must—

1. Track the results of each kidney transplant center referral;

2. Monitor the status of any facility patients who are on the transplant wait list; and

3. Communicate with the transplant center regarding patient transplant status at least annually, and when there is a change in transplant candidate status.

(d) Standard: Patient education and training. The patient care plan must include, as applicable, education and training for patients and family members or caregivers or both, in aspects of the dialysis experience, dialysis management, infection prevention and personal care, home dialysis and self-care, quality of life, rehabilitation, transplantation, and the benefits and risks of various vascular access types.

The *ESRD Program Interpretive Guidance* document is used by site surveyors when surveying a program under the Conditions for Coverage and provides more details about what type of documentation is needed to demonstrate that a dialysis facility meets federal standards. For example, Figure 5-2 provides an excerpt from the Measures Assessment Tool (MAT) found in the *Interpretive Guidance* document, which highlights documentation that should be present in the record to evaluate elements related to the required patient assessment.

The Forum of ESRD Networks' Quality Assurance Committee has also described a medical record model to improve the quality of the dialysis medical record. Improving the quality of the medical record improves the team's ability to provide care and encourages a consistent approach. The medical record model presents a format for medical records that should contain the

494.80 Patient assessment: The interdisciplinary team (IDT), patient/designee, RN, MSW, RD, physician must provide each patient with an individualized & comprehensive assessment of needs.

Condition/Standard	Measure
- Health status/comorbidities	- Medical/nursing history, physical exam findings
- Dialysis prescription	- Evaluate: HD every mo; PD first mo & q4 mo
- BP & fluid management	- Interdialytic BP & wt gain, target wt, symptoms
- Lab profile	- Monitor labs monthly & as needed
- Immunization & meds history	- Pneumococcal, hepatitis, influenza; med allergies
- Anemia (Hgb, Hct, iron stores, ESA need)	- Volume, bleeding, infection, ESA hypo-response
- Renal bone disease	- Calcium, phosphorus, PTH & medications
- Nutritional status	- Multiple elements listed
- Psychosocial needs	- Multiple elements listed
- Dialysis access type & maintenance	- Access efficacy, fistula candidacy
- Abilities, interests, preferences, goals, desired level of participation in care, preferred modality & setting, outcomes expectations	- Reason why patient does not participate in care, reason why patient is not a home dialysis candidate
- Suitability for transplant referral	- Reason why patient is not a transplant candidate
- Family & other support systems	- Composition, history, availability, level of support
- Current physical activity level & referral to voc & physical rehab	- Abilities & barriers to independent living; achieving educational & work goals

FIGURE **5-2** Excerpt from the Measures Assessment Tool (MAT) found in the ESRD Program Interpretive Guidance. (Permission to reuse in accordance with http://www.cms.gov Content Reuse and Linking Policy.)

Source: http://www.cms.gov/SurveyCertificationGenInfo/downloads/SCletter09-01.pdf.

information necessary for continuity of patient care and qualitative review. Although the 2008 revisions to the Conditions for Coverage are more stringent in some regards than the 2001 version of the medical record model, the medical record model still provides additional guidance for facilities seeking to improve their documentation. For example, the medical record model provides recommendations regarding the contents of progress notes, as outlined in the following excerpt.

"Progress notes should provide an accurate picture of the progress of the patient, which reflects changes in patient status, plans and results of changes in treatment regimen, diagnostic testing, consultations, unusual events, etc. Either single discipline or integrated multidisciplinary progress notes may be utilized. The following are minimal entries:

- Each discipline, physician(s), nurse(s), social worker(s) and dietitian(s) should record the progress of the patient at regular intervals…
- Patient condition and response to treatment noted on daily treatment record
- Regular review of abnormal labs/clinical findings and any action taken
- Monthly review of laboratory results (including adequacy) & hepatitis status
- Vascular Access Assessment" (Forum of ESRD Networks, 2001, p. 4)

REIMBURSEMENT

A person with ESRD is generally eligible for Medicare coverage on the basis of the ESRD diagnosis beginning in the third month after regular dialysis treatments begin, provided that the patient, a spouse, or a parent has made sufficient contributions to the Social Security system. At present, most dialysis patients receive benefits through Medicare's ESRD program. However, for patients with existing group health insurance, Medicare is the secondary payer during the first 30 months of ESRD-based eligibility (National Kidney and Urologic Diseases Clearinghouse, 2009). Even after Medicare has become the primary payer, many patients also receive some benefits from other insurance programs, such as an employer's group insurance policy. Because of this type of dual coverage, dialysis facilities frequently deal with other third-party payers.

Facility Reimbursement

Prior to changes brought about by the Medicare Improvements for Patients and Providers Act of 2008 (MIPPA), Medicare Part A paid the dialysis facility a composite rate per treatment for three treatments per week for each patient on chronic dialysis, with no payment for patients who miss treatments (no-shows). This composite rate included payment for some of the other services the patient received, such as some of the routine laboratory tests. However, certain types of tests and treatments, such as administration of **erythropoietin stimulating agents (ESAs)**, were separately billable and accounted for about 40 percent of Medicare's costs for the ESRD program. MIPPA required the development of a prospective payment system for ESRD services that utilized a single payment for dialysis services, to be phased in beginning January 1, 2011, and fully implemented by January 1, 2014 (CMS, 2010). MIPPA also required that payments be adjusted according to performance measures, described more fully in the quality improvement section of this chapter.

DEFINITION   **erythropoietin stimulating agent (ESA)** stimulates the bone marrow to make red blood cells; used to treat and prevent anemia, a common complication of chronic kidney disease in patients on dialysis.

The prospective payment system for ESRD facilities combines payments for the composite rate and certain services that previously were separately billable into a single base rate. The base rate is then adjusted using patient specific case-mix adjustment factors, including age, body surface area (BSA), low body mass index (BMI), the onset of renal dialysis (new patient), and six comorbidity categories. The comorbidity categories are bacterial pneumonia, gastrointestinal bleeding, hereditary hemolytic and sickle cell anemia, monoclonal gammopathy, myelodysplastic syndrome, and pericarditis (End-Stage Renal Disease Prospective Payment System Final Rule and Proposed Rule, 2010).

Physician Reimbursement

In general, a physician receives a monthly payment from Medicare Part B based on the number of visits for each patient. Physicians may receive additional payments for other services, such as evaluation and management services rendered to inpatients.

INFORMATION MANAGEMENT

Coding and Classification

The ESRD facility codes diagnoses using the current version of the *International Classification of Diseases* approved for use in the United States, *ICD-9-CM* until October 1, 2013, and *ICD-10-CM* thereafter. Coding in an ESRD facility is mainly used for reimbursement. For Medicare, the code submitted to the ESRD network and ultimately to CMS when dialysis is first initiated must be a code that CMS recognizes as end-stage renal disease. The proposed ESRD prospective payment system (PPS) also utilizes diagnostic codes submitted on claim forms to identify comorbidities. If a patient has more than one comorbidity, only the comorbidity with the highest adjustment factor affects the payment. Table 5-2 lists all of the case-mix variables, including the comorbidity categories, from the ESRD PPS rule for 2011.

Physicians who see ESRD patients must also code their encounters with the patient for reimbursement purposes. For physician reimbursement, diagnoses are coded with the current U.S. version of *ICD*, and the services performed by the physician are coded with the Healthcare Common Procedural Coding System (HCPCS).

At the national level, CMS maintains coded data submitted by dialysis providers that can be used for purposes other than reimbursement, including research. This is discussed more completely in the section on Data and Information Flow.

Data and Information Flow

Data and information flow can be viewed at the level of the individual patient and at the aggregate level of many patients in a given area.

TABLE 5-2

Case-Mix Adjustment from ESRD Prospective Payment System
Final Rule (2010)

Variable	Modeled Case-Mix Adjustment
Age	
18–44	1.171
45–59	1.013
60–69	1.000
70–79	1.011
80+	1.016
Body surface area (per 0.1 m²)	1.020
Underweight (BMI < 18.5)	1.025
Time since onset of renal dialysis < 4 months	1.510
Comorbidity	
Pericarditis	1.114
Bacterial pneumonia	1.135
Gastrointestinal tract bleeding	1.183
Hereditary hemolytic or sickle cell anemia	1.072
Myelodysplastic Syndrome	1.099
Monoclonal Gammopathy	1.024
Low volume facility adjustment	1.189

Individual Patient Data

At the level of the individual patient, the initial information on a dialysis patient is gathered when the patient is admitted to the dialysis facility. Information flows into the patient record from many sources. The caregivers document their interactions with, and assessments of, the patient. The patient contributes to portions of the record, such as the plan of care. The facility also receives copies of portions of the patient's hospital record whenever the patient is admitted to the hospital. Information from reference laboratories and other facilities that have treated or tested the patient are also included in the patient's record.

When a dialysis patient is transferred to another facility, the transfer of information between the two facilities is very important. Federal regulation 42 C.F.R. 494.170 requires that all requested medical record information be transmitted to the receiving facility within one working day. A transfer agreement between the dialysis facility and a local hospital can facilitate the transfer of information when a dialysis patient is admitted to or discharged from one location and transferred to another.

Because hemodialysis patients should dialyze at least three times per week, planning a vacation or an extended trip out of town involves the ESRD facility. The local dialysis facility must contact another facility in the city to which the patient is traveling. The distant facility must agree to treat the patient while the patient is in that location. The transfer of referral information back and forth between the distant and the local facility is important in providing quality patient care.

Aggregate Data

As previously mentioned, the ESRD networks are responsible for collecting and analyzing data on ESRD patients in their areas. The facilities treating patients are responsible for submitting information on each patient and on the facility itself to the appropriate network. In 2010, electronic submission of information through a system named **Consolidated Renal Operations in a Web-enabled Network (CROWNWeb)** began to be phased in (CMS, 2008). The network processes the data, which are also electronically transmitted to CMS, where they are aggregated on a national scale. CMS created CROWNWeb to collect data from patient records, clinical performance measures, and information about each dialysis facility.

Using these data and other beneficiary-specific data, CMS has developed a comprehensive database called the End-Stage Renal Disease (ESRD) Program Management and Medical Information System (PMMIS). The ESRD PMMIS includes medical and demographic information for the Medicare ESRD population. CMS uses the data for program analysis, policy development, and epidemiologic research. The **Renal Management Information System (REMIS)** determines Medicare coverage periods for ESRD patients and serves as the chief means for storing and accessing information in the ESRD PMMIS Database. REMIS tracks both Medicare and non-Medicare ESRD patients. It also includes interfaces to the Medicare Beneficiary Database and to the ESRD Network Organizations' Standard Information Management System (SIMS) (CMS, 2009).

Electronic Health Record (EHR) and Information Systems

To plan a successful dialysis treatment program, the physicians and nurses need data on the patient's condition and response to treatment. Because of the large amount of clinical information collected on dialysis patients, dialysis facilities were among the first health care providers to adopt electronic health records.

EHR applications in the dialysis setting may include the ability to track patient data from each treatment session, electronic charting at the patient chair-side, electronic patient flow sheets, tracking of prescriptions, progress notes for various disciplines, reports, graphing capability, calculations to measure the adequacy of dialysis, and, in some instances, the ability to collect data through an interface with dialyzer equipment. Some EHR systems also facilitate CROWNWeb reporting.

By maintaining medication records and data from each dialysis session electronically, clinicians can track the patient's response to treatment.

The EHR system can generate reports showing the patient's weight, blood pressure, and so forth, before and after each treatment and can compute monthly averages for various clinical data elements. These simple reports can be used to educate the patient and to encourage compliance with the prescribed diet and medication regimen. The caregivers also learn more about each patient from studying the accumulated data available in EHR-generated reports.

Even though this important clinical information is often stored in an electronic system, most dialysis facilities find it necessary to maintain a portion of the patient's record on paper. A hybrid record is often needed to maintain consents, referral information, and so forth, which are frequently maintained in paper format. As in most health care facilities, electronic systems are also used for billing and accounting purposes.

Data Sets

Examples of data sets used by dialysis facilities include the CMS 2728, "End Stage Renal Disease Medical Evidence Report Medicare Entitlement and/or Patient Registration" and the CMS 2746 "ESRD Death Notification." These forms were previously submitted on paper, but are now electronically generated through the electronic reporting process. The "End Stage Renal Disease Medical Evidence Report: Medicare Entitlement and/or Patient Registration" (CMS 2728) is generated from data that are submitted by the dialysis facility for each new dialysis patient. The "ESRD Death Notification" form (CMS 2746) is generated from data submitted for each ESRD patient who expires. The data included in both of these data sets are transmitted electronically through CROWNWeb to the networks and ultimately to CMS. CROWNWeb also provides the capability of printing these data sets as CMS 2728 and CMS 2746 forms. (See Figure 5-3 and Figure 5-4.)

In addition to patient record information, clinical performance measures, and facility data, CROWNWeb also includes a listing of all ESRD facilities within each network, as well as employees and patients within each facility.

The ESRD networks also collect census data from each dialysis facility. In addition, they maintain records on the status each patient, including information on patient follow-up and transplants. Maintenance of patient-specific records requires that the networks maintain an accurate master patient index.

Data on kidney transplants are available from the United Network for Organ Sharing (UNOS). Under a contract with the Health Resources and Services Administration of the U.S. Department of Health and Human Services, UNOS manages the Organ Procurement and Transplantation Network (OPTN). One of the most important functions of OPTN is facilitating the matching of donor organs and transplant recipients. This is accomplished by means of a computer system and an Organ Center that operates 24 hours a day. However, OPTN also collects and manages data about organ donation and transplantation for kidney, pancreas, liver, intestine, heart, and lung procedures. Most candidates on the UNOS waiting list for organs are waiting for kidney donations (UNOS, 2010; OPTN, 2010).

DEPARTMENT OF HEALTH AND HUMAN SERVICES
CENTERS FOR MEDICARE & MEDICAID SERVICES

Form Approved
OMB No. 0938-0046

END STAGE RENAL DISEASE MEDICAL EVIDENCE REPORT
MEDICARE ENTITLEMENT AND/OR PATIENT REGISTRATION

A. COMPLETE FOR ALL ESRD PATIENTS   *Check one:* ☐ Initial   ☐ Re-entitlement   ☐ Supplemental

1. Name *(Last, First, Middle Initial)*

2. Medicare Claim Number	3. Social Security Number	4. Date of Birth ___/___/___ MM DD YYYY
5. Patient Mailing Address *(Include City, State and Zip)*		6. Phone Number ( )

7. Sex   ☐ Male ☐ Female

8. Ethnicity   ☐ Not Hispanic or Latino ☐ Hispanic or Latino (Complete Item 9)

9. Country/Area of Origin or Ancestry

10. Race *(Check all that apply)*
☐ White
☐ Black or African American
☐ American Indian/Alaska Native
Print Name of Enrolled/Principal Tribe _____
☐ Asian
☐ Native Hawaiian or Other Pacific Islander*
*complete Item 9

11. Is patient applying for ESRD Medicare coverage?
☐ Yes ☐ No

12. Current Medical Coverage *(Check all that apply)*
☐ Medicaid ☐ Medicare ☐ Employer Group Health Insurance
☐ DVA ☐ Medicare Advantage ☐ Other ☐ None

13. Height
INCHES _____ OR
CENTIMETERS _____

14. Dry Weight
POUNDS _____ OR
KILOGRAMS _____

15. Primary Cause of Renal Failure *(Use code from back of form)*

16. Employment Status *(6 mos prior and current status)*

Prior Current
☐ ☐ Unemployed
☐ ☐ Employed Full Time
☐ ☐ Employed Part Time
☐ ☐ Homemaker
☐ ☐ Retired due to Age/Preference
☐ ☐ Retired (Disability)
☐ ☐ Medical Leave of Absence
☐ ☐ Student

17. Co-Morbid Conditions *(Check all that apply currently and/or during last 10 years)* *See instructions
a. ☐ Congestive heart failure
b. ☐ Atherosclerotic heart disease ASHD
c. ☐ Other cardiac disease
d. ☐ Cerebrovascular disease, CVA, TIA*
e. ☐ Peripheral vascular disease*
f. ☐ History of hypertension
g. ☐ Amputation
h. ☐ Diabetes, currently on insulin
i. ☐ Diabetes, on oral medications
j. ☐ Diabetes, without medications
k. ☐ Diabetic retinopathy
l. ☐ Chronic obstructive pulmonary disease
m. ☐ Tobacco use (current smoker)
n. ☐ Malignant neoplasm, Cancer
o. ☐ Toxic nephropathy
p. ☐ Alcohol dependence
q. ☐ Drug dependence*
r. ☐ Inability to ambulate
s. ☐ Inability to transfer
t. ☐ Needs assistance with daily activities
u. ☐ Institutionalized
      ☐ 1. Assisted Living
      ☐ 2. Nursing Home
      ☐ 3. Other Institution
v. ☐ Non-renal congenital abnormality
w. ☐ None

18. Prior to ESRD therapy:
a. Did patient receive exogenous erythropoetin or equivalent?   ☐ Yes ☐ No ☐ Unknown If Yes, answer: ☐ 6-12 months ☐ >12 months
b. Was patient under care of a nephrologist?   ☐ Yes ☐ No ☐ Unknown If Yes, answer: ☐ 6-12 months ☐ >12 months
c. Was patient under care of kidney dietitian?   ☐ Yes ☐ No ☐ Unknown If Yes, answer: ☐ 6-12 months ☐ >12 months
d. What access was used on first outpatient dialysis: ☐ AVF ☐ Graft ☐ Catheter ☐ Other
   If not AVF, then: Is maturing AVF present?   ☐ Yes ☐ No
   Is maturing graft present?   ☐ Yes ☐ No

19. Laboratory Values Within **45** Days Prior to the Most Recent ESRD Episode. (Lipid Profile within 1 Year of Most Recent ESRD Episode).

LABORATORY TEST	VALUE	DATE	LABORATORY TEST	VALUE	DATE
a.1. Serum Albumin (g/dl)	__.__		d. HbA1c	__ __.__ %	
a.2. Serum Albumin Lower Limit	__.__		e. Lipid Profile TC	__ __ __	
a.3. Lab Method Used (BCG or BCP)			LDL	__ __ __	
b. Serum Creatinine (mg/dl)	__ __.__		HDL	__ __	
c. Hemoglobin (g/dl)	__ __.__		TG	__ __ __	

B. COMPLETE FOR ALL ESRD PATIENTS IN DIALYSIS TREATMENT

20. Name of Dialysis Facility	21. Medicare Provider Number *(for item 20)*

22. Primary Dialysis Setting
☐ Home ☐ Dialysis Facility/Center ☐ SNF/Long Term Care Facility
☐ CAPD ☐ CCPD ☐ Other

23. Primary Type of Dialysis
☐ Hemodialysis (Sessions per week___/hours per session___)

24. Date Regular Chronic Dialysis Began
Dialysis at Current Facility ___/___/___ MM DD YYYY

25. Date Patient Started Chronic ___/___/___ MM DD YYYY

26. Has patient been informed of kidney transplant options?
☐ Yes ☐ No

27. If patient NOT informed of transplant options, please check all that apply:
☐ Medically unfit
☐ Unsuitable due to age
☐ Psychologically unfit
☐ Patient declines information
☐ Patient has not been assessed
☐ Other

FORM CMS-2728-U3 (06/04)   1

FIGURE 5-3 CMS Form 2728. (Permission to reuse in accordance with http://www.cms.gov Content Reuse and Linking Policy.)

C. COMPLETE FOR ALL KIDNEY TRANSPLANT PATIENTS

28. Date of Transplant MM DD YYYY	29. Name of Transplant Hospital	30. Medicare Provider Number for Item 29

Date patient was admitted as an inpatient to a hospital in preparation for, or anticipation of, a kidney transplant prior to the date of actual transplantation.

31. Enter Date MM DD YYYY	32. Name of Preparation Hospital	33. Medicare Provider number for Item 32

34. Current Status of Transplant *(if functioning, skip items 36 and 37)* ☐ Functioning ☐ Non-Functioning	35. Type of Donor: ☐ Deceased ☐ Living Related ☐ Living Unrelated
36. If Non-Functioning, Date of Return to Regular Dialysis MM DD YYYY	37. Current Dialysis Treatment Site ☐ Home ☐ Dialysis Facility/Center ☐ SNF/Long Term Care Facility

D. COMPLETE FOR ALL ESRD SELF-DIALYSIS TRAINING PATIENTS (MEDICARE APPLICANTS ONLY)

38. Name of Training Provider	39. Medicare Provider Number of Training Provider (for Item 38)
40. Date Training Began MM DD YYYY	41. Type of Training ☐ Hemodialysis a. ☐ Home b. ☐ In Center ☐ CAPD ☐ CCPD ☐ Other
42. This Patient is Expected to Complete *(or has completed)* Training and will Self-dialyze on a Regular Basis. ☐ Yes ☐ No	43. Date When Patient Completed, or is Expected to Complete, Training MM DD YYYY

I certify that the above self-dialysis training information is correct and is based on consideration of all pertinent medical, psychological, and sociological factors as reflected in records kept by this training facility.

44. Printed Name and Signature of Physician personally familiar with the patient's training a.) Printed Name b.) Signature c.) Date MM DD YYYY	45. UPIN of Physician in Item 44

E. PHYSICIAN IDENTIFICATION

46. Attending Physician *(Print)*	47. Physician's Phone No. ( )	48. UPIN of Physician in Item 46

PHYSICIAN ATTESTATION

I certify, under penalty of perjury, that the information on this form is correct to the best of my knowledge and belief. Based on diagnostic tests and laboratory findings, I further certify that this patient has reached the stage of renal impairment that appears irreversible and permanent and requires a regular course of dialysis or kidney transplant to maintain life. I understand that this information is intended for use in establishing the patient's entitlement to Medicare benefits and that any falsification, misrepresentation, or concealment of essential information may subject me to fine, imprisonment, civil penalty, or other civil sanctions under applicable Federal laws.

49. Attending Physician's Signature of Attestation *(Same as Item 46)*	50. Date MM DD YYYY
51. Physician Recertification Signature	52. Date MM DD YYYY

53. Remarks

F. OBTAIN SIGNATURE FROM PATIENT

I hereby authorize any physician, hospital, agency, or other organization to disclose any medical records or other information about my medical condition to the Department of Health and Human Services for purposes of reviewing my application for Medicare entitlement under the Social Security Act and/or for scientific research.

54. Signature of Patient *(Signature by mark must be witnessed.)*	55. Date MM DD YYYY

G. PRIVACY STATEMENT

The collection of this information is authorized by Section 226A of the Social Security Act. The information provided will be used to determine if an individual is entitled to Medicare under the End Stage Renal Disease provisions of the law. The information will be maintained in system No. 09-70-0520, "End Stage Renal Disease Program Management and Medical Information System (ESRD PMMIS)", published in the Federal Register, Vol. 67, No. 116, June 17, 2002, pages 41244-41250 or as updated and republished. Collection of your Social Security number is authorized by Executive Order 9397. Furnishing the information on this form is voluntary, but failure to do so may result in denial of Medicare benefits. Information from the ESRD PMMIS may be given to a congressional office in response to an inquiry from the congressional office made at the request of the individual; an individual or organization for research, demonstration, evaluation, or epidemiologic project related to the prevention of disease or disability, or the restoration or maintenance of health. Additional disclosures may be found in the *Federal Register* notice cited above. You should be aware that P.L.100-503, the Computer Matching and Privacy Protection Act of 1988, permits the government to verify information by way of computer matches.

FIGURE **5-3** (*Continued*)

DEPARTMENT OF HEALTH AND HUMAN SERVICES
CENTERS FOR MEDICARE & MEDICAID SERVICES

Form Approved
OMB No. 0938-0448

ESRD DEATH NOTIFICATION
END STAGE RENAL DISEASE MEDICAL INFORMATION SYSTEM

1. Patient's Last Name	First	MI	2. Medicare Claim Number

3. Patient's Sex

a. ☐ Male   b. ☐ Female

4. Date of Birth

___ / ___ / ___ __
Month   Day   Year

5. Social Security Number

6. Patient's State of Residence

7. Place of Death

a. ☐ Hospital   c. ☐ Home   e. ☐ Other
b. ☐ Dialysis Unit   d. ☐ Nursing Home

8. Date of Death

__ __ / __ __ / __ __ __ __
Month   Day   Year

9. Modality at Time of Death

a. ☐ Incenter Hemodialysis   b. ☐ Home Hemodialysis   c. ☐ CAPD   d. ☐ CCPD   e. ☐ Transplant   f. ☐ Other

10. Provider Name and Address (Street)

11. Provider Number

Provider Address (City/State)

12. Causes of Death (enter codes from list on back of form)

a. Primary Cause __ __ __

b. Were there secondary causes?

☐ No

☐ Yes, specify: __ __ __ . __ __ __ . __ __ __ . __ __ __

C. If cause is other (98) please specify: _____

13. Renal replacement therapy discontinued prior to death: ☐ Yes ☐ No

If yes, check one of the following:

a. ☐ Following HD and/or PD access failure

b. ☐ Following transplant failure

c. ☐ Following chronic failure to thrive

d. ☐ Following acute medical complication

e. ☐ Other

f. Date of last dialysis treatment __ __ / __ __ / __ __ __ __
Month   Day   Year

14. Was discontinuation of renal replacement therapy after patient/family request to stop dialysis?

☐ Yes   ☐ No

☐ Unknown   ☐ Not Applicable

15. If deceased ever received a transplant:

a. Date of most recent transplant __ __ / __ __ / __ __ __ __   ☐ Unknown
Month   Day   Year

b. Type of transplant received
☐ Living Related   ☐ Living Unrelated   ☐ Deceased   ☐ Unknown

c. Was graft functioning (patient not on dialysis) at time of death?
☐ Yes   ☐ No   ☐ Unknown

d. Did transplant patient resume chronic maintenance dialysis prior to death?
☐ Yes   ☐ No   ☐ Unknown

16. Was patient receiving Hospice care prior to death?

☐ Yes   ☐ No

☐ Unknown

17. Name of Physician (Please print complete name)	18. Signature of Person Completing This Form	Date

This report is required by law (42, U.S.C. 426; 20 CFR 405, Section 2133). Individually identifiable patient information will not be disclosed except as provided for in the Privacy Act of 1974 (5 U.S.C. 5520; 45 CFR Part 5a).

Form CMS-2746-U2 (08/06) EF 08/2006

FIGURE **5-4** CMS Form 2746. (Permission to reuse in accordance with http://www.cms.gov Content Reuse and Linking Policy.)

QUALITY ASSESSMENT, PERFORMANCE IMPROVEMENT, AND UTILIZATION MANAGEMENT

Individual dialysis facilities must engage in quality assessment, performance improvement, and utilization management. These are also major responsibilities of the ESRD networks. Federal regulation 42 C.F.R. 405.2112 charges the ESRD networks with:

(a) Developing network goals for placing patients in settings for self-care and transplantation.

(b) Encouraging the use of medically appropriate treatment settings most compatible with patient rehabilitation and the participation of patients, providers of services, and renal disease facilities in vocational rehabilitation programs.

(c) Developing criteria and standards relating to the quality and appropriateness of patient care and, with respect to working with patients, facilities, and providers of services, for encouraging participation in vocational rehabilitation programs.

(d) Evaluating the procedures used by facilities in the network in assessing patients for placement in appropriate treatment modalities.

....

(g) Evaluating and resolving patient grievances.

(h) Appointing a network council and a medical review board (each including at least one patient representative)...

(i) Conducting on-site reviews of facilities and providers as necessary, as determined by the medical review board or CMS...

(j) Collecting, validating, and analyzing data...(ESRD Network Organizations, 2009, pp. 258–259).

Quality Improvement

The Conditions for Coverage require each dialysis facility to conduct its own internal **quality assessment and performance improvement (QAPI)** program. The following excerpt from the Conditions for Coverage, § 494.110 provides important details regarding the QAPI program:

The dialysis facility must develop, implement, maintain, and evaluate an effective, data-driven, quality assessment and performance improvement program with participation by the professional members of the interdisciplinary team. The program must reflect the complexity of the dialysis facility's organization and services (including those services provided under arrangement), and must focus on indicators related to improved health outcomes and the prevention and reduction of medical errors. The dialysis facility must maintain and demonstrate evidence of its quality improvement and performance improvement program for review by CMS.

(a) Standard: Program scope.

1. The program must include, but not be limited to, an ongoing program that achieves measurable improvement in health outcomes and reduction of medical errors by using indicators or performance measures associated with improved health outcomes and with the identification and reduction of medical errors.

2. The dialysis facility must measure, analyze, and track quality indicators or other aspects of performance that the facility adopts or develops that reflect processes of care and facility operations. These performance components must influence or relate to the desired outcomes or be the outcomes themselves. The program must include, but not be limited to, the following:
    (i) Adequacy of dialysis.
    (ii) Nutritional status.
    (iii) Mineral metabolism and renal bone disease.
    (iv) Anemia management.
    (v) Vascular access.
    (vi) Medical injuries and medical errors identification.
    (vii) Hemodialyzer reuse program, if the facility reuses hemodialyzers.
    (viii) Patient satisfaction and grievances.
    (ix) Infection control....

MIPPA also required the establishment of quality incentives in the ESRD program. Provider payment rates are affected by specific performance-based measures that assess iron management (avoiding anemia), adequacy of dialysis, mortality, albumin levels, bone mineral metabolism (e.g., calcium and phosphorus control), and vascular access, including maximizing the placement of arterial venous fistulas. Providers not meeting performance standards will experience a payment reduction of up to 2 percent. (Gadzik & Raney 2010; MIPPA 2008).

The ESRD networks also perform quality improvement activities for their regions. For example, the ESRD **Clinical Performance Measures (CPM) Project** collects clinical data on ESRD patients and other performance data related to dialysis facilities and clinicians (CMS, 2009, December 24). According to the *Medicare ESRD Network Organizations Manual*, the networks are responsible for developing and conducting quality improvement projects based on the CPMs for "adequacy of dialysis, anemia management, and vascular access, or other CPMs developed or adopted by CMS" (CMS, 2003, p. 2). The CPM project has resulted in significant quality improvement over the years. For example, in 2003, 87 percent of patients received adequate hemodialysis compared to only 43 percent in 1994. Also in 2003, 80 percent of patients had a mean hemoglobin greater than 11, compared to only 46 percent in 1994 (CMS, 2006). Figure 5-5 lists the CPMs being collected and monitored as of 2008. In the past, data were collected on a statistically significant sample of patients, but the implementation of CROWNWeb allows data needed for the CPMs to be electronically submitted to the networks and to CMS for all patients. Other projects include the Elab project and the Fistula First breakthrough initiative. Large dialysis organizations submit data for both of these projects electronically, and independent facilities may submit data using manual processes. The Elab project collects values for 12 different lab tests for 100 percent of the dialysis facility population for performance improvement purposes. The Fistula First project collects data regarding vascular access on a monthly basis, with a goal of increasing the number of hemodialysis patients using arteriovenous fistulas for dialysis access.

Anemia Management
- Assessment of Iron Stores—Facility Level
- Hemoglobin control for ESA therapy—Facility Level
- Monitoring hemoglobin levels below target minimum—Facility Level
- Hematocrit control for ESA therapy—Facility Level
- Monitoring hematocrit levels below target minimum—Facility Level

Hemodialysis Adequacy
- Hemodialysis Adequacy—Monthly measurement of delivered dose
- Method of Measurement of Delivered Hemodialysis Dose
- Minimum delivered hemodialysis dose for ESRD hemodialysis patients undergoing dialytic treatment for a period of 6 months or greater—Facility Level
- Minimum delivered hemodialysis dose for ESRD hemodialysis patients undergoing dialytic treatment for a period of 90 days or greater—Facility Level
- Percentage of the facility's hemodialysis patients with a urea reduction ratio (URR) of 65% or greater in the calendar year—Facility Level

Peritoneal Dialysis Adequacy
- Measurement of total Solute Clearance at regular intervals—Facility Level
- Delivered Dose of peritoneal dialysis above the minimum of 1.7—Facility Level

Mineral Metabolism
- Measurement of Serum Calcium Concentration—Facility Level
- Measurement of Serum Phosphorus Concentration—Facility Level

Vascular Access
- Minimizing use of catheters as Chronic Dialysis Access—Facility Level
- Maximizing Placement of Arterial Venous Fistula (AVF)—Facility Level
- Functional Autogenous AV Fistula Access or referral to vascular surgeon for placement—Clinician Level
- Catheter Vascular Access and referred to vascular surgeon for evaluation for a permanent access—Clinician Level
- Decision-making by Surgeon to Maximize Placement of Autogenous Arterial Venous Fistula—Clinician Level

FIGURE **5-5** ESRD Clinical Performance Measures in effect April 1, 2008. "Facility Level" means that performance will be measured at the level of the facility. "Clinician Level" means that performance will be measured at the level of the clinician. (Permission to reuse in accordance with http://www.cms.gov Content Reuse and Linking Policy.)

Source: CMS ESRD CPM Project. http://www.cms.gov/CPMProject/Downloads/ESRDPhaseIIICPM04012008Final.pdf

> **Influenza Vaccination**
> - Influenza Immunization—Clinician Level
> - Influenza Vaccination in the ESRD Population—Facility Level
>
> **Patient Education, Perception of Care, and Quality of Life**
> - Patient Education Awareness—Facility Level
> - Patient Education Awareness—Clinician Level
> - CAHPS In-Center Hemodialysis Survey—Facility Level
> - Assessment of Health-related Quality of Life (Physical & Mental Functioning)—Facility Level
>
> **Patient Survival**
> - Facility Patient Survival Classification (based on Standardized Mortality Ratio)—Facility Level

FIGURE **5-5** (*Continued*)

Clinical practice guidelines represent another quality improvement mechanism. The National Kidney Foundation (NKF) has developed evidence-based guidelines as a component of a project called the Kidney Disease Outcomes Quality Initiative (KDOQI). KDOQI has published four sets of clinical practice guidelines for dialysis care: for hemodialysis adequacy, for peritoneal dialysis adequacy, for vascular access, and for cardiovascular disease in dialysis patients. Additionally, there are nine sets of KDOQI guidelines for care of patients with chronic kidney disease (CKD), including treatment of anemia in chronic kidney disease, bone metabolism and disease in chronic kidney disease, and so on. KDOQI has an established process for maintenance and revision of guidelines as well as principles for determining when new guideline topics are needed (NKF, 2010). CMS has incorporated outcome measures from the KDOQI guidelines into their clinical performance measures projects.

Utilization Management (UM)

In each dialysis facility, an interdisciplinary team assesses and develops a plan of care for each individual dialysis patient. As a part of this process, the team must consider the suitability of the patient for a transplant referral. Patients who have kidney transplants generally have higher survival rates, a better quality of life, and lower overall medical costs than patients on dialysis. Therefore, one aspect of utilization management in a dialysis program involves making it possible for patients to leave dialysis by referring them for transplant when appropriate. The interdisciplinary team must consider the criteria developed by the prospective transplantation center when making recommendations for transplant referral. The patient is a vital member of the interdisciplinary team as well, and the patient's desires regarding transplantation are an important consideration. However, it is still incumbent upon the clinicians on the team to educate the patient about the advantages and disadvantages of various modalities of renal replacement therapy. The patient's nephrologist, a registered dietitian, a qualified social worker, and a registered nurse participate with the patient in determining the type of treatment that would be best for him or her.

Data submitted to the ESRD networks are also used by the networks and CMS to study overall utilization patterns. For example, the networks may examine laboratory values submitted through CROWNWeb to evaluate trends in their regions regarding the appropriateness of initiation of dialysis.

RISK MANAGEMENT, LEGAL, AND ETHICAL ISSUES

Many of the legal issues in a dialysis facility are the same as in any other health care facility. The patient must give consent to treatment, must authorize the release of medical information, and has the right to expect that the confidentiality of clinical information will be protected. Records must also be protected against loss, destruction, or unauthorized use (42 C.F.R. 494.170). Dialysis facilities are "covered entities" under the Health Insurance Portability and Accountability Act of 1996 (HIPAA) and so must comply with all of HIPAA's privacy, security, and transactions standards. Dialysis treatment facilities may release protected health information to the ESRD networks as public policy disclosures required by law for health oversight. However, because the facilities must be able to provide an accounting of disclosures to its patients as mandated by HIPAA and the HITECH Act (see Chapter 1), facilities should maintain records of their disclosures to the ESRD networks and other regulatory authorities and facilities with an EHR should develop systems to provide the necessary accounting for all disclosures.

The retention period for clinical information on dialysis patients, according to federal statute, is six years following the patient's discharge, transfer, or death. Of course, when the requirements of state law are more stringent than the federal regulations, the state retention statutes must be followed.

Because the success of dialysis treatment depends largely on patient compliance, it is especially important that clinical professionals document patient education. They should also record action taken when the patient is not complying with the treatment regimen.

As a long-term life-sustaining treatment, renal replacement therapy has been a focal point for numerous ethical issues. For example, a disruptive, abusive patient can create unsafe conditions for other patients in a dialysis facility. An ethical and legal dilemma in this situation arises in determining whether or how the health care provider may transfer or discharge such a patient, given that the patient's life depends on continued dialysis. Kidney transplant is also a type of renal replacement therapy, and, unlike many other types of transplants, a kidney may be obtained from a living donor. This brings its own unique set of ethical issues, ranging from the competency of the prospective donor to the suitability of the prospective recipient (Friedman, 2000). As with other life-saving measures, there are also ethical issues surrounding the initiation of and withdrawal from dialysis. The Renal Physicians Association and the American Society of Nephrology have addressed this subject through the development of a comprehensive clinical practice guideline and tool kit entitled *Shared Decision-Making in the Appropriate Initiation of and Withdrawal from Dialysis* (RPA/ASN, 2000).

ROLE OF THE HEALTH INFORMATION MANAGEMENT PROFESSIONAL

Health information management (HIM) professionals practice in a variety of roles in ERSD health care. A health information manager may work full-time for an organization providing dialysis services or as a consultant. In this role, the HIM professional is concerned with procedures related to the documentation, storage, retrieval, and security of individual patient records. The consultant provides advice on the development of systems to provide timely, appropriately accessible patient information to caregivers and administrators. A consultant visits the dialysis unit periodically to review a sample of records and to discuss procedures for record maintenance with facility staff. Often, several dialysis units are owned by a single entity, such as a corporation. In this type of arrangement, the company headquarters may employ an HIM professional on a full-time basis to assist all of the units with HIM issues.

The ESRD networks also employ health information professionals. A health information manager may work as a data coordinator, quality improvement coordinator, quality manager, or even as an executive director in an ESRD network.

SUMMARY

Dialysis facilities treat patients who are experiencing renal failure as a result of Stage 5 chronic kidney disease (also known as end-stage renal disease or ESRD). The two types of dialysis are hemodialysis and peritoneal dialysis. Hemodialysis is usually administered by nurses and technicians in a dialysis facility, but it may also be self-administered by the patient at home. Peritoneal dialysis is a portable process that can be self-administered by the patient at home or in a variety of locations.

Interdisciplinary teams of registered and licensed nurses, technicians, physicians, dietitians, and social workers, along with the patient, plan and administer the dialysis treatment regimen. Health information management professionals can assist in ensuring that the patient records are properly documented and preserved.

Most freestanding dialysis units must meet the federal guidelines for ESRD facilities, because Medicare is the chief source of funding for these facilities. Therefore, the federal documentation requirements in the Conditions for Coverage represent the minimum guidelines for quantity and quality of documentation for dialysis patient records. Other federal regulations include the ESRD prospective payment system, which bundles services into a single per-treatment rate and standardized data set reporting, which is accomplished electronically through CROWNWeb.

Information management for dialysis facilities requires the implementation of systems to meet a variety of needs. Not only must information be coded and transmitted for reimbursement purposes, but data must be submitted to the ESRD networks for quality improvement and utilization management. Dialysis facilities also conduct their own quality assessment and performance improvement (QAPI) programs. Medicare's quality incentive program affects reimbursement through payment reductions to facilities that do not meet standards. Electronic health record systems are commonly used for information management in the dialysis facility setting.

A health information manager can play several roles in the dialysis health care system. HIM professionals provide services both in treatment settings (ESRD dialysis units) and in regulatory settings (ESRD networks). HIM professionals work in positions extending from medical record supervisor to executive director.

KEY TERMS

chronic kidney disease (CKD) a gradual loss of kidney function classified into five stages, with mild loss of kidney function in the early stages and severe or total loss in the later stages. In the final stage (Stage 5) the individual's kidneys are no longer able to perform the job of excreting the body's wastes or promoting homeostasis, and the patient requires dialysis or kidney transplant to survive.

Clinical Performance Measures (CPM) Project an ongoing project of CMS, implemented through the ESRD networks, to measure and report the quality of renal dialysis services provided under the Medicare program.

Consolidated Renal Operations in a Web-enabled Network (CROWNWeb) CMS Internet-based software application that is the required method by which dialysis facilities submit data about patients and facility operations.

continuous ambulatory peritoneal dialysis (CAPD) a form of peritoneal dialysis in which the patient is able to dialyze him or herself three or four times per day without special assistance and with a minimum amount of equipment.

continuous cycling peritoneal dialysis (CCPD) a form of peritoneal dialysis in which the

patient uses a cycler machine to dialyze once a day for nine or ten hours, generally while sleeping.

dialysate a solution used to filter products across a semipermeable membrane by the process of diffusion. Waste products filter into the dialysate from the blood, while certain other products, such as bicarbonates, filter into the blood from the dialysate.

dialysis "the process of artificially removing metabolic end products and water across a semipermeable membrane by diffusion" (McAfee, 1987). The two most common types of dialysis are hemodialysis and peritoneal dialysis. (See also *hemodialysis and peritoneal dialysis*.)

dialysis facility "an entity that provides (1) outpatient maintenance dialysis services; or (2) home dialysis training and support services; or (3) both. A dialysis facility may be an independent or hospital-based unit... or a self-care dialysis unit that furnishes only self-dialysis services" (*Conditions for Coverage*, 2008, 20476)

end-stage renal disease (ESRD) is Stage 5 of chronic kidney disease. At this stage the patient has irreversible renal failure with little or no kidney function. When a patient is in end-stage renal disease, he or she requires either dialysis or a kidney transplant to maintain life.

erythropoietin stimulating agent (ESA) stimulates the bone marrow to make red blood cells and is used to treat and prevent anemia, a common complication of chronic kidney disease in patients on dialysis.

ESRD networks 18 organizations that have contracted with the Centers for Medicare & Medicaid Services (CMS) to assess the quality of care rendered to ESRD patients and to collect and analyze ESRD data.

hemodialysis (HD) cleansing of the blood as it circulates through an artificial kidney machine outside the patient's body.

Kt/V a means of measuring the adequacy of dialysis (i.e., a way to determine whether the patient is dialyzing long enough or often enough to remove sufficient waste and excess fluid from the body). Target Kt/V values in the *Conditions for Coverage* are 1.2 for hemodialysis and a weekly Kt/V of at least 1.7 for peritoneal dialysis.

peritoneal dialysis (PD) filling of the patient's abdominal cavity with a solution (dialysate); the semipermeable membrane across which the products diffuse is the patient's own peritoneal membrane. The fluid containing the wastes is later withdrawn from the peritoneal cavity.

quality assessment and performance improvement (QAPI) The *Conditions for Coverage* require each dialysis facility to adopt a data-driven performance improvement program that utilizes indicators or performance measures associated with improved health outcomes and with the identification and reduction of medical errors.

Renal Management Information System (REMIS) a system that determines Medicare coverage periods for ESRD patients and serves as the primary mechanism to store and access information in the ESRD Program Management and Medical Information System (PMMIS) Database. REMIS tracks the ESRD patient population for both Medicare and non-Medicare patients.

renal replacement therapy (RRT) a treatment that replaces kidney function. The treatment may be some type of dialysis or it may be kidney transplantation.

validation survey a survey conducted by a regional office of the CMS to determine whether the surveys being conducted by state agencies (or other groups) are appropriately assessing the facility's operations.

REVIEW QUESTIONS

Knowledge-Based Questions

1. Explain the following types of care given to end-stage renal disease patients: hemodialysis, CAPD, and CCPD.
2. Who performs regular surveys of dialysis facilities? Who performs validation surveys of dialysis facilities?
3. What items of information should be documented for each dialysis patient?
4. What is the source of payment for most patients who have been on dialysis for more than 30 months?
5. What role do the ESRD networks play in the collection and aggregation of data on dialysis patients?

6. What types of QAPI activities take place in dialysis facilities?
7. What are possible roles for the health information manager in organizations dealing with end-stage renal disease?

Critical Thinking Questions

1. Compare and contrast ESRD Networks with quality improvement organizations.
2. What resources would a health information consultant find helpful in consulting for ESRD facilities?

WEB ACTIVITY

1. Visit the Web site http://www.medicare.gov.
2. Scroll down and select "Dialysis Facilities" (under "Resource Locator").
3. Under "How would you like to find a Dialysis Facility?" see "By Proximity" and select "Zip Code."
4. Type in a zip code and select an appropriate "distance," depending upon the density of population in the geographic area you selected.
5. At the next screen, you will be presented with a list of all of the dialysis facilities within the geographic area you selected. Select several facilities in the area by clicking the check box beside the facility name, then the "Next Step" button to compare these dialysis facilities.
6. At the next screen, note the information available. *How would this information assist a patient in selecting a dialysis facility?*
7. Click "Compare Quality" for one of the facilities displayed.
8. Scroll down and find the list of quality measures for which comparative data are available. *What quality measures are currently reported?*
9. Select "Show All" to display the quality information for each of the facilities. *How would this information assist a patient in selecting a dialysis facility?*
10. *If you were selecting a dialysis facility for yourself or a family member, which facilities would you visit in narrowing your list of choices? Why did you select these facilities?*

CASE STUDY

Kay Carnes has begun consulting for a dialysis facility that began using an electronic health record system approximately six months ago. On her first consultation visit, she examined both the electronic and paper portions of the patient record. She found that certain portions of the record, which were not included in the electronic health record, were maintained in sturdy three-ring binders. These binders were labeled on the spine with the patient's name and the patient's treatment schedule (e.g., John Doe, M-W-F, or Mary Smith, T-T-S). The paper-based portion of the record included signed consent forms, assessment forms, outside lab reports, history and physical examination reports from the patient's physician or last hospital visit, identification data, CMS data collection forms, and patient care plans. The electronic portion of the record included data from each dialysis treatment and progress notes from the nurses, the dietitian, and the social worker. On some of the older records in which all of the progress notes were handwritten, Kay noticed that the physicians had recorded monthly progress notes. However, there were no progress notes from the physicians in the electronic portion of the record that covered the past six months. Kay asked the unit director, a registered nurse, about this. The director answered that all of the other disciplines were entering their own progress notes into the electronic health record during or after each patient contact. However, the physicians were accustomed to handwriting their progress notes and, therefore, did not use the computer. The physicians had continued to see each patient on a monthly basis, but there was very little documentation in the chart to indicate this after the electronic health record had been implemented.

1. What issues should Kay address in her consultation report to this facility?
2. What recommendations would you make if you were in her place?

REFERENCES AND SUGGESTED READINGS

[CMS] Centers for Medicare & Medicaid Services. (2003). Chapter 5—Quality improvement. *Medicare ESRD Network Organizations Manual.* [Online]. http://www.cms.gov/ manuals/downloads/eno114c5.pdf [2010, July 5].

[CMS] Centers for Medicare & Medicaid Services. (2006, January 27). *Summary of the ESRD Network Program.* [Online]. http://www.cms. gov/ESRDNetworkOrganizations/Downloads/ ESRDNetworkProgramBackgroundpublic.pdf [2010, May 8].

[CMS] Centers for Medicare & Medicaid Services. (2008, April 15). 42 C.F.R. pts. 405, 410, 413, 414, 488, & 494. Medicare and Medicaid Programs; Conditions for Coverage for End-Stage Renal Disease Facilities; Final Rule. [Online]. http://www.cms.hhs.gov/CFCsAndCoPs/downloads/ESRDfinalrule0415.pdf.

[CMS] Centers for Medicare & Medicaid Services, Office of Public Affairs. (2009, September 15) Press Release: CMS proposes new prospective payment system for renal dialysis facilities. [Online]. http://www.cms.hhs.gov/apps/media/press_releases.asp.

[CMS] Centers for Medicare & Medicaid Services. (2009, December 24). Clinical Performance Measures (CPM) Project. [Online]. http://www.cms.gov/CPMProject.

[CMS] Centers for Medicare & Medicaid Services. (2010). End-stage renal disease (ESRD) payment. [Online]. http://www4.cms.gov/ESRDPayment

Conditions for Coverage for End-Stage Renal Disease Facilities; Final Rule, 73 Fed. Reg. 20370- 20484 (2008) (to be codified at 42 C.F.R. pt. 494.)

End-Stage Renal Disease Prospective Payment System, Final Rule and Proposed Rule, 75 Fed. Reg. 49030–49214 (August 12, 2010).

ESRD network organizations. *Code of Federal Regulations*, Title 42, Part 405, Section 405.2112, 2009 ed.

Forum of ESRD Networks. (2001). Medical record model. [Online]. http://esrdnetworks.org/resources/medicalrecordsmodel.pdf.

Friedman, E. A. (2000). *Legal and Ethical Concerns in Treating Kidney Failure: Case Study Workbook*. Dordrecht, The Netherlands: Kluwer Academic Publishers.

Gadzik, D., & Raney, D. A. (2010, March 25). Procedural coding for dialysis services. AHIMA Audio Seminar.

McAfee, L. (1987). A consultant's guide to renal dialysis units. *Journal of the American Medical Record Association, 58*(7), 44–46.

National Kidney and Urologic Diseases Clearinghouse. (2009, April). *Financial Help for Treatment of Kidney Failure*. [Online]. http://kidney.niddk.nih.gov/kudiseases/pubs/financialhelp/#medicare [2010, May 24].

[NKF] National Kidney Foundation. (2010). *The National Kidney Foundation Kidney Disease Outcomes Quality Initiative (NKF KDOQI ™)*. [Online]. http://www.kidney.org/professionals/KDOQI/ [2010, July 6].

[OPTN] Organ Procurement and Transplantation Network. (2010). *About OPTN*. [Online]. http://optn.transplant.hrsa.gov [2010, May 8].

[RPA/ASN] Renal Physicians Association & American Society of Nephrology. (2000). *Shared Decision-Making in the Appropriate Initiation of and Withdrawal from Dalysis* (Clinical Practice Guideline No. 2). Washington, DC: Authors.

[UNOS] United Network for Organ Sharing. (2010). *Data*. [Online]. http://www.unos.org/data/ [2010, May 8].

[USRDS] U.S. Renal Data System. (2009). Treatment modalities. *2009 USRDS Annual Data Report*, Vol. 3, Sec. D. [Online]. http://www.usrds.org/2009/ref/D_Ref_09.pdf.

KEY RESOURCES

American Association of Kidney Patients
http://www.aakp.org

American Nephrology Nurses Association
http:// www.annanurse.org

American Society of Nephrology
http://www.asn-online.org

American Society of Transplantation
http://www.a-s-t.org

American Society of Transplant Surgeons
http://www.asts.org

Association of Organ Procurement Organizations
http://www.aopo.org

Forum Clearinghouse
Forum of End-Stage Renal Disease Networks
http://www.esrdnetworks.org

National Association for Nephrology Technicians/Technologists
http://www.dialysistech.net

National Renal Administrators Association
http://www.nraa.org

Project CROWNWeb
http://www.projectcrownweb.org

Renal Physicians Association
http://www.renalmd.org

United Network for Organ Sharing
http://www.unos.org

CHAPTER 6

Correctional Facilities

NINA DOZORETZ, MA, RHIA, CCHP

BARBARA MANNY, MS, RHIA

BRIANNA MCCLOE ROGERS, RHIA

LEARNING OBJECTIVES

Upon successful completion of this chapter, you should be able to:

- Identify the types of correctional facilities that exist and the responsible authority for each.

- Identify the various health care delivery models that exist in correctional institutions.

- Distinguish between the various types of licensure and certification available for correctional professionals.

- Recognize the different accrediting organizations and the strengths and weaknesses of each.

- Identify the role of HIPAA in correctional facilities.

- Identify situations where the application of technology can help reduce costs and increase access to health care.

Setting	Description	Synonyms/Examples
Prisons	Individual facilities operated by a unit of a state or the federal government for the confinement of adults 18 years or older convicted of a felony, whose sentence exceeds one year (Anno, 1992).	There are three different classifications for prisons: maximum, medium, and minimum security.
Jails	Institutions intended for adults, usually administered by local units of government (i.e., cities or counties) with the authority to detain for a period of 48 hours or longer (ACA, 1985). Some adult facilities hold juveniles for less than one year or hold them pending trial, awaiting sentencing, or awaiting transfer to other facilities after a conviction (BJS, 2009).	In various locations these facilities may also be known as detention centers, county prisons, or workhouses.
Juvenile Detention Facilities	Facilities operated by a unit of government for the confinement of individuals younger than 18 years of age.	
Bureau of Immigration and Customs Enforcement (ICE)	ICE owned, operated, or contracted detention centers are used to hold individuals placed into administrative detention during periods of investigation into their legal status or resolution of a removal order.	
Correctional facilities operated by the Army, Navy, Air Force, or Marines	All branches of the U.S. military operate their own correctional facilities in the United States and overseas.	
Shelters or Halfway Houses	Incarcerated individuals may be released to community residential facilities as a means of completing their sentences or making the transition back to society by receiving substance abuse, rehabilitative, and/or vocational services.	

INTRODUCTION TO SETTING

As crime rates increased over the past century, the correctional industry in the United States underwent dramatic changes and experienced enormous growth in the **inmate** population. The greatest increase occurred between 1980 and 1990, when the total prison population increased more than 200 percent (ACA, 1993). The Bureau of Justice Statistics reported that 1,613,656 prisoners were held in prisons and jails nationwide as of December 31, 2009 (BJS, 2009).

U.S. correctional institutions are complex organizations. Their purpose is to enhance public safety by keeping separate those persons deemed a threat to other individuals or their property. Each level of government—federal, state, county, and city—is responsible for the operation of some type of correctional facility. The various levels of government operate independently of each other. Even the operation of facilities within the same system varies. This chapter provides health information managers with a general understanding of the nature of correctional institutions and, specifically, the role of health information management in the delivery of health care in correctional settings.

The operation of correctional institutions and, more specifically, the delivery of health care to inmates was not of great concern to many individuals or organizations until fairly recently. It was not until the early 1970s, when civil rights advocates and health professionals began taking a serious look at the lack of health care services available to inmates, that the conditions under which inmates lived became widely known.

Before 1970, few efforts were made to identify and change the status of health care delivery in correctional facilities. A common misconception was that **prisons** provided better health care than did **jails**. Jails typically lacked the funds necessary to maintain an infirmary, so treatment was often provided by the emergency departments of community hospitals. But prison inmates were rarely sent outside the system for care, because prisons were more likely to have some type of medical care available on-site. Prison health care staff were usually not as well trained as their peers working in private or public institutions. The health staff practicing in correctional institutions were often physicians with restricted licenses or unlicensed foreign medical graduates. Support staff often included unlicensed former medical corpsmen and untrained inmate "nurses" (Anno, 1992).

Health services in prisons today are generally given by providers who are licensed, certified, or registered to practice, in the same manner as required in the community (Anno, 2004).

Both federal and state laws affect prisoners' rights. In general, prisoners lose some of their civil rights, such as the right to vote, when they are incarcerated. However, the Eighth Amendment to the U.S. Constitution prohibits cruel and unusual punishment, which means that prisons must provide a minimum standard of living for prisoners. Also, the Fourteenth Amendment's Equal Protection Clause protects prisoners against unequal treatment on the basis of race, sex, and creed. Prisoners also have limited rights to speech and religion. Other constitutional rights that apply to prisoners include due process in the right to administrative appeals and a right of access to the parole process (Legal Information Institute, n.d.).

In 1976, the landmark case *Estelle v. Gamble* created a "right" to health care for inmates. The case applied a two-prong test to determine the extent of the medical care duty owed to inmates. Correctional institutions would be in violation of inmates' constitutional rights if (1) correctional officials showed a "deliberate indifference" to inmates' medical needs and (2) the inmates' needs were "serious." The vagueness of the language used in the court's ruling and the creation of a "right" to health care has created enormous difficulties for correctional institutions, including a continuous rise in inmate petitions claiming violations of their "right" to health care (Posner, 1992).

Today inmates receive treatment for AIDS (acquired immune deficiency syndrome), cardiovascular disease, and even rehabilitation services. The physical settings have changed substantially and can range from small infirmaries to large medical facilities with specialty clinics. The typical prison clinic today looks much like an ambulatory health facility outside the prison. It usually has a trauma room, exam rooms, a laboratory, a radiological suite, a pharmacy or medication room, and dental operatories—all of which are reasonably supplied and equipped (Anno, 2004). Advocates for correctional health care seek the availability of even more extensive and expensive treatment and facilities.

Organizational structure and methods of administration vary depending on the level of government operating a facility, corresponding laws and court orders, and characteristics of the incarcerated populations. Health information management professionals should fully understand the structure of the correctional facility and government with which they intend to work.

There is still relatively little empirical data available about the correctional health care delivery systems in operation around the United States. Several organizations have conducted studies and continue to examine the state of correctional health care delivery systems, but large-scale research efforts are needed to provide current, accurate information about the state of correctional health care.

State Departments of Correction

The traditional organizational model places responsibility for health services with wardens. In this model, health professionals must report directly to the warden, which does not promote consistency in the policies and procedures used to operate a health care delivery system. It can also be a source of conflict and ethical concern for health care professionals if the warden is not sympathetic to the health care needs of inmates. The placement of a health services program within a state **department of corrections (DOC)** may be an indication of the perceived importance of health services (Anno, 2001). Such placement provides centralized fiscal management, standardized operations, and reduces potential for conflict between health professionals and prison administration.

The use of a statewide **health services director (HSD)** is common. An HSD is responsible for overseeing the health care delivery system, developing statewide policies and procedures, and approving the health services budget. An ideal arrangement would have an HSD as head of a separate division, with direct access to the head of the DOC. To be hired, an HSD must have had clinical and administrative experience (Anno, 1992).

In the late 1980s, several state DOCs still used the traditional organizational model, meaning that they had no one at the central office with full-time responsibility for overseeing health services, and the health professionals reported to the warden. Historically, there might have been an individual responsible for "programs," which could include anything from food service to mental and medical health care. The problem with health professionals reporting to wardens is not just that the wardens are nonmedical personnel and might not understand the need for expensive equipment. If the wardens are not progressive correctional administrators, the focus of the health staff could be shifted away from providing adequate care (Anno, 1992).

A survey conducted in 1999 by the National Commission on Correctional Health Care (NCCHC) received responses from 28 (54 percent) of the 52 prison systems surveyed. Because of the low response rate, no definitive conclusions can be drawn about the extent to which states have abandoned the traditional model. However, all but one of the 28 prison systems had at least one full-time person operating a central health office for the DOC, and some systems had more than 75 persons employed in the DOC central health office. Twenty-one of the 28 systems operated health services with contracted staff instead of or in addition to DOC employees. Only seven prison systems operated their DOC health services solely with their own employees (Anno, 2001).

Operation by State versus Contracted Firms

Correctional facilities have used contracted services for many years, mainly for ancillary services. The first such contract occurred in 1978 at a state correctional facility. Some correctional facilities have begun contracting all health services, including mental health, dental, and clinical services. Supporters of contract firms claim cost reductions to the state and improvements in the efficiency and quality of care. Critics claim that state-operated services can be cost-effective and that savings realized by firms are accomplished at the expense of inmates (Anno, 2001).

Critics also argue that for-profit correctional facilities have no incentive to spend money on adequate health services or appropriate facilities and that it is the responsibility of the government alone to punish criminals. Supporters of private enterprise cite profit as their motive for providing inmates with adequately equipped facilities and appropriate medical care, thus reducing their risk of litigation. Profit is also their incentive for using proactive policies and programs to hold costs down, something government bureaucracies have been reluctant and unable to do.

Prisons

A prison confines, houses, feeds, clothes, educates, and polices its population. Responsibility for the operation of most prisons falls under the authority of a state DOC. Within a state system, individual prisons are run by wardens or superintendents. Wardens have more or less complete control over the operation of their prison, so administrative policies and procedures may differ greatly from facility to facility.

Prisons are classified by their level of security. *Maximum security prisons* have heavily armed guards and high fences and walls, as well as very restrictive rules for controlling the movement of inmates. These facilities house the inmates who have the longest sentences. *Medium security prisons* have slightly less restrictive rules and facilities. Individuals convicted of misdemeanors—offenses less serious than felonies—are kept in medium security prisons. *Minimum security prisons* offer the least restrictive rules and facilities. They house individuals convicted of nonviolent crimes such as forgery and obstruction of justice.

The physical structure of prisons is determined in part by the population and the security measures required for their confinement. Common configurations

Photo courtesy Linda Manny

FIGURE **6-1** Fishkill Correctional Facility, Beacon, New York. (Photo courtesy of Linda Manny)

include structures that resemble a wheel hub and spokes. The hub usually houses a main security center and the spokes contain the cells. Other common designs resemble a long pole with intersecting shorter poles with cells, or a campus resembling small groups of apartment buildings (*World Book Encyclopedia*, 1996). Figure 6-1 shows an example of one type of prison design.

The **Federal Bureau of Prisons (FBP)** was established in 1930 by an act of Congress and operates under the direction of the U.S. Department of Justice. There are more than 100 federal facilities operated by the FBP, including penitentiaries, prison camps, and metropolitan correctional/detention centers. The FBP encourages inmates to participate in a range of programs that will help them live crime-free upon their release (USDOJ, n.d.). Federal prisons house individuals charged and convicted of crimes against the United States, such as kidnapping. The FBP is headquartered in Washington, DC, but the administration of facilities is divided into six regions across the country (ACA, 1996). Figure 6-2 shows one of these facilities.

An individual awaiting trial in federal courts may be free on bond or may be detained by the U.S. Marshals Service. A person who has not been sentenced but is incarcerated while awaiting trial is a *detainee*, whereas a *prisoner* has been tried and sentenced to a period of incarceration. The U.S. Marshals Service must place detainees in custody in an appropriate facility, but cannot place detainees in a federal prison. The U.S. Marshals Service ordinarily contracts with local jails, which must meet certain criteria, to house detainees.

Photo courtesy Barbara Manny

FIGURE **6-2** Federal Bureau of Prisons Metropolitan Correctional Center, Chicago, Illinois. (Photo courtesy of Barbara Manny.)

Initial health screenings of inmates are carried out within 24 hours of admission to correctional facilities. The screening begins the inmate's health record. The treatment available to inmates during their confinement varies greatly by the type and location of the facility. Variations in levels of care may result from financial considerations, characteristics of the inmate population, or availability of resources. Some correctional institutions have little more than an examination room and a visiting physician, whereas others have on-site hospitals with mental health, rehabilitation, and substance abuse services.

Jails

Jails are generally the responsibility of local governments. Most jails are administered by sheriffs who are elected officials. Reporting to the sheriff is a county administrator or a board of county commissioners. A police chief reports to the administrator or board and oversees law enforcement, while a corrections director oversees administration of the jails. In some areas, a DOC may have been developed to administer county and/or municipal jails. The FBP has its own jails in several cities, which hold individuals awaiting trial in federal courts. Some areas of the United States have federal courts but no federal detention facility. For these areas, the FBP contracts with the local jail to house the federal pretrial prisoners.

The three primary purposes for jails are (1) to detain those awaiting trial after arrest; (2) to hold those being transferred to a state or federal prison or mental facility; and (3) to incarcerate those serving a sentence of less than a year for a minor crime (misdemeanor). There are three types of jails: detention, sentenced, and detention sentenced. A *detention jail* is solely for the confinement of those awaiting trial. *Sentenced jails* are for those serving misdemeanor sentences, and *detention-sentenced jails* house both detainees and individuals who have been sentenced (Miller, 1978).

Occasionally jails are used to house inmates in an effort to alleviate overcrowding in prisons. Typically, a prison will have a contractual agreement with a jail for a specific number of beds. As soon as space becomes available at the prison, the inmates are transferred out of the jail. Housing prisoners in jails is only a temporary solution to the problem of overcrowding in prisons.

The provision of health services in jails is the responsibility of the sheriff. Some jurisdictions require screening (upon intake) for communicable diseases such as tuberculosis and venereal diseases, but all jails perform medical examinations after booking procedures have been completed. Some courts have required the screening of intoxicated persons and continuous monitoring throughout the detoxification period. This is an important precaution, because intoxication often masks symptoms of fractures, diabetes, and illnesses that could be mistaken for drunkenness. Most jails do not have on-site medical facilities. Those that do usually have only an examination room and an office. Most large urban jails have a separate infirmary with beds that are used for inmates who are too ill to remain in their cells but not ill enough to be transferred to a hospital. Inmates can be isolated in an infirmary bed to prevent the spread of communicable diseases and sometimes when their treatment includes devices that could be used as weapons, such as crutches.

Juvenile Facilities

Before the nineteenth century, juveniles were confined with adults, and, in some jails, this still occurs. Today, there are two main types of **juvenile detention facilities**: short term and long term. Responsibility for juvenile facilities belongs either to the state department of corrections or the local county.

Short-term facilities include detention centers, shelters, and reception and diagnostic centers. *Detention centers* are similar to county jails in appearance and function. These centers are used to hold juveniles awaiting jurisdictional or dispositional hearings. *Shelters* are used for dependent and neglected juveniles and are usually not secure buildings. Public shelters typically house only children awaiting an order of the court or those confined by a public welfare agency. *Reception* and *diagnostic centers* are basically way stations for juveniles moving from short- to long-term facilities. Juveniles received are screened, diagnosed, and sent to an appropriate facility based on the diagnosis. Short-term facilities are often part of state-operated juvenile systems (Klempner, 1981).

Long-term facilities include training schools, ranches, group homes, and halfway houses. *Training schools* are typically located in rural areas. The primary purpose of training schools is the reeducation and development of juvenile offenders. Juveniles learn vocational skills and can complete their high school equivalency examination (GED). *Ranches*, *camps*, and *farms* are also in rural settings and tend to offer fewer academic and vocational programs. *Group homes* are generally found in urban environments and house approximately 15 to 30 juveniles. These facilities are not secure, and residents usually attend school or have jobs. *Halfway homes* are similar to group homes. They are generally used for first-time offenders, those almost ready for release, and sometimes for juveniles with no other available living arrangements (Klempner, 1981).

Responsibility for health services at juvenile facilities rests with the authority responsible for their operation. Some juvenile facilities are within the jurisdiction of the state DOC, and others are run by a county authority. Health care services in juvenile facilities are similar to those found in other types of correctional institutions. Depending on the size of the facility, characteristics of the inmate population, and budgetary resources, the health care services may be extensive or almost nonexistent. Accredited facilities generally have disease prevention and health promotion programs that address issues such as sexually transmitted and blood-borne diseases as well as the use of tobacco products and family planning services. Counseling and mental health services are considered critical by advocates of the juvenile justice system.

Bureau of Immigration and Customs Enforcement

The United States has operated some form of immigration control since 1882. From 1940 until 2003, the Immigration and Naturalization Service (INS) was the agency responsible for enforcing immigration laws. In 2003, the border and security functions of the former INS were transferred to the Directorate of Border and Transportation Security within the Department of Homeland Security and reorganized as a part of the **Bureau of Immigration and Customs Enforcement (ICE)**. INS immigration service functions were placed into a separate **Bureau of Citizenship and Immigration Services (USCIS)**. Generally, a person applying to become a naturalized citizen of the United States must have been a person of good moral character for the given statutory period. An applicant is permanently barred from naturalization if he or she has been convicted of murder or of an aggravated felony (USCIS, 2006).

The **Division of Immigration Health Services (DIHS)**, formerly of the Health Resources and Services Administration (HRSA), was transferred to ICE's Office of Detention and Removal Operations (DRO) in October 2007. The DIHS is staffed with United States Public Health Service Officers, civil servants, and contract personnel to provide medical, dental, and mental health services to individuals in ICE custody.

Within 12 hours of admission to a detention facility, individuals receive an initial screening for tuberculosis and an intake health screening. A history and physical examination, which include a dental and mental health assessment, are conducted within 14 days of arrival at the facility. Medical emergencies are addressed immediately, and most treatment is provided on-site at the detention facilities, with referrals for nonroutine and specialty services to the community. Usually, detainees remain at detention facilities until their legal status is resolved.

On-Site versus Off-Site

A great deal of effort and research must go into the decision to provide health services on-site or off-site, and the type of services that must be available at the facility. Planning is the critical step in the process of designing a health care delivery system. Experts suggest creating a planning committee with a project director and representatives from the medical, custody, budgeting, information systems, and administrative divisions. The committee must have current, accurate data to determine to what extent health services are to be provided.

This setup involves many variables, not the least of which includes a health profile of the facility's current and expected population. Examples of information in a health profile include the expected inmate volume, health needs of the population, resources of the correctional system, resources available from other public agencies, staffing needs, and costs of transportation services, to name only a few.

Types of Patients

Inmates as patients present challenges for health care professionals. The goal of medicine to diagnose and cure and the goal of corrections to punish are sometimes in conflict. Security and personal safety are always the priority. Yet there are serious and legitimate problems that health care professionals must face when treating inmates. Legislation stressing more-stringent sentencing restrictions ensures that inmates will stay in the correctional system longer. This and other factors have a direct impact on the types of services and staffing required.

The inmate population overall is not well educated and enters the correctional system already in poor health. Inmates may make attempts to manipulate health staff, creating a difficult and potentially dangerous work environment. Inmates represent all age groups and a growing population of females. Age, sex, and offense can all have an effect on the delivery of health services in correctional settings.

Age

The age of the inmate population will affect the type of care, professionals, and staffing required. Younger populations are generally healthier and should require less staff. However, more juvenile offenders are entering correctional institutions in need of psychiatric and drug treatments. Older populations will have chronic conditions that require certain types of care. Inmates older than age 40 are a growing segment of the population. In 2005, one of every 23 inmates in prison was age 55 or older (Sentencing Project, 2006). Geriatric issues may be faced earlier than expected in correctional settings because of the related stress of incarceration and the generally poor health of inmates. Older inmates are also more likely to suffer from chronic illnesses such as hypertension, asthma, and diabetes. Conditions that are part of the aging process, such as hearing and vision loss and mental confusion, must also be addressed. Correctional facilities will have to be modified or built to accommodate the disabled and elderly.

Palliative care and hospice programs are becoming more common in prison systems, but there are institutional obstacles to their effective implementation as well. These include institutional policies that often limit prescribing narcotics to prisoners, specify limits on family visitation, prohibit visits from other inmates when a patient is in the infirmary, and prohibit inmates from serving as volunteers or workers in any "care giving" capacity (Anno, 2004). Terminally ill inmates have been treated in a number of ways. Some DOCs house terminally ill inmates in separate units; others offer hospice care (Bauersmith & Gent, 2002). Some facilities also allow for compassionate release or medical furlough programs when inmates are known to be terminally ill (Anno, 2001).

Sex

Gender also affects the type of health care services and professionals that must be available. Women will require access to gynecological services and obstetric and prenatal care if they are pregnant. The intake history for female inmates should include questions about menstrual cycles, pregnancy history, and gynecological problems. Female inmates need access to personal sanitary supplies, education on breast self-examinations, and annual Pap smears. Where state law allows, pregnant inmates retain the right to choose abortion services.

Pregnant inmates pose a special problem for correctional facilities and should be housed together with other pregnant inmates. Their work assignments must be limited to protect their condition, and special attention should be paid to their diet.

Offense

The type of offense an inmate has committed may affect the treatment received if the inmate poses a threat to security or the safety of staff. In correctional facilities, custody and security are the primary concerns, and health care is provided in a manner that does not compromise those primary concerns. Inmates are classified and confined based on the type of offense committed, and although the offense cannot be used as a reason for refusing inmates treatment, it may affect decisions to transfer inmates off-site for treatment. During periods of heightened security such as lock-downs, health staff members treat inmates in their cells.

Nature of Illness

The health status of incarcerated populations reflects and magnifies the worst trends in public health today—namely the dramatic rise in previously controlled diseases such as tuberculosis, as well as in sexually transmitted diseases, especially AIDS. This section briefly examines some of the trends health professionals working in correctional settings face today and the corresponding administrative difficulties.

After intake examinations, many inmates are found to be in the acute stages of respiratory ailments and sexually transmitted diseases. Acute conditions may also include traumas. Although prison violence is generally well controlled by correctional officers and facility rules, some inmates still suffer stab wounds, blunt trauma, and other acute or urgent conditions.

Chronic conditions are on the rise in correctional institutions for several reasons, including the rise in incarceration of individuals over age 40. From 1995 to 2005, there was an 85 percent increase in the inmate population over age 55 in both state and federal facilities (Sentencing Project, 2006). Cardiovascular diseases, end-stage renal disease, and complications from AIDS are not uncommon in correctional facilities.

Communicable diseases are commonly found in inmate populations, most notably tuberculosis and sexually transmitted diseases. The lifestyle chosen by many inmates before their incarceration includes heavy drug and alcohol use and indiscriminate sexual behavior, including prostitution. Their health is worsened by smoking cigarettes and maintaining poor nutritional habits. The treatment of chronic conditions is complicated by incarceration.

Trips to on-site or off-site appointments require the use of correctional officers for escort and the use of transportation in the case of treatment that is provided outside of the facility. Basic medical information must accompany each prisoner treated. Figure 6-3 shows a health transfer summary form completed by health professionals for prisoners who are treated off-site or transferred. Educating inmates on proper administration of their medication is also difficult.

Types of Caregivers and Services

A variety of health care professionals can be found working in a wide range of correctional settings. The extent to which services, and therefore professionals, will be available at a facility is a constant challenge for correctional administrators.

Clinical Professionals

A well-structured, adequately funded health care delivery system can employ any number of professionals. Professionals include psychiatrists, physicians, nurses (both RNs and LPNs), physician assistants, dentists, and optometrists. Other professionals encountered may have nonclinical roles, such as those of

DEPARTMENT OF CORRECTIONS
Office of the Secretary
DOC-2077 (Rev. 1/2009)

HEALTH TRANSFER SUMMARY
CONFIDENTIAL – Purpose: For Continuity of Care

WISCONSIN
Wisconsin Statute
Section 302.388 and 51.30 (4)

INSTRUCTIONS: Per §302.388 (2), Wis. Stats.: If the person initially completing this form is not a health care provider, within 24 hours of the transfer, a health care provider must review the form, sign in section #7, and forward to the receiving facility.

SENDING FACILITY _____

Street Address: _____

City, State, Zip: _____

Phone # _____ Fax # _____

HEALTH OFFICE (If not located at sending facility)

Facility/Agency _____

Phone # _____

Fax # _____

1. OFFENDER NAME _____ DOC# _____ DOB _____ SEX ☐ Male ☐ Female

TRANSFER DATE _____ RECEIVING FACILITY _____

☐ **Copy of Medical Information Sent**   Booking Date (If less than 30 days): _____

2. PRECAUTIONS: BEHAVIORAL / MENTAL HEALTH INFORMATION AND OBSERVATIONS

NOTE: Check boxes describing behaviors observed at the time of transfer or within 2 weeks prior to the transfer. Explain as needed in "Other".

☐ Disoriented / Confused   ☐ Self-Abusive Behaviors   ☐ Suicide Attempts / Threats   ☐ Hyper / Anxious
☐ Violent, Aggressive, Angry   ☐ Sad, Crying, Withdrawn   ☐ Unusual / Bizarre Behavior   ☐ **None Observed**
☐ Suicide Watch (within past 12 months), if known. If checked, give date(s) _____
☐ Other (Attach additional sheets or call phone number above) _____

Suspect Drug / Alcohol Use Within Past 7 Days? ☐ Yes ☐ No   If Tested, Date And Results: _____

Withdrawal History ☐ Yes ☐ No - If Yes, Withdrawal Symptoms Within Past Two Weeks? ☐ Yes ☐ No

3. MEDICAL CONDITIONS:

☐ Heart Disease   ☐ Diabetes   ☐ Prescribed Diet   ☐ **None Known**
☐ High Blood Pressure   ☐ Asthma   ☐ Seizure Activity

☐ Currently Pregnant, Expected Delivery Date _____
☐ Pregnancy Within Past Six Weeks – If checked, list any health complications _____
☐ **Allergies (List)** _____   ☐ **No Known Allergies**
☐ Hospitalizations / ER Visits / Surgeries (Within last 6 months) Date/Reason _____
☐ Special Needs – If checked, list _____
☐ Future Health Care Appointments (Dates, Physician/Clinic, Phone #) _____
☐ **Other:**

4. TUBERCULOSIS HISTORY ☐ Unknown

Date Last PPD Test	Result (mm)	Date Last Chest X-Ray	Result

Last Quantiferon TB Gold	Results	Check Box If INH Preventive Treatment Completed	Check Box If Treatment Completed For Active TB
		☐ Date Completed:	☐ Date Completed:

5. CURRENT MEDICATIONS AT SENDING FACILITY

☐ Copy of Medication Sheet Attached   ☐ Medications Sent   ☐ **No Prescribed Medications**

Medication Name, Dose, Frequency	Medication Name, Dose, Frequency

6. PRINT NAME AND TITLE OF PERSON COMPLETING FORM   SIGNATURE   DATE

7. HEALTH CARE PROVIDER REVIEW (Required within 24 hours of transfer if person completing form is not a health care provider)

PRINT NAME AND TITLE OF HEALTHCARE PROVIDER   SIGNATURE OF HEALTHCARE PROVIDER   DATE

Offender Seen by Health Care Provider During Current Incarceration ☐ Yes ☐ No
Form Reviewed: ☐ Accurate as Initially Completed ☐ Revisions Made ☐ Supplemental Documents Provided

8. HEALTH TRANSFER SUMMARY ACKNOWLEDGMENT (To be Completed by Receiving Facility)

Receiving Facility: _____ HAS RECEIVED HTS INFORMATION REGARDING ABOVE OFFENDER

DATE / TIME   PRINT NAME OF PERSON RECEIVING HEALTH TRANSFER INFORMATION

FIGURE **6-3** Health Transfer Summary. (Courtesy Wisconsin Department of Corrections. Used with permission.)

HEALTH TRANSFER SUMMARY INSTRUCTIONS

Sec. 302.388, Wis. Stats., requires jails, houses of corrections and prisons to provide health care information when an inmate transfers from one facility to another. The sending facility shall provide either a fully completed Health Transfer Summary (HTS) <u>or</u> the complete medical record and a partially completed at HTS *at the time of transfer*. The HTS and medical records are protected by confidentiality laws.

PLEASE PRINT LEGIBLY IN ALL FIELDS

1. **Inmate Information:**
   - Only DOC inmates have an assigned DOC#.
   - When a sending facility is forwarding an inmate's medical record to the receiving facility, check the box labeled "Copy of Medical File Sent" and attach an HTS with <u>Sections 1 and 6</u> completed, **except** that DOC completes an alternative form for inmates transferred from a DOC facility to a county jail contract bed.
   - Complete the entire HTS when the medical record is <u>not</u> being sent.
   - Note that DOC and other multi-facility jurisdictions do not need to complete an HTS when transferring an inmate within their system.

2. **Precautions: Behavioral/Mental Health Information and Observations**
   - Check boxes to indicate observed behaviors at the time of transfer or within 2 weeks prior to transfer.
   - Check "Suicide Watch" box if the inmate was on suicide watch at time of transfer or within <u>12 months prior</u> to transfer, if known by person completing the HTS.
   - Check "None Observed" box for an inmate without precautions, concerns or observations.

3. **Medical Conditions**
   - Check boxes to indicate known medical conditions.
   - Include information on recent traumas/injuries, special diets, or problems/complications.
   - "Other" may include a known disability, or prosthetic devices such as canes/walkers, eyeglasses/contacts, dentures, wheelchairs and any other special equipment.
   - Check "None Known" for an inmate with no known medical conditions.

4. **Tuberculosis History**
   - Check "Unknown" box if person completing HTS does not know the TB information.
   - Enter date of most recent PPD test and the result in mm when known.
   - Enter date of most recent Chest X-ray and result when known.
   - Enter date of most recent Quantiferon TB Gold test and result when known.
   - Check box and enter date of completion of preventive (INH) treatment or treatment for active TB when applicable.

5. **Current Medications**
   - Attach a list of medications inmate is receiving <u>at the time of transfer</u> including name of medication, and dose/frequency <u>or</u> enter the information on the HTS. Attaching a list is preferred.
   - Check the "Medications Sent" box when medications are being sent with the inmate.
   - Check the "No Medications" box when the inmate was not taking medications at the time of transfer.

6. **Person Completing Health Transfer Summary**
   - Complete this section for all transfers.
   - Print name and title of person completing the HTS.
   - Sign and date.

7. **Health Care Staff Review: <u>Required</u> if person completing the HTS is not a health care professional.**
   - Complete review within **24 hours** of receipt of the inmate.
   - Print name/title, date of review, and sign.
   - Check "YES" or NO" to indicate whether a health professional saw the inmate during the stay at sending facility.
   - Check the appropriate box to indicate whether the original HTS was accurate.

8. **Health Transfer Summary Acknowledgment: To be completed at receiving facility by jailer or health care staff.**
   - Complete this section immediately upon receipt of inmate including the date and time.
   - File the HTS in the inmate medical file.

FIGURE **6-3** (*Continued*)

social workers and counselors. Sophisticated delivery systems provide case management and other support services.

Previous shortages of physicians often reflected shortages existing in the surrounding communities. Correctional facilities were often built in rural areas, and many had insufficient funds to attract qualified professionals. Still other facilities refused to hire women, thus eliminating a potential source of applicants, and sometimes the working conditions discouraged clinicians from seeking employment in correctional health care (Anno, 1992). However, health services in prisons today are generally given by providers who are licensed, certified, or registered to practice—the same as is required in the community (Anno, 2004).

Physicians perform the physical examinations and order medications and referrals to specialists. Some of the physician's time is spent on administrative tasks. Nurses, and sometimes physician assistants, are responsible for triaging patients, recording health histories and vital signs, and taking samples for laboratory analysis. Dental services must also be included in basic health services, and optometry services should be provided as well.

Ancillary Services

Pharmacy, radiology, laboratory, and dietetics are considered ancillary services. Laboratory and radiology services may or may not be performed on-site. Medications must be administered to inmates at least twice a day, 365 days a year, and some antibiotics require more frequent administration. Some correctional facilities have been successful with "keep-on-person" medication programs that allow some inmates to maintain their own small supply of medications. It is common for facilities to have a central area where inmates go to receive their daily medications (Anno, 1992).

Emergency Services

The availability of emergency services is subject to the same variables as other health services. At a minimum, however, correctional facilities must have a plan for handling medical emergencies. Facilities must designate one or more hospital emergency departments to which inmates will be transported in case of medical emergencies. The plan must also specify arrangements, including security, for emergency evacuation and identify modes of transportation to be used. Because of the remote location of many facilities, transportation can be one of the biggest problems. Some state DOCs have their own emergency medical technicians (EMTs) and/or ambulances (Anno, 2001).

Specialty Services

Depending on a facility's population, specialty health care services may include mental health, speech and rehabilitative therapies, and more extensive dental services. Some prisons must include provisions for physically handicapped inmates or those who are vision or hearing impaired. To avoid victimization of these inmates, some prisons provide separate housing (Anno, 2001).

Mental health services available at correctional facilities often come under attack for their inadequacies. Mental health screening should be part of the intake process to identify those inmates with immediate mental health needs. Aggressive mentally ill and self-mutilating inmates require careful handling and can cause extreme management problems. Many prison and jail systems now have special programs to manage aggressive mentally ill inmates (Anno, 2001).

Mentally ill offenders also receive short shrift regarding treatment for their serious health needs in a number of prison systems. One study indicated that self-reported prevalence rates for serious mental illness among state prison inmates were at 16 percent (Ditton, 1999). While the aggressive mentally ill offender is usually identified and treated, those who may be quietly mentally ill often are not (Anno, 2004). It is of note that the accrediting agency, CARF International, publishes specific standards in its Behavioral Health program for "Criminal Justice" and "Juvenile Justice" (CARF, 2010).

Licensure

State licensing boards establish standards that control the number of professionals practicing in a state and determine minimum standards of competence. The licensing boards also define what activities may be legally performed under each type of license. Licensing standards do not set staffing ratios, but their requirements have staffing implications for health care facilities. Licensed independent practitioners employed by the federal government who provide services at federally designated locations need only be licensed in any state. This allows federal agencies staffing flexibility to meet patient care demands and changes to facility organizational needs. It also represents a valuable recruitment tool to attract physicians and other professional health care practitioners.

REGULATORY ISSUES

Regulations for correctional facilities come in many forms. Those dealing with health care services and professionals are most often found in professional licensing statutes and court orders. Correctional facilities that have hospitals, satellite facilities, mental health programs, and so on must follow established legal and professional standards. Regulation of health services is usually the responsibility of the state department of health, and applicable rules can be found in state statutes.

Accreditation programs provide an opportunity for correctional institutions to evaluate their operations against national standards, identify and correct problems, and continually improve the quality of living conditions and services. Benefits most often recognized include improved management, additional defense against lawsuits, enhanced credibility, a safer environment for inmates and staff, and the establishment of objective, measurable criteria for improving the quality of programs, staff, and the physical structure of correctional facilities.

The accreditation process is initiated by completing an application with basic information about the facility. Facilities are usually encouraged to complete a self-assessment before the on-site survey. At the conclusion of the on-site survey, members of the survey team review their findings and submit a report to an accreditation committee within the accrediting organization (Anno, 1992).

The evolution of correctional standards is significant in that they enable evaluation of correctional facilities based on compliance with objective, measurable standards. Currently, the **National Commission on Correctional Health Care (NCCHC)**, the **American Correctional Association (ACA)**, and the **American Public Health Association (APHA)** publish health care standards for correctional institutions. Except for the APHA, these associations offer voluntary accreditation for the administration of health care services in correctional institutions.

National Commission on Correctional Health Care (NCCHC)

The National Commission on Correctional Health Care (NCCHC) standards were developed by a wide range of professional health care associations, including the American Health Information Management Association (AHIMA). The NCCHC used correctional health care standards developed by the American Medical Association (AMA) in the 1970s as a template and developed separate standards for jails, prisons, and juvenile detention facilities. The NCCHC standards are the most comprehensive health standards of accrediting organizations, are more measurable, and provide the most comprehensive guidance for implementation, because they take into account the size and complexity of facilities and are complemented by an accreditation process. The major disadvantage to NCCHC standards is the lack of comprehensive standards addressing environmental and occupational health issues (Anno, 2001).

American Correctional Association (ACA)

The ACA was founded in 1870 as the National Prison Association. In 1954, the name was changed to the American Correctional Association. The ACA standards are advantageous in that they were developed and promoted by the nation's leading professional correctional association. The ACA is a private, nonprofit organization and the only organization that provides accreditation for all components of adult and juvenile correctional facilities, whereas the NCCHC standards' primary focus is health services.

The Joint Commission

Of the various standards available from the Joint Commission, its ambulatory care standards are the most applicable to health services provided in correctional facilities. An advantage of these standards is that they reflect community standards and emphasize quality improvement. The greatest disadvantages are that the standards are not specific to corrections and do not address important concerns of the health staff. The standards also do not cover dental health services (Anno, 2001).

American Public Health Association

The American Public Health Association (APHA) is not listed as an accrediting agency along with the other associations that publish health care standards because it has no corresponding accreditation program for its standards. The absence of an accreditation component makes compliance with the standards difficult to verify. The APHA standards were developed by health care professionals, and they are comprehensive, specific to corrections, and provide some guidance for implementation. A significant disadvantage of APHA standards is their attempt to apply to large and small institutions simultaneously, even when this is unwarranted or impractical (Anno, 2001).

DOCUMENTATION

Published standards recognize the importance of documentation in correctional institutions, whether for health care or administrative purposes. However, reality is sometimes very different. Documentation of factual information is essential for successful management of any organization, and is particularly crucial in the correctional setting. Inmates are a litigious group, and clear, precise, factual documentation is critical to a correctional facility's defense.

The Correctional Health Record

Managing correctional health information will challenge the best health information management (HIM) professional. The test of a truly successful and effective information system is its ability to adapt to the ever-changing needs of a growing inmate population.

The APHA standards require that health records be kept as a unit record. There is resistance to this method of organization from some mental health and other allied health professionals. When psychiatric and medical services operate separately, copies of psychiatric consultations and treatment reports should be provided to the health services department and kept in an envelope in the health record. This enables the physician to have access to important information but restricts the HIM professionals from releasing the reports. The original documentation is physically maintained at another site by the counselor or psychiatrist, and any requests for copies of the information must be directed to him or her.

The primary purpose of the health record, regardless of the setting, is to enhance communication among health professionals providing care to patients and to document the course of a patient's treatment and outcome. The secondary purpose of the health record is to serve as a legal document to protect both the facility and the patient. It also serves as an educational tool and is the basis for most quality assurance and utilization management activities (Gannon, 1988).

Format

Where facility or systemwide procedures are lacking, it is recommended that the health staff assist in establishing a standardized format for the health record. The format chosen should be based on the unique needs of the facility. HIM professionals can play an important role in educating other staff about the advantages and disadvantages of the source-oriented, problem-oriented, and integrated record formats. HIM professionals are reminded to remain flexible and open to new ideas, as must the health staff who use the record. The format should also facilitate retrieving information from the record. Abstracting is still a widely used method of accessing the wealth of information contained in health records. Neglecting to consider retrieval of information when designing the health record format and forms may hinder future efforts for automation or research.

Numbering and Filing

Inmates in state and federal prisons are assigned identification numbers upon admission to some facilities. Some large jails or detention facilities also may use ID numbers. Most state DOCs have a central office and a computer system that assigns numbers. Other methods of assigning numbers are manual and require the use of ledgers, files, and logs. Some facilities give inmates a new number if they leave and reenter the correctional system, but most assign a number that is retained for all subsequent admissions to the correctional system. The federal system also assigns inmates a computer-generated number that the inmate keeps throughout his or her confinement, even if transferred to a federal facility in another state (Gannon, 1988). In very small rural facilities, HIM professionals may be more likely to find alphabetic filing systems, whereas terminal digit filing may be used in more populated urban facilities.

Retention and Destruction

Retention and storage requirements for inactive health records are usually found in law and jurisdictional policies. In order to retain the records for the required length of time, some state prisons place records on microfilm or use imaging technology, whereas others store older paper records off-site in a central storage facility. In the federal system, inactive records remain in the facility for one year after an inmate's release. The records are sent to a central storage facility, where they are maintained for 30 years and then destroyed. Methods of destruction vary by facility. When contracting with a vendor, the responsibilities of all parties must be clearly defined. Accurate accounts of records sent for destruction must be kept to ensure that the destruction is carried out according to the terms of the agreement.

Written policies governing retention and destruction are essential. HIM professionals must ensure that retention and destruction policies follow state laws and guidelines. The state department of archives or similar authority should know the applicable regulations for retention and destruction of correctional and health-related records. Careful thought should also be given to disaster policies, such as what should be done to protect records from or restore those with fire and water damage. Some companies specialize in helping facilities recover records after disasters causing such damage. Consideration should also be given to the potential for different types of natural disasters, such as tornadoes or floods.

Health records in corrections present an interesting opportunity for the energetic HIM professional. There is a great need for data analysis in the evolving field of correctional health care, and HIM professionals should lead the way in abstracting and using the information from these records.

Transfer

Transferring inmates is a regular occurrence in correctional settings and often necessitates the transfer of health records. In some systems, a copy of pertinent information is sent with the inmate; other facilities complete a separate health summary form that may include lab results, medications, allergies, scheduled appointments, and major medical conditions such as seizure disorders. Still other facilities send the entire original record. Generally, the health record will follow the inmate. The health record must be protected from physical damage, and the confidentiality of the information must be protected as well. Frequently, copies of inmate medical records are placed into secure bags or envelopes to ensure their security during the inmate's transfer.

Detailed logs should be kept for tracking records that have been transferred and for copies that have been released. The records should be securely sealed by the transferring facility. The receiving facility should document the condition of the seal and record upon arrival to verify that no tampering has occurred. Correctional officers must not have access to inmates' health information, but they should be informed of a physical condition if the situation warrants.

Confidentiality

It is imperative that HIM professionals stay current on changes affecting the confidentiality of inmate health information. Current political trends often have a direct impact on the protection and release of inmate health information. Diseases such as AIDS and the mental health status of inmates may further complicate already difficult situations. HIM professionals must know under what conditions an inmate's record may be released and what constitutes a valid authorization. HIM professionals can face hostile attorneys, inmates, and other parties that may or may not be legally entitled to know the content of health records. The HIM professional must therefore have clear, precise policies, written in strict adherence to current law.

Privacy provisions of the Health Insurance Portability and Accountability Act (HIPAA) apply to correctional facilities that are deemed to be covered entities. However, there are some special provisions of HIPAA for correctional institutions. See the discussion of HIPAA in correctional health care later in this chapter.

Correctional officers and administrative personnel sometimes pose a special problem. Health and legal professionals agree that inmate health records must be maintained separately from any confinement records kept by the facility. For the protection of the inmate and the institution, correctional personnel should be prohibited from accessing the record. Statutory directives require reporting medical conditions to particular authorities and agencies, and these directives must be followed.

Using inmates to supplement staffing in the health services area may create additional threats to confidentiality and the safety of some inmates. Correctional organizations have standards that detail when inmates may be used as employees. The NCCHC, ACA, and AHPA standards all prohibit inmates from providing or assisting in direct patient care, determining access of other inmates to health services, or handling medical records (Anno, 2001).

There is no substitute for careful, thorough research. Policies and procedures must be unambiguous and current. Consents and authorizations make up a large part of the inmate health record. HIM professionals must be well versed in informed consent statutes and current case law, which differ from state to state and between jurisdictions.

Issues surrounding inmates' right to refuse treatment and consents by juveniles arise frequently. Forms must adhere strictly to legal requirements and should not be used without approval by an attorney. Correctional settings face additional problems of handling inmates with substance abuse problems and mentally incompetent inmates. HIM professionals must know the legal ramifications such conditions have on individuals' ability to give consent.

Administrative Information

During litigation, considerable weight is given to the administration's ability to demonstrate compliance with institutional policies and procedures and monitor staff compliance. Well-written policies and procedures imply a thoughtful and well-documented organizational philosophy. For any facility, well-written policies and procedures can help reduce training time for new employees and can reduce the potential conflicts resulting from a lack of clear direction.

The first step toward a complete set of policies is to evaluate what is currently available. The policies should be read thoroughly. It is easy for busy staff members to neglect updating procedures when a modification is necessary. It is even easier for badly written procedures to be ignored. The administration must be confident that the institution's policies are consistent with current practices.

Financial Data

Accurate financial data are essential in successfully managing correctional institutions. Because of the current method of funding (i.e., taxation), correctional facilities have difficulty receiving adequate resources to meet escalating demands for health services. Careful, accurate documentation of costs and expenditures is crucial. Once allocated, funds should be tracked and reported regularly (Anno, 2001).

Statistical Reports

Health administrators require statistical information on health care activities for budgeting, planning, and operating correctional health services. Reports should regularly reflect the number of patients served each month by each of the primary programs and information on ancillary and support services. A detailed breakdown of specific activities enhances the utility of statistical data. Statistics for off-site contracted services should be reported and monitored regularly.

Logs, Checklists, and Inspection Forms

Developing tools to monitor and measure compliance is an important contribution that HIM professionals can make. Checklists may be designed to verify compliance with other policies such as routine equipment checks. Daily operation requires tracking of patients scheduled for sick call, chronic clinics, or appointments outside the correctional facility. Logs are important for documenting supply use and release-of-information requests for health records.

REIMBURSEMENT AND FUNDING

There is no counterpart in corrections to the reimbursement arrangements that exist in other health care settings. Funding for all corrections-related activities comes from taxes appropriated by federal and state legislatures.

The management of health care costs is often more difficult for correctional institutions than for other health care facilities. Needs frequently exceed resources. This can be true even during initial stages of budget planning if the legislature rejects the budget and allocates less funding. Budget shortfalls can also occur at any time of the year because original estimates were wrong or conditions changed unexpectedly.

There are limited options for financing correctional health services. Potential sources of funding include federal government sources, private sources, payments from prisoners for care, and appropriations from state legislatures. Of these, the latter is the only funding source of any substance. Medicaid and Medicare payments generally are not available to state prisoners, and few of them carry private health insurance (Anno, 2004).

The vast majority (if not all) of the operating funds used to pay for inmates' health care comes from appropriations from state legislatures. In 2005, health care expenditures for state prison inmates represented an average of 13.3 percent of DOC total costs (ranging from 21 percent in Kansas to 6 percent in Maine) (ACA, 2006). Correctional institutions are increasingly turning to managed care arrangements as a method of paying for care received by inmates. Decision makers view managed care systems as a way to meet inmates' increasing health care needs while containing costs. Many states have contracted with private managed care organizations (MCOs) to provide health care for incarcerated individuals. An MCO that agrees to capitation payments based on the number of inmates in the system will have more incentive to deliver care efficiently than a health care organization that is paid on a fee-for-service basis.

Charging inmates for health care has been hotly debated over the years. Those arguing for collecting fees from inmates cite the astronomical cost of correctional health care as a burden to citizens that should rightfully belong to inmates. They also cite overutilization of health services and malingering as incentives for instituting a fee or copayment structure. Charging fees or copayments based on the facility's economy is thought to control abuse of health services. Supporters also argue that paying for their health care forces inmates to become responsible for their health and money. Inmates who spend their money to buy cigarettes rather than save it in case they become ill will continue making the same irrational choices once they are released.

Critics of this issue argue that if health care is a right, all inmates should have access to services at the continued expense of taxpayers. Another argument is that basing copayments on a facility's economy will not even begin to cover the cost of health services. Payments may constitute a high fee for some inmates, while clearly not compensating the facility for the cost of care. Critics claim that copayments or fees would create a tiered system favoring "wealthy" inmates (NCCHC, 1996). Opponents of fee-for-service correctional health care argue that the use of a clinically trained "gatekeeper" would help prevent abuse of the health system by malingerers without impeding access to inmates who need health care services (Anno, 2001).

The trends in **inmate self-pay** or **copayment** are illustrated by survey data collected over an 11-year period. At the end of 1994, the NCCHC conducted a survey of 206 jail jurisdictions. Of the 117 systems that responded, 35 percent charged inmates for health care and 15 percent were exploring it as an option. The majority of the programs required fixed payments between $2 and $10, and every jail system made provisions for providing emergency services (Legal issues in correctional health care, 1995). A National Institute of Corrections Survey in 1997 found that 33 state legislatures (almost two-thirds) had authorized imposition of fees on inmates for health services (Anno, 2001). By 2005, 90 percent of states responding to an American Correctional Association survey indicated that their departments of correction were charging inmates some sort of copay for specified health care services (ACA, 2006).

INFORMATION MANAGEMENT

Careful information management is essential to providing health professionals with necessary information on which to base their treatment decisions. In principle, health information management in correctional facilities is similar to that of other health care settings.

Data and Information Flow

External data are provided to correctional facilities from local governments, government agencies such as the Federal Bureau of Investigation (FBI) and the Centers for Disease Control and Prevention (CDC), and from health care facilities such as hospitals and community health clinics. Internally, data are collected by various departments during the performance of daily activities, special projects, internal audits, and so forth. Most data specific to health services come from sick call slips completed by inmates and from treatment reports provided by health staff.

One of the biggest barriers to providing inmates with adequate health care comes from a lack of access to inmate health information from hospitals and clinics. Uninformed or misinformed staff often refuse to release inmate health records to correctional facilities for the continued treatment of inmates.

In most states, release of health information is ordinarily allowed only with the prior written consent of the patient. However, information may be released without prior consent to a health professional directly involved in the care and treatment of the inmate in an emergency situation or when the inmate is unable to sign. Health information management professionals must know under what conditions inmate health information can and cannot be released. HIM professionals working in corrections should develop relationships with other professionals working in facilities with which the correctional system might contract for services. Fostering good relations will facilitate the release of information.

Coding and Classification

Coding of diseases and procedures is not routinely done in DOCs, jails, or juvenile detention centers, but the FBP does utilize the current modification of *ICD* for tracking morbidity and mortality. Classification in correctional facilities relates to the categorization of offenders according to established criteria for making housing and job assignments as well as determining security status and developing educational or rehabilitation programs. Typically, the criteria include age, sex, legal status (e.g., pretrial, detention, sentenced), and inmates' physical and mental health status (Miller, 1978).

Electronic Information Systems

A fundamental challenge to corrections is the integration of twenty-first-century information technology into nineteenth-century organizational structures. The primary purpose of current organizational structures is to maintain the integrity and hierarchy of legitimate authority positions that give bureaucratic organizations their strength. These same directives, however, tend to inhibit the flow of information within the organization (Archambeault, 1987).

The number of prisons and jails adopting electronic health record (EHR) systems is growing, although paper systems are still quite common. Even if a full-blown EHR is not in use, correctional facilities will often use electronic systems for specific functions, such as various types of logs for tracking (Paris, 2009). Although some of the incentives to convert to an EHR system do not apply to correctional health care, many of the benefits of EHR systems can be reaped in correctional health care when appropriate systems are well implemented.

HIPAA

As the privacy provisions of HIPAA were being implemented in 2003, many correctional institutions were still unsure of their status under HIPAA. A correctional facility that provides health care services and transmits health information electronically in connection with a standard transaction would be considered an HIPAA-covered entity. However, because many correctional institutions provide self-funded health care, they do not transmit health information in electronic form and therefore would not be considered covered entities. When a correctional facility is considered a covered entity, it may designate itself as a **hybrid covered entity**, which is an organization whose activities include both covered and noncovered functions. Any correctional institution that is deemed to be a covered entity would need to appoint a privacy officer, to promulgate policies and procedures protecting the privacy of inmate health information, and to allow inmates access to their health records as a general rule (Orr & Hellerstein, 2002). Correctional institutions are granted an exception to the access rule when such access would "jeopardize the health, safety, security, custody, or rehabilitation of the individual or of other inmates, or the safety of any officer, employee, or other person at the correctional institution or responsible for transporting of the inmate" (DHHS, 2000, p. 82823).

Figure 6-4 provides excerpts from the HIPAA privacy rule that pertain to correctional institutions, inmates, and health care providers that work with them. For example, a health care provider may release an inmate's

---

§ 164.512 Uses and disclosures for which an authorization or opportunity to agree or object is not required....

(j) *Standard: Uses and disclosures* to *avert a serious threat to health or safety.*

(1) *Permitted disclosures.* A covered entity may, consistent with applicable law and standards of ethical conduct, use or disclose protected health information, if the covered entity, in good faith, believes the use or disclosure....

(ii) Is necessary for law enforcement authorities to identify or apprehend an individual....

(B) Where it appears from all the circumstances that the individual has escaped from a correctional institution or from lawful custody, as those terms are defined in §164.501....

(k) *Standard: Uses and disclosures for specialized government functions....*

(5) *Correctional institutions and other law enforcement custodial situations.*

(i) *Permitted disclosures.* A covered entity may disclose to a correctional institution or a law enforcement official having lawful custody of an inmate or other individual protected health information about such inmate or individual, if the correctional institution or such law enforcement official represents that such protected health information is necessary for:

(A) The provision of health care to such individuals;

(B) The health and safety of such individual or other inmates;

(C) The health and safety of the officers or employees of or others at the correctional institution;

(D) The health and safety of such individuals and officers or other persons responsible for the transporting of inmates or their transfer from one institution, facility, or setting to another;

(E) Law enforcement on the premises of the correctional institution; and

(F) The administration and maintenance of the safety, security, and good order of the correctional institution....

FIGURE **6-4** Excerpts from HIPAA privacy regulations concerning correctional institutions and inmates. (DHHS, 2000; DHHS, 2002)

(iii) No *application after release.* For the purposes of this provision, an individual is no longer an inmate when released on parole, probation, supervised release, or otherwise is no longer in lawful custody.

§ 164.520 Notice of privacy practices for protected health information.

(a) *Standard: notice of privacy practices....*

(3) *Exception for inmates.* An inmate does not have a right to notice under this section, and the requirements of this section do not apply to a correctional institution that is a covered entity....

§ 164.524 Access of individuals to protected health information....

(2) *Unreviewable grounds for denial.* A covered entity may deny an individual access without providing the individual an opportunity for review, in the following circumstances....

(ii) A covered entity that is a correctional institution or a covered health care provider acting under the direction of the correctional institution may deny, in whole or in part, an inmate's request to obtain a copy of protected health information, if obtaining such copy would jeopardize the health, safety, security, custody, or rehabilitation of the individual or of other inmates, or the safety of any officer, employee, or other person at the correctional institution or responsible for the transporting of the inmate....

§ 164.528 Accounting of disclosures of protected health information.

(a) *Standard: Right to an accounting of disclosures of protected health information.*

(1) An individual has a right to receive an accounting of disclosures of protected health information made by a covered entity in the six years prior to the date on which the accounting is requested, except for disclosures....

(vii) To correctional institutions or law enforcement officials as provided in § 164.512(k)(5) (DHHS, 2000; DHHS, 2002)

FIGURE **6-4** (*Continued*)

health information to a correctional institution without the inmate's authorization under certain circumstances. However, when an inmate is released from custody, he or she regains all privacy rights (DHHS, 2000; DHHS, 2002). With regard to providing inmates with a "notice of privacy practices," correctional institutions are exempt from this HIPAA requirement. They should, however, make a good-faith effort to provide such a notice to former inmates who have been paroled (Orr and Hellerstein, 2002). Health care providers who do not have an EHR do not have to account for disclosures to correctional institutions as they do for other disclosures. (See Chapter 1 for the impact of the HITECH Act on accounting of disclosures when the covered entity has an EHR.) HIM professionals can play an active role in implementation and maintenance of HIPAA standards by providing expertise and guidance relating to the privacy, security, and transactions rules and regulations.

QUALITY MANAGEMENT, PERFORMANCE IMPROVEMENT, AND UTILIZATION MANAGEMENT

Over time, different terms have been used to describe the processes of quality management, performance improvement (PI), and utilization management (UM), but the basic purposes of these processes have remained the same. The goal has always been the constant improvement of the quality of health care services and the control of costs. Today, the functions of PI and UM overlap considerably and are most effective when they are coordinated with one another and with risk management programs.

Quality Management and Performance Improvement

Quality management (QM) and performance improvement (PI) involve a process of ongoing monitoring and evaluation to assess the adequacy and appropriateness of care provided and to offer a means of initiating effective corrective action when needed.

The infrastructure of correctional facilities in large part determines health professionals' ability to deliver quality care. HIM professionals can play an important role in monitoring and improving the systems that support the efforts of health professionals by assisting with the development of the QM/PI program and objectives, defining the scope and process. Critical to the success of the QM/PI program is the ability to monitor and measure the program's effectiveness and gain the support of administrators.

Services that are provided for the correctional system by contracted professionals, organizations, or other health care facilities should also be monitored. Maintenance of statistical and other data should be forwarded to the medical director and other appropriate authorities to determine whether the terms of the agreement are being met.

Accreditation is a preferred method of external review, because it provides comprehensive, objective analysis of the facility's operations, with a comparison to the facility's policies and procedures. The three accrediting agencies previously cited offer self-assessment and pre-survey consultation services. After an on-site survey, the survey team reviews its findings with the appropriate individuals of the correctional facility. Finally, a written report is submitted to the correctional facility and to an accreditation committee. The accreditation committee makes the final decision regarding the facility's accreditation status.

Utilization Management

Utilization management (UM) focuses on controlling the use of resources by reviewing a facility's efficiency in providing heath care services. The objective of UM is to maintain quality while ensuring appropriate utilization of services. The UM program should be a component of the organization-wide QM/PI effort. Accurate data are crucial for a successful UM program. A facility must be able to accurately determine the costs of providing care and assess current levels of utilization. Careful monitoring of staff time and supply and equipment costs must be done initially in order to establish a baseline figure for health service costs. HIM professionals should be instrumental in the development of an effective UM program.

RISK MANAGEMENT AND LEGAL ISSUES

Risk management (RM) and QM share similar beginnings. Both existed in other industries before emerging in health care. RM used to be distinguished from QM by its involvement with financial issues, protection of assets, and limiting professional and general liability. The legal issues faced by correctional facilities necessitate the application of RM principles and techniques.

Risk Management

The primary purpose of RM is to protect the resources of the facility and its staff. The strategies of RM and QM may sometimes overlap. Generally, QM/PI focuses on aggregate data to identify patterns and improve care; risk management focuses on individual events that may involve patients, employees, or visitors. Correctional institutions are charged with the enormous responsibilities of providing a secure environment for inmates and protecting the public, both of which expose them to substantial liability that must be managed.

When the Supreme Court required correctional facilities to provide health care to inmates, it immediately exposed the facilities to additional risk. One risk management tool that has been used by correctional facilities is the inmate **grievance process**. Grievances identify and document areas of potential risk exposure and allow corrective action to be taken to improve operations and reduce the incidence of litigation. The major objectives of a grievance process are to (1) improve institutional management and problem identification, (2) reduce inmate frustration and the potential for violence, (3) increase prospects for inmate rehabilitation, (4) hold down the volume of litigation, and (5) promote justice in institutional procedures (Brakel, 1983).

Common Legal Issues

There is no limit to the number and types of lawsuits that correctional facilities may be forced to address. In the realm of correctional health care, these issues will also raise significant ethical questions.

Inmate lawsuits take up a considerable amount of time and money. Even with grievance procedures, the number of inmate lawsuits continues to rise. Lawsuits brought by inmates claiming "deliberate indifference" to their needs are common in all correctional facilities. Defining deliberate indifference is a frequently and often hotly debated legal issue. Some professional organizations are arguing for a broader definition, and others for a more specific and limited definition.

Forced medication is also a frequent topic of ethical debate in corrections. In some instances of general psychiatric emergencies, state laws allow the use of psychotropic medications without the consent of the patient. Accrediting agencies have specific guidelines for the use of such medications and clearly defined rules under which they may be used. Inmates' refusal of treatment is also a topic of concern for many professionals working in correction facilities.

Perhaps the ultimate ethical issue for physicians is judging inmates' competency for execution. Physicians vow to "do no harm," but some insist this situation places them in direct conflict with that oath. The remedy offered by accreditation agencies is to use an independent expert and not a health care professional employed or under contract with the correctional facility.

Other Areas of Risk

Correctional health care delivery systems are at risk in other ways. Care delivered by contracted firms must be overseen and constantly reviewed for adequacy by the correctional facility. Reporting to the National Practitioner Data Bank and monitoring credentialing are other issues correctional facilities must address.

ROLE OF THE HEALTH INFORMATION MANAGEMENT PROFESSIONAL

HIM professionals will find their role in correctional settings clearly defined. They will be expected to manage the inmate health records as they would manage health records in any other setting.

Correctional facilities generate and receive enormous amounts of data, but relatively little data are being converted into useful information. Even less data are shared through electronic networks and databases. Statistical information is routinely requested and used by a variety of organizations and government agencies, but in too many cases the collection and retrieval of basic data must be done manually. Correctional facilities interested in surviving despite dwindling financial resources must look to technology and effective use of information.

The existing databases that collect correctional information usually reside in well-funded federal agencies such as the National Institute of Corrections and the U.S. Bureau of Justice Statistics. HIM professionals can find the greatest opportunities for improving the management of correctional data at the regional, local, and facility levels.

In 1990, the NCCHC established the **Certified Correctional Health Professional (CCHP) Program** to elevate the level of professionalism in the field of correctional health care. After an individual submits an application, the candidate participates in a proctored, written examination composed of 80 to 100 multiple-choice questions. An advanced certification, CCHP-A, is available to individuals who achieve the CCHP. Many HIM professionals have attained the CCHP credential. AHIMA continues to provide a representative to participate on NCCHC's board of directors. In 2009, the NCCHC Board voted AHIMA's representative as their chairman for 2009–2010, which is the first time in the history of NCCHC that an RHIA was elected to chair the board.

Another group that offers professional development and support for correctional health care professionals is the **American Correctional Health Services Association (ACHSA)**. ACHSA provides "education, skill development and support for personnel, organizations and decision makers involved in correctional health services . . ." (ACHSA, Online).

The American Correctional Association (ACA) also offers certification to health service personnel through its **Correctional Certification Program (CCP)**, but its programs are limited to nurses and individuals who serve in a management capacity. The ACA launched the Healthcare Professional Interest Section as well as the Correctional Certification Program in 2007 (ACA, n.d.).

Every setting that provides health services, without exception, can benefit from the expertise of HIM professionals. Working in correctional settings will demand the consistent application of all the principles of health information management. Ethical issues are magnified by the politically charged atmosphere. A successful HIM professional must stay current on a wide variety of legal issues and must be able to support decisions with documentation from any number of sources, including the state and federal laws, court rulings, and guidelines published by professional associations.

Opportunities for careers in corrections will continue to grow along with the industry. Mandatory sentencing, truth in sentencing, and more-restrictive drug laws continue to increase the number of inmates housed in correctional facilities. Excellent opportunities are available in corrections for HIM professionals who exhibit a high degree of excellence and maintain their professional and ethical standards. Once employed, HIM professionals should make every effort to foster relationships with educational programs and publish their experiences in professional journals.

Research is another area in which HIM professionals can excel by taking an aggressive leadership role in the proper collection and use of correctional information. It should be noted that prisoners themselves are considered a "protected class" and can rarely participate as research subjects (National Commission for the Protection of Human Subjects, 1979). Many health information managers are trained in research methods, and this knowledge is beneficial to their institutions in planning and implementing research projects appropriate to the correctional setting.

TRENDS

As the correctional industry continues to grow, various professions will continue to define their roles within the industry. Substantial improvements have been made in prison health care delivery systems over the past 30 years, resulting in better treatment for those incarcerated (Anno, 2004).

Technology improves the quality of life and allows health care professionals to be more productive by eliminating redundant tasks. Each new application of a technology creates opportunities for new professional fields. As new technologies prove to be beneficial, increased use will lower costs. Some states have implemented the electronic health record (EHR), which automates the operations of health information management in twenty-first-century correctional facilities. Because there is no formal process for sharing health information from community providers, to jail health staff, to prison health staff, and back to community providers, millions of health dollars are wasted each year repeating the same tests, exams, and information-gathering processes on the same people (Anno, 2004). Electronic health information exchange could help to avoid some of these costs.

Correctional health care has seen the introduction of technology in recent years that, as proven in private industry, has become more affordable and accessible. One technology in particular—telemedicine—is bringing the benefits of improved access to health services and cost savings to corrections. An independent experiment and evaluation of telemedicine conducted in 1999 by the U.S. Department of Justice's National Institute of Justice (NIJ), through the cooperation of the Federal Bureau of Prisons and the U.S. Department of Defense, determined that providing long-distance health care to inmates was feasible. Several federal prisons with different missions and security levels were connected via a telemedicine network. One of the federal prisons was a medical center. A Veterans' Administration hospital in Lexington, Kentucky, was also part of the network (NIJ, 2002).

In the twenty-first century, **telemedicine** or **telehealth** is widely used to provide specialist consultations and digital radiology services to inmates housed in rural to urban correctional and detention facilities—for example, in Texas, Arizona, and Wisconsin. Teleradiology is used at the majority of the DIHS clinic locations located across the country. The Federal Bureau of Prisons uses telepsychiatry at many of their prison facilities. The University of Texas Medical Branch has an extensive telemedicine program that supports its correctional health care programs. Primary care physicians are on-site to treat most medical problems, but specialists are sometimes needed to treat more complicated conditions. By using satellite links and computer networks, specialists are able to provide consultations, examinations, and evaluations to inmates while reducing the tremendous cost and risks associated with transporting inmates to off-site health care facilities. The technology also allows remote areas to have more consistent access to specialists and supplements staffing where health care personnel shortages exist. Telemedicine will not eliminate the need for inpatient care, and there is a distinct disadvantage to the specialist in not being able to touch the patient, but the programs currently in operation are viewed as highly successful.

HIM professionals can make a tremendous contribution to the application of technology in correctional health care. HIM professionals can have a huge impact on the way technology is introduced and applied in correctional settings.

SUMMARY

Corrections is a rapidly growing industry, and correctional health care is growing along with it. Working in a correctional setting creates exciting and challenging opportunities for HIM professionals. Correctional health care has a long and challenging history, with continually increasing emphasis on providing accessible health services of high quality. In this evolving field, the roles and responsibilities for managing correctional health information are still being defined. Bright, articulate, energetic HIM professionals can achieve any measure of success they desire, while creating additional opportunities for themselves and their peers as the true leaders in health information management.

KEY TERMS

American Correctional Association
a professional association of correctional administrators, wardens, superintendents, and other individuals and institutions that promotes improved correctional standards and studies causes of crime and juvenile delinquency as well as methods of crime control and prevention, offering voluntary accreditation for all components of adult and juvenile corrections.

American Correctional Health Services Association (ACHSA) a professional association of health care providers, individuals, and organizations interested in improving the quality of correctional health services.

American Public Health Association (APHA) a professional association of health care workers, administrators, epidemiologists, planners, community and mental health specialists, and interested individuals who seek to protect and promote personal, mental, and environmental health through promulgation of standards, establishment of uniform practices and procedures, and research.

Bureau of Citizenship and Immigration Services (USCIS) a division of the Department of Homeland Security responsible for the immigration service functions that were formerly performed by the Immigration and Naturalization Service (INS).

Bureau of Immigration and Customs Enforcement (ICE) a division of the Department of Homeland Security responsible for the border and security functions of the former Immigration and Naturalization Service (INS).

Certified Correctional Health Professional Program (CCHP) a certification program for health care professionals working in corrections, administered by the National Commission on Correctional Health Care.

Correctional Certification Program (CCP) a certification program offered by the American Correctional Association to correctional officers, correctional staff, staff nurses, and nurse managers working in corrections.

department of corrections (DOC) a division of state government responsible for the operation of prisons.

detainee a person held in custody awaiting trial or disposition.

Division of Immigration Health Services (DIHS) an organizational component of ICE responsible for providing health care services to individuals placed in ICE custody.

Federal Bureau of Prisons (FBP) a division of the U.S. Department of Justice responsible for the administration and operation of federal correctional facilities, including penitentiaries, prison camps, and metropolitan correctional centers.

grievance process a formal, administrative process whereby inmates may file complaints against a correctional facility for review by a panel. Institutional policies, and sometimes state statutes, determine time frames for the review process, decisions, and appeals.

health services director (HSD) an individual responsible for the administration and operation of health services within a prison system or DOC.

hybrid covered entity an organization whose activities include both covered and noncovered functions under HIPAA

inmate a person confined to a correctional institution such as a prison.

inmate self-pay or **copayment** the practice of requiring inmates to pay a (small) fee for predetermined, nonemergency medical treatments.

jail an institution administered by local units of government (i.e., cities or counties) with the authority to detain adults for a period of 48 hours or longer and to confine adults convicted of misdemeanors whose sentence does not exceed one year.

juvenile detention facility a facility operated by a unit of government for the confinement of individuals under 18 years of age.

National Commission on Correctional Health Care (NCCHC) a national association that offers voluntary accreditation of the health services in correctional facilities.

prisons facilities operated by a unit of the state or federal government for the confinement of

adults convicted of a felony whose sentence exceeds one year.

telemedicine or telehealth the application of technology where a video camera, a high-speed line, and monitoring and imaging equipment are installed at both a correctional facility and a medical facility. The telehealth equipment is linked either by high-speed communication lines, computer networks, or satellite hookups, thus allowing videoconferencing and digital images to be transmitted and received by either site.

REVIEW QUESTIONS

Knowledge-Based Questions

1. List the different types of correctional facilities.
2. What is the significance of *Estelle v. Gamble* to correctional health care?
3. What are the advantages of placing the health services program within the state department of corrections under a health services director (HSD) as opposed to placement under individual wardens?
4. Briefly describe the accreditation process. Explain options for accreditation of correctional health care programs.
5. What certifications can health professionals working in corrections receive, and through which organizations are the programs administered?

Critical Thinking Questions

1. Explain the different arguments for and against the use of contracted health services and privately operated correctional facilities.
2. What are the factors that will determine the type of health services that correctional facilities may need over the next 10 years?
3. How are correctional institutions affected by the Health Insurance Portability and Accountability Act of 1996 (HIPAA)? In what ways do HIPAA rules apply differently to the correctional setting?

WEB ACTIVITY

Visit the Web site of the National Commission on Correctional Health Care (NCCHC) at http://www. ncchc.org and click on their "Accreditation" link. How many institutions are currently accredited by NCCHC? What other helpful information about

their accreditation program is located here? Next click on the "CCHP Certification" link. What benefits are listed for a person who obtains the Certified Correctional Health Professional (CCHP) credential?

CASE STUDY

It is your first week as the health information supervisor of a reception facility in a prison system. During your initial interviews with staff, you hear

complaints of staffing shortages and poor relationships with other facilities in the system. There are so few trained medical staff that guards and some record technicians have taken on responsibility for documenting inmate histories. Members of the medical staff know they are performing duplicate lab tests, but the medical records are not available to verify previous tests and corroborate inmate complaints. You also learn that several inmates are filing lawsuits claiming deliberate indifference because a tuberculosis test was not performed on another inmate who infected his cellmates after being transferred from your facility. Because the medical records are stored by the discharging facility, they are not available to the reception center. You know by law that the staff must complete a health status within 24 hours and a physical exam within seven days, but most inmates are transferred after four days, which does not provide enough time to transfer records. A cursory examination of the electronic information system indicates that it lacks relevant data on prescription drugs, dates of tests, HIV (human immunodeficiency virus) status, and allergies, and therefore cannot compensate for a lack of medical records. The staff turnover rate at the facility averages 40 percent.

1. How will you prioritize the issues you identify?
2. What recommendations would you make?

REFERENCES AND SUGGESTED READINGS

American Correctional Association. (1985). *Jails in America: An overview of issues*. College Park, MD: author.

American Correctional Association. (1993). *Standards for the administration of correctional agencies (central office)* (2nd ed.). Laurel, MD: author.

American Correctional Association. (1996). *Directory of Juvenile and Adult Correctional Departments, Institutions, Agencies and Paroling Authorities*. Laurel, MD: author.

American Correctional Association. (2006). Inmate health care and communicable diseases. *Corrections Compendium*. [Online]. http://www.aca.org/hpis/pdf/Survey%20Summary_Tables.pdf [2010, July 16].

American Correctional Association. (n.d.). [Online]. http://aca.org [2010, July 16].

[ACHSA] American Correctional Health Services Association. [Online]. http://www.achsa.org

Anno, B. J. (1992). *Prison Health Care: Guidelines for the Management of an Adequate Delivery System*. Chicago: NCCHC.

Anno, B. J. (2001). *Correctional Health Care: Guidelines for the Management of an Adequate Delivery System*. Chicago: NCCHC.

Anno, B. J. (2004). Prison health services: An overview. *Journal of Correctional Health Care*, 10(3), pp. 287–301.

Archambeault, W. (1987). Emerging issues in the use of microcomputers as management tools in criminal justice administration. In *Microcomputers in Criminal Justice: Current Issues and Applications*. Cincinnati, OH: Anderson Publishing Co.

Bauersmith, J., and Gent, R. (2002). The Broward County Jails hospice program: Hospice in the jail. *Journal of Palliative Medicine*, 5(5), 667–670.

Brakel, S. (1983). Ruling on prisoners' grievances. *American Bar Foundation Research Journal*, 2, 393–422.

[BJS] Bureau of Justice Statistics. (2009). *Statistics of December, 2009*. [Online]. http://bjs.ojp.usdoj.gov/ [2010, July 17].

CARF International. (2010). *Behavioral Health Program Descriptions*.[Online]. http://www.carf.org/Programs/ProgramDescriptions/.

[DHHS] Department of Health and Human Services (2000). Standards for privacy of individually identifiable health information. *Federal Register*, 65(250), December 28, 82461–82829.

[DHHS] Department of Health and Human Services (2002). Standards for privacy of individually identifiable health information. *Federal Register*, 67(157), August 14, 53181–53273.

Gannon, C. (1988). *Health Records in Correctional Health Care: A Reference Manual*. Chicago: NCCHC.

Klempner, J. (1981). *Juvenile Delinquency and Juvenile Justice*. New York: F. Watts.

Legal Information Institute. (n.d.). Prisoners' rights. [Online]. http://topics.law.cornell.edu/wex/prisoners_rights [2010, March 3].

Legal issues in correctional health care to be addressed at national conference. (1995, January/February). *CorrectCare*, 9, 1, 7.

Miller, E. E. (1978). *Jail Management Problems, Programs, and Perspectives*. Lexington, MA: D. C. Heath & Co.

National Commission for the Protection of Human Subjects of Biomedical and Behavioral Research. (1979, April 18). *The Belmont Report: Ethical Principles and Guidelines for the Protection of Human Subjects of Research*. [Online]. http://ohsr.od.nih.gov/guidelines/belmont.html [2010, July 10].

[NCCHC] National Commission on Correctional Health Care. (1996). *Position Statement: Charging Inmates a Fee for Health Care Services*. Chicago: NCCHC.

[NIJ] National Institute of Justice (2002). *Implementing Telemedicine in Correctional Facilities*. [Online]. http://www.ojp.usdoj.gov/nij/pubs-sum/190310.htm [2010, July 17].

Orr, D., and Hellerstein, D. (2002). Controversy, confusion herald HIPAA. *CorrectCare*, 16(4), 1, 22. [Online]. http://www.ncchc.org/pubs/CC/hipaastudy.html [2010, March 3].

Paris, J. E. (2009). The litmus test of electronic health record performance. *CorrectCare*. [Online]. http://www.ncchc.org/pubs/CC/EHR_litmus.html [2010, July 16].

Posner, M. (1992). The Estelle medical professional judgement standard: The right of those in state custody to receive high-cost medical treatment. *American Journal of Law and Medicine, 18*(4), 347–368.

Sentencing Project. (2006, December). *New Incarceration Figures: Growth in Population Continues*. [Online]. http://www.sentencing-project.org/doc/publications/inc_newfigures.pdf [2010, July 16].

[USCIS] U.S. Bureau of Citizenship and Immigration Services. (2006). *Naturalization Eligibility Worksheet* (M-480 form). [Online]. http://www.uscis.gov/files/nativedocuments/M-480.pdf [2010, July 17].

[USDOJ] U.S. Department of Justice, Federal Bureau of Prisons. *About the Bureau of Prisons*. [Online]. http://www.bop.gov/about/index.jsp [2010, March 3].

World Book Encyclopedia. (1996). Chicago: World Book, Inc.

KEY RESOURCES

American Correctional Association (ACA)
http://www.aca.org

American Correctional Health Services Association (ACHSA)
http://www.achsa.org

American Health Information Management Association
http://www.ahima.org

American Medical Association
http://www.ama-assn.org

American Public Health Association
http://www. apha.org

Bureau of Justice Statistics
http://www.ojp.usdoj.gov

Centers for Disease Control and Prevention
http://www.cdc.gov

Division of Immigration Health Services
http://www.icehealth.org

Federal Bureau of Prisons
http://www.bop.gov

National Commission on Correctional Health Care
http://www.ncchc.org

National Criminal Justice Association
http://www.ncja.org

National Institute of Corrections (NIC), U.S. Department of Justice
http://www.nicic.org

Society of Correctional Physicians
http://www.corrdocs.org

CHAPTER 7

Mental Health: Long-Term and Acute Services

C. HARRELL WEATHERSBY, MSW, PHD

LEARNING OBJECTIVES

Upon successful completion of this chapter, you should be able to:

- Describe the various settings and caregivers commonly associated with provision of mental health services.

- Evaluate the impact of state and federal laws and regulations on the treatment of mentally ill persons.

- Describe the components of a "typical" mental health treatment record, both inpatient and outpatient.

- Discuss current reimbursement issues related to mental health treatment.

- Discuss quality improvement and utilization management within mental health facilities.

- Discuss the role of the health information manager in a mental health facility.

- Discuss the current state and use of electronic information systems in managing mental health treatment information.

- Identify the specific legal and ethical considerations associated with the confidentiality of mental health treatment records.

Setting	Description	Synonym/Examples
Outpatient Mental Health Facility	A facility where clients receive regularly scheduled outpatient mental health treatment	Community Mental Health Center
Group Home	Residential facility providing 24-hour supervision and daily living skills training on a time-limited basis to prepare clients for a less restrictive environment	Halfway House
Personal Care Home	A permanent living facility offering some supervision and meals, but no training, for persons who are too severely impaired to live completely independently	
Psychiatric Crisis Facility	A facility for short-term treatment of psychotic symptoms in an early stage	Acute Care
Inpatient Psychiatric Hospital	A facility providing long-term inpatient treatment for persons whose symptoms do not respond sufficiently to medication to allow them to live successfully in a less restrictive environment	Institution

INTRODUCTION TO SETTING

The principal setting for treatment of serious mental illness is the **community mental health center (CMHC)**. CMHCs are publicly funded entities established nationally by the Mental Health Act of 1965. This congressional legislation provided the initial funding for CMHCs on a gradually decreasing scale over a period of years, with increased funding from county and state monies intended to eventually replace the majority of the federal grants. The community mental health system was conceived as the conduit for affordable mental health services, to be provided to the public in much the same way as the state departments of health were established earlier to provide a broadly based health care system to all segments of the population.

Over time, however, this service system became increasingly focused on the more chronic segment of the mentally ill population, both adults and children. The increased need for a large-scale effort to provide supportive services for this population grew out of the discovery of **psychotropic medications** in the late 1960s, which reduced the symptoms of **psychosis** and disordered thinking. Although the medications were not universally successful, the majority of persons who previously had been destined to spend their lives in mental institutions were rendered capable of living in community settings. There followed in the 1970s and 1980s a major push to restore to the community those patients who responded well to the new medications. The process of **outpatient commitment** became feasible, making it possible for courts to place persons in need of psychiatric care in outpatient programs, with stipulations regarding taking medications and maintaining scheduled psychiatric appointments. This mass deinstitutionalization movement resulted in the downsizing of most large mental hospitals where people had been confined, as lack of any effective restorative treatment necessitated their removal from

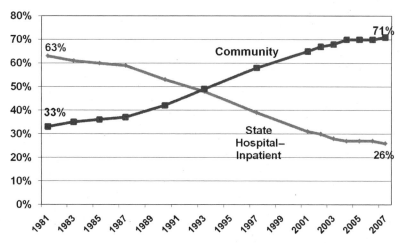

FIGURE **7-1** State mental health agency-controlled expenditures for state psychiatric hospital inpatient and community-based services as a percent of total expenditures: 1981 to 2007.

Source: NASMHPD Research Institute, Inc., under contract to SAMHSA.

society for their own safety as well as that of the public. Figure 7-1 illustrates this trend, demonstrating how the percentage of State Mental Health Authority expenditures for inpatient care has decreased, while the percentage of expenditures for community-based services has increased since 1981. To a limited extent, some private psychiatric hospitals also provide outpatient services, but seldom on the scale and of the variety that are offered by CMHCs.

The enthusiasm with which this medical breakthrough was hailed proved, however, to be somewhat premature. The medications often had rather unpleasant, and in some cases dangerous, side effects. Nor did they always work as precisely as had been hoped. Additionally, many of the persons discharged into the community had lived most of their adult lives in the structured environment of the hospital. They had little idea of how to carry on daily life within society at large. Consequently, many of them experienced extremes of stress that necessitated their return to the hospital. Or worse, they skirted the mental health system and became part of the growing homeless population that burgeoned in the 1980s and has persisted to a lesser degree ever since. Although it is difficult to get accurate statistics because of the hidden nature of the homeless persons, it is thought that approximately 20 to 25 percent of the homeless population is seriously mentally ill (National Institute of Mental Health, 2008). This group consists largely of persons who are unwilling to receive treatment principally because of the unpleasant side effects of psychotropic medications, or who are incapable of accessing the mental health system because of their disordered thinking.

A second site for provision of mental health services is the acute care inpatient hospital. The two types of acute facilities are short-term psychiatric crisis facilities and traditional inpatient psychiatric hospitals where patients who do not respond to medication can be treated for a lengthier period of time.

As the effectiveness of medication continues to improve, it has become less necessary in recent years for persons with mental illness to undergo long periods of hospitalization. Often during a period of florid psychosis, they are able to access short-term acute psychiatric care that lasts on average three to four weeks. Admittance to facilities providing this care is either voluntary or involuntary, depending on the ability of the potential patient to recognize the need for treatment. (An **involuntary commitment** is a legal process whereby individuals may be admitted to an inpatient facility even though they refuse or cannot consent to the treatment if they are legally adjudicated to be a "danger to self or others.") These inpatient facilities operate in many ways similar to long-term psychiatric hospitals. Most offer the same highly structured environment, with emphasis on group therapy and recreational activities, provided in the more traditional long-term facilities. As in the case of long-term psychiatric hospitals, they generally maintain capacity for restraint and isolation in case of violent behavior that poses a threat to the patient or to others. Their chief distinction is in the brevity of treatment. Patients who do not respond to this type of therapy fairly quickly are usually transferred to long-term hospitals for involuntary treatment through the usual legal commitment procedures.

Types of Clients

Although there are some similarities between services for adults and those designed for children and adolescents, there are also some differences. As one might expect, the different points within the life cycle occupied by these two groups make for some fundamental differences in status, both legal and educational, and in life tasks. In some cases, the illness also manifests itself differently within these two groups.

Adults

The two types of mental or emotional illness that adults are likely to experience are temporary emotional crisis related to traumatic event(s) or chronic, long-term mental illness. Temporary mental problems result from some traumatic event or series of events in a person's life, such as loss of a loved one, divorce, or bankruptcy. These emotional upheavals manifest most often in the form of extreme depression and/or suicidal tendencies. In these cases mental anguish and sad feelings can be clearly traced to a causal factor that has triggered the crisis and that can usually be dealt with through counseling or at times with mood-altering medication that can aid in lifting depression.

Long-term mental illness, on the other hand, cannot be traced so easily in a causal fashion. Its onset is a result of chemical changes in the brain, which the mental health profession is becoming increasingly skilled—with rapidly advancing technology—at observing and describing. We are as yet unable, however, to say in general what causes these changes to take place. This type of mental illness is chronic in nature, in that it can often be controlled with medication, but it cannot be cured. It receives the heaviest funding and greatest research support within the public sector, based on the concept that persons with serious, persistent mental illness are those "most in need" of the insufficient resources available for mental health treatment.

Because there are many myths about this type of mental illness, persons who have it prefer the use of terms in describing the illness that are free of the traditional connotations that arouse pity, fear, or rejection. For this reason, they particularly dislike the use of *chronic* as a descriptive term. They prefer either *long-term*, *severe*, or *serious* as descriptors of the illness, with persons with **serious mental illness (SMI)** currently being the most preferred epithet. They also favor what is known as "person first" language—that is, "a person with schizophrenia" rather than "a schizophrenic," or "persons with **manic depression**" rather than "manic-depressives." This group also has a preference in terms describing their status as service recipients. Since the 1970s there has been a movement toward political and social empowerment of persons with mental illness as part of the campaign against public stigmatization. Most service recipients prefer to be known as "mental health service consumers" (usually shortened to "consumers" once the context has been established) or "users of mental health services." Some persons also have chosen to be recognized as "psychiatric survivors," so that the term "consumer/survivor" has recently come into use. As a group they prefer this type of terminology over the more traditional "client" or "patient" (except in an inpatient situation or medical relationship, as with a doctor or nurse). They feel that these latter terms connote a "one-down" relationship and imply a dependency and inability to participate in treatment planning, as opposed to the implication of a customer relationship suggested by the terms *consumer* and *service user.*

The most common forms of serious mental illness are schizophrenia, clinical depression, and bipolar disorder, which has become the favored term for what has more widely been known as manic depression. There is another large category that encompasses persons with **dual diagnoses** (two diagnoses). These persons may be dually diagnosed mentally ill with intellectual/developmental disability (mental retardation) or mentally ill with alcohol and/or chemical addiction.

Schizophrenia is a type of psychosis, a state of extremely disordered thinking, manifesting as a break with reality. Persons with schizophrenia are unable to distinguish reality from **hallucinations** or **delusions** within their own minds. Hallucinations are false perceptions of the five senses (e.g., seeing images that are not present, hearing internal voices, feeling skin sensations that are not the result of external stimuli, tasting or smelling things that are not real). Delusions are false ideas that have no basis in fact (e.g., belief that the FBI is pursuing a person, that food is being poisoned, that the person has been chosen by a supreme being as the recipient of a divine message for the world). The root causes for the chemical changes in the brain that result in schizophrenic psychoses are not yet known.

Clinical depression appears as a deep feeling of melancholy and futility that is not situational in nature. It too results from chemical imbalances in the brain that are stress induced, but the reason for this reaction to stress in some persons and not in others remains unknown.

Bipolar disorder presents a spiral of behavior that typically begins with an episode of extreme euphoria, which in its early stages may even be highly creative, but that degenerates into hallucination and/or delusional thinking.

This phase is usually followed by a very deep depression, often reaching suicidal proportions, from which only medication can lift a person.

As indicated previously, there are two types of dually diagnosed persons within the mentally ill population. Persons with developmental disabilities may become mentally ill also, in which case they will carry a diagnosis of mental illness with mental retardation/intellectual disability. The treatment modes for this group are largely behavioral shaping techniques. The chief intervention regarding the mental illness is administration of psychotropic medication. Because of the low functioning abilities that result from the retardation, persons with this dual diagnosis often have to be followed carefully to ensure that the medication is actually being taken and in the correct dosage.

The other type of dual diagnosis occurs in persons with mental illness and an alcohol/chemical addiction. Treatment programs for these individuals are often referred to as **MICA (mental illness with chemical addiction)** services. This type of dual diagnosis is on the rise within the mental health system. Because of the wide availability of illegal recreational drugs, many young persons in particular begin to experiment, sometimes as a way to cope with the onset of the symptoms of the mental illness. Traditionally, there has been a battle waged between substance abuse service providers and mental health professionals as to who should serve this group. Consequently, members of this group have been shuttled back and forth between the two providers, depending on which illness was most in evidence at a given time, and ill served by both. There has also been a fundamental difference in treatment philosophy between the two providers, further reducing the likelihood of successful outcomes.

Substance abuse service providers typically take a confrontational approach to the addiction, with the idea that the client must face up to the addiction before help can begin. This approach often produces negative results in dually diagnosed persons because of the low self-esteem and inability to handle stress that generally accompany the mental illness. However, there has been a tendency on the part of mental health professionals to ignore the substance abuse altogether, which is equally counterproductive to a successful treatment outcome. Thus, this group has tended to have a high incidence of repeated hospitalizations: People in this group travel the cycle from achievement of sobriety in the hospital, to resumption of drug usage in the community, to onset of a psychotic episode that returns them to inpatient care—beginning the cycle all over again.

In the past several years, however, there has been a growing trend toward melding elements of both substance abuse and mental health treatment modes that are designed specifically for this population. As this cross-training occurs, it appears that an educational model is emerging. This model eschews confrontation in favor of an openness to discussion of the nature of mental illness and symptom management that incorporates material about detrimental effects of substance abuse on the efficacy of the psychotropic medications. Concomitantly, the persons with mental illness are repeatedly presented with nonconfrontational invitations, in both individual and group counseling sessions, to examine the detrimental effects that the addiction has produced in their lives.

The major symptoms for these types of serious mental illness, as well as less common ones, are described in the American Psychiatric Association's *Diagnostic and Statistical Manual of Mental Disorders,* **fourth dition, text revision** (*DSM-IV-TR*) (2000). The American Psychiatric Association has currently assembled a cluster of working groups made up of mental health experts to produce a new edition of the manual (*DSM-V*), available in draft form for comment in 2010, with final publication scheduled for 2013 (American Psychiatric Association, 2010).

In the 1970s, mental health professionals and politicians began to realize that deinstitutionalization would not work without **continuity of care,** with particular emphasis on providing a smooth transition from inpatient to outpatient services. What was needed was a service system designed to maintain mentally ill persons outside the hospital. This led to the establishment of the Community Support Program (CSP) at the federal level, an initiative that originated within the National Institute of Mental Health (NIMH), the federal center at that time for research around mental health issues. This branch of the institute undertook studies of what services were needed to adequately support mentally ill persons who were attempting to live independently and how those services could best be delivered. Concurrently, the federal funding streams for mental health were diverted to this population as the group "most in need." Disability benefits were provided in the form of **Supplemental Security Income (SSI)** for those who had not been able to establish a work history and as **Social Security Disability Income (SSDI)** for those who had sufficient investiture in the Social Security system to be eligible. Additionally, Medicaid benefits have been tied to SSI eligibility, and Medicare benefits are also available based on age or SSDI eligibility. Because these benefits are linked to diagnosis, documentation in this area becomes an extremely important part of the person's medical history. In addition to the medical diagnoses determined through use of the *Diagnostic and Statistical Manual (DSM)*, federal guidelines have been set up based on criteria of physical and psychological functioning. According to these criteria:

> adults with a serious mental illness are persons age 18 and over, who currently or at any time during the past year have had a diagnosable mental, behavioral, or emotional disorder of sufficient duration to meet diagnostic criteria specified within DSM-III-R [DSM-IV or V] that has resulted in functional impairment which substantially interferes with or limits one or more major life activities. (*Federal Register,* May 20, 1993)

CSP efforts to determine the best practice treatment methods for the maintenance of mentally ill persons outside the hospital gave rise to some changes in the traditional methods of aftercare following discharge from the hospital. The older concepts centered on partial hospitalization, which provided a setting in which former patients could continue during the day with nonstressful activities similar to those provided during hospitalization, such as handicrafts, group therapy, and recreational activities. Over time this emphasis on maintenance gradually changed to a focus on rehabilitation, the concept of moving the mental health consumer to a routine more nearly in keeping with that of a person without the illness, whose day is devoted primarily to meaningful activity. Wherever possible, the goal here is to provide actual employment, even if just part-time, because work provides to the general population one of the most powerful of all psychological connections to the society as a whole. As such, it is a major source of self-esteem. More recently, the term *recovery* has become preferred over *rehabilitation* as a descriptor for the periods of time that persons with mental illness experience when the illness is brought under control. This concept, borrowed from the treatment language for persons with drug or alcohol addictions, suggests a greater potential for long periods of enfolding into routine community life similar to that experienced by addicts during successful attainment of sobriety.

This change in vision resulted in part also from a growing demand by the consumers to have an active voice in the design and purpose of mental health programming. In time the concept of **psychosocial rehabilitation** arose. This treatment modality consists of an array of support services designed to meet the changing needs of consumers based on the degree of moribundity or floridity of their symptoms at any given point in time. Because the course of the illness and the medication side effects cannot always be predicted with perfect precision, it is essential to be able to individualize treatment plans with a great deal of flexibility. The system must be designed to meet the service needs of each person as his or her needs change with regard to more structure in times of increased psychosis or sensitivity to medication and less structure as he or she becomes more stable.

Figure 7-2 provides a concept of the ideal system of support services for the mentally ill (Parrish, 1987).

The variety of services shown that are outside the mental health system per se indicates the necessity for a holistic approach to service provision to maximize the time period that a person may remain in the community without rehospitalization. Within the mental health setting, the following options are generally considered core services likely to be needed by the majority of seriously mentally ill persons at some point in the course of their treatment (Stroul & Friedman, 1994):

- *Diagnostic evaluation and psychiatric medication management.* These services are provided by a psychiatrist, nurse practitioner, and/or nurse. If medical conditions unrelated to mental illness are present, the person is typically referred to appropriate medical personnel within the community for treatment.
- *Case management.* This service area provides linkage and brokerage to other services. Its primary function is to obtain access for the consumer to services both within and outside the mental health setting. It is thus the "glue" that provides coordination of support across the continuum and mitigates fragmentation of the service delivery system.
- *Day programming.* This area varies somewhat from system to system. The goal is to provide an opportunity for consumers to interact with both peers and professional staff. Some programs offer the more traditional partial hospitalization activities described previously. Others take a more

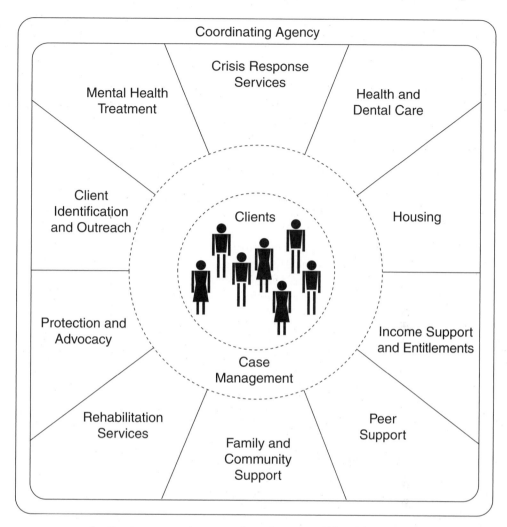

FIGURE **7-2** A client-centered comprehensive mental health system published by the National Institute of Mental Health (Parrish, 1987).

rehabilitative approach, actively preparing and encouraging the consumer to move toward employment in the job market or volunteer work in the community and more independent functioning outside the mental health system.

- *Residential living.* This alternative is offered to consumers whose level of functioning has been impaired to the extent that they are not able upon remediation of their psychotic symptoms to maintain themselves initially in an independent setting. They are placed in group home settings (sometimes referred to as halfway houses), where they typically stay for six months to a year and practice such necessary daily living skills as cooking, money management, and personal hygiene. Acquisition of these skills will then allow them to function successfully in more independent settings such as personal care homes, where they receive some assistance with meals and medication monitoring, or in apartments or houses of their own.

- *Screening and evaluation.* Determination as to the need for short-term acute psychiatric care and/or recommendation to the courts for involuntary hospitalization is generally provided through the CMHC professional staff.
- *After-hours crisis services.* Emergency services for psychiatric crises are generally provided on a 24-hour basis through a system of on-call personnel. Where necessary, screening and evaluation for involuntary hospitalization can also be provided in this way.

Adolescents and Children

Approximately 9 to 13 percent of children ages 9 to 17 have a **serious emotional disturbance (SED)** with considerable functional impairment, and 5 to 9 percent have a serious emotional disturbance with extreme functional impairment (Friedman, 1996). A federal definition for this population has also been developed, as with mentally ill adults:

> Children with a serious emotional disturbance are persons from birth to 18 who currently or at any time during the past year have had a diagnosable mental, behavioral, or emotional disorder of sufficient duration to meet diagnostic criteria specified within DSM-III-R [DSM-IV or V] that resulted in functional impairment which substantially interferes with or limits the child's role or functioning in family, school, or community activities. (*Federal Register*, 1993)

The first initiative to examine the extent of need for mental health services for this population was the Joint Commission on the Mental Health of Children in 1969 (Stroul & Friedman, 1994). As further studies were conducted and advocacy groups formed, Congress funded a federal initiative to address the gap in services. The National Institute of Mental Health (NIMH) established the **Child and Adolescent Service System Program (CASSP)** in 1984. As a result of the dispersion of NIMH programs in the late 1980s, this program, currently known as **system of care** grants, is now under the auspices of the **Center for Mental Health Services (CMHS)** of the **Substance Abuse and Mental Health Services Administration (SAMHSA)**, U.S. Department of Health and Human Services. The goal of the program is to assist states in creating systems of care for children and youth who have severe emotional disturbances. According to CMHS, a "system of care" is "an organizational philosophy and framework that involves collaboration across agencies, families, and youth for the purpose of improving access and expanding the array of coordinated community-based, culturally and linguistically competent services and supports for children and youth with a serious emotional disturbance and their families. Research has demonstrated that systems of care have a positive effect on the structure, organization, and availability of services for children and youth with serious mental health needs" (CMHS, 2009, para 2).

Core services needed within the mental health system itself were initially identified as follows (Stroul & Friedman, 1994) (although *children* is used to describe the clientele, it should be understood to include adolescents unless otherwise specified):

- *Early identification and intervention.* This effort necessarily crosses several service systems (e.g., health, education), but mental health has a role to play. The earlier that identification of problems occurs, the better the chance for successful treatment. However, sometimes the problems or their seriousness may not become manifested clearly until latency age or adolescence. Identification of multiproblem families who seek mental health services, regardless of the age of the child, may be a first step.
- *Diagnosis and evaluation.* Again, this area may include several systems. It will usually include assessments of physical health, intelligence level, and academic achievement or potential; social and behavioral functioning; family dynamics; and environmental factors, such as degree of poverty and type of housing.
- *Outpatient treatment.* This intervention usually entails regularly scheduled appointments for individual, group, and/or family therapy, with a frequency based on need. Although there is some question as to the effectiveness of this type of treatment, some studies seem to indicate that it can be helpful (Sowder, 1979; Casey & Burman, 1985).
- *Day treatment.* This service involves an integration of educational and mental health services, whether established formally between agencies or not. Intensive treatment includes carefully integrated components of education, counseling, and family therapy and is generally provided during school hours. Service provision may occur in a variety of settings, from regular schools, to special schools, to the mental health center. This service is much like the partial hospitalization program for adults, except for the usual inclusion and particular emphasis on the educational component.
- *Emergency services.* Crisis response is similar to that for adults, although somewhat rarer for children (Stroul & Friedman, 1994). Such services for children also may include runaway shelters and home-based services that are unique to this population.
- *Home-based services.* Other terms for this type of intervention include in-home services, family-centered services, intensive family services, and family preservation services. This category encompasses a rather wide range of services provided. The commonality among them all is that they are family rather than individual centered (Hutchinson et al., 1983), and, as the term implies, the majority of the services are delivered in the home. Most of these programs have the following goals in common: "preserving the integrity of the family and preventing unnecessary out-of-home placement; linking the child and family with appropriate community agencies and individuals to create an ongoing community support system; and strengthening the family's coping skills and capacity to function effectively in the community" (Stroul & Friedman, 1994).

- *Therapeutic foster care.* This service "provides treatment for troubled children within the private homes of trained families" (Stroul & Friedman, 1994). It provides a homelike atmosphere in which treatment interventions can be applied. It looks similar to traditional foster care, but the families receive special training in how to cope with the extreme emotional disturbance that has led to removal of the child from the family. In terms of removal from the home of origin, this setting is considered the least restrictive in the continuum of alternative placements because of its capacity to most nearly duplicate a home environment.

- *Therapeutic group home.* This type of residential setting involves congregate care somewhat similar to that of the adult group home. Some group homes exist primarily to serve less severely disturbed children who need care of a protective nature because of abuse or neglect. These children typically need a mental health treatment component as well as the highly structured environment typical of these programs. Generally, a therapeutic group home is defined as "a single home, located in the general community, that serves no more than eight children" (Stroul & Friedman, 1994). These entities can vary greatly in staff-to-child ratio, depending on severity of psychological impairment and intensity of treatment. Two distinct models of care are used. The teaching family model employs a married couple who live with the children in family-like arrangements, with relief help to provide time off. The other model employs shifts of workers who rotate to provide 24-hour care and supervision. Treatment approaches vary, but they generally include individual and group counseling along with a behavior modification program.

- *Inpatient hospitalization.* This setting is utilized in extreme situations. Children who demonstrate signs that they might seriously harm themselves or others are referred for hospitalization. With increasing frequency, as the home-based services become more generally available, such hospital stays are of short duration, usually a matter of days or a few weeks at most. Occasionally, however, there are situations where a child's difficulties are so severe that long-term hospitalization becomes the only option. This setting is also used for conducting comprehensive evaluations, particularly where the possible presence of neurological or other physiological complications may require extensive testing and observation over time.

As the core services have become more developed, a new concept, known as **wrap-around services**, has become the predominant method of service delivery for emotionally disturbed children and adolescents. Wrap-around services are community-based services that attempt to prevent the necessity for more restrictive levels of care. As the term *wrap-around* suggests, this is a comprehensive array of professional services that includes the child's home and/or school setting. The essential features of this service approach entail individualization of services to fit the specific needs of each child and family, maximization of the strengths of the child's family and natural support systems as resources, and attention to the cultural values of the child's family and community in the way that services are developed and delivered (Furman, 1997).

As an almost necessary adjunct to wrap-around services, the notion of flexible funding has come into use. This concept allows for funding to be used for development of nontraditional services such as respite care, which allows for brief "cooling off" periods during times of high emotional crisis when the child can temporarily be cared for outside the home. Mentoring programs are another example of highly successful nontraditional services in which successful members of the community are encouraged to volunteer as companions to troubled youths of similar culture and background, as a means of providing guidance and stability through the relationship.

Types of Caregivers

There are many professional and educational backgrounds and requirements for caregivers within the mental health system. With only a few exceptions, the types of workers providing both adults' and children's services tend to be the same. Likewise, the types of staff found in both the inpatient and outpatient settings tend to be similar, although their actual daily duties and responsibilities may differ in the degree of structure and control provided.

Medical Personnel

Because psychotropic medication is generally essential to the maintenance of stability in serious mental illness, the psychiatrist plays a central treatment role in performing diagnosis and evaluation and providing medication management. Many of the medications prescribed for the illness can have severe and in some cases fatal consequences if their levels are not carefully monitored at regular intervals. Dosages may also have to be adjusted from time to time because of increases or decreases in the amount of stress a person is experiencing or because of metabolic changes in the body over time. It is the role of the physician to oversee these matters. In most settings there is also a nurse to assist the physician, providing follow-up care as prescribed. These duties would typically include monitoring of blood work and medication levels, provision of injections if the psychotropic medication is prescribed in this form, and assistance with minor side effects of the medication. Although somewhat less frequently found at present in the mental health field, there is a growing number of nurse practitioners who can, under supervision of a physician, perform some of the physician's functions, including the prescription of medication.

Therapists

This category includes a wide diversity of workers. It encompasses psychologists, master's-level and bachelor's-level social workers, and community counselors. Each of these disciplines has a certification mechanism at the national level, and most states also require a state license to practice. Persons at the master's level or higher in social work and psychology are usually allowed to perform diagnostic and evaluation screening for mental illness.

In some cases, this function is provided under supervision of a psychiatrist. In some states, psychologists have gained the authority to prescribe some drugs on a limited basis and with a physician's oversight.

Where short-term, situational emotional disturbance exists, the therapist—either bachelor's or master's level—performs a counseling function. It is generally thought that persons with serious mental illness who are in a stable mental state do not benefit greatly from traditional talk therapy, and that in fact it may sometimes produce negative effects by increasing stress when discussion turns to unhappy events. However, one symptom of mental illness that is not always as readily apparent as the psychoses is called "poverty of thought." This symptom is characterized by an inability to generate alternative solutions to a problem. It is therefore sometimes useful to have available a person who can counsel the consumer who is experiencing a current life crisis and cannot seem to find a viable solution. In some settings, the therapist will also conduct group therapy, especially where the traditional partial hospitalization model is used as a day care program. In the inpatient setting, group therapy is a standard form of treatment and is generally conducted by a therapist.

Case Managers

The case manager's credentials vary widely from state to state. Most possess a bachelor's degree, but there is generally great latitude as to the field of study. The chief responsibility of the case manager is to provide the consumer in the community with access to services across the spectrum of support services, as indicated in Figure 7-2. Thus the chief functions of this position are referral to needed services, coordination among service providers, and monitoring for escalation of psychotic symptoms. In general, case managers are prohibited from offering counseling and therapy because of licensure and Medicaid restrictions. In rare cases, appropriately licensed persons are used in intensive case management programs that include a counseling component for which the target population is a small caseload of consumers (usually no more than 10) who tend to be high users of inpatient hospitalization. Persons providing the intensive home-based services to families of emotionally disturbed children would also perform many of the same functions as case managers for adults.

Aides/Direct Care Workers

This group of workers goes by different appellations within the various settings where they work: direct care workers (DCWs), residential living technicians, or certified nursing aides (CNAs). Their primary duties revolve around providing assistance with daily living skills to persons in the inpatient setting or in community group homes. In each of these settings, 24-hour care and supervision are generally provided. Levels of certification vary, but generally a high school diploma or general equivalency diploma (GED) is required.

Recreation Therapists

Recreation therapists are more likely to be found in the inpatient setting than in the community mental health setting, unless the program is conducting a partial hospitalization component. They are employed most often in the structured setting to provide an antidote for the lassitude that often accompanies the illness, especially in its acute state, and to provide activity and distraction, which generally ameliorate psychotic symptoms.

Occupational Therapists

Occupational therapists typically work in the inpatient setting. They assess functioning abilities and prescribe programs designed to restore the patients' capacities to work, where feasible, and they teach daily living skills that will increase the likelihood of the patients' successful transitions to community living. They may also be found occasionally in rehabilitative roles within the community setting where the outpatient day program has an emphasis in this direction.

REGULATORY ISSUES

Mental health centers typically receive certification from a designated state regulatory agency, usually a department or office of mental health. These agencies establish licensure standards and perform monitoring functions accordingly. As mental health consumers and their family members have become increasingly politicized in recent years, the agencies have engaged in a steady effort to make the regulations for licensure more outcome based. The thrust is more toward measurement of quality of services than of quantity or frequency of delivery.

Another regulatory mechanism exists at the state level for both inpatient and outpatient facilities that wish to receive Medicaid. They must comply with the Medicaid guidelines set and monitored by the state agency designated as the regulatory body for this funding. Similarly, facilities that receive Medicare reimbursement must comply with the applicable Conditions of Participation. The Conditions of Participation for hospitals include special provisions applying to psychiatric hospitals in sections 482.60–482.62, including special medical record requirements for psychiatric hospitals. The "Interpretive Guidelines and Survey Procedures" for psychiatric hospitals are found in Appendix AA of the *State Operations Manual* (CMS, n.d.). These guidelines provide state surveyors with detailed explanations for interpreting and applying the Conditions of Participation during the survey of a psychiatric hospital. Medicare and Medicaid coverage is tied to diagnosis and to a physician's prescription for the entire array of services to be provided as "medically necessary." Thus accuracy of documentation in this area is extremely important.

Several other regulatory entities set standards for mental health service delivery by virtue of their accrediting processes. A mental health service provider may seek accreditation by one or more of the following groups: the Joint Commission (TJC), CARF International (formerly the Commission on Accreditation of Rehabilitation Facilities), the National Committee for Quality Assurance (NCQA), or URAC (formerly the Utilization Review Accreditation Commission).

The Joint Commission provides accreditation for both inpatient and outpatient mental health facilities. A facility licensed as a hospital is surveyed under the *Comprehensive Accreditation Manual for Hospitals (CAMH)*. If the hospital offers residential treatment, partial hospitalization, or supervised living programs, the Joint Commission conducts a tailored survey using selected standards from the *Comprehensive Accreditation Manual for Behavioral Health Care (CAMBHC)* in addition to the standards in the *CAMH*. Other mental health service providers that are freestanding (i.e., that are not affiliated with a hospital) are surveyed by the Joint Commission under the *CAMBHC* only.

CARF provides an accrediting process for mental health and psychosocial rehabilitation programs. Programs that can be accredited include case management, crisis intervention, outpatient treatment, partial hospitalization, residential treatment, community housing, inpatient treatment, assertive community treatment, and many other services. A mental health facility seeking accreditation from CARF would be surveyed under its *Behavioral Health Standards Manual* (CARF, n.d.).

NCQA offers an accreditation program to managed behavioral health care organizations (MBHOs). An MBHO may be a managed behavioral health care company or a behavioral health program or department within a managed care organization (MCO). At the request of an MCO or MBHO, NCQA surveys mental health services under the *MBHO Standards and Guidelines* (National Committee for Quality Assurance, n.d.).

Clinical services of MBHOs are also often accredited by URAC. URAC also accredits case management services.

DOCUMENTATION

There is considerable similarity among mental health case records, whether inpatient or outpatient, and other medically oriented records. Although content and arrangement vary, certain information is basic to all treatment of individuals with mental illness and appears in some form in the mental health record. This includes assessment, treatment plan, progress notes, and discharge summary with plans for aftercare (Conditions of Participation, 2009).

Assessment

At the first contact between a consumer/patient and a mental health facility, an initial assessment is performed. This could occur in a telephone contact or in an emergency encounter. The initial assessment focuses on the patient's apparent needs and whether those needs can be appropriately addressed by the facility. In some instances, the result of the initial assessment is that the patient is referred elsewhere for further services. If it is determined that the patient should be admitted to the original facility, the initial assessment serves as a basis for determining which services of the facility are most appropriate.

The assessment process continues with the completion of the intake or general assessment. The mental health professional performing the intake gathers any remaining demographic information that has not yet been collected.

A history of previous hospitalizations or other medical difficulties is elicited. If the consumer or patient is in a psychotic state that renders him or her unreliable, the professional seeks this information from collateral contacts where possible. Regardless of the patient's mental status, some time should be spent gaining the consumer's perception of why he or she is present for the interview. If possible, the professional should determine the presenting problem from the point of view of the consumer/patient. It is important that the assessment be holistic in nature, so that possible physically based problems can be ruled out as contributory or ancillary to the interviewee's mental problems. For instance, diabetes can cause mania-like symptoms similar to those of bipolar disorder when insulin dosages are not accurate.

A complete assessment may include any or all of the following: physical, emotional, behavioral, social, recreational, legal, vocational, and/or nutritional components (Huffman, 1994). It should also be noted that assessment is an ongoing process. It may often take several interviews for the consumer/patient to gain sufficient trust to fully state the nature of his or her problem(s). Also, these concerns may change over time as some problems reach resolution or, in some cases, unfortunately prove to be unsolvable. Certain events or circumstances—such as the use of restraints or seclusion, a recommendation for electroconvulsive therapy, or a recommendation for a therapeutic pass— may trigger a new assessment. Most facilities have policies stating how often assessments will be routinely repeated. Comments from patients or significant others may trigger a new assessment at a date earlier than scheduled.

The federal Conditions of Participation outline specific medical record requirements for psychiatric hospitals. One of these standards requires that each inpatient receive a psychiatric evaluation. The psychiatric evaluation must be completed within 60 hours of admission and must cover specific content areas such as medical history, mental status, the onset of illness, attitudes and behavior, intellectual and memory functioning, orientation, and an inventory of the patient's assets. For other federal requirements specific to psychiatric hospital records, see Figure 7-3 (Conditions of Participation, 2009).

Treatment Plan

Traditionally the assessment process has been a procedure by which the interviewer or team evaluates the consumer/patient's level of functioning. The problems have thus been defined essentially as deficits in functioning that need to be addressed in the treatment plan, with steps to mitigate or eliminate the problem outlined. As consumers have embraced the notion of empowerment, however, they have become more insistent on participation in the treatment planning process. Particularly in the outpatient setting, consumers have complained that the established method placed them in a position of inferiority in relationship to the interviewer and often resulted in a treatment plan in which they had little interest and no investiture. To expedite and encourage the consumer's participation, a strengths model of treatment planning has emerged in the community mental health sector. Using this approach, the interviewer determines from the consumer what goals he or she is interested in pursuing. The interviewer and the consumer then work out a mutual plan whereby the

§ 482.61 Condition of participation: Special medical record requirements for psychiatric hospitals.

The medical records maintained by a psychiatric hospital must permit determination of the degree and intensity of the treatment provided to individuals who are furnished services in the institution.

(a) *Standard: Development of assessment/diagnostic data.* Medical records must stress the psychiatric components of the record, including history of findings and treatment provided for the psychiatric condition for which the patient is hospitalized.

(1) The identification data must include the patient's legal status.

(2) A provisional or admitting diagnosis must be made on every patient at the time of admission, and must include the diagnoses of intercurrent diseases as well as the psychiatric diagnoses.

(3) The reasons for admission must be clearly documented as stated by the patient and/or others significantly involved.

(4) The social service records, including reports of interviews with patients, family members, and others, must provide an assessment of home plans and family attitudes, and community resource contacts as well as a social history.

(5) When indicated, a complete neurological examination must be recorded at the time of the admission physical examination.

(b) *Standard: Psychiatric evaluation.* Each patient must receive a psychiatric evaluation that must—

(1) Be completed within 60 hours of admission;

(2) Include a medical history;

(3) Contain a record of mental status;

(4) Note the onset of illness and the circumstances leading to admission;

(5) Describe attitudes and behavior;

(6) Estimate intellectual functioning, memory functioning, and orientation; and

(7) Include an inventory of the patient's assets in descriptive, not interpretative, fashion.

(c) *Standard: Treatment plan.*

(1) Each patient must have an individual comprehensive treatment plan that must be based on an inventory of the patient's strengths and disabilities. The written plan must include—

(i) A substantiated diagnosis;

(ii) Short-term and long-range goals;

(iii) The specific treatment modalities utilized;

(iv) The responsibilities of each member of the treatment team; and

(v) Adequate documentation to justify the diagnosis and the treatment and rehabilitation activities carried out.

FIGURE **7-3** Excerpt from the Conditions of Participation (2009) outlining special medical record requirements for psychiatric hospitals.

(2) The treatment received by the patient must be documented in such a way to assure that all active therapeutic efforts are included.

(d) *Standard: Recording progress.* Progress notes must be recorded by the doctor of medicine or osteopathy responsible for the care of the patient as specified in § 482.12(c), nurse, social worker and, when appropriate, others significantly involved in active treatment modalities. The frequency of progress notes is determined by the condition of the patient but must be recorded at least weekly for the first 2 months and at least once a month thereafter and must contain recommendations for revisions in the treatment plan as indicated as well as precise assessment of the patient's progress in accordance with the original or revised treatment plan.

(e) *Standard: Discharge planning and discharge summary.* The record of each patient who has been discharged must have a discharge summary that includes a recapitulation of the patient's hospitalization and recommendations from appropriate services concerning follow-up or aftercare as well as a brief summary of the patient's condition on discharge.

[72 FR 60788, Oct. 26, 2007]

FIGURE **7-3** (*Continued*)

goal may be achieved. If the goal is a result of unrealistic thinking, the interviewer typically does not discourage the goal, but rather creatively attempts to find some facet of the goal that may be achievable. For instance, if a consumer sets as a goal the fulfillment of a lifelong dream to be a concert pianist but has never had a piano lesson, the interviewer may suggest as a first step attendance of a music appreciation class.

In most instances, the consumer will recognize an unattainable goal, and the goal can then be relinquished in favor of a more realistic one. At the same time, the professional's acquiescence to and participation in goals of interest to the consumer may open him or her to eventual consideration of goals that the professional may believe they need to work on together. If the consumer enjoys the music appreciation class, he or she may be more willing to stay on medication to avoid a relapse and the need to give up attending it. This model, and the underlying concept of client empowerment, is increasingly becoming the preferred treatment mode nationwide. A sample treatment plan form for case management using the strengths model is shown in Figure 7-4.

This model poses something of a challenge for health information managers, however, because it is not as easy to document progress using this model as it has been with the functional assessment approach. In using the older model, the professional typically identifies a deficit; prescribes a treatment solution and a time frame for success; and documents either a successful outcome, in which case the goal is eliminated, or a failure, in which case the goal is either dropped as unattainable or a different intervention strategy is proposed.

LIFE DOMAINS ASSESSMENT

Consumer Name: _____ Case # _____ Dx Code _____ Date _____

Admitted to Case Management: _____ Yes _____ No

Frequency of Contact: _____ High _____ Moderate _____ Low _____ Follow Along

_____   _____

       Consumer Signature   Staff Signature

LIFE DOMAINS	CURRENT STATUS (Include Strengths and Barriers)	PERSONAL COAL (What do I want?)
LIVING ARRANGEMENTS		
Location		
Safety		
Adequacy		
LIFE SKILLS		
Home Management/Bill Paying		
ADL's		
Transportation		
Utilization of Resources		
SOCIAL SUPPORTS		
Family/Friends/Spiritual		
Interpersonal Relationships		
VOC/ED		
Education/Employment		
Skills		
FINANCIAL/LEGAL		
Monthly Income		
Money Management/Debts		
HEALTH/MENTAL HEALTH		
Physical Symptoms/Needs		
Psychological Symptoms/Needs		
Medication/Tx. Compliance		
Substance Abuse		
Physical/Emotional Abuse		
LEISURE/RECREATIONAL		
Exercise		
Recreation/Socialization		

CONSUMER STRENGTHS SUMMARY:

FIGURE 7-4 Sample assessment form for case management using the strengths model. (From the Case Record Guide produced by the Mississippi Department of Mental Health.)

Although there is an increased attempt to involve the patient within an institution in treatment planning, the degree of the illness makes necessary the continued use of the functional assessment methodology to a large extent. The chief goal within the inpatient setting is virtually always stabilization to the point that the patient can be discharged into the community. Accomplishment of this aim often requires a highly structured approach to changing behaviors that are not contributory to that end. Therefore, the strengths model must be utilized in a somewhat modified form.

Progress Notes

Progress notes mark the achievement or lack thereof in the attempts of the consumer or patient to reach the goals stated in the treatment plan. Accreditation surveyors often check to see that every goal in a treatment plan has corresponding progress notes. There may be some general progress notes that do not relate to a specific treatment plan goal. However, most progress notes are tied directly to the treatment plan.

Progress notes are often also extremely important as documentation that a service was performed as a basis for reimbursement from Medicaid, Medicare, or client insurance ("If it isn't written, it didn't happen."). As a basis for reimbursement, the timeliness of the note also becomes a central issue, as most regulatory agencies place considerable emphasis on regular intervals of review and updates of the treatment plan, which are also generally recorded in a progress note.

One of the advantages of an electronic mental health record is that the documentation of progress notes can be electronically monitored. Some systems prompt the clinician with treatment plan goals when the clinician is writing progress notes. Some organizations prepare automated reports that indicate treatment plan goals for which no progress notes have yet been written. The same type of report can also indicate services billed that lack progress notes, or the reverse—progress notes for services performed but not billed.

For psychiatric hospitals, the Conditions of Participation specify that physicians, nurses, social workers, and others involved in active treatment of the patient must record progress notes. These standards require progress notes at least weekly for the first two months and at least once a month thereafter (see Figure 7-3) (Conditions of Participation, 2009). Because of the importance of progress notes to the care of the patient, accreditation, and reimbursement, there is great incentive in a psychiatric hospital to properly document progress notes.

Special Procedures

Certain procedures may be necessary in the mental health setting that may not be used in the treatment of other types of disorders. For example, a patient who is threatening injury to self or to others may be placed in restraints or in seclusion. Examples of other types of special procedures include psychosurgery and electroconvulsive therapy. When special procedures are used, proper documentation of their use is extremely important (Huffman, 1994).

The documentation regarding the use of seclusion or restraints serves as an example of the extensive documentation necessary when special procedures are used. Following a public advocacy campaign for stricter oversight of policies and procedures with regard to use of restraints and seclusion, Congress initiated an investigation of the use of these emergency safety interventions. Findings indicated an unacceptably high rate of death and injury to both staff and patients as a result of improper use or poorly planned procedures for implementation of these interventions. Accordingly, Congress called for stricter regulations governing the use of restraints and seclusion for both children and adults in facilities receiving Medicaid or Medicare funding.

As a result, the Centers for Medicare & Medicaid Services (CMS)—formerly the Health Care Finance Administration (HCFA)—proposed rules in 1999 that granted patients protection from inappropriate restraint or seclusion. The latest version of these rules was promulgated in the Final Rule, Hospital Conditions of Participation of Patients' Rights, effective January, 2007. These guidelines strengthened the rules for conditions under which these interventions could be used, the procedures to be followed prior to and during use, and the training required for personnel qualified to administer them (*Federal Register*, 2006). Accordingly, documentation must begin upon the patient's entry to the facility with "notification of the right to be free from the inappropriate use of restraint and seclusion with requirements that protect the patient when use of either intervention is necessary" (p. 71378) and continue surrounding the entire event in the case of utilization of such emergency safety interventions—from the decision-making process through implementation of the procedure and including follow-up evaluative measures.

Restraints are defined as being of two types: physical and chemical. **Physical restraint** is described as:

> mechanical or personal restriction that immobilizes or reduces the ability of an
> individual to move his or her arms, legs, or head freely, not including devices . . .
> for the purpose of conducting routine physical examinations or tests or
> to protect the resident from falling out of bed or to permit the resident to
> participate in activities without the risk of physical harm to the resident. . . ."
> (P. L. 106-310, 2000, pp. 1195–1196).

Chemical restraint is defined as the use of a drug or medication not part of a person's usual medical regimen that is administered to control behavior or restrict freedom of movement (P. L. 106-310, 2000).

The rules for applying restraint or seclusion require an order from a board-certified psychiatrist or a physician with specialized training and experience in diagnosis and treatment of mental disorders. Assessment of the need for such procedures must include consideration of all possible alternatives and rationale for the chosen intervention. At bottom, the issue must be the safety of the patient. Such intervention must also be the least restrictive possible in order to achieve the desired outcome. Within one hour of initiation of such an emergency safety intervention, there must be a face-to-face assessment of the psychological and physical well-being of the patient conducted by a physician, registered nurse, or other professionals qualified by special training in the use of emergency safety interventions (*Federal Register*, 2008).

The regulations emphasize in particular the issue of training for all staff who are involved in any way in the process of emergency safety intervention. Such training must be conducted upon hire and updated semiannually. Documentation of the type of training developed and staff in attendance at each session is required. Time limits for the procedure have also been changed: The physician's order may not exceed four hours for patients ages 18 to 21, two hours for patients ages 9 to 17, and one hour for residents under age 9. The Final Rule also expands the category of practitioners who may carry out patient evaluation during the first hour of implementation: In addition to physicians, a trained registered nurse (RN) or physician assistant (PA) may conduct the face-to-face observation but must consult with the physician as soon as possible thereafter. Distinction is also made between time-out, which by definition implies that the patient is not physically restrained from leaving the area, and the more restrictive nature of emergency safety interventions, although staff is also required to monitor persons placed in time-out. In the case of minors, parents or guardians must also be notified of the intervention as soon as possible, and notification must be documented. During restraint, trained staff must be physically present and continually monitoring the physical and psychological well-being of the patient and the safety of the restraining device. Use of seclusion requires trained staff either physically present or just outside the seclusion room, continually monitoring and assessing the patient's physical and psychological well-being. Staff administering the procedure must document its use in the patient's record by the end of the shift in which the intervention has taken place. A physician or appropriately trained registered nurse must conduct an evaluation of the patient's well-being immediately after cessation of restraint or seclusion. Within 24 hours after the use of an emergency safety intervention, involved staff and the patient must have a face-to-face discussion. Within the same time frame, a second debriefing is to occur with all involved staff and appropriate supervisory and administrative staff. A chief topic in both meetings is to see how such an intervention might be avoided in the future. Staff must document both of these meetings. If a patient is seriously injured or dies during or possibly because of use of restraint or seclusion, the facility must report the incident to both the state Medicaid agency and the state-designated protection and advocacy agency by no later than close of business the next business day (*Federal Register*, 2001).

Additionally, Congress enacted the Children's Health Act of 2000. This legislation applied specific restrictions to utilization of emergency safety interventions with children and youth, particularly those residing in nonmedical community-based residential facilities receiving Medicaid. Most notably, use of mechanical restraints with children was altogether prohibited in these facilities. Also defined is the concept of "physical escort," which is contrasted with "physical restraint." Whereas *physical restraint* is defined as a restriction that immobilizes an individual or severely limits his or her ability to move arms, legs, or head freely (as defined previously), *physical escort* is defined otherwise and is permitted. The latter is "temporary touching or holding of the hand, wrist, arm, shoulder, or back for the purpose of inducing a resident who is acting out to walk to a safe location" (P. L. 106-310, 2000, p. 1196). Distinction is also made between time-out and restraint. Time-out is described as a separation of a resident from his or her peers for the purpose of calming; most important, the separation is within an unlocked setting, so that no physical limitation is imposed.

A two-sided form, such as the one depicted in Figure 7-5, may be used to help meet the special documentation requirements of emergency safety interventions.

Discharge Summary and Aftercare Plans

The discharge summary contains the reason for discharge, noting whether the person left in a timely manner or against program advice, and if the person is living in the community. Hospital discharge in the case of an involuntary commitment includes the doctor's orders certifying that the person is no longer a danger to self or others and is therefore ready for discharge. Although some hospitals have begun to make the determination of readiness for discharge a decision of an interdisciplinary team, the treating physician has ultimate responsibility for discharge. Documentation related to discharge summarizes what the goals of the treatment plan have been and the progress made. It includes linkages with other programs, including mental health, to which the person has been referred, any appointments that have been made, and a prognosis statement as to future expectations for the person's physical and mental health. Other details documented in the discharge summary in a psychiatric hospital include the final diagnoses, medications and instructions, disabilities (if any), dietary instructions, and with whom the patient was discharged.

Although discharge summary documentation is important in both institutional and community settings, it is especially important to have it completed in a timely manner in the inpatient setting. Community programs often have policies that prohibit recently discharged patients from participating in their programming until they have received the discharge summary from the hospital. There are several reasons for this policy. First, it is more difficult to assist with a treatment plan if the worker does not know where the potential candidate for the program fits on the scale of recovery. Also, the program workers need to be aware of any special conditions or needs that were discovered in the hospital, particularly related to physical health needs. It is also vital to identify linkages for funding, such as Supplemental Security Income (SSI) or food stamp eligibility, or for entering the community mental health system via an appointment set up before discharge. These continuity of care issues are of absolute importance in preventing immediate relapse and return to the hospital. How quickly and how well the former patient is reoriented to community living is a key factor in successful transition from the institution. The discharge summary, with its delineation of aftercare plans, provides community mental health professionals with invaluable information with which to assist in that process.

MISSISSIPPI STATE HOSPITAL
SECLUSION/RESTRAINT/PROTECTIVE DEVICE OBSERVATION REPORT

Addresssograph

DATE:	TIME STARTED:	BUILDING:	Explanation of initiation and goal for discontinuation of seclusion/restraint given to patient/significant other: Time: _____ Nurse's Signature: _____

TYPE OF BEHAVIOR WARRANTING SECLUSION/RESTRAINT/PROTECTIVE DEVICE:
☐ Agitated/Combative   ☐ Self Destructive   ☐ Invasion of Other's Personal Space   other:
☐ Confusion   ☐ Threatening

CRITERIA FOR DISCONTINUATION:
☐ Maintains relaxed, non threatening posture   ☐ Cease verbal threats
☐ Can discuss alternative behavior   ☐ Agrees to follow plan for safety (Contracts)   ☐ Other:

PRIOR INTERVENTION:
☐ Time Out   ☐ Visual Contact   ☐ I:I Observation   ☐ Behavior Management   ☐ Medication
☐ Limit Setting   ☐ Family Participation   ☐ Supervised Physical Activity   ☐ Reduced Stimulation   ☐ Redirection
☐ Frequent Reorientation   ☐ Peer Isolation   ☐ Other:

TYPE OF INTERVENTION
☐ Seclusion
☐ Restraint
☐ Protection Device
☐ Behavior Management Program

TYPE OF DEVICE
☐ Restraint Bed   ☐ Helmet   ☐ Sleeved Jacket/Vest
☐ Wrist Restraint   ☐ Mittens   ☐ Papoose Board
☐ Ankle Restraint   ☐ Pelvic Holder   ☐ Restraint Chair
☐ Lap Belt   ☐ Jump Suit   ☐ Other:

CODE - OBSERVATION (More than one may be used)
1. Yelling or Screaming
2. Attempting Self Harm
3. Kicking
4. Threatening Violence
5. Mumbling Incoherently
6. Talking Coherently
7. Biting
8. Restless
9. Requesting Release
10. Sleeping
11. Quiet/Calm/Resting
12. Attempting Removal of Restraint
13. Other _____
14. Other _____

CODE - INTERVENTIONS (More than one may be used)
A. Offered Fluids (q 1 hour)
B. Offered Bathroom (q 2 hours)
C. Circulation/Skin Check (q 2 hours)
D. "A,B,C"
E. Refused Fluids
F. Refused Bathroom
G. Released from Seclusion
H. Released from Restraints
I. Released from Protective Device
J. Restraints Reapplied
K. Did not meet criteria for d/c, renew restraints up to 4 hrs.
L. Other: _____
M. Other: _____

BEHAVIORAL CARE ONLY:
Observation documentation required Q 15 minutes..... Reassessment for release/renew documentation Q 4 hours

Initials	O	I	Initials	O	I	Initials	O	I
12:00 am			8:00 am			4:00 pm		
12:15 am			8:15 am			4:15 pm		
12:30 am			8:30 am			4:30 pm		
12:45 am			8:45 am			4:45 pm		
1:00 am			9:00 am			5:00 pm		
1:15 am			9:15 am			5:15 pm		
1:30 am			9:30 am			5:30 pm		
1:45 am			9:45 am			5:45 pm		
2:00 am			10:00 am			6:00 pm		
2:15 am			10:15 am			6:15 pm		
2:30 am			10:30 am			6:30 pm		
2:45 am			10:45 am			6:45 pm		
3:00 am			11:00 am			7:00 pm		
3:15 am			11:15 am			7:15 pm		
3:30 am			11:30 am			7:30 pm		
3:45 am			11:45 am			7:45 pm		
4:00 am			12:00 pm			8:00 pm		
4:15 am			12:15 pm			8:15 pm		
4:30 am			12:30 pm			8:30 pm		
4:45 am			12:45 pm			8:45 pm		
5:00 am			1:00 pm			9:00 pm		
5:15 am			1:15 pm			9:15 pm		
5:30 am			1:30 pm			9:30 pm		
5:45 am			1:45 pm			9:45 pm		
6:00 am			2:00 pm			10:00 pm		
6:15 am			2:15 pm			10:15 pm		
6:30 am			2:30 pm			10:30 pm		
6:45 am			2:45 pm			10:45 pm		
7:00 am			3:00 pm			11:00 pm		
7:15 am			3:15 pm			11:15 pm		
7:30 am			3:30 pm			11:30 pm		
7:45 am			3:45 pm			11:45 pm		

MSH 31B (04/05)

FIGURE 7-5 Front of Seclusion/Restraint/Protective Device Observation Report. (Courtesy of Mississippi State Hospital.)

Pre-Seclusion/Restraint Search and Removal Of Items

Items Removed	Description	Disposition	Initials
☐ Clothes	_____	_____	_____
☐ Belt	_____	_____	_____
☐ Shoes	_____	_____	_____
☐ Smoking Materials	_____	_____	_____
☐ Money	_____	_____	_____
☐ Other	_____	_____	_____

☐ **Patient Wishes Family/Correspondent to be Notified**
☐ **Patient Does Not Want Family Notified**
☐ **Family Does Not Want to be Notified**

Date/Time of Notification, if Applicable:

Notified By: _____ _____ at _____ AM/PM
　　　　　　　Signature/Title　　　　　　　　　　Date　　　　　　　　　Time

Date/Time Released:

Date: _____　Time: _____ AM/PM

Trauma Experienced?

☐ Yes　Explain: _____
☐ No

Patient Debriefing: (To be Completed within 24 Hours After Episode

What could you have done differently to have prevented/avoided seclusion/restraint?

_____

Do you feel like hurting yourself?
☐ Yes　Explain: _____
☐ No

Do you feel like hurting anyone else?
☐ Yes　Explain: _____
☐ No

Debriefed By: _____ _____ at _____ AM/PM
　　　　　　　Signature/Title　　　　　　　　　Date　　　　　　　　Time

Staff Debriefing:

Can staff identify factors that may reduce the risk of future episodes?
☐ Yes　Explain: _____
☐ No
Debriefed By: _____ _____ at _____ AM/PM
　　　　　　　Signature/Title　　　　　　　　　Date　　　　　　　　Time

Treatment Plan Modification Needed and documentation of need placed on Accountability?
☐ Yes　Explain: _____
☐ No

First Name	Last Name	Title	Initials	First Name	Last Name	Title	Initials

FIGURE **7-5** Reserve side of Seclusion/Restraint/Protective Device Observation Report. (Courtesy of Mississippi State Hospital.)　(*Continued*)

REIMBURSEMENT AND FUNDING

The principal sources of funding for CMHCs are client fees, Medicaid, Medicare, and block grant funding for special projects. Client fees are calculated on a sliding scale based on income and account for a small percentage of the overall budget. The majority of the income for community mental health comes from Medicaid and Medicare reimbursement. Some funding comes from federal block grants, which is typically distributed through the state mental health agency to support special initiatives. CMHCs also receive a prescribed millage (local property tax) from the counties they serve. The great variety of funding streams makes for a complex billing and accounting system that could well become a specialized area into which health information managers might wish to venture.

The larger inpatient institutions have traditionally been supported for the most part by state funds, with a small percentage coming from patient fees. The trend in recent years, however, has been toward becoming accredited, leading to eligibility for the institutions to receive payment through Medicaid funding.

In 2003, CMS published a proposed rule to create an **inpatient psychiatric facility prospective payment system (IPF PPS)** for Medicare payments to both freestanding psychiatric hospitals and psychiatric units in acute care hospitals. The final rule was issued in 2004, and the new payment system took effect January 1, 2005. Under the IPF PPS, inpatient psychiatric facilities (IPFs) receive per diem payments that are adjusted up or down by four patient-level factors, as follows:

- the patient's age (increasingly higher rates for patients age 45 and older through age 80 and above)
- variable per diem adjustments (higher per diem payments for the first days of the patient's stay, gradually decreasing through the 22nd day of hospitalization, with no further decrease beyond that point)
- the Medicare Severity diagnosis related group (MS-DRG) for the stay
- certain comorbidities. (Only one comorbidity adjustment is made for each comorbidity category, but adjustments for more than one comorbidity category are possible.)

Because coded data are used to determine the MS-DRG as well as the additional comorbidity factors, the health information department plays an important role in providing accurate and complete coding for the IPF PPS.

The proposed rule issued in 2003 also included a Case Mix Assessment Tool (CMAT), a data collection instrument designed to capture additional information about the patient's psychiatric symptoms, level of cognitive functioning, and ability to perform activities of daily living, along with limited information on services or treatments provided and diagnostic studies performed. As of 2010, the CMAT had not been implemented in the IPF PPS, but CMS has continued research in this area, and some type of assessment instrument may eventually help to determine Medicare payment amounts for inpatient psychiatric facilities.

Managed care is becoming more prevalent as a payer. States have begun to contract with MCOs to provide mental health services for their Medicaid programs. Such a program may be capitated, meaning that payment is made based on the number of program participants in the service area. In other types of managed care arrangements, the MCO may authorize the number of services that will be paid during a certain period. This period could be six months or a year, or it could be defined as an **episode of care**. An episode of care involves a variety of services (inpatient and/or outpatient) provided by an organization to an individual during a given episode of illness.

The growing concern of politicians and the public regarding health care costs has motivated some states to move mental health services to a system of managed care more driven by economic concerns than quality assurance issues. The focus within a managed care system becomes the number of services and length of time that services are performed. This approach has been quite controversial when applied to the seriously mentally ill population because of the erratic and unpredictable nature of psychosis. The uncertainty of prognosis renders very difficult any reliable prediction as to the number and types of services a person may need over extended periods of time. Nevertheless, states have begun programs of managed care within mental health, with mixed results. Of particular concern to mental health consumers and their advocates is the tendency of managed care organizations to define narrowly the range of services that are seen as "medically necessary." This concept allows selective provision, usually limited to medication management during stable periods and hospitalization during psychotic episodes, rather than the full range of treatments and services such as case management and vocational rehabilitation options that are necessary for most persons with mental illness to maintain themselves in a community setting.

INFORMATION MANAGEMENT

Beginning in 1975 there was a movement toward creation of a uniform, integrated statistical reporting system for mental health at the national level. In 1975, the Division of Biometry and Epidemiology (DBE) proposed an undertaking to create such a system (Patton & Leginski, 1983). As a result, the **Mental Health Statistics Improvement Program (MHSIP)**, became an early initiative within the National Institute of Mental Health (NIMH) to create a uniform data system nationwide for reporting of mental health statistics. MHSIP suggested that the State Mental Health Authorities work cooperatively with NIMH to create a broad-based data collection spearheaded by state efforts. The goals were to be as follows:

> (a) Enhance state, local, and national mental health agencies' capacity to respond to local, state, and national needs for mental health program management data; (b) train sufficient systems and statistical personnel to collect, process, and analyze the data generated by these systems; (c) provide an ongoing cost sharing mechanism for the production of data required by the federal system. (Patton & Leginski, 1983)

An ad hoc advisory group made up of personnel from local, state, and federal programs undertook the early work of establishing data sets that were widely accepted as appropriate and useful. Following the reorganization of NIMH, this initiative was placed with the Center for Mental Health Services (CMHS) branch of the Substance Abuse and Mental Health Services Administration (SAMHSA).

In 1984, the initiative received a second strong impetus with a mandate from Congress to create a system for data collection regarding mental health and substance abuse. Unlike the substance abuse system, where the move toward uniformity was translated into a set of federally mandated standards for data collection, the mental health system chose to promote guidelines rather than specific standards. Thus, participation in the initiative continued to be voluntary. The congressional directive led NIMH to publish, the next year, the *Data Standards for Mental Health Decision Support Systems* "FN 10". This manual became the basis for all subsequent work in the effort to create a compatible data reporting system. It produced a significant impact on the direction and scope of the current thinking about mental health data, as it made a strong case for including more than just client service data. The case was made for expanding the data collection into such areas as finances and human resources as "auxiliaries" to the direct service arena (Leginski et al., 1989). The MHSIP/FN-10 initiative later entered a second phase, termed Decision Support 2000+, which was to include incorporation of the HIPAA regulations regarding confidentiality as well as other recent developments in the field. The move toward data standards has continued with submission by State Mental Health Authorities of aggregate information to SAMHSA through the **Uniform Reporting System (URS)** and eventually through the reporting of client-level data by the states. For example, in 2001 the first Data Infrastructure Grants (DIGs) were awarded noncompetitively. The goal of this initiative was to have all State Mental Health Authorities enabled to report performance measures in their Community Mental Health Services Block Grant (CMHSBG) applications. The emphasis on performance measures accompanied new terminology for the block grants, which were to transition to "Performance Partnership Grants" (PPGs). The guiding intention was that state mental health agencies and SAMHSA would collaborate on setting goals and reporting data. The following excerpt from a National Association of State Mental Health Program Directors (NASMHPD) Research Institute report provides information on the evolution of this system: "As part of the federal government's effort to change federal block grants into performance-based systems, P.L. 106-310 (2000) required the U.S. Department of Health and Human Services Secretary to submit a Report to Congress on the legislative and other steps required to implement a performance partnership model. This plan would have grown out of the Mental Health Statistics Improvement Program (MHSIP) and data infrastructure grant projects, and would have specified what performance measures would be imposed under a performance partnership. Instead, SAMHSA has required core data elements as part of its annual instructions which phased in de facto uniform performance criteria" (NASMHPD Research Institute, 2007, p. 3).

Several other factors have also affected the move toward a uniform data system. In recent years, the cry for increased democratization of the mental health service delivery system has broadened to include the ways in which those services are measured and quantified. This movement has occurred within the societal context of the growing popularity of consumer service orientation in management. Such an information system would arise from an entirely different paradigm from the traditional collection and analysis of data, shifting the focus "from persons *served within* individual specialty mental health *organizations* toward *persons with significant needs* for mental health services and supports, *regardless of* the number or type of *organizations* that may or may not serve them" (Campbell & Frey, 1993). The emphasis would become one of identifying need across systems and organizations in a much broader context than just that of the mental health system. Obviously, such a system, where highly individualized data are being sought and shared in a variety of settings, raises special concern around issues of confidentiality. (See Confidentiality, further on.) Yet it can be done. South Carolina is one state that has achieved creation of an information system for mental health consumers that reaches across agencies in this way.

With regard to sharing data for the purpose of treatment, several states have laws that make it difficult to include mental health information in broad-based health information exchanges (HIE). Also, mental health facilities were not included in the original ARRA bill as among those eligible for incentives for meaningful use of EHR technology and the accompanying goal of being able to participate in health information exchange. (Note that psychiatrists, as physicians, are considered to be eligible providers for the ARRA incentives.) As individual states began setting up their statewide health information exchanges, the idea of including mental health in HIE began to be discussed, as well as how it could be accomplished while still protecting the privacy and rights of the consumers and patients being served.

With regard to the protection of confidentiality in data collection for planning purposes, CMHS implemented a successful pilot project in which client-level data from nine states were submitted in a fashion that did not compromise confidentiality. This was accomplished by submitting the data without the use of identifiers that would allow the data to be associated with an individual. For example, age was submitted instead of date of birth. Also, specific dates for admission and discharge were not used, but time frames were provided that indicated the duration of service and that could also be used to capture changes in the client's status over time. De-identifying the data in this manner protects the patient's confidentiality, but also provides more useful data for analysis than does the submission of aggregate data. In 2010, CMHS announced plans to expand client-level reporting for five specific outcome measures to all states within three years.

The other, and quite antithetical, influence on current discussions of data standards and information systems development springs from the managed care system. Here, of course, the driving force is economic considerations. The emphases on fiscal responsibility and cost/benefit considerations of this model of service delivery place paramount value on the very type of data supporting organizational accountability that the proponents of "person-centered" information systems find unsatisfactory. The debate within the managed care camp has focused on use of outcome measures versus performance indicators. Outcome measures are more suitable to situations where an illness has a usual duration and generally ends in a cure. Obviously, there is a measurable outcome in such cases. Because of the chronic nature of mental illness, it is difficult to measure outcome with accuracy. So many factors enter into the possibility of relapse that mental health professionals are hard-pressed to say what particular factors prevent or produce recidivism. Nor can they always predict the duration of a psychotic episode and its aftermath, much less the long-term prognosis of the illness. For these reasons there is a strong belief among mental health professionals that a much more accurate way of measuring success is by using performance indicators. Such indicators focus on consumer satisfaction with services delivered, rather than on treatment outcomes. To some extent this approach also bows in the direction of consumer empowerment, as it provides a vehicle by which the consumer can register his or her satisfaction or unhappiness with the mental health system.

Many players within the mental health system have taken divergent routes in incorporating newer and more efficient technologies for their data collection, many of which include categories and methods of reporting not compatible with SAMHSA's ongoing developments for a uniform reporting system. Lack of funding for these efforts has also been a concern. Nevertheless, it appears that uniform reporting is moving forward, despite the fact that the process of deliberation and experimentation has taken so long.

Data and Information Flow

Intake procedures vary within the community mental health system. Because of staff constraints, few CMHCs are able to take walk-ins except those in emergency situations—usually defined as persons in need of inpatient commitment due to danger to self or others. Typically, applications are received and screened as to the seriousness of the case, and appointments are established, including an appointment with a psychiatrist if it is clear from the application that one is needed for medication issues. Priority is generally given to persons who have been discharged from inpatient care; these appointments are generally set up by the social worker at the institution before the person's discharge.

A file for recording service delivery, billing data, and other pertinent information is usually established just before the intake interview. Intake provides an opportunity to gather additional demographic information not included or unclear on the application form. Assessment is conducted and an initial plan of treatment is agreed on by consumer and therapist, with the understanding that it can be modified as needed as the treatment progresses. If necessary, an appointment is made to see a psychiatrist for possible medication. If appropriate, other services are offered, such as participation in the case management program; attendance at a day program; either psychosocial rehabilitation aimed at vocational opportunity or partial hospitalization; and/or placement in a group home designed to increase daily living skills for a more independent living arrangement in the future. In most cases, these services will be paid for by Medicaid and/or Medicare, so the psychiatrist will need to certify under signature that they are "needed services." From this point, the course of treatment becomes individualized, based on the consumer's needs and preferences as to the services available.

There is no universal standard for content or order of arrangement of information in the consumer's file. (See Figure 7-6 for sample items from a large psychiatric hospital.) If the services are offered in a satellite office, the essential, most up-to-date information will, quite naturally, be contained in the record at that site. Some CMHCs have a central file for all clients in their main office, with copies of material sent periodically from the satellite file for inclusion in the central record. Others have only the one record at the satellite office. Billing information, in particular reporting of units of service (15-minute increments in the case of Medicaid) provided, is contained in the record. Surveyors and auditors are thus able to match billing information with documentation of service delivery in the progress notes section of the record.

Voluntary admission to a hospital would follow much the same process as that for admission for treatment in the community. The documentation process for involuntary admission to an inpatient facility begins, of course, with the information assembled during the commitment proceedings, from screening and evaluation through the legal order of commitment. This documentation usually arrives with the patient. It typically becomes the responsibility of the institutional social worker to assemble and augment the information received by performing a social history, including contact with family members whenever possible. In most inpatient settings, the patient's treatment plan is developed by an interdisciplinary team that usually includes at least a psychiatrist, a nurse, a psychologist, and a social worker. The patient is encouraged to participate in the planning to whatever extent possible. An attempt is made to provide a highly structured atmosphere, as activity often alleviates the psychotic symptoms and the debilitating side effects of some of the medications. Progress notes are entered into the case file by the various disciplines in the same way it is done for persons who are followed in the outpatient setting. The team meets periodically and decides whether the patient's condition indicates long-term hospitalization or whether progress is being made toward release. The social worker usually begins to develop a tentative discharge plan very early in treatment so that the necessary steps are in place when the time comes to put them into action. As the actual time of discharge nears, the social worker takes steps to ensure continuity of care beyond the hospital. At a minimum these steps include assurance of housing, establishment of monetary benefits if the patient is eligible, and contact with the community mental health system to set up an initial appointment.

Coding and Classification

Behavioral health organizations use a variety of coding systems. The system used will depend on the purpose of coding and other factors. Psychiatric diagnoses have commonly been coded using the *Diagnostic and Statistical Manual*

Identification and Personal Data
  Demographic Data
  Legal Status (commitment vs. voluntary
    admission)

Physician's Orders

Treatment Plan and Behavioral Documentation
  Treatment Plan
  Treatment Plan Update/Review Note
  Anger Management Assessment
  Psychiatric Intervention History
  Patient/Family Education Record
  Individual Patient Schedule
  Behavior Modification Plan

Progress Notes, including...
  Initial Integrated Summary
  Admission Note
  Transfer Notes
  Elopement Notes
  Diagnostic Summary or Addendum to
    Diagnostic Summary
  Audiology Alert Sheet
  Discharge Summary

Nurses' Notes, including...
  Nursing Assessment
  Child/Adolescent Addendum
  Abnormal Involuntary Movements
  Fall Assessment
  Nursing Discharge Summary

Medication Records
  Monthly Medication Administration
    Records (MARs)
  Monthly PRN medications
  Medication Information Documentation
    Form
  Specialized Medication Records (for example,
    for patients with diabetes mellitus)

Other Health Records
  Vital Signs Record
  Menstrual Record
  Intake/Output
  Fluid Accountability Record

Other Health Records (*continued*)
  Seizure Record
  Immunization and TB Record
  Summary of Ambulatory Visits
  Outpatient Procedure Report

Ancillary Services
  Lab Reports
  X-ray Reports
  EKG

Consultations
  Medical
  CT Scans
  EEC
  Outpatient Unscheduled Visit

Physical Exam

Alcohol and Drug Abuse Needs
  Assessment/Aftercare Plan

Psychology
  Psychology General Assessment
  Psychology Progress Notes
  Psychological Evaluation

Social Service
  Social Service Assessment/Plan
  Social Service Clinical Progress Notes
  Spiritual Assessment
  Social History

Dietary
  Nutritional Assessment
  Dietary Clinical Progress Notes

Pharmacy Medication Review

Activities
  Therapeutic Recreation Assessment
  Rehab Clinical Progress Notes
  Leisure Assessment

Rehabilitation
  Rehabilitation Services Screening
    Assessment
  Rehabilitation Clinical Progress Notes

FIGURE **7-6** Examples of items that may be found in the records of a large psychiatric hospital. (Excerpted and adapted from procedures of Mississippi State Hospital, Whitfield, MS. Used with permission.)

Rehabilitation (*continued*)
    Restorative Therapy Note
    Physical Therapy Evaluation Report
    Kinesiotherapy Evaluation Report
    Occupational Therapy Evaluation
    Feeding Evaluation
    Upper Extremity Evaluation
    Splint Information
    Speech, Language, Pathology Assessment
    Dysphagia Assessment

Education
    Education Clinical Progress Notes
    Patient Education Progress Report
    Psychosocial Education Program
    Functional Needs Assessment
    Psychosocial Education Program
    Art Assessment
    Music Evaluation
    Hearing and Vision Screening Results

Dental
    Dental Record
    Dental Treatment Plan

Residential Living
    Patient Care Flow Sheet
    Patient Observation Reports

Legal
    Advance Directives
    Admission Checklist
    Patient's Rights Statement

Legal (*continued*)
    Smoking Policy
    Ethics Fact Sheet
    Notice of Privacy Practices
    Consent Forms
    Contraband Search, Seizure, Disposition
    Admission Papers (Commitment orders)
    Legal Guardianship
    Legal Correspondence

Miscellaneous
    Visitors' Permits
    Patient Transfer Form
    Transfer and Referral Form
    Patient's Valuable Form
    Missing Patient Reports
    Hearing Reports
    Patient's Pass/Discharge Record
    Pass Evaluation Checklist
    Vocational Rehab
    Sheltered Workshop forms
    Work Opportunity forms
    Transitional Living Forms and Progress
      Reports

Electroconvulsive Therapy (ECT)
    ECT Checklist
    Progress Report
    Anesthesia Record
    Electroconvulsive Nursing Care Plans
    Consent for ECT
    Referral for ECT

FIGURE **7-6** (*Continued*)

of Mental Disorders, fourth edition, text revision (*DSM-IV-TR*), published by the American Psychiatric Association, with *DSM-V* scheduled as a replacement system in 2013. This publication provides not only a classification system but also diagnostic criteria to assist clinicians in making psychiatric diagnoses. More information on the structure and utilization of this classification system may be found in Chapter 8.

For billing purposes, behavioral health organizations submitting electronic bills must use the HIPAA standard code sets, which do not include *DSM-IV-TR* or *DSM-V*. Therefore the current modification of *ICD* and *CPT/HCPCS* codes are used as appropriate.

Data Sets

The key data sets in mental health are found in the reporting requirements that the State Mental Health Authorities must follow in the annual grant application and funding process. The Data Infrastructure Grants support these efforts. In the following excerpt from the 2010 Request for Applications (RFA) for the State Mental Health Data Infrastructure Grants for Quality Improvement (State DIGs), CMHS explained its data collection efforts as follows:

> Building on the results of the CMHS Client Level Data Pilot, CMHS will work with the States through the Data Infrastructure Grants (DIGs) to enable collection and reporting of client level data for five Mental Health Block Grant National Outcome Measures (NOMS) over the next three years. These NOMS are Employment/School Attendance, Stability in Housing, Criminal Justice Involvement, Readmission to State Hospital, and Access/Capacity: Number of Persons Served with Demographic Characteristics. The additional NOMS and Uniform Reporting System (URS) Tables, which do not require direct State or client level data, will continue to be reported, and will add value in decision support at the national and State levels. The population of focus will include mental health consumers served within the purview of the State Mental Health Authorities (SMHAs), as defined in the URS Tables. The project supports the reporting requirements for the National CMHS Mental Health Block Grant Program.
>
> The purpose of the State Mental Health Data Infrastructure Grants for Quality Improvement (DIGs) is to support client level data reporting by the States by 2012 for 5 NOMS. Building upon the Federal/State partnership established through the development of the URS..., this mechanism will be used for collecting client level data for more than 6 million mental health consumers. In addition, by receiving SAMHSA/CMHS funds through the DIGs over the grant period, States will engage in T1 and T2 (to include Admission and Discharge) client level data collection and reporting.
>
> The project supports State Mental Health Authorities (SMHAs) in their continuing implementation and strengthening of the annual collection of URS data through focus on selected NOMS for client level reporting. Historically, great strides have been made in data infrastructure development in the States for reporting the URS and NOMS at the national level. Over a period of years in the DIG grant effort, the States have achieved uniform URS reporting so that by 2008, eight of the 10 NOMS were being reported by 85% of grantees (48 States). The effort has additionally strengthened State and local data infrastructure for reporting and decision support. The future of the SAMHSA/CMHS mental health data reporting program continues to evolve in refining the reporting of NOMS, using the framework of the CMHS Client Level Pilot in which 9 States piloted the feasibility of implementing client level NOMS reporting in the States through FY 2009. In the new grant cycle, the effort will be made to strengthen quality of reporting and performance accountability for selected NOMS, including developing capability to report assessment of service provision and improvement of individual clients from Time 1 to Time 2 (including admission and discharge). (SAMHSA, 2010, para. 1–3)

TERMINOLOGY RELATED TO MENTAL HEALTH DATA SETS

CMHS Client Level Data Pilot – A pilot study in which nine states tested the feasibility of reporting certain data to SAMHSA at the level of the individual client rather than in aggregate as in the URS tables

Data Infrastructure Grants (DIGs) – Federal grants to assist states in developing infrastructure for reporting performance measures for mental health

National Outcome Measures (NOMS) – Mental health outcome measures collected nationally. Examples of NOMS for which CMHS is seeking to collect client-level data include:

- Employment/School Attendance
- Stability in Housing
- Criminal Justice Involvement
- Readmission to State Hospital
- Access/Capacity: Number of Persons Served with Demographic Characteristics

Uniform Reporting System (URS) Tables – A set of tables by which each State Mental Health Authority (SMHA) reports aggregate data to SAMHSA

State Mental Health Authorities (SMHAs) – The agency in each state that is responsible for oversight of mental health programs in that state.

Time 1 to Time 2 (T1 to T2) – Two points in time for which data are reported, allowing comparison of progress or outcomes over the time period, as well as duration of the time period, without reporting the exact dates, thus avoiding the submission of protected health information (PHI) such as dates of admission and discharge

Historically, the emphasis has been on producing guidelines for the development of relevant data standards, rather than promulgation of a uniform system of data fields and collection procedures. In part the reluctance to mandate uniformity has stemmed from the enormous impact of the consumer empowerment movement, which changed not only the programming for service delivery but also the perception of what constitutes success in the rendering of those services. The implementation of client-level data reporting brings about a measure of uniformity in data collection for the targeted outcomes measures.

QUALITY IMPROVEMENT AND UTILIZATION MANAGEMENT

The mental health field has been at least as susceptible as other segments of our society to the current focus on total quality management (TQM), or its more recent manifestation as **continuous quality improvement (CQI)**. The focus that both of these management techniques place on customer satisfaction and sharing of decision-making power between administrative and line staff make a natural fit with the mental health consumer movement toward empowerment. These concepts have been for the most part well accepted by now and in general incorporated into both the outpatient and the inpatient systems of care. Client-centered approaches permeate the mental health system, affecting all aspects of service delivery, from programming that encourages self-determination, emphasizing consumer strengths rather than functional deficits, to data collection that focuses on client satisfaction and feedback mechanisms. Performance improvement is an important component in Joint Commission accreditation of inpatient facilities. Because this accreditation is generally accepted by major funding sources such as Medicare and Medicaid, it is frequently sought after by inpatient facilities.

Utilization management has led over the years to the downsizing of large public mental institutions. The move to deinstitutionalization, while resulting in part from the improvement in stabilization through medication, has also been driven in part by economic considerations. It has proved much less expensive, generally speaking, to maintain consumers in the community with a variety of support services than to keep them in the hospital, with its more costly medical orientation. Because the funding from the hospitals did not always follow the consumer to the community, however, some would argue that the consumers have received uneven and often inadequate support outside the hospital. Thus, the lowered cost of community services may in part be a reflection of the inadequate funding that could deprive its customers of a decent quality of life, and may in this sense be somewhat deceptive as to what the actual costs ought to be.

In both the outpatient and inpatient settings, steps have been taken to further reduce costs. Many CMHCs have created a staff position that serves as the "single point of entry" (SPOE) for emergency hospitalization in either the acute care psychiatric units or the long-term institution. Data are sometimes gathered regarding high users of inpatient services, with an eye to providing more or different supports to those who fall into this category. Bed allocation is a further device, particularly within institutions, to encourage utilization of community resources to the fullest before resorting to hospitalization. This method assigns beds on a regional basis, using formulas that take into account such factors as total population and past usage of the facility. Then a certain amount of "borrowing" of beds among regions is allowed to take care of emergencies.

RISK MANAGEMENT AND LEGAL ISSUES

Risk management as an organized program exists more frequently in the inpatient than in the outpatient treatment sector. The function of this program is to predict and thereby reduce or eliminate sources of likely injury and accident or of other potential financial loss to the institution. Such responsibility obviously includes avoidance of litigation, which leads to involvement in treatment issues that carry a high risk of violation of patients' rights, such as the use of restraints, informed consent regarding administration of medications, and timely discharge when stabilization has occurred. Additionally, protection of confidentiality is of particular importance, especially since implementation of the Health Insurance Portability and Accountability Act (HIPAA) regulations. (See Chapter 1, for details regarding HIPAA.) This concern has direct impact on the duties of the health information manager, who has ultimate responsibility for protection of such information.

Confidentiality

Patient information in mental health settings has always been highly confidential. It was more restricted than other types of medical information until passage of HIPAA, which tightened restrictions on all types of medical information and brought confidentiality more in line with practices already largely in place within mental health. For example, before HIPAA, in settings outside mental health, information such as patient name and dates of service was considered nonconfidential and could be disclosed in the absence of a specific request by the patient to prohibit disclosure (Huffman, 1994). However, in mental health facilities, such information has traditionally been legally protected; even acknowledging that a patient has been treated at a facility has been considered a breach of confidentiality. Mental health facilities have always placed great emphasis on strictest confidentiality, and long before HIPAA have generally required all employees and vendors to sign confidentiality agreements prohibiting staff and vendors alike from disclosing any information regarding patients who have been treated at the facility.

HIPAA provides a greater degree of protection to psychotherapy notes than to other types of protected health information. The use or disclosure of psychotherapy notes requires a valid authorization even for treatment, payment, or health care operations, with the following exceptions: (1) The originator of the notes may use them for continuing treatment; (2) students, trainees, or practitioners may use psychotherapy notes in supervised mental health training programs; (3) the covered entity may use the notes when necessary to defend itself in a legal action brought by the individual; and (4) notes may be used as needed for health oversight activities or other activities as required by law (Standards for privacy of individually identifiable health information, 2002).

As a general rule, the mental health consumer's right to strictest confidentiality regarding matters of illness and treatment is carefully guarded. Legal protections of this right have been enacted legislatively in every state as well as at the federal level. Traditionally, the relationship of mental health professionals to the consumer/patient has been considered privileged in the same way as that of lawyer to client or priest to confessing parishioner. The only way in which such information can be released is through a formal, documented procedure whereby the consumer, patient, or patient's guardian provides written consent. The consent form should state the specific type of information to be released, the exact recipient of the information, and should specify the time period for which the consent is valid.

Although these strictures continue to hold true in general, certain court decisions have somewhat eroded the concept of nearly absolute confidentiality. Perhaps the most profound impact on the traditional notion of the inviolability of the therapist–client relationship has been the emergence of the concept of **"duty to warn."** This idea stems from a 1976 court decision (*Tarasoff v. Regents of the University of California*), which held that a therapist has an obligation to warn persons against whom their clients make threatening statements, regardless of the fact that such threats are made within a privileged context. The theory behind the decision appears to be that safety from violent assault outweighs the breach of confidentiality and the risk of erroneous warnings. Since this court decision, there has been a trend to legislate "duty to warn" clauses into the states' laws regarding confidentiality.

There are other instances where case information may be required, such as in determining client eligibility for benefits, but these vary somewhat from state to state. Frequently the courts will accept release of a summary of the case record along with specific sections that pertain directly to the legal questions of the case. In cases where specific designation of information to be released is not provided by the court, responsibility for such summaries and/or selections of pertinent material will most often fall to the information manager, with possible collaboration with risk management and/or legal counsel staff.

Technological advances have also complicated the maintenance of confidentiality. Organizations must take an aggressive approach to security to protect information stored on computer networks from mischievous or malicious "hackers." Widespread use of facsimile (fax) machines has likewise created a potential source of information leakage, through human error of misdialing the correct fax machine number or through machine malfunction, in either case resulting in transmission of confidential information to unintended recipients. Public concern over these issues was a major factor in passage of the HIPAA legislation, which now mandates many of the policies and procedures that were previously left to the discretion of the mental health system. These concerns are even more critical in an era of health information exchange as providers, consumers, and the public endeavor to determine the extent to which mental health can be included in health information exchange and still ensure the patient's or consumer's right to confidentiality.

Court-Ordered Treatment

One of the most tragic aspects of serious mental illness is that persons who are in the grips of psychosis are victims of disordered thinking, which prevents their recognition of the fact that they are indeed ill. They are often unable to make decisions that are in their best interest, such as recognizing their need for psychotropic medication, and may be led by their delusions to acts that are dangerous to themselves or to others. In such cases, the mentally ill person may be in need of court-ordered treatment.

Treatment under court order is generally predicated by a procedure that is similar throughout the nation, with slight variations from state to state, and in some states even from county to county. Generally, there is an examination of the person deemed in need of treatment by a physician and/or mental health professional (at least a master's-level psychologist or social worker). The usual criterion for court-ordered commitment to an inpatient institution is the professional's certification that the person is "a danger to self and/or others." In recent years there has been an effort to broaden the rationale for commitment to include "person in need of care." Such a concept provides greater latitude for the court's decision as to whether institutionalization would be a means of improving a person's quality of life even if that person does not pose a direct threat to anyone. It takes into account the ill person's quality of life around such issues as homelessness resulting from the inability to access resources because of disordered thinking, or the degree of mental misery inflicted by paranoia and delusional thinking that might be remediated by medication. While family members and the general public support this concept, particularly as a means of dealing with the homeless population, some consumer groups are opposed. They fear that such latitude can be misused and would return us to the era of widespread abuse of the commitment laws as a means of removing undesirables from the community who were not actually mentally ill, resulting in the "snake pit" conditions of mental institutions widely publicized by the media in the 1930s and 1940s.

Yet another solution to the dilemma of recognizing persons who are in need of supervision but who do not pose a threat to anyone is the outpatient commitment, which consists of a court order that outlines guidelines for behavior (e.g., regularly taking prescribed medication, refraining from abusing nonprescribed drugs or alcohol, reporting for mental health appointments) and may include commitment to a particular residence located in the community (e.g., a group home, a family residence). Failure to abide by the prescribed conditions may result in a new court appearance and the likelihood of inpatient commitment if the person's condition has deteriorated.

ROLE OF THE HEALTH INFORMATION MANAGEMENT PROFESSIONAL

Increased interest in technological advances in data management is expanding the potential role of health information managers in the field of mental health as in other areas of health care. The traditional role function of the profession has been in the institutional sector of mental health services, where the recording, storing, and monitoring of patient information have been the chief responsibilities. Frequently, however, community mental health centers are finding that decision making around management information systems is growing increasingly complex and requires an expertise of its own. This area would seem a logical extension of the domain of the health information manager in the era of electronic information systems.

Outside the domain of client data collection, another major potential for the expansion of the traditional role of the health information manager within CMHCs is in the area of reimbursement and the revenue cycle. Because of the multiple and disparate nature of the sources of funding for community mental health services, this is a complex arena for information storage and management (refer back to Reimbursement and Funding for further details).

Health information managers may also assume roles in quality improvement and risk management, or they may work as consultants to mental health facilities. A health information management (HIM) consultant could advise a mental health facility on issues related to accreditation, information management, or automation of patient information. A consultant assisting with the automation of patient information could have responsibilities ranging from helping to write requests for proposals for new information systems to assisting with the actual implementation of a new system.

A health information manager who chooses a career in mental health can find opportunity for advancement within the field. Some have moved into positions of increased responsibility such as oversight of all information systems. With additional education (e.g., attainment of an appropriate graduate degree), HIM professionals with experience in the financial and administrative aspects of the mental health system have moved into other managerial positions, such as director of a community mental health center.

TRENDS

One of the continuing major efforts in the area of mental health information management is the attempt to create nationally standardized data sets along with a universal system of data collection. Several mutually antagonistic factors have somewhat impeded this movement, although some progress has been made. The thrust toward managed care has created interest in data that in essence justifies an organization's decision making in service delivery based on cost/benefit issues. On the other hand, the interest in "client-centered" information systems that focus largely on client satisfaction rather than on treatment efficacy per se predicates moving in another direction in the development of data collection and analysis. The emphasis at the national level had therefore been more on the quality of the standards for data management than on uniformity. Lack of funding at the federal level for a uniform reporting system had also hampered this endeavor. However, the continuation of the State Data Infrastructure Grants and the move to client-level reporting points toward the possibility of more robust data for planning, decision support, and research in mental health.

The movement toward use of electronic information systems has increased tremendously in the past decades, particularly in the community mental health sector. However, the level of sophistication of the technology varies widely from locale to locale, as does the capacity for linkages, whether interagency or to statewide systems. Adoption of electronic health records (EHRs) is increasing in mental health settings, even though behavioral health facilities were not initially included in the EHR incentive program of the American Recovery and Reinvestment Act. Because of the need to coordinate mental health care among various providers, advocates have pushed to make mental health facilities eligible for the incentive program, which already includes psychiatrists, who are eligible for the program as physicians. Regardless of federal incentives, the almost universal dependence on electronic information technology has implications for health information managers. As the level of complexity of these systems continues to climb, there will be a call for increased sophistication and specialization in their utilization as a tool for data collection. Decisions about a multitude of data-related questions will need to be addressed, from which information system best suits the needs of the particular agency to which programs will best capture the information needed by a particular service provider. Such questions are clearly within the purview of the HIM profession.

In terms of treatment innovations, there have also been several developments in recent years. There has been an emphasis placed on client strengths, rather than on functional deficits. This change in focus results in a shift in the type of data collected, with increasing emphasis on satisfaction with services, as opposed to specific goals accomplished or failed. As a part of this trend, the concept of "recovery" has been borrowed from substance abuse to contrast with the older mental health concept of "stabilization," which means a reduction of symptomology but does not imply return to the level of functioning before the illness. To capture progress in this type of program emphasis is rather difficult and calls for creative and innovative approaches to data collection and analysis.

Telepsychiatry and tele-mental health offer opportunities to bring mental health services to individuals who may have difficulty accessing services otherwise, because of a remote or rural location or for some other reason. Because videoconferencing is often the only technology needed for the use of telemedicine in mental health, there have been very few barriers to its implementation. Tele-mental health may not be appropriate in every situation, but in some circumstances it has proven valuable in overcoming a lack of access to mental health services. In some instances, the consumer may present for an encounter in a specific location staffed by nurses or other care providers for a videoconference with a psychiatrist at a distant site (Tschirch, Walker, & Calvacca, 2006). In other instances, a consumer may use his or her own personal computer with a Web camera and high-speed Internet connection, providing the opportunity to receive mental health services in the privacy of the consumer's home (Ikelheimer, 2008). There are several different ways that tele-mental health services can be delivered that have proven to be successful under appropriate circumstances.

These are some of the challenges facing health information managers in the area of developing client data systems. There are also other areas opening for exploration in the profession. Collection of other types of data besides the client service information is also a possible area of expansion for the profession. As mentioned earlier, the billing process in outpatient facilities is a complicated weave of funding sources that also requires a knowledge of electronic information storage and retrieval.

Additionally, there is the possibility of entrepreneurial enterprise in developing and marketing software designed to meet the growing and changing data collection needs of the mental health system. Consultation around data system development targeted at specific program needs is also a possible avenue for the skills of health information managers.

SUMMARY

As in other areas of health care, treatment of mental health service consumers has shifted from the inpatient to the outpatient setting because of advances in treatment methodologies and other factors. Mental health services consumers may also be called clients or patients. Among adults, the most common forms of serious mental illness are schizophrenia, clinical depression, and bipolar disorder. Adolescents and children may also suffer from mental disorders, and specific services have been identified to benefit these categories of mental health services consumers. A variety of caregivers, including medical personnel, therapists, case managers, aides, recreation therapists, and occupational therapists, provide services to clients.

Mental health service providers are licensed by the state. Voluntary accreditation is available from the Joint Commission for both inpatient and outpatient providers. CARF offers accreditation for programs that offer rehabilitation services. Managed behavioral health care organizations may seek NCQA or URAC accreditation for some services. Medicare and Medicaid guidelines apply to facilities that receive payment from these sources.

Documentation is very important in mental health services. Various assessments help determine the patient's treatment plan. To demonstrate that every goal in the treatment plan is being addressed, there must be progress notes documenting services provided and the patient's progress toward achieving the treatment goals. Discharge summaries and aftercare plans are also important in the continuing care of the patient.

Several forces have helped mental health service providers improve the quality of data and information. The Center for Mental Health Services has worked with state agencies to improve, broaden, and standardize data collection activities. The increase in managed care in the mental health arena has also caused providers to pursue high-quality data and information. High-quality information in the individual patient's record is also important to the patient and the provider. Mental health information is extremely confidential, and the health information manager must ensure that appropriate HIPAA-compliant policies and procedures are in place to safeguard it. The health information manager can find opportunities in mental health hospitals and community mental health centers in a traditional information management role or in risk management, quality assurance, reimbursement, or information services. The increasing use of aggregate data for mental health services also presents opportunities for health information managers as data analysts in a variety of agencies.

KEY TERMS

bipolar disorder a form of serious mental illness in which a person alternates between states of ecstatic mania and severe depression. Also known as *manic depression.*

Center for Mental Health Services (CMHS) the federal agency that oversees administration of demonstration and research grants and other initiatives at the federal level related to mental health issues. This entity and its parent organization, the Substance Abuse and Mental Health Services Administration (SAMHSA), were created within the U.S. Department of Health and Human Services upon the reorganization of the National Institute of Mental Health (NIMH), which formerly carried these responsibilities.

chemical restraint the use of a drug or medication not part of a person's usual medical regimen that is administered to control behavior or restrict freedom of movement (P. L. 106-310, 2000).

Child and Adolescent Service System Program (CASSP) an initiative begun by the National Institute of Mental Health to create a comprehensive network of services for emotionally disturbed children and adolescents through a series of demonstration grants. The program is now overseen by the Substance Abuse and Mental Health Services Administration (SAMHSA) within the U.S. Department of Health and Human Services.

clinical depression a serious mental illness appearing as a deep feeling of melancholy and futility that is not situational in nature.

community mental health centers (CMHC) publicly funded mental health organizations established in communities throughout the United States by the Mental Health Act of 1965.

continuity of care a concept that refers to creation of a comprehensive system of care for persons with serious mental illness, with particular emphasis on smooth transition from inpatient to outpatient services.

continuous quality improvement (CQI) a management concept that focuses on customer involvement in planning services and obtaining feedback as to satisfaction with service delivery. This concept has been an important feature of the mental health consumer empowerment movement. Also known as total quality management (TQM).

Data Standards for Mental Health Decision Support Systems **("FN-10")** an early reference source for creation of a national mental health services database. Also referred to by its series number, "FN-10."

delusion a form of disordered thinking in which a person holds unrealistic beliefs (e.g., that they are receiving communications from aliens in outer space or that their food is being poisoned). See *psychosis.*

Diagnostic and Statistical Manual of Mental Disorders, **fourth edition, text revision (*DSM-IV-TR*)** a classification system and nomenclature of mental disorders developed by the American Psychiatric Association (APA) with a stated purpose of providing "clear descriptions of diagnostic categories in order to enable clinicians and investigators to diagnose, communicate about, study, and treat people with various mental disorders" (APA, 1994, p. xxiii). It is also used as a coding system for mental disorders. The APA scheduled *DSM-V* for implementation in 2013.

dual diagnoses two diagnoses. Most commonly refers to diagnoses in persons with mental illness and chemical or alcohol addiction, but may also refer to persons who are diagnosed as developmentally disabled and seriously mentally ill.

"duty to warn" a legal concept that holds that it is the duty of a mental health professional to warn a person whom a mentally ill client has threatened to harm, despite the usual protections of confidentiality in the client–professional relationship.

episode of care a period during which a variety of services (inpatient and/or outpatient) are provided to an individual for a given episode of illness.

hallucination a form of disordered thinking in which a person reports sensory experience that is not valid, such as seeing, hearing, smelling, or feeling things that are not real. See *psychosis.*

inpatient psychiatric facility prospective payment system (IPF PPS) Medicare's method of payment for both freestanding psychiatric hospitals and psychiatric units in acute care hospitals. Under the IPF PPS rule, inpatient psychiatric facilities (IPFs) receive per diem payments that are adjusted up or down by patient-level factors such as age, the MS-DRG, and certain comorbidities, with earlier days of the stay paid at higher rates than later days.

involuntary commitment a legal process by which individuals who are deemed to be a danger to themselves or to others may be admitted to an inpatient facility even though they refuse or cannot consent to the treatment.

manic depression   see *bipolar disorder.*

Mental Health Statistics Improvement Program (MHSIP)   an early initiative begun by the National Institute of Mental Health and continued by the Substance Abuse and Mental Health Services Administration to create a uniform data system nationwide for reporting of mental health statistics. MHSIP's work was largely done by a voluntary ad hoc group made up of local, state, and federal personnel.

MICA (mental illness with chemical addiction)   common acronym for programs for persons dually diagnosed with mental illness and chemical/alcohol addiction. Also sometimes written as MIDA or MICAA. Not considered correct when used to refer to individuals or to indicate a population.

outpatient commitment   judicial diversion, from inpatient to outpatient care, of a person who has been certified as in need of psychiatric care, with stipulations regarding behaviors such as taking medications, remaining sober, and maintaining residence in a designated place. Failure to abide by the stipulations generally results in involuntary commitment to an inpatient facility.

physical restraint   "mechanical or personal restriction that immobilizes or reduces the ability of an individual to move his or her arms, legs, or head freely, not including devices . . . for the purpose of conducting routine physical examinations or tests or to protect the resident from falling out of bed or to permit the resident to participate in activities without the risk of physical harm to the resident. . . ." (P. L. 106-310, 2000, pp. 1195–1196).

psychosis   state of extreme disordered thinking in which a person demonstrates such symptoms of serious mental illness as hallucinations and delusions. (See *hallucination* and *delusion.*)

psychosocial rehabilitation   mode of treatment for serious mental illness that focuses on provision of an array of community support services (e.g., development of job skills, if needed) for persons with mental illness, sufficient to allow them to live in the least restrictive environment possible outside an institution.

psychotropic medication   a variety of medications designed to reduce psychotic symptoms by altering the chemical processes within the brain. Also sometimes referred to as "neuroleptics."

schizophrenia   a psychosis represented by a state of extremely disordered thinking, manifesting as a break with reality.

serious emotional disturbance (SED)   a condition in which a young person (from birth to age 18) has a diagnosable mental, behavioral, or emotional disorder resulting in functional impairment that substantially interferes with or limits the child's role or functioning in family, school, or community activities.

serious mental illness (SMI)   a condition in which a person has a diagnosable mental, behavioral, or emotional disorder resulting in functional impairment that substantially interferes with or limits one or more major life activities.

Social Security Disability Income (SSDI)   federal benefits paid to persons with disability who have worked a sufficient length of time to qualify to receive Social Security benefits. A frequent source of income for persons with serious mental illness who are not able to work.

Substance Abuse and Mental Health Services Administration (SAMHSA)   an agency created in 1992 under the umbrella of the U.S. Department of Health and Human Services. The purpose of SAMHSA is to "reduce the impact of substance abuse and mental illness on America's communities."

Supplemental Security Income (SSI)   federal benefits paid to persons with disability who have not worked a sufficient length of time to qualify for Social Security benefits. A common, and often only, source of income for the seriously mentally ill who are unable to work.

system of care "an organizational philosophy and framework that involves collaboration across agencies, families, and youth for the purpose of improving access and expanding the array of coordinated community-based, culturally and linguistically competent services and supports for children and youth with a serious emotional disturbance and their families" (CMHS, 2009, para 2).

Uniform Reporting System (URS) a system by which each State Mental Health Authority (SMHA) reports aggregate data to SAMHSA

wrap-around services predominant method of mental health service delivery to emotionally disturbed children and adolescents and their families. The concept consists of a comprehensive array of professional services that may include home and/or school settings and are tailored to meet the specific needs of the child and his/her family.

REVIEW QUESTIONS

Knowledge-Based Questions

1. Explain the difference between serious emotional disturbance and serious mental illness.
2. Name the three most prevalent types of serious mental illness.
3. What are two categories of dual diagnoses?
4. Give a term by which persons with mental illness who are living in the community prefer to be called.
5. Define "outpatient commitment."
6. Name the main components of the mental health consumer case record.
7. What is the basis for payment in the inpatient psychiatric facility prospective payment system (IPF PPS)?
8. What is the relationship between the treatment plan and progress notes, and why is it important?

9. How did the "duty to warn" originate, and how does it affect confidentiality of mental health information?
10. What are the URS tables?
11. Provide examples of the national outcome measures (NOMs) for which client-level data are reported.

Critical Thinking Questions

1. Discuss how the mental health consumer empowerment movement may have affected development of mental health data collection systems.
2. Discuss some of the areas in mental health services into which health information managers may expand their roles.

WEB ACTIVITY

Visit the Substance Abuse and Mental Health Services Administration (SAMHSA) National Mental Health Information Center Web site at http://www.samhsa.gov/

a. Select "Data, Outcomes & Quality."
b. Under "Mental Health Statistics," select "Uniform Reporting System (URS) Output Tables."
c. At the next page, select the latest year for which data are available.
d. Select a report for your state and review the information it contains. Can you find consumer

survey results within the report? How does your state compare to the U.S. national average on various measures surveyed?

e. Select a report for another state and compare the two state reports. To what extent do they report the same categories of information? Is some optional information reported by one state and not by the other?

CASE STUDY

You are the director of health information services for a community mental health center that is planning to expand its use of electronic information systems. You have been asked to serve on the steering committee that will be guiding this initiative. What types of electronic systems might the committee investigate and what special considerations might there be for a community mental health center embarking on this project?

REFERENCES AND SUGGESTED READINGS

American Psychiatric Association. (2000). *Diagnostic and statistical manual of mental disorders*, fourth edition (text revision). Washington, DC: Author.

American Psychiatric Association. (2010). *DSM-5 overview: The future manual.* [Online]. http://www.dsm5.org/about/Pages/DSMVOverview.aspx [2010, July 24].

Campbell, J., & Frey, E. (1993). Humanizing decision support systems. Unpublished position paper.

Casey, R., & Berman, J. (1985). The outcome of psychotherapy with children. *Psychological Bulletin, 98,* 388–400.

CARF. (No date). Behavioral health publications. http://www.carf.org. [2010, July 17].

[CMHS] Center for Mental Health Services. (2009). *Request for Applications (RFA): Cooperative Agreements for Comprehensive Community Mental Health Services for Children and Their Families Program.* [Online]. http://www.samhsa.gov/Grants/2010/SM-10-005.aspx [2011, February 27].

[CMS] Centers for Medicare & Medicaid Services. (n.d.). Appendix AA: Psychiatric hospitals—Interpretive guidelines and survey procedures. State Operations Manual [Online]. http://cms.gov/manuals/Downloads/som107ap_aa_psyc_hospitals.pdf [2010, July 24].

Conditions of participation for hospitals. *Code of Federal Regulations*, Title 42, Pt. 482, Subpart E—Requirements for Specialty Hospitals, Section 61 Condition of participation: Special medical record requirements for psychiatric hospitals. 2009 ed.

Federal Register. (1993, May 20). Definitions of adults with a serious mental illness and children with a serious emotional disturbance, pp. 29422–29425.

Federal Register. (2001, January 22). Psychiatric residential treatment facilities providing psychiatric services to individuals under age 21; use of restraint and seclusion, pp. 7147–7164.

Federal Register. (2006, December 8). Medicare and Medicaid programs; hospital conditions of participation; patients' rights, pp. 71378–71380.

Friedman, R., Katz-Leary, J., Manderscheid, R., & Sondheimer, D. (1996). Prevalence of serious emotional disturbance in children and adolescents. In R. Manderscheid and M. Sonnenschein (Eds.), *Mental Health: United States* (pp. 71–98). Washington, DC: U.S. Government Printing Office, DHHS Publication Number (SMA) 96-3098.

Furman, R. (1997). Wrap-around services: A comprehensive approach to adolescent mental health services. *Advocates Forum, 4*(1), 8–9.

Huffman, E. (1994). *Health Information Management* (10th ed.). Berwyn, IL: Physicians' Record Company.

Hutchinson, J., Lloyd, J., Landsman, M., Nelson, K., & Bryce, M. (1983). *Family-centered social services: A Model for Child Welfare Agencies.* Iowa City, IA: The University of Iowa School of Social Work, National Resource Center on Family Based Services.

Ikelheimer, D. M. (2008). Treatment of opioid dependence via home-based telepsychiatry. *Psychiatric Services, 59,* 1218–1219.

Leginski, W., Croze, C., Driggers, J., Dumpman, S., Geertsen, D., Kamis-Gould, E., Namerow, M., Patton, R., Wilson, N., & Wurster, C. (1989). *Data Standards for Mental Health Decision Support Systems. Series FN No. 10.* Rockville, MD: U.S. Department of Health and Human Services.

NASMHPD Research Institute, Inc. (2007, December 3). Task 25a report: Identifying, collecting and comparing each state's expenditures for use of mental health block grant allocations. *How State Mental Health Agencies Use the*

Community Mental Health Services Block Grant to Improve Care and Transform Systems: 2007. [Online]. http://download.ncadi.samhsa.gov/ken/pdf/MHBGReportSection508-5-6-08.pdf [2010, July 19].

National Committee for Quality Assurance. (n.d.). 2010 NCQA MBHO Accreditation Requirements Link. [Online].http://www.ncqa.org [2010, July 17].

National Institute of Mental Health. (March, 2009). "Statistics." Available at http://www.nimh.nih.gov

P. L. 106-310. (2000). Children's Health Act of 2000.

Parrish, J. (1987). *Ideal Community-Based Mental Health Service System for Adults with Long-Term, Disabling Mental Illness.* Washington, DC: Substance Abuse and Mental Health Services Administration.

Patton, R., & Leginski, W. (1983). *The Design and Content of a National Mental Health Statistics System. DHHS Publication (ADM) 83-1095.* Rockville, MD: U.S. Department of Health and Human Services.

Sowder, B. (1979). *Issues Related to Psychiatric Services for Children and Youth: A Review of Selected Literature from 1970–1979.* Bethesda, MD: Burt Associates.

Standards for privacy of individually identifiable health information; final rule. (2002, August 14). *Federal Register,* pp. 53181–53273.

Stroul, B., & Friedman, R. (1994). *A System of Care for Children and Youth with Severe Emotional Disturbances.* Washington, DC: Georgetown University Child Development Center.

[SAMHSA] Substance Abuse & Mental Health Services Administration. (2010). *Request for Applications (RFA): State Mental Health Data Infrastructure Grants for Quality Improvement.* [Online]. http://www.samhsa.gov/Grants/2010/SM-10-009.aspx [2010, July 24].

Tarasoff v. Regents of the University of California, 17 Cal 3d 425, 131 Cal Rptr 14, 551 P 2d 334 (1976).

Tschirch, P., Walker, G., & Calvacca, L. T. (2006). Nursing in tele-mental health. *Journal of Psychosocial Nursing & Mental Health Services,* 44(5), 20–27.

KEY RESOURCES

Center for Mental Health Services
http://mentalhealth.samhsa.gov/cmhs

CARF International
http://www.carf.org

Joint Commission
http://www.jointcommission.org

National Alliance for the Mentally Ill
http://www.nami.org

National Association of State Mental Health Program Directors (NASMHPD)
www.nasmhpd.org

National Committee for Quality Assurance (NCQA)
http://www.ncqa.org

National Institute of Mental Health (NIMH)
http://www.nimh.nih.gov

URAC
http://www.urac.org

CHAPTER 8

Substance Abuse

MELISSA KING, MPPA, RHIA

FRANCES WICKHAM LEE, DBA, RHIA

KIMBERLY D. TAYLOR, RHIA

LEARNING OBJECTIVES

Upon successful completion of this chapter, you should be able to:

- Describe the various settings and caregivers commonly associated with substance abuse treatment.

- Evaluate the impact of state and federal laws and regulations on the treatment of substance abuse clients.

- Describe the role of the Commission on Accreditation of Rehabilitation Facilities (now CARF International) and the Joint Commission (TJC) in setting substance abuse treatment standards.

- Describe the components of a "typical" substance abuse client record, both inpatient and outpatient.

- Discuss current reimbursement issues related to substance abuse treatment.

- Compare *DSM* and the current version of *ICD* as they relate to the coding of substance abuse client records.

- Discuss quality improvement and utilization management within substance abuse facilities.

- Discuss the role of the health information manager in a substance abuse facility.

- Discuss the use of electronic information system technology in managing substance abuse client information.

- Identify the specific legal and ethical considerations associated with the confidentiality of substance abuse client records.

Setting	Description	Synonyms/Examples
Outpatient Substance Abuse Facility	A facility where clients receive regularly scheduled outpatient substance abuse treatment	Substance abuse treatment program or center
Intensive Outpatient Substance Abuse Facility	A facility where clients spend at least nine hours per week in substance abuse treatment but do not stay overnight	Partial hospitalization Day treatment IOP (Intensive Outpatient Program)
Residential Inpatient Substance Abuse Treatment Setting	A setting where clients are treated for substance abuse in a nonmedical residential setting	Rehabilitation 28-day program Residential treatment program Chemical dependency unit
Medically Managed Intensive Inpatient Substance Abuse Treatment Setting	A setting where clients are treated for substance abuse under the direction of a physician, which includes all services of an acute care hospital	Acute inpatient treatment Inpatient detoxification
Substance Abuse Education and Prevention Program	A program designed to prevent substance abuse problems in individuals or families	Early intervention School intervention programs Children of addicted families programs Alcohol and other drug prevention programs
Self-Help Recovery Groups	Support groups established to assist individuals in maintaining sobriety and a drug-free lifestyle	Alcoholics Anonymous Narcotics Anonymous 12-step programs and other recovery support groups
Aftercare	Usually follows intensive in/outpatient treatment; weekly individual and group sessions; lasts up to two years	Continuing Care Program Relapse Prevention Program

INTRODUCTION TO SETTING

The American Psychiatric Association's *Diagnostic and Statistical Manual of Mental Disorders, fourth edition, text revision (DSM-IV-TR)*, has traditionally divided various substance use disorders (e.g., alcohol use disorder, cocaine use disorder) into the broad categories of substance abuse and substance dependence, depending on the severity of the condition and the presence of withdrawal and other symptoms of addiction. General synonyms for substance abuse include *alcohol and other drug abuse* and *psychoactive substance abuse.* Alternate terms that are commonly used in place of substance dependence include *alcohol and other drug dependence, psychoactive substance dependence, drug addiction, alcoholism,* or *chemical dependency.* These terms may be substituted where appropriate for *substance abuse* throughout the various care settings discussed in this chapter. It is also important to note that individuals seen in substance abuse treatment settings are often referred to as clients or individuals receiving services (IRS), rather than patients, because the term *patient* implies a more medically oriented model of care.

Substance abuse is a major health problem in the United States. Many different types of treatment settings are available to substance abuse clients seeking assistance, including public and private facilities that provide a full range of services, from educational programs to medically managed intensive inpatient care. In 2006, 23.6 million people aged 12 or older needed substance abuse treatment. Of those, 2.5 million people received treatment in a specialized facility for substance abuse issues (SAMHSA, 2007b). The National Center on Addiction and Substance Abuse (CASA) at Columbia University found federal, state, and local government spending as a result of substance abuse and addiction to be $467.7 billion or more in 2005 (2009). The public sector has traditionally assumed a major responsibility for the operation of substance abuse treatment centers, particularly outpatient treatment centers. According to the *National Survey of Substance Abuse Treatment Services (N-SSATS): 2007,* 58 percent of all clients in treatment were in private non-profit facilities. Private for-profit facilities accounted for the treatment of 29 percent of substance abuse clients (SAMHSA, 2009). Publicly owned treatment centers generally receive their funds from state, city, and county governments; federal grants and contracts; and some client fees and third-party reimbursement. Private substance abuse treatment facilities, on the other hand, rely primarily on direct client payments and third-party reimbursement for their funds. Figure 8-1 shows the distribution of substance abuse clients by facility ownership and primary focus of facility.

The evolution of modern substance abuse treatment in the United States began in the 1950s with the development of freestanding residential programs for the treatment of alcohol dependency and with the continued growth and recognition of **Alcoholics Anonymous (AA)** and its 12-step recovery philosophy. Early alcohol treatment programs were not considered by the medical community to be truly part of the health care system and were often staffed and run by nonprofessionals, some of whom were recovering alcoholics themselves. Treatment for drug addiction was even more removed from mainstream health care, and clients were often referred to drug treatment centers by the criminal justice system. Although the American Medical Association classified alcoholism as a disease in 1956, it was not until the 1970s that the public began to recognize alcoholism as a disease and third-party payers began to offer some reimbursement for inpatient treatment. Outpatient treatment became more prevalent in the 1980s and 1990s as providers and third-party payers realized that substance abuse clients needed a full range of treatment options. In 2007, outpatient rehabilitation was the most widely available type of care, with non-intensive and intensive rehabilitation offered by 74 percent and 44 percent of all facilities, respectively. Residential rehabilitation was offered by 27 percent of all facilities, while hospital inpatient rehabilitation was offered by 7 percent

Facility Operation			Clients in Treatment on March 31, 2009			
	Facilities		All Clients		Clients Under Age 18	
	No.	%	No.	%	No.	%
Private non-profit	7,826	57.9	630,579	53.3	56,034	66.4
Private for-profit	3,959	29.3	375,256	31.7	16,280	19.3
Local government	795	5.9	75,126	6.4	7,044	8.4
State government	401	3.0	42,761	3.6	2,980	3.5
Federal government	341	2.5	46,282	3.9	440	0.5
Dept. of Veterans Affairs	210	1.6	37,381	3.2	18	<.05
Dept. of Defense	91	0.7	6,877	0.6	88	0.1
Indian Health Service	38	0.3	1,982	0.2	332	0.4
Other	2	0.0	42	<.05	2	<.05
Tribal government	191	1.4	12,073	1.0	1,548	1.8
Total	**13,513**	**100.0**	**1,182,077**	**100.0**	**84,326**	**100.0**

Primary Focus of Facility			Clients in Treatment on March 31, 2009			
	Facilities		All Clients		Clients Under Age 18	
	No.	%	No.	%	No.	%
Substance abuse treatment services	8,257	61.1	792,815	67.1	47,528	56.4
Mental health services	878	6.5	43,137	3.6	5,508	6.5
Mix of mental health & substance abuse treatment services	4,091	30.3	327,166	27.7	30,656	36.4
General health care	169	1.3	13,933	1.2	232	0.3
Other/unknown	118	0.9	5,026	0.4	402	0.5
Total	**13,513**	**100.0**	**1,182,077**	**100.0**	**84,326**	**100.0**

FIGURE 8-1 Substance abuse treatment clients by facility ownership and by primary focus of facility.
Source: Office of Applied Studies, Substance Abuse and Mental Health Services Administration, National Survey of Substance Abuse Treatment Services (N-SSATS), 2009.

of facilities. Fifteen percent of all facilities provided partial hospitalization programs. Outpatient detoxification was available at 11 percent of facilities, while residential detoxification and hospital inpatient detoxification were each provided by 6 percent of all facilities (SAMHSA, 2009).

Care Settings

The following list represents some of the more common settings for substance abuse treatment and services; however, it should not be considered an exhaustive list. For simplicity, the programs discussed in this chapter have been grouped by care setting under the following general headings:

1. Outpatient treatment
2. Intensive outpatient or partial hospitalization treatment
3. Inpatient/residential treatment
4. Aftercare/continuing care
5. Educational/prevention programs
6. Self-help recovery groups

Within the substance abuse treatment community, however, similar programs can sometimes be found in an inpatient, outpatient, or community setting. For example, the Alcoholics Anonymous (AA) 12-step philosophy and program originated as part of a self-help recovery network, but over the years this philosophy has also been incorporated into programs at both inpatient and outpatient treatment facilities.

The discussion of the first three care settings in this section is based on the levels of care as defined in *American Society of Addiction Medicine Patient Placement Criteria*, second edition revised (*ASAM PPC-2R*) (ASAM, 2001). The levels of care are:

- Level 0.5, Early Intervention
- Level I, Outpatient Treatment
- Level II, Intensive Outpatient/Partial Hospitalization
- Level III, Residential/Inpatient Treatment
- Level IV, Medically Managed Intensive Inpatient Treatment

Within these broad levels of service is a range of specific levels of care. As a general rule, clients should be treated at the lowest or least intensive level of care that will accomplish their treatment goals. The levels are discussed in this chapter as discrete entities, but in reality they represent the continuum of substance abuse treatment services available to clients in most areas of the country.

Outpatient Treatment

ASAM describes Level I **outpatient treatment** as follows:

> Level I encompasses organized services that may be delivered in a wide variety of settings. Addiction or mental health treatment personnel provide professionally directed evaluation, treatment and recovery service. Such services are provided in regularly scheduled sessions and follow a defined set of policies and procedures or medical protocols.

> Level I outpatient services are designed to treat the individual's level of clinical severity and to help the individual achieve permanent changes in his or her alcohol- and drug-using behavior and mental functioning. To accomplish this, services must address major lifestyle, attitudinal and behavioral issues that have the potential to undermine the goals of treatment or inhibit the individual's ability to cope with major life tasks without the non-medical use of alcohol or other drugs. (ASAM, 2001, p. 2)

Outpatient providers, such as mental health centers, hospital-based outpatient centers, and freestanding drug and alcohol treatment centers, currently treat substance abuse clients through a variety of treatment modalities, including individual, group, and family therapy. Individual therapy is currently the most common form of outpatient treatment, accounting for 81 percent of all treatment sessions (SAMHSA, 2009). Specialized outpatient programs are also found throughout the substance abuse treatment system. Some examples of specialized outpatient treatment programs are methadone maintenance programs for heroin addicts, organized school intervention programs for adolescents, court-related programs for individuals convicted of substance abuse–related offenses, and employee assistance programs that contract with companies within the community to provide care to their employees. The Types of Clients section in this chapter provides more information on these and other specific client populations. Outpatient therapy is typically a long-term commitment for a client, lasting up to a year or more.

Intensive Outpatient or Partial Hospitalization Treatment

ASAM defines **intensive outpatient or partial hospitalization treatments** as follows:

> Level II is an organized outpatient service that delivers treatment services during the day, before or after work or school, in the evening or on weekends. For appropriately selected patients, such programs provide essential education and treatment components while allowing patients to apply their newly acquired skills within "real world" environments. Programs have the capacity to arrange for medical and psychiatric consultation, psychopharmacological consultation, medication management, and 24-hour crisis services (ASAM, 2001, p. 3).

Intensive outpatient treatment requires a minimum of nine hours of weekly attendance, usually in increments of three to eight hours a day for five to seven days a week. This treatment is often recommended for patients in the early stages of treatment or those transitioning from residential or hospital settings. This environment is suitable for patients who do not need full-time supervision and have some available supports but need more structure than is usually available in less intensive outpatient settings. This treatment encompasses day treatment or group programs that may offer a full range of services. Some of these include outpatient detoxification. The frequency and length of session is usually tapered as patients demonstrate progress, less risk of relapse, and a stronger reliance on drug-free community supports. An evening program can provide clients with an alternative to inpatient treatment, thus avoiding an extended leave from home, work, or school. Intensive outpatient treatment programs allow adult clients to continue working and adolescent clients to continue schooling, while providing a structured treatment environment. Partial hospitalization programs are generally day treatment programs that provide a greater number of treatment hours for clients with a more severe level of illness. Clients spend all day in the treatment program, but return home each evening (American Psychiatric Association, 2006).

Inpatient/Residential Treatment

Under certain circumstances a substance abuse client may require an inpatient stay at a hospital or residential treatment facility. These clients may be in need of medically managed detoxification, have substance abuse-related medical problems, or come from environments that make outpatient treatment ineffective. ASAM recognizes two levels of inpatient treatment: **residential/inpatient treatment** and **medically managed intensive inpatient treatment**. Both levels require a planned regimen of 24-hour professionally directed evaluation, care, and treatment.

Residential/Inpatient Treatment   Residential/inpatient treatment is directed at clients with subacute medical, behavioral, or emotional problems. Residential treatment provides a live-in facility with 24-hour supervision. This type of treatment is better than outpatient treatment for consumers with an overwhelming substance abuse problem. The consumers in this program typically are without the motivation or social supports to abstain from abusing. The length of stay in these facilities ranges from short term to long term. There are programs that offer less restrictive types of treatment, such as halfway and quarter-way houses, to help the consumer's transition back into the community (American Psychiatric Association, 2006).

Medically Managed Intensive Inpatient Treatment   In a medically managed environment, the clients' problems are acute, and a full range of medical and support services that can be found in a general hospital should be available to them. The treatment settings for medically managed intensive inpatient treatment include acute care general hospitals, acute psychiatric hospitals or units, and chemical dependency specialty hospitals that have the appropriate medical and nursing services available (ASAM, 2001). According to the American Psychiatric Association (2006), this level of inpatient hospitalization includes around-the-clock treatment and supervision by a multidisciplinary staff that emphasizes medical management of detoxification or other psychiatric crises. The length of stay at this level of care is usually short term.

Educational/Prevention Programs/Early Intervention

Society places a significant emphasis on awareness and prevention of substance abuse problems. Substance abuse facilities, particularly those in the public sector, are frequently involved in providing structured prevention, education, and awareness programs. The clients served by these programs differ from those who receive substance abuse treatment; these clients do not necessarily have substance abuse or dependence diagnoses, but are considered to be at risk for problems in the future. Many participants in educational programs are children or adolescents who have been identified by the schools, social service agencies, or legal system as having the potential to develop substance abuse problems or who have family members with existing substance abuse problems. A program that targets children of addicted families is one example of a service that might be offered by a substance treatment facility to help children who are affected by substance abuse within their families.

SAMHSA's **Center for Substance Abuse Prevention (CSAP)** administers a number of grant programs aimed at reducing the incidence of substance abuse. Recognizing the cost-effectiveness of prevention programs, CSAP provides national leadership for community-based prevention programs. Research has demonstrated the effectiveness of various interventions for substance abuse prevention. Over 60 prevention interventions are listed at the National Registry of Evidence-based Programs and Practices (NREPP—discussed later) that meet evidence-based practice criteria for effectiveness.

Self-Help Recovery Groups

It can be argued that it is not appropriate to include the self-help recovery groups in a list of substance abuse care settings, because they are designed to be voluntary and to provide support rather than treatment for the recovering addict. However, these groups provide lifelong assistance to many individuals with substance abuse problems and are considered a significant factor in many successful recoveries. The most widely recognized self-help organization is Alcoholics Anonymous, a program in which members follow a 12-step program that leads to recovery. AA was founded in 1935 and had reached national prominence by the 1950s (Alcoholics Anonymous World Services, Inc., 1957). Since that time, AA has spawned other self-help groups, such as Narcotics Anonymous (NA), that adhere to a similar 12-step philosophy. No records are kept by 12-step support groups, because anonymity is a key element in the recovery programs. However, 12-step programs have reached such prominence in the substance abuse treatment community that many providers actually integrate the philosophy into their treatment services, and this will be reflected in client records.

AA is the most widely accepted network of substance abuse self-help groups, but other approaches are also available. For example, some programs offer support groups based on various adaptations of cognitive behavioral therapy as a means to recovery. Client participation in a support group, regardless of the group's philosophy, improves the chances that the client will stay sober. Clients are more likely to participate in groups when they feel a connection to the group's general beliefs. Because various support groups have differing philosophical underpinnings, it is helpful for the treatment professional to assist the client in finding a group that is a good fit for him or her (Atkins & Hawdon, 2007).

Types of Clients

Within the various types of substance abuse settings and programs, the clients served may range in age from infants to the elderly and come from all socioeconomic backgrounds. In addition to identifying broad categories of clients, such as inpatients and outpatients, facilities will often further identify segments of their client populations by factors such as age, sex, type of referral, or legal status. This categorization facilitates program planning and administration. In many cases, educational and treatment programs can be tailored to meet the needs of particular client groups. Some examples of client groups served by specific programs or protocols because of their special needs are adolescents, women, clients referred to employee assistance programs, clients who have been dually diagnosed with a mental disorder and a substance abuse disorder, and clients who have been court referred. A recent trend is to provide group sessions to individuals who are incarcerated. The sessions are provided to the individuals while they are in a jail or other correctional setting. Many other special programs are offered in substance abuse treatment centers throughout the United States, but examining this sample will provide an overview of the scope of clients served.

Adolescents

In addition to potentially causing problems with family, friends, and schoolwork, use of alcohol and other drugs by adolescents can lead to dangerous patterns of lifelong abuse. The 2007 national Youth Risk Behavior Survey indicated that around 75 percent of high school students had tried alcohol (CDC, Online). Health care providers, teachers, and parents now recognize that an adolescent can develop serious abuse and addiction problems as a result of this early experimentation. In 2007, the National Survey on Drug Use and Health reported that an estimated 19.3 million adolescents between the ages of 12 and 17 needed treatment for alcohol problems. This does not include the number that sought treatment for drug issues (SAMHSA, 2009). The majority of these clients are treated in a clinical setting that is specifically structured for treating adolescents. Treating an adolescent substance abuse problem is quite different from treating an adult problem. The youthful client's unique emotional, social, and educational needs must be addressed by his or her treatment plan. To highlight the need to use care in selecting a treatment program for adolescents, the American Academy of Pediatrics (AAP) developed a list of program selection criteria that addresses, among other concerns, such issues as:

- Knowledge of the clinicians about adolescent behavior and development, in addition to chemical dependency treatment
- Low staff-to-patient ratio
- Separation of the adolescent unit from an adult unit
- Availability of academic and vocational activities (Muramoto & Leshan, 1993)

Other factors, such as family involvement in treatment, have also been found to produce better outcomes in adolescent substance abuse treatment programs (Brannigan et al., 2004). The treatment settings for adolescents span all levels of care and include in-school intervention programs, outpatient therapy, intensive outpatient programs, short-stay inpatient treatment, and extended-stay inpatient treatment.

Women

There is growing awareness within the substance abuse treatment community that women, particularly pregnant women and women who are parents of young children, have special care and support needs, as do their children. In 2006, 6 percent of women of childbearing age who entered publicly funded substance abuse treatment were pregnant when admitted (SAMHSA, 2009). Treatment of pregnant women should be made a priority, because the welfare of both the mother and the unborn baby are at stake. Fetal alcohol syndrome and cocaine addiction in newborns can lead to serious health and developmental problems for children. Pregnant women with substance abuse problems need prenatal care along with substance abuse treatment, and their children need monitoring for potential medical and emotional problems. Programs developed for pregnant women might include child care that incorporates therapeutic activities to assist the children in learning to deal with issues related to living with an addicted parent and easy access to intensive prenatal care and case management services. The levels of service provided in women's substance abuse programs include outpatient, intensive outpatient, and inpatient treatment, depending on the severity of the substance abuse and the individual's treatment plan.

EAP Clients

Many substance abuse agencies and treatment facilities have established **employee assistance programs (EAPs)** to serve working adults and their employers. Businesses contract with local substance abuse organizations to provide services to their employees. Employers have come to recognize that substance abuse problems will have a negative impact on job performance, and that it is in their best interest and that of their employees to encourage treatment of these problems. The actual scope of the substance abuse services provided by the EAP is specified in a contract negotiated between the business and the provider. The contract generally includes at least an assessment, at little or no out-of-pocket cost for the employee and, if needed, referral to one of the education or treatment options available through the provider's existing programs. Employees can be referred to the EAP by their employers, or in some cases the employees will seek out the EAP services for themselves. As in other substance abuse treatment programs, the strict confidentiality of EAP client information is maintained, regardless of the referral source.

Dually Diagnosed Clients

A growing portion of the substance abuse client population is **dually diagnosed** with both a substance abuse or dependency disorder and a chronic mental illness. These clients typically have difficulty succeeding in traditional alcohol and drug treatment programs and self-help groups, which has led to the development of programs designed to meet their special care needs. By using assessment tools specifically designed to identify dually diagnosed individuals, treatment facilities can better plan the course of treatment for clients. In some states, and in some private facilities, substance abuse and mental health services are offered in the same location or by a single organizational unit, allowing dually diagnosed clients access to treatment for both their substance abuse and their mental health disorders. However, states do not have to provide mental health and substance abuse services through one agency in order to develop programs for dually diagnosed clients. For example, the New Hampshire Division of Mental Health and Developmental Services, in collaboration with the state's Office of Alcohol and Drug Abuse, has been offering integrated treatment services for dually diagnosed clients since 1987 (Drake et al., 1991).

Court-Referred Clients

Individuals who are arrested and convicted of alcohol- and other drug-related offenses are frequently referred to substance abuse treatment programs for drug and alcohol awareness education, a substance abuse assessment, or substance abuse treatment. For additional information on court-ordered treatment, refer to the Risk Management and Legal Issues section. When an individual is convicted of driving while intoxicated (DWI) or driving under the influence (DUI) of alcohol or drugs, the court may, for example, order that individual to enroll in an awareness program and to obtain a substance abuse assessment to determine whether treatment would be required. In some states, the assessment or education program may actually be required by law, creating a situation in which law enforcement, the court system, and the substance abuse treatment center must work closely together. DUI clients are not the only court-related clients seen by substance abuse facilities; persons arrested and convicted of other alcohol- or drug-related offenses may also be referred or ordered to obtain assessment and treatment.

Types of Caregivers

The types of caregivers who work with substance abuse clients are quite varied. They include individuals who possess a wide range of educational and professional backgrounds, from residential aides to psychiatrists and other physicians. Each of these caregivers is an important member of the substance abuse treatment team, bringing unique experience and expertise to the overall treatment process. The following discussion includes a representation of direct caregivers who work with substance abuse clients; however, there may be several others who are involved in the clients' care. Clients treated in an acute inpatient setting are cared for by the various ancillary departments and other medical and allied health specialists found in the hospital. It is not unusual to see professionals such as occupational therapists, recreation therapists, and dietitians working in substance abuse programs.

Physicians

Some physicians specialize in the treatment of chemically dependent patients. However, there are also psychiatrists, family practitioners, or other physicians with a general practice orientation involved in substance abuse treatment. Any treatment plan that requires a medical intervention, such as prescription medications or detoxification services, is monitored, if not managed, by a physician. Medical services may be provided by full-time staff physicians or by part-time contract physicians, depending on the level of care and the treatment setting, for example, public or private, inpatient or outpatient.

Physician Assistants and Nurse Practitioners

As in other segments of health care, the role of physician extenders or mid-level providers—physician assistants (PAs) and nurse practitioners (NPs)—varies from state to state and from facility to facility. As a general rule, these professionals treat clients under the supervision of a physician; however, some states allow more independent practice.

Nurses

In addition to medical care and substance abuse treatment, clients in inpatient substance abuse facilities require nursing care. The extent of nursing service provided by a facility depends on the level of care it offers. An acute care hospital setting provides 24-hour nursing care to its substance abuse patients, just as it does to other patients.

Counselors

Substance abuse counselors are professionals such as social workers and psychologists, with special training and experience in the treatment of clients with substance abuse problems. The educational background of these individuals varies and may depend in part on the state's facility licensure, practitioner licensure, and Medicaid regulations. The counselor provides individual, group, and/or family therapy to the client and the client's family according to the treatment plan. Frequently, the counselor is recognized as the client's primary therapist, particularly in an outpatient setting. The primary therapist is the caregiver responsible for coordinating the treatment of the client, including ensuring that all documentation requirements are met.

Case Managers

As with substance abuse counselors, substance abuse case managers come from a variety of professional and educational backgrounds. They may be nurses, social workers, or educational specialists. The role of the case manager in substance abuse treatment depends on the level of care and the particular care setting. In an inpatient setting, the case manager may focus primarily on reimbursement issues and organizing follow-up care. The case manager in an outpatient setting assists the client with these and other nontreatment activities, such as obtaining adequate housing, securing financial assistance, keeping medical and counseling appointments, and so on. A case manager differs from a counselor in his or her relationship with the client; the case manager provides assistance with obtaining and coordinating services for clients rather than actual therapy.

Recreational Therapists

Long-term inpatient and other residential treatment programs often employ recreational therapists to work with clients. Recreational therapists design therapeutic recreational activities for residents while they are undergoing treatment. For example, a residential treatment program for adolescents might incorporate a challenge course or other outdoor activities designed to build trust and self-esteem.

REGULATORY ISSUES

Several public and private agencies regulate or set standards for substance abuse treatment facilities and programs. One important set of federal regulations, **42 C.F.R. Part 2, Confidentiality of Drug and Alcohol Abuse Records,** mandates that strict confidentiality guidelines and legal procedures be adhered to by any federally assisted substance abuse treatment program. Substance abuse treatment records historically have been the only category of health-related record—except those created in government-operated health care facilities such as Veterans Affairs and Indian Health Service hospitals—whose security and confidentiality are specifically protected by a comprehensive federal law. A detailed discussion of 42 C.F.R. Part 2 is in the Risk Management and Legal Issues section of this chapter. As discussed in an earlier chapter, HIPAA also provides guidelines for confidentiality of protected health information (PHI). The federal law that protects substance abuse programs and their information is more comprehensive than the HIPAA requirements in many ways. Therefore, the substance abuse programs have not fundamentally changed their approach to maintaining confidentiality.

The other regulatory agencies that are discussed in this section set standards for substance abuse treatment facilities, along with other health care facilities, with the intent of promoting high-quality care. There are two major private, not-for-profit, voluntary accrediting agencies that set standards for substance abuse facilities: The Joint Commission (TJC) and CARF International (the Commission on Accreditation of Rehabilitation Facilities). The government standards that are most frequently applied to substance abuse treatment programs are state Medicaid guidelines. Facilities treating Medicare clients also have to comply with the applicable Conditions of Participation.

As the best-known voluntary health care accreditation agency in the United States, the Joint Commission's original focus was on improving the quality of hospital-based patient care. Over the years, however, the Joint Commission has developed distinct accreditation programs for nonhospital settings, such as outpatient mental health and substance abuse treatment, ambulatory care, long-term care, and others. Although Joint Commission accreditation is voluntary, in some states substance abuse treatment facilities, particularly inpatient facilities and hospital-based programs that are accredited, do not have to undergo additional surveys for licensure and certification. Inpatient substance abuse facilities, as well as hospital-based ambulatory, residential, or partial hospitalization substance abuse programs, follow the standards outlined in the Joint Commission's *Comprehensive Accreditation Manual for Hospitals (CAMH).* This is the same manual that is used by acute care hospitals, but specific standards within the *CAMH* address services to behavioral health patients, including substance abuse clients. Community-based outpatient substance abuse programs follow the standards outlined in a separate Joint Commission accreditation program manual, the *Comprehensive Accreditation Manual for Behavioral Health Care (CAMBHC).* This manual and its corresponding accreditation program are designed to meet the needs of nonhospital programs serving mental health, substance abuse, and developmentally delayed clients. Hospital-based and inpatient substance abuse programs are more likely to seek Joint Commission accreditation, often as a part of an organization-wide effort, than are community outpatient programs. Although there are definite advantages for substance abuse treatment programs in seeking Joint Commission accreditation, it can be a costly process, and many publicly funded outpatient programs often choose not to participate.

The mission of **CARF International (Commission on Accreditation of Rehabilitation Facilities)** is "to promote the quality, value, and optimal outcomes of services through a consultative accreditation process that centers on enhancing the lives of the persons served" (CARF, Online). CARF's core values emphasize the rights of the individuals served by rehabilitation facilities. These values address the importance of treating individuals with respect and empowering them to make their own informed choices. Substance abuse programs can be accredited under several of CARF's core programs, including detoxification, drug court treatment, employee assistance, outpatient treatment, partial hospitalization, prevention, or residential treatment, to name a few. Two CARF standards manuals are relevant to substance abuse programs: the *Behavioral Health Standards Manual* and the *Opioid Treatment Program Standards Manual* (CARF, Online).

Another major category of regulators of substance abuse treatment is the various state agencies that are responsible for state Medicaid programs. Medicaid is a federally mandated program that provides medical assistance to low-income individuals, as authorized by Title XIX of the Social Security Act of 1965. However, the actual Medicaid costs are shared by the federal government and the states. The percentages for this cost sharing and the actual dollar amount spent for Medicaid vary significantly from state to state. State Medicaid agencies are granted a fair amount of independence in determining the levels of coverage and the payment mechanisms they will employ, provided the basic services as required by the federal regulations are covered. Consequently, most of the standards governing Medicaid providers are developed at the state level and also vary from one state to another. One basic tenet of Medicaid is that it provides for reimbursement of care that is "medically necessary." For substance abuse treatment programs, this translates into the need for physician involvement and clear documentation of the medical necessity of the prescribed substance abuse treatment for Medicaid clients. Figure 8-2 details the number and percentage of substance abuse facilities licensed, approved, certified, or accredited by various agencies.

Facility Licensing, Approval, Certification, or Accreditation	Facilities[1]	
	No.	**%**
Any listed agency/organization	12,838	95.0
State substance abuse agency	11,085	82.0
State mental health department	4,644	34.4
State department of health	5,490	40.6
Hospital licensing authority	935	6.9
The Joint Commision	2,665	19.7
CARF[2]	2,932	21.7
NCQA[3]	357	2.6
COA[4]	660	4.9
Other state/local agency/org	1,159	8.6

[1]Facilities may be licensed by more than one agency/organization.
[2]Commission on Accreditation of Rehabilitation Facilities
[3]National Committee for Quality Assurance
[4]Council for Accreditation

FIGURE **8-2** Types of licensing, approval, certification, or accreditation held by substance abuse facilities.
Source: Office of Applied Studies, Substance Abuse and Mental Health Services Administration, National Survey of Substance Abuse Treatment Services (N-SSATS), 2009.

DOCUMENTATION

As in other health care settings, substance abuse facilities require clear and consistent documentation. Good-quality documentation of care, whether it is done manually or electronically, is essential. The primary purpose for maintaining client records is to support client treatment. Other purposes for the records include: to improve communication among care providers, to serve as legal records of care provided, to support reimbursement claims, to monitor the quality of care, and to provide data for research and education. Records are increasingly important for documenting evidence-based practices and outcome measures. It is becoming more important to support the treatment program through documentation. Facilities need to demonstrate that a client's treatment was successful. Documentation can help to support this by indicating an increase in an Axis V diagnosis (which is explained later in this chapter) or by documenting recidivism rates.

Although the federal government mandates that a standard set of information be submitted on each client that is treated, the types of documents, computer systems, files, and forms vary considerably from organization to organization. However, each facility should develop and maintain standards, policies, and procedures governing its specific documentation requirements (Ohio Administrative Code, 2005). The following list, adapted from South Carolina Department of Alcohol and Other Drug Abuse Services' *Uniform Clinical Records*, represents typical information that might be found within a substance abuse client's record, divided into two general groups: legal/administrative documentation and clinical documentation.

Legal/Administrative Documentation

The legal/administrative portion of the client record typically includes essential nonclinical information such as demographic and identifying information, along with any required legal documentation. Some examples include:

- Admission information
- Commitment papers
- Fee agreement and financial assessment
- Insurance authorization
- Special-program enrollment forms
- Program or agency rules
- Consents to treatment
- Consents to release of information
- Client rights information

Clinical Documentation

The clinical portion of the client's record documents the direct care provided and might include such items as:

- Clinical assessments
- Medical assessment, if necessary
- Individualized treatment plan
- Clinical service notes or progress notes (They may be daily or weekly summary notes, depending on the type of program and applicable standards.)
- Discharge summary/aftercare plan
- Follow-up information
- List of medications

Two key documents in the substance abuse record are the **clinical assessment** and the **individualized treatment plan**. (See Figure 8-3 and Figure 8-4.) Each client should receive a thorough clinical assessment before the development of his or her individualized treatment plan. This assessment typically includes documentation of:

- Identifying information
- Presenting problem
- Health, medical, and/or developmental history
- Family and social history
- History of psychoactive substance use
- History of psychological factors impacting the client's condition

Clinical Assessment Outline

Client Name (Last, First, MI)	ID#

Presenting Problem: Include reason for entry, source of referral, legal Involvement, self-identified problems and recent stressors.

_____

_____

_____

_____

_____

_____

Health/Medical History: Describe general health, nutrition, medical problems, medications, hospitallza-tions, disabilities, tuberculosis screening and HIV-risk behaviors.

_____

_____

_____

_____

_____

_____

Page 1 of 4

FIGURE 8-3 Sample clinical assessment forms. (Delmar/Cengage Learning)

Family/Social Interaction: In chronological order, describe family of origin and present family, including relationships with all family members. Include family history of substance use/abuse and current family use. Describe other intimate and social relationships. Include peer group functioning. Include cultural, ethnic and spiritual factors and expectations. Include any physical and/or sexual abuse history.

_____

_____

_____

_____

_____

_____

_____

_____

_____

_____

_____

_____

_____

_____

_____

_____

FIGURE **8-3** (*Continued*)

Client Name (Last, First, MI)	ID#

Drug	Age at First Use	Frequency (last 6 months)	Quantity (specify time frame)	Last Use	How Used
Alcohol					
Amphetamine					
Caffeine					
Cannabis					
Cocaine					
Hallucinogen					
Inhalant					
Nicotine					
Opioid					
PCP					
Sedative Hypnotic					

Psychoactive Substance Use: Include other relevant substance use factors such as loss of control, tolerance, treatment history, patterns of use and problems related to use. Include data to differentiate between use, abuse and dependence.

_____

_____

_____

_____

_____

_____

_____

FIGURE **8-3** (*Continued*)

Page 4 of 4

Psychological: Include mental status, activities of daily living, communication skills/abilities, present emotional state, management of emotions, violence, suicide attempts/thoughts and psychiatric history (to include history of eating disorder behaviors).

_____

_____

_____

_____

_____

Educational/Vocational: Include years of education, military service, job history, financial status and leisure activities.

_____

_____

_____

Strengths and Needs: Describe client and clinician perceptions and unique factors affecting the course of treatment.

_____

_____

_____

Sources of Information other than client:

Name _____   Relationship_____

Name _____   Relationship_____

Assessment Interview Information		
Assessment Date	Client Time	Clinician Signature and Title
_____	_____	_____
_____	_____	_____
_____	_____	_____

FIGURE **8-3** (_Continued_)

Clinical Assessment Outline

Client Name (Last, First, MI)	ID#

Identifying Information

DOB _____ Age _____ Sex _____ Ethnic Group _____

Marital Status _____ Occupation _____ Education _____

Multiaxial Diagnosis

Code #   Description

Axis 1:   _____   _____

Axis II: _____   _____

Axis III: _____   _____

Axis IV: Psychosocial Stressors: _____

              Severity: _____

Axis V: GAP -   _____(current)

Master Problem List: In concise statements, list the most immediate problems the client is presenting. Indicate whether each problem will be addressed on the Treatment Plan (T); whether it will be referred (R) for services elsewhere; or whether it will be monitored (M). Place the letter that corresponds to the appropriate disposition in the space provided to the left of each problem statemen

_____ 1) _____

_____ 2) _____

_____ 3) _____

_____ 4) _____

_____ 5) _____

_____ 6) _____

_____ 7) _____

_____ 8) _____

Admitted to services _____ yes _____ no Reason for non-admission _____

_____

FIGURE **8-3** (*Continued*)

Interpretive Summary: Include an integration and interpretation of all pertinent assessment information; the client's perception of his/her needs, strengths, limitations or problems; clinical judgments regarding the course of treatment; recommended treatments; and anticipated level and length of care.

_____

_____

_____

_____

_____

_____

_____

_____

_____

_____

_____

_____

Clinician Signature and Title	**Date**

FIGURE **8-3** (*Continued*)

Six Month Individualized Treatment Plan

1. Client Name (Last, First, MI)	ID#

2. Diagnosis and Justification for Treatment or Continuation of Treatment

3. Proposed Treatment Process

a. Date Service Ordered	b. Type Service	c. Estimated Frequency	d. Goals	e. Expected Achievement Date

4. Client Signature	Date
5. Clinician Signature and Title	Date

FIGURE **8-4** Sample individualized treatment plan forms. (Delmar/Cengage Learning)

6. Summary of FIRST 90 Day Progress	
(Address progress on goals, appropriateness of service being provided, and need for continued treatment.)	
7. Clinician Signature and Title	Date
8. Summary of SECOND 90 Day Progress	
(Address progress on goals, appropriateness of service being provided, and need for continued treatment.)	
9. Clinician Signature and Title	Date

FIGURE **8-4** (*Continued*)

- Educational/vocational history
- Client abilities, strengths, needs, and preferences
- Preliminary diagnoses
- Admission-to-program information, including specific reasons when admission is denied
- Initial problem list
- Clinical assessment summary

The severity and unique treatment considerations of substance abuse problems vary significantly from one client to another, so an individualized plan of treatment must be established for every case, even if the clients' diagnoses are the same. For example, one client with a diagnosis of cocaine abuse might require both an inpatient stay and outpatient therapy, whereas another client might only need outpatient therapy. The individualized treatment plan (ITP) is the document in the client's record that is intended to guide the clinician and the client through the treatment process; therefore, the ITP must be based on the client's comprehensive clinical assessment. An ITP typically includes:

- Identifying information
- *DSM-IV-TR* diagnoses (*DSM-V* to replace *DSM-IV-TR*)
- Strengths of the individual
- Justification or reason for treatment, including duration and frequency of the problem
- Proposed treatment process, including type of service and frequency
- Treatment goals and objectives that are measurable, with target achievement dates

The ITP is updated periodically to reflect changes in the client's condition and revised treatment goals. The ITP should be a flexible document designed to meet the treatment needs of the individual client. Both CARF and TJC have developed standards for the ITP.

REIMBURSEMENT AND FUNDING

The reimbursement issues facing inpatient substance abuse facilities are essentially the same as those for other types of inpatient mental health services. However, the funding stream for outpatient substance abuse treatment is complex, involving several government agencies at both the state and federal levels, as well as private insurance companies and client fees.

In a community (outpatient or residential) substance abuse treatment center, for example, revenues may come from any combination of the following sources:

- *Client Fees.* In the public sector, client fees do not account for a major portion of revenue, but they are collected, generally on a sliding-scale basis (i.e., clients' out-of-pocket fees are set according to their ability to pay). Both family size and income are taken into consideration in determining the clients' copayments.
- *Private Insurance.* Individual insurance policies may cover substance abuse services at the inpatient or outpatient level. In public facilities, the insurance company is generally billed first, before any federal insurance is billed or any applicable sliding-scale copayment is determined.
- *Medicaid.* Medicaid program costs are shared by the federal and state governments. Therefore, eligibility, reimbursement rates, and payment mechanisms (fee-for-service, capitation, etc.) for substance abuse treatment vary from state to state. Most publicly supported substance abuse facilities rely heavily on Medicaid as a source of revenue.
- *Medicare.* Medicare covers a limited amount of substance abuse treatment for eligible clients. Services such as inpatient treatment, outpatient treatment, and detoxification are covered for a preset number of days or visits.
- *Other Government Funding Sources.* Several federal agencies administer a variety of block grants and contracts to support substance abuse treatment or prevention. The agency that administers the federal substance

abuse prevention and treatment (SAPT) grants is the Substance Abuse and Mental Health Services Administration (SAMHSA). These grants, and others, are generally awarded to individual states, which in turn distribute the money to eligible community agencies. In some of these agencies, federal funding may account for up to 75 percent or more of total revenue. Certain community-based treatment programs, such as school-based intervention programs, may actually be funded up to 100 percent by specific grants or contracts—for example, from SAMHSA's Center for Substance Abuse Prevention (CSAP) or Center for Substance Abuse Treatment (CSAT).

INFORMATION MANAGEMENT

Many of the information management issues facing substance abuse facilities are shared by other types of health care settings. This makes sense, because the purpose of maintaining client information in substance abuse facilities is basically the same as in other facilities: to facilitate the documentation of care and services provided; to support quality review activities; to ensure appropriate financial reimbursement; to meet all legal requirements; and to meet a variety of administrative, research, and educational needs. There are, however, a few issues that are either unique to substance abuse or are more commonly found in this setting. The following sections describe some of these issues related to the areas of data and information flow, coding and classification, data sets for substance abuse, and computerization of client information.

Data and Information Flow

Each substance abuse facility has its own distinct flow of client information, from the time of admission through discharge and follow-up care. This information flow may or may not include computer-based information, but it should reflect the course of treatment provided to the clients. Figure 8-5 represents a typical flow of information in an outpatient substance abuse center. Once a client enters the system, whether as a court-ordered admission or as a voluntary admission, the intake process is the first step in collecting client information and determining the appropriate treatment. During intake, clerical personnel gather all necessary demographic and financial information, as well as the necessary consent to treatment and release-of-information forms. After the intake, designated clinical staff members conduct a complete substance abuse assessment to determine the level of care and program that is most appropriate for the client. The client's program-specific, individualized treatment plan is then developed by his or her treatment team. This treatment plan lists, among other things, the client's individualized treatment goals and objectives and serves as a "blueprint" to his or her care. While the client is involved in active treatment, all other documentation is tied to the treatment plan and should reflect progress toward the treatment goals. Most substance abuse programs have aftercare staff members who follow up on their discharged clients to evaluate their continued progress once active treatment has been completed.

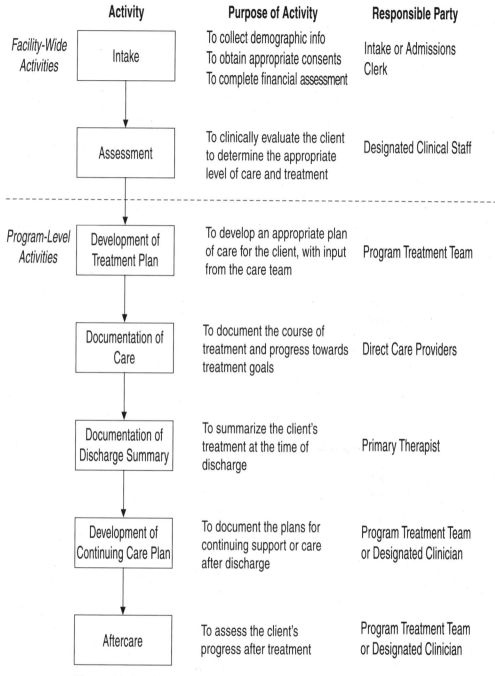

FIGURE 8-5 Flow of information within a client's record. (Delmar/Cengage Learning)

Coding and Classification

The selection of a coding or classification system for a substance abuse treatment facility depends on the level of care provided by that facility and the type of funding that is used to support its programs. In general, when *ICD-9-CM* and *CPT* codes are required for reimbursement purposes, they are assigned following the same rules that apply to other inpatient and outpatient settings. The one significant difference in substance abuse coding is the availability of the *Diagnostic and Statistical Manual of Mental Disorders*, fourth edition, text revision (*DSM-IV-TR*). *DSM-IV-TR* is a classification system and nomenclature of mental disorders that was developed by the American Psychiatric Association with a stated purpose of providing "clear descriptions of diagnostic categories in order to enable clinicians and investigators to diagnose, communicate about, study, and treat people with various mental disorders" (American Psychiatric Association, 2000, p. xxxvii). The term *mental disorders* in *DSM-IV-TR* includes conditions related to substance abuse and dependence. In addition to providing diagnostic criteria sets for clinicians to use in assigning mental health diagnoses, *DSM-IV-TR* includes a five-character coding system that is based on *ICD-9-CM*. Although there is a high degree of compatibility between the codes found in *DSM-IV-TR* and those in *ICD-9-CM*, there are some significant differences.

Another interesting feature of *DSM-IV-TR* is that it offers clinicians the option of assessing clients and recording their findings in a multiaxial format. According to the American Psychiatric Association, a multiaxial system is one that "involves an assessment on several axes, each of which refers to a different domain of information that may help the clinician plan treatment and predict outcome" (American Psychiatric Association, 2000, p. 27). The first three axes in *DSM-IV-TR* are generally thought of as the basic components of the multiaxial reporting system. They are described in the following table (Lee, 1995).

Axis	Title	Used for Reporting...
Axis I	Clinical Disorders Other Conditions That May Be a Focus of Clinical Attention	All the disorders or conditions found within *DSM-IV-TR* (including substance abuse and dependence diagnoses), except personality disorders and mental retardation/intellectual disabilities
Axis II	Personality Disorders Mental Retardation	Personality disorders and mental retardation/intellectual disabilities
Axis III	General Medical Conditions	General medical conditions that impact the treatment of the client. *ICD-9-CM* codes are used for reporting diagnostic codes on Axis III

The remaining axes—Axes IV and V—are less frequently used in assessing substance abuse clients:

Axis	Title	Used for Reporting...
Axis IV	Psychosocial and Environmental Problems	Psychosocial and environmental problems that may affect the treatment of the client, such as unemployment, victim of child neglect, etc.
Axis V	Global Assessment of Functioning	The client's overall level of functioning. Clinicians may report this using the Global Assessment of Functioning (GAF) scale contained within the *DSM-IV-TR* or another appropriate functioning scale. The GAF scale is reported as a number between 0 and 100, with 100 representing the highest level of functioning.

The advantage of using *DSM-IV-TR* in a substance abuse treatment setting is that it represents the latest research findings and acceptable diagnostic terms associated with mental health and substance abuse disorders. The disadvantage is that most third-party payers do not accept *DSM-IV-TR* codes in lieu of *ICD-9-CM* codes. To offset this disadvantage, the American Health Information Management Association (AHIMA) published the *DSM-IV Crosswalk: Guidelines for Coding Mental Health Information*, which provides an easy-to-use tool for translating *DSM-IV* codes to the equivalent *ICD-9-CM* codes (Albaum-Feinstein, 1999).

As explained in Chapter 7, *DSM-V* has been scheduled to replace *DSM-IV-TR* in 2013, coinciding with the United States' conversion to *ICD-10-CM*.

Data Sets

In 1988, Congress passed Public Law 100-690, which required the collection of data on the national incidence and prevalence of both mental illness and substance abuse. The message that Congress sent by passing this law was that states had to be able to substantiate the need for federal block grant money. The National Institute of Drug Abuse (NIDA) and the National Institute of Alcohol Abuse and Alcoholism (NIAAA) were the federal agencies charged at that time with the administration of a national database of substance abuse client information to meet the substance abuse reporting component of the law. In 1995, this function was taken over by the Substance Abuse and Mental Health Services Administration (SAMHSA), which has developed the **Drug and Alcohol Services Information System (DASIS)**, an evolution of the earlier reporting systems. The goal of DASIS is to provide one data system that provides national and state-level data on substance abuse clients and on the facilities that receive federal grants or contracts to provide substance abuse treatment. DASIS includes three components: the **Treatment Episode Data Set (TEDS)**, the **National Survey of Substance Abuse Treatment Services (N-SSATS)**, and the **Inventory of Substance Abuse Treatment Services (I-SATS)**. I-SATS (formerly the National Master Facility Inventory) is a listing of all known public and private substance abuse treatment facilities in the United States and its territories. TEDS, which was previously called the Client Data System, collects from states uniform data that are client specific, but not client identifiable, including demographic and substance abuse characteristics. Facility-specific information is collected through N-SSATS, an annual survey of all substance abuse treatment facilities known to SAMHSA (i.e., in I-SATS). N-SSATS, formerly known as the Uniform Facility Data Set (UFDS), collects information on location, characteristics, services offered, and utilization for each facility. Information from the N-SSATS is used to maintain the National Directory of Drug and Alcohol Abuse Treatment Programs and the Substance Abuse Treatment Facility Locator.

Electronic Information Systems

It is difficult to generalize about electronic information systems that exist within the substance abuse treatment community today, because they vary greatly from facility to facility. There are treatment programs in the United States that have sophisticated electronic client information systems, and there are programs where electronic applications are very limited. Some of this variability comes from the differences in levels of care and funding sources. A substance abuse treatment unit within a progressive acute care hospital, for example, will benefit from the hospital-wide information systems that are in place. On the other hand, a public community treatment program with limited funds may not have much in the way of computer development. One generalization that can be made, however, is that as the health care industry moves toward more integrated delivery systems and electronic health records, client information systems within the substance abuse treatment community will take on new importance. Substance abuse treatment facilities will be competing with other health care entities for scarce health care dollars, and the government and other payers are demanding outcomes-oriented data to support continued direct funding or reimbursement. This increased need for timely, accurate data should lead to increased development of electronic substance abuse client information systems. Public community treatment programs are working together to develop a standardized electronic record. This will allow the agencies to pool their resources and create a set of electronic forms that are standardized throughout the state. With the increased use of electronic records, the intake process for clients has become more efficient. Also, the flow of information throughout the course of treatment is more effective.

QUALITY IMPROVEMENT AND UTILIZATION MANAGEMENT

Quality improvement (QI) and utilization management (UM) are two additional areas within substance abuse facilities about which it is difficult to make general statements. Substance abuse treatment organizations do include the QI and UM functions, but the level of sophistication of the QI and UM processes depends on the level of care provided by that facility, its primary funding source, and its accrediting organization.

Quality Assessment and Improvement

Providers of substance abuse treatment must ensure that they offer quality care and service. The quality assessment and improvement activities found within substance abuse treatment facilities are often related to the level of care provided and whether the facility seeks Joint Commission or CARF accreditation. Some states have specific Medicaid standards that also address the need for an organized quality assessment and improvement process. A substance abuse treatment unit in a Joint Commission-accredited hospital would participate in the hospital-wide performance improvement program. Regardless of the setting, a substance abuse treatment program looking for processes to improve may consider consensus-based and evidence-based treatment guidelines available at SAMHSA's **Center for Substance Abuse Treatment (CSAT)** as a means to identify effective treatment practices to which its own processes can be compared. Another source for evidence-based interventions for both substance abuse and mental health is SAMHSA's **National Registry of Evidence-based Programs and Practices (NREPP)**, an online searchable database of interventions and treatments that have been demonstrated to be effective.

Utilization Management

Providers of substance abuse treatment, just as other health care providers, must demonstrate fiscal responsibility and solid clinical decision making that is based on the individual needs of the client. It is important that facilities ensure that each client receives the level of care appropriate to his or her severity of illness. As a general rule, clients should be served at the least intensive level that will meet their treatment objectives, such as outpatient therapy, and should move on to a more intensive level, such as residential treatment, only when it is justified by their specific treatment needs.

Severity indexes and other treatment review instruments have also been developed for evaluating treatment and the utilization of services within the substance abuse treatment community. As discussed earlier, the American Society of Addiction Medicine (ASAM) publishes a placement criteria manual that defines levels of care and the specific criteria that should be used in placing both adolescent and adult clients in the appropriate treatment setting. The Care Settings section of this chapter describes these levels of care. Managed care organizations have endeavored to use these or similar levels of care to place patients in the most cost-effective settings, yet still achieve the desired treatment results (Kosanke et al., 2002). Another instrument that is used in utilization management and to facilitate client care is the **Addiction Severity Index (ASI)**, which was developed in 1979. ASI is designed to be administered through an interview process by a trained technician to measure seven substance abuse-related problem areas: medical condition, drug use, alcohol use, employment, illegal activity, social relations, and psychological findings. The data from the client interview are tabulated and result in a severity "score" for the client. The score can be stated as a 10-point severity rating for clinical use or as a mathematically weighted score for use as an outcomes measure in research studies (Grissom, 1991).

RISK MANAGEMENT AND LEGAL ISSUES

Risk management is defined as "a four step process designed to identify, evaluate and resolve the actual and possible sources of loss. The four steps are risk identification, risk evaluation, risk handling, and risk monitoring" (Roach et al., 2006, p. 556). Formal risk management programs are found in inpatient substance abuse treatment settings more often than they are found in outpatient settings. There are, however, many other important legal issues—such as confidentiality and release of information, court-ordered treatment, and commitments—commonly associated with all levels of substance abuse treatment.

Confidentiality and Release of Information

Confidentiality of client information is extremely important in substance abuse treatment facilities. Clients seeking alcohol and drug abuse prevention and treatment services must be assured of the greatest possible privacy because of the stigma attached to "alcoholic" and "addict" labels and because use of illicit drugs and underage minors' use of alcohol constitute crimes. Clients must feel that they will not be subject to a law enforcement investigation if they seek treatment. In the early 1970s, the federal government enacted two laws that were written to guarantee this strict level of confidentiality: the Comprehensive Alcohol Abuse and Alcohol Prevention, Treatment and Rehabilitation Act of 1970 and the Drug Abuse and Treatment Act of 1972 (Legal Action Center, 1991). The federal regulations—known as 42 C.F.R. (*Code of Federal Regulations*) Part 2, Confidentiality of Alcohol and Drug Abuse Patient Records—that implemented these confidentiality statutes were issued in 1975 and revised in 1987 and 1995.

The regulations in 42 C.F.R. Part 2 are more restrictive than the privacy provisions of the Health Insurance Portability and Accountability Act (HIPAA). Except under certain specified conditions, disclosure of information concerning any client who is seen in a federally assisted alcohol or drug abuse program is strictly prohibited. A program is defined as "any person or organization that, in whole or in part, provides alcohol or drug abuse diagnosis, treatment or referral for treatment" (42 C.F.R. pt. 2). There are a few exceptions to this general prohibition written into the regulations. Disclosure can be made:

- With the written consent of the patient
- For internal communications on a need-to-know basis
- When there is no patient-identifying information
- In a bona fide medical emergency
- With a court order (with special procedures)
- When a crime is committed at the treatment program or against program personnel
- For research and audits
- In child and vulnerable adult abuse reporting, under the provisions of the applicable state law
- Under the provisions of a **qualified service organization agreement (QSOA)**, through which an organization, such as a commercial laboratory or a private occupational therapy group, has a written agreement to provide services to the substance abuse program. (A qualified service organization can also provide services such as data processing, bill collecting, dosage preparation, legal, medical, accounting, and other professional services.)

No information about a substance abuse client should be disclosed unless the facility can state how these exceptions permit disclosure. Certain exceptions are very rarely encountered and therefore rarely used as a basis for release of information. Confidential substance abuse information can be released with a written authorization from the patient (Legal Action Center, 2003), but this authorization must contain specific items to be considered valid. Figure 8-6 outlines the required elements for an authorization to release drug and alcohol treatment information. Other elements, such as the signature of a witness, may be added to the authorization form at the discretion of the facility. When the information is released, it must be accompanied by a written statement notifying the recipient that the information is "protected by federal confidentiality rules" and that the recipient may not redisclose the records to a third party (42 C.F.R. pt. 2).

Court-Ordered Treatment

A portion of the substance abuse client population enters treatment as a result of a court order. The court order may come from a conviction for driving under the influence of alcohol or drugs (DUI). In some states, substance abuse assessment is mandated by law for all persons with a DUI conviction, and if the assessment indicates that the individual needs further treatment, this treatment is also mandated. Typically, if the DUI client fails to fulfill an established court-ordered assessment and treatment protocol, he or she will not be reissued a driver's license. Thus, it is necessary to establish a good working relationship between the substance abuse treatment centers and the legal system. One common practice, for example, is the development of an active partnership with the municipal court system.

- The name or general designation of the program(s) making the disclosure
- The name of the individual or organization that will receive the disclosure
- The name of the patient who is the subject of the disclosure
- The purpose or need for the disclosure
- How much and what kind of information will be disclosed
- A statement that the patient may revoke the consent at any time, except to the extent that the program has already acted in reliance on it
- The date, event, or condition upon which the consent expires if not previously revoked
- The signature of the patient (and/or other authorized person)
- The date on which the authorization is signed

FIGURE 8-6 Required elements for an authorization to release information from an alcohol or drug program, from 42 C.F.R. Part 2, *Confidentiality of Alcohol and Drug Abuse Patient Records.*

A treatment center employee may be assigned to be present in court during the DUI hearings to facilitate the enrollment of court-ordered clients. All necessary consents and authorizations to release information back to the court can be signed and appropriate fees collected before the client leaves the courthouse.

DUI convictions are not the only court procedures that lead to court-ordered substance abuse treatment. Examples of situations that might result in a court order for treatment are child abuse, possession of illegal drugs, sexual assault, underage alcohol consumption, burglary, or assault, when the court feels that the perpetrator's substance abuse was a factor. Typically, the judge will order the client to seek substance abuse treatment as a stipulation in a suspended or reduced sentence or probation. On occasion the court might actually order an incarcerated individual to obtain appropriate substance abuse treatment, if it is available through the correctional facility.

Involuntary Commitments

Involuntary commitment is a legal process by which individuals who are deemed to be a danger to themselves or to others may be admitted to a treatment program even though they refuse or cannot consent to the treatment. Involuntary commitment is governed by state statutes, and the criteria and procedures vary from state to state. All states require that the person being committed have a mental illness or mental disorder; however, many states do not define the terms *mental illness* or *mental condition*, or they define them very broadly. Several states, such as North Carolina, Louisiana, and Hawaii, specifically cite substance abuse as a mental disorder or as a potential cause for involuntary commitment (Bazelon Center for Mental Health Law, 2004).

In states where involuntary commitment for substance abuse treatment is permitted, the actual procedure varies depending on the state laws, but the following steps represent a typical series of events in the overall process:

- A petitioner, law enforcement officer, or other responsible person files a petition that states that the client meets the criteria for involuntary admission (i.e., he or she is a danger to himself or herself or to others).
- The client is detained for an evaluation by a physician or other qualified clinician for a period of time that may vary from state to state.
- The clinician certifies that the client meets the standard for involuntary commitment.
- The petition and the certificate are filed with the court and a hearing date is set.
- The court determines whether or not the client meets the standard for involuntary admission.
- The court will require that the client be admitted if the client meets the standard (this admission may be to an inpatient or outpatient program, depending on the needs of the client and the state guidelines) (Beis, 1984).

See Figure 8-7 for an example of a form used to evaluate individuals in a commitment recommendation screening process.

ROLE OF THE HEALTH INFORMATION MANAGEMENT PROFESSIONAL

The role of the health information manager is becoming increasingly important in substance abuse treatment settings. The changing health care environment requires that substance abuse facilities collect, analyze, and maintain timely and reliable client information. Managed care organizations and other payers, including the federal government, want "proof" that their enrollees are receiving quality services at the lowest possible cost.

Opportunities for the health information manager within substance abuse facilities are found in the areas of traditional client record management, risk management, utilization management, quality improvement, release-of-information services, client rights coordination, and especially in electronic client records systems. Even though electronic health records first appeared in 1960, they are still underutilized in many treatment facilities (Asp & Peterson, 2003). As the need to be more efficient in providing treatment—and the need to be more cost effective with the funding that is utilized by a facility—becomes more apparent, the need for adequate electronic records will also become more important. The health information manager will play an important role in planning, development, and implementation of the electronic health records. Another challenging aspect for the health information manager working in substance abuse treatment is being an advocate for client confidentiality. Most health information managers in substance abuse facilities fill the role of the

DEPARTMENT OF MENTAL HEALTH **Community Counseling Services** *Pre-evaluation Screening Form* DMH/013 5/02	Name:_____ Case #:_____

IN THE_____COURT OF _____COUNTY   RE:_____
       (Type of Court)   *(Name of County)*

CASE NO. _____ SERVICE CODE _____ UNITS OF SERVICE _____DATE_____

Respondent having been evaluated and pre-screened for commitment pursuant to M.C.A. Section 41-21-67, Region_____ Mental Health Center Offers the following:

Legal Charges Pending: Yes ☐   No ☐

PERSONAL DATA INFORMATION

NAME: _____ SOCIAL SECURITY NO: _____ DOB: _____

RACE: _____   MARITAL STATUS: ☐Single   ☐Married   ☐Divorced   ☐ Widowed   SEX: ☐Male   ☐Female

ADDRESS: _____

_____

_____

NAME OF SPOUSE/NEXT OF KIN: _____ COUNTY OF RESIDENCE: _____

MEDICAID # _____   MEDICARE # _____

EDUCATION *(Circle Highest Grade Completed)* 1 2 3 4 5 6 7 8 9 10 11 12 13 14 15 16 17 18 GED

OCCUPATION: _____   PRESENTLY EMPLOYED: ☐ Yes   ☐ No

EMPLOYER: _____   LENGTH OF EMPLOYMENT: _____years ____ months

HOUSEHOLD COMPOSITION *(Mark All That Apply)*

☐ Lives Alone   ☐ With Siblings   ☐ With Parents   ☐ With One Parent   ☐ With Children
☐ With Spouse   ☐ With Relatives   ☐ With Legal Guardian ☐ With Others   ☐ Others

NUMBER OF DEPENDENT(S): _____

NAME OF AFFIANT (Person Filing Papers)

Name: _____ Relationship: _____ Phone: (H) _____ (W) _____

Address: _____ City _____ State _____ Zip Code _____

FAMILY CONTACT

Name: _____ Relationship: _____ Phone: (H) _____ (W) _____

Address: _____ City _____ State _____ Zip Code _____

PERSON WITH <u>LEGAL CUSTODY</u>, GUARDIANSHIP, and /or Conservatorship

Name: _____ Relationship: _____ Phone: (H) _____ (W) _____

Address: _____ City _____ State _____ Zip Code _____

FIGURE **8-7** Pre-commitment evaluation screening form. (Courtesy of Community Counseling Services, Starkville, Mississippi.)

MEDICAL HISTORY INFORMATION

PREVIOUS MENTAL HEALTH HOSPITALIZATION, SERVICE, A&D TREATMENT (*List Where & When*)_____

_____

_____

_____

_____

CURRENT MEDICATIONS (*List Names and Dosage*)

Name	Dosage
_____	_____
_____	_____
_____	_____
_____	_____
_____	_____
_____	_____
_____	_____

COMPLAINT WITH MEDICATIONS: ❐ Yes   ❐No   ❐Unknown

ALLERGIES: ❐ Yes   ❐ No   If Yes, Explain _____

PREVIOUS SURGERY: ❐ Yes   ❐ No   If Yes, Explain _____

CONCURRENT PHYSICAL CONDITIONS (*Mark all that apply*)

❐ Diabetes   ❐ Emphysema/Cold   ❐ Heart Condition   ❐ Seizures
❐ Hypertension   ❐ S.T.D.   ❐ TB   ❐ Cancer
❐ Contagious Disease ❐ Other Chronic Illness ❐ (Please State) _____
❐ Hepatitis
Elaborate on acute medical conditions of conditions marked (if needed) _____

FAMILY PHYSICIAN: _____

BEHAVIORS EXHIBITED BY RESPONDENT
Also consider information from affiant and/or affidavit.
(*Mark appropriate answer and/or write in additional pertinent descriptions.*)

History or Present Danger to Self   ❐ Yes   ❐ No   (*If Yes, Mark Appropriate Statements Below*)

❐ Thoughts of suicide   ❐ Threats of suicide   ❐ Plan for suicide   ❐ Preoccupation with death
❐ Suicide gesture   ❐ Suicide attempts   ❐ Family history of suicide   ❐ Self-mutilation
❐ Inability to care for self ❐ High risk behavior   ❐ Provoking harm to self from others
❐ Other _____

Describe: _____

History or Present Danger to Others   ❐ Yes   ❐ No   (*If Yes, Mark Appropriate Statements Below*)

❐ Thoughts to harm others   ❐ Threats to harm others   ❐ Plans to harm others
❐ Attempts to harm others   ❐ Stalking   ❐ Has harmed others
❐ Felt like killing someone   ❐ Inability or unwillingness to care for dependents
❐ Other _____

Describe: _____

FIGURE **8-7** (*Continued*)

Pre-evaluation Screening Form *(page three)*   Name:_____   Case#:_____

Failure to Care for Self   ☐ Yes   ☐ No   *(If Yes, Mark Appropriate Statements Below)*

Failure or inability to provide necessary: ☐ Food   ☐ Clothing   ☐ Shelter   ☐ Safety   ☐ Medical care for self

☐ Other _____

Antisocial/Criminal Behavior   ☐ Yes   ☐No   *(If Yes, Mark Appropriate Statement Below)*

☐ Frequent lying   ☐ Stealing   ☐ Running away from home   ☐ Excessive fighting
☐ Destroys property   ☐ Fire setting   ☐ Cruelty to other   ☐ Cruelty to animals
☐ Arrests   ☐ Gang membership   ☐ Brandishing weapons   ☐ Convictions
☐ Imprisoned   ☐ Promiscuity   ☐ Exhibitionism   ☐ Family desertion
☐ Uses assumed name   ☐ Identify any legal charges which may be pending

☐ Other _____

Describe: _____

Drug Use/Abuse   ☐ Yes   ☐No   *(If Yes, Mark Appropriate Statement Below)*

☐ Has abused   ☐ Is abusing   ☐ Narcotics   ☐ Amphetamines ☐ Barbiturates   ☐ Hallucinogens
☐ Cocaine   ☐ Marijuana   ☐ Absenteeism ☐ Job loss   ☐ Arrests
☐ Has required hospitalization ☐ Family problems due to drug use   ☐ Currently under the influence of drugs

☐ Other _____

Describe: _____

Alcohol Use/Abuse   ☐ Yes   ☐No   *(If Yes, Mark Appropriate Statement Below)*

☐ Drinking problem suspected   ☐ Intoxicated Now   ☐ Has required hospitalization
☐ D.T. s   ☐ Black-outs   ☐ Absenteeism
☐ Job loss   ☐ Arrests/DUI   ☐ Family problems due to drinking
☐ Currently under the influence of alcohol (BAL, if available)
☐ High-risk behavior occurs primarily when under the influence of alcoholic beverages, including beer.

☐ Other _____

Describe: _____

Depressive-Like Behaviors   ☐ Yes   ☐No   *(If Yes, Mark Appropriate Statement Below)*

☐ Sadness   ☐ Fatigue   ☐ Low Energy   ☐ Loss of interest   ☐ Extreme Withdrawal
☐ Crying   ☐ Poor Concentration   ☐ Weight loss or gain   ☐ Guilt feelings
☐ Feelings of worthlessness   ☐ Hopelessness about the future   ☐ Hypoactive
☐ Thoughts/threats of suicide   ☐ Sudden drop in grades or change in friends (especially in adolescents)

☐Other _____   _____

Describe: _____

Manic-Like Behavior   ☐ Yes   ☐No   *(If Yes, Mark Appropriate Statement Below)*

☐ Euphoria   ☐ Hyperactivity   ☐ Grandiosity   ☐ Over-talkativeness and/or pressured speech
☐ Irritability   ☐ Sexual promiscuity   ☐ Sleep disturbance ☐ Extravagance with money

☐ Other _____

Describe: _____

Dementia-Like Characteristics   ☐ Yes   ☐No   *(If Yes, Mark Appropriate Statement Below)*

☐ Confusion   ☐ Wanders off   ☐ Disorientation   ☐ Impaired judgement
☐ Absent-mindedness   ☐Getting lost   ☐ Confusion   ☐ Significant short- and/or long-term memory
☐ Decline in activities of daily living *(Consider age of respondent)*   ☐Impaired Abstract Thinking

☐ Other _____

Describe: _____

FIGURE **8-7** *(Continued)*

Psychotic-Like Behavior ☐ Yes ☐No *(If Yes, Mark Appropriate Statement Below)*

☐ Poor personal hygiene ☐ Loose Association ☐ Suspiciousness ☐ Bizarre or obscene acts
☐ Withdrawn ☐ Incoherence ☐ Unmanageable ☐ Flat or inappropriate affect
☐ Talks often ☐ Wanders off ☐ Illusions ☐ Disorientation (time, place, people)
☐ Delusions ☐ Confusion ☐ Forgetfulness ☐ Poor judgment
☐ Doesn t make sense ☐ Irritability ☐ Hallucinations
☐ Emotional turmoil ☐ Disorganized speech or behavior

☐ Other _____

Describe: _____

ADDITIONAL INFORMATION

Child/Adolescent Conduct Disturbance ☐ Yes ☐ No *(If Yes, Mark Appropriate Statement Below)*
(Current Behavior or During Childhood)

☐ Theft ☐ Firesetting ☐ Cruelty to people ☐ Cruelty to animals ☐ Destruction of property
☐ Aggression ☐ Arrest/detainment ☐ Sexual misconduct ☐ Combativeness/aggression
☐ Refusal to attend school ☐ Running away ☐ Defiance of authority and rules
☐ Possession/Use of weapons
☐ Other _____

Mental Retardation ☐ Yes ☐No *(If Yes, Mark Appropriate Statement Below)*

☐ History of special education placement ☐ Documented IQ below a70
☐ Inability to care for self or activities of daily living ☐Significantly sub-average intellectual functioning before age 18
☐ Substantial limitations in adaptive skills *(communication, self-care, home living, social skills, community use, self-direction, health and safety, leisure and work)*
☐ Other _____

Other ☐ Yes ☐No *(If Yes, Mark Appropriate Statement Below)*

☐ Anxiety ☐ Panic ☐Eating disorders ☐Sexual disorders ☐ Impulsive disorders
☐ Obsessive disorders ☐ Other _____

RECOMMENDATIONS

Examination for Commitment: ☐ Yes ☐ No

If yes, is outpatient commitment currently an option for the respondent? ☐ Yes ☐No Explain:

_____
_____
_____

If no, explain why outpatient commitment is not an option for the respondent:_____
_____
_____

SPECIFIC RECOMMENDATIONS
(Include Treatment Options)

_____
_____
_____

_____
Screener/Credentials   Date   Print Name

FIGURE **8-7** *(Continued)*

confidentiality "expert" and must be thoroughly familiar with the federal regulations governing alcohol and drug abuse treatment records. Health information managers can assist in developing policies to meet the requirements of existing and newly developed regulations.

TRENDS

The trends in substance abuse treatment can be divided into treatment trends and economic or funding trends. The current trends in treatment include many innovative approaches, some of which are discussed in this chapter. Examples of current treatment trends include the growth of programs for women, adolescent prevention programs, and treatment for the dually diagnosed. Substance abuse treatment centers are involved with an increasing number of Employee Assistance Programs (EAPs) and are also becoming more active in identifying needs of inmates in city or local jails. The economic trends are related to the changing health care environment and to the government's continuing struggle to spend taxpayers' dollars wisely.

Because government support is an essential source of revenue to many substance abuse treatment facilities, the changing political and economic climate will affect the future of the delivery of substance abuse services. Substance abuse education, prevention, and treatment have been important social issues in the United States for several decades. Congress, in partnership with state governments, has directed a substantial amount of government funds toward increasing awareness of substance abuse issues, as well as toward increasing the availability of treatment services across the socioeconomic spectrum. The national political and economic climate, however, has changed considerably since the 1970s, as taxpayers are asking for validation that their tax dollars are spent appropriately and are questioning the high cost of health care.

One of the most significant trends to affect health information management within the substance abuse treatment community is the government's increased emphasis on the need for data to substantiate the effectiveness of government-funded programs. Programs are being held accountable for the government dollars they are awarded, and this accountability means providing supporting data to the funding agency. In many cases, the information systems within substance abuse facilities are inadequate to provide this type of outcome-oriented data in a timely and accurate manner. To thrive in the current climate, substance abuse facilities will need improved information systems.

Another political and economic factor that is impacting substance abuse treatment services, along with the other segments of the health care delivery system, is the increase in the role of managed care organizations (MCOs). Not only are private MCOs increasing their services across the United States, but many states are opting to develop managed care models for Medicaid. Dealing with MCOs will necessitate significant changes in the way substance abuse facilities have traditionally operated. The need for more sophisticated information systems that can provide financial and client outcomes data will be an important part of this change.

Along with changes in government funding procedures and the increase in the number of MCOs, substance abuse facilities will also be affected by the trend of multiple health care organizations building alliances and partnerships to develop integrated health delivery systems and health information exchanges. Hopefully, substance abuse treatment will be valued as an important component of any comprehensive health delivery system. However, this raises important issues related to integrated client information systems, access to this information, and client confidentiality that will need to be addressed. To this end, SAMHSA (2010) released a "Frequently Asked Questions" document, *Applying the Substance Abuse Confidentiality Regulations to Health Information Exchange (HIE)*, explaining under what circumstances substance abuse treatment facilities could participate in health information exchange without violating the confidentiality provisions of 42 C.F.R. Part 2 or HIPAA. Among other considerations, one component that would have to be in place is that the HIE would have to be a qualified service organization (QSO) with a written agreement requiring the HIE to follow the 42 C.F.R. regulations.

This is an era of significant change in health care delivery systems, of which substance abuse treatment services are an important element, and it is important that substance abuse clients be afforded the benefits of these changes without compromising their rights to confidentiality.

SUMMARY

Modern substance abuse treatment emerged in the 1950s as residential facilities for the treatment of alcohol dependency began to develop across the United States. Since that time, the number of different treatment settings for clients with alcohol and other drug problems has grown to include outpatient treatment, intensive outpatient and partial hospitalization treatment, residential/inpatient treatment, and medically managed intensive inpatient treatment settings. The number of programs within the treatment settings has also grown to include special programs for women, adolescents, court-referred clients, children of addicted families, and many others. Substance abuse treatment settings can be either publicly funded or privately funded. Substance abuse treatment and prevention has been a national issue for several decades, with the government granting to states significant amounts of money that are specifically targeted for substance abuse treatment and prevention programs. Public substance abuse treatment settings have traditionally assumed a major responsibility for providing substance abuse treatment services to the community, and they receive the majority of their funds from the federal and state governments. However, reimbursement from private insurance companies and client fees also account for a portion of their revenue.

Health information managers working in substance abuse treatment facilities not only provide the traditional services associated with health information management, but they must gain expertise in several other areas as well. For example, substance abuse treatment is regulated by federal and state governments and by voluntary accreditation organizations such as TJC and CARF. Many state regulations, and the CARF and Joint Commission standards, address quality of care and information management issues. Health information managers working in substance abuse treatment facilities need to be aware of all relevant regulations and standards, as they are often seen as the information management and quality assurance experts within the facilities. Another very important aspect of managing substance abuse client information is maintaining strict client confidentiality. The federal regulations 42 C.F.R. Part 2, *Confidentiality of Alcohol and Drug Abuse Records*, mandate that all federally assisted substance abuse programs follow certain procedures before releasing client information. The health information manager often oversees compliance with 42 C.F.R. Part 2.

The national trends in health care—such as cutting government spending on health care, the growth of managed care, and the development of integrated delivery systems—have had an impact on substance abuse treatment facilities. Centers that had few financial worries when government substance abuse grants were plentiful are now faced with competing for scarce dollars with other segments of the health delivery system. One potentially positive development to result from this changing environment may well be the growth in the use of computer technology to develop and maintain integrated client information systems that provide data that are timely, accurate, complete, legible, and accessible.

KEY TERMS

42 C.F.R. Part 2, Confidentiality of Drug and Alcohol Abuse Records federal regulations that mandate strict confidentiality of drug and alcohol patient information in federally assisted substance abuse treatment programs.

Addiction Severity Index (ASI) a rating scale that was developed to be used by clinicians to measure the severity of a client's substance abuse problems. The ASI measures seven substance abuse–related problem areas: medical condition, drug use, alcohol use, employment, illegal activity, social relations, and psychological findings.

Alcoholics Anonymous (AA) a worldwide organization of self-help recovery groups that support individuals in maintaining sobriety. AA is based on a 12-step recovery process, and AA and other programs that follow the 12-step recovery process are sometimes referred to as 12-step programs.

CARF International (Commission on Accreditation of Rehabilitation Facilities) a voluntary accreditation agency that sets standards that promote "the delivery of quality services to people with disabilities" (CARF, 1994). CARF standards include a section devoted to alcohol and other drug treatment programs.

Center for Substance Abuse Prevention (CSAP) an agency of SAMHSA that provides national leadership for community-based substance abuse prevention programs. Among other activities, CSAP administers a number of grant programs aimed at reducing the incidence of substance abuse.

Center for Substance Abuse Treatment (CSAT) an agency of SAMHSA that "promotes the quality and availability of community-based substance abuse treatment services for individuals and families … [working]with States and community-based groups to improve and expand existing substance abuse treatment services under the Substance Abuse Prevention and Treatment Block Grant Program" (CSAT, n.d., para. 1).

clinical assessment a clinical assessment is conducted by a clinician for every client that enters a substance abuse treatment program.

The clinical assessment is used as a basis for the client's diagnosis and individualized treatment plan.

Diagnostic and Statistical Manual of Mental Disorders, **fourth edition, text revision** (*DSM-IV-TR*) a classification system and nomenclature of mental disorders developed by the American Psychiatric Association with a stated purpose of providing "clear descriptions of diagnostic categories in order to enable clinicians and investigators to diagnose, communicate about, study, and treat people with various mental disorders" (American Psychiatric Association, 2000, p. xxxvii). It is also used as a coding system for mental health disorders. Each diagnosis is assigned a unique code number that is based on *ICD-9-CM*. *DSM-V* is scheduled to replace *DSM-IV-TR* in 2013.

Drug and Alcohol Services Information System (DASIS) a data system managed by SAMHSA that provides national and state-level data on substance abuse clients and on the facilities that receive federal grants or contracts to provide substance abuse treatment. DASIS includes three components: the Treatment Episode Data Set (TEDS), the National Survey of Substance Abuse Treatment Services (N-SSATS), and the Inventory of Substance Abuse Treatment Services (I-SATS).

dually diagnosed clients with both a substance abuse disorder and a chronic mental illness are considered to be dually diagnosed. These clients typically have special treatment needs.

employee assistance programs (EAPs) substance abuse assessment and treatment programs established through a contractual arrangement between an organization and a substance abuse treatment facility to serve the employees within the organization.

individualized treatment plan (ITP) a written plan developed by the client's treatment team that is used to identify the type and frequency of services needed by the client. It includes measurable goals and objectives that address the problems identified in the clinical assessment and should be updated periodically (usually every six months) as the client's treatment needs change.

intensive outpatient or partial hospitalization treatment "an organized outpatient service that delivers treatment services during the day, before or after work or school, in the evening or on weekends" (ASAM, 2001, p. 3).

Inventory of Substance Abuse Treatment Services (I-SATS) a listing of all known public and private substance abuse treatment facilities in the United States and its territories.

involuntary commitment a legal process by which individuals who are deemed to be a danger to themselves or to others may be admitted to a substance abuse (or mental health) treatment program even though they refuse or cannot consent to the treatment.

medically managed intensive inpatient treatment substance abuse treatment programs that "provide a planned regimen of 24-hour medically directed evaluation, care and treatment of mental and substance related disorders in an acute care inpatient setting. They are staffed by designated addiction-credentialed physicians, including psychiatrists, as well as other mental health- and addiction-credentialed clinicians" (ASAM, 2001, p. 4).

National Registry of Evidence-based Programs and Practices (NREPP) sponsored by SAMHSA, NREPP is an online searchable database of treatments and interventions that have been demonstrated to be effective for substance abuse and mental health treatment and prevention programs.

National Survey of Substance Abuse Treatment Services (N-SSATS) an annual survey of all substance abuse treatment facilities known to SAMHSA. N-SSATS collects facility-specific information on location, characteristics, services offered, and utilization.

outpatient treatment "professionally directed evaluation, treatment and recovery services...

provided in regularly scheduled sessions" (ASAM, 2001, p. 2).

qualified service organization agreement (QSOA) an exception to the 42 C.F.R. Part 2 *Confidentiality of alcohol and drug abuse patient records* that permits disclosure of patient record information to an organization providing services to the substance abuse program, such as laboratory, data processing, bill collecting, dosage preparation, legal, medical, or accounting services. The qualified service organization (QSO) has a written agreement to provide professional services to the substance abuse program, and that agreement requires the QSO to follow the 42 C.F.R. regulations.

residential/inpatient treatment substance abuse treatment "services staffed by designated addiction treatment and mental health personnel who provide a planned regimen of care in a 24-hour live-in setting.... They are housed in, or affiliated with, permanent facilities where patients can reside safely. They are staffed 24 hours a day. Mutual and self-help group meetings generally are available on site" (ASAM, 2001, p. 3).

Treatment Episode Data Set (TEDS) one of the components of DASIS, TEDS collects from states uniform data that are client specific, but not client identifiable, including demographic and substance abuse characteristics.

REVIEW QUESTIONS

Knowledge-Based Questions

1. Describe three different settings in which substance abuse treatment can take place.
2. Define the role of a case manager versus the role of a counselor in substance abuse treatment settings.
3. What is Alcoholics Anonymous? How does it relate to substance abuse treatment?
4. List the key elements that should be included in an individualized treatment plan.
5. Name two voluntary accreditation organizations that set standards for substance abuse treatment facilities. What standards are used for outpatient centers? Inpatient programs?
6. Define involuntary commitment. What are the basic steps to obtain an involuntary commitment?

Critical Thinking Questions

1. Why is it important for a health information manager to be familiar with the ASAM *Patient Placement Criteria Manual*? What is the purpose of this manual?
2. The role of the health information manager in a substance abuse treatment facility often involves serving as the confidentiality expert. Why is confidentiality of special concern in a substance abuse treatment program?
3. Briefly discuss current trends in the overall health care delivery system that you believe will impact substance abuse treatment services.

WEB ACTIVITY

1. Go to the U.S. Government Printing Office's Federal Digital System Web page at http://www.gpo.gov/fdsys to search the *Code of Federal Regulations* for a sample consent form in 42 C.F.R. Part 2, "Confidentiality of Alcohol and Drug Abuse Patient Records." Upon arriving at the site, locate the hyperlink for the Code of Federal Regulations. At the next page, choose a year (the previous year is recommended). When the Titles for the year selected appear, scroll down to Title 42—Public Health, then select

"Download" and choose a file type (e.g., "PDF") to download Volume 1. After downloading Volume 1, locate Part 2, then Subpart C. Find the sample consent form in Subpart C, and use it to begin developing a consent form for the fictitious facility Seven Acres Substance Abuse Treatment Services. Find the notice of prohibition of rediscolosure in the same subpart, and use it in developing a form to accompany information released from the Seven Acres facility.

2. Visit the Web site of the Legal Action Center at http://www.lac.org to view the sample forms available there. Under "Resources," select the "Free Publications" hyperlink, which opens a new set of hyperlinks. From these links, select "Drug & Alcohol." Scroll down to find the sample forms. Select "Sample Consent - Basic," which is a consent for the release of confidential information. How does this form compare to the form you developed in Web Activity 1?

CASE STUDY

Sarah Johnson is the health information manager for the Columbus County Alcohol and Drug Treatment Center, a CARF-accredited, publicly funded treatment facility. As a member of the quality improvement (QI) committee, Sarah has been reviewing client records, focusing on written clinical assessments and treatment plans. The QI committee is interested in evaluating how consistently the clinicians document appropriate treatment goals based on the information found in the clinical assessment. One of the records that Sarah reviewed is an outpatient record for Ann Wilson, a 24-year-old female client enrolled in the center's women's program. Based on the following summaries of Ms. Wilson's clinical assessment and treatment plan, what specific feedback should Sarah give to the committee? Do the treatment goals and objectives relate to the person's goals? Are they written in measurable terms? Do they specify treatment interventions and their frequency?

Clinical Assessment

Presenting Problem: The 24-year-old, white female with a history of alcohol and cannabis abuse was referred by the county inpatient alcohol and drug treatment program. She is in need of continuing treatment for her longstanding problem with alcohol and drugs.

Health/Medical History: No current health problems. Client has two children, aged 2 years and 4 years. Other than childbirth and her recent substance abuse treatment, this client has not had any previous hospitalizations.

Family/Social Interaction: Client was raised in a physically abusive environment by her mother and alcoholic stepfather. Natural father was killed in a nightclub when the client was 10 years old. Client indicates that her natural father was also an alcoholic. She is currently living in public housing with her two children. She has little family or other emotional support. Her boyfriend of several years (father of her 2-year-old child) recently moved in with another woman.

Psychoactive Substance Use History

Drug	Age at First Use	Frequency (last 6 mo)	Quantity	Last Use	How Used
Alcohol	11	Daily	Pint of bourbon per day	One month ago	Oral
Cocaine	18	Once in the last year	Unknown	6 months ago	Smoked
Cannabis	15	Weekly	Two per week	One month ago	Smoked

DSM-IV Diagnoses

Axis I	Alcohol Dependence
	Cannabis Abuse
	Cocaine Use
Axis II	Diagnosis deferred
Axis III	None Currently

Clinical Impression: This client recently completed a 28-day inpatient rehabilitation program. Client realizes she has a problem and is ready to seek treatment on a voluntary basis. Client feels relapse risks are high due to her lack of support. She will be admitted to the womens' program so her children can benefit from the day care services and she can benefit from the support network. Anticipated level of care is weekly individual counseling sessions, as well as participating in group therapy twice a week.

Individualized Treatment Plan

Justification for Treatment: Referred by inpatient program.

Goals: Date Service Ordered: 8/20/XX Expected Achievement Date: 2/22/XX

1. Client will improve her knowledge of addiction by:

    a. Read chapters 2 and 3 from the book on addiction behavior and list 10 addictive behaviors.

    b. Remember a drug is a drug.

    c. Acknowledge problems related to alcohol use.

2. Improving self-esteem

    a. Client shall report three personal strengths about herself.

    b. Client will use at least three "I statements" per day.

REFERENCES AND SUGGESTED READINGS

[42 C.F.R. Part 2] Confidentiality of alcohol and drug abuse patient records. *Code of Federal Regulations*, Title 42, pt. 2, 2009 ed.

Albaum-Feinstein, A. L. (1999). *DSM-IV crosswalk: Guidelines for coding mental health information*. Chicago, IL: American Health Information Management Association.

Alcoholics Anonymous World Services, Inc. (1957). *Alcoholics Anonymous comes of age: A brief history of A.A.* New York: Author.

American Psychiatric Association. (2000). *Diagnostic and statistical manual of mental disorders* (text revision). Washington, DC: Author.

American Psychiatric Association. (2006). Practice guideline for the treatment of patients with substance use disorders (2nd ed.). Available at http://www.psychiatryonline.com/pracGuide/loadGuidelinePdf.aspx?file=SUD2ePG_04-28-06

[ASAM] American Society of Addiction Medicine. (2001). *American Society of Addiction Medicine Patient Placement Criteria,* 2nd ed., revised *(ASAM PPC-2R)*. Chevy Chase, MD: Author.

Asp, L., & Petersen, J. (2003). A conceptual model for documentation for clinical information in the EHR. *International Clinical Documentation Models*. National Board of Health, Denmark.

Atkins, R. G., Jr., & Hawdon, J. E. (2007). Religiosity and participation in mutual-aid support groups for addiction. *Journal of Substance Abuse Treatment, 33*, 321–331.

Bazelon Center for Mental Health Law. (2004, June). Summary of state statutes on involuntary outpatient commitment. Available at http://www.bazelon.org/issues/commitment/ioc/iocchart.html.

Beis, E. B. (1984). *Mental health and the law.* Rockville, MD: Aspen.

Brannigan, R., Schackman, B., Falco, M., & Millman, R. B. (2004). The quality of highly regarded adolescent substance abuse treatment programs: Results of an in-depth national survey. *Archives of Pediatric and Adolescent Medicine, 158*, 904–909.

[CSAT] Center for Substance Abuse Treatment. (n.d.). [Online.] http://csat.samhsa.gov [2010, July 28].

[CDC] Centers for Disease Control and Prevention. (n.d.). Trends in the prevalence of alcohol use. National YRBS: 1991–2007. Available at http://www.cdc.gov/HealthyYouth/yrbs/pdf/yrbs07_us_alcohol_use_trend.pdf.

[CARF] Commission on Accreditation of Rehabilitation Facilities. [Online.] http://www.carf.org.

Drake, R. E., Antosca, L. A., Noordsy, D. L., Bartels, S. J., & Osher, F. C. (1991). New Hampshire's specialized services for the dually diagnosed. *New Directions for Mental Health Services, 50*, 57–67.

Grissom, G. R. (1991). Addiction severity index: Experience in the field. *International Journal of the Addictions, 26*(1), 55–64.

Kosanke, N., Magura, S., Staines, G., Foote, J., & DeLuca, A. (2002). Feasibility of matching alcohol patients to ASAM levels of care. *American Journal on Addictions, 11*, 124–134.

Lee, F. Wickham (1995). *Using the DSM-IV to ICD-9-CM Crosswalk*. Chicago, IL: American Health Information Management Association.

Legal Action Center. (2003). *Confidentiality and communication: A guide to the Federal Alcohol & Drug Confidentiality Law and HIPAA, 2003 Revised Edition*. New York: Author.

Muramoto, M. L., & Leshan, L. (1993). Adolescent substance abuse. Recognition and early intervention. *Primary Care: Clinics in Office Practice, 20*(1), 141–154.

National Center on Addiction and Substance Abuse (CASA) at Columbia University. (2009, May). Shoveling Up II: The impact of substance abuse on federal, state and local budgets. Available at http://www.casacolumbia.org/absolutenm/articlefiles/380-ShovelingUpII.pdf.

Ohio Administrative Code. (2005, November 17). 3793:2 Program Standards. Chapter 3793:2-1 Alcohol and Drug Addiction Programs 3793:2-1-06 Client records. Available at http://codes.ohio.gov/oac/3793:2-1-06

Roach, W. H., Hoban, R.G., Broccolo, B. M., Roth, A. B., & Blanchard, T. P. (2006). *Medical records and the law* (4th ed.). Sudbury, MA: Jones and Bartlett.

[SAMHSA] Substance Abuse and Mental Health Services Administration, Office of Applied Studies. (2007a). *Pregnant women in substance abuse treatment*. Available at http://www.samhsa.gov/oas/2k2/pregTX/pregTX.cfm.

[SAMHSA] Substance Abuse and Mental Health Services Administration. (2007b). Results from the 2006 National Survey on Drug Use and Health: National Findings (Office of Applied Studies, NSDUH Series H-32, DHHS Publication No. SMA 07-4293). Rockville, MD: Author.

[SAMHSA] Substance Abuse and Mental Health Services Administration, Office of Applied Studies. (2009). *2009 State Profile—United States: National Survey of Substance Abuse Treatment Services (N-SSATS)*. [Online]. http://wwwdasis.samhsa.gov/webt/state_data/US09.pdf [2010, July 28].

[SAMHSA] Substance Abuse and Mental Health Services Administration. (2010). *Frequently Asked Questions: Applying the substance abuse confidentiality regulations to Health Information Exchange (HIE)*. [Online]. http://www.samhsa.gov/HealthPrivacy/docs/EHR-FAQs.pdf [2010, July 28].

KEY RESOURCES

Alcoholics Anonymous
http://www.aa.org

American Psychiatric Association
http://www.psych.org

American Society of Addiction Medicine
http://www.asam.org

CARF International (Commission on Accreditation of Rehabilitation Facilities)
http://www.carf.org

Drug Enforcement Administration
http://www.usdoj.gov/dea/index.htm

The Joint Commission
http://www.jointcommission.org

Legal Action Center
http://www.lac.org

Narcotics Anonymous
http://www.na.org

National Institute on Alcohol Abuse and
Alcoholism (NIAAA)
http://www.niaaa.nih.gov

National Institute on Drug Abuse
http://www.nida.nih.gov

Substance Abuse & Mental Health Services
Administration

General information
http://www.samhsa.gov

Center for Substance Abuse Prevention (CSAP)
http://prevention.samhsa.gov

Center for Substance Abuse Treatment (CSAT)
http://csat.samhsa.gov

National Clearinghouse for Alcohol and Drug
Information
http://ncadi.samhsa.gov

Office of Applied Studies
http://www.oas.samhsa.gov

CHAPTER 9

Facilities for Individuals with Intellectual or Developmental Disabilities

NAN R. CHRISTIAN, MED

JUDY S. WESTERFIELD, MED

ELAINE C. JOUETTE, MA, RHIA

LEARNING OBJECTIVES

Upon successful completion of this chapter, you should be able to:

- Identify the major differences in services provided to an individual living in an ICF/MR as compared to other settings.

- Explain various methods of record keeping and the natural separation of information into sections or divisions for individuals in an ICF/MR setting.

- Explain the need for utilizing various coding systems for capturing and classifying data from the records of individuals with intellectual and developmental disabilities.

- Discuss the process involved in risk management in the tracking of accident/incident reports.

- Discuss technical aspects of health information management in an ICF/MR.

Setting	Description	Synonyms/Examples
ICF/MR	Intermediate care facilities for mentally retarded and developmentally disabled individuals (now known as intellectually and developmentally disabled individuals) May be operated as private, religious, or governmental	Services for persons classified with autism spectrum disorders, cerebral palsy, dual diagnoses, and intellectual or developmental disabilities; parameters set for services based on age, functioning level, and condition Special education

INTRODUCTION TO SETTING

Federal regulations classify an organization providing specialized services for persons with mental retardation (in many environments known as intellectual and developmental disabilities) as an **intermediate care facility for the mentally retarded (ICF/MR)**. In addition to routine medical and nursing care, this type of facility must be responsive to the unique needs of its population and provide individualized training in such areas as sensorimotor, cognitive, emotional, communicative, vocational, and social development. An organization licensed as an ICF/MR is eligible to receive payment for its services from Medicaid (Title XIX). These facilities may be called schools, training centers, development centers, or some other similar name.

Individuals who live on the premises of an ICF/MR may have a wide range of needs, so a particular ICF/MR may provide a wide range of living arrangements. A typical center may have a campus with several homes or dormitories in which persons live. It may provide one building that resembles a small nursing home, with 24-hour nursing care for individuals with severe physical and mental disabilities. The same center may house persons with less severe disabilities in a group home setting where direct care staff members with no nursing background provide supervision. Federal regulations encourage the grouping of individuals by age and developmental level but prohibit segregating them solely on the basis of physical disability. For example, persons who are deaf or blind must be integrated with others of comparable social and intellectual development (Conditions of participation, 2009).

Typically, each building or home houses a small number of individuals—in the range of three to 24. A common standard is six persons per group home. However, the total number of individuals served by an ICF/MR facility can be quite large, ranging from less than 100 to more than 1,000. Although this chapter deals largely with the ICF/MR facility, it should be noted that many ICF/MR organizations also offer community-based services for individuals who do not reside at the facility. In some states almost all services are community based.

The ICFs/MR differ from other settings in that individuals are on a 24-hour training schedule. Tasks that can be easily accomplished by the "normal" population, such as tying one's shoes, may take months and even years to master by these special needs individuals, and the ICF/MR is required to include such **training objectives** (measurable outcomes expected to be achieved by the individual within one year) in its plans for each person. ICFs/MR are committed to helping individuals reach their fullest potential. These facilities strive for the best quality of life for persons by providing care, treatment, training, and a safe environment for those for whom they are responsible.

Types of Individuals Served

Persons receiving services from an ICF/MR are affected by an **intellectual disability** (formerly known as **mental retardation**), which is "a disability characterized by significant limitations both in intellectual functioning and in adaptive behavior as expressed in conceptual, social, and practical adaptive skills. This disability originates before age 18" (AAIDD, 2010). The term **developmental disability** is used almost interchangeably with the terms *intellectual disability* and *mental retardation*, although it has been defined slightly differently. A developmental disability is caused by either a mental or physical impairment that begins before age 22 (AAMR, 1992).

The admission of persons with this type of disability may be voluntary, court ordered, or the result of an emergency situation. The parent/family, the state, and/or regional departments usually make the referrals of the individual to the ICF/MR facility.

The facility conducts a preliminary examination (preadmission screening) of the referred individual. This evaluation can be conducted by an admission committee that focuses on two major areas: (1) Do the facility's services meet the needs of the individual? and (2) is this the least restrictive environment for the individual?

The individual admitted to an ICF/MR facility must be in need of receiving **active treatment** services. Therefore, the facility's primary responsibility is to provide health care, training, and habilitative services for individuals with intellectual or developmental disabilities, under the supervision of qualified professionals.

These individuals, over the years, have been referred to as patients, students, residents, clients, individuals, or customers. The synonyms have changed over time for these individuals as there has been a move away from the medical model toward the person-centered approach. The medical model leans toward institutions, "patients," basic needs, clinicians, and restoration to health with the emphasis on good care. The developmental model stresses deinstitutionalization. In this model, generally preferred terms are *individual* or *person*. Services are offered to promote skill development or behavior change using the interdisciplinary team approach in the active treatment process. The individual supports model is more community based, with the individual/consumer obtaining support services based on self-determination that is outcome oriented. Also, facilities may be under different departments and services, and the synonyms tend to favor the service the department renders. For instance, individuals with cerebral palsy may come under the Department of Special Education; therefore, *students* may be the preferred term. However, coauthors Amy Hewitt and Susan O'Nell, in addressing labels for persons with developmental disabilities, remind us that "it's the person, not the service, that matters. It's a sign of respect" (1998, p. 5).

Types of Caregivers

Personnel vary from facility to facility, depending on the size and scope of the services the facility provides. However, all ICFs/MR must focus on activities that build or strengthen the person's skills (Janicki, 1992). To this end, an **interdisciplinary (ID) team** identifies and addresses each person's needs. The members of an individual's interdisciplinary team should represent the professions, disciplines, or service areas that are relevant to the person's needs (Conditions of participation, 2009). Any of the following may serve on an interdisciplinary team: physician, psychologist, social worker, registered nurse, pharmacist, dietitian, physical therapist, occupational therapist, speech-language pathologist, audiologist, dentist, recreational staff member, vocational staff member, education staff member, or resident services staff member. The individual also participates as a member of the team, as well as family members and friends or advocates invited by the individual.

In the traditional planning approach established in the Conditions of Participation, the interdisciplinary team reviews and discusses the past progress and current status of the individual. From this review, a program is developed exclusively for the individual, based on individual **assessments** and identification of needs by the interdisciplinary team. A summary of essential assessment information that facilitates the identification of needs and provides necessary information to staff members who are responsible for working with the person is developed along with the goals, objectives, and a service plan for meeting the individual's prioritized needs. This document becomes the product of the interdisciplinary team process, which is a review and revision of services provided. Although federal regulations governing this process have not changed, the expectation for including the expressed needs and desires of the individual receiving services is critical. Several self-advocacy models can be incorporated into the team process that allow persons and their families to make choices and have a major role in the development of the program plan. This shift in the planning process toward more personal choice is based on the belief that every person has the right to plan a life that is meaningful and satisfying and is known as **person-centered planning**.

A **qualified mental retardation professional (QMRP)** is responsible for coordinating and monitoring each person's active treatment program. A QMRP must have at least one year of experience working directly with individuals with intellectual or developmental disabilities and is a physician, an RN, or a person with a bachelor's degree in a relevant profession (Conditions of participation, 2009).

Health Care Staff

Members of the health care staff are responsible for providing and administering proper health care in order to maintain the physical and mental well-being of the person receiving services. These caregivers include, but are not limited to, the following:

- Physicians
- Dentists

- Podiatrists
- Nursing service staff
- Health information staff
- Laboratory technicians
- X-ray technicians
- Respiratory therapists
- EEG technicians
- EKG technicians
- Occupational therapists
- Physical therapists
- Dietary staff
- Pharmacists
- Central supply staff

Habilitative Staff

An ICF/MR provides **habilitation**, which is a process by which a person is assisted to acquire and maintain life skills that enable him or her to cope more effectively with personal and environmental demands and to raise the level of physical, mental, and social efficiency. Habilitation includes, but is not limited to, programs of structured education and training. The operative force in the habilitation process is often accomplished by the "person first" philosophy. Employees are involved in creating an environment for individuals that encourages continuous improvement. The person-centered approach has been instrumental in improving the services rendered and identifying the least restrictive program alternative—meaning that the program is the least confining for the person's condition, service, and treatment, and is also provided in the least intrusive manner reasonably and humanely appropriate to the individual's needs and preferences. The habilitative staff members include, but are not limited to, the following:

- Qualified mental retardation professional (QMRP)
- Social service workers
- Psychologists
- Speech-language pathologists
- Audiologists
- Special education staff
- Vocational/life skills coaches
- Recreational therapists
- Music therapists
- Direct care staff

Administrative Staff

Members of the administrative staff work within the guidelines of the ICF/MR federal regulations to produce positive outcomes for individuals receiving services. They manage funds in order to provide quality care. They are responsible for the smooth operation of the facility in order to maintain the health, safety, and quality of life for the individuals being served. Administrative staff members include, but are not limited to, the following:

- Administrator
- Finance officer
- Human resources staff
- Health information services staff
- Home life directors/managers/supervisors
- Housekeeping staff

Types of Settings

Facilities for individuals with intellectual or developmental disabilities may be operated by a variety of groups, such as the government, religious groups, private interests, and everything in between. Also, the facilities may be designated by the type of services rendered. Some facilities may provide services to individuals based on an age range, such as from the age of 3 to 22. Some may provide services only to individuals with a specific diagnosis, such as those with cerebral palsy, autism spectrum disorders, and dual diagnoses.

In general, no admission should be considered permanent. The facility provides the individual with the training and guidance necessary to develop and acquire the skills needed to function in a less restrictive setting. This normalization training model has been a major force for individuals with intellectual and developmental disabilities.

Once these goals have been reached, the discharge planning objectives are obtained by referring the person to the appropriate setting, such as a group home, supervised living, or supported living (where the person chooses where and with whom he or she will live, with assistance as needed).

REGULATORY ISSUES

Most ICF/MR facilities are funded by Title XIX (Medicaid) and must therefore meet the standards in the Conditions of Participation for Intermediate Care Facilities for the Mentally Retarded. As in other settings, a state agency surveys facilities to determine whether they meet federal and any applicable state standards. This annual survey may be conducted by the state department of health, mental health, or hospital licensing division. Because funding is tied into the survey process, it is the goal of all facilities to meet regulatory requirements the first time around. However, if deficiencies are noted that may endanger the safety of the client, the facility can be fined several hundreds to thousands of dollars per day, depending on the infraction, until the deficiency has been rectified.

Voluntary accreditation is also available to facilities serving persons with intellectual or developmental disabilities. The Joint Commission offers accreditation for such organizations through its behavioral health care division. The standards that are used to survey these organizations are found in the *Comprehensive Accreditation Manual for Behavioral Health Care*.

Another accrediting body, The Council on Quality and Leadership (formerly the Accreditation Council on Services for People with Developmental Disabilities), has also set standards for facilities serving persons with intellectual or developmental disabilities. There are currently around 185 organizations accredited by the Council (CQL). The Council is sponsored by the following organizations and service providers: American Association on Intellectual and Developmental Disabilities, American Network of Community Options and Resources, The Arc (formerly Association for Retarded Citizens of the United States), Autism Society of America, Mosaic, National Association of QMRPs, Self Advocates Becoming Empowered, and United Cerebral Palsy Associations, Inc. The accreditation standards of the Council on Quality and Leadership are found in its publication *Personal Outcome Measures* (2005).

Generally, voluntary accreditation surveys performed by the Council or the Joint Commission are more stringent than the states' ICF/MR surveying processes. Usually when accreditation is obtained, the facility is considered to be performing above and beyond the state licensing requirements. Although the majority of ICFs/MR may not undergo voluntary accreditation by the Council or the Joint Commission, they sometimes use the publications of these organizations to improve the quality of the services they offer.

DOCUMENTATION

Individual records are the official files on each person at an ICF/MR facility. Although in theory they should consist of only one chart, these records are often divided into administrative, health, and habilitation/training sections. All sections must be kept confidential in secure areas when not in use.

A number of documentation requirements are found in the Conditions of Participation. For example, the standards for admissions, transfers, and discharge include the following requirements in 42 C.F.R. § 483.440 under Standard (b):

(2) Admission decisions must be based on a preliminary evaluation of the client that is conducted or updated by the facility or by outside sources.

(3) A preliminary evaluation must contain background information as well as currently valid assessments of functional developmental, behavioral, social, health and nutritional status to determine if the facility can provide for the client's needs and if the client is likely to benefit from placement in the facility.

(4) If a client is to be either transferred or discharged, the facility must—
    (i) Have documentation in the client's record that the client was transferred or discharged for good cause; and
    (ii) Provide a reasonable time to prepare the client and his or her parents or guardian for the transfer or discharge (except in emergencies).

(5) At the time of the discharge, the facility must—
    (i) Develop a final summary of the client's developmental, behavioral, social, health and nutritional status and, with the consent of the client, parents (if the client is a minor) or legal guardian, provide a copy to authorized persons and agencies; and
    (ii) Provide a post-discharge plan of care that will assist the client to adjust to the new living environment.

One very important documentation requirement in the ICF/MR setting is the **individual program plan (IPP)**. Standards for this document are also detailed at C.F.R. § 483.440 as follows:

(c) Standard: Individual program plan.

    (1) Each client must have an individual program plan developed by an interdisciplinary team that represents the professions, disciplines or service areas that are relevant to—

        (i) Identifying the client's needs, as described by the comprehensive functional assessments required in paragraph (c)(3) of this section; and

        (ii) Designing programs that meet the client's needs.

    (2) Appropriate facility staff must participate in interdisciplinary team meetings. Participation by other agencies serving the client is encouraged. Participation by the client, his or her parent (if the client is a minor), or the client's legal guardian is required unless that participation is unobtainable or inappropriate.

    (3) Within 30 days after admission, the interdisciplinary team must perform accurate assessments or reassessments as needed to supplement the preliminary evaluation conducted prior to admission. The comprehensive functional assessment must take into consideration the client's age (for example, child, young adult, elderly person) and the implications for active treatment at each stage, as applicable, and must—

        (i) Identify the presenting problems and disabilities and where possible, their causes;

        (ii) Identify the client's specific developmental strengths;

        (iii) Identify the client's specific developmental and behavioral management needs;

        (iv) Identify the client's need for services without regard to the actual availability of the services needed; and

        (v) Include physical development and health, nutritional status, sensorimotor development, affective development, speech and language development and auditory functioning, cognitive development, social development, adaptive behaviors or independent living skills necessary for the client to be able to function in the community, and as applicable, vocational skills.

    (4) Within 30 days after admission, the interdisciplinary team must prepare for each client an individual program plan that states the specific objectives necessary to meet the client's needs, as identified by the comprehensive assessment required by paragraph (c)(3) of this section, and the planned sequence for dealing with those objectives. These objectives must—

        (i) Be stated separately, in terms of a single behavioral outcome;

        (ii) Be assigned projected completion dates;

        (iii) Be expressed in behavioral terms that provide measurable indices of performance;

        (iv) Be organized to reflect a developmental progression appropriate to the individual; and

        (v) Be assigned priorities.

(5) Each written training program designed to implement the objectives in the individual program plan must specify:
  (i) The methods to be used;
  (ii) The schedule for use of the method;
  (iii) The person responsible for the program;
  (iv) The type of data and frequency of data collection necessary to be able to assess progress toward the desired objectives;
  (v) The inappropriate client behavior(s), if applicable; and
  (vi) Provision for the appropriate expression of behavior and the replacement of inappropriate behavior, if applicable, with behavior that is adaptive or appropriate.

(6) The individual program plan must also:
  (i) Describe relevant interventions to support the individual toward independence.
  (ii) Identify the location where program strategy information (which must be accessible to any person responsible for implementation) can be found.
  (iii) Include, for those clients who lack them, training in personal skills essential for privacy and independence (including, but not limited to, toilet training, personal hygiene, dental hygiene, self-feeding, bathing, dressing, grooming, and communication of basic needs), until it has been demonstrated that the client is developmentally incapable of acquiring them.
  (iv) Identify mechanical supports, if needed, to achieve proper body position, balance, or alignment. The plan must specify the reason for each support, the situations in which each is to be applied, and a schedule for the use of each support.
  (v) Provide that clients who have multiple disabling conditions spend a major portion of each waking day out of bed and outside the bedroom area, moving about by various methods and devices whenever possible.
  (vi) Include opportunities for client choice and self-management.

(7) A copy of each client's individual program plan must be made available to all relevant staff, including staff of other agencies who work with the client, and to the client, parents (if the client is a minor) or legal guardian.

(d) Standard: Program implementation.

(1) As soon as the interdisciplinary team has formulated a client's individual program plan, each client must receive a continuous active treatment program consisting of needed interventions and services in sufficient number and frequency to support the achievement of the objectives identified in the individual program plan.

(2) The facility must develop an active treatment schedule that outlines the current active treatment program and that is readily available for review by relevant staff.

(3) Except for those facets of the individual program plan that must be implemented only by licensed personnel, each client's individual program plan must be implemented by all staff who work with the client, including professional, paraprofessional and nonprofessional staff.

(e) Standard: Program documentation.

(1) Data relative to accomplishment of the criteria specified in client individual program plan objectives must be documented in measureable terms.

(2) The facility must document significant events that are related to the client's individual program plan and assessments and that contribute to an overall understanding of the client's ongoing level and quality of functioning.

(f) Standard: Program monitoring and change.

(1) The individual program plan must be reviewed at least by the qualified mental retardation professional and revised as necessary, including, but not limited to situations in which the client—
   (i) Has successfully completed an objective or objectives identified in the individual program plan;
   (ii) Is regressing or losing skills already gained;
   (iii) Is failing to progress toward identified objectives after reasonable efforts have been made; or
   (iv) Is being considered for training towards new objectives.

(2) At least annually, the comprehensive functional assessment of each client must be reviewed by the interdisciplinary team for relevancy and updated as needed, and the individual program plan must be revised, as appropriate, repeating the process set forth in paragraph (c) of this section.

The major difference between individual records in an ICF/MR and other long-term settings relates to the fact that some type of training is occurring on a 24-hour basis. For example, persons may practice toileting or grooming skills in their living areas. Thus, it is important that the records are housed in the living units or homes. This also makes the records more accessible for the authorized chart handlers who follow the 24-hour schedules for daily observation and documentation of training factors for their monthly statistics. The statistics are gathered for annual meetings of the interdisciplinary team (sometimes informally called **annual staffings**). They are needed to demonstrate the accomplishment or failure of goals set forth for each individual.

Likewise, the health section of the record documents the health/medical needs of the person, the content of which meets the standards of practice for the caregivers. Table 9-1 is a generic listing of data that may be maintained on an individual in an ICF/MR facility. The tabular arrangement is based on what meets the needs of the facility and the user of the various sections of the document. Often forms are designed to meet several types of charting needs, such as two-sided copies for efficiency, multipart forms for distribution purposes, and forms that can meet the requirements of two or more departments/services. For example, a weight chart could

TABLE **9-1**
Generic Listing of Individual Data in a ICF/MR Facility

Administrative Data

Personal Account

Personal Funds Ledger

Savings Accounts

Long-Term Care Certification

Medicare/Medicaid

Insurance

    Funeral Home Preference/Verification

Financial Agreements

Admission Agreements

Legal Data

Guardianships

Interdictions

Court Commissions

Authorizations

    Authorizations for Release of Information

    Authorizations for Administration of Long-Term Estrogen Substances

Consents

    Consents for Disclosure of Information

    Consent to Medical Treatment/Therapy/Surgery Procedures

    Consent Regarding Emergency Medical Treatment

Consents for Off-Campus Visits/Activities with Authorized Individuals

Consent for Seizure Medications

Consent to Photograph or Record

Consent for Behavior Program Using Restricted Procedures

Consent for Psychotropic Medications and Treatment Plan

Consent for Religious Activities

Consent for Off-Campus Activities

Correspondence

    Letters, Memos, Forms

Resident's Rights

    Bill of Rights

    Explanation of Rights of Individuals Served

    Review/Approval by Behavior Management Committee

    Human Rights Committee Review or Approval Data

    Abridgement of Rights

Office of Family Services Notifications

Pre-Admission Data

Birth Certificate

Discharge and Follow-up

Discharge Summary

Training Data

Individual Habilitative Program (IHP) Addenda

Psychological (Comprehensive/Annual) Behavior Treatment Plans

Individual Education Plan (IEP)

Special Education Assessments

    Education Correspondence

Activity Schedule (24 hours)

Training Assessments

    Core Team Notes

    QMRP Monthly Reviews

    Monthly Core Team Progress Notes

    Social Service Assessments

    Vocational (Life Skills) Assessment/Evaluations

    Speech and Language Updates

        Comprehensive Evaluations

(Continued)

TABLE 9-1 *(Continued)*

Audiology Evaluations and Screenings	Physical Therapy Evaluations and Updates
Occupational Therapy Evaluations and Updates	Recreation Therapy Evaluations and Updates
Wheelchair Evaluations	Music Therapy Evaluations and Updates
Adaptive Equipment Evaluations	

Health Care Data (Medical and Nursing)

Medical	*Nursing*
Major and Minor Problem Lists	Height/Weight/Head Circumference
Physician Orders	Nursing Assessments
Health Care Progress Notes	Quarterly
Consultations	Initial
Neurology/EEGs	Medication Administration Records
Occupational	Medication History
Ophthalmology	Pharmacy Medication/Drug Reviews
Orthopedic	Medication Destruction Records
Physical Therapy	Medication on Leave of Absence Form (Visits)
Psychiatry	Seizure Records
Physical Exams	Restraint Checklist
Referrals	Accident/Incident Report Forms
Off-Campus Clinics/Health Care Facilities	Graphic Data
Laboratory	Female Health Care Records (Copies of Consents for Oral Contraceptives and Estrogen Usage)
Hematology	Diabetic Record
Chemistry	Immunization Record
Medication Levels	Dietary Data
Urinalysis	Nutritional Evaluations
Microbiology	Dietary Notes
Serology	Tube Feedings
Parasitology	Growth Graph (under 18 years of age)
Miscellaneous	Death Certificate
Radiology	Autopsy Reports
X-rays	Death Summary
EKGs	
Dental	
Progress and Treatment Received	

meet both dietary and nursing requirements. Forms should be designed to keep the bulk of the chart down while meeting the appropriate documentation standards.

REIMBURSEMENT AND FUNDING

Medicaid is the primary source of funding for most ICFs/MR. A facility that meets the requirements of the federal Conditions of Participation is certified to receive payment from Medicaid for persons who have been determined to need its services. A state's mental health or intellectual disability authority determines whether a particular individual needs the type of specialized services provided by an ICF/MR (Preadmission Screening and Annual Review of Mentally Ill and Mentally Retarded Individuals, 2009). When the person has been determined to need active treatment in a facility setting, then the ICF/MR receives a per diem payment for each day of care provided to that individual. Other sources of funding include state offices of family services, Veterans Affairs, railroad retirement funds, and so on. Some persons qualify for services covered by Medicare as well.

In some states, the level of care needed by each person determines the amount of the per diem payment received by the facility. Individuals with more medical complications, behavior problems, and disabilities would be funded at higher levels, because they need more specialized treatment and service modalities provided by a variety of professionals and caregivers. Various methods for determining the level of care needed are used in different states. Standardized assessment tools that can be used for diagnostic and planning purposes can also be used to determine the level of services needed. Some states have begun using these assessment instruments to establish case-mix reimbursement systems. Under such a system, the provider typically receives a case-mix-adjusted per diem payment for each individual receiving services. For example, the **Inventory for Client and Agency Planning (ICAP)** is an example of an assessment instrument used by some states that provides service scores that can be used to adjust payments to providers.

Managed care proposals have been offered as a mechanism for paying for services for persons with mental retardation or developmental disabilities. Managed care proposals should consider some of the differences between care for the subject population and the other types of care that are usually provided in a managed care program. For example, unlike the typical managed care population, people with intellectual/developmental disabilities need more than just health care—they need training and other types of supports. States considering managed care proposals may find it difficult to determine an appropriate capitation rate because of these differences. Advocates for persons with intellectual or developmental disabilities are urging attention to the special needs of these individuals in any managed care programs developed for them (Goel & Keefe, 2003).

INFORMATION MANAGEMENT

Data and Information Flow

Chronologically, data tend to flow as follows:

Admission of the Individual

↓

Comprehensive Diagnostics

↓

Interdisciplinary Team Assessments/Updates

↓

Receipt of Treatment/Services
Documentation of these in the individual record

↓

Discharge/Death of the Indvidual

↓

Follow-up Documentation

The physical flow of the record varies from facility to facility. However, Figure 9-1 depicts a typical flow of information in a paper-based system from decentralized storage in the person's living unit to centralized storage in the health information department.

In a paper-based system, information is filed in the centralized comprehensive record as it is received from the living units and other sources. For ease of reference, the centralized record is usually maintained in sections, such as the administrative section, the habilitative or training section, and the health section. Because the active records can be voluminous, some facilities may use

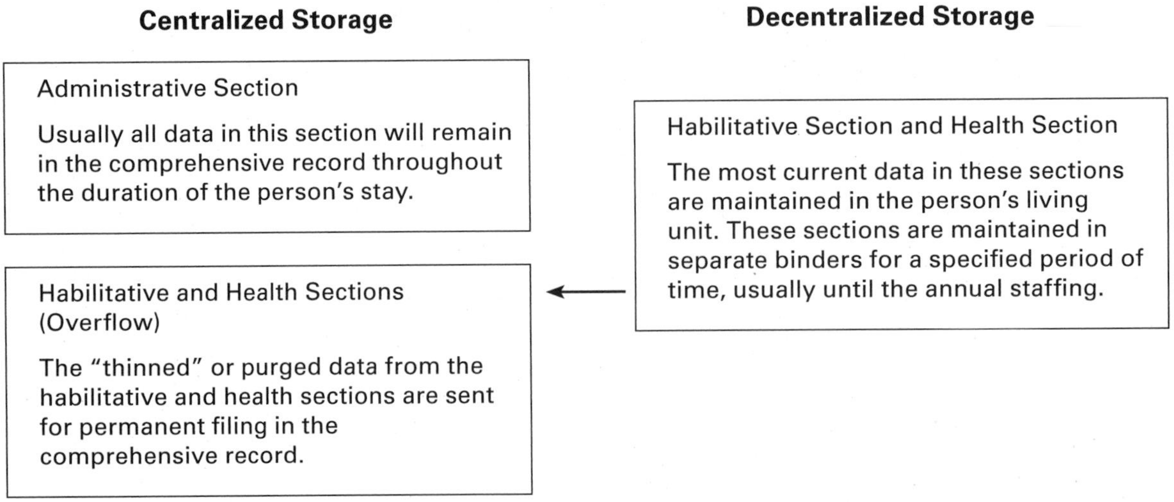

Centralized Storage   **Decentralized Storage**

Administrative Section

Usually all data in this section will remain in the comprehensive record throughout the duration of the person's stay.

Habilitative Section and Health Section

The most current data in these sections are maintained in the person's living unit. These sections are maintained in separate binders for a specified period of time, usually until the annual staffing.

Habilitative and Health Sections (Overflow)

The "thinned" or purged data from the habilitative and health sections are sent for permanent filing in the comprehensive record.

FIGURE **9-1** Relationship between centralized and decentralized record storage.

imaging technology to store portions of the paper record while the individual is still being served by the facility. Some facilities may have a hybrid system in which an electronic record system is used for a portion of the active record.

At the death or discharge of the individual, the active record is closed and retained for the duration of the statute of limitations. If a facility utilizes an imaging program for active records, the remaining portions of the closed records are often imaged at the death or discharge of the person. However, some facilities prefer to avoid the additional cost of imaging the entire record and may image only selected portions for research or administrative purposes. The remainder of the paper record in these facilities is destroyed upon reaching the statute of limitations or other legal retention period.

Coding and Classification

In the ICF/MR facilities, employees may need to become familiar with three types of coding systems, depending on established policies and procedures. Various coding systems serve different purposes helpful in the care of the individual and in research into the causes of intellectual and developmental disabilities.

ICD-9-CM and ICD-10-CM

The current clinical modification of the *International Classification of Diseases* (*ICD-9-CM*, replaced by *ICD-10-CM* in 2013) is the more widely used coding system. Codes may be assigned on an accumulative basis or based on individual "infirmary," "sick call," or "acute care" stays or visits. Coded data may be useful when a survey is in process so that individual records containing specific diagnoses or conditions can be obtained for tracking during the survey. Traditionally, this type of coding often appears in the summary sheet, which encompasses infirmary screenings, sick call, or acute care stays whenever these services are rendered in the ICF/MR facility. Facilities often prefer to use an accumulative type of diagnoses/procedures sheet that is chronological in nature and is an inclusive listing of the individual's conditions and procedures, coded for reference purposes. However, diagnoses and procedures may also be required on identification sheets for quick reference and may be used as well on the order sheets because the condition for which the medication is being ordered is also required. Whatever format is utilized, it should be developed in conjunction with facility services and with reference needs in mind. One format, which could be used in the infirmary section, is as follows:

Mental Retardation [mild, moderate, severe, profound]
Etiology: Due to _____

Additional diagnoses and conditions could then be listed.

DSM-IV (1994)/DSM-IV-TR (2000)

The Diagnostic and Statistical Manual of Mental Disorders, fourth edition, text revision (*DSM-IV-TR*), is mainly used by psychologists and psychiatrists in their evaluations and consultations. (For more information on *DSM-IV*, see Chapter 8.) Mental Retardation is coded in Axis II of *DSM-IV-TR*, which recognizes four degrees of severity of mental retardation: mild, moderate, severe, and profound. IQ test results are used to determine the degree of severity (American Psychiatric Association, 1994). This information may be recorded on the consultation, evaluation, or data sheet for retrieval purposes and/or stored electronically for access by authorized individuals through the facility network.

Manual on Terminology and Classification in Mental Retardation, 1983 Edition

The *Manual on Terminology and Classification in Mental Retardation* was published by the American Association on Mental Retardation, now the American Association on Intellectual and Developmental Disabilities (AAIDD), in 1983 and is still cited as the source of definitions of mental retardation in the *Code of Federal Regulations* (Preadmission Screening and Annual Review of Mentally Ill and Mentally Retarded Individuals, 2009). The AAIDD has replaced this reference with a publication called *Intellectual Disability: Definition, Classification, and Systems of Supports*, 11th edition. However, the older publication is still used for classification purposes in many ICFs/MR.

This manual attempts to provide a definitive classification system for use in the mental retardation field. Classifications generally provide a systematic arrangement of individuals, units, or events into groups with one or more common denominators. They may be useful for administrative purposes and for preliminary planning for groups identified by the system. Classifications can assist with the allocation of funds and personnel to provide special services. Once an individual is classified as mentally retarded, it is imperative to periodically reassess the diagnosis, classification, and service needs.

The manual includes ten major categories and seven secondary categories, both with sublistings, as well as tertiary categories. Coding is usually done at the time of admission to encompass the necessary information for establishing the comprehensive plan of care required of the facility. An example of this type of coding would be as follows:

Primary

Secondary

Tertiary

    Genetic
    Cranial anomaly
    Sensory impairment
    Perception
    Convulsive disorder
    Psychological impairment

The major and minor categories of this classification system include a variety of helpful levels in both the behavioral and medical classifications to standardize the data needed for statistical reporting. The major medical divisions in this manual follow those listed in the *ICD* and the *DSM* coding systems.

Intellectual Disability: Definition, Classification, and Systems of Supports, Eleventh Edition

The Manual on Terminology and Classification in Mental Retardation has continued to evolve over time and is now known as *Intellectual Disability: Definition, Classification, and Systems of Supports*, 11th edition. The 11th edition of the AAIDD Definition Manual contains current and authoritative information on defining, classifying, and diagnosing intellectual disability and planning lifelong supports for individuals with this condition. The manual includes discussion of 10 dimensions of support areas; a five-step process for assessing, planning, and delivering supports to a person with intellectual disability; and various approaches to individualized service planning.

Electronic Information Systems

Electronic information systems may vary from facility to facility and/or within the facility. Acute health care settings are, in general, more advanced than ICF/MR facilities, but, with additional requirements of various licensing and accreditation agencies, the use of electronic information systems is becoming more prevalent. Some ICF/MR facilities use off-the-shelf programs, but the majority of facilities have customized programs to meet the needs and types of persons served.

Private ICF/MR facilities are considered to be businesses. Electronic systems with various functions and features needed to accomplish the business aspects of the overall facility operation are seen as vital to the business's survival. The need to control the "paper tiger" has grown to encompass a variety of other areas including, but not limited to, the individual record.

Benefits of electronic systems may range from financial reports to program planning, or from timekeeping to rapidly producing all information requested during a survey. The first priority in many facilities is to begin to integrate the various systems that have been developed over time to address specific needs. As various departmental systems begin to interface with each other or with a central system, a partially electronic, or hybrid, record can be achieved. Attempting to go to a completely paperless record would probably not be cost effective in most facilities at present. More benefits are likely to be achieved by developing databases to help manage individual data and information. A completely electronic record is not possible until computers or workstations are available on all units and in all services.

For facilities pursuing an imaging system, it is imperative that the health information director become an active participant in the establishment of standardized forms and reports. With the ease of formatting and designing forms using readily available software, every department or service may tend to develop their own forms or records. Some type of facility-wide forms control, however, is vital to the success of an imaging program.

Data Sets

Data collection varies from state to state, with certain standard items required by *Conditions of Participation*. For discussion and illustration purposes, a conservative selection of forms and specific features of typical data sets has been made here, to share some of the information tools beneficial to the operation of a 24-hour ICF/MR.

The listing that follows is not exhaustive. Many variables can affect the choice of forms and the management of their use, such as variations in state laws, survey requirements, types of facilities, and even the choice of computer hardware and software. The selected forms serve a twofold purpose. One is to meet requirements, and these forms have a filing designation on them to ensure that they are filed in the correct sequence and under the correct tab heading. Other selected forms are simply tools that may not become part of the permanent file and can be shredded once they have met their service needs.

Assessment Data

Assessment of the individual is a requirement in most states to determine eligibility for services. Assessment processes vary from state to state and may include psychological, psychiatric, and medical evaluations. To assist in determining the services that the individual may need, many states use standardized assessment instruments. For example, adaptive and maladaptive behavior can be assessed with a variety of instruments, such as the Scales of Independent Behavior—Revised (SIB-R), the Vineland Adaptive Behavior Scales, the AAIDD Diagnostic Adaptive Behavior Scale (DABS), and the Inventory for Client and Agency Planning (ICAP). The use of such instruments can assist with both diagnosis and program planning. Some states use this type of instrument to provide data for case-mix reimbursement systems as well.

Annual Assessments   When the full interdisciplinary team conducts its annual assessments, forms for such categories as nutritional assessment, recreational assessment, and vocational assessment are used to summarize and address the services rendered by these specialty areas.

Administrative Data

Authorizations/Consent Forms   A variety of consent and authorization forms—such as those for psychotropic drug use and birth control pills—can be generated for each individual using data from the facility's electronic information system.

Individual Information Release   A record is maintained for the control and authorized release of requested information in the individual records, thus providing an audit tool of this task area.

Ongoing Inventory of Individual Belongings   This inventory is one of the most useful computer-generated forms, making it easy to update inventories by the touch of a key to add, delete, and/or change the information. There is still manual labor involved in the inventory process, of course, because just keeping up with each person's clothes is a monumental task in itself. Clothing is listed by long sleeves, short sleeves, and a variety of identifying features that can be noted in a specific area of the form.

Identification Data   Generally, identification sheets illustrate a variety of information/features vital to the care and management of the individual's records. The design of the form provides for a view of the individual's information at a glance. This form is usually reviewed and updated as required—at least yearly at the annual staffing.

A second form is a baseline information sheet applicable at the time of admission that maintains the same information throughout the person's stay. It is very important for the completion of vital records such as death certificates.

A third form is used at the time of death/discharge and provides necessary information for tracking and follow-up and is basically used to officially close out the individual's record.

Individual Program Plan (IPP) and Related Training Data

This section of the individual record is unique to an ICF/MR. The following specific forms are described as examples of training data forms.

The Individual Program Plan   As described previously, the individual program plan (IPP) is a composite summary of the goals and the objectives that the staff will assist the individual to attain during the coming year. This individualized program plan is used in the overall care of the person and outlines how the program will guide the individual toward achieving the set goals. The program includes brief summaries of all services rendered for the past year and the establishment of goals for the coming year. Figure 9-2 is an excerpt from an individual program plan, illustrating the portion of the plan that summarizes the person's current status and progress. Figure 9-3 is an excerpt that demonstrates how goals and plans to accomplish them may be documented in the individual program plan.

The Updating Worksheet   This worksheet is an electronic application used by the interdisciplinary team at the full team meetings for updating the person's record in specific service areas. This tool not only captures the services rendered and the responsible staff member providing each service, but also provides the capability of immediately making these changes in the person's individual program plan.

The Draft Referral to Staffing   This form is used throughout the year to provide updates to the current individual program plan. It eventually becomes a part of the permanent record as an addendum to the current staffing, which illustrates that program updates have been initiated and approved by appropriate staff members.

Core Team Summary Sheet   The core team summary sheet (Figure 9-4) is a tracking form used to implement the individual program plan. As needs are identified by the staff, they are added to the sheet. Because this is a working tool used by the staff, there is no problem if there are "write-overs" and strike-outs to indicate when goals have been met or when new information is added.

PECAN GROVE TRAININC CENTER
INDIVIDUAL PROGRAM PLAN
April 24, 20YY

NAME:

PGTC: # A-Unit

DATE OF ADMISSION: 7-22-YY

RELIGION: Catholic

BIRTHDATE: 11-23-YY

AGE: 25 years and 6 months

TYPE OF ADMISSION: Family

LEGAL STATUS: Noninterdicted Major

HOME OF RECORD: Anywhere, LA

CURRENT STATUS AND PROGRESS:

MEDICAL: _____ is currently monitored through a Medical Care Plan. Her condition is considered to be chronic stable due to her convulsive disorder. _____ remains in optimal physical health. She has had no serious illnesses or injuries during the past year. _____ had one chronic medication change, when Surfak was discontinued. _____'s bowel movements are monitored and she is given a suppository for relief of constipation as needed. _____ has quarterly head circumferences taken, as she has a shunt, and there has been no change. _____ is seen by her podiatrist for routine care. Because of her lack of cooperation, she required sedation before her visit. _____ has a prescriptive behavioral program, and she required manual restraint thirty-one times since her last review as part of her prescriptive behavioral program, to promote relaxation when positive and less restrictive measures failed to control behavior endangering self and others.

DENTAL: _____'s recent dental examination revealed her oral hygiene is at its highest level. She is void of any carious lesions, and her periodental support tissues are healthy. No other dental treatment is indicated for her at this time. _____ is scheduled for fluoride treatment next month. She receives dental treatment as needed at Dr. Doe's office in the community.

FIGURE 9-2 Individual program plan (excerpt).

A new summary sheet for review purposes is printed at or before a 90-day interval, with the recommended revisions. Because care is rendered on a 24-hour basis, the summary sheets are also used in developing the 24-hour active treatment schedules, described as follows.

The 24-Hour Active Treatment Schedule The 24-hour active treatment schedule works in conjunction with the individualized program plan and the summaries (see Figure 9-5). It specifically sets into time frames the who, what, why, when, and where of the individual's treatment program. Although the IPP and the 24-hour schedules are developed for a period of one year, periodic revisions/summaries/assessments are done at a minimum of 90-day intervals and more frequently if warranted by the service and treatment modalities of the IPP and schedule changes. Often surveyors use this form to ensure that a service or activity is being followed by the **direct care staff** (personnel whose

RECREATION:

1. Promote effective use of leisure time and improve socialization skills.

2. Maintain high level of participation in community-based activities.

3. Expand range of interests and activities.

---

1. Continue to organize small-group activities and encourage participation through 4-30-YY.

2. Continue to provide outings into community through 4-30-YY.

3. Provide a variety of activities for a broader recreational program through 4-30-YY.

DIETARY:

1. Maintain adequate nutritional status. Gain weight of approximately 2 pounds to help reach her ideal weight range of 137–147.

2. Increase intake of fiber.

---

1. Provide present diet as ordered by physician: regular high fiber diet, with no seconds and low-fat milk.

2. Provide foods high in fiber at meals.

FIGURE 9-3 Individual program plan (excerpt).

daily responsibility is to manage, supervise, and provide direct care to individuals in the residential living units). If the facility is not adhering to the individualized program based on the time frame set forth, it can be cited for a deficiency in that particular area of care or service.

Physician Data

Standing orders are individualized forms listing medications, contraindications, allergies, and so forth (see Figure 9-6).

Orders sheets list every medication the person is taking along with a corresponding diagnosis. For example, if the person is a diabetic, there must be supporting documentation for the diagnosis in order for medication to be provided for the control of this condition.

Physician progress notes may be handwritten or may be generated electronically.

Because most ICF/MR facilities do not maintain full-time medical staff members but must utilize available community medical services, the use of the transfer and referral record is vital not only for the individual's care but for the communication of the care rendered. This is especially true in emergency transfer situations. The front of the form deals with information that the facility furnishes when the person is transferred, and the reverse side provides for communication of the treatment, evaluation, and consultation rendered.

CORE TEAM REVIEW SUMMARY FOR X

(Based Upon Client & Staff Interviews and 20–25% Random Sampling of Daily Documentation)

COVERING THE REVIEW PERIOD 02/02/YY THROUGH 04/19/YY

RTA MEMO: SEIZURES: Monitor closely and report to Nursing. Wash hair every Wednesday. Apply activator daily. Encourage her to carry purse.

1. Praise good behavior and give extra attention when good. Give attention to dress and appearance.
2. Offer (when patting stomach) to take X to bathroom often (each half hour).
3. Direct her to bathroom and offer shower when highly upset.
4. Remove from loud areas when upset.
5. When agitated and aggressive, contact supervisor.
6. Call for help as needed.
7. Do not "back off" from X; this increases problems.
8. Monitor closely when around Y (may bite when upset).

Time:	Location:	Code:	Current Training Objective:				Flags:	Recommendations:
08:15 AM	DAYROOM/GYM	BC61L-005AAAD	**BASIC COMMANDS**/Also scheduled: 04:45 PM					
			Will remain dressed in same outfit for half					
			hour (RTA to reward with edible)					
			does this on verbal command 1 out of 3 trials					
			to be completed by 08/30/YY					DATE
			PERIOD ENDING:	09/01/XX	11/17/YY	02/02/YY	04/19/YY	
			PROGRESS:	82.30 %	79.76 %	80.00 %	78.90 %	DECLINE
			OBJECTIVE:	BC53G	BC53G	BC53G	BC53G	
			LEVEL:	005 D	005 D	004 D	004 D	

FIGURE 9-4 Core team summary sheets (excerpt).

08:30 AM BEDROOM   HK125N-005 D

HOUSEKEEPING/Also scheduled: 04:30 PM

Will carry two items of dirty clothing

to dirty clothes bucket in bathroom

does this on verbal command

to be completed by 09/30/YY

PERIOD ENDING:	09/01/YY	11/17/YY	02/02/YY	04/19/YY	
PROGRESS:	0.00 %	0.00 %	85.19 %	86.14 %	RECENT OBJECTIVE CHANGE
OBJECTIVE:			HK79B	HK79C	
LEVEL:			011AAAD	011D	RECENT LEVEL CHANGE

08:30 AM BATHROOM [At Workshop]
BATHROOM TO15F-005AMAS

TOILETING/Also scheduled: 10:00 AM 12:15 PM

Will wash hands after toileting for

30 seconds (RTA to monitor closely)

does this on verbal command to be trained throughout day

to be completed by 10/31/YY

PERIOD ENDING:	09/01/YY	11/17/YY	02/02/YY	04/19/YY	
PROGRESS:	81.15 %	94.23 %	83.03 %	76.67 %	DECLINE
OBJECTIVE:	TO19G	TO19G	TO3B	TO3B	
LEVEL:	011 D	011 D	005AMAD	005AMAS	RECENT LEVEL

FIGURE **9-4** (Continued)

Weekday Client Active Treatment Schedule 12:00 A.M.—11:45 P.M.		
TIME:	**LOCATION:**	**SCHEDULED TRAINING:**
06:00 AM	BEDROOM/BR	Rise; Personal Hygiene Care
06:15 AM	BEDROOM/GYM	TOILETING SKILL Formal Training
07:00 AM	BEDROOM	GROOMING Formal Training
07:30 AM	DINING ROOM	Scheduled Mealtime
08:15 AM	BATHROOM	ORAL HYGIENE Formal Training
08:30 AM	BEDROOM/GYM	TOILETING SKILL Formal Training
09:00 AM	GYM/CR 7	STIMULATION Formal Training
09:15 AM	GYM/CR 7	READING Formal Training
09:30 AM	CLASSROOM 6	KITCHEN MANAGEMENT Formal Training
09:45 AM	BEDROOM/GYM	TOILETING SKILL Formal Training
10:00 AM	CANTEEN	Snack/allowance on Thursdays
10:15 AM	GYM/CR 7	DISCRIMINATION Formal Training
10:30 AM	GYM/CR 7	TIME KNOWLEDGE Formal Training
10:45 AM	BATHROOM	BATHING Formal Training
11:00 AM	BEDROOM	Leisure time until 11:30 AM
11:30 AM	BEDROOM	PERSONAL INFORMATION Formal Training
12:00 PM	BEDROOM/GYM	TOILETING SKILLS Formal Training
12:15 PM	BATHROOM	GROOMING Formal Training
12:30 PM	DINING ROOM	Scheduled Mealtime
01:15 PM	BATHROOM	ORAL HYGIENE Formal Training
A.M. Medication Times: None		
P.M. Medication Times: None		
PGTC #		CLIENT:

FIGURE **9-5** 24-hour schedule—weekday. (The weekend schedule is separate.)

HUDSPETH REGIONAL CENTER
PHYSICIAN'S STANDING ORDERS

1. PASSES: To include therapeutic leaves: Individualized activities, school and programing; off-campus consultations, appointments and follow-up visits with physicians in clinic, and other diagnostic studies done off campus and other purposes.

2. ROUTINE TREATMENT FOR WOUND CARE AND INJURIES:
   1. Superficial wounds: clean with saline twice a day and apply antibiotic ointment (Neosporin or Bacitracin) until healed.
   2. Ice pack as needed.
   3. For sutures: clean with saline twice a day and apply antibiotic ointment and remove sutures in 7 days, unless otherwise ordered.

3. FEVER/PAIN:

   For fever greater than 100.5° F rectally (99.5° oral, 98.5° axillary) and/or for Pain give:

   1. Tylenol 10 mg. per kg up to 650 mg. q. 4 hours as needed or
   2. Tylenol suppository 325 mg. per rectum for clients weighing less than 45 pounds and 650 mg. per rectum for clients weighing more than 45 pounds q. 4 hours as needed.

   For fever not relieved by Tylenol within t hour:

   May give Ibuprofen 10 mg. per kg up to 800 mg. q. 6 hrs. PRN.

   For temperature of 103° rectally (102° oral, 101° axillary) or above:

   3. Use a cooling blanket.
   4. Give tepid sponge bath and Tylenol/Ibuprofen as noted above.
   5. CBC with differential on A shift closest to occurrence of fever
   6. Check complete set of vital signs and Notify MD.

4. HYPOTHERMIA: (temp less than 96° rectal, 95° oral, 94° axillary)
   1. Put socks and cap on client.
   2. Wrap client up with a regular blanket.
   3. If temperature does not respond, put on heating blanket.

5. NAUSEA AND VOMITING: (New Onset)
   1. Check for fecal impaction.
   2. If positive, follow orders for impaction. If negative, and after vomiting 2 times, give Phenergan suppository 2.5 mg., 1 whole one for clients over 45 pounds, $1/2$ for clients under 45 pounds.

NAME:_____   CASE NUMBER:_____

FIGURE 9-6 Physician's standing orders. (Courtesy Hudspeth Regional center, Whitfield, MS. Used with permission.)

6.   DIARRHEA: (New Onset)

   1. Hold any laxatives or prune juice for 48 hrs.

   2. Immodium 2 mg. P.O. after 3rd loose stool. May repeat once within an hour.

7.   SEIZURES:

   After 2nd Grand Mal seizure:

   1. Check for impaction.

   2. Give Ativan 2 mg. IM for clients weighing greater than 50 pounds or 1 mg. IM for clients weighing less than 50 pounds.

   3. Check complete set of vitals and notify MD if seizures not resolved.

   4. If impaction was positive, follow orders for impaction.

8.   IMPACTION:

   1. Give one Dulcolax or Bisacodyl Suppository per rectum.

   2. May manually disimpact as needed.

9.   CONSTIPATION:

   1. Give MOM 30 cc by mouth or PEG.

10.   MOUTH INJURIES:

   1. Glyoxide application 3 times a day for 5 days.

   2. Refer to the physician or dentist as needed.

11.   RUNNY NOSE: Nalex-A:

   1. Age greater than 12, give 1 tablet or 2 teaspoons 3 times a day × 5 days, or

   2. Age less than 12, give 1 teaspoon or $1/2$ tablet 3 times a day × 5 days with first and last dose being at least 12 hours apart and middle dose being at least 4 hours from first and last. (Ex. 7am, 4pm, 8pm, or 8am, 12am, 8pm)

   OR

   Rondec:

   1. Age greater that 6, give 1 tablet or 1 tsp. three times a day × 5 days, or

   2. Age less that 6, give $1/2$ tsp. of the liquid three times a day × 5 days with first and last dose being at least 12 hours apart and middle dose being at least 4 hours from first and last. (Ex. 7am, 4pm, 8pm, or 8am, 12am, 8pm)

NAME: _____   CASE NUMBER: _____

FIGURE **9-6** (*Continued*)

12. FOR RED EYES WITH DRAINAGE/CONJUNCTIVITIS: Bacitracin or Neosporin Ophthalmologic Ointment 3 times a day for 5 days with first and last dose being at least 12 hours apart.

13. DIAPER RASH: A & D Ointment as needed and with every diaper change.

14. PURULENT EAR DRAINAGE: Cortisporin Otic Suspension or Cortaine-B, 4 drops in affected ear 4 times a day for 7 days. Do not use if there is a known tympanic membrane perforation or PE Tubes.

15. COUGH:

   1. For clients 12 and above, give Robitussin DM 3 teaspoons 4 times a day for 7 days.

   2. For clients 12 and under, give 2 teaspoons of Robitussin DM 4 times a day for 7 days.

16. EAR WAX (REMOVAL: (Do not use if there is a known tympanic membrane perforation or PE Tubes.)

   1. Cerumenex 3 or 4 drops in affected ear at 8 PM and repeat again at 8 AM the next morning. OR

   2. For more stubborn cerumen: Cerumenex 3 to 4 drops in affected ear 3 times a day for 5 days

   3 Then irrigate with warm water after the Cerumenex treatment.

17. FINGER STICK GLUCOSE: Do a finger stick glucose for signs and symptoms of hypoglycemia or hyperglycemia (nausea, diaphoresis, shakiness, decreased level of consciousness).

   1. If glucose is less than 70, give juice and sugar or Instaglucose and reiheck in 15 minutes. If still less than 70, continue with juice and sugar and/or Instaglucose, check complete set of vitals and notify MD.

   2. If glucose is greater than 400, check complete set of vitals and notify MD.

18. ROUTINE MEDICATION ORDERS THAN RUN OUT ON THE WEEKENDS OR HOLIDAYS: Continue same medications and dosages until the next working day.

19. For any acute illness or change in status, check a complete set of vitals (Blood Pressure, Temperature, Pulse, Respirations) and notify MD.

DO NOT GIVE ANY OF THE ABOVE MEDICATIONS IF ALLERGIC. ANY SPECIFIC ORDERS ON ANY CLIENT SUPERCEDES THESE STANDING ORDERS.

| Physician | Date | Nurse | Date |

NAME:_____   CASE NUMBER:_____

FIGURE **9-6** (*Continued*)

Specialty services such as x-rays and laboratory work are often provided by outside sources. When they are requested and the facility documentation of the service rendered is recorded on this form, it is also used for accounting purposes.

The transportation request form is used when the individual must obtain health care services in the community. This is not only a request but is required for accounting purposes.

The physical exam form is used at the time of the annual staffing. As noted, the primary and additional diagnoses, as well as personal information, are furnished to the physician, enabling him or her to screen more methodically. For example, if the individual has a heart problem, it would be in the diagnosis section, and the physician could address the status of the heart with a cardiovascular entry.

Nursing assessments are performed throughout the year and with the physical exam provide the data needed to annually summarize the overall medical and nursing care rendered.

Nursing Data

The chronological drug regimen review is a form used on a monthly basis by the consultant pharmacist, who conducts a review not only of the medication and administration of drugs but also of specific protocols that the staff are required to follow in the use of the medications prescribed for the individual.

The medication administration record (MAR) is a tool used by the nursing staff to initial for the medication administered during their shift. The reverse side of the form is used to explain why medications were not administered—for example, the person was out on pass, NPO (nothing by mouth) prior to surgery, or the person refused medication.

The director of nursing and the pharmacist use this form in their medication reviews to check for problem areas, for incidents in medication administration, and in guidelines when in-service training or more severe corrective measures are required in reference to the issues noted in the review.

The individual medication and chart audit review summary is used on a monthly basis to audit services provided to the person, such as medications and behavior monitoring activities. This form is used primarily by the director of nursing in medication reviews for checking problem areas, such as incidents in medication administration and in guidelines when in-service training or more severe corrective measures/actions are required. The information could be noted on the medication administration record or on the individual medication and chart audit review summary. Some facilities and nursing staffs may elect to conduct their medication review and chart audit on a separate form.

The medication worksheet is a computerized summary used by the nursing staff to assist in the review and audit of medication administration and may be used in conjunction with the process covered in this section.

A self-administration of medication progress form is valuable for recording an individual's skill in self-medication administration.

The medication destruction record is used when the medication becomes outdated or unused quantities of medications must be destroyed.

The discharge from facility release of responsibility and medication form is vital when individuals leave the facility and medication is being administered.

Often medication issues can be addressed and staff alerted to possible medication problems by the use of this form. The medication count can reveal if the individual was overdosed, underdosed, or the medication was not given correctly.

The seizure chart provides documentation on individuals with convulsive disorders. This form allow recording of the frequency, time of day, and kinds of seizures, and can assist the staff in medication adjustments for the control of seizures.

Behavior modification is often a major concern in an ICF/MR. In order to meet the legal and medical needs set forth, forms such as restraint documentation are required in the tracking of restraint use and become valuable in addressing such issues on a timely basis, such as in quarterly summary reviews.

Graphic records, such as weight, are important to various services. For example, the dietary department must provide menus based on the individual's diagnoses and nutritional needs. Nursing may need to check the weight records for the administration of medications, especially for children. Monitoring of vital signs and menstrual information is also tracked.

The influenza vaccine authorization and administration record serves a dual purpose. The form is sent to the family to obtain permission or refusal for giving the person the flu vaccine. In the event that the response is affirmative, the second portion of the form is used to document the administration of the vaccine.

QUALITY IMPROVEMENT AND UTILIZATION MANAGEMENT

To continue providing excellent care and supports to individuals, every area of a facility must be involved in continuous quality improvement. To make sure that individuals are in the right setting, utilization management is essential.

Quality Improvement

The quality improvement (QI) function includes each department and service in order to accomplish its mission completely. This task is ultimately a facility-wide endeavor. Quality must be incorporated into all of the services provided and measured according to acceptable standards. These standards are usually developed as guidelines in meeting licensing and accrediting requirements.

QI can involve a wide range of activities: studies conducted by the Infection Control Committee; comparisons of the frequency of accidents/incidents, medication errors, or seizure frequency; and review of yearly required training in universal precautions and cardiopulmonary resuscitation. Review of the various drills for fire, weather conditions, and toxic spills can be included in the QI function. Audits of documentation requirements on a monthly, quarterly, and yearly basis are other examples of QI in action.

Utilization Management

Utilization management (UM) relates to caring for each individual in the most appropriate setting and also to the efficient use of resources. The interdisciplinary team reviews the person's progress at regular intervals and places the individual in the most appropriate care setting. UM is also part of the work of various standing committees. For example, the formulary committee attempts to obtain the medications recommended by the medical and dental staff at the most reasonable price. Department heads and supervisors can also practice UM techniques in their daily activities as they strive to provide efficient, quality services.

RISK MANAGEMENT AND LEGAL ISSUES

Risk management includes, but is not limited to, reviewing deaths, studying incidents and accidents, correcting errors, changing records properly, and using new technology correctly. Legal issues that must be considered are confidentiality, production of records, policies and procedures for health information, and record retention.

Risk Management

Depending on the organization of the ICF/MR, the governing body, along with its legal counsel, oversees the legal issues and sets the parameters under which the facility must operate. The records maintained by the facility can be risk management's best friend or worst enemy, depending on the documentation contained within the record. The following are some of the areas in which risk management may be involved in the ICF/MR.

Deaths

Usually every death is automatically reviewed in depth, no matter if the death occurred in-house or in another health care facility. The risk management committee leaves no stone unturned in verifying that all necessary steps were taken to prevent the death from occurring. This investigation is very important in deaths that have occurred unexpectedly or without a previous disease process.

Incidents and Accidents

Risk management may study every incident and accident report to see if the situation could possibly have been avoided. Often, computer programs are designed to study the incident/accident and the time of day (by shift and hour), place, cause of incident, most effective interaction, and the injury sustained. This information is placed on a grid. From the computer printout, the staff may ascertain something as simple as a hole in a shower curtain allowing puddles of water to accumulate. With this information, the staff can correct the situation and prevent individuals from being placed in an unsafe environment.

Method of Correcting Errors

In order to eliminate any suspicion of fraudulent documentation, staff must use the proper method to correct documentation errors. A single line through an incorrect entry without completely obliterating it is the correct method for changing an entry. The person making the correction should also date and initial the correction.

Editing Documentation in Records

Addenda should be used when information in a person's record is incorrect. By retaining the original form and including an addendum, legal questions about a change should be reduced. An addendum should include the date, time, reason for the change, and the signature of the person entering the addendum, followed by professional credentials such as MD, RN, or other.

Use of Technology

The risk management staff may want to investigate the possible legal issues in the use of technology and its various features, such as electronic signatures and faxing of information. The facility's policies and procedures should address potential risks in the use of technology. Watching for changes in the laws governing the high-tech equipment of the present and future is definitely a major function of risk management.

Legal Issues

Confidentiality

Confidentiality issues are a major concern in an ICF/MR. Medical professionals and other professional staff generally receive training in the safeguarding of confidential information during their formal educational programs. As records are made more user-friendly and placed in the areas where individuals live, direct care workers must be provided with in-depth in-service training in protecting confidential information. All chart handlers should sign statements agreeing to protect the confidentiality of individual information, and a breach of this responsibility would make the employee subject to disciplinary action, up to and including dismissal.

The confidentiality statement should be obtained from all authorized record handlers before their first handling of any records. All data contained within the record may not be discussed with anyone who has not obtained the appropriate clearance for use of the record. As a rule of thumb, no person should be allowed to review an individual's record who does not have a job-related need to do so.

With the easy availability of copiers and printers, unnecessary copies of records are sometimes made. All data produced by the facility (originals) should become a part of the person's permanent record. Copies of information from other health services and copies of data retained for reference and/or proof of work completed should be stamped with a "copy" indicator, which would signal to the staff that this information is to be retained as a permanent record. All unnecessary data should be destroyed by shredding.

The Health Insurance Portability and Accountability Act (HIPAA) and related legislation such as the HITECH Act intensified the need for scrutiny in maintaining confidentiality of protected information in ICF/MR facilities. Facilities have taken steps to ensure compliance with both the privacy and security standards of HIPAA. In taking the protection of confidentiality to a higher level, facilities have typically appointed privacy and security officers and enhanced staff training programs. Policies involving actions such as release of records to third parties, use of photos on bulletin boards, persistence in obtaining parental permissions, and labeling personal articles have been reviewed and brought into compliance. Training procedures have been put into place for business associate activities that require identification of individuals. Maintenance of these higher standards will require that facilities make compliance with the federal law everyone's responsibility through continued staff training and advocacy for individual rights. Health information managers have a vital role in this process.

Protection of Records

Individual records are the property of the facility and as such should be protected from loss, damage, tampering, or use by unauthorized individuals. Records may be removed from the facility's jurisdiction and safekeeping only in accordance with court order, subpoena, or statute.

Written Policies and Procedures

There should be written policies and procedures governing access to, publication of, and dissemination of information from individuals' records. Some points to consider in the management of information are as follows.

Policies should be inclusive and applicable on a facility-wide basis. Training sessions should also be implemented to provide in-service for new employees and serve as a reminder and reference to tenured employees. Procedures can be department/service specific and are not necessarily applicable on a facility-wide level.

Policies and procedures may vary in the ICF/MR setting, depending on the type of facility and the services rendered, but there must be established guidelines. Some infractions in the day-to-day handling (mishandling) of an individual's records could lead not only to dismissal of the employee for not performing his or her job according to policy/procedure but also fines, imprisonment, and even the loss of license, certification, or accreditation, depending on the severity of the offense.

Record Retention

Laws vary from state to state; therefore, the retention schedule should be consistent with the state statute of limitations.

For historical and research purposes, it is recommended that if the individual's records are not retained in their entire original format after the retention period, at least a "skeleton" of the most vital data be considered for retention for archival purposes.

Health information managers should work with administration, legal staff, or state research centers (e.g., genetic research) to determine the most useful information to retain to enhance specialty study areas and general population data requirements.

On average, an ICF/MR may receive from five to 10 requests annually for information about a family member who was in the facility. Today, the public is more aware of genetic conditions, and many individuals want to know whether they are at risk of having a child who could be mentally and/or physically challenged. In working with genetic specialists, family members often find that the cause of disability was simply a "fluke"; but if this is not the case, they can, with the genetic information, make an informed decision as to the risks of producing a child with inheritable conditions.

The "overretention" of beneficial information in essence becomes a judgment call. The cost of maintaining the data in the original, imaged, or electronic format is an important decision factor that must be weighed against the need to have this helpful information.

ROLE OF THE HEALTH INFORMATION MANAGEMENT PROFESSIONAL

The role of the HIM professional may be either as a regular employee or as a consultant to the facility. The health information manager serving as a regular employee performs duties and responsibilities relevant to all levels of management. When issues and problems in the management of the records arise, the expertise of this professional is sought facility-wide. This is doubly true because the most active portion of the individual's record is not housed in the HIM department, but rather in the living unit. Development of policies and procedures in the handling of records must consider activities more far-reaching than the processes occurring in the centralized department of health information services.

Major duties and responsibilities fall into the following categories:

- Management
- Risk management/legal aspects
- Supervision
- Implementation and maintenance of health information systems
- Designing health care records to address the health needs of the facility and the individuals it serves
- Retrieval and storage of health information
- Maintenance of statistical data
- Coding and indexing of records
- Quality improvement
- Completion of all phases of the record including:
  - Active records
  - Overflow
  - Closed records
  - Maintenance and storage of imaged records
- Data analysis

The health information manager consultant assists the administration in establishing policies and procedures to address the maintenance, preservation, completion, and confidentiality of records and the release of information. In order to accomplish facility objectives for this service, the consultant trains personnel assigned to record-keeping services, using methods including on-the-job training and in-service education.

The major function of the consultant involves quality management in the review and auditing of the facility records. This task includes all facility-wide records—administrative, habilitative, and health records.

TRENDS

The provision of services for individuals with intellectual disabilities (mental retardation) or developmental disabilities is in a state of constant change. As mentioned in the introduction of this chapter, the number of persons receiving services in large public or private facilities is decreasing. As noted by Braddock et al. in 2002, "Since the 1970s many states have vigorously reduced their reliance on institutional facilities and developed community residential settings including group homes, foster care, and supported living options" (p. 1). This trend has continued in the twenty-first century. The number of individuals living in an ICF/MR setting decreased by 25 percent between 1998 and 2008, while the number of individuals receiving home and community based services increased by 118.5 percent over the same time period (Lakin et al., 2010). Reasons for the expansion of community services are varied. The number of persons needing services is increasing partly because of the aging of our society and the increased longevity of persons with developmental disabilities. Many individuals and their families are becoming vocal in expressing their needs and desires and want more choices in the types of supports made available.

The **Home and Community Based Services (HCBS) Waiver** became available in 1981, enabling states to expand support for community-based services through Medicaid funding. By 2008 there were 525,119 HCBS recipients nationwide. Between 1998 and 2008 Medicaid HCBS program expenditures for persons with intellectual and developmental disabilities increased from $7.133 to $22.310 billion—a 213 percent increase (Lakin et al., 2010). Services provided by the waiver—such as respite care, home health aides, supported employment, transportation, and various health therapies—can delay or prevent placement in a facility.

Litigation is another factor influencing the growth of community-based programs: In a landmark case decided in 1999, *Olmstead v. Lois Curtis and Elaine Wilson*, the United States Supreme Court ruled that requiring individuals with disabilities to reside in institutions in order to receive support services may constitute discrimination based on disability. The court determined that the Americans with Disabilities Act called for states to provide community-based services for individuals with disabilities when such services were more appropriate than institutional placements (National Disability Rights Network, 2009). Lawsuits based on *Olmstead* and other class action suits have been filed to force states to expand services to persons on waiting lists and to those who have been found eligible for Medicaid services but who did not receive them (Braddock et al., 2002). As states often struggle with a weak economy and limited funds to initiate new services, progress toward implementing the provisions of *Olmstead* have not occurred as rapidly as some would like. Care in an institutional setting is one option that may be appropriate for certain individuals with intellectual or developmental disabilities; however, future growth is most likely to occur in the provision of supports that enable individuals to remain in their home communities.

SUMMARY

The ICF/MR setting serves individuals with intellectual disabilities. This chapter has reviewed the technical aspects of ICF/MR services and how they apply to the practical daily work environment. With the guidelines, suggestions, and recommendations furnished in this chapter, the health information manager has at his or her fingertips basic information that should serve as a quick reference in the management of individual records.

In the ICF/MR, health care, habilitative, and administrative staff work with or on behalf of individuals to help them achieve their goals. The ICF/MR must meet federal standards and may choose to meet voluntary accreditation standards. Providing community-based services is the trend for individuals with intellectual disabilities.

This chapter should provide health information managers, as members of an interdisciplinary team, with a solid foundation from which to build their skills, talents, and knowledge to best meet the needs, objectives, and goals of individuals receiving services in an ICF/MR.

KEY TERMS

active treatment   each individual must receive a continuous, active treatment program that includes aggressive, consistent implementation of specialized and generic training, treatment, health services, and related services.

annual staffing   informal term for the annual meeting of the interdisciplinary team during which the individual program plan is reviewed and revised for the coming year; not to exceed 365 days from the previous annual or initial staffing.

assessment   the process of identifying an individual's functional level, strengths, needs, causes of disabilities, and conditions hindering development.

developmental disability   a disability "attributable to a mental or physical impairment that begins before age 22 and is likely to continue indefinitely and that results in substantial functional limitation in three or more areas of major life activity" (AAMR, 1992).

direct care staff   personnel whose daily responsibility is to manage, supervise, and provide direct care to individuals in their residential living unit.

habilitation   the process by which a person is assisted to acquire and maintain life skills that enable the person to cope more effectively with personal and environmental demands and to raise the level of his or her physical, mental, and social efficiency. Habilitation includes, but is not limited to, programs of structured education and training.

Home and Community Based Services (HCBS) Waiver   a federal program that allows states to use Medicaid funding to serve persons in their own homes and communities, not just in institutional settings.

individual program plan (IPP)   a comprehensive written document that states the specific objectives necessary to meet the individual's needs, as identified by a comprehensive individualized assessment. The IPP is the major tool in planning and implementing the care and services rendered to the individual.

intellectual disability   significant limitations in both intellectual functioning and adaptive behavior expressed in conceptual, social, and practical adaptive skills and age of onset before the age of 18.

interdisciplinary (ID) team a group that develops an integrated habilitation or program plan that provides individualized services to the individual.

intermediate care facility for the mentally retarded (ICF/MR) a facility that provides care and training for persons with mental retardation in order to increase their adaptive skills, such as self-care skills, language skills, social skills, vocational skills, and so on.

Inventory for Client and Agency Planning (ICAP) a standardized assessment instrument that can be used for program planning and is also used in several states as a data collection tool for case-mix reimbursement to ICF/MR organizations.

mental retardation low intelligence with significant disabilities in two or more adaptive skill areas and age of onset before age 18. Mental retardation may be classified in terms of etiology or causal factors, including conditions caused by infection, intoxication, brain injury, disorders of metabolism, and neoplasms.

person-centered planning a process that focuses on the preferences of the individual receiving services in planning the type of future life the individual wishes to live.

qualified mental retardation professional (QMRP) a person assigned to monitor and coordinate all activities related to development and implementation of the individual program plan.

training objective single outcome expected to be achieved by the individual within one year as a result of training. Measurable outcome, criteria for measuring progress, and projected completion date should be specified relative to strengths, needs, and established goals.

REVIEW QUESTIONS

Knowledge-Based Questions

1. What types of coding may be utilized in an ICF/MR?
2. Name the sections into which the individuals' charts may be divided.
3. Is an admission to an ICF/MR facility permanent? Why or why not?
4. Who performs regular surveys of an ICF/MR facility?
5. How did the U.S. Supreme Court's *Olmstead* decision affect provision of services in an ICF/MR?

Critical Thinking Questions

1. What would you consider to be one of the major issues in an ICF/MR facility? Why?
2. The HIM professional employed on a regular basis and the HIM consultant would have different job roles. How would their jobs be different?
3. Describe how the services rendered to an individual in an ICF/MR are different from those in other health care settings.
4. Explain why accident and incident situations are important to study.

WEB ACTIVITY

At the CMS Web site, http://www.cms.gov/, make the following selections:

1. Select "Regulations & Guidance."
2. Under "Legislation," select "Conditions for Coverage (CfCs) & Conditions of Participation (CoPs)."
3. Select "Intermediate Care Facilities for Persons with Mental Retardation (ICF/MR)."
4. Select the "Related Link Outside CMS," "CONDITIONS OF PARTICIPATION: ICF/MR (483.400-480)."
5. Select either the text (TXT) or PDF version of section 483.25, Quality of Care.

What specific areas (*a* through *m*) are addressed in this section of the regulation?

CASE STUDY

The interdisciplinary team in the XYZ facility was experiencing problems with the habilitative portion of the individuals' records in that changes in the program were not being addressed by the direct care staff. Recommendations were being made on the quarterly team reviews but were not getting into the program records to be instituted by the direct care staff as required for the continuity of care.

Jean Deaux, a health information management professional, was contacted about this discrepancy in the program. She noted the recommended program changes and that the revised program was not being carried out, along with the lack of some type of documentation to tie these two together.

After studying the problem and the frequency with which it was occurring, she made the following recommendation: The suggested changes were to be covered in an addendum format so that at any time throughout the year when a major change in the individual's program was instituted, the change would be reflected in the 24-hour schedule, thus alerting the direct care staff of the addition, deletion, and/or change in the program.

In order to better track the documentation requirements, Ms. Deaux elected to monitor in her monthly audit of the records whether program changes were being documented appropriately and to submit any variance in the program to the assigned QMRP.

1. Who is the "assigned QMRP"? Why do you think Ms. Deaux elected to report variances to the QMRP?

2. How could electronic health records or electronic information systems have made a difference in this situation?

3. Is there anything different or additional that you would have done had you been in Ms. Deaux's place? If so, what would it be?

REFERENCES AND SUGGESTED READINGS

American Association on Intellectual and Developmental Disabilities. (2010). *Intellectual disability: Definition, classification, and systems of supports* (11th ed.). Washington, DC: Author.

American Association on Mental Retardation. (1983). *Manual on terminology and classification in mental retardation* (1983 ed.). Washington, DC: Author.

American Association on Mental Retardation. (2002). *Mental retardation: Definition, classification, and systems of supports* (10th ed.). Washington, DC: Author.

American Psychiatric Association. (2000). *Diagnostic and statistical manual of mental disorders* (text revision). Washington, DC: Author.

Braddock, D., Hemp, R., Rizzolo, M. C., Parish, S., & Pomeranz, A. (2002, June). *The state of the states in developmental disabilities: 2002 study summary*. Boulder, CO: University of Colorado, Coleman Institute for Cognitive Disabilities and Department of Psychiatry.

Centers for Medicare & Medicaid Services. (n.d.) *Interpretive Guidelines—Intermediate care facilities for the mentally retarded.*[Online]. http://

www.cms.gov/manuals/Downloads/som107ap_j_intermcare.pdf [2011, March 17].

Conditions of participation for intermediate care facilities for the mentally retarded. *Code of Federal Regulations*, Title 42, Pt. 483, Subpart I, 2009 ed., § 483.400 through § 483.480.

Council on Quality and Leadership. (2005). *Personal outcome measures*. Towson, MD: Author.

Council on Quality and Leadership. Accredited Organizations. [Online]. http://www.thecouncil.org [2010, August 7].

Goel, N.L, & Keefe, R.H. (2003). Medicaid managed care meets developmental disabilities: Proceed with caution. *Journal of Health & Social Policy, 16*(3), 75–90.

Hewitt, A., & O'Nell, S. (1998, August). Preface. *I Am Who I Am* Y. Bestgen (Ed.). [Online]. http://www.acf.hhs.gov/programs/pcpid/docs/help4.pdf [2010, August 7].

Janicki, M. P. (1992). Lifelong disability and aging. In L.Rowitz (Ed.), *Mental retardation in the year 2000*. New York: Springer-Verlag.

Joint Commission. (2009). *2010 portable comprehensive accreditation manual for behavioral health care*. Oak Brook, IL: Author.

Lakin, K.C., Scott, N., Larson, S., & Salmi, P. (2010).Changes in service recipients and expenditures in Medicaid long-term services and supports programs for persons with intellectual and developmental disabilities, 1998-2008. *Intellectual & Developmental Disabilities, 48*(1), 80–83.

National Disability Rights Network. (2009, September 30). *A decade of "little progress" implementing Olmstead: Evaluating federal agency impact after 10 years.* [Online]. http://www.napas.org/Decade_of_Little_Progress_Implementing_Olmstead.pdf [2010, August 7].

Preadmission screening and annual review of mentally ill and mentally retarded individuals. *Code of Federal Regulations*, Title 42, Pt. 483, Sec. 112, 2009 ed.

KEY RESOURCES

American Association on Intellectual and Developmental Disabilities
http://www.aamr.org or http://www.aaidd.org

The Arc of the United States
http://TheArc.org

Council on Quality and Leadership
(formerly Accreditation Council on Services for People with Developmental Disabilities)
http://www.thecouncil.org

The Joint Commission
http://www.jointcommission.org

CHAPTER 10

Long-Term Care

BARBARA A. GORENFLO, RHIA

KRIS KING, MS, RHIA, CPHQ

LEARNING OBJECTIVES

Upon successful completion of this chapter, you should be able to:

- Describe the type of care typically associated with long-term care facilities.

- Discuss the impact of stringent state and federal regulation on the long-term care industry and its effect on information management and documentation content.

- Identify the significance of state and federal surveys to long-term care facilities.

- Describe the types of reimbursement and payer relationships within a long-term care facility.

- Describe the purpose of the *minimum data set* and its use in the federal survey process and in case-mix payment systems.

- Identify the priorities for health information management in the long-term care setting.

Setting	Description	Synonym/Examples
Freestanding Nursing Facility	A facility or a portion of a facility licensed by the state as a nursing facility or nursing home, where the majority of patients are regarded as permanent residents for long-term nursing care	Nursing facility (NF) Nursing home Long-term care facility (formerly called intermediate care facility)
Freestanding Skilled Nursing Facility	A facility or a portion of a facility licensed by the state as a skilled nursing facility and certified, either wholly or in part, as a Medicare Part A skilled nursing facility provider	Skilled nursing facility (SNF) Skilled nursing unit
Acute Care Hospital	A designated area, attached wing, or a separate structure on the hospital campus that is licensed for skilled nursing care	Distinct part SNF Skilled nursing facility (SNF) Skilled nursing unit SNF unit

INTRODUCTION TO SETTING

Long-term care typically describes care of the frail, institutionalized elderly or those who are permanent residents of a nursing facility. For purposes of this chapter, long-term care does not include boarding care; assisted living; residential care; long-term care for the mentally ill; mentally retarded; developmentally disabled (ICF/MR); or other types of institutionalized care settings that are not subject to the federal long-term care regulations or the state licensure regulations for **nursing facilities (NFs)**, or **skilled nursing facilities (SNFs)**. With the exception of ICF/MR facilities, which are discussed in Chapter 9, these other components of the care continuum are less regulated and do not have the broad range of caregivers found in the typical long-term care facility. (Also note that long-term acute care hospitals [LTCHs] are not included in this chapter, but are discussed in Chapter 2.) With regard to federal regulations, the term *nursing facility* is a facility that is qualified for reimbursement under the Medicaid program. A *skilled nursing facility* meets the requirements for reimbursement under Medicare (CMS, 2002e).

The discussion of the long-term care setting in this chapter relates to nursing facilities and skilled nursing facilities. However, there is another type of long-term care facility—the long-term acute care hospital (abbreviated LTAC, LTACH, or LTCH)—which is discussed in Chapter 2, Hospital-Based Care. Although both nursing facilities and LTCHs are considered "long-term care," LTCHs and skilled nursing facilities represent two distinctly different levels of care, with different licensing and different payment systems. LTCH facilities are licensed as hospitals and have their own prospective payment system (PPS) under Medicare.

As the percentage of our population age 65 and older continues to grow, there will likely be several different care settings that will fall under the global term of *long-term care*; however, this chapter addresses long-term care as it applies to the settings and care descriptions identified.

Types of Patients

In the long-term care setting, *patient* is often replaced with *resident*, because the person receiving care is not only a recipient of nursing care but in many cases is also permanently residing in the facility. The nursing facility becomes the home or place of residence, and, as such, the facility is responsible for providing quality of care as well as high quality of life under the long-term care regulations. Within the broad category of *long-term care*, more specific distinctions can be drawn to describe the types of residents and the care they receive. As specialization of services increases within the long-term care industry, facilities find the need to categorize levels of care and often physically separate types of care to distinct units or floors within the same facility. Therefore, residents can be placed in areas with other residents of similar care needs.

Permanent Residents Receiving Nonskilled Care

These residents are distinguished by their need for general oversight and supervision in performing **activities of daily living (ADL)** (e.g., bathing, eating, dressing); however, their needs can generally be met without the direct care or services of a licensed professional on a 24-hour basis. While a licensed practical nurse or registered nurse supervises their general care under the direction of the attending physician, their immediate care needs do not involve direct skilled treatment on a daily basis, such as injections, intravenous therapy, parenteral feeding, or skilled wound care. From a level of care perspective, these residents require a higher level of care than those in a residential, boarding or assisted living environment, either due to cognitive impairment or as a result of physical incapacity. For example, these residents could not, either due to physical or cognitive impairment, negotiate their way to safety in the event of an emergency. However, their daily care needs do not require continual intervention by a licensed nurse or other skilled health care professional.

Permanent Residents, Special Care

Special care units (SCUs) are often found as a distinct part within a long-term care facility. For example, some of these units are designed to specifically care for the Alzheimer's residents who benefit from a physical environment that is quiet, homelike, and adapted to their specific cognitive impairment. The physical separation of the unit assures that these residents are afforded the opportunity to move throughout the area without fear of wandering off the property. In addition, staff members assigned to these units generally receive special training in the care of Alzheimer's residents, because their needs are typically more behavior oriented than medically oriented. Other special care units may be designed for patients using ventilators or those with special needs.

Permanent Residents, Skilled Care

In contrast to the permanent residents who do not receive daily skilled care, permanent residents requiring skilled care receive services from one or more licensed professionals on a frequent and often daily basis. Typically, these residents have received as much benefit from rehabilitation services as can be reasonably expected, and their improvement or progression has plateaued. As a result, their potential to be discharged is not good. Types of care would include the need for continuous tube feeding, long-term ventilator care, complex wound care, and/or an aggregate combination of nursing and restorative professionals to meet the daily care needs of feeding, performing ADLs, and maintaining the highest functional level for as long as possible. Often, the term *heavy care* is used to describe the care needs of these residents because of the intensity of their dependence on the staff for mobility, toileting, bathing, eating, and performing all ADLs. Their care can be described as more custodial in nature.

Short-Term Patients (less than 100 days)

A short-term patient in a long-term care facility would generally be considered one who has a length of stay of less than 100 days and in the traditional health care sense would be regarded as a patient, because the intent is to ultimately discharge the patient to a more independent level of care. In some long-term care facilities, the distinct unit in which these patients are found is categorized as a **subacute care** unit, where patients are provided with a higher level of care than that associated with the traditional skilled nursing setting. Care in these distinct units is skilled care for treatment of a specific condition, and often placement is temporary because the goal of treatment is rehabilitation to discharge the patient home or to a lower level of care. In some situations, discharge from this unit may correlate with an internal transfer to a long-term care bed within the same facility.

Respite Care

Respite care is a short stay for the purpose of providing relief or "respite" to the primary caregivers of the frail elderly who cannot live in an independent environment and do not require the intensity of services and supervision required of the traditional long-term care facility. The period of respite care may range anywhere from overnight to several weeks, depending on the caregiver's needs. In a respite care admission, a long-term care facility is providing meals and general supervision to assure that necessary medications are administered and is also providing a safe environment for the respite resident, with opportunities for socialization and no need for active care intervention.

Types of Caregivers

Licensed Physicians

Doctors of medicine and osteopathy are responsible for the overall medical supervision in the long-term care facility; however, their physical presence in the nursing facility is generally limited. Frequency of visits to a long-term care resident can range from once a month to once a year, depending on the level of care required of the resident. In some instances, the physician does not actually visit the nursing facility but requires that the resident be transported to his or her office for necessary medical examinations. Therefore, the majority of communication with the physician is done through the nursing staff via telephone as opposed to face-to-face encounters with the physician. In the SNF or subacute units of long-term care facilities, frequency of physician involvement is generally greater and can range to several visits a week, with monthly visits being the outside range, depending on the level of acuity of the SNF/subacute unit. The minimum visit requirement for physician visits in the SNF and subacute units is once every 30 days for the first 90 days and then every 60 days thereafter.

Physician Extenders

Nurse practitioners, clinical nurse specialists, and physician assistants work with physicians to assist in caring for their patients who reside in long-term care facilities. Particularly in rural settings, the addition of these personnel to the physician office practice affords greater contact with the resident than may occur if only the physician were making visits to the nursing facility.

Registered Nurses

Registered nurses are the primary coordinators of daily care within the long-term care facility. Because physicians ordinarily do not visit residents on a daily basis in most long-term care settings, care is nursing driven. The director of nursing in most regulatory environments is required to be a licensed, registered nurse. Depending on the number of beds, the facility will employ additional registered nurses for supervisory positions or as charge nurses on specific nursing units.

Licensed Practical Nurses

Licensed practical nurses are the most predominant caregivers among the licensed professionals in the long-term care nursing facility setting. Their responsibilities range from administering medications, tube feedings, and treatments to charging a nursing division and serving in a supervisory capacity within the nursing department.

Nursing Assistants

Nursing assistants comprise the bulk of the nursing department in a long-term care nursing facility. They are nonlicensed staff members who have completed a basic training course for providing daily care needs to the geriatric patient, including basic skills in bathing, transfer training, lifting, range of motion, and related supportive services that would be provided under the general supervision of a licensed nurse.

In some facilities, a distinction is made for nursing assistants who strictly provide restorative therapy, called restorative aides or rehabilitation aides. With additional training from the licensed therapists, the restorative or rehabilitation aides are given responsibility for providing maintenance services to residents after skilled rehabilitation has been discontinued. At this point in the resident's care, a plateau has been reached and no active improvement is expected from continued skilled therapy. The restorative therapy is intended to maintain the level of functioning that has been achieved from skilled therapy and/or to prevent further functional decline.

Certified Medication Technicians

In some states, a certified medication technician (CMT) is a distinct type of caregiver in the long-term care setting, provided for in the state long-term care regulations. Requirements for this position are generally a minimum of nursing assistant training with an additional course in medication administration, the scope of competency requirements varying with the individual state regulations. The purpose of this caregiver category is to recognize a lower-cost health care position with limited responsibilities that can lessen the workload of the licensed nursing professionals.

Social Services

Provision of medically related social services to residents is assigned to the department that is typically described as "social services" in the long-term care setting. Depending on the size of the facility, this department may or may not be staffed with a credentialed social worker (BSW or MSW). Federal long-term care regulations require that a facility with more than 120 beds employ a full-time social worker or a person with qualifications outlined in the federal requirements.

These requirements describe a qualified social worker as an individual with a bachelor's degree in social work or a bachelor's degree in a human services field such as sociology, special education, rehabilitation counseling, and psychology and with one year of supervised social work experience in a health care setting working directly with individuals.

In the long-term care setting, the social services staff take on many responsibilities that affect the care and well-being of the resident, such as making arrangements for adaptive equipment, clothing, and financial assistance; coordinating discharge planning; coordinating and initiating referrals and appointments with outside services; providing counseling to residents, family members, and facility staff as it relates to the care needs of individual residents; and providing any other services that promote the psychosocial well-being of the resident. Social services staff members are advocates for many residents who are no longer able to protect their rights to decision making, fair treatment, dignity, respect, and so on or who cannot realize what their rights are.

Activities/Therapeutic Recreation

Although therapeutic recreation is not a direct care service in the same category as administration of a treatment or a medication, providing stimulating activities or therapeutic recreation services is extremely important in the long-term care setting. In most long-term care facilities, the activity program is not necessarily directed by a licensed or credentialed individual. Licensing of activity professionals other than recreational therapists is not universal in each state, and federal regulations provide several alternative options as qualifications for an activity professional, including two years of direct experience in a patient activities program in a health care setting and/or completion of a training program approved by the state agency.

The activities staff is responsible for assessing the therapeutic recreational needs and preferences of each resident and developing an individualized program that responds to those needs. This includes providing sufficient group and individual activity and recreational programs to respond to the needs of the various levels of care within the facility. The types of activity programs that fall within the scope of the typical long-term care facility include planning and providing for outings such as shopping and recreational activities off the premises of the facility; planning and providing supplies and materials for independent, in-room activities; establishing small group programs for the cognitively impaired, such as reminiscence therapy; conducting in-room, one-on-one activities for the room-bound and unresponsive resident, such as music therapy and tactile stimulation; and planning and conducting facility-wide social events for residents and their families.

If a facility population consists of mostly alert and oriented residents with limited physical impairments, the recreational program will be far different than that for the population that consists of semicomatose residents or residents with severe dementia. As a result, the therapeutic activities program must be responsive to the varying needs of the resident population.

Independent Contractors

In the long-term care facility, most of the ancillary services and many of the professional services are provided through independent contracts with outside resources such as those of laboratory, radiology, pharmacy, and rehabilitation, including physical, occupational, speech, and respiratory therapy services. As independent contractors, these providers are not employees of the facility and are generally not physically present within the facility on a full-time basis.

Laboratory and Radiology   Laboratory and radiology services may be necessary to further evaluate or treat chronic or acute medical conditions, and these services are performed in accordance with physician orders. Laboratory and radiology services are evaluated in terms of their timeliness of response to stat and routine calls and for the additional services they provide for enhancing the overall quality of health information. For example, laboratory services generally provide the facility with a monthly computerized report outlining the types of tests performed in the previous month, patterns and trends with respect to nosocomial infections, use of antimicrobial agents, and related infection control issues.

Rehabilitation Services   Rehabilitation services (physical therapy, occupational therapy, and speech therapy) are most often provided through independently contracted arrangements, because the volume of rehabilitation cases in the typical long-term care facility does not warrant full-time employees in any of the respective rehabilitation disciplines. Registered physical and occupational therapists visit the facility based on the volume of skilled therapy services required by the resident population. Often, services are supplemented with physical therapy and occupational therapy assistants, who provide the daily therapy under the general supervision of the registered therapist. Speech therapists provide daily skilled therapy for dysphagia and dysphasia, primarily in postacute care of patients suffering from a cerebrovascular accident.

Respiratory Therapists Respiratory therapists are more prevalent in facilities with long-term ventilator patients or facilities with a high number of residents requiring daily suctioning and respiratory therapy treatments.

Registered Dietitians Federal regulations and many licensure regulations require the services of a registered dietitian on either a full-time or consulting basis. In the larger long-term care facilities of more than 150 beds, a registered dietitian may be a full-time employee of the facility, particularly if the resident population predominantly requires skilled care and has more complex nutritional care needs. If a registered dietitian is not employed in the facility on a full-time basis, the day-to-day management of the dietary service is the responsibility of a food services manager, while the dietitian, during regularly scheduled consultation visits, approves menus for therapeutic diets and provides individual clinical assessments for those residents with high risk or clinically complex nutritional needs. Diet technicians may also be utilized to assist with nutritional care under the supervision of a registered dietitian.

Registered Pharmacists With rare exception, pharmaceutical services are not available directly within a long-term care facility and are provided by a supplier that is remote to the facility. The services of a pharmacist are also required by the long-term care federal regulations, either on a full-time, part-time, or consulting basis. The consulting pharmacist role may or may not be provided by the same entity that services the facility as the pharmaceutical supplier. The provider of drugs and biologicals or the actual pharmaceutical service is responsible for ensuring that medications are dispensed to the facility in a timely and appropriate manner. The responsibilities of the facility pharmacy consultant are somewhat different, in that consultation extends to all aspects of the provision of pharmacy services within the facility and includes performing a monthly drug regimen review for each resident in the facility to evaluate potential irregularities in medication administration. This includes monitoring for unnecessary drugs, evaluating proper dosages and indications for psychotropic medications, and evaluating internal storage and administration procedures within the facility. This review is required in the federal regulations and can be accessed by long-term care surveyors in the event of a question regarding the medication profile of a particular resident.

REGULATORY ISSUES

The long-term care industry is one of the most, if not the most, highly regulated industries in the United States. In addition to federal regulations for long-term care facilities participating in Medicare and Medicaid, each state has separate licensure laws for long-term care facilities. In the case of overlapping or conflicting laws, the facility is obligated to abide by the more stringent of the two. **Standard surveys** are unannounced and conducted at least every 15 months. The two general survey outcomes are termed "substantial compliance" and "substandard quality of care." **Substantial compliance** means that any deficiencies found by the surveyors were deemed to be of minimal potential for harm to the residents. **Substandard quality of care** means that surveyors found one or more deficiencies that constitute either immediate jeopardy to resident health or safety; a pattern of widespread actual harm that is not immediate jeopardy; or a widespread potential for more than minimal harm but less than immediate jeopardy, with no actual harm (CMS, 2002a). Results of all surveys are accessible to the public, with federal regulations requiring that the most recent survey be posted in a public area of the facility for easy access by residents, family members, and the general public. In addition to the certification and **licensure surveys**, long-term care facilities are subject to surveys conducted in response to complaint investigations, which result from calls to the state agency concerning care concerns and potential regulatory violations. These survey findings are also subject to public access and can affect the facility license in the event of substantial noncompliance. Table 10-1 provides examples of several surveys to which a long-term care facility may be subject.

In 1995, federal enforcement regulations were implemented by the Health Care Financing Administration (now CMS) that outline remedies, including **civil money penalties** of up to $10,000 per day, for findings of substantial noncompliance and substandard quality of care. In addition to federal enforcement regulations, individual states may pass legislation that also gives the state agency authority for fines and civil money penalties. Therefore, findings of substandard quality during a facility survey can result in civil money penalties from both the federal and the state licensing agency. Furthermore, federal enforcement regulations also provide for mandated temporary management of a facility, termination from the Medicare/Medicaid program, and denial of Medicare/Medicaid payment for new admissions and/or for all current nursing facility residents in addition to the civil money penalties. As a result, the regulatory environment and impact of state and federal regulation on the long-term care facility is without comparison in other sectors of the health care industry.

State Licensure

If a long-term care facility does not participate in the Medicare or Medicaid program, federal regulations do not apply, and the facility is subject only to the state licensure requirements. These requirements are passed by the respective state legislative bodies, and, consequently, there is great variability among the 50 states with regard to the scope of issues promulgated in their long-term care requirements.

Joint Commission Accreditation

The number of long-term care facilities seeking Joint Commission accreditation is relatively insignificant. There is no clear advantage for a long-term care facility in seeking Joint Commission accreditation, unless it is required as

TABLE **10-1**

Types of Surveys Unique to a Long-Term Care Facility

Surveying Agency/Entity	Purpose and Frequency	Potential Impact and Outcome
State licensing agency	Annual licensure renewal and interim review, depending on state law (unannounced)	Written deficiencies requiring a plan of correction and revisit Monetary fines Ban on admissions and other penalties and restrictions, depending on state law
State licensing agency	Complaint investigation in response to state hotline calls concerning abuse and/or neglect (unannounced)	Written deficiencies requiring a plan of correction and revisit Monetary fines Ban on admissions and other penalties and restrictions, depending on state law Full survey in response to findings of substantial noncompliance
Centers for Medicare & Medicaid Services (CMS)	Annual certification for participation in Title XVIII or XIX federal programs (unannounced)	Written deficiencies requiring a plan of correction and letter of credible allegation stating date corrections will be implemented Revisit may or may not be conducted to determine facility compliance Federal agency may conduct follow-up survey to validate findings of state agency Civil money penalties, temporary ban on admissions, and denial of payment for Medicare/Medicaid admissions or current residents, depending on scope and severity of noncompliance
The Joint Commission (TJC)	Optional survey for long-term care facilities and special care and subacute units within long-term care facilities (unannounced survey between 18–39 months after previous survey)	Accredited Provisional accreditation Conditional accreditation Preliminary denial of accreditation Denial of accreditation Preliminary accreditation

part of an overall hospital accreditation for hospital-owned and -operated long-term care facilities. The Joint Commission has sought deemed status from the Centers for Medicare & Medicaid Services that would present long-term care facilities with the option of choosing between the current survey system by state and federal agencies or applying for Joint Commission long-term care accreditation. However, at this writing no such option is available for long-term care.

DOCUMENTATION

Documentation in the resident's record has tremendous significance to the nursing facility. Documentation is vital in the evaluation of how a facility has contributed to and/or affected the **quality of care** and **quality of life** of individual residents, strongly linking documentation with regulatory compliance. In addition, accuracy and appropriateness of documentation affects facility reimbursement by Medicare, Medicaid, and commercial insurance. Finally, as litigation involving negligence for poor care outcomes becomes more pervasive in the long-term care industry, proper documentation can be crucial in defending a provider against a wrongful claim for failure to provide quality care and services.

Although documentation of key information is important when a resident is transferred or discharged, the primary emphasis on routine documentation monitoring should be concurrent for detecting significant omissions in individual records as well as in identifying key training issues for ongoing staff education and quality improvement.

Federal Requirements

The quality of documentation is highly significant in the **federal survey** process, in that the resident record is used as a means of validating positive and negative care outcomes both in the annual survey and in complaint investigations. Survey procedures for the federal long-term care survey process include two items under Task 5C, Resident Review, in which the record is used for evaluating compliance with care issues: Part F—Closed Record Review and Part I—Record Review (CMS, 2009a).

The **comprehensive resident assessment** is the primary vehicle for evaluating care outcomes in the federal long-term care survey process. Comprehensive resident assessment refers not only to the actual resident assessment document but also to the federally mandated **resident assessment instrument (RAI)** process. The RAI consists of three basic components: the **minimum data set (MDS); care area assessment (CAA) process**, formerly **resident assessment protocols (RAPs)**; and **utilization guidelines** as specified in the *Resident Assessment Instrument Manual*. As a process, each of the three basic components flows into the next. The MDS is a core set of screening, clinical, and functional status elements that constitutes a standardized means of assessing all residents in Medicare and/or Medicaid certified facilities.

The Omnibus Budget Reconciliation Act (OBRA) "regulations have defined a schedule of assessments that will be performed for a nursing facility resident at admission, quarterly, and annually, whenever the resident experiences a significant change in status, and whenever the facility identifies a significant error in a prior assessment. These are known as '**OBRA assessments**.' MDS assessments are also required for Medicare payment purposes.... When the OBRA and Medicare assessment time frames coincide, one assessment may be used to satisfy both requirements. When combining OBRA and Medicare assessments, the most stringent requirement for MDS completion must be met. It is important for facility staff to fully understand the requirements for both types of assessments in order to avoid unnecessary duplication of effort" (CMS, 2009, p. 2–1).

Components of the CAA process include care area triggers (CATs), CAA resources, and the CAA summary. The CAA process provides structure for assessing social, medical, and psychological problems by providing a systematic method of reviewing key components of the MDS and directing caregivers to evaluate causes, interrelationships, and particular strengths that affect the development of the **care plan**. A key element of this process involves **care area triggers (CATs)**, "specific resident responses for one or a combination of MDS elements. The triggers identify residents who have or are at risk for developing specific functional problems and require further assessment" (CMS 2010, p. 1–5). As of this writing there are 20 CATs:

1. Delirium
2. Cognitive loss/dementia
3. Visual function
4. Communication
5. ADL functional/rehabilitation potential
6. Urinary incontinence and indwelling catheter
7. Psychosocial well-being
8. Mood state
9. Behavioral symptoms
10. Activities
11. Falls
12. Nutritional status
13. Feeding tubes
14. Dehydration/fluid maintenance
15. Dental care
16. Pressure ulcer
17. Psychotropic drug use
18. Physical restraints
19. Pain
20. Return to Community Referral (an assessment to assist nursing facility residents interested in transitioning back to their communities)

Based on the resident data entered on the MDS, care areas may or may not be triggered. If a care area is triggered, this means there is a potential need to address the issue in the care plan. At this point, the interdisciplinary team can use the utilization guidelines to evaluate the problem and determine whether or not to continue to care plan for it. **CAA resources** are a list of resources that may be helpful in performing the assessment of a triggered care area. The interdisciplinary team must document the outcome of their assessment process for that particular care area and their decision regarding care planning for a particular problem or need. The **care area assessment (CAA) summary** (formerly RAP summary) form is used to document the location within the resident's record where the assessment information may be found. Surveyors then use the CAA summary to locate pertinent assessment information within the record in order to evaluate whether nursing facility staff members have properly utilized MDS information to assess and plan care for avoidable negative outcomes and to recognize resident strengths in the development of a comprehensive care plan. (See Figure 10-1 for an example of a Care Area Assessment Summary form.)

Resident **TEST1 MDS 1**   Identifier _____   Date _____

Section V	Care Area Assessment (CAA) Summary

V0200. CAAs and Care Planning

1. Check column A if Care Area is triggered.
2. For each triggered Care Area, indicate whether a new care plan, care plan revision, or continuation of current care plan is necessary to address the problem(s) identified in your assessment of the care area. The <u>Addressed in Care Plan</u> column must be completed within 7 days of completing the RAI (MDS and CAA(s)). Check column B if the triggered care area is addressed in the care plan.
3. Indicate in the <u>Location and Date of CAA Information</u> column where information related to the CAA can be found. CAA documentation should include information on the complicating factors, risks, and any referrals for this resident for this care area.

A. CAA Results

Care Area	A. Care Area Triggered	B. Addressed in Care Plan	Location and Date of CAA Information
	↓ Check all that apply ↓		
01. Delirium	☐	☐	
02. Cognitive Loss/Dementia	☐	☐	
03. Visual Function	☒	☒	1/25/2010 CARE PLAN
04. Communication	☒	☒	1/26/2010 CARE PLAN
05. ADL Functional/Rehabilitation Potential	☒	☒	
06. Urinary Incontinence and Indwelling Catheter	☒	☒	1/26/2010 URINARY
07. Psychosocial Well-Being	☐	☐	
08. Mood State	☐	☐	
09. Behavioral Symptoms	☐	☐	
10. Activities	☐	☐	
11. Falls	☒	☒	1/25/2010 ADL
12. Nutritional Status	☒	☒	1/27/2010 DIETARY
13. Feeding Tube	☐	☐	
14. Dehydration/Fluid Maintenance	☒	☒	
15. Dental Care	☐	☐	
16. Pressure Ulcer	☒	☒	1/26/2010 CARE PLAN
17. Psychotropic Drug Use	☐	☐	
18. Physical Restraints	☐	☐	
19. Pain	☐	☐	
20. Return to Community Referral	☐	☐	

B. Signature of RN Coordinator for CAA Process and Date Signed

1. Signature

2. Date

0	1	–	2	7	–	2	0	1	0
Month			Day			Year			

C. Signature of Person Completing Care Plan and Date Signed

1. Signature

2. Date

0	1	–	2	7	–	2	0	1	0
Month			Day			Year			

FIGURE **10-1** Care Area Assessment (CAA) Summary.

According to federal regulations, a comprehensive assessment must be completed for each resident admitted to a certified bed within 14 days of admission or after any significant change in condition and on at least an annual basis thereafter. Between comprehensive assessments, staff must complete a quarterly review of specific assessment categories of physical, mental, and psychosocial information.

Although the comprehensive assessment (MDS form) and the quarterly reviews are actual data sets, they are regarded as a permanent part of the long-term care resident record. Therefore, these documents are not only valuable in providing aggregate care information concerning intensity of services and ongoing care outcomes, but they are also used to track individual resident care outcomes in the long-term care survey process. As changes occur with regard to assessed categories on the MDS, there should be explicit documentation in the resident record to explain and individualize these changes in condition, particularly if negative outcomes such as unplanned significant weight loss or acquired pressure ulcers are reflected in the course of care.

The data from the MDS have a variety of uses in the long-term care industry. Depending on the state, the MDS data may be used as the basis for Medicaid reimbursement for the nursing facility. In many states MDS data are required to be submitted to the state agency on a monthly basis, either in paper or electronic form. The state agency uses the data to evaluate care trends and may use the information as a presurvey evaluation tool for targeting potential care concerns before a formal survey. For example, MDS data can be used to track the number of residents with facility-acquired pressure sores, urinary tract infections, increased use of indwelling catheters, decline in functional ability, increased use of antipsychotic medications, and increased use of physical restraints, as well as the number of residents receiving rehabilitation and restorative services. Consequently, the data are valuable not only to the state agencies and surveyors but also to the individual provider. As a result, accurate and focused documentation is extremely important in its relationship to the comprehensive assessment. Documentation must support the assessment information in the MDS and should explain and describe how this information affects the individual resident.

The record review portion of the long-term care federal survey procedures instructs surveyors to evaluate the care and outcome of care provided to residents as portrayed through direct observation of staff and assessed through improvement/decline as noted on the MDS. In this phase of the survey, the record is used as a source of information to determine if the assessment process is accurate and consistent with what is actually observed with the residents and to evaluate if the staff are properly planning and implementing care goals and interventions to avoid decline and/or to facilitate improvement in physical or psychosocial well-being (CMS, 2011). If there is an identified negative care outcome with a particular resident, documentation of the CAA process and other elements of the resident record would be used as a means of validating whether the negative outcome was facility related as compared to clinically unavoidable.

Care Plan

The care plan content and use is linked to the comprehensive assessment in the federal long-term care survey process. Depending on the individual state licensure regulations, additional emphasis may be placed on care plan documentation; however, this varies from state to state. In some states, care plans are not specifically required for residents who are not in Medicare or Medicaid certified beds.

In the federal long-term care regulations, the care plan is a subcategory of the comprehensive assessment regulation [483.20(d)]. These requirements specify content as well as timeliness guidelines. The care plan must be completed within seven days of the comprehensive assessment and should be an interdisciplinary process that involves not only the professional disciplines involved in the care of the resident but also the attending physician and the resident or resident's legal representative.

Specific documentation guidelines for the comprehensive care plan include the following items:

- Measurable objectives and timetables to meet medical, nursing, and mental and psychosocial needs that are identified in the comprehensive assessment
- Description of the services that are to be furnished to attain or maintain the resident's highest practicable physical, mental, and psychosocial well-being
- Description of the services that would otherwise be required but are not provided due to the resident's exercise of rights, including the right to refuse treatment (CMS, 2011)

Because the care plan is an inherent part of federal regulatory compliance, it is not only viewed as a tool for direct caregivers, but it also has far-reaching implications from a legal point of view. If the content of the care plan does not show that appropriate and individualized care was provided to a resident, the facility has increased vulnerability to claims of poor and/or inappropriate care if there are avoidable negative care outcomes (Sullivan, 1996). It is very important that care plans be individualized to the residents' care needs, strengths, and individual preferences. Standardized care plans that do not list the caregiver's daily care responsibilities for the individual resident are not regarded as resident-centered. Furthermore, if the facility has a survey record of noncompliance with care plan requirements that can be correlated with quality of care deficiencies, the legal vulnerability of the facility is heightened.

The care plan is viewed as the focal point for communicating significant care findings and goals for the individual long-term care resident. For that reason, a well-documented care plan should reflect an individualized view of the resident, such that it introduces the resident to each caregiver on the interdisciplinary team, from the nursing assistant on each tour of duty to the licensed therapists and physicians who care for the resident on a less frequent basis. Consequently, standardized or computerized care plans that do not reflect individualization of care routines based on specific resident strengths and care priorities are not regarded as individualized or resident specific.

Individualization of care information is the single most important content characteristic of a care plan in the long-term care setting from the perspective of a long-term care survey.

Discharge/Transfer

In the closed record review, documentation is evaluated in reference to the circumstances surrounding the transfer and/or discharge of the resident from the facility. Particular emphasis is placed on whether federal regulations were followed concerning involuntary transfer or discharge of a resident to another health care facility. Federal regulations outline specific circumstances in which a facility may transfer or discharge a resident involuntarily, and proper documentation is critical in demonstrating compliance with these requirements:

(1) The transfer or discharge is necessary for the resident's welfare and the resident's needs cannot be met in the facility;

(2) The transfer or discharge is appropriate because the resident's health has improved sufficiently so the resident no longer needs the services provided by the facility;

(3) The safety of individuals in the facility is endangered;

(4) The health of individuals in the facility would otherwise be endangered;

(5) The resident has failed, after reasonable and appropriate notice, to pay for (or to have paid under Medicare or Medicaid) a stay at the facility. For a resident who becomes eligible for Medicaid after admission to a nursing facility, the nursing facility may only bill a resident those charges allowable under Medicaid.

When the facility transfers or discharges a resident under any of the circumstances specified in paragraphs (a) (2) (i) through (v) of this section, the resident's clinical record must be documented. The documentation must be made by:

(i) The resident's physician when transfer or discharge is necessary under paragraph (a)(2)(i) of this section; and

(ii) A physician when transfer or discharge is necessary under paragraph (a)(2)(iv) of this section. (CMS, 2011)

In addition, circumstances leading to the transfer, discharge, or death are evaluated to identify if any specific avoidable negative care outcomes or lapses in care contributed to the final status of the resident. Consequently, discharge and transfer documentation is crucial in determining key quality of care and quality of life compliance issues.

Resident Rights

Resident rights represent a major focus in the long-term care setting, and often documentation becomes crucial in the evaluation of potential resident rights issues and whether a facility has properly acknowledged and recognized the rights of residents in the provision of care and services. Documentation affects the evaluation of compliance with resident rights requirements in a variety of ways. In addition to providing each resident or resident's legal representative with a written explanation of his or her basic rights under state and federal law, ongoing documentation of care preferences and explanations for various care outcomes becomes essential in determining compliance with resident rights requirements.

For example, if a resident has a particular diet order (such as an order for a diabetic diet) but the resident is not compliant with that diet and is frequently eating candy and other items that are restricted on that diet, documentation becomes essential as a resource for determining whether staff members are aware of this dietary compliance concern and how they manage the situation and balance clinical priorities with observance of residents' rights. Ideally, documentation would reflect that staff had advised the resident of the adverse complications associated with dietary noncompliance. If the resident knowingly chooses to continue with a behavior that has potentially negative consequences, documentation should reflect ongoing attempts to educate and reverse the behavior as well as the ongoing assessment of the resident's ability to understand and participate in this decision-making process. Although the need to recognize the rights of residents to participate in their own care and care planning is significant, there is an equally important need for the facility to demonstrate that staff acted appropriately and responsibly to supervise the care needs of the resident and to inform appropriate individuals of the consequences of their actions or inactions. Often, these types of situations are portrayed differently depending on the perspective—that is, resident or caregiver. Therefore, documentation plays a crucial role in the balance between observing resident rights and providing necessary care and services for the well-being of the resident.

In addition to ongoing documentation by caregivers, various consents are necessary in order to document that permission has been obtained for specific activities that are specified in the federal regulations, and additional resident rights issues may also be included in state-specific requirements. These include, but are not limited to, permission to open mail, designation of attending physician and pharmacy service, permission to be photographed, handling of funds deposited with the facility, and informed consent for use of physical and chemical restraints. New resident rights under the Health Insurance Portability and Accountability Act (HIPAA) include the residents' right to know what information is obtained about them and how it is used and disclosed. Residents have the right to review and amend their information and have an accounting of all disclosures.

State Licensure Requirements

As stated earlier in this chapter, the scope and intensity of state long-term care licensure requirements varies. In some states, the need for specific documentation above and beyond the content of the federal regulations may be extensive, whereas in other states the focus may be less stringent. From a health information management standpoint, it is essential that the long-term care facility evaluate documentation needs from the perspective of both state and federal requirements. If a facility is not certified for Medicare or Medicaid, state licensure requirements provide the regulatory structure for documentation standards. If, however, a facility is certified for Medicare or Medicaid, both the federal and the state requirements must be met. In some cases, the state requirements may require more stringent documentation than the federal requirements. For example, in the state of Missouri, the state licensure requirements specify that telephone orders must be signed within seven days. There is no federal requirement specifying a time frame for signature of telephone orders; however, long-term care facilities in Missouri would be obligated to both understand and comply with this separate licensure requirement during a state licensure survey.

Joint Commission Long-Term Care Accreditation Requirements

The emphasis on comprehensive assessments and care plans is reflected equally in the long-term care accreditation requirements of the Joint Commission. In many respects, Joint Commission long-term care requirements are quite similar to the federal long-term care requirements. The standards refer to the need for the facility to establish and follow specific care protocols depending on the scope and intensity of services provided in a particular facility or unit.

In addition to long-term care accreditation standards, the Joint Commission also offers disease-specific care certification programs. For example, a long-term care facility with a special care unit for the care of Alzheimer's-type dementia residents could elect to seek certification for this unit with or without seeking accreditation for the entire facility (Joint Commission, n.d.). However, if a facility is seeking both facility accreditation and certification for one of its disease-specific programs, both sets of standards must be utilized in determining compliance. From the facility perspective, compliance with multiple Joint Commission standards and federal and state long-term care standards presents a significant challenge to all clinical disciplines.

REIMBURSEMENT AND FUNDING

Reimbursement ranges from the very simple to the extremely complex in the long-term care setting because of the various sources of payment, the type and level of care provided by the facility, and whether a facility participates in Medicare and/or Medicaid. Within the industry as a whole, Medicaid reimbursement methodology varies from state to state. Moreover, depending on the type of long-term care facility, care and services may be billed to Medicare Part A and B, Medicaid, managed care, commercial insurance, and private pay, depending on the licensure and certification of the facility and the type and scope of services provided. A general overview of the various payment categories that are typically found in a long-term care facility is provided in Table 10-2. Depending on the degree to which a long-term care facility participates in each of these types of payer options, the complexity of documentation and information systems increases proportionally. The most simplistic environment is the strictly private pay facility in which all care and services are billed to the resident or resident's guarantor on a monthly basis. The most complex setting is one in which the facility participates in both Medicare Part A and Medicaid, has managed care contracts for subacute care, bills directly for Medicare Part B

TABLE **10-2**
Basic Reimbursement Categories and Pay Sources

ITEM	Medicaid	Medicare Part A	Medicare Part B	Managed Care	Commercial Insurance	Private Pay
Daily room and board	If all other financial resources have been exhausted and resident meets state criteria, basic care services are reimbursed at a daily rate.	If resident meets eligibility and level of service criteria, pays up to 100 days per period of illness.	Does not apply to subacute patients.	For rehabilitation and policy, daily care individual and/or provider contracts are negotiated for room and board and other services.	Depending on the patient or is reimbursed at the skilled level or at a daily cap outlined in the individual policy.	Paid by family funds.
Durable medical equipment	Coverage varies from state to state; most equipment is expected to be provided by the facility as a part of the daily rate. Medicaid will pay as a secondary payer for care/ services billed and paid under Medicare Part B.	Daily Medicare Part A rate is all inclusive for the period of certification. Use and cost of supplies and equipment is tracked for cost-reporting purposes.	Ancillary services such as physician visits, use of rehabilitation services outside of a Part A bed, some durable medical equipment, injections.	Reimbursement for durable medical equipment may be a part of the daily negotiated rate or negotiated and reimbursed separately by the managed care payer.	Coverage of durable medical equipment varies with individual policy.	Billing for use of special equipment and services over and above room and board varies from facility to facility.
Drugs	Specific coverage of drugs in the Medicaid program varies from state to state.	Cost of pharmaceuticals during care under Medicare Part A is included in the daily rate.	Coverage of medication is limited to that reimbursed under Part B.	Reimbursement for medications and treatments may be a part of the daily negotiated rate or negotiated and billed separately to the managed care payer.	Coverage for medications varies with individual policy.	Generally, the supplier bills the facility, which in turn bills the resident or guarantor on a monthly basis.

services, and has residents with commercial insurance policies that pay on a fee-for-service basis for daily care.

Medicaid per Diem Based on Overall Facility Costs

The Medicaid program is an indigent health care program that is promulgated by individual state legislation. Therefore, Medicaid reimbursement for nursing facilities varies from state to state, depending on the type of reimbursement methodology adopted by the state agency and the type of Medicaid coverage available in a given state. A common methodology is to calculate an overall facility per diem rate based on basic facility cost reporting. In these types of systems, there is no level of care distinction, and all residents are reimbursed at a flat daily rate based on facility-specific cost data using a reimbursement formula developed by the state agency.

Medicare Part A Skilled Nursing Facility Benefit

Medicare Part A coverage is limited in that a resident must first be eligible for Medicare Part A coverage and qualify with a three-day hospital stay within the previous 30 days of admission to a Medicare-certified bed and require the services of a skilled professional on a daily basis. If these criteria are met, the duration of the SNF coverage is limited to the need for daily skilled care up to a maximum of 100 days per period of illness. Therefore, not every admission to a nursing facility will qualify for Part A benefits, and not every long-term care facility chooses to participate in the Medicare Part A program. Consequently, if a resident chooses to utilize the Medicare SNF benefit following discharge from an acute care facility, he or she must select a facility/provider that is certified to participate in the Medicare program unless the resident is covered under a Medicare risk contract with a health maintenance organization.

Beginning in 1998, Medicare payments to SNFs changed from a cost-based reimbursement to a prospective payment system (PPS). Medicare Part A payment rates now utilize a case-mix adjusted per diem rate. The per diem payments for each qualified admission are based on **resource utilization groups (RUGs)**, a case-mix methodology driven from the MDS. One of the 53 groups is assigned, and that payment is reimbursed to the facility for a specific period of time or until the next MDS is completed according to the defined schedule.

The SNF PPS also assigns billing responsibility to the SNF for the entire package of care that residents receive during a stay. This concept is called **consolidated billing**. For example, physical therapy services are billed by the SNF (not by the physical therapy provider) as part of the package of care. The physical therapy provider, in turn, receives payment from the SNF. There are some exceptions to the consolidated billing requirement. For example, Medicare does make separate payments for physicians' professional services, certain dialysis-related services, and other items (CMS, n.d.).

From a health information management perspective, a **case-mix reimbursement** system such as the SNF PPS is greatly affected by documentation and accurate submission of MDS data. Therefore, the quality and accuracy of documentation has a direct relationship with the financial viability of a facility heavily dependent on Medicare reimbursement.

Medicaid per Diem Based on Level of Care

In some states, a Medicaid per diem or daily rate is established based on a level of care distinction for intermediate or skilled care or on a case-mix methodology developed by the state agency. In some states, the MDS is used as a resource document for calculating the level of care and extent of resources utilized for individual residents and for the facility as a whole. Depending on the state methodology, additional reimbursement may be recognized for intensity of services, such as may be the case with the care of AIDS, or for specific quality of care outcomes, such as would apply for improvement in functional independence as a result of rehabilitation and restorative services.

Resource Utilization Groups in Medicaid Reimbursement

Resource utilization groups (RUGS) reimbursement methodology is a specific case-mix payment system used in a growing number of states for long-term care Medicaid reimbursement. Using the MDS as the foundation for the data collection, states categorize reimbursement for individual residents based on their characteristics and service needs. From a very general perspective, the methodology is based on the premise that if a resident has special or heavy care needs, the facility will be reimbursed at a higher rate than that for a resident who is more independent in care and requires less skilled or clinically complex services. In addition to a direct care rate, the facility is also reimbursed a nondirect rate that includes cost of administrative services, capital costs, and other financial categories that are not directly related to the provision of individual care and services. As with the Medicare SNF PPS, attention to documentation and the accuracy of MDS data is crucial when RUGs form the basis of a large portion of a provider's reimbursement.

Commercial Insurance

Commercial insurance coverage for long-term care services is growing and is projected to increase with the aging of our population. There is great variability, however, in terms of the type and duration of services that are covered, because there is no standard definition of long-term care coverage as there is, to some degree, with *major medical* in relation to acute hospitalizations. In some instances, coverage mirrors the Medicare Part A SNF benefit and will reimburse the beneficiary only for a maximum of 100 days or for the period of time that daily skilled care is needed. In other instances, room and board expenses are reimbursed for a predetermined period of time regardless of level of care. Often, the commercial insurance carrier will request copies of the resident medical record on a monthly basis to verify services rendered and to substantiate the level of care required by the beneficiary. Depending on the specific policy coverage, documentation of the level of care and scope/intensity of services is essential for assuring reimbursement from the third-party payer.

Managed Care Payers

Although the penetration of managed care into the long-term care industry is likely to increase over time, the predominant influence at this time is in the Medicare SNF and subacute sector of the long-term care industry. Managed care payers have entered into Medicare **risk contracts** (a contract between an HMO and CMS to provide services to Medicare beneficiaries, under which the health plan receives a monthly payment for enrolled Medicare members) and therefore assume responsibility for the SNF benefit for their enrollees. In addition, an increasing number of managed care payers are contracting with long-term care facilities for the care of non-Medicare enrollees who require the intensive postacute rehabilitation and nursing services provided by SNF and subacute units. In order to control cost of care, managed care payers are seeking affiliations with long-term care facilities that can provide the same or higher-quality outcomes at a lesser cost per care episode than can the acute care setting. Consequently, managed care reimbursement is projected to increase in the long-term care setting for the low-cost, high-quality providers.

Managed care reimbursement can occur as a result of a variety of affiliations with a long-term care facility. For those facilities that are a part of a large, multifacility chain, managed care payers and health maintenance organizations (HMOs) may enter into national agreements on an exclusive basis. Facilities that are a part of an integrated delivery system may be involved in a managed care payment situation for an entire episode of care for enrollees. An example might be a workers' compensation claim in which the global care episode is reimbursed at a designated rate that includes acute care, postacute care, and related physician or other outpatient services. On an individual facility basis, negotiation with a managed care payer is done on both an individual or patient-to-patient basis and on a capitated basis based on predetermined levels of care and reimbursement. These negotiated rates may or may not include separate charges for pharmaceuticals, durable medical equipment, and/or rehabilitation services beyond a designated minimum number of units per day. As the term *negotiation* implies, there is a certain degree of bargaining on both sides, in that the managed care payer is looking for the lowest price and the provider is looking for the highest price for the same outcome. For this reason, information becomes essential to the successful managed care negotiator. If a provider has insufficient or inaccurate information from which to understand where specific care costs can be controlled, profits maximized, and losses minimized, a capitated rate can be financially devastating if care needs exceed reimbursement.

Private Pay

Private pay in the long-term care setting denotes payment by the individual without any third-party payer. In some facilities, a global daily rate is billed to the resident on a monthly basis, including all meals, treatments, and supplies, with no additional line item charges other than medications supplied by the pharmacy. In other facilities, a basic daily rate includes only room, board, and a nominal list of supplies/services, with additional services being charged for restorative services, incontinent care, specialized therapeutic activity programs, feeding assistance, and other services that are regarded as nonroutine by the facility. The degree to which additional services are charged over and above routine services varies from provider to provider.

INFORMATION MANAGEMENT

Management of information is an area of growing significance in the long-term care setting not only from a reimbursement perspective but also from a regulatory compliance and risk management perspective. This need is seen more dramatically in facilities participating in Medicare and Medicaid because of the information emphasis in the survey process and successful management of information-based reimbursement.

Coding and Classification

Although coding has a place in tracking various types of care, reimbursement is not dictated by codes in the residential long-term care setting. As a general rule, ICD codes have limited value in describing the level of care or intensity of services required for a long-term, chronically ill institutionalized resident. Consequently, while coding is used for billing of services and tracking clinical information in NFs and SNFs, its role is somewhat diminished when compared to the acute care environment.

ICD

The current clinical modification of the *International Classification of Diseases* diagnosis codes must be used for submitting Medicaid, Medicare Part A SNF, and Medicare Part B claims; however, their role is not significant in dictating the level of reimbursement the facility receives for an individual resident. Although inaccurate or incomplete codes may affect the timely processing of claims or increase the chances of a claim being isolated for medical review, reimbursement decisions are not solely linked to *ICD* codes. *ICD* codes may be used by the individual facility to track reasons for admission and hospitalization and to monitor clinical care issues such as incidence of acquired pressure ulcers, urinary tract infections, fractures, and other care outcomes that would be relevant to the overall monitoring and surveillance of quality. The use of *ICD* codes for tracking of clinical information beyond basic admission and discharge data varies from provider to provider.

ICD codes are also a part of the diagnosis reporting information included in the minimum data set (Section I). In this section, diagnoses are to be recorded in relation to current ADL status, cognitive status, mood and behavior status, medical treatments, nursing monitoring, or risk of death. A minimum amount of space is provided for recording actual *ICD* codes, because the majority of diagnosis information is entered by checking the relevant box on the form. If a diagnosis code provides more specific information relative to intensity of care or level of skilled services, then a code should be entered in preference over the checked box. For example, if a resident has insulin-dependent diabetes mellitus or uncontrolled diabetes, there is a greater degree of skilled supervision and monitoring required than with a resident whose diabetes is diet controlled. Consequently, an *ICD* code would provide greater information concerning that resident's level of care than would the simple description "diabetes mellitus." However, diagnoses and/or diagnosis codes are not adequate to describe the level and intensity of care required by the long-term care resident. Therefore, there is less focus on use and value of *ICD* codes in the long-term care setting, because they have less direct impact on facility reimbursement and monitoring of quality of care.

Current Procedural Terminology

Current Procedural Terminology (CPT) codes are used for billing Medicare Part B services for rehabilitation (PT, OT, speech) and for physician visits to residents in a nursing facility. For the rehabilitation services, *CPT* codes indicate the type of therapy provided. For physician visits, the *CPT* codes describe the level of service provided, which thereby dictates the reimbursement for the visit performed. In a retrospective review of claims by the Medicare carrier, physician documentation must support that the level of service billed was actually performed and was medically justified. Therefore, if a *CPT* code is used that correlates with a more intensive visit, documentation should support that a greater amount of time was involved than for a routine physician visit.

Often, billing for Part B physician services is not done directly by the nursing facility, because these services are billed through the private practice. Therefore, nursing facility staff members have much less familiarity with *CPT* codes as compared to *ICD* codes.

Data and Information Flow

Management of data and use of automation for data management has increased dramatically in the long-term care industry in the twenty-first century. In large part this has been due to the efforts of the Centers for Medicare & Medicaid Services to mandate automation of the MDS for all facilities participating in the Medicare and/or Medicaid programs. Also, individual state agencies are increasing their own requirements for electronic submission of MDS data on a monthly basis. Consequently, discussion of data and flow of information is relevant not only from the internal facility viewpoint but also from the perspective of reporting information to external agencies.

Data and Information Flow within the Facility

MDS Data In the Medicare- and/or Medicaid-certified facility, data and information flow centers around the MDS, which is not only a vehicle for a clinical assessment process but is also a mandated data set linked to regulatory compliance. Therefore, timeliness and accuracy of assessment information must be coordinated between the various disciplines and is a significant activity within the facility. From a data management perspective, the facility must ensure that systems are in place to monitor timeliness of completion of the MDS and accuracy of reported items (see Table 10-3). Furthermore, a system must be in place to ensure that significant changes in condition are properly

TABLE **10-3**
Monitoring Assessment Timeliness and Content

Time	Content of Information
Within 14 days of admission	MDS information is consistent with interdisciplinary assessment information recorded in the resident record.
Within 14 days of significant change in condition	Care plan content reflects appropriate use of care area triggers for development of goals and interdisciplinary interventions.
At least annually	Documentation explains the clinical reason(s) for not completing a new comprehensive assessment if some significant change criteria are met based on a quarterly review and/or at any time between scheduled assessment or review intervals.
Review of specific data elements quarterly	

identified, assessed, and communicated to the appropriate individuals, as this represents an area of federal regulatory compliance.

Once the MDS is completed, information is used to establish which care areas are triggered, either through an automated RAI process or through manual review of the MDS trigger legend. Therefore, coordination of completion among the various disciplines is an ongoing process within the nursing facility. In addition, information regarding changes in resident condition must be monitored continually to determine if specific criteria are met that indicate a possible need for a new comprehensive assessment. The criteria for determining if a resident has experienced a significant change in condition, either through improvement or decline, are included in the federal long-term care regulations and as such are a significant part of evaluating compliance with the resident assessment regulations. Consequently, concurrent information regarding resident condition must be communicated and evaluated on an ongoing basis.

Federal regulations define a "significant change" as a major change in the resident's status that is:

1. Not self-limiting
2. Impacts on more than one area of the resident's health status
3. Requires interdisciplinary review and/or revision of the care plans (CMS, 2011)

According to this definition, a significant change reassessment would be indicated if decline or improvement is consistently noted in two or more areas of decline or two or more areas of improvement. Following are examples that *could* indicate a significant change:

Decline

- Any decline in ADL functioning for which a resident is newly coded as 3, 4, or 8 (extensive assistance, total dependency, activity did not occur)
- Increase in the number of areas in which behavioral symptoms are coded as "not easily altered"
- Resident's decision making changes from 0 to 1, 2, or 3
- Resident's incontinence pattern changes from 0 or 1 to 2, 3, or 4, or to placement of an indwelling catheter
- Emergence of sad or anxious mood as a problem that is not easily altered
- Emergence of an unplanned weight loss problem (5 percent in 30 days or 10 percent in 180 days)
- Begin to use trunk restraint or a chair that prevents rising for a resident when it was not used before
- Emergence of a condition/disease in which a resident is judged to be unstable
- Emergence of a pressure ulcer at Stage II or higher when no ulcers were previously present at Stage II or higher
- Overall deterioration of resident's condition; received more support (e.g., in ADLs or decision making)

Improvement

- Any improvement in ADL physical functioning where a resident is newly coded as 0, 1, or 2 when previously scored as a 3, 4, or 8
- Decrease in the number of areas in which behavioral symptoms or sad or anxious mood are coded as "not easily altered"
- Resident's decision making changes from 2, 3, or 4 to 0 or 1
- Overall improvement of resident's condition; resident receives fewer supports (CMS, 2011)

Level of Care Evaluation   There are different reasons for residents requiring permanent care in a long-term care facility. Some require a higher level of skilled intervention on a daily basis, whereas others may need less intensive care. Depending on their diagnoses and overall condition, residents may decline rapidly and require more intensive services. For this reason, facilities develop methods for defining individual resident acuity and care needs and will attempt to place residents with similar needs in the same physical area or unit of the facility. As residents' conditions change, their care needs change, and relocation to more appropriate areas within the facility may be required. Generally, the type of information that would be utilized for this assessment would depend on the care issues outlined in Figure 10-2.

Utilization of Supplies and Services   Regardless of the pay source of the resident, information regarding utilization of central supply items and special services must be maintained for cost-accounting purposes. Some facilities manage supply information with the use of scanners, a system in which charge

Skilled Nursing Requirements	Dependence on staff for Activities of Doily Living
• Enteral feedings	• Supervised feeding or totally fed by staff
• Wound care	• Number of staff required for transfer and/ or mobility
• Ostomy care	• Number and extent of staff assistance required for dressing and personal hygiene
• Acute, unstable condition requiring skilled monitoring	

FIGURE **10-2** Information needs for level-of-care evaluation.

information is automatically captured at the point of use. In other instances, supply utilization is managed totally by a manual tracking system. Improper management of this key area of the facility operations can result in tremendous amounts of lost revenue to the long-term care facility.

For those facilities participating in managed care contracts with capitated payments, concurrent monitoring of supply utilization is essential to the successful provider. If the facility is paid a negotiated rate of a certain amount per day, it is important that the facility have a system in place that ensures effective monitoring of actual facility cost versus what the managed care payer will reimburse. This also applies to use of pharmaceuticals and durable medical equipment.

External Data Reporting

Facilities participating in the Medicare and/or Medicaid programs are required to submit MDS data to the state agency. In compliance with the individual state requirements, facilities submit individual resident MDS data to the state agency electronically. Both the state and federal agencies utilize individual resident and aggregate facility data to monitor quality by individual provider and to evaluate trends in care throughout various regions of the country. In some states, MDS data are also used to establish the facility Medicaid reimbursement.

Electronic Information Systems

With the advent of mandated electronic submission of MDS data, the long-term care industry has seen a growing number of vendors specializing in long-term care software. However, the degree to which facilities are able to totally computerize clinical and financial data is still dependent on the financial constraints of the average long-term care provider. As a result, there are wide ranges of utilization of electronic information systems within the industry, from stand-alone systems used strictly for processing MDS data to systems that successfully integrate all financial and clinical information within the facility.

Some of the more common electronic software applications are as follows:

- Electronic physician orders, medication, and treatment records either within the facility or provided by the pharmacy service off-site
- Electronic financial information (census, payroll, billing, cost-reporting data)
- Electronic MDS system, care area triggering system, and care plans
- Integration of care plan with nurse aide assignments
- Electronic interdisciplinary progress notes
- Electronic assessment templates
- Electronic tracking of incidents/accidents, infections, and other significant events

Often, these systems are not integrated and/or are not designed such that the facility has full advantage of the data in a repository. As the impact of concurrent information management grows within the long-term care industry, there will be an increasing demand for effective and affordable automated systems.

CMS provides free software, called RAVEN, for entering and transmitting MDS assessment data. The RAVEN software "imports and exports data in standard MDS record format, maintains facility, resident, and employee information, enforces data integrity via rigorous edit checks, and provides comprehensive on-line help" (CMS, 2002g, p. 1). . Facilities may also choose to submit MDS data using software purchased commercially through a vendor, provided that the software meets the CMS standards.

President Obama's economic stimulus package of 2009 encourages implementation of electronic health care records by 2014. This contributes to opportunities for increased computerization in long-term care and in other health care settings and at the same time increases regulation of privacy and security.

Data Sets

MDS has become the universal data set for the long-term care industry. Although some states have made additional data submission requirements to accommodate their Medicaid reimbursement systems, the MDS 2.0 became the universal basic reporting instrument for all 50 states effective January 1, 1996, with MDS 3.0 taking effect October 1, 2010. The initial goal of CMS in establishing MDS was to combine the benefits of a standardized clinical assessment tool with a universal data set for monitoring key information within the long-term care industry.

Now that the MDS also supplies information important to reimbursement, CMS is concerned with the potential for fraudulent reporting of MDS data. The MDS form includes a formal statement certifying accuracy of information for all MDS sections. Each staff member completing a portion of the MDS document must certify the accuracy of that portion by signing an attestation statement, which includes verbiage warning of criminal, civil, and/or administrative penalties for submitting false information. Figure 10-3 includes an example of the attestation statement as incorporated into the MDS form.

For the PPS/Medicare covered admission, the MDS is required to be completed on a 5-day, 14-day, 30-day, 60-day and 90-day schedule to acquire Medicare payment. (Refer to item A0310.B in Figure 10-4.) Deviation from this schedule while the resident is covered under Medicare results in the default or lowest payment rate.

Resident **TEST1 MDS 1**   Identifier   Date

Section Z	Assessment Administration

Z0400. Signature of Persons Completing the Assessment or Entry/Death Reporting

I certify that the accompanying information accurately reflects resident assessment information for this resident and that I collected or coordinated collection of this information on the dates specified. To the best of my knowledge, this information was collected in accordance with applicable Medicare and Medicaid requirements. I understand that this information is used as a basis for ensuring that residents receive appropriate and quality care, and as a basis for payment from federal funds. I further understand that payment of such federal funds and continued participation in the government-funded health care programs is conditioned on the accuracy and truthfulness of this information, and that I may be personally subject to or may subject my organization to substantial criminal, civil, and/or administrative penalties for submitting false information. I also certify that I am authorized to submit this information by this facility on its behalf.

Signature	Title	Sections	Date Section Completed
A.			
B.			
C.			
D.			
E.			
F.			
G.			
H.			
I.			
J.			
K.			
L.			

Z0500. Signature of RN Assessment Coordinator Verifying Assessment Completion

A. Signature:	B. Date RN Assessment Coordinator signed assessment as complete:
	0 1 – 2 7 – 2 0 1 0
	Month Day Year

FIGURE **10-3** MDS attestation and signatures.

Resident **TEST1 MDS 1** _____ Identifier _____ Date _____

MINIMUM DATA SET (MDS) - Version 3.0
RESIDENT ASSESSMENT AND CARE SCREENING
Nursing Home Comprehensive (NC) Item Set

Section A	Identification Information

A0100. Facility Provider Numbers

A. National Provider Identifier (NPI):

1	1	2	2	3	3	4	4	5	5

B. CMS Certification Number (CCN):

2	9	5	7	0	1						

C. State Provider Number:

C	M	C	A	I	D								

A0200. Type of Provider

Enter Code [1]

Type of provider
1. **Nursing home (SNF/NF)**
2. **Swing Bed**

A0310. Type of Assessment

Enter Code [0][1]

A. **Federal OBRA Reason for Assessment**
- 01. **Admission** assessment (required by day 14)
- 02. **Quarterly** review assessment
- 03. **Annual** assessment
- 04. **Significant change in status** assessment
- 05. **Significant correction** to **prior comprehensive** assessment
- 06. **Significant correction** to **prior quarterly** assessment
- 99. **Not OBRA required** assessment

Enter Code [9][9]

B. **PPS Assessment**
PPS Scheduled Assessments for a Medicare Part A Stay
- 01. **5-day** scheduled assessment
- 02. **14-day** scheduled assessment
- 03. **30-day** scheduled assessment
- 04. **60-day** scheduled assessment
- 05. **90-day** scheduled assessment
- 06. **Readmission/return** assessment
PPS Unscheduled Assessments for a Medicare Part A Stay
- 07. **Unscheduled assessment used for PPS** (OMRA, significant or clinical change, or significant correction assessment)
Not PPS Assessment
- 99. **Not PPS** assessment

Enter Code [0]

C. **PPS Other Medicare Required Assessment - OMRA**
- 0. **No**
- 1. **Start of therapy** assessment
- 2. **End of therapy** assessment
- 3. **Both Start and End of therapy** assessment

Enter Code [ ]

D. **Is this a Swing Bed clinical change assessment?** Complete only if A0200 = 2
- 0. **No**
- 1. **Yes**

Enter Code [1]

E. **Is this assessment the first assessment** (OBRA, PPS, or Discharge) **since the most recent admission?**
- 0. **No**
- 1. **Yes**

Enter Code [9][9]

F. **Entry/discharge reporting**
- 01. **Entry** record
- 10. **Discharge** assessment-**return not anticipated**
- 11. **Discharge** assessment-**return anticipated**
- 12. **Death in facility** record
- 99. **Not entry/discharge** record

FIGURE **10-4** First page of the MDS, including time frames for assessments.

QUALITY IMPROVEMENT AND UTILIZATION MANAGEMENT

Quality Improvement

Researchers at the University of Wisconsin developed the first MDS-derived quality indicators. These indicators can be utilized to monitor quality, both in process and outcome, through the automated use of MDS data. Figure 10-5 provides examples of quality indicators based on MDS data. From a facility perspective, many of these indicators also correlate directly with compliance monitoring for key federal quality of care and quality of life regulations (F-tags) as noted in Figure 10-5. (Note: An "F-tag" is an alphanumeric label that identifies a federal regulation and the associated interpretive guidelines used by surveyors. When a survey team cites a facility for a deficiency, it is cited by the appropriate tag number.)

Quality Indicator	Quality of Care and Quality of Life Requirement (F-tags)
Accidents	F323, F324—The facility must ensure that (1) the resident environment remains as free of accident hazards as is possible; and (2) each resident receives adequate supervision and assistance devices to prevent accidents.
Behavioral and emotional patterns	F319, F320—Based on the comprehensive assessment of a resident, the facility must ensure that (1) a resident who displays mental or psychosocial adjustment difficulty receives appropriate treatment and services to correct the assessed problem; and (2) a resident whose assessment did not reveal a mental or psychosocial adjustment difficulty does not display a pattern of decreased social interaction and/or increased withdrawn, angry, or depressive behaviors, unless the resident's clinical condition demonstrates that such a pattern is unavoidable.
Infection control/ prevalence of UTIs	F315—A resident who is incontinent of bladder receives appropriate treatment and services to prevent urinary tract infections and to restore as much normal bladder function as possible.
Prevalence of weight loss	F325—Based on a resident's comprehensive assessment, the facility must ensure that a resident maintains acceptable parameters of nutritional status, such as body weight and protein levels, unless the resident's clinical condition demonstrates that this is not possible.
Prevalence of tube feeding	F321, F322—Based on the comprehensive assessment of a resident, the facility must ensure that (1) a resident who has been able to eat enough alone or with assistance is not fed by nasogastric tube unless the resident's clinical condition demonstrates that use of a nasogastric tube was unavoidable; (2) a resident who is fed by a nasogastric or gastrostomy tube receives the appropriate treatment and services to prevent aspiration, pneumonia, diarrhea, vomiting, dehydration, metabolic abnormalities, and nasal-pharyngeal ulcers and to restore, if possible, normal eating skills.
Prevalence of dehydration	F327—The facility must provide each resident with sufficient fluid intake to maintain proper hydration and health.

FIGURE 10-5 **MDS-derived quality indicators.**

Quality Indicator	Quality of Care and Quality of Life Requirement (F-tags)
Incidence of decline in late loss ADLs	F310—A resident's abilities in activities of daily living do not diminish unless circumstances of the individual's clinical condition demonstrate that diminution was unavoidable. This includes the resident's ability to (1) bathe, dress, and groom; (2) transfer and ambulate; (3) toilet; (4) eat; and (5) use speech, language, or other functional communication systems.
Incidence of contractures	F317, F318—Based on the comprehensive assessment of a resident, the facility must ensure that (1) a resident who enters the facility without a limited range of motion does not experience reduction in range of motion unless the resident's clinical condition demonstrates that a reduction in range of motion is unavoidable; and (2) a resident with a limited range of motion receives appropriate treatment and services to increase range of motion and/or to prevent further decrease in range of motion.
Psychotropic drug use	F329—Each resident's drug regimen must be free from unnecessary drugs. Based on a comprehensive assessment of a resident, the facility must ensure that residents who have not used antipsychotic drugs are not given these drugs unless antipsychotic drug therapy is necessary to treat a specific condition as diagnosed and documented in the clinical record. Residents who use antipsychotic drugs receive gradual dose reductions, and behavioral interventions, unless clinically contraindicated, in an effort to discontinue these drugs.
Quality of life: prevalence of daily physical restraints	F221—The resident has the right to be free from any physical or chemical restraints imposed for purposes of discipline or convenience and not required to treat the resident's medical symptoms.
Prevalence of stage 1–4 pressure ulcers	F314—Based on the comprehensive assessment of a resident, the facility must ensure that (1) a resident who enters the facility without pressure sores does not develop pressure sores unless the individual's clinical condition demonstrates that they were unavoidable. (2) resident having pressure sores receives necessary treatment and services to promote healing, prevent infection and prevent new sores from developing.

FIGURE **10-5** (Continued)

As part of the CMS Nursing Home Quality Initiative, CMS hosts a "Nursing Home Compare" Web site that provides information about nursing homes in the form of quality measures. This information is posted for nursing homes in all states, with the intent of assisting potential residents and their families in making an informed selection if they need to consider nursing home placement. Quality measures are derived from the MDS, with some being adjusted per facility profile. Providers can utilize the information to compare themselves to similar nursing homes in a QI process.

Since 2008, the Nursing Home Compare Web site has included a Five-Star Quality Rating System for all Medicare or Medicaid certified nursing homes. CMS intends for this system to be a tool to assist consumer decision making. The rating is updated monthly with any new information. The five-star rating includes three categories of performance measures: health inspections, staffing, and quality measures. The three measures determine a facility's overall composite rating. A rating of one to five stars in each of the three categories as well as a composite star rating is assigned. One star indicates much below average and five stars indicate much above average quality. The health inspections category is based on three years of data including standard health surveys, complaint investigations, and on-site revisits. Data are weighted most heavily toward the most recent survey.

The staffing measure takes currently reported staffing information from nursing homes and case-mix adjusts the information according to the resource utilization group classification system. RN staffing and overall staffing is looked at and converted into a single one- to five-star rating. The staffing measure distributes nursing homes nationally along a quintile distribution.

The performance measure in the initial rating system incorporated 10 quality measures (seven long-stay measures and three short-stay measures) that were believed to be the most appropriate and reliable for the purpose of the Five-Star Quality Rating System. Long-stay measures included activities of daily living, mobility, pressure ulcers, restraints, urinary tract infections, pain, and catheterization. For the short-stay measures, delirium, high-risk pressure ulcers, and pain were included. (See end-of-chapter Web Activity to obtain the most current list of quality measures.) The quality measures distribute nursing homes nationally along a quintile distribution. Both staffing and quality measures use a national distribution, but the health inspections measure uses a state-based distribution.

The composite or overall rating begins with the health inspections rating, and this is moved up or down based on whether the staffing and quality measures ratings are extreme (meaning either one star or five stars). The purpose of the system is to separate high-performing nursing homes from low-performing nursing homes.

Utilization Management

In the long-term care setting, utilization management applies to the Medicaid, Medicare Part A, and managed care residents who may be in an SNF or subacute unit of a facility. Each state has individual requirements for qualifying for Medicaid nursing home payments, and the manner in which this process is monitored varies from state to state. In some instances, qualification is monitored through the MDS data in conjunction with additional state-specific information submission. In other instances, a separate review process is adopted by the state agency to determine initial and continuing Medicaid eligibility.

For the Medicare Part A SNF benefit, utilization must be monitored to ensure that the condition of the resident meets ongoing criteria for daily skilled care. In addition, the facility must be aware of SNF days that the resident may have used before being admitted to the SNF unit to ensure that the stay does not exceed the maximum benefit of 100 days per period of illness. If the level of care of the resident changes such that the facility feels that care no longer meets Medicare skilled criteria, an internal denial letter must be issued to the beneficiary (or the beneficiary's representative). In addition, the beneficiary must be advised of the right to submit an appeal to the intermediary if the denial decision is questioned or challenged.

Utilization management for managed care residents, typically those in an SNF or subacute bed, is a dynamic process that requires frequent monitoring by the facility case manager to ensure that care needs and progress are communicated to the managed care case manager on an ongoing basis. The facility must be in a position to communicate changes in resident status and discharge plans to the managed care payer. If care needs increase such that additional services must be ordered or are recommended by the attending physician, this must be communicated and generally approved through the managed care case manager. Most often, this monitoring and communication process is the responsibility of the facility RN case manager who serves as the primary communicator of care progress to the managed care payer.

RISK MANAGEMENT AND LEGAL ISSUES

Risk management and legal issues in the long-term care setting are similar to those in other health care settings. Proper tracking and documentation of incidents or potentially compensable events is important in the long-term care facility as it is in other settings. Clinical issues that present risk to the facility include pressure ulcers, falls, fractures, medications errors, infections, and dehydration. Long-term care facilities can use quality management techniques and monitor quality indicators to improve the quality of care and lower the level of legal risk.

ROLE OF THE HEALTH INFORMATION MANAGEMENT PROFESSIONAL

Credentialed health information managers (i.e., RHIT, RHIA) are not required in the federal long-term care regulations but may be required on either a part-time or consulting basis in some of the state long-term care licensure laws. The trend toward automation and use of health information in long-term care reimbursement has increased the importance of the credentialed health information manager in the long-term care setting. As a result, independent facilities and long-term care management corporations are increasing their use of full-time registered health information technicians (RHITs) and registered health information administrators (RHIAs). RHITs and RHIAs have formal education in health information management that can equip them for several roles in long-term care. Many long-term care facilities employ credentialed health information managers as full-time directors of health information services. Another role would be that of a health information management consultant. A consultant may focus on a specific area of information management such as auditing documentation. Whatever the role, it is important that the health information manager understand, apply, and stay abreast of pertinent regulations as well as follow professional best practices.

Auditing

One role of the health information manager in long-term care is in designing and implementing auditing systems. Of significant importance to the long-term care facility is the content, completion, accuracy, and timeliness of medical record documentation. Documentation affects the quality of care provided. Assessment and ongoing care planning are determined in part by what is written in the medical record. Documentation is also an important factor in outcomes for reimbursement systems, survey compliance, and in the event of legal action. The medical record serves as a tool in QI studies and is used in facility planning.

Health information managers and other trained staff can be a valuable asset to the long-term care organization by conducting routine documentation audits against established criteria. Results of such audits can be used to help ensure quality care, survey readiness, and proper reimbursement. Additionally, audit outcomes can be utilized as measures in training health care staff and for system evaluation and improvement.

Audits can be quantitative or qualitative in nature. Quantitative audits include review of whether medical record forms are complete, timely, and signed by the authors of the forms. Qualitative audits generally require more training, because they are a more in-depth look at the actual content of the medical record as compared to regulations and standards of practice.

Typical intervals for auditing records in long-term care are when admission assessments are complete, concurrently at regularly scheduled intervals throughout the resident/patient stay (such as quarterly), and upon discharge. The purpose of regular ongoing monitoring is to identify any problems or trends in documentation while correction is possible or when changes can be made. In many cases, because of the extended length of stay and volume of the record, delaying review of documentation until discharge is not as effective as employing an ongoing review system. Incomplete documentation often cannot legally be completed at a time well after the event and most likely would not be to anyone's benefit.

Utilizing a defined set of criteria for auditing or a review form promotes consistency and objectivity. Audit forms can be created by giving consideration to regulatory requirements and what the facility defines as useful information to collect. Some typical items on a long-term care audit form might include the following:

- Timeliness of MDS assessments
- Physician orders signed
- Advance directives addressed
- Allergies identified
- Assessments completed by each discipline
- Medication orders are consistent with medication records
- Physician progress notes coincide with required visit schedule
- Laboratory results are in the record for all lab testing ordered

The auditor can review several items in a sample of records or focus on one issue in a larger sample of records. In order to be effective, it is important in any type of auditing to accurately report the results in a timely manner. Problems or trends should be identified, a plan of correction developed, and further monitoring done to measure improvement.

External Consultant versus Full-Time Employee

As a consultant, the HIM professional conducts periodic visits ranging from monthly to quarterly to monitor documentation trends within the facility, particularly as this relates to potential regulatory compliance concerns. The HIM professional brings expertise in terms of resident confidentiality and release of confidential information, and also serves as an ongoing resource for development of forms and documentation systems and procedures that facilitate compliance and promote proper reimbursement. With the increase in automation, the HIM consultant is also a useful resource in selection of electronic information systems that are suited to the needs of the facility while also meeting specific state and federal requirements pertaining to automation of resident information. From that perspective, the HIM professional offers expertise in terms of evaluating the adequacy of existing traditional paper systems and provides valuable insight as to the necessary steps for streamlining and preparing manual systems for the gradual transition to an electronic resident record.

Because of the resident's length of stay and the scrutiny that nursing home documentation receives, HIM staff must ensure that the medical record, whether automated or paper, is safeguarded throughout the resident's stay as well as thereafter. HIM staff members must be diligent in protecting privacy and confidentiality by adhering to proper release-of-information standards.

Whether as a full-time employee or as an independent consultant to the long-term care facility, the HIM professional is often the key resource for monitoring federal regulatory compliance and alerting the facility to potential survey compliance concerns. Key quality of care concerns are often detected through the monitoring of current documentation in residents' records. As a result, the HIM professional can serve as an ongoing compliance monitor for the facility.

In some long-term care facilities, the documentation of assessments and progress notes by social services, activities, and dietary staff is the responsibility of noncredentialed personnel who have limited training for their jobs. As a result, the HIM professional is a valued resource for training these personnel in the proper methods and procedures of charting and for emphasizing the importance of their documentation as a part of the permanent medical record.

Training and education of long-term care facility staff is ongoing with respect to the various documentation requirements affecting long-term care reimbursement and regulatory compliance. This need is seen in all of the departments of the nursing facility as new graduates in nursing enter the long-term care setting and as more personnel from the acute care setting are moving into the long-term care and subacute care facilities. The HIM professional is a valuable resource for ongoing in-service with all disciplines and for providing initial training as to the role of the MDS and the proper procedures to follow in the RAI and care planning processes.

The expertise of the HIM professional offers numerous opportunities in the long-term care environment, particularly as information management becomes more crucial to monitoring regulatory compliance and ensuring proper reimbursement from Medicare, Medicaid, and managed care payers. Skills in streamlining work flow, management of information for QI initiatives, and data collection and analysis for critical pathways are growing areas in the SNF and subacute care settings in which the HIM professional can offer tremendous value.

TRENDS

Across the United States, a growing number of nursing homes and other residential care facilities are embracing the philosophy and values of a culture change. The residents, staff, and other stakeholders associated with these facilities are on a journey to transform traditional institutions into places where people are proud to live and work. This effort is a person-directed model called the **culture change movement**. This movement challenges the institution-centered culture traditionally found in nursing homes, where control is in the hands of facility leadership and staff. This conventional hospital-type model treats residents as patients who are sick and unable to care for themselves or make decisions. The traditional model emphasizes efficient operation of the facility rather than the physical, social, and spiritual needs of the residents. On the other hand, the culture change movement gives emphasis to the social model rather than the medical model in the way that care is rendered to elders. In the words of the culture change movement, it is about "creating home." A person-directed or self-directed model of care is one in which elders make their own decisions about their care and daily activities (Doty et al., 2008). Caregivers are still involved in decisions that are relevant to their jobs and to the individuals to whom they provide care. The elders, their families, and the staff form a community where relationships are important.

Under the leadership of the Pioneer Network and culture change organizations such as the Eden Alternative, Action Pact, Wellspring, and the Live Oak Institute, the culture change movement has been gaining recognition for its successes in creating a better world for the elders, staff, and leadership of many nursing homes. This movement has regulatory support. The Centers for Medicare & Medicaid Services (CMS) released new interpretive guidance for several quality of life and environmental F-tags in April of 2009. CMS and the Pioneer Network have also cosponsored "Creating Home" national meetings promoting self-directed living and other concepts of the culture change movement. These meetings have served to identify changes to the interpretive guidelines that CMS has used to enhance instructions to surveyors, with a sharpened focus on elements of quality of life. Some of the areas include F242 Self-Determination and Participation, which addresses resident choices about daily schedules; F172 Access and Visitation Rights; F241 Dignity; and F252 Homelike Environment.

SUMMARY

As the population continues to age, the demand for long-term care facilities will continue to grow. Often referred to as one of the most regulated industries in the country, long-term care has unique information system needs and documentation requirements. Consequently, health information managers have valuable skills to offer this growing segment of the health care industry. Prior federal regulations required the services of a credentialed health record practitioner as either an employee or a consultant of long-term care facilities participating in the Medicare or Medicaid programs. Although this regulation was deleted in the early 1990s, there has been a growing trend for long-term care facilities to employ credentialed health information managers as a result of the increasing demand for efficient and effective documentation and information systems. In the culture-changed environment, health information managers will find new challenges and at the same time will likely find pleasant features in their workplace, including interacting with the elderly and the aspects of their everyday living.

KEY TERMS

activities of daily living (ADL) for purposes of the federal long-term care regulations, activities of daily living include the resident's ability to (1) bathe, dress, and groom; (2) transfer and ambulate; (3) toilet; (4) eat; and (5) use speech, language, or other functional communication systems (CMS, 2011). Federal regulations include ADL as a component part of the quality of care requirements, and information concerning individual resident ADL capability is a significant portion of the monitoring information in the minimum data set.

CAA resources "a list of resources that may be helpful in performing the assessment of a triggered care area" (CMS, 2010, p. 1–5).

care area assessment (CAA) process a process that helps the assessor and clinician interpret and utilize MDS data by focusing on key issues. Components of the CAA process include care area triggers (CATs), CAA resources, and the CAA summary.

care area assessment (CAA) summary "(Section V of the MDS 3.0) provides a location for documentation of the care area(s) that have triggered from the MDS and the

decisions made during the CAA process regarding whether or not to proceed to care planning" (CMS, 2010, p. 1–5).

care area triggers (CATs) "specific resident responses for one or a combination of MDS elements. The triggers identify residents who have or are at risk for developing specific functional problems and require further assessment" (CMS, 2010, p. 1–5).

care plan a documented plan developed by an interdisciplinary team that includes measurable objectives and timetables to meet a resident's medical, nursing, and mental and psychosocial needs identified in the comprehensive assessment. A care plan must describe (1) the services that are to be furnished to attain or maintain the resident's highest practicable physical, mental, and psychosocial well-being; and (2) any services that would otherwise be required but are not provided because of the resident's exercise of rights including the right to refuse treatment (CMS, 2011).

case-mix reimbursement a long-term care reimbursement methodology designed to provide a mechanism for facilities to be paid in a manner that reflects the types of residents served and the types of services provided. The system is also designed to provide greater access to nursing facility beds for heavier care residents and to improve the quality of care for all nursing facility residents. Payment is based on a specific methodology that considers direct care costs, care-related costs, administrative and operating costs, and property.

civil money penalties   penalties or fines levied by the federal government against providers who are found to be in substantial noncompliance with federal regulations. These penalties may be as much as $10,000 per day.

comprehensive resident assessment   as defined by the long-term care federal regulations, a comprehensive resident assessment describes the resident's ability to perform daily life functions and significant impairments in functional capacity. Specifically, it includes at least the following information: (1) medically defined conditions and prior medical history; (2) medical status measurement; (3) physical and mental functional status; (4) sensory and physical impairments; (5) nutritional status and requirements; (6) special treatments or procedures; (7) mental and psychosocial status; (8) discharge potential; (9) dental condition; (10) activities potential; (11) rehabilitation potential; (12) cognitive status; and (13) drug therapy (CMS, 2011).

consolidated billing   under Medicare, a skilled nursing facility is responsible for billing the entire package of care that residents receive during a stay, with certain specified exceptions such as physicians' professional services.

culture change movement   a person-centered philosophy that creates a more homelike environment for residents of a nursing facility. Culture change involves providing individuals with privacy and the ability to make choices similar to what they would experience were they living in their own homes.

federal survey   a survey based on the federal long-term care requirements and using the federal long-term care survey procedures required for long-term care facility participation in the Medicare and/or Medicaid programs.

licensure survey   a survey conducted by the state agency to determine long-term care facility compliance with state licensure laws.

minimum data set (MDS)   a core set of screening and assessment elements, including common definitions and coding categories, that forms the foundation of the comprehensive resident assessment for all residents of long-term care facilities certified to participate in Medicare or Medicaid. The items in the MDS standardize communication about resident problems and conditions within facilities, between facilities, and between facilities and outside agencies (CMS, 2011). MDS data also serve as the basis for RUG assignment in the long-term care prospective payment system.

nursing facility   an institution or a distinct part of an institution that provides skilled nursing care, rehabilitation services, or health-related care to individuals who because of their condition require services above the level of room and board. Either a registered nurse or a licensed practical nurse is on active duty at all times. If properly licensed and certified, a nursing facility may receive reimbursement under the Medicaid program.

OBRA assessments   a schedule of assessments performed for a nursing facility resident at admission, quarterly, annually, whenever the resident experiences a significant change in status, and whenever the facility identifies a significant error in a prior assessment.

quality of care   a broad category of the long-term care federal regulations that requires a facility to provide the necessary care and services to attain or maintain the highest practicable physical, mental, and psychosocial well-being, in accordance with the comprehensive assessment and plan of care. Substantial noncompliance with quality of care requirements subjects a facility to potential civil money penalties and other punitive measures in the federal enforcement regulations.

quality of life a broad category of the long-term care federal regulations that requires a facility to care for its residents in a manner and in an environment that promotes maintenance or enhancement of each resident's quality of life. Substantial noncompliance with quality of life requirements subjects a facility to potential civil money penalties and other punitive measures in the federal enforcement regulations.

resident assessment instrument (RAI) an instrument that requires for completion the performance of a standardized assessment system, comprised of the MDS, CAA process, and utilization guidelines. This assessment system provides a comprehensive, accurate, standardized, and reproducible assessment of each long-term care facility resident's functional capabilities and identifies medical problems (CMS, 2011).

resident assessment protocols (RAPs) structured, problem-oriented frameworks for organizing MDS information and additional clinically relevant information about an individual that identifies medical problems and forms the basis for individual care planning (CMS, 2011). Although RAP terminology is still in common use, CMS now uses the term *care area assessment (CAA) process* to describe this concept.

resource utilization groups (RUGs) a case-mix methodology based on data submitted on the MDS. RUGs are used to adjust per diem payments to SNFs under the Medicare PPS and to NFs under some state Medicaid programs.

risk contract also known as a Medicare risk contract. A contract between an HMO and CMS to provide services to Medicare beneficiaries, under which contract the health plan receives a monthly payment for enrolled Medicare members and must then provide all services on an at-risk basis (Kongstvedt, 1993).

skilled nursing facility an institution or a distinct part of an institution that provides skilled nursing care or rehabilitation services. Either a registered nurse or a licensed practical nurse is on active duty at all times. If properly licensed and certified, a skilled nursing facility may obtain a Medicare provider agreement and be reimbursed under the Medicare program.

standard survey a periodic, resident-centered inspection that gathers information about the quality of service furnished in a facility to determine compliance with the requirements of participation in the federal Medicare and Medicaid programs (CMS, 2011).

subacute care a transitional type of care that represents a level of service that is less intensive than traditional acute care but more goal oriented and resource intensive than what is generally regarded as skilled nursing care.

substandard quality of care one or more deficiencies related to participation requirements under 42 C.F.R. 483.13, resident behavior and facility practices; 42 C.F.R. 483.15, quality of life; or 42 C.F.R. 483.25, quality of care. These constitute either immediate jeopardy to resident health or safety; a pattern of widespread actual harm that is not immediate jeopardy; or a widespread potential for more than minimal harm, but less than immediate jeopardy, with no actual harm (CMS, 2011).

substantial compliance a level of compliance with the Conditions of Participation, such that any identified deficiencies pose no greater risk to resident health or safety than the potential for causing minimal harm. Substantial compliance constitutes compliance with participation requirements (CMS, 2011).

utilization guidelines CMS guidelines that provide instructions for when and how to use the RAI. These include instructions for completion of the RAI as well as structured frameworks for synthesizing MDS and other clinical information. The utilization guidelines can be used to evaluate a care area that has been triggered and to determine whether or not to continue to care plan for it.

REVIEW QUESTIONS

Knowledge-Based Questions

1. What two primary agencies regulate long-term care facilities?
2. What are the primary reimbursement categories for care of residents in long-term care facilities?
3. Who determines how long-term care facilities are reimbursed under the Medicaid program?
4. What are the three categories for which ratings are provided in the Five-Star Rating System for nursing homes? What are some of the specific long-stay and short-stay quality measures used in this system?
5. What is the single most important content characteristic of a care plan in a long-term care facility that is subject to federal regulations?
6. List common electronic software applications in long-term care.

Critical Thinking Questions

1. How is ICD coding of relevance to the long-term care setting? Compare its impact in long-term care to acute care.
2. Why is there a greater focus on concurrent documentation monitoring in the long-term care setting as compared to evaluating documentation in the closed medical record?
3. Conduct additional research as necessary to discover the principal uses of the MDS in the long-term care industry (a) by the individual provider, (b) by the state agency, and (c) by CMS.

WEB ACTIVITY

Go to the CMS Nursing Home Quality Initiatives Web site at http://www.cms.gov/NursingHome QualityInits/.

Explore some of the links at the Nursing Home Quality Initiative Web site to answer the following questions:

1. What version of the MDS is currently in use?
2. Click on the "Quality Measures" link.
3. What items are included in the current long-stay and short-stay quality measures? How many additional measures have been added since the initial list of 10 measures?

CASE STUDY

You are the consultant for a long-term care facility that has recently undergone a long-term care survey in which the facility received several deficiencies for noncompliance with federal requirements. The most significant deficiency involved a noted pattern (7 of 10 examples reviewed in the surveyor sample) in which comprehensive assessments (MDS) were not completed within the required time frame (within 14 days of admission). In addition, surveyors identified that there was no documentation to support that the triggered care areas were being used in the assessment and care-planning process. This resulted in related quality of care deficiencies for failure to adequately assess and manage urinary incontinence and psycho-social needs. In three additional examples, surveyors identified that residents had experienced a significant change in condition without evidence of a new

assessment being done. Within the statement of deficiencies, surveyors noted that the director of nursing stated that she was unaware that assessments had not been done. It was also noted that the nursing staff stated that they did not understand what the care area triggers were, and that they were unaware of the federal criteria for determining when a significant change had occurred. The administrator of this facility has asked you to help develop a plan to correct these deficiencies.

1. What would be your recommendations for overall system evaluation and revision?
2. What would be your recommendations for staff education?
3. How could the facility medical records designee be utilized to prevent similar problems from occurring in the future?

REFERENCES AND SUGGESTED READINGS

[CMS] Centers for Medicare & Medicaid Services. (2004). Appendix R: Resident Assessment Instrument for Long Term Care Facilities. *State Operations Manual*. [Online]. http://cms.hhs.gov/manuals/Downloads/som107ap_r.pdf.

[CMS] Centers for Medicare & Medicaid Services (2009). *RAI User Manual* [Online]. http://www.cms.gov/NursingHomeQualityInits/20_NHQIMDS20.asp.

[CMS] Centers for Medicare & Medicaid Services. (2010a). Chapter 2—The Certification Process. *State Operations Manual*. [Online]. http://www.cms.hhs.gov/manuals/downloads/som107c02.pdf.

[CMS] Centers for Medicare & Medicaid Services. (2010b). Chapter 7—Survey and Enforcement Process for SNFs and NFs. *State Operations Manual*. [Online]. http://www.cms.hhs.gov/manuals/downloads/som107c07.pdf.

[CMS] Centers for Medicare & Medicaid Services (2010c). *CMS's RAI Version 3.0 Manual* [Online]. *http://www.cms.gov/NursingHomeQualityInits/45_NHQIMDS30TrainingMaterials.asp.*

[CMS] Centers for Medicare & Medicaid Services. (2011). Appendix PP: Guidance to Surveyors—Long Term Care Facilities. *State Operations Manual*. [Online]. http://cms.hhs.gov/manuals/Downloads/som107ap_pp_guidelines_ltcf.pdf.

[CMS] Centers for Medicare & Medicaid Services. (n.d.). Nursing Home Compare. [Online]. http://www.medicare.gov/NHCompare/home.asp.

[CMS] Centers for Medicare & Medicaid Services. (n.d.). RAVEN Software. [Online]. http://www.cms.hhs.gov/MinimumDataSets20/07_RAVENSoftware.asp.

[CMS] Centers for Medicare & Medicaid Services. (n.d.). Consolidated Billing for Skilled Nursing Facility (SNF) Residents Claims Billed to Medicare Carriers or DMERCS by Physicians, Non-physician Practitioners, and Suppliers. *Medicare Learning Network*. [Online]. http://www.cms.hhs.gov/medlearn/snfcode.asp.

Doty, M. M., Koren, M. J., & Sturla, E. L. (2008, May). Culture Change in Nursing Homes: How Far Have We Come? Findings from the Commonwealth Fund 2007 National Survey of Nursing Homes. *Commonwealth Fund*. [Online]. http://www.commonwealthfund.org/Content/Publications/Fund-Reports/2008/May/Culture-Change-in-Nursing-Homes--How-Far-Have-We-Come--Findings-From-The-Commonwealth-Fund-2007-Nati.aspx.

Joint Commission. (n.d.). *Certification: Disease-Specific Care*. [Online]. http://www.jointcommission.org/NR/rdonlyres/2933D499-84CC-4EC1-83A2-6990DDC7D977/0/Mktg_DSC_Brochure.pdf.

Kongstvedt, P. (1993). *The Managed Health Care Handbook*. Gaithersburg, MD: Aspen.

Sullivan, J. G. (1996, March). Long term care on trial. *Contemporary Long Term Care*, p. 46.

KEY RESOURCES

American Association of Homes and Services for the Aging
http://www2.aahsa.org

American College of Health Care Administrators
http://www.achca.org

American Health Care Association
http://www.ahca.org

American Medical Directors Association
http://www.amda.com

Assisted Living Facilities Federation of America
http://www.alfa.org

The Joint Commission
http://www.jointcommission.org/

National Association for Directors of Nursing Administration in Long Term Care (NADONA/LTC)
http://www.nadona.org

CHAPTER 11

Rehabilitation

TERRY WINKLER, MD

ANN H. PEDEN, PHD, RHIA, CCS

LEARNING OBJECTIVES

Upon successful completion of this chapter, you should be able to:

- Identify and describe the various levels of rehabilitative care.

- Describe the major accrediting agencies for rehabilitation.

- List the members of an interdisciplinary rehabilitation team.

- Describe key features of the inpatient rehabilitation facility prospective payment system (IRF PPS).

- Explain classification systems used to grade severity of injury/ disability and relate them to outcome measures.

- Define basic rehabilitation terms and distinguish between the concepts of impairment, disability, and handicap.

- Review sample forms used to track a person's progress in rehabilitation.

- Explain current trends in rehabilitation.

Setting	Description	Synonyms/Examples
Acute Care Hospitals	Inpatient facilities that provide acute medical care	Community hospitals Regional or tertiary care centers
Long-Term Acute Care Hospitals	Inpatient rehabilitation services to the patient who has an acute illness superimposed on chronic disability or for medically complicated patients	Long-term acute care
Freestanding Rehabilitation Centers	A center for rehabilitation that stands alone and is not physically part of another health care center	Physical therapy clinics Rehabilitation centers
Skilled Nursing Programs	Inpatient rehabilitation for patients who are progressing too slowly to meet criteria for standard rehabilitation programs	Nursing home rehabilitation Skilled nursing facilities
Outpatient Rehabilitation	Programs where therapy is provided but patient does not stay overnight	Day treatment centers Work hardening programs Occupational rehabilitation Chronic pain treatment centers Therapy clinics
Home Health Rehabilitation	Rehabilitation services provided to patients in their home by a home health care agency	Area agency on aging Various county health department programs Hospital-owned/operated home health National home health agencies

INTRODUCTION TO SETTING

Rehabilitation is the development of a person to the fullest physical, psychological, social, vocational, avocational, and educational potential consistent with his or her physiological or anatomic impairment and environmental limitations. Rehabilitation should begin when the patient enters a hospital with an injury or illness that is going to result in some limitations of the patient's functional status. The end result of comprehensive rehabilitation should be increased independence, increased overall functional status, and improved quality of life.

Types of Rehabilitation Settings

Rehabilitation is a continuum of care that begins with the patient's stay in the acute care hospital setting, extends throughout the postacute hospital phase, and, in many cases, continues through outpatient treatment. The types of rehabilitation facilities expanded greatly in the late twentieth century. Rehabilitation is now provided in numerous types of settings.

Acute Rehabilitation

Acute rehabilitation units in hospitals are the most common settings and have more than doubled since around 1990. These rehabilitation wards usually have a set number of beds, ranging from 10 to 30, designated in one ward of a hospital where patients are transferred for their acute care rehabilitation. Length of patient stays can vary from two to four weeks. When a patient is medically stable and has reached his or her maximum short-term improvement, the patient is then transferred to a different setting based on his or her needs at that point.

Long-Term Acute Care (LTAC)

Long-term acute care (LTAC) facilities provide services to the patient who has an acute illness superimposed on chronic disability or for medically complicated patients. These facilities bridge the gap between acute hospitals and rehabilitation programs. (For more information on long-term acute care, see Chapter 2.)

Freestanding Rehabilitation Hospitals

In the 1990s, several national corporations were created to operate rehabilitation hospitals. These facilities are freestanding, but usually in proximity to larger medical centers to guarantee a referral base. **Freestanding rehabilitation hospitals** include both acute rehabilitation centers and postacute rehabilitation centers.

Rehabilitation Provided in Skilled Nursing Settings

Skilled nursing rehabilitation centers are usually located in a wing of a nursing home or a hospital and serve a skilled-level patient. These facilities can accommodate a patient with multiple problems or older patients who are progressing more slowly than would be acceptable in an acute rehabilitation setting.

Due to economic factors, patients are being discharged earlier from the hospital, which has resulted in some patients being discharged who are not yet completely recovered and are unable to care for themselves. In many instances, due to age, multiple medical problems, or other factors, the patient may not be considered a good candidate for an acute rehabilitation center. On the other hand, if it appears that the patient would still continue to make some progress given proper rehabilitation, then the patient is an ideal candidate for skilled-level rehabilitation. Skilled rehabilitation centers serve the population of patients who would benefit from inpatient rehabilitation but do not meet the criteria for rehabilitation admissions and acute or postacute centers.

Outpatient Rehabilitation Facilities

Most rehabilitation centers, whether acute or postacute, have outpatient components. In addition, some freestanding outpatient rehabilitation facilities are independent and not affiliated with larger hospitals. These facilities provide therapies and rehabilitation strategies to patients who do not require hospitalization or overnight stays. Most commonly, these facilities provide care for workers' compensation or sports injuries and/or services to patients who have progressed through acute and postacute rehabilitation facilities.

A comprehensive outpatient rehabilitation facility (CORF) is a type of outpatient rehabilitation program certified by Medicare as a Part A provider. According to the Conditions of Participation, a CORF is "established and operated exclusively for the purpose of providing diagnostic, therapeutic, and restorative services to outpatients for the rehabilitation of injured, disabled, or sick persons, at a single fixed location, by or under the supervision of a physician..." (42 C.F.R. 485.51). At a minimum, a CORF must provide physicians' services, physical therapy services, and social or psychological services in a comprehensive and coordinated manner.

Home Health Care Rehabilitation

Home health care agencies provide rehabilitation services to the homebound patient who does not require hospitalization and who is unable to obtain transportation to an outpatient rehabilitation facility. The definition of *homebound* is that it is substantially difficult for the patient to be mobile in the community. A person with tetraplegia, for example, who requires a power wheelchair and a handicap van would have substantial difficulty being mobile in the community. This is interpreted differently from agency to agency and in different regions.

Types of Caregivers

A **rehabilitation team** can be organized along a multidisciplinary approach, meaning team members evaluate the patient in their specific discipline, or in an interdisciplinary approach, which means that the team members work together in a synergistic fashion to solve specific problems for the patient. An interdisciplinary approach, used in goal setting, problem solving, and coordination of treatment, provides a more cost-effective and nonfragmented treatment to the patient and is generally considered to be best. The interdisciplinary approach also improves patient learning, because all team members are reinforcing the learned concepts to approach the specific problems of the patient. In 2009, CMS changed the wording in its regulations from *multidisciplinary* to *interdisciplinary* to reflect the most common and best practice for rehabilitation teams (CMS, 2009).

Several clinical specialists might be part of a patient's rehabilitation team. These include the physiatrist, occupational therapist, physical therapist, speech pathologist, psychologist, social worker, and rehabilitation nurse, as well as vocational rehabilitation counselors, recreational therapists, kinesiotherapists, music therapists, audiologists, and chaplains.

Physiatrist

A **physiatrist**, or physical medicine and rehabilitation physician, is generally the head of the rehabilitation team. A physiatrist is a physician who has completed four years of approved residency training after medical school in physical medicine and rehabilitation. The American Academy of Physical Medicine and Rehabilitation is the specialty board for physiatry and is recognized by the American Board of Medical Specialties. Physiatry is a small specialty, with some states having as few as a half-dozen physiatrists. However, the specialty has been in existence for some time, with the first specialty boards being given in 1947.

Occupational Therapist

An **occupational therapist (OT)** has completed a master's degree in an OT program that is accredited by the American Occupational Therapy Association (AOTA). Occupational therapists address several areas in their rehabilitation of a patient. These include activities of daily living (ADLs) such as dressing, bathing, grooming, toileting, and transfers. OTs are also the members of the team who focus on upper-extremity movement and function, including fine motor control and hand-eye coordination. For example, they may fashion various splints for the upper extremity to preserve range of motion and improve function. OTs also address higher cognitive skills and community skills, such as homemaker chores, driving, and money handling.

Occupational therapists assist in evaluating future equipment needs such as wheelchairs, cushions, and bathtub benches, and assist in recommendations for home modifications.

Physical Therapist

The **physical therapist (PT)** is a member of the rehabilitation team who has completed a graduate program in physical therapy from a college or university program accredited by the American Physical Therapy Association's (APTA's) accrediting body, the Commission on Accreditation of Physical Therapy Education (CAPTE). In keeping with APTA's vision, most training programs now lead to a doctoral degree, with some master's-level training still available. Physical therapists are licensed by the state in which they practice. The physical therapist is the member of the team who is primarily responsible for improving the patient's strength, range of motion, balance, and mobility. The physical therapist specializes in appropriate strength and endurance exercises, assisting in controlling pain, providing skin care treatment, and providing modalities (such as ultrasound, diathermy, hot packs, and whirlpool treatments). When rehabilitating injured workers, the physical therapist will teach proper lifting techniques, offer ergonomic suggestions, and conduct work hardening programs and functional capacity evaluations. Work hardening programs are outpatient treatment programs that assist an injured worker in maximizing his or her strength, range of motion, and functional status. They improve a worker's chances of returning to the job and avoiding future injuries. These treatment programs try to simulate activities that the worker would have to do in the workplace. A functional capacity evaluation is a formalized series of tests, usually with some parts computerized, that helps the physician determine what is a safe level of lifting, pushing, toting, bending, and climbing to which an injured worker would be able to return.

Speech-Language Pathologist

The **speech-language pathologist** has a master's level of education and is certified by the American Speech-Language-Hearing Association (ASHA). Almost all states have a licensure process for speech-language pathologists. The speech pathologist evaluates and treats patients who have aphasias, apraxias, dysarthrias, dysphasias, communication disorders, and cognitive deficits. A speech pathologist would primarily be concerned with three broad areas: (1) swallowing problems, (2) communication problems, and (3) cognitive deficits.

Psychologist

A **psychologist** has a PhD level of training from a school accredited by the American Psychological Association (APA) and has completed the necessary requirements for licensure within his or her state. The primary role of the psychologist is to assist the newly disabled person and his or her family in adjustment to the disability and to develop a relationship of cooperation between the patient and the rehabilitation team. The psychologist has two primary roles in the rehabilitation team: (1) testing to identify problem areas in cognition or behavior on which the rehabilitation team should focus and (2) counseling for the patient and his or her family members. When the person performing these roles has a master's degree instead of a doctorate, the position is usually termed *counselor*, *specialist*, or *clinician* rather than psychologist.

Social Worker

The **rehabilitation social worker** has a master's level of training with specific training and knowledge in the area of social work and may be certified by the National Association of Social Workers. Social workers are also licensed by the state in which they are practicing. The social worker assists the rehabilitation team by providing background information about the patient and his or her family situation, and in coordinating funding resources for the patient. The social worker also assures a smooth transition from the rehabilitation program back to the community.

Rehabilitation Nurse

The **rehabilitation nurse** is an RN who has completed a two-year or four-year accredited nursing program, is licensed in the state in which he or she practices, has completed additional training in rehabilitation nursing, and may be certified by the Association of Rehabilitation Nurses. The rehabilitation nurse plays a key role in the patient's rehabilitation by teaching the patient information about proper bowel and bladder management programs and skin care. The rehabilitation nurse is also responsible for teaching the patient about medications, their indications, and their side effects. This member of the rehabilitation team teaches the patient about the most common complications and problems associated with a disability—such as deep vein thrombus, skin breakdown, or heterotopic ossification—and how to monitor them.

Kinesiotherapist

The **kinesiotherapist** has received specialized training in the proper techniques to maximize range of motion, strength, balance, and gait, which is similar to the physical therapist's role within the rehabilitation team. Typically, kinesiotherapists are employed in the VA system or in professional sports and training programs.

Other Health Care Workers

Numerous other health care professionals can contribute to the rehabilitation team, including dietitians, vocational rehabilitation counselors, recreational therapists, music therapists, audiologists, and chaplains.

Rehabilitation programs vary in which members of the rehabilitation team are essential, depending on the setting of the rehabilitation, the type of facility, and the types of rehabilitation patients that are accepted. In general, core members of the rehabilitation team for almost any program would include the physiatrist, occupational therapist, physical therapist, and speech pathologist at a minimum. An inpatient program would also require a rehabilitation nurse and a social worker. The ratio of therapists to patients is critically important. The therapist should not be required to have more than approximately four to six hours of hands-on therapy time per day, to allow the opportunity for adequate medical record documentation by the therapist and staffing time.

Types of Patients

Numerous diseases and injuries lead to a variety of disabling conditions. These disabilities can be divided into several general categories, including patients who require rehabilitation to treat injuries or disorders in the following areas:

- orthopedic
- neurologic
- medical
- pediatric
- involving management of acute or chronic pain
- sensory impairment

Patients requiring orthopedic rehabilitation have injuries such as fractured hips, total joint replacements, multiple fractures, amputations, or soft tissue injuries. Pain management patients include those with acute pain and chronic pain such as back pain or cervical pain, cumulative trauma disorders, or reflex sympathetic dystrophy. Patients with neurologic injuries or diseases include those who have conditions such as stroke, traumatic brain injuries, spinal cord injuries, multiple sclerosis, or muscular dystrophy. A sensory-impaired patient has hearing or visual disabilities. Medical disabilities include chronic obstructive pulmonary disease (COPD), myocardial infarction, diabetes mellitus and its complications, and cancer.

Pediatric rehabilitation patients are generally viewed as a separate category because of their special needs. These patients are often considered to be *habilitation* patients rather than *rehabilitation* patients. Conditions that are commonly treated include cerebral palsy, spina bifida, and various genetic disorders. Similarly, the aged population often has different rehabilitation issues and goals, and tends to be treated in a geriatric rehabilitation setting.

Because of the subspecialization required by rehabilitation team members, rehabilitation hospitals or programs tend to evolve around specific types of injuries. For example, there are rehabilitation centers that treat only brain injuries, spinal cord injuries, or burn survivors.

Spinal cord injury treatment centers have evolved to treat the 7,000 to 10,000 new cases of spinal cord injury each year in the United States. There are model system spinal cord injury treatment centers that specialize in treating the spinal cord-injured patient, such as Craig Hospital in Englewood, Colorado, Rehabilitation Institute of Chicago, Texas Institute of Rehabilitation in Houston, and Shepherd Rehabilitation Center in Atlanta. In the 2006–2011 funding cycle, there are 14 regional model system spinal cord injury treatment centers that are funded by grants from the National Institute of Disability Research, a branch of the National Institutes of Health (NIH).

Similarly, there are rehabilitation centers that focus on traumatic brain injury (TBI), such as Timber Ridge Ranch in Bentonville, Arkansas; the Greenery in Dallas, Texas; and Rancho Los Amigos in Downy, California. It is estimated that approximately 50,000 to 75,000 people per year in the United States have severe traumatic brain injury. There are four to five times as many who have mild to moderate TBI.

It has been estimated that approximately 14 percent of Americans have a disability; this is approximately 35 to 43 million people with disabilities. Of these individuals with a disability, as many as one-third have functional limitations that can be classified as severe.

Understanding proper terminology regarding this population is important. The World Health Organization (WHO) developed an international standard of definitions for terms that are used to discuss individuals with functional limitations. **Impairment** is any temporary or permanent loss or abnormality of a body structure or function, whether physiological or psychological. **Disability** is a restriction or inability to perform an activity in the manner or within the range considered normal for a human being, mostly resulting from impairment. **Handicap** is the result of an impairment or a disability that limits or prevents the fulfillment of one or several roles that are regarded as normal (depending on age, sex, social, and cultural factors) for that individual. Stated differently, the impairment might be the disease or diagnosis; the disability is how the impairment (i.e., the disease or diagnosis) affects the person. Finally, the handicap is an interaction between the impairment or disability and the person's socioeconomic environment. In other words, how does the problem affect the person's life? What functional limitations or problems are posed by the impairment or the disability? For example, amputation of a distal segment of the index finger and the long finger of a hand would result in an impairment (i.e., partial amputation of digits) and some disability (decreased range of motion, decreased grip strength). In most situations, this injury would not result in a major handicap. Given some rehabilitation and time, the individual would learn how to adapt quite well to a relatively minor impairment. Now suppose that the individual is a concert classical pianist. The handicap is overwhelming in this situation, and the person would be totally disabled from pursuing his or her occupation.

Consider an example of an individual with a spinal cord injury resulting in paraplegia. This person then attends college, medical school, and residency training to become a rehabilitation physician. The impairment is spinal cord injury with paraplegia; the disability is a mobility impairment with an inability to walk. However, in this situation the handicap is mild or moderate, because the hospital is an accessible environment and the individual is able to practice rehabilitation medicine in the environment of a hospital. Remember that the handicap is defined by the socioeconomic environment and the interaction of the impairment. The same individual would be severely handicapped if he were a tree surgeon or a mountain climber.

Durable Medical Equipment Commonly Used

Assistive devices fall into many different categories depending on the type of function the device is intended to supplement or augment. They can be divided into several broad categories: orthotics, prosthetics, ambulation aids, wheelchairs, and high-tech assistive devices such as computers. Refer to Table 11-1 for examples of the various types of durable medical equipment used in rehabilitation.

TABLE **11-1**

Examples of Durable Medical Equipment Used in Rehabilitation

Device	Definition	Examples
Orthotics	An orthopedic appliance to support, align, prevent, or correct deformity or to improve function	AFO, KAFO, WHO, neck, back, or spine braces*
Ambulation aids	A device to provide stability and support for walking	Straight cane, walker, quad cane, crutches
Prosthetics	A device to replace a missing body part	Mechanical arm or leg, artificial eye, dentures, myoelectric arms
Wheelchairs/ mobility devices	A wheeled chair to provide mobility when ambulation is difficult or not possible	Standard wheelchair, power wheelchair, power scooter
High-technology assistive devices	Computer to control environments and wheelchairs	Kurzweil readers, Peachtree control systems

*AFO (ankle-foot orthosis); KAFO (knee-ankle-foot orthosis); WHO (wrist-hand orthosis)

Orthotics

An **orthotic device** is an external appliance or brace that can supplement an extremity's function or improve stability and positioning. Orthotics have been in existence for more than 300 years and come in a variety of shapes, sizes, and styles from leather to metal to polyethylene plastics. The most commonly seen is a spinal brace, either cervical or lumbar. Cervical orthoses are commonly prescribed after trauma to the cervical spine, such as a motor vehicle accident, or after surgery. A variety of devices are available, from the Philadelphia collar, which is a soft foam-like collar that provides very little restriction of head movement and serves only as a proprioceptive reminder to the person to limit range of motion, to the halo, which is placed by the surgeon and provides the greatest level of stability for an unstable cervical spine. The most commonly seen cervical orthosis is a SOMI-type brace, named for the body part that it contacts and its function (sternal occipital mandibular immobilizer).

Similarly, thoracolumbar orthoses come in a variety of styles and shapes, the most common being the Jewett brace, which provides support in the upper sternal, midthoracic, and lower anterior abdominal area, and a chair-back-type brace that resembles a straight-back chair, with straps to keep it positioned properly on the back. For scoliosis, the Milwaukee brace is most commonly used to limit the progression of scoliotic spine. Thoracolumbar orthoses tend to be named for the city in which they were developed.

Several devices exist to stabilize or assist function of an upper extremity that has impairment. These devices can be static or dynamic. A static device assists in positioning; the dynamic orthosis assists in replacing some function. A sling suspension orthosis, or ball-bearing feeder orthosis, assists a quadriplegic who has limited strength in the upper extremities, allowing this person to perform functional activities such as feeding himself or herself. A Cock-up splint, or flexor hinge splint, can be used in the C6 quadriplegic to replace the lost pinch grasp between the forefingers and the thumb.

Extremity orthoses are named for the body part with which they interact. For example, an orthosis that crosses the wrist and hand is a WHO (wrist-hand orthosis). One that goes over the back of the leg and around the bottom of the foot is an AFO (ankle-foot orthosis). If that same brace extends up the leg and just above the knee, it is a KAFO (knee-ankle-foot orthosis).

The most common lower-extremity orthotic is an AFO to replace weakened muscles in the leg and prevent the foot from dropping when ambulating. An additional brace that is commonly seen is the Swedish knee cage, which is used for athletes who have suffered injury to the ligaments in their knee.

Ambulation Aids

Ambulation aids provide additional stability and support for an individual who has trouble walking. These range from a straight cane to a walker. Wheels may be added to the walker to allow the person to move at a faster pace without having to pick up the walker. A variety of canes exist, from a straight cane to a quad cane, a device that has four feet to broaden the base of support. Crutches, such as wooden axillary crutches, are commonly used. A Lofstrand (forearm) crutch is also commonly used, and sometimes platform crutches are required depending on the person's functional level.

Prosthetic Devices

Prosthetic devices are divided into upper-extremity and lower-extremity devices. A **prosthesis** is a device that is designed to replace a missing extremity or partially missing extremity. Prosthetics are divided into several categories: mechanical prostheses (body-powered prostheses), which are the most common; myoelectric prostheses, which are high tech and use a series of electric motors to replace the missing action; and cosmetic prostheses, which improve appearance for social reasons and are usually less functional than body-powered or myoelectric prostheses. Lower-extremity amputations are much more common than upper-extremity amputations. Amputations are further defined by the level of amputation. A major body joint is used to make this distinction. For example, if the person is missing a portion of the hand and wrist, the amputation is said to be a BE (below-the-elbow) amputation. If the amputation is above the elbow, it is an AE amputation. In the lower extremity, if it is below the knee, it is a BKA (below-the-knee) amputation. Above the knee is an AKA amputation.

A variety of prosthetic devices are available depending on the functional status and age of the patient. Terminology regarding prosthetics is presented in a standardized form. The prosthetic device is described based on the type of suspension, the type of skeleton, the type of joint, and the type of terminal devices. For example, a below-the-knee prosthesis is a PTB (patellar tendon-bearing) socket endoskeleton. The ankle is specified as a multi-axis or single-axis ankle, and the type of foot is a SACH foot, Flex foot, or Seattle foot. Upper-extremity prosthetics terminology is presented in the same fashion. A description of the socket that fits over the amputated extremity, the type of skeleton support (endoskeleton or exoskeleton), the type of joint, and the type of terminal device is used.

Wheelchairs

Many different types and styles of wheelchairs exist. The choice depends on the patient's age, size, and intended use of the device. There are two general categories for wheelchairs: manual wheelchairs and power wheelchairs.

Manual wheelchairs are divided into lightweight sports-type wheelchairs and standard wheelchairs. A number of companies manufacture both; the most common companies are Quickie, InvaCare, and E&J. The lightweight sports-type chairs are used by those who pursue an active lifestyle, whereas the standard chairs are more commonly seen in hospitals and nursing homes and are often used by the elderly population.

Power wheelchairs (they should not be referred to as "electric chairs") and mobility devices are available and manufactured by the same companies that make manual wheelchairs. A variety of configurations are available depending on the functional status of the person. Chairs are available that bring the person to a standing position, lay the person down, or tilt him or her in space if these functions are required. Chairs are also available that have ventilator support. Extremely advanced power wheelchair control systems are now available, such as the Peachtree system, which has a sensory array behind the chair user's head, and movement of the head controls the chair. Looking to the left will make the chair turn left and looking to the right will make it turn right.

High-Technology Assistive Devices

There has been an explosion of computer technology designed to assist the disabled person. **Environmental control units (ECUs)** are now available that allow a person who has limited mobility to run many everyday functions in the home, at work, or at school, such as turning on lights, using appliances, and opening and closing doors and windows. Recently, there have been many devices on the market that allow the disabled person greater access to the computer. Prior to this time, computer technology was limited to individuals who had hand dexterity and could type on a keyboard. Now computers can be run with a variety of switching systems such as an eye-blink switch, an infrared beam that is able to catch a reflex from the eye, head control systems such as Head Master by Ultraphonics, and voice recognition systems such as Dragon NaturallySpeaking®.

Computer systems are available to assist visually impaired people. These devices, such as a Kurzweil reader, are able to scan print and convert it to spoken language. Augmentative communication devices are available to replace speech for individuals who are unable to communicate verbally.

REGULATORY ISSUES

Medical rehabilitation is both medical and rehabilitative in nature. The dual nature of medical rehabilitation has resulted in two independent accreditation options. The Joint Commission and CARF International (Commission for Accreditation of Rehabilitation Facilities) are the nationally recognized voluntary agencies that review care. The Centers for Medicare & Medicaid Services (CMS) regulate rehabilitation for Medicare recipients. The *Code of Federal Regulations* contains Conditions of Participation for hospitals, comprehensive outpatient rehabilitation facilities (CORFs), and clinics and other agencies providing inpatient/outpatient physical therapy and speech-language pathology services. In addition, because inpatient rehabilitation facilities have their own prospective payment system for Medicare, CMS has outlined criteria that an inpatient facility must meet to be classified as a rehabilitation hospital. State licensure agencies generally use these regulations and criteria as basic components in the process of licensing rehabilitation facilities. Other criteria for state licensure may vary from state to state.

The Joint Commission

The Joint Commission (TJC) surveys facilities according to standards that are intended to promote quality and improve outcomes in rehabilitation at all levels of medical care. In order to receive Medicare reimbursement, a facility must have Joint Commission accreditation or otherwise be deemed to meet the Conditions of Participation. The Joint Commission no longer has specific guidelines for rehabilitation facilities or rehabilitation units in an acute care hospital. However, Joint Commission standards have become more "rehabilitation-like," focusing on outcomes and outcome management, and applying to all settings of the inpatient and outpatient areas of patient care.

CARF International

CARF International (formerly Commission on Accreditation of Rehabilitation Facilities) standards and criteria for full accreditation are comprehensive and specific in regard to the rehabilitation care of patients. CARF accreditation is difficult to attain; thus, many rehabilitation centers fail to apply for CARF accreditation. The quality of care in a rehabilitation program, however, is markedly affected by meeting the standards of CARF. In the managed care market, insurance companies seek out CARF-accredited programs to ensure the best patient care.

The standards (Section A) for a comprehensive inpatient rehabilitation program require the medical director to be a physical medicine and rehabilitation physician (physiatrist) or a physician who is qualified by virtue of his or her training and experience in rehabilitation and who is board certified in his or her area of specialty and has the appropriate experience and training necessary to provide rehabilitation physician services through one of the following:

1. Formal residency in physical medicine and rehabilitation
2. A fellowship in rehabilitation for a minimum of one year
3. A minimum of two years of experience in providing rehabilitation services for patients

Accrediting agencies and third-party payers strongly advocate that the medical director of a rehabilitation facility be a board-eligible or board-certified physiatrist. In cases where a physiatrist is not available, then board-eligible or board-certified neurologists or orthopedists may serve.

The rehabilitation physician has the responsibility for the care of the patient who has the potential for continuing, unstable, or complex medical conditions or must make arrangements for the care to be provided through other physicians (consults).

In addition, general inpatient standards may be applied to specific programs in brain injury, spinal cord injury, stroke, and amputation.

Centers for Medicare & Medicaid Services (CMS)

The Centers for Medicare & Medicaid Services (CMS) promulgate regulations affecting several types of rehabilitation providers. There are Conditions of Participation for hospitals (inpatient rehabilitation services), as well as for outpatient services (physical and occupational therapists in independent practice, outpatient physical therapy, occupational therapy, and speech pathology services) and comprehensive outpatient rehabilitation facilities (CORFs).

The 60 Percent Rule

One set of CMS regulations provides criteria that determine whether a hospital or unit can be classified as an inpatient rehabilitation facility. A hospital that meets the criteria can receive Medicare reimbursement under the inpatient rehabilitation facility prospective payment system (IRF PPS) rather than under the diagnosis related group (DRG) system of reimbursement applied to short stay acute care hospitals. One of the criteria, known as the 60 percent rule, defines the types of conditions that should comprise the caseload of a rehabilitation hospital. The original rule, which took effect in 1983, was used to determine whether a hospital or unit was exempt from the DRG-based inpatient prospective payment system and required that certain conditions comprise 75 percent of the caseload for classification as an IRF. After implementation of the IRF PPS in 2002, CMS suspended enforcement of the 75 percent rule in order to evaluate whether changes were needed in the regulation. The study commissioned by CMS showed that the majority of IRFs did not meet the criteria specified in the 75 percent rule. The Medicare, Medicaid, and SCHIP Extension Act of 2007 (MMSEA) established the threshold at 60 percent and allowed secondary conditions to be counted as qualifying conditions. The conditions that count toward the 60 percent are as follows:

(A) Stroke.

(B) Spinal cord injury.

(C) Congenital deformity.

(D) Amputation.

(E) Major multiple trauma.

(F) Fracture of femur (hip fracture).

(G) Brain injury.

(H) Neurologic disorders, including multiple sclerosis, motor neuron diseases, polyneuropathy, muscular dystrophy, and Parkinson's disease.

(I) Burns.

(J) Active, polyarticular rheumatoid arthritis, psoriatic arthritis, and seronegative arthropathies resulting in significant functional impairment of ambulation and other activities of daily living that have not improved after an appropriate, aggressive, and sustained course of outpatient therapy services or services in other less-intensive rehabilitation settings immediately preceding the inpatient rehabilitation admission or that result from a systemic disease activation immediately before admission, but have the potential to improve with more intensive rehabilitation.

(K) Systemic vasculitides with joint inflammation, resulting in significant functional impairment of ambulation and other activities of daily living that have not improved after an appropriate, aggressive, and sustained course of outpatient therapy services or services in other less-intensive rehabilitation settings immediately preceding the inpatient rehabilitation admission or that result from a systemic disease activation immediately before admission, but have the potential to improve with more intensive rehabilitation.

(L) Severe or advanced osteoarthritis (osteoarthrosis or degenerative joint disease) involving two or more major weight-bearing joints (elbow, shoulders, hips, or knees, but not counting a joint with a prosthesis) with joint deformity and substantial loss of range of motion, atrophy of muscles surrounding the joint, significant functional impairment of ambulation and other activities of daily living that have not improved after the patient has participated in an appropriate, aggressive, and sustained course of outpatient therapy services or services in other less-intensive rehabilitation settings immediately preceding the inpatient rehabilitation admission but have the potential to improve with more intensive rehabilitation. (A joint replaced by a prosthesis no longer is considered to have osteoarthritis, or other arthritis, even though this condition was the reason for the joint replacement.)

(M) Knee or hip joint replacement, or both, during an acute hospitalization immediately preceding the inpatient rehabilitation stay and also . . . one or more of the following specific criteria:

(1) The patient underwent bilateral knee or bilateral hip joint replacement surgery during the acute hospital admission immediately preceding the IRF admission.

(2) The patient is extremely obese with a Body Mass Index of at least 50 at the time of admission to the IRF.

(3) The patient is age 85 or older at the time of admission to the IRF. (42 C.F.R. 412.23)

The health information department has an important role to play in ensuring correct coding and data quality so that the percentage of patients falling into the various condition categories can be accurately calculated.

Medical Supervision and Other Services   CMS also requires that patients in an inpatient rehabilitation facility receive "close medical supervision" (Excluded hospitals: Classification, 2009). Other services needed in a rehabilitation hospital are rehabilitation nursing, physical therapy, occupational therapy, speech therapy, social or psychological services, and orthotic and prosthetic services. A qualified physician must serve as full-time director of rehabilitation.

Preadmission Screening   CMS requires that the rehabilitation hospital have a preadmission screening procedure to determine whether a prospective patient is likely to benefit from inpatient rehabilitation. Figure 11-1 is an example of part of a patient database form that collects pertinent functional information about the patient to help define areas of functional deficit and thus assist in goal development. Each inpatient selected for admission must have a plan of treatment established, with an interdisciplinary team approach, and the preadmission screening must be validated by the admitting physician.

Bar Code	PATIENT DATABASE PHYSICAL REHABILITATION UNIT	Patient Sticker

Rehab Problem/Diagnosis _____ Initial Evaluation Date _____ Expected Admit Date _____
Patient Address (City/State) _____ Date of Onset _____

To be completed at preadmit   INFORMANT: ☐ SELF   ☐ OTHER: _____

I. Status Prior to Admission:

How were you doing the following activities at home?	Preadmission*	Current* (prescreening)
1. Grooming (care of hair, teeth, nails, face)		
2. Dressing (shirts, underwear, pants, shoes/socks on/off)		
3. Walking (inside/outside/distance/device)		
4. Cooking (home/out/microwave/self/others)		
5. Bathing (indep/assist, tub/shower, sink/equip)		
6. Toileting (indep/assist, equip)		
7. Housekeeping (indep/services)		
8. Transportation (self/others, where [Dr./store/church/beauty shop])		
9. Animal/pet care (self/others, describe)		
10. Caregiver responsibilities (who/how many/freq./what)		
11. Medication management (equi/self/others)		
12. Business Mgmt (POA/family/self/decision maker)		
13. Swallowing		
14. Bowel/Bladder Management		
15. Communication		
16. Memory Problems		
17. Safety		

* **Key for Indepndence or Assistance scale: I** = 100% independent; **S** = Supervision (requires no more help than standby cueing or coaxing); **Min** = expends 75% or more of the effort; **Mod** = expends 50–75% of the effort; **Max** = expends 25–50% of the effort; **D** = dependent, expends less than 25% of the effort

II. Description of Home: ____ house ____ apartment ____ trailer ____ retirement home ____ nursing home

Number of floors	Stairs inside home? ___ Yes ___ No How many? ___	Steps to gain access to home? ___ Yes ___ No	Number	Floors carpeted? ___Yes ___ No	Which rooms?
Are hallways carpeted? ___ Yes ___ No	Type of carpet ___ Low ___ Medium ___ High ___ Shag			Are there throw rugs or area rugs? ___ Yes ___ No	

Comments: _____
_____

_____
recorder signature   date

FIGURE 11-1 An excerpt from a patient database that covers all CARF criteria. This form promotes interdisciplinary assessment of the patient.

| Bar Code | PATIENT DATABASE PHYSICAL REHABILITATION UNIT | Patient Sticker |

III. **TO BE COMPLETED AT PRESCREENING:** **INFORMANT:** ☐ **SELF** ☐ **OTHER:** _____

1. Do you live alone? ____ Yes ____ No   With whom?: _____

2. Expected assistance and/or limitation from person living with you: _____
_____

3. Expected assistance from persons outside your home: _____
_____

4. Who will perform the following activities?
   a. Meal Preparation _____
   b. Cleaning/Washing dishes _____
   c. Heavy Housework (scrubbing, floors, cleaning bathrooms, washing laundry, ironing, yard work, etc.)
   _____
   d. Light housework (dusting, folding/putting clothes away, etc.) _____
   e. Shopping _____
   f. Child care _____
   g. Driving _____
   h. Other areas of concern: (farming, etc.) _____

5. What was/is your occupation? _____
   a. How long have you been there? _____
   b. What do you do? _____
   c. Is it full or part time? _____
   d. Is it days or nights? _____

6. Referral Source _____ Episode _____ Patient/Family Tour: Date _____
   Referring Physician _____ Other Acute Care Physician(s) _____
   _____

   Program: Evaluation   Limited Services   Comprehensive
   Services Requested: PT / OT / SP / PSY / NPSY / REC / RN / NUT / MSW / PM
   ELOS: _____ Patient Goals: _____
   Trauma: Yes   No   Recommendations: _____ Date _____

IV. Did you have any in-home or community services assisting you before this hospitalization?

_____
_____

_____
recorder signature   date

FIGURE **11-1** (*Continued*)

Bar Code	PATIENT DATABASE PHYSICAL REHABILITATION UNIT	Patient Sticker

III. TO BE COMPLETED WITHIN 2 HOURS OF ADMISSION TO REHAB UNIT:

INFORMANT: ☐ SELF ☐ OTHER: _____

V. Medical Database

Admission Time: _____ Informant: _____ Relationship (if not patient): _____

Family Physician: _____ Person to be contacted in case of emergency: _____

Relationship: _____ Phone: day (____) _____ night: (____) _____

ADMISSION VITAL SIGNS: T____ P____ R____ BP____ L R Height ____ Weight ____ kg lb. Type scale____

Reason for admission: (patient's own words) _____

_____

List and give dates of pertinent surgeries, senous illnesses or injuries, depression/emotional problems:

_____

_____

Cardiovascular: _____

Endocrine: _____

Renal: _____

Respiratory: _____

Flu/Pneumonia immunizations up to date? ____Yes ____No

Have you ever had a blood transfusion? ____Yes ____No   Reaction: ____Yes ____No

Describe: _____

Medications brought to hospital

____Yes ____No

Disposition of medications:

____ Home ____ Pharmacy ____ Bedside

ALLERGIES: (meds, foods, skin, resp, etc.):

____ None   ____ Allergy band

List Allergy and reaction: ____

_____

_____

_____

_____

LATEX ALLERGY SCREEN:

____ History of multiple catheterizations

____ Occupational exposure to latex

____ Allery to kiwi, avocado, banana, potato

List Medications: Pills, Patches, Inhaler, O2, etc. ( ) NONE ( ) Unavailable	Dose & how taken: P.O., Injected, Inhaled	Time of last dose

VI. Medical History:

a. How has your overall health been in the past year? _____

b. What pharmacy do you use? _____

c. Do you take your medicines as prescribed? _____

d. Do you utilize anything to help organize your medications (pill organizer)? _____

e. Do you have a family doctor that follows your care? _____

f. Do you use alcohol? Yes ____ No ____   Intake (daily/weekly) _____ Ouit _____

g. Do you use tobacco? Yes ____ No ____   Type _____

   # years _____ Quit? Yes ____ No ____ When? _____

h. Do you use street drugs? Yes ____ No ____ Type _____ Amt./Freq. _____

i. Do you wear glasses/contacts? Yes ____ No ____   For Distance _____ For Reading _____

j. Do you have visual problems not treated by glasses? _____

k. Do you have a hearing aid? _____   Do you wear your hearing aid? _____

l. Do you have any cultural or spiritual beliefs that we need to be aware of that would affect your care? _____

FIGURE **11-1** (*Continued*)

Bar Code

**PATIENT DATABASE
PHYSICAL REHABILITATION UNIT**

Patient Sticker

m. How long has it been since your vision/hearing has been tested? _____

n. Who do you see for your eye exams? _____ hearing exams _____

o. Do you wear dentures? _____

P. Do you have chewing problems? _____

Communicable Disease Screening: Recent exposure to infectious disease?   _____Yes _____No

   MRSA: (Check those that apply)

     _____ Known MRSA positive   _____ Has open wound

     _____ from nursing home or other hospital   _____ IV drug user

     _____ hospitalized or on antibiotic therapy for 14 days or more within 30 days

If "yes" on any of above MRSA questions, please culture according to policy for MRSA screening.

CULTURE: Date: _____ Time: _____ Site: _____

TB: (Check those that apply)   **Hepatitis A:**   (Check those that apply)

Family member with TB?   _____Yes   _____ No   Family member with Hep A?   _____Yes _____ No

Exposed to anyone with TB?   _____Yes   _____ No   Exposed to anyone with Hep A? _____Yes _____ No

Positive skin test?   _____Yes   _____ No

VII. General Nutrition/Swallowing Screen

a. What type of diet are you on?. _____

b. Do you follow your special diet recommendation? _____

c. Prescribed snacks: _____

d. Recent weight change: _____ Loss _____ Gain _____pounds over _____weeks/months

e. Reason for weight change: _____

f. Do you take any vitamins or minerals?   Yes _____ No _____

g. Swallowing Screen: _____ Normal _____ See "Dysphagia Consult" Protocol, #s 1, 2, 6, 9,12

h. Patient currently on swallowing program?   Yes _____ No _____

VII. Elimination

IX. Sleep/Rest Patterns: (Ask patient to describe sleeping pattern/problems and check/complete those that apply.)

No difficulty _____   Hours per night _____   Naps _____   Sleep aids _____

History of insomnia _____   Norma sleep time frame _____

History of orthopnea _____   Sleep apnea _____   Number of pillows _____

Comments: _____

What time do you go to bed? _____   Time you get up? _____

Do you get up in the night? _____   Reason? _____

Do you take a nan during the day? _____   What time? _____

X. Integumentary Status:

Mark drawing with appropriate
letter at exact location:

A - Amputation   L - Laceration

B - Burn   O - Ostomy

BR - Bruise   P - pressure

D - Dry patches   R - Rash

DS - Dressing   S - scar

I - Incision   W- Wound

Stages of breakdown:

O - potential

1 - Reddened

2 - Disruption/Ulceration

3 - Complete destruction of skin
   layers (exposed fat, muscle, bone)

4 - Invasion by ulceration of bone
   structure

Front   Back

Other Comments/descriptions:

_____
_____
_____
_____
_____
_____
_____

If stage 1 or greater, pull skin care flow
sheet and take a picture.

Circumference Measurements:

Thigh (18 cm above patella)

   Left _____ Right _____

Calf (13 cm below patellar tendon)

   Left _____ Right _____

FIGURE **11-1** (*Continued*)

Bar Code	PATIENT DATABASE PHYSICAL REHABILITATION UNIT	Patient Sticker

PAIN ASSESSMENT: Document history of pain and associated symptoms. Make current pain assessment on the Patient Care Record.

_____

_____

_____

_____

XI. Health Care Directive:

It is mandated by law that we ask, "Do you have an Advance Directive or Durable Power of Attorney for health care?"

_____Yes _____No

If "yes," we need a copy for the chart. If "no" is checked, information was given regarding Self-Determination Act. _____Yes

RN Signature _____ **Date** _____ **Time** _____

To be completed within 2 to 24 hours of admission to Rehab unit:

INFORMANT: ☐SELF ☐OTHER:

XII. Description of Home:

Description of Bedroom:

Is there room for walker to maneuver? _____Yes _____NO	Explain:
Is there room for commode seat, dressing chair? _____Yes _____NO	Explain:
Description of bed: _____ High ____ Low ____ Single ____ Double ____ Waterbed	S.O. sleep in same room? _____Yes _____No
Other areas of concern:	

Description of Bathroom:

Do you have?: ____Tub ____ Walk-in shower (no threshold) ____ Shower stall ____ Tub/shower combo ____ Grab bars		
Do you have glass doors or a curtain? _____Glass doors _____Curtain	Do you prefer to take: _____ shower _____bath	Do you have handheld shower attachment? _____Yes _____No
Is bathroom on the same floor as bedroom? _____Yes _____No	Is toilet standard height? _____Yes _____No	Comment:
Is there a supported sink or tub adjacent to toilet? _____Yes _____No	If so, can the supported sink/tub be used for getting on/off the toilet? _____Yes _____No	
Is there room for a walker or wheelchair to maneuver to toilet? _____Yes _____No	Do you have a non-slip surface in the tub/shower? _____Yes _____No	How wide is the bathroom door?_____
Do you have any other equipment for the bathroom? Explain:	Other areas of concern:	

Where are your phones located? _____

Do you have a portable phone? _____Yes _____No

Do you have: _____ Rotary _____ Touch-tone _____ Memory redial

Do you have lifeline? _____Yes _____No

Describe the chair or couch you usually sit in: _____ Straight chair _____ Recliner _____Couch

Occupational Therapist Signature _____ **Date** _____

FIGURE **11-1** (Continued)

Bar Code	**PATIENT DATABASE** **PHYSICAL REHABILITATION UNIT**	Patient Sticker

DISCHARGE PLANNING

XIII. Emotional/Social:

1. Which family members do you see most frequently? _____
2. How often do you see them? _____
3. What activities do you do with your family? _____
4. Does your spouse/significant other/family work? _____
   a. What do they do? _____
   b. Is it full time or part time? _____
   c. Is it days or nights? _____
5. Have you had recent episodes of depression or anxiety that persist for more than a few days? _____
6. Have you required services of a mental health professional (psychologist/psychiatrist)? _____
   If so, for what? _____
7. What medications have you taken for emotional or psychiatric problems? _____
   For what purpose? For how long? _____
8. Do you have to have things "just so" or in perfect order? _____
9. Would you describe yourself as easygoing, quick tempered, high strung, or happy-go-lucky? _____
10. Have you had any major stressors in your life in the past year? _____

11. How do you handle stress? _____
_____

To be completed within **24–72** hours of admission to Rehab unit:

INFORMANT: ☐ SELF ☐ OTHER: _____

XIV. Financial/Community Resources

a. Who manages your financial affairs at home? _____
b. If it is you, is there someone who could assist you if needed? _____
c. Have you had financial issues in the past in regards to health care? _____
d. Purchasing medications _____   Purchasing equipment _____
e. What is your understanding of how Medicare/private insurance pays for your hospital rehab stay? _____

XV. Social History

1. Education
   a. What is the highest grade you completed in school? _____
   b. Did you like school? _____
   c. How well did you do in school? _____
   d. Do you have difficulties reading or writing? _____
2. Family
   a. ____ Married   ____ Single   ____ Widowed   ____ Divorced   ____ Previous marriage
   b. Do you have children? ____ Yes ____ No   Any children living in your home? ____ Yes (How many? ____)
      ____ No

XVI. Hobbies/Leisure Activities

a. What do you do for fun? _____
b. List your three favorite things to do _____
   1. _____
   2. _____
   3. _____
c. Who do you spend recreational time with? _____
d. Do you ____ travel   ____ fish   ____ garden   ____ woodwork
   ____ sports   ____ eat out   ____ other
e. Do you enjoy?: ____ church activities   ____ crafts   list types: _____
   ____ television   ____ cards/games   other: _____

Social Worker Signature _____   **Date** _____

FIGURE **11-1** (*Continued*)

DOCUMENTATION

As in all health care facilities, there are specific guidelines regarding the documentation that must be completed in a patient's medical records. It is not the purpose of this chapter to cover this topic in its entirety; refer to other chapters in this text for basic medical record documentation guidelines. This chapter focuses on additional or specific documentation requirements in the rehabilitation facility as it applies to specific sections of the records.

The admission history and physical includes a functional history. The functional history should cover the patient's functional status before the onset of the illness or injury. If the person had a preexisting disability and is now returning to rehabilitation because of a change in condition, then a discussion of the patient's functional status before the onset of the new illness or change is required. The functional history addresses activities of daily living, required assisted devices, reliance on other caregivers, and a discussion of community mobility.

The history also includes a discussion of equipment that the person has at home. A full description of braces, orthoses, prosthetics, or durable medical equipment is required. Also included is a description of the type of vehicle the individual has, because this will affect in many ways the type of wheelchair that can be prescribed for the patient.

The social history must include a discussion of available family members or caregivers, a description of the home (i.e., multilevel, single level, number of steps at entrance, accessibility of bathroom, etc.), educational status, employment status, and previous hobbies, in addition to standard social history information such as alcohol and drug abuse.

The physical examination includes a comprehensive neurologic and musculoskeletal exam, adequate documentation of the condition of the skin, and a description of interventional devices such as a catheter, feeding tube, or tracheostomy. The neurologic exam includes cranial nerves, motor strength, reflexes, and sensory nerves. It also includes a mention of the patient's cognitive, speech, and language capabilities. The examination must clearly describe the functional status of the individual both cognitively and physically. The musculoskeletal exam should document the range of motion of all joints and extremities, note contractures, amputations, or missing body parts, and indicate the presence or absence of complications such as deep vein thrombosis or heterotopic ossification.

The physiatric history and physical diagnosis section includes standard medical diagnoses as well as functional rehabilitation diagnoses. For example, a spinal cord-injured patient's admission diagnoses may be (1) T9 spinal cord injury, (2) decreased strength and endurance, and (3) dependence for ADL activities. Stating the functional limitations or problems in the diagnostic sections helps focus the rehabilitation team on the primary issue of concern that has led to the rehabilitation treatment.

The history and physical also includes a specific discussion of goals as they relate to the interdisciplinary team. For example, a physician notes that occupational therapy is to focus on dressing, bathing, grooming, and equipment needs or that physical therapy is to address decreased strength, transfer skills, balance, and range of motion. The plan section is specific and outlines the goals in quantitative terms for the entire rehabilitation team. The plan is concluded with a statement of the estimated length of stay for the hospitalization.

In summary, the history and physical by the physician should provide identification of presenting problems, goals and expected benefits, initial estimated time frames for accomplishing goals, and services needed. The individual's pathological diagnosis, impairment, and functional limitations must be thoroughly discussed in the physician history and physical. This serves as basis for the initial plan of care for the interdisciplinary team to follow. With regard to team conferences, in general, the physician documents in each of the areas of concern the comments that the interdisciplinary team makes regarding the patient's progress. In addition, the team conference sets goals to be accomplished in the rehabilitation stay.

Federal regulations outlining coverage criteria include requirements for information that must be documented regarding the type and frequency of services that are received by the patient, documentation of the preadmission screening, a post-admission physician evaluation, and an individualized overall plan of care, including weekly team meetings, as follows:

42 CFR § 412.622 Basis of payment.

(a) *Method of payment . . .*

(3) *IRF coverage criteria.* In order for an IRF claim to be considered reasonable and necessary under section 1862(a)(1) of the Act, there must be a reasonable expectation that the patient meets all of the following requirements at the time of the patient's admission to the IRF—

    (i) Requires the active and ongoing therapeutic intervention of multiple therapy disciplines (physical therapy, occupational therapy, speech-language pathology, or prosthetics/orthotics therapy), one of which must be physical or occupational therapy.

    (ii) Generally requires and can reasonably be expected to actively participate in, and benefit from, an intensive rehabilitation therapy program. Under current industry standards, this intensive rehabilitation therapy program generally consists of at least 3 hours of therapy (physical therapy, occupational therapy, speech-language pathology, or prosthetics/orthotics therapy) per day at least 5 days per week. In certain well-documented cases, this intensive rehabilitation therapy program might instead consist of at least 15 hours of intensive rehabilitation therapy within a 7 consecutive day period, beginning with the date of admission to the IRF. Benefit from this intensive rehabilitation therapy program is demonstrated by measurable improvement that will be of practical value to the patient in improving the patient's functional capacity or adaptation to impairments. The required therapy treatments must begin within 36 hours from midnight of the day of admission to the IRF.

      (iii) Is sufficiently stable at the time of admission to the IRF to be able to actively participate in the intensive rehabilitation therapy program that is described in paragraph (a)(3)(ii) of this section.

      (iv) Requires physician supervision by a rehabilitation physician, defined as a licensed physician with specialized training and experience in inpatient rehabilitation. The requirement for medical supervision means that the rehabilitation physician must conduct face-to-face visits with the patient at least 3 days per week throughout the patient's stay in the IRF to assess the patient both medically and functionally, as well as to modify the course of treatment as needed to maximize the patient's capacity to benefit from the rehabilitation process.

(4) *Documentation.* To document that each patient for whom the IRF seeks payment is reasonably expected to meet all of the requirements in paragraph (a)(3) of this section at the time of admission, the patient's medical record at the IRF must contain the following documentation—

    (i) A comprehensive preadmission screening that meets all of the following requirements—

      (A) It is conducted by a licensed or certified clinician(s) designated by a rehabilitation physician described in paragraph (a)(3)(iv) of this section within the 48 hours immediately preceding the IRF admission. A preadmission screening that includes all of the required elements, but that is conducted more than 48 hours immediately preceding the IRF admission, will be accepted as long as an update is conducted in person or by telephone to update the patient's medical and functional status within the 48 hours immediately preceding the IRF admission and is documented in the patient's medical record.

      (B) It includes a detailed and comprehensive review of each patient's condition and medical history.

      (C) It serves as the basis for the initial determination of whether or not the patient meets the requirements for an IRF admission to be considered reasonable and necessary in paragraph (a)(3) of this section.

      (D) It is used to inform a rehabilitation physician who reviews and documents his or her concurrence with the findings and results of the preadmission screening.

      (E) It is retained in the patient's medical record at the IRF.

    (ii) A post-admission physician evaluation that meets all of the following requirements—

      (A) It is completed by a rehabilitation physician within 24 hours of the patient's admission to the IRF.

      (B) It documents the patient's status on admission to the IRF, includes a comparison with the information noted in the preadmission screening documentation, and serves as the basis for the development of the overall individualized plan of care.

      (C) It is retained in the patient's medical record at the IRF.

    (iii) An individualized overall plan of care for the patient that meets all of the following requirements—

        (A) It is developed by a rehabilitation physician, as defined in paragraph (a)(3)(iv) of this section, with input from the interdisciplinary team within 4 days of the patient's admission to the IRF.

        (B) It is retained in the patient's medical record at the IRF.

  (5) *Interdisciplinary team approach to care.* In order for an IRF claim to be considered reasonable and necessary under section 1862(a)(1) of the Act, the patient must require an interdisciplinary team approach to care, as evidenced by documentation in the patient's medical record of weekly interdisciplinary team meetings that meet all of the following requirements—

    (A) The team meetings are led by a rehabilitation physician as defined in paragraph (a)(3)(iv) of this section, and further consist of a registered nurse with specialized training or experience in rehabilitation; a social worker or case manager (or both); and a licensed or certified therapist from each therapy discipline involved in treating the patient. All team members must have current knowledge of the patient's medical and functional status.

    (B) The team meetings occur at least once per week throughout the duration of the patient's stay to implement appropriate treatment services; review the patient's progress toward stated rehabilitation goals; identify any problems that could impede progress towards those goals; and, where necessary, reassess previously established goals in light of impediments, revise the treatment plan in light of new goals, and monitor continued progress toward those goals.

    (C) The results and findings of the team meetings, and the concurrence by the rehabilitation physician with those results and findings, are retained in the patient's medical record.

The physical therapist and occupational therapist as well as other disciplines are required to document daily notes regarding their treatment, interactions with the patient, and the results. This documentation should be made in functional terms and be clearly related to the specific goals identified for the hospitalization. The number of hours the patient has actually participated in therapy should be clearly indicated in the therapist's documentation.

Nursing documentation includes information about the patient's skin status; bowel and bladder status; knowledge of medications, uses, and side effects; information regarding the patient's functional status in terms of self-care and skin care; and documentation of the patient's knowledge regarding common complications given the disability.

At the conclusion of hospitalization, the discharge summary includes a discussion in quantifiable terms of the patient's functional status at the time of admission and his or her functional status at the time of discharge, and should reflect the patient's progress or lack of progress. Recommendations regarding equipment needs or home support services are specifically addressed in the discharge summary.

The discharge recommendations and a discharge conference should be held with the patient and/or responsible family members. The discharge summary and recommendations should contain specific warnings or limitations for the patient. Safety issues and other concerns should be discussed, such as driving, preparing meals, and the need for attendant care.

CARF-accredited facilities are required to have a set of policies that clearly address how the rehabilitation patient may gain access to his or her own records. In addition, there must be documentation that the patient has been provided with orientation to the rehabilitation facility, which includes a statement of the organization's mission and philosophy, participation in goal setting, and a patient's rights and responsibilities list.

CARF further requires that individual program planning be performed and documented. The plans must be individualized, establish the goals and objectives for the admission, and incorporate the unique strengths, needs, abilities, and preferences of the person served. There must be documentation that the patient understands the goals, and this must reflect the person's informed choice.

Functions of the interdisciplinary team that must be documented in the record include (1) the assessment of the person served; (2) determination, modification, and implementation of the individual plan and the discharge plan of the person served; (3) provision of direct services consistent with needs; (4) active participation in care planning of the person served; and (5) promotion of interdisciplinary functions and mutual support among all members of the team. Medical records systems can be established in such a way as to meet these requirements and minimize the number and types of forms required. Examples are provided later in the chapter.

The rehabilitation assessment must document (1) the needs of the person from a rehabilitation perspective; (2) desired outcomes and expectations of the patient; (3) outcomes anticipated by the interdisciplinary team; (4) the use of assistive technology as needed; and (5) the use of assessment findings to direct the development of the individual's plan.

REIMBURSEMENT AND FUNDING

Equitable reimbursement for rehabilitation cannot be made on the basis of diagnosis related groups (DRGs), because many factors other than those considered by the DRG system determine the patient's functional level and thus the recovery of the patient. In other words, two patients with an identical diagnosis can have different functional problems and handicaps based on a host of factors. (Recall the previous discussion of the definitions of *impairment, disability,* and *handicap.*) These factors include age, weight, gender, comorbidities, psychological factors, premorbid personality, educational status, and occupation, to name a few. Implemented in January 2002, the Medicare inpatient rehabilitation facility prospective payment system (IRF PPS) does consider more than the patient's diagnoses and procedures, but it does not take into account every factor that affects the patient's recovery.

Under the IRF PPS, a rehabilitation hospital is reimbursed for each patient admission. Patient stays are classified into **case-mix groups (CMGs)**, which determine the payment the facility will receive from Medicare. The factors that influence the assignment of a case into a particular CMG include rehabilitation impairment categories (RICs), functional measurements, age, and comorbidities. Diagnosis codes determine the RICs, which group cases that are similar in clinical characteristics and resource use. Functional measures that influence CMG assignment are motor and cognitive scores. Some CMG categories also consider the patient's age. Finally, comorbidities, or secondary diagnoses, affect CMG assignment and are classified into three categories, or tiers, based on whether the costs are considered high, medium, or low. Most of the CMGs are subject to four relative weights—the three that reflect the comorbidity tiers and one for patients with no comorbidities. Comorbidity tiers do not apply to the CMG for patients discharged before the fourth day (short-stay outliers) or to the CMGs for the relatively unusual cases in which patients expire in a rehabilitation facility. The IRF PPS has increased emphasis on *ICD-9-CM* coding (*ICD-10-CM* after 10/1/13); this is because the CMG payment is influenced by RICs, which correspond to certain categories of codes, and also by comorbidities, which are reported directly as diagnosis codes.

In addition, a length of stay is assigned to each CMG under the payment system. Providers know that these lengths of stay are merely averages, and many patients have longer or shorter lengths of stay than the time outlined in the regulations. However, CMGs have required rehabilitation hospitals to give attention to the length of time it takes to treat patients. See Figure 11-2 for an excerpt from the CMG table demonstrating the assignment of relative weights and average lengths of stay for selected CMGs (CMS, 2009).

The CMG assignment is based on information recorded on the patient assessment tool, the **Inpatient Rehabilitation Facility Patient Assessment Instrument (IRF-PAI)** (see Figure 11-3). This tool captures all of the information necessary to assign a CMG, including codes for up to 10 comorbidities. The IRF-PAI must be completed upon the patient's admission and again at discharge, with the admission and discharge data transmitted together after the patient has been discharged. The data from the IRF-PAI must be **encoded** (i.e., entered into a specified computer program) before transmission. CMS has published an assessment schedule in the IRF PPS rule that specifies dates by which the admission and discharge assessments must be performed, encoded, and transmitted. There is a 25 percent penalty deducted from the IRF PPS payment for data transmitted more than 10 calendar days late. For example, IRF-PAI data must be transmitted within 17 calendar days of discharge; therefore, an IRF-PAI transmission 28 days after discharge would result in a penalty (CMS, 2005).

CMG	CMG Description	(M=motor, C=cognitive, A=age)	Relative Weight				Average Length of Stay			
			Tier 1	Tier 2	Tier 3	None	Tier 1	Tier 2	Tier 3	None
101	Stroke	M>51.05	0.8035	0.7197	0.6454	0.6096	10	10	9	8
102	Stroke	M>44.45 and M<51.05 and C>18.5	0.9917	0.8883	0.7966	0.7524	12	12	11	10
103	Stroke	M>44.45 and M<51.05 and C<18.5	1.1439	1.0245	0.9188	0.8678	13	14	12	12
104	Stroke	M>38.85 and M<44.45	1.2393	1.11	0.9954	0.9402	15	15	13	12
105	Stroke	M>34.25 and M<38.85	1.4613	1.3088	1.1737	1.1086	15	15	15	14
106	Stroke	M>30.05 and M<34.25	1.6711	1.4968	1.3422	1.2678	20	19	17	16
107	Stroke	M>26.15 and M<30.05	1.8917	1.6943	1.5193	1.4351	21	21	18	18
108	Stroke	M<26.15 and A>84.5	2.2976	2.0579	1.8454	1.7431	28	24	22	22
109	Stroke	M>22.35 and M<26.15 and A<84.5	2.2017	1.9719	1.7683	1.6703	23	23	20	21
110	Stroke	M<22.35 and A<84.5	2.7847	2.4941	2.2366	2.1126	35	29	26	25
201	Traumatic brain injury	M>53.35 and C>23.5	0.7712	0.6244	0.5824	0.5226	10	10	7	8
202	Traumatic brain injury	M>44.25 and M<53.35 and C>23.5	1.0413	0.843	0.7864	0.7056	14	13	10	10
203	Traumatic brain injury	T M>44.25 and C<23.5	1.1997	0.9713	0.906	0.813	16	14	11	11
204	Traumatic brain injury	M>40.65 and M<44.25	1.3484	1.0917	1.0183	0.9138	18	16	14	12
205	Traumatic brain injury	M>28.75 and M<40.65	1.6052	1.2996	1.2122	1.0878	18	16	15	14
206	Traumatic brain injury	M>22.05 and M<28.75	2.0205	1.6359	1.5259	1.3692	24	20	18	18
207	Traumatic brain injury	M<22.05	2.7619	2.2361	2.0858	1.8716	37	29	26	22

FIGURE **11-2** Examples of relative weights for case-mix groups (CMGs).
Source: CMS.

INPATIENT REHABILITATION FACILITY — PATIENT ASSESSMENT INSTRUMENT

Identification Information*

1. Facility Information
   A. Facility Name
   _____
   _____
   _____

   B. Facility Medicare
      Provider Number _____

2. Patient Medicare Number _____

3. Patient Medicaid Numbe _____

4. Patient First Name _____

5A. Patient Last Name _____

5B. Patient Identification Number _____

6. Birth Date
   _____ / _____ / _____
   MM   DD   YYYY

7. Social Security Number _____

8. Gender (1 - Male; 2- Female) _____

9. Race/Ethnicity (Check all that apply)
   American Indian or Alaska Native   A. _____
   Asian   B. _____
   Black or African American   C. _____
   Hispanic or Latino   D. _____
   Native Hawaiian or Other Pacific Islander   E. _____
   White   F. _____

10. Marital Status _____
    (1 - Never Married; 2- Married; 3 - Widowed;
    4 - Separated; 5 - Divorced)

11. Zip Code of Patients Pre-Hospital Residence _____

Admission Information*

12. Admission Date
    _____ / _____ / _____
    MM   DD   YYYY

13. Assessment Reference Date
    _____ / _____ / _____
    MM   DD   YYYY

14. Admission Class _____
    (1 - Initial Rehab; 2 - Evaluation; 3- Readmission;
    4 - Unplanned Discharge; 5 - Continuing Rehabilitation)

15. Admit From _____
    (01 - Home; 02 - Board & Care; 03 - Transitional Living;
    04 - Intermediate Care; 05 - Skilled Nursing Facility;
    06 - Acute Unit of Own Facility; 07- Acute Unit of Another
    Facility; 08- Chronic Hospital; 09 - Rehabilitation Facility;
    10 - Other; 12 - Alternate Level of Care Unit; 13 — Subacute
    Setting; 14 - Assisted Living Residence)

16. Pre-Hospital Living Setting _____
    (Use codes from item 15 above)

17. Pre-Hospital Living With _____
    (Code only if item 16 is 01 - Home;
    Code using 1 - Alone; 2 - Family/Relatives;
    3- Friends; 4 - Attendant; 5 - Other)

18. Pre-Hospital Vocational Category _____
    (1 - Employed; 2- Sheltered; 3- Student;
    4 - Homemaker; 5- Not Working; 6- Retired for
    Age; 7- Retired for Disability)

19. Pre-Hospital Vocational Effort _____
    (Code only if item 18 is coded 1 - 4; Code using
    1 - Full-time; 2-Part-time; 3-Adjusted Workload)

Payer Information*

20. Payment Source
    A. Primary Source _____

    B. Secondary Source _____
    (01 - Blue Cross; 02 - Medicare non-MCO;
    03 - Medicaid non-MCO; 04 - Commercial Insurance;
    05 - MCO HMO; 06 - Workers' Compensation;
    07- Crippled Children's Services; 08— Developmental
    Disabilities Services; 09 - State Vocational Rehabilitation;
    10 - Private Pay; 11 - Employee Courtesy;
    12- Unreimbursed; 13- CHAMPUS; 14 - Other;
    15- None; 16— No-Fault Auto Insurance;
    51 — Medicare MCO; 52 - Medicaid MCO)

Medical Information*

21. Impairment Group _____ _____
    Admission   Discharge
    Condition requiring admission to rehabilitation; code
    according to Appendix A, attached.

22. Etiologic Diagnosis _____
    (Use an ICD-9-CM code to indicate the etiologic problem
    that led to the condition for which the patient is receiving
    rehabilitation)

23. Date of Onset of Impairment
    _____ / _____ / _____
    MM   DD   YYYY

24. Comorbid Conditions; Use ICD-9-CM codes to enter up to
    ten medical conditions

    A. _____   B. _____
    C. _____   D. _____
    E. _____   F. _____
    G. _____   H. _____
    I. _____   J. _____

Medical Needs

25. Is patient comatose at admission? _____
    0 - No; 1 - Yes

26. Is patient delirious at admission? _____
    0 - No; 1 - Yes

27. Swallowing Status _____ _____
    Admission   Discharge

    3 - _Regular Food_: soilds and liquids swaiowed safely
        without supervision or modified food consistency
    2- _Modified Food Consistency/Supervision_: subject
        requires modified food consistency and/or needs
        supervision for safety
    1- _Tube /Parenteral Feeding_: tube/parenteral feeding
        used wholiy or partially as a means of sustenance

28. Clinical signs of dehydration _____ _____
    Admission   Discharge

    (Code 0 — No; 1 — Yes) e.g., _evidence of oliguria, dry
    skin, orthostatic hypotension, somnolence, agitation_

*The EIM data set, measurement scale and impairment codes
incorporated or referenced herein are the property of U B
Foundation Activities, Inc. ©1993, 2001 U B Foundation Activities,
Inc. The FIM mark is owned by UBFA. Inc.

FIGURE **11-3** Inpatient Rehabilitation Facility Patient Assessment Instrument (IRF-PAI). The FIM data set, measurement scale and impairment codes incorporated or referenced herein are the property of UB Foundation Activities, Inc. © 1993, 2001 UB Foundation Activities, Inc. The FIM mark is owned by UBFA, Inc. Used with permission.

Source: Centers for Medicare & Medicaid Services.

INPATIENT REHABILITATION FACILITY — PATIENT ASSESSMENT INSTRUMENT

Function Modifiers*

Complete the following specific functional items prior to scoring the FIM™ Instrument:

	ADMISSION	DISCHARGE
29. Bladder Level of Assistance (Score using FIM Levels I - 7)	☐	☐
30. Bladder Frequency of Accidents (Score as below)	☐	☐

7 - No accidents
6 - No accidents; uses device such as a catheter
5 - One accident in the past 7 days
4 - Two accidents in the past 7 days
3 - Three accidents in the past 7 days
2 - Four accidents in the past 7 days
1 - Five or more accidents in the past 7 days

Enter in Item 39G (Bladder) the lower (more dependent) score from Items 29 and 30 above.

	ADMISSION	DISCHARGE
31. Bowel Level of Assistance (Score using EIM Levels 1 - 7)	☐	☐
32. Bowel Frequency of Accidents (Score as below)	☐	☐

7 - No accidents
6 - No accidents; uses device such as an ostomy
5 - One accident in the past 7 days
4 - Two accidents in the past 7 days
3 - Three accidents in the past 7 days
2 - Four accidents in the past 7 days
1 - Five or more accidents in the past 7 days

Enter in Item 39H (Bowel) the lower (more dependent) score of Items 31 and 32 above.

	ADMISSION	DISCHARGE
33. Tub Transfer	☐	☐
34. Shower Transfer	☐	☐

(Score Items 33 and 34 using EIM Levels 1 - 7; use 0 if activity does not occur) See training manual for scoring of Item 39K (Tub/Shower Transfer)

	ADMISSION	DISCHARGE
35. Distance Walked	☐	☐
36. Distance Traveled in Wheelchair	☐	☐

(Code items 35 and 36 using: 3- 150 feet; 2-50 to 149 feet; 1 - Less than 50 feet; 0— activity does not occur)

	ADMISSION	DISCHARGE
37. Walk	☐	☐
38. Wheelchair	☐	☐

(Score Items 37 and 38 using FIM Levels 1 - 7; 0 if activity does not occur) See training manual for scoring of Item 39L (Walk/Wheelchair)

*The FIM data set, measurement scale and impairment codes incorporated or referenced herein are the property of U B Foundation Activities, Inc. ©1993, 2001 U B Foundation Activities, Inc. The FIM mark is owned by UBFA. Inc.

39. FIM™ Instrument*

	ADMISSION	DISCHARGE	GOAL
SELF-CARE			
A. Eating	☐	☐	☐
B. Grooming	☐	☐	☐
C. Bathing			
D. Dressing - Upper	☐	☐	☐
E. Dressing - Lower	☐	☐	☐
F. Toileting	☐	☐	☐
SPHINCTER CONTROL			
G. Bladder	☐	☐	☐
H. Bowel			
TRANSFERS			
I. Bed, Chair, Whlchair	☐	☐	☐
J. Toilet	☐	☐	☐
K. Tub, Shower	☐	☐	☐

LOCOMOTION

W-Walk
C-wheelChair
B-Both

	ADMISSION	DISCHARGE	GOAL
L. Walk/Wheelchair	☐	☐	☐
M. Stairs	☐	☐	☐

COMMUNICATION

A - Auditory
V - Visual
B - Both

	ADMISSION	DISCHARGE	GOAL
N. Comprehension	☐	☐	☐
O. Expression	☐	☐	☐

V - Vocal
N - Nonvoca
B - Both

SOCIAL COGNITION

	ADMISSION	DISCHARGE	GOAL
P. Social Interaction	☐	☐	☐
Q. Problem Solving			
R. Memory	☐	☐	☐

FIM LEVELS

No Helper
7 Complete Independence (Timely, Safely)

6 Modified Independence (Device)

Helper - Modified Dependence
5 Supervision (Subject = 100%)

4 Minimal Assistance (Subject = 75% or more)

3 Moderate Assistance (Subject = 50% or more)

Helper - Complete Dependence
2 Maximal Assistance (Subject = 25% or more)

1 Total Assistance (Subject less than 25%)

0 Activity does not occur; Use this code only at admission

FIGURE **11-3** (*Continued*)

INPATIENT REHABILITATION FACILITY — PATIENT ASSESSMENT INSTRUMENT

Discharge Information*

40. Discharge Date _____ / _____ / _____
    MM / DD / YYYY

41. Patient discharged against medical advice? _____
    (0-No, 1-Yes)

42. Program Interruption(s) _____
    (0-No, 1-Yes)

43. Program Interruption Dates
    (Code only if Item 42 is 1 - Yes)

    A. 1st Interruption Date   B. 1st Return Date
    [_____]   [_____]
    MM / DD / YYYY   MM / DD / YYYY

    C. 2nd Interruption Date   D. 2nd Return Date
    [_____]   [_____]
    MM / DD / YYYY   MM / DD / YYYY

    E. 3rd Interruption Date   F. 3rd Return Date
    [_____]   [_____]
    MM / DD / YYYY   MM / DD / YYYY

44A. Discharge to Living Setting _____
     (01 - Home; 02- Board and Care; 03- Transitional
     living; 04- Intermediate Care; 05- Skilled Nursing
     Facility; 06- Acute Unit of Own Facility; 07- Acute Unit of
     Another Facility; 08- Chronic Hospital; 09 - Rehabilitation
     Facility; 10- Other; 11 - Died; 12- Alternate Level of Care Unit;
     13 - Subacute Setting; 14- Assisted Living Residence)

44B. Was patient discharged with Home Health Services? _____
     (0-No, 1-Yes)
     (Code only if Item 44A is 01 - Home, 02- Board and Care,
     03- Transitional Living, or 14 - Assisted Living Residence)

45. Discharge to Living With
    (Code only if Item 44A is 01 - Home; Code using 1 - Alone;
    2- Family/Relatives; 3-Friends; 4- Attendant; 5- Other

46. Diagnosis for Interruption or Death _____
    (Code using ICD-9-CM code)

47. Complications during rehabilitation stay
    (Use ICD-9-CM codes to specify up to six conditions
    that began with this rehabilitation stay)

    A. _____   B. _____

    C. _____   D. _____

    E. _____   F. _____

Quality Indicators

RESPIRATORY STATUS
(Score items 48 to 50 as 0- No; 1 - Yes)

	Admission	Discharge
48. Shortness of breath with exertion	_____	_____
49. Shortness of breath at rest	_____	_____
50. Weak cough and difficulty clearing airway secretions	_____	_____

*The FIM data set, measurement scale and impairment codes
incorporated or referenced herein are the property of U B Foundation
Activities, Inc. ©1993, 2001 U B Foundation Activities, Inc. The FIM
mark is owned by UBFA. Inc.

Quality Indicators

PAIN

51. Rate the highest level of pain reported by the patient within the
    assessment period:
    Admission: _____ Discharge: _____

    (Score using the scale below; report whole numbers only)

    0   1   2   3   4   5   6   7   8   9   10
    | | |
    No   Moderate   Worst
    Pain   Pain   Possible Pain

Pressure Ulcers

52A. Highest current pressure ulcer stage
     Admission _____ Discharge _____

     (0 - No pressure ulcer; 1 - Any area of persistent skin
     redness (Stage 1); 2 - Partial loss of skin layers
     (Stage 2); 3 - Deep craters in the skin (Stage 3); 4 - Breaks
     in skin exposing muscle or bone (Stage 4); 5 - Not
     stageable (necrotic eschar predominant; no prior
     staging available)

52B. Number of current pressure ulcers
     Admission _____ Discharge _____

PUSH Tool v. 3.0 ©

SELECT THE CURRENT LARGEST PRESSURE ULCER TO CODE THE
FOLLOWING. Calculate three components (C through E) and code
total score in F.

52C. Length multiplied by width (open wound surface area)
     Admission _____ Discharge _____

     (Score as 0 - 0 cm²; 1 - <0.3 cm²; 2 - 0.3 to 0.6 cm²;
     3 - 0.7 to 1.0 cm²; 4 - 1.1 to 2.0 cm²; 5 - 2.1 to 3.0 cm²;
     6 - 3.1 to 4.0 cm²; 7 - 4.1 to 8.0 cm²; 8-8.1 to
     12.0 cm²; 9 - 12.1 to 24.0 cm²; 10 - >24cm²)

52D. Exudate amount
     Admission _____ Discharge _____
     0 - None; 1 - Light; 2- Moderate; 3 - Heavy

52E. Tissue type
     Admission _____ Discharge _____
     0 - Closed/resurfaced: The wound is completely covered with
     epithellum (new skin); 1 - Epithelial tissue: For superficial ulcers,
     new pink or shiny tissue (skin) that grows in from the edges
     or as islands on the ulcer surface. 2 - Granulation tissue: Pink
     or beefy red tissue with a shiny, moist, granular appearance.
     3 - Slough: Yellow or white tissue that adheres to the ulcer bed
     in strings or thick clumps or is mucinous. 4 - Necrotic tissue
     (eschar): Black, brown, or tan tissue that adheres firmly to the
     wound bed or ulcer edges.

52F. TOTAL PUSH SCORE (Sum of above three items -- C, D and E)
     Admission _____ Discharge _____

SAFETY

	Admission	Discharge
53. Balance problem	_____	_____
(0- No; 1 - Yes)		
e.g., dizziness, vertigo, or light-headedness		
54. Total number of falls during the rehabilitation stay		_____

FIGURE **11-3** *(Continued)*

INFORMATION MANAGEMENT

Information Flow

The medical record is initiated during admission to the rehabilitation care system and is maintained as an interdisciplinary unit. Each member of the interdisciplinary team records observations on a daily basis. If the treatment areas are in separate parts of the hospital, then the medical record goes with the patient to the treatment areas.

Coding

The system utilized for diagnostic coding is the current clinical modification of the *International Classification of Disease*. The codes most frequently reported include those that classify neurologic conditions, musculoskeletal disorders, and amputations. Diagnoses encountered frequently in rehabilitation include neurogenic bladder, fibromyalgia, decubitus ulcer (or pressure sore), spasticity, urinary tract infection, cerebral palsy, and below-the-knee amputation.

Physicians use *Current Procedural Terminology* (CPT) for reporting services provided. Rehabilitation physicians generally address a host of issues on a follow-up visit, frequently utilizing time spent in counseling and coordination of care or complexity of medical decision making as major criteria for coding evaluation and management services. Other common rehabilitation services that would be coded are trigger point injections, motor point blocks, final reports and ratings, medical management conferences, and physician review of care plan.

For inpatient rehabilitation facilities, the diagnostic coding rules differ for the IRF-PAI and the facility's billing form, the UB-04. Unlike the UB-04, the IRF-PAI does not capture the principal diagnosis, but reports the etiologic diagnosis instead. For example, consider the case of a patient who had previously suffered an intracerebral hemorrhage treated at an acute care hospital and who was subsequently admitted to the IRF for rehabilitation for the late effects of the hemorrhage. For the UB-04, the IRF would report the principal diagnosis as a "V code" for admission for rehabilitation. However, on the IRF-PAI, the code for intracerebral hemorrhage would be reported as the etiologic diagnosis. No V code would be reported on the IRF-PAI, and intracerebral hemorrhage would not be reported on the UB-04 (Trela, 2002). (Note that the V code is an *ICD-9-CM* code. After October 1, 2013, the *ICD-10-CM* coding structure in many instances reports the underlying condition with an appropriate seventh character extension to indicate a subsequent encounter.)

The World Health Organization (WHO) publishes the *International Classification of Functioning, Disability and Health* (ICF). (An earlier version of this publication was known as the *International Classification of Impairments, Disabilities and Handicaps* [ICIDH]). The ICF classifies disability concepts by body functions and structure, activities and participation, and environmental factors (World Health Organization, 2001).

Electronic Information Systems

Electronic information systems are used administratively in rehabilitation facilities in much the same manner as in other types of health care facilities. However, inpatient rehabilitation facilities have the unique requirement to submit IRF-PAI data to fiscal intermediaries. CMS provides software called **Inpatient Rehabilitation Validation and Entry (IRVEN)** free of charge to facilities that wish to use it to submit the IRF-PAI data. Vendors and other organizations also license software for submission of IRF-PAI data and often include other capabilities, such as the ability to transmit ORYX data to the Joint Commission or the ability to benchmark performance against peer facilities. Some commonly used systems are E-Rehab or Uniform Data Systems (UDS).

National Databases

National databases on spinal cord injury and traumatic brain injury are examples of systems that provide efficient, large-scale collections of data that facilitate research in rehabilitation and promote uniform treatment, thereby leading to improved functional outcomes.

The National Spinal Cord Injury Data Base is maintained in Birmingham, Alabama, and collects its data from the Model Spinal Cord Injury System. The model system's uniform database is the largest longitudinal data set on spinal cord injury in the world and has collected data since June 1973. Information is collected on 472 variables in each spinal cord injury case, and the model system's database captures approximately 15 percent of all new spinal cord injury cases in the United States.

A similar national database is maintained on traumatic brain injury. Due to the multiple types of brain injuries, it is much more difficult to compare brain injury data than to compare spinal cord injury data.

Other databases track all admissions to rehabilitation units and therapy clinics. A variety of data is collected related to demographics, diagnosis, and outcomes. Specific information collected and the amount varies by providers.

Classification and Rating Systems Used in Rehabilitation

Numerous classification schemes have developed for both spinal cord-injured individuals and traumatic brain-injured individuals. It is extremely important that a standardized nomenclature system be utilized to facilitate research in spinal cord injury and brain injury.

American Spinal Injury Association Classification System

The international standards for neurologic and functional classification of spinal cord injury have been developed by the American Spinal Injury Association in cooperation with the International Medical Society of Paraplegia. This system of classification standardizes the neurologic motor and sensory examination. It further requires that the diagnosis be stated giving both a sensory and motor neurologic level and a qualifying statement regarding the completeness of the spinal cord injury. For definitions utilized in the development of classification systems, see Table 11-2.

TABLE **11-2**
Standardization Classification System Definitions

Classification	Definition
Tetraplegia (or quadriplegia)	Spinal cord injury of the cervical level that leads to neurologic and functional damage of the upper extremities and the lower extremities
Paraplegia	Impairment or loss of motor and/or sensory function in the thoracic, lumbar, or sacral segments of the spinal cord affecting the lower extremities only
Tetraparesis or paraparesis	A relative weakness of the extremities (tetraparesis) or the lower extremities (paraparesis) but not complete paralysis
Central cord syndrome	A lesion occurring in the central region of the spinal cord at the cervical level that produces greater weakness in the upper extremities than in the lower extremities
Brown-Sequard syndrome	A lesion that produces a greater motor and proprioception loss ipsilateral and a contralateral loss of sensitivity to pinprick and temperature
Anterior cord syndrome	A spinal lesion that is vascular in origin and produces a loss of motor function and a deficit in sensitivity to pinprick and temperature while preserving proprioception
Conus medullaris syndrome	This injury occurs when there is damage to the conus of the spinal cord, resulting in an areflexic bladder and bowel and areflexic lower extremities
Cauda equina syndrome	Injury to the lumbosacral nerve roots inside the neurocanal before exiting to the peripheral nerves, resulting in an areflexic bladder and areflexic lower extremities

Besides the classifications of tetraplegia, paraplegia, tetraparesis, and paraparesis, spinal cord injuries must be further classified as to whether they are: complete, meaning there is total absence of sensory and motor functions below the level of the lesion; or incomplete, meaning there is partial preservation of sensory and/or motor functions below the neurologic level of injury.

Of the incomplete spinal cord injury syndromes, several can and do occur with a high degree of frequency and have been assigned to specific nomenclature. These are defined in Table 11-2. Central cord syndrome is more common in the elderly population. Brown-Sequard syndrome is said to occur when there is a relative hemisection of the spinal cord, with the contralateral side of the spinal cord being preserved. Others are anterior cord syndrome, conus medullaris syndrome, and cauda equina syndrome. The American Spinal Injury Association also publishes a handbook of spinal cord injury classification and nomenclature. See the Key Resources section of this chapter for information on how to obtain this document.

It is crucial that accurate spinal cord injury classification be performed by physicians who are caring for a spinal cord-injured person so that physicians who come in contact with the patient later on will be able to accurately determine if there has been a change in the neurologic status of the patient.

Traumatic Brain Injury Classification Systems

Traumatic brain injury classification systems have evolved, and two primary systems are useful in rehabilitation. One is the Glasgow Coma Scale, used early after injury in the emergency room (ER) and in the first few days of hospitalization. The other is the Rancho Los Amigos Levels of Cognitive Function Scale, which is useful in communicating the patient's recovery from traumatic brain injury.

The Glasgow Coma Scale measures three areas: eye opening on a scale of 4 to 1, best motor response on a scale of 6 to 1, and verbal response on a scale of 5 to 1. The range for a Glasgow Coma Scale is 3 to 15 (the lowest score possible is 3; a person dead on arrival at an ER would score a 3). The Glasgow Coma Scale scores recorded upon arrival at the ER and on the second, third, fourth, and seventh post-injury days are extremely predictive of the patient's outcome. Glasgow Coma Scale scores of 8 or less are associated with poor outcomes (see Figure 11-4).

The Rancho Los Amigos Scale goes from 1 to 8. A level of 1 or 2 is consistent with a coma or near-coma state. A level 8 is purposeful and appropriate behavior. The Rancho Los Amigos Scale is extremely beneficial in communicating to other members of the rehabilitation team the patient's level of

---

GLASGOW COMA SCALE

Best Eye Response (4)	1. No eye opening
	2. Eye opening to pain
	3. Eye opening to verbal command
	4. Eyes open spontaneously
Best Verbal Response (5)	1. No verbal response
	2. Incomprehensible sounds
	3. Inappropriate words
	4. Confused
	5. Orientated
Best Motor Response (6)	1. No motor response
	2. Extension to pain
	3. Flexion to pain
	4. Withdrawal from pain
	5. Localizes pain
	6. Obeys commands

FIGURE **11-4** The Glasgow Coma Scale (Graham Teasdale & Bryan J. Jennett, University of Glasgow, 1974.)

I. No response

II. Generalized response to stimulation

III. Localized response to stimuli

IV. Confused and agitated behavior

V. Confused with inappropriate behavior (non-agitated)

VI. Confused but appropriate behavior

VII. Automatic and appropriate behavior

VIII. Purposeful and appropriate behavior

FIGURE **11-5** Rancho Los Amigos Levels of Cognitive Function Scale.

recovery, and thereby infers what level of treatment is appropriate at that point. In general terms, once a patient has reached level 6 or above, he or she is ready for discharge to home. However, the patient may continue to require some outpatient services. A person who has a Rancho Los Amigos Scale of 3 or less is not considered an inpatient rehabilitation candidate and would be better served in a coma stimulation program (see Figure 11-5).

Self-Care Assessment Scales and FIM® Scores

A number and variety of tools have been developed to assist in assessing the functional status of the patient in areas addressing bathing, grooming, toileting, and so forth. Some common scales include the Katz index, the Barthel index, and the FIM® rating scale. Deciding which functional assessment tool is most useful depends on the individual institution and patient population that is served.

The **Functional Independence Measure or FIM**® instrument evolved from a task force of the American Congress of Rehabilitation Medicine and the American Academy of Physical Medicine and Rehabilitation, and has established itself as an extremely reliable and valid tool for documenting the severity of disabilities as well as outcomes in rehabilitation. FIM® is the most commonly used measure of independence, and, due to its reliability and validity, it has been incorporated into the IRF-PAI (see page 2 of the IRF-PAI in Figure 11-3). FIM® scores are issued in 13 motor areas and 5 cognitive areas. The motor areas include self-care (e.g., eating, grooming, bathing, dressing, and toileting), sphincter control (e.g., bowel and bladder management), mobility transfers, and locomotion. The cognitive areas include comprehension, expression, social interaction, problem solving, and memory.

Each area receives a score that ranges from 1 to 7. A score of 1 means that the individual requires total assistance, and 7 means that the individual is totally independent. In any given functional category, a score of 1 to 5 means that the patient requires the assistance of another person for that function.

FIM® is a highly reproducible and reliable measure of the patient's independence. FIM® scoring is repeated on a routine basis to help document the progress or lack of progress of the patient in rehabilitation. If FIM® scores do not show an improvement, then the treatment plan must be reevaluated and modified to meet current needs, or the patient must be placed at maximum medical improvement and discharged from rehabilitation. All members of the rehabilitation team should receive specific training in the proper way to assess the patient and assign FIM$^®$ scores.

FIM$^®$ is an excellent technique for almost all rehabilitation problems, including traumatic brain injury, spinal cord injury, stroke, amputations, and medical disability. The reason FIM$^®$ works well for the various types of disabilities is because it is a measure of the functional status of the patient, irrespective of the etiology of the disability.

There are some subsets of patients for which FIM$^®$ does not work well, including patients who are progressing extremely slowly and pediatric patients. A separate scale called WeeFIM$^®$ has been developed for pediatric patients. (FIM$^®$ and WeeFIM$^®$ are registered trademarks of the Uniform Data System for Medical Rehabilitation, a division of UB Foundation Activities, Inc.)

FIM$^®$ scores or some other reliable, reproducible measure of functional outcome is required in rehabilitation. It allows the rehabilitation interdisciplinary team to (1) assess functional improvement of the patient and response to the treatment plan; (2) document functional status and thereby needs for discharge planning; (3) establish the beneficial role of the rehabilitation service; (4) justify the treatment and cost incurred; (5) allow rapid communication of a patient's functional status to other interested parties such as third-party payers or other rehabilitation teams that may become involved in the patient's score; and (6) standardize the nomenclature system regarding functional outcome.

QUALITY IMPROVEMENT AND UTILIZATION MANAGEMENT

Quality Improvement and Program Evaluation Systems

The primary product of rehabilitation is improvement in the patient's functional status. There are three components of quality care: appropriateness of care, technical competence with which the care was given, and patient dignity and involvement. Quality assessment may be done on a multidisciplinary basis by monitoring the different departments and outcomes. For example, an increase in ADL skills can be used to measure the quality of services provided by the occupational therapy department; an increase in physical functioning indicates an improved outcome for the physical therapy department; and an increase in cognitive and emotional adaptation by the patient and the family can be used to assess the quality of services from the psychology staff. Quality of outcome is also viewed in terms of the absolute level of independence of the patient, a reduction in the need for caregivers, and the setting to which the patient was discharged.

FIM scores lend themselves readily to quality and outcome measurements. In addition, costs can be analyzed in light of changes in FIM scores. For example, a patient's FIM score could improve from 50 to 75—a gain of 25 points—after several weeks of rehabilitation. If the cost of providing rehabilitation services during that time period was $25,000, then the cost per point-change in FIM score would be $1,000 for that patient.

Program evaluation systems are best organized along diagnostic and functional groups such as general inpatient medical rehabilitation and stroke, spinal cord injury, or traumatic brain injury. Program evaluation and assessments of quality in outcome should continue after discharge. The patient should be seen for a follow-up visit to determine how he is functioning at home, which is the true indicator of the effectiveness of the rehabilitation program.

Utilization Management

Elements of utilization management have been discussed throughout this chapter. In the discussion of various types of rehabilitation settings (inpatient, outpatient, skilled nursing, etc.), factors that affect the appropriateness of different types of rehabilitation for different types of patients were mentioned. In an inpatient rehabilitation facility (IRF), the preadmission screening is very important in determining whether the patient is a suitable candidate for inpatient rehabilitation. For example, a patient that is too acutely ill would not be able to participate in therapy at a level that would be beneficial. In addition to determining the appropriateness of admission, the IRF must also determine when the patient is ready for discharge. As previously noted, FIM® scores may be calculated at routine intervals to measure the progress of rehabilitation. When it appears that the patient has achieved optimum benefit from inpatient rehabilitation and that continued inpatient rehabilitation would improve the patient's status only slightly, then a decision to discharge the patient may be in order. When the patient is ready for discharge, appropriate plans for follow up or continuing outpatient therapy should be in place.

RISK MANAGEMENT AND LEGAL ISSUES

The rehabilitation team, its records, and physiatrists are often called on to provide information in legal proceedings regarding the disability, functional status, and future needs of an individual with a handicapping condition. This is entirely understandable, because the rehabilitation team is the primary caregiver for individuals who have permanent injuries and disabilities. Some of these people have been injured as a result of a motor vehicle accident, a work-related injury, or malpractice. The rehabilitation professional is responsible for maximizing the quality of life and functional status, and follows the individual over a lifetime to meet his or her needs related to the injury and the disability. As a result, the physiatrist is frequently called on to render opinions in these areas as an expert witness. The physiatrist is uniquely qualified to provide this service to his or her patient because of the specific training in recovery from injuries, an understanding of the natural history of the disease process, and a working knowledge of the types of equipment and supplies necessary to maximize functional status and preserve health.

The rehabilitation medical records, FIM scores, discharge recommendations, medications, and equipment recommendations are useful to help prepare a **life care plan**. The International Academy of Life Care Planners has defined a life care plan as a "dynamic document based upon published standards of practice, comprehensive assessment, data analysis, and research, which provides an organized concise plan for current and future needs with associated cost, for individuals who have experienced catastrophic injury or have chronic health care needs" (IALCP, n.d., p. 1). The life care plan is developed on an individualized basis, given that person's unique presentation. It lists the items required over a lifetime for the individual, their cost, and the frequency of replacement. This document serves as a medical legal document that may guide court decisions regarding a settlement. The document could also be used as a guide to provide future medical services for the individual.

Medicare Set-Aside Trust

In 2001, CMS addressed guidelines regarding settlement of claims for individuals with work-related injuries or injuries covered under other general liability insurance plans. The objective was to ensure that third-party payers do not shift the responsibility for payment of medical services to Medicare (Lump-sum payments, 2009). CMS guidelines require that a life care plan be used to assess future medical care in cases where a high level of future care is likely to be required. As of 2010, CMS is requiring that a set-aside analysis be made in the case of everyone with a recovery in litigation who may reasonably be expected to qualify for Medicare services.

ROLE OF THE HEALTH INFORMATION MANAGER

The health information professional in a rehabilitation setting may manage traditional types of services related to the creation, development, storage, and retrieval of the patient record and patient information, and, as in other settings, has an important part to play in obtaining and maintaining accreditation of the rehabilitation facility. In addition, the health information manager may assist in selecting or developing appropriate forms to track patient outcomes and may work with others to develop and implement quality improvement programs. The health information manager may monitor rates of complications, early discharges, or failures to improve, and present findings that can help target processes for improvement. In inpatient rehabilitation facilities, the health information manager may play a role in managing coding for the IRF-PAI and the UB-04. This role may extend to other aspects of the revenue cycle of the facility, including timely submission of both of these forms. Some of the trends described in the next section call for the skills of a health information manager. For example, the possibility of the implementation of a bundled payment for postacute care could involve the HIM professional in managing related systems.

TRENDS

Acute Rehabilitation, Skilled Nursing, and Other Postacute Care Providers

Since 1990, a continuum of nonhospital-based postacute rehabilitation facilities has evolved that has been driven by economic factors in the American health care delivery system. Earlier discharges from the hospital have resulted in patients being discharged who are unable to care for themselves. Skilled rehabilitation facilities provide a cost-effective, economic system that allows the patient to develop a functional level of independence that would make returning home safe. The level of care offered by rehabilitation units in skilled nursing facilities is generally more cost effective for older patients who often cannot participate in the intensive rehabilitation programs offered at more acute levels of care. The resulting trend has been toward increasing the number of skilled rehabilitation beds and decreasing the number of acute inpatient rehabilitation beds.

All of the following settings provide various types of postacute care (PAC): skilled nursing facilities (SNFs), home health agencies (HHAs), long-term care hospitals (LTCHs), and inpatient rehabilitation facilities (IRFs). The Medicare Payment Advisory Commission (MedPAC) has noted the following concerns about postacute care:

- Payments are not accurately calibrated to costs in each sector.
- Services overlap among settings.
- The PAC (postacute care) product is not well defined.
- Assessment instruments differ among settings. (MedPAC, 2010, p. 165)

One proposal has been to develop a payment system that would bundle payments for postacute care for all types of PAC providers with the acute care hospital payment for a given episode of care. The rationale is that such a system would give all providers an incentive to provide the right mix of services for each patient. Another proposal addressing these concerns has been to develop a uniform assessment instrument for postacute care to be completed at hospital discharge and integrated into PAC assessments. Pilot testing of such an instrument was scheduled for completion in 2011 (MedPAC, 2010). There are significant challenges in developing a bundled payment system as well as an appropriate uniform assessment tool. However, movement in this direction continues, as evidenced by the provision in Title III, Sec. 3023, of the Patient Protection and Affordable Care Act enacting a "National Pilot Program on Payment Bundling."

Outpatient Rehabilitation

The cost savings are substantial when rehabilitation services—PT, OT, and speech pathology—can be provided in an outpatient setting. The number of outpatient rehabilitation settings and freestanding rehabilitation clinics has continued to increase in the twenty-first century.

Independent Living

At one time, individuals who had limiting conditions that reduced their functional status had little option except discharge to nursing homes. The independent living movement advocates for funding to provide support services to an individual with a disability, at the level required to keep the person in his or her home, resulting in decreased morbidity and mortality for the patient and increasing the likelihood that the individual will be employable.

The independent living movement will continue to progress because of its cost-effectiveness, and therefore health care providers will need to adopt strategies that promote independent living. Health information management specialists can help develop systems of documentation that promote good health care in the independent living situation. Along these lines, Title III, Sec. 3024, of the Patient Protection and Affordable Care Act enacted an Independence at Home Demonstration Program that will utilize electronic health records and telehealth methodologies.

Technology

There is a rapid explosion of technology in rehabilitation. Electronic systems are being developed that may some day replace lost vision, and computer-assisted ambulation systems are becoming much more functional and smaller. Robotic devices are now in existence and are able to supplement the missing function of upper extremities. This technology is in its infancy and will continue to grow.

Small pacemaker neurostimulation devices (Neuro-Control) are now commonly implanted in the brachial plexus to replace lost motor function in the upper extremities, and similar devices can be used to cause a neurogenic bladder to function appropriately.

Upper-extremity amputees now have high-tech I-hands available that allow individual finger movement. Persons with above-the-knee amputation now have an option of using the C-leg prosthesis, a computerized prosthesis that increases safety while allowing infinite variability in walking cadences. The modern power wheelchair has infrared and other communication technologies integrated into the chair, allowing the user to interface with home environmental control unit systems (ECUs), home entertainment systems, and telephones via the wheelchair's joystick. Home ECUs can be controlled from anywhere in the world with a smart-phone technology interface.

Care paths were once used to cover the expected course during rehabilitation and to document outcomes. Due to regulations and pressure from third-party payers, this has given way to uniform data sets such as those required by CMS. The Inpatient Rehabilitation Facility Patient Assessment Instrument (IRF-PAI) has previously been discussed in the context of payment and the IRF PPS, but it is also an important component in assessing the patient for clinical purposes and developing an individualized overall plan of care (see Figure 11-3).

SUMMARY

Rehabilitation is a continuum of care that spans the entire gamut of disabling conditions, involves all age groups, and is provided in numerous types of health care settings. It will be challenging for the health care information specialist to assist in developing health information systems that improve the quality of care and enhance full-team interdisciplinary communication.

KEY TERMS

60 percent rule one of the criteria for defining a hospital as an inpatient rehabilitation facility (IRF). The 60 percent rule requires that at least 60 percent of the patients treated have at least one of 13 qualifying medical conditions.

acute rehabilitation unit a designated unit in a hospital to which patients can be transferred for rehabilitation after treatment for the original acute illness or injury. Length of stay in these units is typically two to four weeks.

ambulation aids devices that provide additional stability and support for an individual who has trouble walking.

case-mix group (CMG) any of 100 categories into which an inpatient rehabilitation stay can be classified based on data submitted on the IRF-PAI. The CMG is determined by factors such as rehabilitation impairment category (RIC), functional measurements, age, and comorbidities

disability a restriction or inability to perform an activity in the manner or within the range considered to be normal for a human being, mostly resulting from impairment

encoding With regard to the IRF-PAI, encoding refers to using a specified computer program to enter data that will subsequently be transmitted to the Centers for Medicare & Medicaid Services (CMS).

environmental control units (ECUs) equipment that allows a person who has limited mobility to perform many everyday functions in the home, at work, or at school, such as turning on lights, using appliances, and opening and closing doors and windows.

freestanding rehabilitation hospitals inpatient rehabilitation facilities that may operate both acute and postacute rehabilitation units.

**Functional Independence Measure or FIM®
instrument** a rating tool for measuring function in motor and cognitive areas; FIM documents the severity of disabilities as well

as outcomes in rehabilitation and has been incorporated into the IRF-PAI

handicap the result of an impairment or a disability that limits or prevents the fulfillment of one or several roles that are regarded as normal (depending on age, sex, social, and cultural factors) for that individual.

impairment any temporary or permanent loss or abnormality of a body structure or function, whether physiological or psychological.

**Inpatient Rehabilitation Facility Patient
Assessment Instrument (IRF-PAI)** an instrument used to gather data regarding each patient stay that will be used to determine the payment for that stay under the Medicare inpatient rehabilitation facility prospective payment system.

**inpatient rehabilitation facility prospective
payment system (IRF PPS)** the prospective payment system by which inpatient rehabilitation facilities are paid for services provided to Medicare beneficiaries. Each patient stay is categorized into a case-mix group (CMG) that determines the payment that will be received by the facility from Medicare.

**Inpatient Rehabilitation Validation and Entry
(IRVEN)** software provided by CMS for entry of IRF-PAI data.

kinesiotherapist a person with specialized training in the proper techniques to maximize range of motion, strength, balance, and gait.

life care plan a dynamic document that details current and future health care needs based on published standards of practice.

occupational therapist (OT) a therapist who has completed an educational program accredited by the American Occupational Therapy Association at the bachelor's level or higher. OTs address activities of daily living, upper-extremity movement, higher cognitive processes, and community skills, among other areas of rehabilitation.

orthotic device   an external appliance or brace that can supplement an extremity's function or improve stability and positioning.

physiatrist   a physical medicine and rehabilitation physician.

physical therapist (PT)   a therapist who has completed an educational program accredited by the American Physical Therapy Association at the bachelor's level or higher. PTs help patients improve their strength, range of motion, balance, and mobility, among other things.

prosthesis   a device designed to replace a missing extremity or partially missing extremity.

psychologist   a person trained in psychology at the doctoral level who is certified by the American Psychological Association. In rehabilitation, a psychologist tests patients to identify problems in cognition or behavior and counsels the patient and family. A master's-level counselor may also perform some of these duties.

rehabilitation   the development of a person to the fullest physical, psychological, social, vocational, avocational, and educational potential consistent with his or her physiological or anatomic impairment and environmental limitations.

rehabilitation nurse   a registered nurse who has received training and credentialing as a rehabilitation nurse.

rehabilitation social worker   a member of the rehabilitation team who has specific training and knowledge in the area of social work and who may be certified by the National Association of Social Workers. The social worker provides background information on the patient and family, coordinates funding resources, and helps the patient with the transition back to the community.

rehabilitation team   an interdisciplinary team made up of numerous allied health professions.

speech-language pathologist   a rehabilitation team member with a bachelor's or master's level of education who is certified by the American Speech, Language, and Hearing Association. The speech pathologist evaluates and treats patients with swallowing problems, communication problems, and cognitive deficits.

REVIEW QUESTIONS

Knowledge-Based Questions

1. Define the term *rehabilitation.*
2. List and describe various settings in which rehabilitative care may take place.
3. List and describe the two ways of organizing rehabilitation teams. Which method of organization for rehabilitation teams is generally considered best and why?
4. List the various medical and other specialists that might be part of a rehabilitation team.
5. List the major categories of disabling conditions.
6. List and describe the World Health Organization's definitions of three major terms used to discuss individuals with functional limitations.
7. List, define, and give examples of the five main classes of durable medical equipment used in rehabilitation.
8. List two voluntary accrediting agencies for rehabilitation facilities.
9. What are some of the CMS criteria for inpatient rehabilitation facilities?
10. List the functions of the interdisciplinary team that must be documented in a patient's medical records under CARF guidelines.
11. List the five items the rehabilitation assessment must document under CARF guidelines.
12. Briefly describe the inpatient rehabilitation prospective payment system (IRF PPS).
13. What are FIM scores and how are they used?
14. List six advantages rehabilitation teams reap from using FIM scores.
15. What are the possible roles of the health information manager in rehabilitation facilities?

Critical Thinking Questions

1. Why is accreditation by CARF important to rehabilitative facilities and their patients? What role might the health information manager play in the CARF accreditation process for a rehabilitative facility?

2. How might the practice of health information management in various settings be affected by the implementation of a bundled payment system for postacute care?

3. Discuss changes in the delivery of rehabilitative care

WEB ACTIVITY

The idea of a bundled payment for postacute care was proposed as early as the 1990s. Conduct your own Internet search for the latest information on the status of payment bundling for postacute care or postacute care payment reform. Write a brief report on what you learn through your search for up-to-date information on these concepts.

CASE STUDY

In monitoring for various complications at XYZ Rehabilitation Hospital, health information manager Mary Moore discovers that in many instances patients with deep vein thrombosis or pressure sores are being admitted to the hospital with those conditions. Because rehabilitation cannot proceed until these medical conditions are resolved, these patients may be discharged from rehabilitation to another type of care after a short stay and later readmitted to rehabilitation. Or these conditions may prolong the patient's length of stay in the rehabilitation facility. Mary plans to report these findings to the quality improvement committee.

What recommendations might the committee make regarding these findings? What role can Mary play in improving this situation?

REFERENCES AND SUGGESTED READINGS

[CMS]Centers for Medicare & Medicaid Services. (2005, July 29). Section 140.3.4: Payment Adjustment for Late Transmission of Patient Assessment Data. *Medicare Claims Processing Manual* [Online]. https://www.cms.gov/manuals/downloads/clm104c03.pdf [2010, August 28].

[CMS]Centers for Medicare & Medicaid Services. (2009, August 7). 42 C.F.R. pt. 412: Inpatient Rehabilitation Facility Prospective Payment System for Federal Fiscal Year 2010; Final Rule. *Federal Register, 74*(151), 39762–39838.

Excluded Hospitals: Classifications, *Code of Federal Regulations*, Title 42, § 412.23, 2009 ed.

[IALCP] International Academy of Life Care Planners (n.d.). Introduction. *Standards of Practice.* [Online].

http://www.rehabpro.org/sections/ialcp/focus/standards/section-i-introduction [2010, August 28].

Lump-Sum payments, *Code of Federal Regulations*, Title 42, § 411.46, 2009 ed.

Medicare Payment Advisory Commission. (2010). Report to the Congress: Medicare payment policy. Washington, DC: MedPAC.

Trela, P. (2002). Inpatient Rehabilitation PPS Presents New Challenges, Opportunities. *Journal of the American Hospital Information Management Association, 73*(1), 48A–48D.

World Health Organization. (2001). *International Classification of Functioning, Disability and Health (ICF).* Geneva, Switzerland: World Health Organization.

KEY RESOURCES

American Academy of Physical Medicine
and Rehabilitation
http://www.aapmr.org

American Medical Rehabilitation Providers
Association
http://www.amrpa.org

American Spinal Injury Association (ASIA)
http://www.asia-spinalinjury.org

CARF International (Commission on
Accreditation of Rehabilitation Facilities)
http://www.carf.org

International Academy of Life Care Planners
http://www.rehabpro.org/sections/ialcp

International Association of Rehabilitation
Professionals
http://www.rehabpro.org

The Joint Commission
http://www.jointcommission.org

National Institute of Neurological Disorders
and Stroke
http://www.ninds.nih.gov

National Institute on Disability Research
and Rehabilitation (NIDRR)
*http://www2.ed.gov/about/offices/list/
osers/ nidrr*

CHAPTER 12

Home Health Care

IDA BLEVINS, RHIA

GWEN D. SMITH, RHIA

KIM A. BOYLES, MS, RHIA

LEARNING OBJECTIVES

Upon successful completion of this chapter, you should be able to:

- Explain the basic operations of a home health care agency and identify potential future trends of the industry.

- Discuss the importance of data collection, analysis, and reporting to be competitive in the current payment environment.

- Identify the types of services provided by home health care agencies.

- Explain the growth of home health care.

- List the agencies or organizations that develop standards for home health care.

- Explain the purpose of the Outcome and Assessment Information Set-C (OASIS-C).

- Discuss the importance of outcome-based quality improvement (OBQI) and outcome-based quality management (OBQM) in the home care setting.

Setting	Description	Synonyms/Examples
Home Health Care	A service to the recovering, disabled, or chronically ill person, providing for treatment and/or effective functioning in the home environment	Home care, visiting nurses, visiting staff

INTRODUCTION TO SETTING

Home health care encompasses a wide range of health and social services delivered at home to recovering, disabled, and chronically or terminally ill persons in need of medical, nursing, social, or therapeutic treatment and/or assistance with the essential activities of daily living.

According to the National Association for Home Care and Hospice, "home care is appropriate whenever a person prefers to stay at home but needs ongoing care that cannot easily or effectively be provided solely by family and friends. More and more older people, electing to live independent, non-institutionalized lives, are receiving home care services as their physical capabilities diminish. Younger adults who are disabled or recuperating from acute illness are choosing home care whenever possible. Chronically ill infants and children are receiving sophisticated medical treatment in their loving and secure home environments. Adults and children diagnosed with terminal illness also are being cared for at home, receiving compassionate care and maintaining dignity at the end of life. As hospital stays decrease, increasing numbers of patients need highly skilled services when they return home. Other patients are able to avoid institutionalization altogether, receiving safe and effective care in the comfort of their own homes" (NAHC 2010, p. 1).

Throughout this chapter and in the real world, the term **home health care** is synonymous with home care, visiting nurses, and visiting staff. Home care may be considered as an alternative to some inpatient and outpatient procedures and treatments routinely performed in the traditional hospital or clinic setting. Although it may seem to be a new means of delivering care to patients, home care has been around for years. The concept of caring for patients at home was common in earlier days but was not considered an industry.

Over the years, there has been substantial growth in the home care industry. The reasons for this growth can be attributed to cost savings, changes in reimbursement, technology, and advances in patients' right to choose. With the implementation of the inpatient prospective payment system, government regulations have motivated hospitals to contain their costs, compelling them to consider utilizing other methods to deliver care to their patients. Home care is among solutions to aid in minimizing hospital expenses while maintaining continuity of care and preventing expensive patient rehospitalizations.

Advances in technology and medical equipment allow patients to receive treatment in the home versus a visit to the hospital or a stay within a long-term care facility. For example, intravenous (IV) bags and pumps can be used to administer IV treatments such as pain medication, chemotherapy, enteral feedings, and antibiotics at a patient's place of residence.

Many patients choose to receive their treatments at home, because it gives them a greater sense of independence and comfort, which are vital aspects in healing many disease processes. If the patient's condition warrants home care, it is important for the patient, the physician, the hospital, and the home care provider to realize that the selection of the home care agency, by regulation, is the patient's choice.

Types of Patients

Home visitation services are provided to those individuals identified by a physician as having a medical necessity for skilled services. Some payer sources, such as Medicare and many private insurance companies, require the patient be **homebound** (i.e., confined to the home except for infrequent or relatively short absences that require considerable and taxing effort) to receive home health services. It is important to note, however, that not all payers have this requirement. Patient referrals can be received from a variety of services, such as hospital discharge planners, patients, patients' physicians, insurance companies through their case management programs, preferred provider organizations (PPOs), and health maintenance organizations (HMOs). Once the agency receives the referral, it is required to have physician orders to provide services.

Upon referral to a home health agency, a staff person from the home care agency will generally visit the patient's home to identify needs and to perform a comprehensive assessment. The agency staff works with the patient's physician to begin the patient's plan of care for **home care visits** based upon the results of this assessment. The preliminary work includes identifying the types of services the patient requires, which disciplines are required (e.g., physical therapy, speech therapy, occupational therapy, home health aide, social worker), as well as supplies/medical equipment the patient may need. Further, it is determined how often these disciplines should visit the patient and what special orders are required to ensure continuity of care for the patient.

Types of Caregivers

Many services can be offered to patients in a home care setting. An organization can be selective in determining what services it offers to its patients; however, an agency has a competitive advantage in the home care market if it offers a variety of services. The following discussion explains some of the available home health care options. Most options are paid by Medicare and third-party payers, with a few exceptions.

Skilled Nursing Agencies

Skilled nursing agencies employ health care personnel with a variety of skill levels. Individuals employed by these agencies may include nurses trained in medical-surgical nursing, intravenous therapy, enterostomal therapy, psychiatric or mental health, maternity, or restorative nursing. The level of nursing care used depends on individual patient need. In the event that a Medicare-certified agency provides psychiatric nursing care, the agency must certify that the psychiatric nurse has met additional qualifying criteria to perform this function.

Home health aides are also employed by skilled nursing agencies. A home health aide is a certified staff person who is able to enhance patient care by assisting with activities of daily living such as checking vital signs, bathing, grooming, and preparing meals. Aides may also provide limited services such as routine wound care (uncomplicated) and prescribed exercise monitoring, depending upon limitations as described by state regulations related to the home health aide's practice.

Specialty Services

Home health care also encompasses a range of specialty services, again depending on the level of care required by the patient. These may include the following **disciplines** and services: physical therapy, occupational therapy, speech-language pathology, medical social services, nutrition (dietitian) services, respiratory therapy, patient transportation, respite care, homemaking services, medical equipment, Meals on Wheels, and so on.

Physical therapists establish a home exercise and maintenance program for the patient, assisting with exercise routines and ambulating devices. Occupational therapists assist the patient to become independent with personal care duties such as dressing, bathing, and other normal activities of daily living. Speech-language pathologists assist patients who suffer from a stroke or adverse effects of feeding tubes or endotracheal tubes. Speech-language pathologists teach proper swallowing techniques, word formation, and word enunciation.

Medical social services help patients and family members cope with a patient's disease process through placement and involvement with community services. They also help find appropriate resources and make suggestions for long-range planning.

Nutrition (dietitian) services are not typically covered by Medicare, but patients always have the option to pay privately for special assistance with dietary needs. However, Medicare does pay for skilled nurses who monitor the patient's diet during a home care treatment period, and it also pays for teaching those who need help with special feeding equipment.

For special respiratory conditions, respiratory therapists teach techniques to increase efficiency in the lungs, such as pursed-lip breathing, and safety precautions when using oxygen equipment in the home.

Patient transportation services will pick up patients and transport them to their desired destination, such as the physician's office. This service is available for those who are willing to pay the fee.

In home respite care is a fee-for-service option not paid by Medicare. Those delivering respite care relieve the primary caregiver of his or her duties for an extended time. During this time, the home respite caregiver monitors the patient as the caregiver would. Home respite care simply allows the primary caregiver to have some free time.

Durable medical equipment (DME), such as a wheelchair or hospital bed, is leased or purchased to aid in the healing of the patient within the home setting. The use of durable medical equipment in the home is covered under Medicare Part B. If coinsurance is used, the patient pays a deductible and 20 percent of the bill.

Meals on Wheels is a charitable organization that provides food services for those unable to leave the home.

REGULATORY ISSUES

Home care agencies may be not-for-profit or they may be proprietarily owned. They can operate as stand-alone companies, often referred to as "freestanding." They can also participate in a partnership or operate as an **affiliate** to another institution, often a hospital. In the latter case, the home care headquarters can be physically separate from its affiliate, or it can be affiliate based.

There are only a few accrediting and certifying agencies that home care organizations need to consider:

- Medicare/Medicaid programs—the latter is sometimes referred to as a medical assistance program
- Individual state licensing agencies
- **The Joint Commission (TJC)**
- **Community Health Accreditation Program (CHAP)**
- **Accreditation Commission for Health Care (ACHC)**

The **National Association for Home Care and Hospice (NAHC)**, while not an accrediting or certifying body, also offers current information at its Web site (www.nahc.org) on regulatory issues affecting home care providers.

In 1997, the Centers for Medicare & Medicaid Services (CMS, known at the time as the Healthcare Financing Administration, or HCFA), offered **deemed status** to home health agencies that had been accredited by TJC or CHAP. *Deemed status* means that the voluntary accrediting agency's standards (e.g., TJC's or CHAP's standards) are deemed to be equivalent to the standards found in the Medicare and Medicaid programs' **Conditions of Participation (COP)**. If the agency chooses to accept deemed status, that deemed status exempts the accredited home health agency from routine surveys under the COP. In 2006, CMS granted deeming authority for home health care to a third voluntary accrediting organization, the Accreditation Commission for Health Care (ACHC).

Medicare/Medicaid

The **Centers for Medicare & Medicaid Services (CMS)**, a federal agency within the Department of Health and Human Services, was created in 1977 as the Health Care Financing Administration (HCFA) to administer the Medicare and Medicaid programs. CMS maintains its headquarters in Baltimore, Maryland, and has regional offices nationwide. The headquarters administers the national direction of the Medicare and Medicaid programs, while the regional offices provide CMS with the local presence necessary for quality customer service and oversight.

CMS mainly acts as a purchaser of health care services for the Medicare and Medicaid beneficiaries. Four key principles for Medicare/Medicaid standards are:

1. Assuring that Medicare and Medicaid are properly administered by their contractors and state agencies
2. Establishing policies for the reimbursement of health care providers
3. Conducting research on the effectiveness of various methods of health care management, treatment, and financing
4. Assessing the quality of health care facilities and services

Medicare Conditions of Participation, manuals, interim manual instructions, and Medicare transmittals are distributed to Medicare administrative contractors (intermediaries, carriers), CMS regional offices, federal agencies, state agencies, and congressional offices via the Internet at the CMS Web site (www.cms.gov).

The Joint Commission

TJC has been in existence since 1951 and is currently the largest accrediting body in the health care industry. It established its Home Care Accreditation Program in 1988. The scope of accreditation for home care encompasses many types of organizations, such as Medicare-certified home health agencies, hospices, private duty agencies, durable medical equipment companies, and infusion therapy companies.

TJC is a well-known accrediting body for those in the home care industry. To receive the Joint Commission seal of approval, an agency must apply for a survey and prepare to be evaluated on performance, functions, and processes aimed at improving patient **outcomes,** or end results. An evaluation is done by TJC, with qualitative and quantitative **standards** or rules. TJC publishes its home care standards in the *Comprehensive Accreditation Manual for Home Care,* which is updated yearly.

Community Health Accreditation Program

The Community Health Accreditation Program (CHAP) was founded in 1965 and is the only accrediting body dedicated exclusively to quality home, community, and public health care. Until 2001, it was a subsidiary of the National League for Nursing and is now an independent, non-profit corporation focusing on improving community-based health care through voluntary programs.

TJC and CHAP have collaborated in an effort to decrease overlaps within their business operations. TJC now recognizes and accepts the accreditation process, findings, and decisions of CHAP for home care institutions.

Four key principles for all CHAP standards are as follows:

1. The organization's structure and function consistently support its consumer-oriented philosophy and purpose.
2. The organization consistently provides high-quality services and products.
3. The organization has adequate human, financial, and physical resources to accomplish its stated mission and purpose.
4. The organization is positioned for long-term viability.

The CHAP *Standards of Excellence* are comprised of *Core Standards* that address broad concepts that apply to all CHAP-accredited organizations and *Service-Specific Standards* that address requirements related to the specific services that may be offered by an organization.

Accreditation Commission for Health Care (ACHC)

The Accreditation Commission for Health Care (ACHC) has deeming authority for Medicare in home health, hospice, and DMEPOS (durable medical equipment, prosthetics, orthotics, and supplies). ACHC was begun by home care providers "endeavoring to create a viable option of accreditation sensitive to the needs of small providers" (ACHC, 2010, para. 1). ACHC is an ISO 9001 certified organization and is integrating ISO concepts into its accreditation processes.

DOCUMENTATION

The primary reasons for documentation, whether electronic or hard copy, are to maintain an accurate record of all care and services provided to the patient in order to provide and maintain high quality patient care and to meet all regulatory requirements in order to obtain reimbursement.

For Medicare-certified agencies, the Medicare Conditions of Participation for home health agencies specify certain documentation requirements. If an agency is interested in becoming accredited by the Joint Commission, CHAP, or ACHC, the agency would need to obtain the appropriate accreditation manuals that outline specific standards regarding content, time frames, and authorized staff.

The Home Health Certification and Plan of Care, also known as the **485**, certifies the patient's need for home health services (see Figure 12-1). The 485 also outlines the patient's plan of care, which must be established by his or her attending physician. This document includes pertinent diagnoses, types of services, frequency and duration of visits, medication and treatments, safety measures, durable medical equipment (DME), nutritional requirements, functional limitations, allergies, mental status, prognosis, activities of daily living, goals, rehabilitation potential, and discharge plans. (NOTE: CMS has dropped the requirement for use of this specific form, stating simply that these elements should be included in the patient's plan of care. In order to make sure that all of these elements are indeed in the patient's plan of care, many agencies have opted to continue using this form.)

Documentation of physician certification of the need for home care is a requirement for payment under Medicare. The Affordable Care Act added a requirement that "the certifying physician must document that he or she, or an allowed **non-physician practitioner (NPP)** has had a face-to-face encounter with the patient.... As part of the certification form itself, or as an addendum to it, the physician must document when the physician or allowed NPP saw the patient, and document how the patient's clinical condition as seen during that encounter supports the patient's homebound status and need for skilled services. The face-to-face encounter must occur within the 90 days prior to the start of home health care, or within the 30 days after the start of care" (MLN Matters, 2010, pp. 1–2). The patient's physician must review, update, and recertify (if necessary) the plan of care at least every 60 days. This time frame is often referred to as the patient's **certification period. Recertification** can continue every 60 days as long as the patient meets Medicare coverage guidelines or agrees to pay privately for services until the patient is discharged from services.

Another important document for home care is the **comprehensive assessment,** which is completed on the first visit. The document should include the patient's present illness; significant past history; review of all systems/

Department of Health and Human Services
Centers for Medicare & Medicaid Services

Form Approved
OMS No. 0938-0357

HOME HEALTH CERTIFICATION AND PLAN OF CARE

1. Patient's HI Claim No.	2. Start of Care Date	3. Certification Period From: To:	4. Medica l Record No.	5. Provider No.

6. Patient's Name and Address

7. Provider's Name, Address and Telephone Number

8. Date of Birth	9. Sex ☐ M ☐ F	10. Medications: Dose/Frequency/Route (N)ew (C)hanged

11. ICD-9-CM	Principal Diagnosis	Date
12. ICD-9-CM	Surgical Procedure	Date
13. ICD· 9-CM	Other Pertinent Diagnoses	Date

14. DME and Supplies

15. Safety Measures:

16. Nutritional Req.

17. Allergies

18. A. Functional Limitations

1 ☐ Amputation
2 ☐ Bowel/Bladder (Incontinence)
3 ☐ Contracture
4 ☐ Hearing
5 ☐ Paralysis
6 ☐ Endurance
7 ☐ Ambulation
8 ☐ Speech
9 ☐ Legally Blind
A ☐ Dyspnea With Minimal Exertion
B ☐ Other (Specify)

18. B. Activities Permitted

1 ☐ Complete Bedrest
2 ☐ Bedrest BRP
3 ☐ Up As Tolerated
4 ☐ Transfer Bed/Chair
5 ☐ Exercises Prescribed
6 ☐ Partial Weight Bearing
7 ☐ Independent At Home
8 ☐ Crutches
9 ☐ Cane
A ☐ Wheelchair
B ☐ Walker
C ☐ No Restrictions
D ☐ Other (Specify)

19. Mental Status:
1 ☐ Oriented
2 ☐ Comatose
3 ☐ Forgetful
4 ☐ Depressed
5 ☐ Disoriented
6 ☐ Lethargic
7 ☐ Agitated
8 ☐ Other

20. Prognosis:
1 ☐ Poor
2 ☐ Guarded
3 ☐ Fair
4 ☐ Good
5 ☐ Excellent

21. Orders for Discipline and Treatments (Specify Amount/Frequency/Duration)

22. Goals/Rehabilitation Potentia/Discharge Plans

23. Nurse's Signature and Date of Verbal SOC Where Applicable

25. Date HHA Received Signed POT

24. Physician's Name and Address

26. I certify/recertify that this patient is confined to his/her home and needs intermittent Skilled nursing care, physical therapy andlor speech therapy or continues to need cccvcauonattherepy. The patient is under my care, and I have authorized the services on this plan of care and will periodically review the plan.

27. Attending Physician's Signature and Date Signed

28. Anyore who misrepresents, falsifies , or conceals essential information required for payment of Federal funds may be subject to fine. imprisonment, or civil penalty under applicable Federal laws.

Form CMS-485 (C-3) (02-94) (Formerly HCFA-485) (Print Aligned)

FIGURE **12-1** Home Health Certification and Plan of Care.

physical assessment; medications; psychological, social, and economic factors; emergency plans; and skilled nursing performed that day. Based on the initial assessment and the patient's needs, the skilled nurse develops a **care plan** that includes goals, objectives, and those responsible for completing the plan. Additionally, CMS expects HHAs to complete the patient's comprehensive assessment *before* assigning the home health diagnoses to the OASIS-C instrument, described later (*OASIS-C Guidance Manual*, 2010).

An authorized staff person, determined by state law, takes verbal orders from the patient's physician. He or she must document, date, and sign the order (either on hard copy or electronically). The order must also be signed by the physician and returned to the home care agency within a certain time frame, determined by state law. Medicare-certified agencies may not bill for services until all orders are signed and returned.

Skilled nursing services must be supervised by a registered nurse and documented at appropriate intervals, determined by state law. Home health aide services require supervisory visits by the registered nurse and documentation at appropriate intervals, also determined by state law. Additionally, physical therapy assistant services and certified occupational therapy assistant services require supervisory visits by the physical therapist or occupational therapist and should be documented at intervals required by regulation.

Additional documents include the patient database, hospital discharge information, information collected upon referral, patient bill of rights, advance directives, DNR (do not resuscitate) orders, medication profile, all initial baseline assessments and progress notes, problem list, care plans, teaching guides, and discharge summary.

A **source-oriented record** (electronic or hard copy) is the traditional way in which a record is organized in sections according to patient care departments and/or disciplines. Within each section, the forms are arranged according to date. The major advantage to the source-oriented format is that it organizes reports from each source together, thus making it easy to determine the assessment, treatments, and observations a particular discipline has provided. One disadvantage of the source-oriented format is that it is not possible to quickly determine all of the patient's problems. It is also difficult to determine all of the treatments being provided for the patient at a given time.

The **problem-oriented record** (electronic or hard copy) provides a systematic method of documentation to reflect logical thinking on the part of the person directing the care of the patient. The individual directing the care of the patient defines and follows each clinical problem individually and organizes the problems for solution. The record must contain four basic components: database, complete problem list, initial plans, and progress notes.

Advantages to this format are that the individual directing the patient care is required to consider all the patient's problems in total context. The record clearly indicates the goals and methods in treating the patient. Medical education is facilitated by the documentation of logical thought processes.

A disadvantage of the problem-oriented record is that the format usually requires training of the professional staff. Also, for this chart format to be effective, the professional staff must be convinced of the system's worth.

In an **integrated format** (electronic or hard copy), the information is organized in strict chronological order. The forms from the various sources are intermingled. An advantage to this format is that the information included reads like a book, providing a clear picture of the patient's illness and response to treatment. However, it is difficult to compare similar information (e.g., fasting blood sugar levels) over a period of time. It also proves difficult for each discipline to quickly determine its treatment regimen and patient outcome.

Outcome and Assessment Information Set-C (OASIS-C)

The **Outcome and Assessment Information Set-C (OASIS-C)** is a group of data items designed to establish a means of systematic measurement of patient home health care outcomes. Outcomes, for the purpose of OASIS-C, measure changes in a patient's health status between two or more time points.

OASIS-C data items address sociodemographic, environmental, support system, health status, functional status, and health service utilization characteristics of the patient. The data is collected at specific time points, including start of care, every 60 days on a follow-up OASIS-C, post-hospitalization, and at transfer or discharge. It is important to note that the OASIS-C data elements alone are not a complete and comprehensive assessment tool and must be incorporated into a comprehensive patient assessment. For example, the OASIS-C data elements do not include such things as vital signs, home safety issues, wound measurements, and so on.

Regulatory Overview

Only home health agencies that participate in the Medicare program are required to follow the OASIS-C regulations, as stated in the Medicare Conditions of Participation. An OASIS-C assessment should be performed on all patients who are adult (over age 18), nonmaternity, and receiving skilled care. TJC also has requirements and standards that address improving organization performance, which can be met by using OASIS-C processes. In addition, state and Medicare surveyors have access to OASIS-generated quality reports, which they may review before an agency's survey. Some reports may be used in the survey process, and surveyors will expect agencies to show how they use OASIS-C data reports for quality monitoring. These quality improvement and quality management uses of OASIS-C are described further on. The OASIS-C is also the data collection tool for the Medicare home health prospective payment system.

Reporting of OASIS Information

There are several methods for gathering and reporting the OASIS-C information. Some home health agencies may gather all of their information electronically in the field and then transmit the data. Others may gather the information on paper and manually enter the data into an electronic file, which is called encoding. Others may gather the data on paper and scan the information.

Data are also submitted in a variety of ways. Some agencies have purchased software specifically for the OASIS-C data and their transmission;

others have elected to use software available at no charge from CMS. The software available from CMS is called **Home Assessment Validation and Entry (HAVEN)** and was developed to provide home health agencies with software for data entry, editing, and validation of OASIS-C data.

The Medicare Conditions of Participation detail the time frames for completion and transmission of the OASIS-C data. Generally, the data must be encoded and "locked" within seven days of completion of the assessment. During this seven-day time frame, the data must be analyzed for accuracy and edited, if needed. Once the data elements have been locked, which prevents subsequent editing and ensures stability of the data, they can be batched in a submission file and transmitted to the state agency.

CMS requires that the data be electronically transmitted at least monthly. Transmissions may occur more frequently at the discretion of the home health agency. Data must be transmitted by the end of the month following the date of collection. For example, an assessment completed in February would have to be transmitted by the end of March. There is no specific date on which the agency must transmit the data, which allows agencies to develop schedules that best meet their needs.

Once the data have been transmitted to the state agency, the home health agency must monitor the state reports for initial and final validation of the submission. If any errors or exceptions occur, the home health agency will receive a message in the final validation report, and errors must be corrected and resubmitted.

REIMBURSEMENT AND FUNDING

When a home care agency receives a request to service a patient, it accepts the responsibility to determine the patient's financial eligibility. A patient may be insured by Medicare, Medicaid, private/third-party payer, or willing to issue payment personally (self-pay). Some organizations may also have a charity fund established for those uninsured and unable to submit payments.

Upon completion of services and documentation and verification that all physician orders are signed and returned to the agency, a bill is submitted. Payment to the home care institution is based on the following:

- Medicare—a home care agency is paid a specific dollar amount for a 60-day period based on the patient's Home Health Resource Group (HHRG), as described in the following section on the prospective payment system (PPS).
- Medicaid—a home care agency is paid based on a rate determined by the state legislature. This rate varies with each state.
- Private insurance—a home care agency is paid based on a percentage of charges.
- Self-pay—a patient opts to acknowledge that he or she understands that Medicare/Medicaid or other payers will not pay for the services and determines that he or she will pay for those services out of pocket.

Medicare Prospective Payment System

On October 1, 2000, the Home Health Prospective Payment System (HHPPS) became effective and changed the way home care agencies were reimbursed for Medicare patients. This system was implemented to promote the same efficiencies and cost savings experienced when Medicare payments to hospitals were converted to a prospective payment system.

Under this payment system, home care agencies are paid a predetermined amount of money that may vary for each 60-day episode of care, depending on the severity of the patient's illness and the services required. Once the assessment of the patient has been performed and the OASIS-C completed, the Home Health Resource Group (HHRG)—based on the answers to certain identified OASIS-C questions—can be determined. The HHRG is represented by an alphanumeric code indicating severity.

Patients are assessed in three areas to determine the HHRG: clinical (C), functional (F), and service utilization (S):

- *Clinical dimension:* Evaluates the patient's medical status by assessing primary diagnosis, vision, level of pain, presence of ulcers or wounds, dyspnea, urinary and bowel status, need for infusion, and behavior
- *Functional dimension:* Assesses the patient's ability to perform activities of daily living (ADLs) such as dressing, bathing, toileting, transferring, and ambulation
- *Service utilization:* Determines what level of service the patient is likely to need based on location at the time of the home care referral (e.g., home, hospital, rehabilitation or skilled nursing facility) and whether there will be a need for 10 or more therapy visits in the next 60 days

There are 157 payment categories relating back to responses from the OASIS-C. Payments are adjusted to accommodate area wage differences, number of visits, and therapy and supply utilization.

Before submitting the claims to Medicare, the HHRG must be converted to a Health Insurance Prospective Payment System code (HIPPS). HIPPS codes are also alphanumeric, but unlike the HHRG are made up of five alpha characters and one numeric position.

Payments for the 60-day episodes are made in two installments: the first when a Request for Anticipated Payment (RAP) is submitted to Medicare, and the second when the final claim is filed. Patients are covered for an unlimited number of episodes as long as they continue to meet the Medicare criteria for skilled care.

There are some exceptions to the 60-day episode payment as follows:

- *Low Utilization Payment Adjustment (LUPA)*—If a patient receives 4 or fewer visits in a 60-day episode, payment will be made by the visit.
- *Partial Episode Payment (PEP)*—Occasionally, a patient may transfer to another agency for care, in which case the first agency would only receive payment for the part of the episode for which it actually provided care to the patient. When the patient starts receiving care from the new agency, a new episode begins.

- *Outliers*—An outlier occurs when the provision of care to a patient results in unusually high costs to the home care agency. Payment adjustments are made for a portion of the costs above the set threshold.
- *Upcodes/Downcodes*—A change in the codes assigned can also affect the payment received.

With the implementation of the prospective payment system, home care agencies have had to evaluate how they provide care to their patients and balance quality care with the efficiency and cost-saving measures the new payment method requires.

Payer Mix

Payer mix is a term that describes the ratio of various types of third-party payers that provide revenue to a health care organization. For example, an agency may have 70 percent of its patients insured by Medicare, 20 percent by Medicaid, and 10 percent by other third-party payers.

This ratio is very important for the financial security of the company. Government programs such as Medicare and Medicaid focus on paying for care on the basis of agency or industry costs. Other third-party payers generally pay contractually on the basis of charges, which can be higher than costs and are set by the agency.

Financial Stability

Within the federal government, CMS and the Department of Health and Human Services administer the Medicare program. They manage the program through rules and regulations described within the Medicare Conditions of Participation. At the state level, the fiscal intermediaries (Medicare administrative contractors), such as Palmetto GBA, CAHABA, and so on, carry out these rules and regulations.

Each agency must submit a yearly cost report to its fiscal intermediary/ Medicare administrative contractor for review. This report includes such things as operating costs, number of visits, and payer mix. Upon review of this report, a rate is determined for cost reimbursement adjustment.

A good business practice is to keep **fixed costs** as low as possible. Fixed costs do not change when the volume of services changes. In a service industry such as home health, rent and utilities are examples of fixed costs. **Variable costs** vary in proportion to the services provided. For example, when visits increase in number, the costs associated with visits, such as labor costs and transportation costs, also increase.

Medicare coverage issues also affect the financial stability of the agency. With regard to Medicare, both Part A and Part B apply. The home health care agency is reimbursed for nursing and other patient care through Part A. However, durable medical equipment is covered under Part B. What is not covered by Medicare?

- 24-hour care at home (unless it is only necessary for one day)
- Meals delivered to the home
- Homemaker services such as shopping, cleaning, and laundry, except that home health aides may do a small amount of these chores at the time they are providing covered services

- Personal care provided by home health aides (such as bathing, toileting, or providing help in getting dressed) *if* this is the only care needed. Medicare classifies this personal care as "custodial" because it could be provided safely and reasonably by people without professional skills and training. However, when skilled services are needed, personal care is covered.

There is a potential for the financial side of an agency to be **audited**. The possible reasons are a cost report that needs further investigation, a high volume of services, or a history of a high denial rate. However, *if* claims are submitted properly as stated in guidelines and further delineated in Medicare Local and National Coverage Determination Policies and documentation exists to support the reimbursement (such as the physician review of the plan of care every 60 days), an audit is not a serious risk to the agency.

A **denial** occurs when a bill amount to Medicare is no longer considered a receivable to an agency (i.e., Medicare notifies the provider that the claim will not be paid). The process begins with Medicare noticing an area in the delivery of care to a patient that does not follow guidelines, such as excessive utilization of a particular service. Medicare then requests documentation. If documentation does not support the utilization, a denial is issued. An agency may appeal by sending written justification and any other data as outlined in Medicare's instructions on responding to denials, additional development requests, and so on. Medicare ultimately remits or denies payment. Most agencies have a low denial rate.

INFORMATION MANAGEMENT

Coding and Classification

Classification systems include diagnosis, procedural, and, if the primary physician chooses to bill Medicare for certification, recertification, and/or care plan oversight, physician procedural codes. Diagnosis and procedural codes for the home health agency are classified using the current modification of *ICD*, and physician procedural codes are classified using *CPT*.

ICD-9-CM/ICD-10-CM

Codes from the current clinical modification of the *International Classification of Diseases* are required for home care agencies to receive payment. Codes must be assigned upon completion of the initial assessment and are vital to determination of the HHRG and HIPPS and may be updated with each certification period, as indicated, to demonstrate changes in the patient's condition.

According to CMS's OASIS manual, HHAs are expected to understand the patient's specific clinical status before selecting and assigning the diagnosis. Each patient's overall medical condition and care needs must be comprehensively assessed before the HHA selects and assigns the OASIS diagnoses. CMS expects HHAs to complete the patient's comprehensive assessment before assigning home health diagnoses (*OASIS-C Guidance Manual*, 2010).

Home care coding generally follows the traditional inpatient coding conventions, with guidelines similar, but not identical, to UHDDS definitions. Just as the diagnoses and procedures coded for the hospital must be relevant to the hospital care provided, diagnoses and procedures coded for home care should be relevant to the care provided within the home. Additional coding direction for home care coders can be found in the CMS *OASIS-C Guidance Manual*.

The items that differentiate home care coding from other coding conventions are as follows:

- Case-mix diagnoses (a diagnosis that determines the Medicare PPS case mix group)
- M1024 (payment diagnoses used when a V code is entered into a case-mix diagnosis field)
- Supplemental codes (V codes in *ICD-9-CM*) replacing case-mix diagnosis

See Figure 12-2 for an excerpt from the OASIS-C document with instructions regarding assignment of diagnosis codes.

(M1020/1022/1024)   Diagnoses, Symptom Control, and Payment Diagnoses: List each diagnosis for which the patient is receiving home care (Column 1) and enter its ICD-9-C M code at the level of highest specificity (no surgical/procedure codes) (Column 2). Diagnoses are listed in the order that best reflect the seriousness of each condition and support the disciplines and services provided. Rate the degree of symptom control for each condition (Column 2). Choose one value that represents the degree of symptom control appropriate for each diagnosis: V-codes (for M1020 or M1022) or E-codes (for M1022 only) may be used. ICD-9-C M sequencing requirements must be followed if multiple coding is indicated for any diagnoses. If a V-code is reported in place of a case mix diagnosis, then optional item M1024 Payment Diagnoses (Columns 3 and 4) may be completed. A case mix diagnosis is a diagnosis that determines the Medicare P P S case mix group. Do not assign symptom control ratings for V- or E-codes.

    Code each row according to the following directions for each column:

Column 1:   Enter the description of the diagnosis.

Column 2:   Enter the ICD-9-C M code for the diagnosis described in Column 1;

    Rate the degree of symptom control for the condition listed in Column 1 using the following scale:

    0 - Asymptomatic, no treatment needed at this time

    1 - Symptoms well controlled with current therapy

    2 - Symptoms controlled with difficulty, affecting daily functioning; patient needs ongoing monitoring

    3 - Symptoms poorly controlled; patient needs frequent adjustment in treatment and dose monitoring

    4 - Symptoms poorly controlled; history of re-hospitalizations

    Note that in Column 2 the rating for symptom control of each diagnosis should not be used to determine the sequencing of the diagnoses listed in Column 1. These are separate items and sequencing may not coincide. Sequencing of diagnoses should reflect the seriousness of each condition and support the disciplines and services provided.

Column 3:   (OPTIONAL) If a V-code is assigned to any row in Column 2, in place of a case mix diagnosis, it may be necessary to complete optional item M1024 Payment Diagnoses (Columns 3 and 4). See OASIS-C Guidance Manual.

Column 4:   (OPTIONAL) If a V-code in Column 2 is reported in place of a case mix diagnosis that requires multiple diagnosis codes under ICD-9-C M coding guidelines, enter the diagnosis descriptions and the ICD-9-C M codes in the same row in Columns 3 and 4. For example, if the case mix diagnosis is a manifestation code, record the diagnosis description and ICD-9-C M code for the underlying condition in Column 3 of that row and the diagnosis description and ICD-9-C M code for the manifestation in Column 4 of that row. Otherwise, leave Column 4 blank in that row.

(Form on next page)

FIGURE **12-2** Excerpt from OASIS-C. (OASIS is the intellectual property of the Center for Health Services Research, Denver, Colorado. Used with permission.)

(M1020) Primary Diagnosis & (M1022) Other Diagnoses		(M1024) Payment Diagnoses (OPTIONAL)	
Column 1	Column 2	Column 3	Column 4
Diagnoses (Sequencing of diagnoses should reflect the seriousness of each condition and support the disciplines and services provided.)	ICD-9-C M and symptom control rating for each condition. Note that the sequencing of these ratings may not match the sequencing of the diagnoses	Complete if a V-code is assigned under certain circumstances to Column 2 in place of a case mix diagnosis.	Complete **only if** the V-code in Column 2 is reported in place of a case mix diagnosis that is a multiple coding situation (e.g., a manifestation code).
Description	ICD-9-C M / Symptom Control Rating	Description/ ICD-9-C M	Description/ ICD-9-C M
<u>(M1020) Primary Diagnosis</u> a. _____	(V-codes are allowed) a. (__ __ __ . __ __) □0 □1 □2 □3 □4	(V- or E-codes NOT allowed) a._____ (__ __ __ . __ __)	(V- or E-codes NOT allowed) a._____ (__ __ __ . __ __)
<u>(M1022) Other Diagnoses</u> b. _____	(V- or E-codes are allowed) b. (__ __ __ __ . __ __) □0 □1 □2 □3 □4	(V- or E-codes NOT allowed) b._____ (__ __ __ . __ __)	(V- or E-codes NOT allowed) b._____ (__ __ __ . __ __)
c. _____	c. (__ __ __ __ . __ __) □0 □1 □2 □3 □4	c._____ (__ __ __ . __ __)	c._____ (__ __ __ . __ __)
d. _____	d. (__ __ __ __ . __ __) □0 □1 □2 □3 □4	d._____ (__ __ __ . __ __)	d._____ (__ __ __ . __ __)
e. _____	e. (__ __ __ __ . __ __) □0 □1 □2 □3 □4	e._____ (__ __ __ . __ __)	e._____ (__ __ __ . __ __)
f. _____	f. (__ __ __ __ . __ __) □0 □1 □2 □3 □4	f._____ (__ __ __ . __ __)	f._____ (__ __ __ . __ __)

(M1030) **Therapies** the patient receives <u>at home</u>: **(Mark all that apply.)**

    □ 1 -   Intravenous or infusion therapy (excludes TPN)

    □ 2 -   Parenteral nutrition (TPN or lipids)

    □ 3 -   Enteral nutrition (nasogastric, gastrostomy, jejunostomy, or any other artificial entry into the alimentary canal)

    □ 4 -   None of the above

(M1032) **Risk for Hospitalization:** Which of the following signs or symptoms characterize this patient as at risk for hospitalization? **(Mark all that apply.)**

    □ 1 -   Recent decline in mental, emotional, or behavioral status

    □ 2 -   Multiple hospitalizations (2 or more) in the past 12 months

    □ 3 -   History of falls (2 or more falls - or any fall with an injury - in the past year)

    □ 4 -   Taking five or more medications

    □ 5 -   Frailty indicators, e.g., weight loss, self-reported exhaustion

    □ 6 -   Other

    □ 7 -   None of the above

FIGURE **12-2** *(Continued)*

The home care primary diagnosis is the diagnosis most related to the plan of care. It may or may not be related to the most recent hospital stay, but must relate to the skilled services being provided. If more than one diagnosis is treated concurrently, the diagnosis that represents the most acute condition and requires the most intensive services should be assigned as primary. This diagnosis is recorded on the plan of care/485 and should mirror the diagnoses listed on the OASIS-C document in item M1020.

If the primary diagnosis has changed by the time of the next recertification (60 days later), the code for the new primary diagnosis is recorded on the recertification plan of care/485 and recertification OASIS-C.

Secondary diagnoses that affect home care are also coded, because several codes may be required to indicate the seriousness of the patient's condition and to explain the care provided in the home. Secondary diagnoses, or other diagnoses, are defined as all conditions that coexisted with the primary diagnosis at the time the plan of care was established or that developed subsequently or that affect the treatment or care of the patient.

Before the fall of 2003, supplemental and external cause of injury codes (V and E codes in *ICD-9-CM*) were not accepted on the OASIS forms. However, with the implementation of the transactions and code sets standards of HIPAA, OASIS forms were required to accept such codes. For example, when the OASIS reports an ICD-9-CM V code (or Z code in ICD-10-CM) as the primary diagnosis, another code that can be used to determine the applicable HHRG must be submitted as a payment (case mix) diagnosis. (See instructions for Column 3 of Figure 12-2.)

ICD-9-CM procedure codes (ICD-10-PCS after October 1, 2013) are also recorded on the 485 or plan of care. Medicare requires that procedure codes be recorded for hospital procedures that have a bearing on the home care provided. For example, a patient who has undergone a laparotomy in the hospital may have a postoperative wound that needs dressing changes. The hospital laparotomy is therefore relevant to the home care plan and should be coded. Since implementation of OASIS-C in January 2010, agencies are required to collect and report procedure data for procedures performed within established time frames. See Figure 12-3 for an excerpt from the OASIS-C document requiring codes related to an inpatient stay.

With the implementation of the PPS in home health, accurate coding has become more important because of the impact of coding on reimbursement and the resulting increased potential for fraud and abuse.

Durable medical equipment (DME) companies are also required to use ICD diagnosis codes for proper payment. The codes must correspond to the type of equipment being billed for per patient. For example, a fractured hip would support the use of ambulating devices, and a respiratory condition would support the use of oxygen equipment.

Current Procedural Terminology (CPT)/Healthcare Common Procedure Coding System (HCPCS)

The physicians who do care planning can use *Current Procedural Terminology (CPT)* or *Healthcare Common Procedure Coding System (HCPCS)* to bill for development of the care plan, as well as for care plan oversight. These codes

(M1010) List each **Inpatient Diagnosis** and ICD-9-C M code at the level of highest specificity for only those conditions treated during an inpatient stay within the last 14 days (no E-codes, or V-codes):

       Inpatient Facility Diagnosis   ICD-9-C M Code

a. _____   __ __ __ . __ __

b. _____   __ __ __ . __ __

c. _____   __ __ __ . __ __

d. _____   __ __ __ . __ __

e. _____   __ __ __ . __ __

f. _____   __ __ __ . __ __

(M1012) List each **Inpatient Procedure** and the associated ICD-9-C M procedure code relevant to the plan of care.

       Inpatient Procedure   Procedure Code

a. _____   __ __ . __ __

b. _____   __ __ . __ __

c. _____   __ __ . __ __

d. _____   __ __ . __ __

☐ NA - Not applicable

☐ UK - Unknown

FIGURE **12-3** Excerpt from OASIS-C, illustrating capture of inpatient codes. (OASIS is the intellectual property of the Center for Health Services Research, Denver, Colorado. Used with permission.)

allow physicians to bill for time spent discussing a patient's care with home health personnel and in the development of a care plan. Although a physician may bill for development of the initial certification and/or subsequent recertifications by following some simple steps, the regulations clearly state that the physician (not the home health agency) must keep his or her own records documenting the time spent per patient on care plan oversight. The rationale for this requirement is that time spent by the physician in this activity provides the basis for payment.

Data and Information Flow

Data collection generally begins upon the referral of the patient to home care. During the initial and subsequent home visits, home care staff members collect data using paper-based systems or computer-based systems that utilize laptop or handheld computers. Data are transmitted to the home care agency's office by manual or electronic means. When the patient is discharged from home care, the complete record is maintained in a central location, in either paper or electronic format.

Electronic Information Systems

Most home care agencies manage data through some type of database management system. Some agencies use their own homegrown systems, and others use systems available from various health care information system vendors. Information system vendors specializing in home care systems generally offer the ability to manage information concerning referral, census, OASIS reporting, medication profiles, orders, scheduling, Medicare certification and recertification, progress and visit notes, and other data and documentation.

The use of electronic health record (EHR) systems has been steadily increasing in home health. According to a study published in the *Journal of the American Medical Informatics Association*, around 40 percent of agencies providing home health services were using an EHR in 2007. This study also showed that over 20 percent of home health providers were using some form of telemedicine (Resnick & Alwan, 2010). Because of the distances traveled to render services to home health patients, the advantages of electronic systems are obvious.

Data Sets

Previous discussion of the OASIS data set has described its documentation and reimbursement features. The OASIS data elements were developed, tested, and refined over a 10-year period through an extensive research and demonstration program funded by CMS. The Center for Health Services Research in Denver, Colorado, developed the OASIS and maintains its copyright but permits the free use of OASIS. This extensive data set is approximately 24 pages when printed. See Figures 12-2 and 12-3 for excerpts from the OASIS in its paper format.

QUALITY IMPROVEMENT AND UTILIZATION MANAGEMENT

Quality Improvement

Outcome measures are the heart of outcome-based quality improvement (OBQI) and outcome-based quality management (OBQM), which are systematic approaches home health agencies use to continuously manage and improve the quality of care they provide. Home health agencies are able to access reports on outcomes for their patients through their state agency, and thus compare their results to the national reference, enabling them to identify areas of strength and weakness in their patient outcomes. OBQI/OBQM requires precise, uniform measures, which can only be obtained from standardized data items. The OASIS was designed to provide the necessary standardized data elements to measure outcomes.

In all health care areas, including home health, outcomes are of interest and importance to many parties. Payers want to know how the patients they insure are benefiting from the dollars they spend on care. On the federal level, outcomes have been stressed in changes to regulations. And, as previously mentioned, accrediting and licensing programs are focusing on outcomes. Consumers and their representatives are requiring outcome information from care providers. For example, data drawn from the OASIS-C are compiled and made available to the public at the Home Health Compare Web site. And last, but not least, home health agencies have always been concerned with measuring their performance relative to other providers.

While gathering, encoding, and submitting the OASIS-C data may seem to be an end in itself, it is merely the means to achieve outcome measurement and only the beginning of the process. OBQI/OBQM is fundamentally a two-stage process. First, the data must be gathered in a uniform manner (OASIS-C). This results in a report showing the agency's performance in terms of outcomes relative to the national sample. During this first step, risk adjustment occurs through grouping or statistical methods to compensate for the potential influence of case-mix variables that can affect outcomes. Risk adjustment is done by the state agency for some data elements. Reports may be printed with and/or without the risk adjustment. In the second step, the agency selects target outcomes for enhancement, evaluates care for the target outcome, develops a plan of action to change the care, and finally monitors the outcome to see if the desired gains are accomplished (see Figure 12-4). CMS has established a Quality Improvement Organization (QIO) for each state. These organizations are available to assist agencies with understanding the OBQI/OBQM process, selecting a target outcome, and developing action plans.

One added advantage of a fully developed OBQI/OBQM program is that agencies are able to move into the domain of managing resources for the explicit purpose of gaining the best outcome. Agencies can improve outcomes in areas of inadequate performance, reinforce outcomes in areas in which they do well, and maintain outcomes in areas where performance is acceptable. By managing outcomes in this way, resources are naturally affected. Staffing patterns as well as frequency of services can be altered with a clear bottom-line assessment of the impact that such alterations have on patients. In the long run, this allows agencies to enhance their quality of care yet manage their resources to become more cost effective, an important goal under the home health prospective payment system.

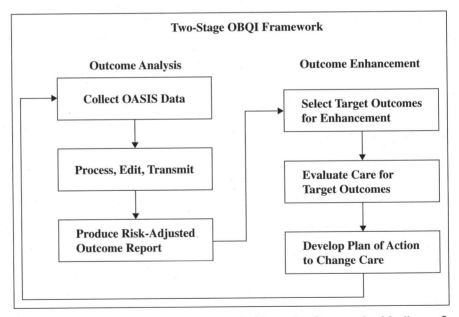

FIGURE **12-4** Two-Stage OBQI Framework. (From the Centers for Medicare & Medicaid Services' *Outcome-Based Quality Improvement (OBQI) Implementation Manual*, pp. 2.4.)

Utilization Management

Utilization management focuses on monitoring the increase and decrease in utilization of services provided to patients. Utilization management seeks to assure that services are appropriate to patients' conditions. For example, a patient may be receiving skilled nursing services for a terminal disease. Offering social and mental health services to such a patient is typical for proper utilization.

A home care agency may have separate written plans for quality improvement and utilization management. It seems that the plans that produce the best results combine the efforts of all information-based areas: quality improvement, utilization management, risk management, information management/systems, and finance. These areas have a common interest—to improve processes that have an impact on the agency's internal and external customer base and to be competitive in price and quality of service within the market of home care.

HIM professionals are increasingly and successfully taking on quality improvement and utilization management duties/roles, using their clinical knowledge and ability to develop tools and reports from the large repositories of clinical data.

RISK MANAGEMENT AND LEGAL ISSUES

Risk Management

Risk management, in general terms, is a program that monitors the liability and accountability of home care services delivered to customers. The areas at risk are measured through clinical analysis by way of incident reporting and financial analysis through the agency's insurance policy. Typically, the health information manager will manage the incident reporting to minimize the risk of injury to patients, visitors, and employees and to delineate procedures for reporting and follow-up of incidents.

An **incident** or **unusual occurrence** is defined as any happening that is not consistent with the routine operations of the agency or routine care of a particular patient. Key elements of the procedure for reporting incidents include the following:

- Establish time frames for reporting and evaluation of the occurrences.
- Establish reporting of occurrences as a positive means of improving the delivery of quality care as opposed to a punitive performance evaluation.
- Record only the facts.
- Narrative description should be written in the first person and recorded by the employee who witnessed or experienced the occurrence.
- Incident reports should not be maintained with the medical record; however, the chart should be documented regarding the occurrence, reflecting the continuation of the treatment provided to the patient.
- Categorize occurrences and utilize reports to identify trends and patterns.
- Share the reports with the appropriate committees, such as the quality improvement committee, to improve processes that are risks and potential risks to the company.

Satisfaction Committee/Monitoring

Another form of proactive risk management is to utilize a satisfaction committee to monitor customer satisfaction issues. During the initial visit, all patients/caregivers should be informed and presented with the patient bill of rights, which includes the toll-free state department of health hotline number and the agency's contact number if there is a problem. This allows patients/caregivers to express concerns and grievances regarding patient care. The committee should monitor issues for all customers, including patients and their caregivers, physicians, and insurance companies, and try to resolve them in a timely manner while maintaining continuity of care for patients.

Legal Issues

Legal issues are important for all departments of home care and are handled best if done proactively. The human resource department is legally required to have certain information on file for new employees. Following is a general list of items to complete when hiring new employees:

- Past employment—dates, employer, salary, and work performance
- Education—license in particular profession
- Criminal background check
- State driver's license
- Credit check for finance employees

The most common requirements for licensed professionals in most states are as follows:

- Cardiopulmonary resuscitation (CPR)—each staff person should be certified when hired and is typically recertified once every two years.
- **Occupational Safety and Health Administration (OSHA)**—in-service educational programs are implemented to provide a safe work environment for employees. Safety topics include ergonomics, first aid, and blood-borne pathogens. OSHA in-service programs are typically presented annually.
- Universal precautions should be practiced at all times.
- Safety in the community should be practiced at all times.
- The Joint Commission requires the original license of all professional staff to be a part of their personnel file.

Other common in-services required by all home care employees are the following:

- An in-service on body mechanics is required and usually completed annually.
- Confidentiality in-services are required at the time of hire and recommended to be done annually.

Policies and Procedures

The health information manager ordinarily develops, or at least updates, particular policies related to medical record procedures. Following is a recommended list of certain policies for review and approval by the agency's legal counsel:

- Advance directives
- Release of medical information
- General treatment
- Alcohol and drug treatment
- HIV/AIDS treatment
- Mental health information
- Procedure for responding to subpoena and court orders
- Procedure for do not resuscitate orders

ROLE OF THE HEALTH INFORMATION MANAGEMENT PROFESSIONAL

HIM positions within home care are still considered nontraditional; however, this career path is becoming more common for recent graduates. The role can be very rewarding, because it usually extends beyond medical records. HIM home care positions require knowledge of finance, quality improvement, utilization review, and information systems.

Now more than ever, agencies must make good use of the information available to them to survive and thrive in the data-driven world of home care. Health information managers can play a key role in developing, implementing, and maintaining effective information systems for home care. Becoming familiar with the home care market and how to be competitive within that market provides HIM professionals with another arena in which to demonstrate their skills in managing information and making that information useful.

TRENDS

Several new types of programs for the delivery of health care in the home have developed in the twenty-first century. Among these innovations are home-based primary care and disease management programs (Turk et al., 2000). Physicians have also shown increased interest in house-call training, education, and practice. In the realm of technology, telemedicine programs for the home will likely expand because of the potential benefits these provide to both patients and providers (Leff & Burton, 2001; Resnick & Alwan, 2010). Home care providers should strive to make effective use of technology without losing the personal touch that homebound patients require.

As noted in Chapter 11, home health agencies are considered a type of postacute care provider. Home health agencies need to stay abreast of proposed policy changes such as the possibility of bundling payments for postacute care. On the other hand, there is also a recognition of the potential for cost savings and improved outcomes offered by home care, as evidenced by the inclusion of the Independence at Home demonstration program in the Patient Protection and Affordable Care Act health reform legislation enacted in 2010. Certainly, the twenty-first century holds both promises and challenges for the home care industry.

SUMMARY

The home health care industry continues to evolve to offer quality care at a reasonable level of operating cost. Changing regulations and rapid growth have forced home care providers to be creative in their business planning to make their agency stand out among the rest. HIM professionals can contribute greatly to the future business planning of home care, especially in light of their training and ability to couple the clinical side with the technical side of information management.

KEY TERMS

485 the document number for a previously required CMS form facilitating a patient's orders for home care. Although the requirement for the form itself has been dropped, the content of the form is still required. Therefore, both the term *485* and the form itself are still in use in many home health agencies. The form provides a plan of care, which must be established and reviewed at least once every 60 days by the patient's attending physician.

Accreditation Commission for Health Care (ACHC) a voluntary accrediting organization with deeming authority for home health, hospice, and suppliers of durable medical equipment, prosthetics, orthotics, and supplies (DMEPOS).

affiliate an associate or member of a particular business.

audit a formal way of checking financial and other records.

care plan an outline for patient care based on a comprehensive assessment and the patient's specific needs that includes goals, objectives, and those responsible for completing the plan.

Centers for Medicare & Medicaid Services (CMS) a federal agency within the Department of Health and Human Services. Its main focus is to administer the Medicare and Medicaid programs. Formerly known as the Health Care Financing Administration (HCFA).

certification period the billing period for which a physician's home care order is valid for patient treatment—60 days—a time frame in which a patient's physician must review, update, and recertify (if necessary) a patient's plan of care.

Community Health Accreditation Program (CHAP) an independent, not-for-profit, accrediting body for community-based health care organizations. Meeting CHAP standards can provide a home health agency with deemed status with regard to the Medicare Conditions of Participation.

comprehensive assessment a document that is completed on the first visit to the patient's home. The document should include the patient's present illness; significant past history; review of all systems/physical assessment; medications; psychological, social, and economic factors; emergency plans; and skilled nursing performed that day, as well as incorporate the required OASIS data elements.

Conditions of Participation federal regulations with which home health agencies must comply in order to participate in the Medicare program. In addition to other regulations, the COP outline documentation requirements for Medicare-certified home health agencies.

deemed status a status conferred by the Centers for Medicare & Medicaid Services (CMS) to health care providers who meet the voluntary standards of an accrediting organization whose standards have been determined by CMS to be the equivalent of the Medicare Conditions of Participation in that particular category. An organization with deemed status is no longer subject to routine surveys under the Medicare Conditions of Participation.

denial lack of payment for home visits/treatments due to failure to meet medical necessity requirements for the services or for some other reason (e.g., provider error, payer error, ineligible patient, and so on). A denial can sometimes be appealed successfully.

disciplines specialty providers offering a variety of treatments or services for patients, for example, physical therapy, maternity services, medical social services, and so on.

durable medical equipment (DME) medical equipment provided to the patient within the home environment.

fixed costs costs that do not change in proportion to changes in volume of services. Office rent and utilities are examples of fixed costs in home health.

Home Assessment Validation and Entry (HAVEN) software available from CMS, developed to provide home health agencies with an electronic application for data entry, editing, and validation of OASIS-C data.

homebound when an individual is physically or mentally limited and is able to leave his or her home only infrequently and with great effort, generally requiring assistance.

home care visit medical and nonmedical treatments provided to patients within the privacy and comfort of their own homes. The home care visit is often used as the unit of measure in home health care for evaluating costs, scheduling, and productivity. For some payers, the visit is the unit of payment for services.

home health aide a certified staff person who is able to enhance the patient's care by assisting with the patient's activities of daily living, such as checking vital signs, bathing, grooming, meal preparation, and so on.

home health care service and treatment provided in the home environment to a recovering, disabled, or chronically ill person to improve health or effective functioning.

incident/unusual occurrence any happening that is not consistent with the routine operations of the agency or routine care of a particular patient.

integrated format a record in which the information is organized in a strict chronological order.

The Joint Commission (TJC) promotes quality in home care by accrediting a variety of organizations that provide home care services. Meeting TJC standards provides a home health agency with deemed status with regard to the Medicare Conditions of Participation.

National Association for Home Care and Hospice (NAHC) an association for organizations and individuals who provide health care and supportive services on an outreach basis to patients in their homes.

non-physician practitioner (NPP) In the context of certifying the necessity of home care services, an NPP is "a nurse practitioner or clinical nurse specialist…, who is working in collaboration with the physician in accordance with State law, or a certified nurse-midwife…, or a physician assistant…, under the supervision of the physician" (MLN Matters, 2010, p. 2).

Occupational Safety and Health Administration (OSHA) a federal agency that develops criteria meant to provide a safe work environment for all employees as part of its mission to enforce occupational safety and health legislation.

outcome end result or consequence; the patient's health and functional status after a period of treatment.

Outcome and Assessment Information Set-C (OASIS-C) a data set requirement under Medicare's Conditions of Participation. Medicare-certified home health agencies collect and use OASIS data when evaluating adult, nonmaternity patients. The intent of OASIS is to make the Conditions of Participation more patient-centered and outcome-oriented while providing home care agencies with more flexibility to operate their programs. It also measures treatment outcomes and provides individual agencies with the ability to compare themselves to the national data set.

payer mix a ratio of an agency's various patient insurers and third-party payers.

problem-oriented record a record organized by the patient's problems; the problem-oriented record follows each clinical problem individually and provides a systematic method of documentation to reflect logical thinking on the part of the one directing the care of the patient.

recertification additional physician orders continuing home health services after the initial 60-day certification period.

skilled nursing agencies agencies that offer nursing services such as trained medical-surgical nursing, intravenous therapy, enterostomal therapy, psychiatric or mental health, maternity, or restorative nursing. Services are provided to patients based on their individual needs.

source-oriented record a record organized in sections according to patient care departments and/or disciplines.

standards rules used as a basis of comparison for measuring quantitative or qualitative value.

variable costs costs that vary in proportion to the volume of service provided.

REVIEW QUESTIONS

Knowledge-Based Questions

1. Identify a few services that home care agencies deliver.
2. Who are the voluntary accrediting bodies that develop the standards for home care?
3. Define a certification period.
4. Explain the importance of documentation and coding for proper reimbursement.
5. What is the OASIS-C and what is its purpose?
6. Explain how Medicare reimburses home care agencies for the provision of care to patients.

Critical Thinking Questions

1. Compare and contrast home care coding with hospital inpatient coding.
2. As home care agencies implement efficiencies to increase their potential profitability under the Medicare PPS, what are some of the issues and concerns they face?

WEB ACTIVITY

Visit the Home Health Agency Center at the CMS Web site at http://www.cms.gov/center/hha.asp. Select a link to one of the many topics available on this page.

Which link did you select? Describe information about home health care that was available through the link that you selected.

CASE STUDY

Mary Jones is the health information supervisor at Somewhere Home Care, which is Medicare certified. As required by Medicare, her agency has been completing and submitting OASIS-C data to their state. They have been accessing their patient data through their OASIS-C reports available from the state, as well as monitoring and documenting visit patterns and frequency by the clinicians in the agency. In addition, they have been monitoring the cost of supplies utilized per patient.

In reviewing their financial data, Mary's director has indicated that the agency has performed marginally under the Medicare prospective payment system. They would like to improve their financial performance and have met with the leadership team of the agency to discuss a possible plan of action. Although some insurers still pay by the visit, Medicare patients are the largest group in the agency's payer mix, and Medicare pays a set amount of money for the provision of care over a 60-day period rather than a per-visit fee.

Mary has some statistics available to her to assist the director with formulating a plan. These include:

- The number of patients the agency has had in each HHRG classification over the past three years
- The number of visits (by clinician type; i.e., RN, LPN, HHA, PT, OT, SLP) made to each patient for each 60-day episode of care
- The average number of visits made to patients in each HHRG classification

- Financial data, including reimbursement amounts for each HHRG and the agency-specific costs per each visit type
- Primary diagnosis for each patient
- OASIS outcome reports printed for OBQI/OBQM, showing how the agency has performed in outcomes as compared to other agencies in the country
- Payer mix report, which shows the percentage of patients the agency has in each payer source (i.e., Medicare, Medicaid, commercial insurance, private pay, etc.). At Somewhere Home Care, 65 percent of their patients are covered by Medicare.

Investigation into care plans and visit patterns indicate that there is wide fluctuation in visit patterns among clinicians. Patients who fall into the same HHRG category, who should basically be very similar, have widely varying visit ranges.

Based on the above information and scenario, answer the following questions:

1. What are some significant factors Mary and her director should consider about their payment sources as they evaluate their financial performance?
2. What statistical data available to Mary would be most helpful in developing an action plan?
3. Where should Mary focus her clinical and medical record expertise?

REFERENCES AND SUGGESTED READINGS

Abraham, P. R. (2001). *Documentation and Reimbursement for Home Care and Hospice Programs.* Chicago: American Health Information Management Association.

[ACHC] Accreditation Commission for Health Care. (2010). About us. [Online]. http://www.achc.org/about_why_achc.php [2010, August 30].

Centers for Medicare & Medicaid Services (2010). *Outcome-Based Quality Improvement (OBQI) Implementation Manual* [Online]. http://www.cms.gov/HomeHealthQualityInits/15_PBQIProcessMeasures.asp [2010, August 30].

Centers for Medicare & Medicaid Services. (n.d.). *OASIS Data Sets* [Online]. http://www.cms.gov/HomeHealthQualityInits/12_HHQIOASISDataSet.asp [2010, August 30].

The Joint Commission (2010). *Comprehensive Accreditation Manual for Home Care.* Oakbrook Terrace, IL: Author.

Leff, B., and Burton, J. R. (2001). The Future History of Home Care and Physician House Calls in the United States. *Journals of Gerontology Series A—Biological Sciences & Medical Sciences,* 56 (10), M603–M608.

MLN Matters. (2010, December 16). Home Health Face-to-Face Encounter: A New Home Health Certification Requirement. Number: SE1038. [Online]. http://www.cms.gov/MLNMattersArticles/downloads/SE1038.pdf [2011, April 2].

National Association for Home Care and Hospice. (2010). *How to Choose a Home Care Agency.* Washington, DC: Author.

OASIS-C Guidance Manual (2010). Appendix D. [Online]. https://www.cms.gov/HomeHealthQualityInits/14_HHQIOASISUserManual.asp [2010, August 31].

Resnick, H. E., & Alwan, M. (2010). Use of health information technology in home health and hospice agencies: United States, 2007. *Journal of the American Medical Informatics Association, 17,* 389–395.

Turk, L., Parmley, J., Ames, A., & Schumacher, K. L. (2000). A New Era in Home Care. *Seminars for Nurse Managers, 8*(3), 143–150.

KEY RESOURCES

Accreditation Commission for Health Care
http://www.achc.org

American Academy of Home Care Physicians
http://www.aahcp.org

Community Health Accreditation Program, Inc.
http://www.chapinc.org

The Joint Commission
http://www.jointcommission.org

National Association for Home Care and Hospice
http://www.nahc.org

CHAPTER 13

Hospice

TERESA SHERFY, RHIT

KAREN M. STASZEL, RHIA

LEARNING OBJECTIVES

Upon successful completion of this chapter, you should be able to:

- Describe the hospice patient.

- Define the term *hospice* and describe the difference between hospice care and traditional acute care.

- Describe the composition and role of the interdisciplinary team in providing hospice care to patients, families, and significant others.

- Define the four reimbursement levels of hospice care—routine home care, respite care, general or acute inpatient care, and continuous care.

- Discuss components of appropriate documentation in the hospice clinical record.

- Describe the use of hospice benefit periods and associated documentation requirements.

- Describe the roles played by volunteers in hospice care and issues relating to the volunteer documentation in the clinical record.

- Discuss the capture of clinical visit information to track the cost of hospice care.

- Discuss the Medicare Conditions of Participation relating to hospice care.

- Discuss Quality Assessment/Performance Improvement in the hospice setting.

- Discuss bereavement care and documentation following the death of the hospice patient.

Setting	Description	Synonyms/Examples
Patient's Residence	The majority of hospice programs provide patient care in the patient's place of residence, which may include the patient's home, a relative's or friend's home, a nursing home, or a senior citizen complex.	
Nursing Home or Hospital	Some hospices contract with major hospital complexes and/or nursing homes to establish hospice units or wings. The hospice wing then becomes the patient's place of residence. These units are used primarily when patients have no primary caregiver in their home, for acute pain and symptom management, if the patient is too sick to leave the existing facility and can just be transferred to another wing, or for respite care.	Hospice inpatient unit, IPU (inpatient unit), care center, hospice wing.
Stand-Alone Hospice	Some hospice programs build their own facilities. These facilities are not associated with an existing hospital or nursing home. Similar to nursing home and/or hospital beds, the bed in the stand-alone hospice becomes patients' place of residence. Again, these facilities are used primarily when there is no primary caregiver in the home, for pain and symptom management, or for respite care.	Freestanding hospice, hospice inpatient unit, hospice care center, IPU (inpatient unit). Depending on the state requirements, hospices may license these facilities as nursing homes, adult foster care homes, or freestanding hospice units (if the state has a category for them).

INTRODUCTION TO SETTING

The history of **hospice** can trace its roots along the same timeline as the history and development of the hospital. Charitable, religious organizations and individuals were caring not only for the sick and diseased throughout history, but also for the dying and those grieving for them. *Hospice* is a French word derived from the Latin *hospitium*, which was a place in which a guest was received. This is very similar to the Latin *hospitalis*, meaning "of a guest," and *hospes*, meaning "a guest," from which *hospital* is derived. It was not until 1967, however, when Dame Cicely Saunders opened St. Christopher's Hospice in London, that caring for the dying patient was recognized and developed as a philosophy and practice. The time period, it appears, was especially ripe for the emergence of the hospice discipline:

> A hundred years ago, doctors cured only a few patients because they lacked the powerful medical tools that exist today. With the advent of safer surgery and the enormous advances in therapeutics, doctors have apparently developed the power to remove problems and effect cures. The relentless pursuit of cures for more and more diseases can lead the blinkered into believing that care of those who are incurable is less important. (Corr & Corr, 1983)

Most hospice programs provide patient care in the patient's **place of residence**, which could be the patient's home, a relative's or friend's home, a nursing home, or a senior citizen complex. In addition to providing care in the patient's place of residence, some hospice programs have built their own facilities and/or contracted with major hospital complexes and/or nursing homes to establish hospice units or wings. The hospice facility or the hospice wing then becomes the patient's place of residence.

Types of Patients

The Terminally Ill

Hospices provide **palliative care** or symptom management rather than **curative therapy** to patients considered **terminally ill**, with a life expectancy of less than six months based on the physician's clinical judgment regarding the normal course of the individual's illness. Terminal diseases range from congenital disorders of children to multiple sclerosis; end-stage renal, respiratory, and cardiac diseases; AIDS (Acquired Immune Deficiency Syndrome); Alzheimer's disease; cancer; and a host of other illnesses. Symptom management not only includes methods to relieve chronic pain and other physical results of the disease process, but it also helps relieve the emotional and mental stress of the dying process. Hospices use non-narcotic analgesics, narcotic analgesics (titrated to manage pain, not cause mental confusion), frequent changes of position, back rubs, massage, oxygen, tranquilizers, antidepressants, music, conversation, and companionship to relieve terminal symptoms. Hospices do not routinely use X-rays, transfusions, chemotherapy, radiation therapy, intubations, cardiopulmonary resuscitation (CPR), or any other therapy that would be considered curative. In general, a hospice allows patients to live as symptom-free as possible and enables them to lead as meaningful a life as possible for the remainder of their illness.

The Unit of Care

In the acute care setting, the focus of care is on treating the patient. Hospice philosophy, on the other hand, recognizes that the dying process is difficult not only for the patient, but also for the patient's family and significant others. Thus hospice care focuses not just on the needs of the patient, but also on the physical, emotional, and mental states of those around the patient. This is such an important part of a hospice treatment plan that the National Hospice and Palliative Case Organization (NHPCO) states, "The unit of care in hospice is the patient/family." Treatment plans and options are discussed with the patient and with family members; goals are written for the patient and family members.

Types of Caregivers

The Interdisciplinary Team

The hospice is similar to other patient care settings in managing the treatment plan using an **interdisciplinary team (IDT)**. The difference, however, is in the composition of the hospice IDT. The team includes:

1. A doctor of medicine or osteopathy (employed by the hospice or under contract)
2. A registered nurse
3. A social worker
4. A pastoral or other counselor

Hospices may also include a volunteer or volunteer coordinator, a pharmacist, a bereavement counselor, or a hospice aide as part of the interdisciplinary team.

The nurse acts as the case manager and coordinates changes to the care plan with other members of the team. The social worker provides psychosocial assessment and social resources that can be utilized by the patient and family. The pastoral or other counselor offers spiritual support and comfort. The bereavement counselor prepares the patient and family for the impending death and provides grief support to the family after the patient's death. **Volunteers** who receive special hospice training offer companionship, comfort, transportation, light housekeeping, and even direct patient care (depending on their professional qualifications). The pharmacist works with the nurse and attending physician to provide adequate symptom relief. The hospice aide is assigned by the nurse to provide bathing, personal care, light housekeeping, and other nonskilled treatments such as dressing changes.

Primary Caregivers

The fact that most hospice care is provided in the patient's home requires that someone from the patient's immediate family and/or friends act as a **primary caregiver**. Members of the patient's interdisciplinary team visit the patient a few times per week, possibly more often, depending on the patient's condition. The team, however, is not with the patient 24 hours per day, so the team members must teach the primary caregiver to give treatments, medications, and baths, and to watch for changes in the patient's condition when hospice personnel are not present.

If the patient can no longer live alone and does not have anyone who can act as the primary caregiver, the hospice has two options. If the hospice has its own facility or contracts with a nursing home or hospital for a hospice unit, the patient could be placed in a bed there. The staff members on these units act as primary caregivers under the direction of the staff and treatment plan of the hospice. The hospice can also arrange to have volunteers and/or hospice aides provide additional hours of care in the patient's home if necessary.

REGULATORY ISSUES

Licensure and Accreditation

A hospice program is licensed by the state in which it is located. In many states, licensure regulations closely follow the Medicare Conditions of Participation for hospice care. In June of 2008, major revisions to the hospice Conditions of Participation were finalized by the Centers for Medicare & Medicaid Services (CMS). This revision marked the first major change in Medicare regulations for hospice since their inception in 1983. Significant changes were made to the requirements for the patient's plan of care, requirements for assessment and reassessment of the patient, and the standards for quality assessment of hospice services. The Joint Commission (TJC), the Community Health Accreditation Program (CHAP), and the Accreditation Commission for Health Care, Inc. (ACHC) can provide deemed status by surveying the hospice organization under the Conditions of Participation for hospice care in addition to their own voluntary accreditation standards.

Licensure issues faced by some hospices in the United States relate to regulations for stand-alone facilities, or hospice facilities that are not directly affiliated with a larger hospital system. These stand-alone facilities have inpatient beds that can be used by hospice patients for management of acute symptoms and/or as a residence if there is not someone in their home to help care for them. The revised Medicare regulations contain many additions to the requirements for hospices that directly provide inpatient care.

The National Hospice and Palliative Care Organization (NHPCO) publishes a book of standards that can be utilized by hospices to validate the quality of care provided. NHPCO, however, does not require hospices to be certified or accredited under these standards to date and has no survey process similar to those of other regulating and accrediting organizations. Staff at the NHPCO are available for questions or concerns regarding interpretation of NHPCO standards and the Conditions of Participation.

All three voluntary accrediting agencies offering the option of deemed status—Accreditation Commission for Health Care (ACHC), the Community Health Accreditation Program (CHAP), and the Joint Commission (TJC)—publish accreditation standards for hospice organizations. The number of hospices seeking voluntary accreditation is increasing; however, many hospices are still not accredited. For this reason, this chapter specifically addresses the Conditions of Participation that all hospices (regardless of size) need to meet in order to receive reimbursement under the Medicare program (and any other third-party reimbursement subsequently).

The Medicare Conditions of Participation for hospice describe regulations pertaining specifically to Medicare patients; however, some third-party payers refer back to the Conditions of Participation when evaluating acceptability of hospice election for their clients. In addition, the Conditions of Participation are commonly utilized by state regulators to assess hospice programs for licensure, making the Conditions of Participation the main standards that hospices follow.

Hospice Medicare Benefit and Regulations

Throughout the Medicare Conditions of Participation, using hospice coverage is referred to as "electing the hospice benefit." Hospice is reimbursed under Part A for Medicare patients. Upon election of the Hospice Medicare Benefit, Medicare will pay for no other Part A services and treatments that are related to the patient's hospice (terminal) diagnosis. The hospice benefit literally is a benefit for patients and families, because coverage includes all hospice services: clinical staff, medications, durable medical equipment, oxygen, supplies, laboratory work, therapy, bereavement support, and so on. There are minimal out-of-pocket expenses in hospice care and the paperwork burden on the family is also minimal.

Certification

To be eligible to elect hospice coverage under Medicare, the patient must be entitled to Medicare Part A and be certified as terminally ill by the attending physician and the hospice medical director. An individual is considered to be terminally ill if he or she has a medical prognosis of six months or less based on the physician's clinical judgment regarding the normal course of the individual's illness.

Health information management (HIM) department staff members are not usually responsible for obtaining the oral certifications, as these must be obtained from a clinical staff member (usually a registered nurse), but they may have significant involvement in obtaining the written certification statements. The certification must be signed by both the certifying physician and the hospice medical director. Hospices are required to have written certification before submission of a claim to Medicare. Hospices focus significantly on this process of obtaining the certification statements in order not to affect reimbursement, which, based on the regulations, cannot be paid without both signatures. Fiscal intermediaries/Medicare administrative contractors for Medicare reimbursement have begun more actively requesting copies of hospice patient clinical records and have requested the return of payment when the above signatures were not in place.

The Hospice Medicare Benefit is structured into benefit periods, the first of which begins on the date of election. Patients have three types of benefit periods: an initial 90-day period, a subsequent 90-day period, followed by an unlimited number of 60-day periods. Patients can **revoke** or leave hospice care and return at a later time with no risk to their Medicare coverage. Patients must continue to be eligible for hospice care at the beginning of each new period. This process is described later in this chapter.

Election of Hospice Care

Medicare regulations require that the patient or his or her legal representative sign an election statement at the time of admission to hospice care. The election statement must include specific requirements described in the Medicare Conditions of Participation. The statement must identify the hospice. It must contain a statement that acknowledges that the patient understands the palliative rather than curative nature of hospice care and that standard coverage for Medicare services related to the patient's terminal diagnosis is waived. The statement must have an effective date and be signed by the patient or legal representative.

The HIM department must ensure that if the election statement is signed by the patient's legal representative, there is documentation (of health care power of attorney, legal guardian, health care surrogate, or patient advocate) in the clinical record reflecting that this person is indeed the legal representative. Many hospice programs in the past have assumed that if the person signing is the patient's primary caregiver, then no other proof is necessary. As an authorization for release of medical information is evaluated for validity, so should the signature on the election form. The HIM department must provide significant clinical education in this area.

Revocation

A patient may choose to revoke the election of hospice care at any time, at which point standard Medicare coverage resumes. There must be a revocation form signed by the patient or legal representative and filed with the hospice, stating that the patient loses the remaining days in the current benefit period and the effective date of the revocation. The effective date may not be earlier than the date on which the form is signed by the patient or legal representative.

The HIM department needs to ensure that the statement is received and filed in the clinical record. Upon revocation of the Medicare hospice benefit, the patient resumes regular Medicare coverage and loses all remaining days within the election period. To elect hospice care again, the patient would be admitted in the subsequent election period. Monitoring the election periods to ensure correct billing practices may be the responsibility of the HIM department or the billing department staff. Verification of the validity of the signature on this form is also appropriate.

Change of Designated Hospice

The patient may change hospices (transfer from one to another) once during each benefit period without needing to revoke. A statement must be filed with the hospice from which care has been received and with the new hospice. The statement must indicate the date the change is effective and must be signed by the patient or legal representative.

The statement must be filed in the patient's record. Verification of the signature is again appropriate. It is important to establish the actual date of change and coordinate it with the other hospice.

Contracting with Other Facilities

When care is provided to hospice patients in hospitals or nursing homes, the hospice must have a written agreement with the facility and must maintain professional management of the patient's plan of care.

The HIM department may be responsible for obtaining documentation from these facilities. It is important that the HIM director is involved in the establishment of any written agreements with a hospital and/or nursing home that will provide acute treatment to hospice patients, so that the issue of obtaining copies of clinical records on hospice patients can be addressed. The sharing of health information for treatment purposes is permitted under HIPAA privacy regulations.

Plan of Care

A plan of care must be established for all hospice patients by the interdisciplinary group, in collaboration with the attending physician, the patient, and the caregiver. The plan of care must include the following components per Medicare Conditions of Participation:

1. Interventions to manage pain and symptoms
2. The scope and frequency of services required to meet the needs of the patient and caregivers
3. Measurable outcomes anticipated from implementing the plan of care
4. Drugs and treatments necessary to meet the patient's needs
5. Medical supplies and equipment necessary to meet the patient's needs
6. Documentation of the patient's involvement, understanding, and agreement with the plan

If the patient's attending physician is not a hospice employee, it will be necessary to document the physician's participation in development and maintenance of the interdisciplinary plan of care. This can be done through documentation of items such as physician orders, clinical staff conferences with the patient's attending physician, communication with the attending physician regarding the patient's status, and the updates made to the plan of care. It is also important that the plan specify the interval until the next review.

Hospice is required to obtain an informed consent that specifies the type of care and services that may be provided. The HIM department must ensure that the signature on the informed consent is valid and any associated documentation of personal representative status is included in the clinical record.

Volunteers

A unique regulation in the Medicare Conditions of Participation is the requirement for volunteers. Hospices must document volunteer hours in both administrative and patient care activities in an amount that equals 5 percent of the total patient care hours of all paid employees and contract staff.

To substantiate that volunteers provide direct patient care, HIM department staff should participate in volunteer orientation programs to provide basic documentation guidelines. Volunteer staff may or may not be clinically oriented. They may never have documented in a patient's record, so basic education on the do's and don'ts of documentation is very important. The capture of volunteer hours may or may not be an HIM department function. It is made easier with the use of volunteer logs, completed by all volunteers regardless of the functions being performed. The log documents the name of the volunteer, the patient seen or activity performed, the number of hours and minutes, and any miles driven if applicable. The data can then be captured in a spreadsheet program or hospice software program. The number of hours of volunteer time is then compared to overall paid staff time in direct patient care to determine if the 5 percent criterion has been met.

Clinical Records

Hospices must establish and maintain a clinical record for every patient receiving hospice care. Services provided by all disciplines should be documented and included in the clinical record. Signatures and dates are required for all entries. The record should include a minimum of the following:

1. Initial and comprehensive assessments
2. Plan of care including interdisciplinary team updates
3. Signed copies of patient rights, hospice election, and informed consent
4. Responses to medications and treatments, with related physician orders
5. Outcome measure data
6. Physician certification and recertification of terminal illness
7. Copies of advance directives

Records must be evaluated to determine if all progress notes have been signed appropriately. In addition, records should be easily accessible. Paper records could be filed numerically or alphabetically, depending on patient volume.

DOCUMENTATION

As stated previously, most hospice care is provided in the patient's place of residence. Clinical staff members (nurses, social workers, hospice aides) visit the patient's home at least once a week, usually more, depending on the condition of the patient. Their visit length varies depending on the condition of the patient and the needs of the family. The patient may or may not be seen by a physician during the entire hospice stay. If the patient has an attending physician outside the hospice, the patient may go to the physician's office if well enough. The hospice physician may visit in an emergency situation or if the patient does not have an attending physician. The registered nurse acts as the case manager, coordinating care from all disciplines and communicating changes in the patient's condition with the physician.

Certification Requirements

Medicare requires that two physicians certify that the patient is terminally ill, with a life expectancy of six months or less based on the physician's clinical judgment regarding the normal course of the individual's illness. One physician can be the patient's attending physician, and the other must be the hospice physician. The certification must include narrative documentation from the hospice physician that serves as an attestation statement of terminal illness. The statement could be incorporated into the initial orders for treatment to reduce the amount of paperwork needing the signature of an outside physician. In either case, the hospice medical director (or a designee) and the certifying attending physician must sign the certification statement. It is important that the HIM staff determine the most effective method to obtain the statement promptly and reduce time spent by the medical staff to sign paperwork. As previously stated in this chapter, no claims can be sent for reimbursement until the certification is signed by both physicians.

Assessment, Interdisciplinary Plan of Care, and Associated Documentation

At the time of admission to the hospice program, a registered nurse visits the patient in the place of residence to perform an initial assessment. At this time, the nurse completes a history of the patient's illness, performs a physical examination, and evaluates the appropriateness of the patient for hospice care. If the nurse assesses that the patient is hospice appropriate, the interdisciplinary care plan will be started. The nurse will establish the plan of care in collaboration with the interdisciplinary team. The care plan is updated a minimum of every 15 days, based on comprehensive assessments of the patient by the team. The interdisciplinary team usually meets every two weeks, or more frequently, depending on the hospice. During the meeting, care plans are reviewed, the hospice physician may recommend new orders, and specific problems may be addressed. These reviews are documented for each individual patient. The interdisciplinary care plan may or may not change depending on the condition of the patient.

The hospice aide provides basic, nonskilled care for patients and may or may not be required in every case. It is the nurse's responsibility to determine the need for a hospice aide, including visit frequency and scope (what is to be performed). Hospices hiring certified nursing assistants can at least be assured of a minimum skill level. Once the case manager has determined that an aide is required, a hospice aide care plan is initiated. The case manager provides specific instructions on the hospice aide plan of care regarding the tasks to be performed and the frequency of the tasks, as well as any potential complications (or signs and symptoms) of which the aide should be aware. The hospice aide must then document completion of the individual tasks according to the specified frequency, as documented by the case manager. Electronic documentation is less common for hospice aides than for other members of the interdisciplinary teams.

It is the responsibility of the case manager to supervise the services provided by the hospice aide. This supervision must be documented in the clinical record. The case manager must assess the skills of hospice aides by watching them provide services to the patient and/or family, as well as evaluate the patient's and/or family's assessment of the hospice aide's services. The case manager can usually document this supervision within routine progress notes or on a separate supervisory visit note. In addition, the nurse should be ensuring that the hospice aide care plan is being carried out as specified for each visit.

The nurse may also identify additional services needed by the patient and family that cannot be adequately covered or provided by paid hospice staff, including companionship, shopping, transportation to the doctor, or respite for family members. The case manager may initiate a request for volunteer services. The hospice volunteer coordinator is then responsible for locating active volunteers who are willing to provide the requested services. Though the regulations do not require specific documentation of supervision of volunteer services, the case manager should ensure that the volunteer care plan is being carried out effectively.

Volunteer Documentation

Volunteers are required to document all contact with hospice patients, including telephone calls. To help volunteer staff complete documentation in a timely manner, most hospices have volunteer offices and/or space available for volunteers to come in and document, or allow the volunteer to document at home, but provide self-addressed envelopes for the volunteer to mail in progress notes. The volunteer coordinator should take an active role to ensure that all visits made are documented by volunteer staff. The HIM department can also help in this process by open and closed chart review.

Inpatient Documentation

A **hospice inpatient unit** can take two forms. The hospice can contract with a facility to utilize designated beds or a wing for hospice patients. The patients are often already in the facility and are identified by the staff as hospice appropriate. The facility staff contact the hospice to admit the patient. By this method, the facility where the patient is staying continues to maintain a clinical record. The hospice creates and maintains a separate clinical record. The hospice nurses will continue to visit the patient on a regular basis, as in the patient's home. Once the patient dies or is discharged, the hospice may supplement the patient's record by taking copies of portions of the facility's clinical record (just the portion during the time the patient was in hospice). Critical to this program is the negotiation of the contract. Administrators as well as staff must know all aspects of the contract relating to caring for the patient. HIM personnel should ensure that they are involved in this process in order to obtain portions of the clinical record after the patient's death and to understand the flow of the documentation.

The second way in which a hospice can be considered an inpatient unit is if it has its own inpatient facility. Patients are admitted directly to the facility, although they may have been referred from a hospital or nursing home. In this facility, all care is given around the clock by hospice employees. The clinical record created here is similar to a hospital or nursing home record, with periodic assessment of the patient's condition.

Documentation at the Close of Care

Upon the death of the hospice patient, all active care plans as well as the interdisciplinary care plan are closed. If the death is in the patient's home, a registered nurse makes a visit. A death in an institutional setting such as a nursing home or hospital may not require the services of a hospice nurse. Depending on the state, and individual cities and counties, a home death may require opening a medical examiner's case file. In addition, state laws may specify who can legally pronounce a patient dead. The hospice usually notifies local police departments or the coroner's office that there is a hospice patient residing in their district, so that upon the patient's death ambulances and police cars do not come with sirens blaring. This is important for the well-being of the family. Regardless of the specific legal requirements, the nurse must document all steps clearly in the clinical record, including (but not limited to) notification of the medical examiner (if applicable), notification of local police, the time the patient was pronounced dead, and contact with a funeral home to pick up the patient's body, as well as the condition of the family and significant others present. In addition to documentation of the death visit, the nurse should also complete a discharge summary documenting the circumstances surrounding the death of the patient and the family's coping abilities.

After the death of the patient, **bereavement** services are available to the patient's family and any significant others for up to one year following the death. The bereavement counselor may have been working with the family before the patient's death to initiate potential care plans. The bereavement counselor performs an assessment to determine the bereavement services needed by the survivors. It is important that HIM department staff continuously monitor the status of bereavement activities to ensure that all bereavement services are documented.

REIMBURSEMENT AND FUNDING

The Medicare Conditions of Participation provide four levels of hospice care (Figure 13-1). All levels of hospice care must be directed by the interdisciplinary team, and the clinical record must document the need for each required level of care. The most common is routine home care. **Routine home care** occurs when a patient is receiving routine (or nonproblematic) care in the place of residence. (The patient's "home" can be a facility such as a nursing home or a facility operated by the hospice if the facility is the patient's designated place of residence.)

Respite care provides an interval of rest for the primary caregiver and is provided to hospice patients in an approved (or contracted) facility (e.g., a nursing home, hospital, or hospice inpatient unit). Respite is provided on an occasional basis, for not more than five days at a time. The regulations are not specific on the definition of "occasional," but they do require hospices to evaluate families who require frequent respite periods to determine if the patient more appropriately belongs in a nursing home or inpatient hospice. When respite services are not provided by the hospice, but in a contracted facility, the hospice maintains a separate record from the facility providing the services. The nurse, social worker, hospice aide, and hospice physician continue to visit the patient and provide services as if the patient were still at home. The contracted facility staff members act as the primary caregivers when hospice staff members are not there. The clinical record must clearly indicate the need for

---

**MEDICARE CONDITIONS OF
PARTICIPATION - LEVELS
OF HOSPICE CARE**

- **ROUTINE HOME CARE**
  - A patient is at "home" and is not receiving continuous care.

- **GENERAL INPATIENT CARE**
  - A patient receives general inpatient care in an inpatient facility for pain control or acute or chronic symptom management that cannot be managed in other settings.

- **CONTINUOUS CARE**
  - A patient receives hospice care consisting predominantly of nursing care on a continuous basis at "home." Must be at least eight hours to be reimbursed at the continuous care rate.

- **INPATIENT RESPITE**
  - A patient receives care in an approved facility on a short-term basis.

FIGURE **13-1** Levels of hospice care.

respite services and also when and where the services are being provided. The hospice must obtain copies of the corresponding record from the facility providing respite care (if not the hospice itself) and incorporate these records in the current hospice clinical record.

General or **acute inpatient care** occurs when a patient receives care in an inpatient facility (a hospice inpatient unit or a facility contracted by the hospice) for pain control or acute or chronic symptom management that cannot be managed in the patient's place of residence. Again, the hospice interdisciplinary team is in charge of the plan of care, even if the services are provided by a nursing home or inpatient hospital. As with respite care, the hospice maintains its own patient record, and the clinical record from the facility providing general inpatient care must be obtained and incorporated into the hospice clinical record. Medicare limits the number of days reimbursed at an inpatient rate (including general inpatient and inpatient respite) to 20 percent of the total patient care days.

Continuous care occurs in the patient's place of residence when a patient requires continuous care for a minimum of 8 hours in a 24-hour period. Continuous care must be predominantly nursing care, although hospice aides may also participate. The clinical record must document at least hourly progress notes confirming the presence of continuous care. Continuous care is only furnished during brief periods of crisis and only as necessary to maintain the terminally ill patient at home.

The levels of hospice care are directly related to the way hospices receive reimbursement. Medicare (Part A), Medicaid, and most commercial insurance companies reimburse hospice care on a *per diem* basis, i.e., for each day the patient is enrolled in a hospice program. This is in contrast to a *service-based* reimbursement (utilized for some nonhospice home care), in which an agency receives payment based on services provided by clinical staff. Per diem payments are paid regardless of whether any services (visits by clinical staff) are actually given each day. Each level of hospice care is reimbursed at a different per diem rate, which is further adjusted based on the geographic location of the patient. These rates are published annually by the Centers for Medicare & Medicaid Services (CMS).

The hospice per diem includes not only visits by hospice clinical staff (nurses, social workers, hospice aides, and chaplains; only the hospice physician can bill separately from the per diem), but also medications (relating to the hospice diagnosis, e.g., pain medication for bone cancer, but not necessarily insulin for long-term diabetes), durable medical equipment, laboratory work, oxygen, supplies, and bereavement services. When the patient expires, reimbursement stops, even though the family and friends may be receiving bereavement services for up to one year. If the patient is seen by the attending physician during the hospice admission, the physician can continue to bill under Medicare Part B (and separately for other insurers as well).

Upon admission to a hospice program, the patient signs an "election of the hospice benefit" statement. This statement not only indicates that the patient is electing the hospice benefit (through Medicare Part A, Medicaid, and most other commercial insurers), but also states that all other services related to the patient's hospice diagnosis—such as skilled home care, inpatient hospitalization, and nursing home care—are not to be paid by the insurer to any other agency. This is an important aspect of hospice reimbursement, especially when a hospice patient receives respite care or general inpatient care in a nursing home or inpatient hospital setting. If a hospice does not have its own inpatient facility, it must contract with an approved nursing home and/or inpatient hospital to provide respite and acute inpatient care. The contract stipulates that only the hospice can bill Medicare for hospice care. The hospital or nursing home can charge the patient (or an insurance company or even the hospice) for room and board only, but cannot bill for the hospice services (even if services are provided by its staff), according to the election statement. As described previously, the hospice patient is still managed by the hospice interdisciplinary team, regardless of the setting for care. The incentive for a nursing home or inpatient hospital to sign such a contract with a hospice would be to fill beds that might otherwise be vacant, to receive room and board payments.

In addition to the levels of hospice care, the Conditions of Participation also describe hospice benefit periods, beginning with one 90-day period, followed by a second 90-day period, then an unlimited number of 60-day periods.

The hospice must evaluate the patient at the end of each benefit period to determine if the patient is still considered hospice appropriate or continues to have a limited life expectancy. At the end of each benefit period, if the patient is still considered hospice appropriate, the hospice medical director (or physician designee) must recertify the patient as requiring hospice care. (The Affordable Care Act requires that a hospice physician or nurse practitioner have a face-to-face encounter with a hospice patient prior to the patient's 180th-day recertification, and each subsequent recertification. The encounter must occur no more than 30 calendar days prior to the start of the hospice patient's third benefit period.) Evaluating that the patient still has a limited life expectancy can be difficult in some diagnoses (congestive heart failure, chronic obstructive pulmonary disease, Alzheimer's disease), because not every diagnosis follows a usual path. NHPCO as well as Medicare intermediaries have developed guidelines to assist hospices in determining the continued appropriateness of a patient for hospice services. Hospices may also use a severity system at the time of admission and when reevaluating the patient for continued services. For example, the Palliative Performance Scale is used by many hospices to assess the patients' decline in physical, functional, and mental status as they near the end of life. An example of the Palliative Performance Scale shown in Figure 13-2.

If the hospice finds, according to available criteria and analysis, that the patient no longer has a limited life expectancy of six months or less, it is the hospice's responsibility to discharge the patient from the hospice benefit. The hospice patient can also choose not to continue with hospice services. The patient's terminal condition may improve slightly and/or the patient and family may choose to seek more aggressive treatment (such as chemotherapy). If the patient chooses to stop receiving hospice services, the patient may revoke the

Palliative Performance Scale (PPSv2)

version 2

PPS Level	Ambulation	Activity & Evidence of Disease	Self-Care	Intake	Conscious Level
100%	Full	Normal activity & work No evidence of disease	Full	Normal	Full
90%	Full	Normal activity & work Some evidence of disease	Full	Normal	Full
80%	Full	Normal activity with Effort Some evidence of disease	Full	Normal or reduced	Full
70%	Reduced	Unable Normal Job/Work Significant disease	Full	Normal or reduced	Full
60%	Reduced	Unable hobby/house work Significant disease	Occasional assistance necessary	Normal or reduced	Full or Confusion
50%	Mainly Sit/Lie	Unable to do any work Extensive disease	Considerable assistance required	Normal or reduced	Full or Confusion
40%	Mainly in Bed	Unable to do most activity Extensive disease	Mainly assistance	Normal or reduced	Full or Drowsy +/- Confusion
30%	Totally Bed Bound	Unable to do any activity Extensive disease	Total Care	Normal or reduced	Full or Drowsy +/- Confusion
20%	Totally Bed Bound	Unable to do any activity Extensive disease	Total Care	Minimal to sips	Full or Drowsy +/- Confusion
10%	Totally Bed Bound	Unable to do any activity Extensive disease	Total Care	Mouth care only	Drowsy or Coma +/- Confusion
0%	Death	-	-	-	-

Instructions for Use of PPS (see also definition of terms)

1. PPS scores are determined by reading horizontally at each level to find a 'best fit' for the patient which is then assigned as the PPS% score.

2. Begin at the left column and read downwards until the appropriate ambulation level is reached, then read across to the next column and downwards again until the activity/evidence of disease is located. These steps are repeated until all five columns are covered before assigning the actual PPS for that patient. In this way, 'leftward' columns (columns to the left of any specific column) are 'stronger' determinants and generally take precedence over others.

> Example 1: A patient who spends the majority of the day sitting or lying down due to fatigue from advanced disease and requires considerable assistance to walk even for short distances but who is otherwise fully conscious level with good intake would be scored at PPS 50%.

> Example 2: A patient who has become paralyzed and quadriplegic requiring total care would be PPS 30%. Although this patient may be placed in a wheelchair (and perhaps seem initially to be at 50%), the score is 30% because he or she would be otherwise totally bed bound due to the disease or complication if it were not for caregivers providing total care including lift/transfer. The patient may have normal intake and full conscious level.

> Example 3: However, if the patient in example 2 was paraplegic and bed bound but still able to do some self-care such as feed themselves, then the PPS would be higher at 40 or 50% since he or she is not 'total care.'

3. PPS scores are in 10% increments only. Sometimes, there are several columns easily placed at one level but one or two which seem better at a higher or lower level. One then needs to make a 'best fit' decision. Choosing a 'half-fit' value of PPS 45%, for example, is not correct. The combination of clinical judgment and 'leftward precedence' is used to determine whether 40% or 50% is the more accurate score for that patient.

4. PPS may be used for several purposes. First, it is an excellent communication tool for quickly describing a patient's current functional level. Second, it may have value in criteria for workload assessment or other measurements and comparisons. Finally, it appears to have prognostic value.

FIGURE 13-2 Palliative Performance Scale version 2 © Victoria Hospice Society, Victoria, BC, Canada (2001). www.victoriahospice.org. (Used with permission.)

Definition of Terms for PPS

As noted below, some of the terms have similar meanings with the differences being more readily apparent as one reads horizontally across each row to find an overall 'best fit' using all five columns.

1. Ambulation
The items '**mainly sit/lie**,' '**mainly in bed**,' and '**totally bed bound**' are clearly similar. The subtle differences are related to items in the self-care column. For example, 'totally bed 'bound' at PPS 30% is due to either profound weakness or paralysis such that the patient not only can't get out of bed but is also unable to do any self-care. The difference between 'sit/lie' and 'bed' is proportionate to the amount of time the patient is able to sit up vs need to lie down.

'**Reduced ambulation**' is located at the PPS 70% and PPS 60% level. By using the adjacent column, the reduction of ambulation is tied to inability to carry out their normal job, work occupation or some hobbies or housework activities. The person is still able to walk and transfer on their own but at PPS 60% needs occasional assistance.

2. Activity & Extent of disease
'**Some**,' '**significant**,' and '**extensive**' disease refer to physical and investigative evidence which shows degrees of progression. For example in breast cancer, a local recurrence would imply 'some' disease, one or two metastases in the lung or bone would imply 'significant' disease, whereas multiple metastases in lung, bone, liver, brain, hypercalcemia or other major complications would be 'extensive' disease. The extent may also refer to progression of disease despite active treatments. Using PPS in AIDS, 'some' may mean the shift from HIV to AIDS, 'significant' implies progression in physical decline, new or difficult symptoms and laboratory findings with low counts. 'Extensive' refers to one or more serious complications with or without continuation of active antiretrovirals, antibiotics, etc.

The above extent of disease is also judged in context with the ability to maintain one's work and hobbies or activities. Decline in activity may mean the person still plays golf but reduces from playing 18 holes to 9 holes, or just a par 3, or to backyard putting. People who enjoy walking will gradually reduce the distance covered, although they may continue trying, sometimes even close to death (eg. trying to walk the halls).

3. Self-Care
'**Occasional assistance**' means that most of the time patients are able to transfer out of bed, walk, wash, toilet and eat by their own means, but that on occasion (perhaps once daily or a few times weekly) they require minor assistance.

'**Considerable assistance**' means that regularly every day the patient needs help, usually by one person, to do some of the activities noted above. For example, the person needs help to get to the bathroom but is then able to brush his or her teeth or wash at least hands and face. Food will often need to be cut into edible sizes but the patient is then able to eat of his or her own accord.

'**Mainly assistance**' is a further extension of 'considerable.' Using the above example, the patient now needs help getting up but also needs assistance washing his face and shaving, but can usually eat with minimal or no help. This may fluctuate according to fatigue during the day.

'**Total care**' means that the patient is completely unable to eat without help, toilet or do any self-care. Depending on the clinical situation, the patient may or may not be able to chew and swallow food once prepared and fed to him or her.

4. Intake
Changes in intake are quite obvious with '**normal intake**' referring to the person's usual eating habits while healthy. '**Reduced**' means any reduction from that and is highly variable according to the unique individual circumstances. '**Minimal**' refers to very small amounts, usually pureed or liquid, which are well below nutritional sustenance.

5. Conscious Level
'**Full consciousness**' implies full alertness and orientation with good cognitive abilities in various domains of thinking, memory, etc. '**Confusion**' is used to denote presence of either delirium or dementia and is a reduced level of consciousness. It may be mild, moderate or severe with multiple possible etiologies. '**Drowsiness**' implies either fatigue, drug side effects, delirium or closeness to death and is sometimes included in the term stupor. '**Coma**' in this context is the absence of response to verbal or physical stimuli; some reflexes may or may not remain. The depth of coma may fluctuate throughout a 24 hour period.

FIGURE **13-2** *(Continued)*

hospice benefit. Discharge is initiated by the hospice; revocation is initiated by the patient. In both circumstances, the patient loses the remainder of days within the current benefit period. If the patient chooses to be readmitted to a hospice, he or she will be readmitted in the next consecutive benefit period. It is critical for HIM departments to monitor the level of care and benefit period status of all admitted patients on a daily basis to ensure that billing is correct. This process can be accomplished through completion of the daily census and cooperative communication with clinical staff.

It is the responsibility of the interdisciplinary team in collaboration with the patient's physician to determine if the patient is appropriate for admission to hospice care, continues to be appropriate at the start of each benefit period, and is receiving services at the correct level of care.

INFORMATION MANAGEMENT

Information management in hospice has much in common with that of all other health care settings. There is a master patient index, diagnosis index, and physician index. Data contained in clinical records are abstracted and utilized for quality assessment, reimbursement, and statistics. This section describes some of the differences in information management that make hospice unique.

Data and Information Flow

The start of any database in hospice begins with the first contact a patient or potential patient has with the hospice—either from the patient or family, a physician, a hospital, or a nursing home. The hospice admissions area can capture the name of the patient, demographic information, diagnosis, referring physician, and all other elements of a standard minimum data set on a paper referral form or in a computerized information system. Many patients and families are not ready for hospice initially, so every contact may not always result in an admission, but many return after time to the hospice for admission, so it is important to retain information from these initial contacts to make any subsequent contact easier.

Once the hospice determines that a patient is to be admitted, a nurse is assigned to the case. At an initial visit, the nurse obtains patient/legal representative signatures on the election of hospice, medical and financial consents, and any other appropriate paperwork. In conjunction with this visit, the nurse obtains information about the patient's primary diagnosis and related diagnoses, determines whether the patient's attending physician wants to continue following the patient or would prefer the hospice physician to act as the attending physician, and obtains any initial physician orders for medication.

The clinical record begins with a referral form or face sheet, the history and physical, consents, and initial physician orders. The HIM department can begin abstracting information for an electronic database from this initial documentation, including the date of admission, benefit period, and level of care, which can be tracked for a daily census and reimbursement.

The nurse coordinates the assignment of additional hospice personnel, social workers, hospice aides, the hospice physician, and volunteers, and begins the interdisciplinary care plan. The clinical record, now housed at the hospice, will be expanded to include the hospice physician's assessment, social work assessment, hospice aide assignment, additional physician orders, and a certification of terminal illness signed by both the attending physician and hospice medical director. As various clinical staff members make assigned visits to the patient and physician orders change, documentation will be added to the clinical record at the hospice. At least every two weeks, the interdisciplinary team will meet as a group to discuss the care of the patient and update the plan of care; the record will document these meetings, as appropriate.

Upon the death (or discharge) of the patient, all open interdisciplinary care plans are closed, the nurse documents a discharge summary (summarizing all care plans initiated, actions taken, and results), and the bereavement assessment is documented. The HIM department at this point should complete a qualitative analysis of the clinical record and abstract additional pertinent information (such as diagnosis codes for symptoms and complications addressed in care plans), date of death (or discharge), and location of death (or reason why the patient was discharged, e.g., revocation, hospice discharge, or transfer to another program). Depending on the state and city of death, the HIM department may also be responsible for initiating the death certificate or providing information to a funeral home to complete the death certificate. This is especially true if a hospice-employed physician has been acting as the patient's attending physician. The death certificate may require the signature of the hospice physician.

Coding and Classification

The primary requirement for hospice admission is the certification of the patient's attending physician that the patient has a limited life expectancy (six months or less). The per diem reimbursement is based solely on the care level and the benefit periods, not on the patient's diagnosis (unlike the prospective payment system used in acute care hospitals). This reimbursement perspective makes hospice diagnosis coding different from that of other settings. The hospice clinical record does not include significant laboratory findings, radiological reporting, or any other ancillary services that could be used to "diagnose" the patient. The hospice clinical record may include copies of records from a hospital if the patient is a direct transfer, or from the physician's office, if the patient has not been to a hospital recently. It is important that the hospice attempt to obtain copies of as many recent records as available on the patient to aid in the coding of the principal diagnosis, but in the end, the code assignment must be the reason the patient has a limited life expectancy.

ICD-9-CM/ICD-10-CM

The coding principles of the current clinical modification of the *International Classification of Disease* should be followed in the assignment of diagnosis codes; however, the specificity of coding may be limited depending on what information is available. Whereas in an acute care setting, resources are often invested in clinical documentation improvement programs and in querying and educating physicians in order to assign highly specific codes because of their importance in DRG payments and in risk-adjustment for quality monitoring, this level of coding specificity is not required for hospice coding. Regulations require only that a valid diagnosis code be included on the claim. This is not to imply that HIM coders should not try to be as specific as possible in the coding assignment; it merely indicates that there is not an incentive to devote resources to assuring that highly specific documentation is available.

The hospice clinical record is significantly nursing documentation. Hospice coding staff should evaluate nursing documentation to look for complications or symptoms that the nurse is trying to manage. Symptoms such as pain (of any body location), constipation (which is a direct result of pain medication such as morphine), respiratory distress, and fatigue are all acceptable to code in hospice. In addition, complications such as urinary tract infections, decubitus ulcers, open wounds or hemorrhage of tumor sites, and thrush are all coded. The coding of these additional signs and symptoms helps build a diagnosis database that can be used internally to evaluate not only the quality of care given (how many catheter patients develop urinary tract infections), but also the components of various diagnosis groups (such as end-stage respiratory diseases).

CPT

Physicians who are employed by the hospice can also bill for their services. Depending on the location of the patient, either in the home or in an inpatient facility, the current procedure terminology (CPT) evaluation and management codes can be used to bill for hospice physician services. Hospice coders should discuss the CPT evaluation and management codes with hospice physicians to educate them on their correct use. If a hospice physician performs a procedure such as a paracentesis (which is common in patients who have abdominal cancers), *ICD-9-CM* (*ICD-10-PCS* after October 1, 2013) and *CPT* can be utilized to assign procedure codes. HIM department staff should coordinate the assignment of procedure codes with hospice billing staff to ensure that physician services are appropriately reimbursed.

Electronic Information Systems

With advancements in technology in recent years, the use of electronic health records in hospice care is increasing. Even small hospices with few staff members are investing in technologies to improve communication and continuity of care for their patients and families. In the past, clinicians may have been required to document visits on paper and leave copies at the patient's residence. Now clinicians are using laptops, handheld devices, and other technologies to document at the patient's bedside. Clinicians can document visits, assessments, care plans, medication orders, medication administration, and other required records into software systems designed specifically for the hospice setting. Information is then readily available to other team members and hospice staff covering patient care after hours and on weekends.

The investment in software and equipment comes with many challenges for hospices, including clinician training, equipment failures, connectivity, security, and initial and ongoing costs. However, the advantages can far outweigh any challenges, because electronic documentation is more current, more accurate, more comprehensive, and more legible than paper records.

Hospices across the country have implemented electronic health records in varying degrees, and most have a combination of both electronic and paper records for their patients. Forms requiring signatures of patients or signatures from physicians may still be maintained in paper format. Whatever the variation of records that each hospice maintains, the HIM department will play a significant role in both the electronic and paper formats and processes. HIM professionals working in the hospice setting should be familiar with using technology and involved in the implementation and ongoing maintenance of any electronic systems.

Data Sets

Several data sets should be captured and maintained within the hospice. These include patient data, resource data, and census data. Software systems designed specifically for hospice can usually provide all these types of data sets within one database. Reports can be generated that show data in whatever manner or summary format requested.

Patient Data

Patient information should include as a minimum those data elements in a standard minimum data set. In addition, the hospice will also want to capture the name of the primary caregiver and any other significant family members (for bereavement tracking), the referral source (this is useful to aid marketing staff), where the patient is or was employed, religion, directions to the home, funeral home, language spoken, location of death, and reason for discharge. NHPCO requests significant statistical information about the patient population from each hospice on a yearly basis. In addition, many hospices are involved with grant writing to obtain additional funding for programs, also requiring significant descriptions of the patient population to be served. Computerized systems make retrieval of patient data for statistical reporting both faster and easier.

Resource Data

Resources are all those clinical staff members and vendors who provide services to a patient. Because hospice is reimbursed on a per diem basis, it is critical that the hospice monitor its actual cost per patient versus reimbursement per patient. A resource database can help provide this information. Resource data and resource utilization should capture the name and specialty (registered nurse, social worker, etc.) of all clinical staff members; the names of all vendors, such as those of durable medical equipment, pharmacy, and supplies; all durable medical equipment dispensed to the patient and associated costs to the hospice; all supplies dispensed to the patient and associated costs to the hospice; the date, clinician, mileage, type of visit, and length of visit for every patient seen; other clinician time associated with the patient, including telephone calls, interdisciplinary team conferences, and staff conferences; the cost of clinician time, using salary plus benefits to obtain a cost per hour; cost of mileage reimbursement; and all medications dispensed to the patient and associated costs. The contents of the resource data set can be utilized in combination with the patient data set to provide total costs per patient, total costs by diagnosis, and total costs by resource. In addition to costs, staff hours by patient, staff hours by diagnosis, and staff hours by resource are examples of other reports that can be created to monitor resource utilization.

Other Data

Census data include the number of admissions, discharges, transfers, and the number of patients under the care of the hospice on a given day. Other statistics that should be captured include patient days, average length of stay, and average daily census not only by patient, but also by insurance, age group, and location (nursing home, inpatient hospital, home care). Many agencies request census information on a yearly basis from each hospice, and the hospice itself monitors census status.

Hospices may also want to create databases or ensure that hospice software contains data elements for the following:

- *Donations*, including type and amount of all monetary and nonmonetary donations, donors, and relationship to any previous patients. (This is useful for fund-raising efforts.)
- *Bereavement*, including names and current addresses of bereaved family members, associated patient and date of patient's death, and status of bereavement efforts (active or inactive).
- *Volunteers*, including names and addresses, training dates, evaluation dates, cost savings attributable to volunteers, special skills (e.g., barber or nurse), availability (days, evenings, weekends), and status (active or inactive).

Ultimately, it is better to collect too much information at least initially than to not collect enough. Once the data entry document is filed, it is very time consuming to retrieve it and go back later to capture the information.

QUALITY ASSESSMENT/PERFORMANCE IMPROVEMENT AND UTILIZATION MANAGEMENT

Quality Assessment/Performance Improvement (QAPI)

Conditions of Participation, as revised in 2008, require that hospices implement a Quality Assessment/Performance Improvement (QAPI) program. QAPI must be an ongoing, hospice-wide, data driven program that involves all hospice services, including those provided by contractors. QAPI can be broken down into two parts that are separate but still related (see Figure 13-3). Quality assessment requires the hospice to develop indicators that measure the quality,

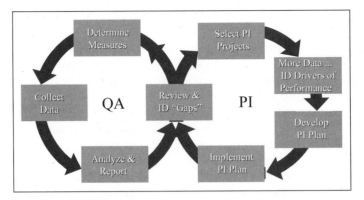

FIGURE **13-3** Quality Assessment and Performance Improvement (QAPI) cycle. (Courtesy of Weatherbee Resources, Inc., Hyannis, MA.)

effectiveness, and safety of its services. An example of a quality indicator for most hospices might be the percentage of patients whose pain is controlled within 48 hours of admission. Hospices must establish benchmarks for each quality indicator and continuously measure to assess performance.

When benchmarks are not being met, the performance improvement part of QAPI begins. Hospices must implement performance improvement projects that address areas of performance that are not meeting standards. These projects must develop and implement strategies to improve performance and ultimately demonstrate the improvement goal. Hospices then continue to monitor the results of performance improvement projects by measurements described in the QA process.

The hospice governing body is responsible for the approval and oversight of the QAPI program, but most hospices also have a QAPI committee that meets regularly and a QAPI manager for day-to-day activities. Committee members may contribute in quality measurement as well as participate in performance improvement projects.

Quality Measures

Patient, family, and physician satisfaction surveys are good examples of quality measures used by many hospices. Satisfaction surveys are geared toward evaluating responses to the specific services offered to patients/families/physicians by the hospice (Did you find volunteers helpful?) as well as those about regulatory requirements (Did you receive a copy of the patient's rights?). Many hospices utilize the Family Evaluation of Hospice Care designed by NHPCO. This national program give hospices the opportunity to submit their survey results and receive quarterly reports summarizing satisfaction with services. The report also gives state and national results for hospices to use as benchmarks in their QAPI measurements. NHPCO also offers a Family Evaluation of Bereavement Services.

Quality Monitoring and HIM

Quality monitoring in the hospice HIM department can take the form of two distinct operations. One is monitoring the contents of the record to ensure compliance with federal, state, and local regulations, as well as standards of accrediting agencies such as the Joint Commission. The second is ensuring the quality and integrity of all data abstracted and captured electronically.

The HIM department evaluates the contents of each clinical record, ensuring compliance with all appropriate regulations. In addition, the review should also monitor compliance with the contents of care plans. If the hospice aide's care plan says that the patient should be bathed at each visit, the record should document that this activity was performed. If the nurse's care plan states that the patient is to be educated on the cleaning of a wound, the clinical record should document that this education was performed. Clinical record review by trained health information professionals looks at the documentation objectively.

HIM departments should continuously monitor all clinicians to determine who is in compliance and who is not. Hospice and home care tend to be high-pressure, high-burnout working environments for clinical staff, with staff turnover high in some areas. Closely monitoring staff compliance to documentation ensures that clinical records are not left incomplete.

Because of the number of outside physicians who continue to follow patients through the hospice, clinical record documentation review also encounters many occasions when it is necessary to obtain progress notes and/or signatures from outside physicians, for example, on physician telephone orders, physician certification of terminal illness, and any related physician office documentation to supplement the hospice record. The physician's office should be contacted or visited (marketing personnel or volunteers are options) to determine the status of any original documents not returned. The original clinical record should not be filed as complete without these documents. Computerization has helped the tracking of signatures and authentication within the clinical record by providing reports that look for unsigned documentation or missing dates for signatures.

Utilization Management

Utilization management activities and criteria are built into hospice regulations. For example, the initial certification by the physician and medical director of the patient's terminal illness provides an assessment of the appropriateness of hospice admission. Another example is that the number of days of inpatient care for which Medicare will pay is limited to not more than 20 percent of total patient care days. A mechanism to monitor a situation in which the combined general inpatient and inpatient respite care days for a patient were approaching 20 percent would help the hospice to avoid exceeding this threshold. Because there are four different levels of care in the Medicare reimbursement system, the hospice needs to take steps to assure that care is being rendered at the appropriate level and that documentation in the clinical record supports the level of care billed.

RISK MANAGEMENT AND LEGAL ISSUES

To decrease risk for legal issues, hospice staff need to be educated on the importance of obtaining proper consents for admission and for procedures. Many hospice patients are unable to consent for themselves and have appointed personal representatives.

Clinical staff should verify that someone is actually a legal representative by reviewing proper legal documents. Ideally, a copy of the documents should be filed in the clinical record. If no representative has been assigned, clinical staff should be educated to help the family obtain legal representative status. The patient should, however, be the first to sign consents; an X is appropriate if witnessed. If the patient is unable to sign, the clinical record should document why the patient was unable to sign (patient in a coma, patient has Alzheimer's disease).

Upon the death of the patient, the HIM department may get requests from insurance companies or attorneys to settle a claim or probate the patient's estate. HIM professionals working in hospice should be knowledgeable of and remain current with HIPAA regulations regarding disclosure of protected health information. No copies of the clinical record should be released without proper authorization from the legal representative of the estate. State laws should be consulted to determine the legal authority to act on behalf of the deceased. Documentation verifying legal authority should be requested and kept in the clinical record. Requests for copies of records may also come from family members, sometimes in dispute of a will or an insurance claim. It is important that HIM department staff verify the legal authority of the requestor or seek proper authorization prior to any disclosure.

ROLE OF THE HEALTH INFORMATION MANAGEMENT PROFESSIONAL

The HIM professional in hospice must be the expert on all documentation standards from all accrediting and licensing agencies. The HIM professional needs to continually offer workshops to clinical staff in basic documentation techniques (including the legal viewpoint on documentation and documentation requirements of accrediting and licensing agencies).

Another role for the HIM professional is that of data manager. Assertiveness in offering to retrieve information at meetings and team conferences is a way to build a reputation as a data manager. The HIM professional can offer to complete statistical reports requested by agencies and compile and distribute a daily census. The admissions or discharges or patient days for a period of time can be graphed. The HIM professional can look at trends and describe them to others. Again, it is important to be assertive in telling people what an HIM professional is able to do. Many hospices are not yet as sophisticated as hospitals in their interpretation and evaluation of data and need an expert who can educate them.

The HIM professional may also serve as a member or chairperson of a QAPI committee or as a HIPAA privacy and/or security officer. In small hospices, HIM professionals may find themselves involved in many aspects of hospice operations in addition to traditional HIM responsibilities.

TRENDS

In the future, hospice will be challenged by issues related to:

- Decreasing lengths of stay
- OIG annual work plan related to hospice care
- Revisions to federal, state, and local regulations
- Expansion of the palliative care specialty
- Increased use of electronic information systems and electronic health records

In the past several years, hospices across the nation have experienced a sharp decline in the average length of stay for hospice patients to the point that one- and two-day lengths of stay are becoming commonplace. A short stay prevents the patient and family from receiving the optimum comfort care and other benefits available through hospice during the final weeks and months of the patient's life. Short stays are also a problem from a financial standpoint because the per diem reimbursement provided by Medicare does not cover all costs associated with an extremely short stay. Increasing the average length of stay is a constant challenge facing hospices. Educational outreaches to both the health care community and the lay community on the benefits of hospice are common approaches to combat this trend.

The Office of the Inspector General (OIG), which is the arm of the Department of Health and Human Services charged with investigating and monitoring the Medicare and Medicaid programs, publishes a new work plan annually at their Web site. All types of health care providers, including hospices, need to be aware of the OIG investigations that could affect their organizations.

Changes to hospice regulations, including the Medicare Conditions of Participation, have been frequent since 2007. Changes in billing requirements, documentation of the certifications and recertifications, and changes in HIPAA regulations have all had an effect on hospices. HIM professionals working in hospice will need to remain current on all regulations related to their field to assist in keeping their organization in compliance.

Many hospices have expanded their scope of practice to include palliative care services that can be provided to patients who are not eligible for hospice benefits. Members of the hospice team work together to provide comfort care through the control of pain and symptoms for patients who are chronically ill or have chronic pain and symptom issues. Certifications are now available for physicians, nurses, social workers, and hospice aides in the specialty of hospice and palliative care.

There is an expanded need for data management and information management personnel. The use of electronic health records, laptops and/or handheld devices, telemedicine, and the Internet requires expertise that some health care professionals do not have. HIM professionals will continue to be in high demand in light of their skills in document management, electronic information systems, privacy, and statistical management.

SUMMARY

Hospice care for terminally ill patients is significantly different from the care provided in other health care settings. It is the only health care setting in which the focus of care is not on curing the patient. It is with this philosophy in mind that the HIM professional must realize that his or her role will also be unique. What is significant about coding in hospitals, outpatient facilities, skilled home care, and other facilities relying on a prospective payment system for reimbursement does not apply in hospice. Furthermore, other settings may have a high volume of requests from insurance companies, attorneys, and patients for clinical records to the degree that a correspondence service is needed to help process the requests; the volume of requests is much lower in hospice. HIM professionals will often play a diversified role when working in hospice, finding themselves involved in quality programs, privacy concerns, and assistance with transitioning to electronic health records and further computerization.

KEY TERMS

bereavement   refers to the time period immediately following the death of the patient. In hospice, clinical staff help family and significant others through this period for up to one year, and longer if requested by the patient's family and friends.

continuous care   care that occurs in the patient's place of residence when a patient requires continuous care for a minimum of 8 hours in a 24-hour period. Continuous care is only furnished during brief periods of crisis and only as necessary to maintain the terminally ill patient at home.

curative therapy   any medical therapy given for the purpose of curing disease.

general or **acute inpatient care**   occurs when a patient receives care in an inpatient facility (a hospice inpatient unit or a facility contracted by the hospice) for pain control or acute or chronic symptom management that cannot be managed in the patient's place of residence.

hospice   a facility or a program designed to provide a caring environment to meet the physical and emotional needs of terminally ill patients and their families and significant others.

hospice inpatient unit   a hospice with a specific set of beds either in its own building or as a wing of a hospital or nursing home, providing round-the-clock clinical staff to care for terminally ill patients. These units provide respite care, pain and symptom management, and/or routine home care for patients who have nobody in their home to help care for them.

interdisciplinary team (IDT)   a patient care team made up of members of two or more clinical disciplines—usually a nurse, social worker, hospice aide, physician, pastoral or other counselor, volunteer, therapist, and dietitian—who plan for the care of the terminally ill patient.

palliative care   the opposite of curative therapy. Clinical measures are taken to reduce the intensity of disease symptoms, rather than providing a cure for the disease. Hospice tries to reduce the intensity of such symptoms as pain, nausea, and anxiety with a variety of pharmacological and nonpharmacological methods.

place of residence   wherever the patient is currently living—his or her own home, a relative's home, a senior citizen's complex, a nursing home, assisted living, etc.

primary caregiver   the person designated to provide care for the patient when hospice staff are not available. This can be any relative, a spouse, a friend, a significant other, a paid caregiver, an adult child, or any other person. The primary caregiver provides a range of care depending on his or her comfort level, from giving medications to changing dressings to emptying catheter bags.

respite care   care that provides an interval of rest for the primary caregiver and is provided to hospice patients in an approved (or contracted) facility.

revoke (revocation)   performed by a hospice patient (or family or legal representative)

to give back or annul his or her hospice benefit. Once a patient has revoked the hospice benefit, the patient returns to standard Medicare or other commercial insurance benefits and loses all remaining days in the current benefit period.

routine home care   care that occurs when a patient is receiving routine (or nonproblematic) care in the place of residence.

terminally ill   a limited life expectancy, usually less than six months.

volunteer   a person who provides a service (clerical, clinical, companionship, etc.) without any monetary or other reimbursement.

REVIEW QUESTIONS

Knowledge-Based Questions

1. True or false: Hospice takes care of only cancer patients.
2. Provide examples of how hospice tries to relieve terminal symptoms for patients.
3. List the members of an interdisciplinary team in hospice.
4. What is the role of the primary caregiver?
5. Describe how a Medicare patient elects to receive hospice care.
6. Describe the role that volunteers play in hospice care.

7. Discuss bereavement services provided by hospice.
8. Describe the four levels of hospice care found in the Medicare Conditions of Participation.
9. Describe aspects of a hospice utilization review program.

Critical Thinking Questions

1. Provide examples of some of the data that can be collected by hospices.
2. Describe the functions of a Quality Assessment/ Performance Improvement program.

WEB ACTIVITIES

1. Access the *Code of Federal Regulations* through the Federal Digital System of the U.S. Government Printing Office at http://www.gpo.gov/fdsys/.

   Follow these steps to find the appropriate section of the regulations:

   - At the Federal Digital System main page, select *Code of Federal Regulations*.

   - At the next page, choose the previous (not the current) year from the drop-down menu and click "Go."
   - Scroll down to Title 42, "Public Health" and click "Download."
   - Hospice regulations are found in Part 418 of Title 42, so click on your preferred format (PDF recommended) for the range of "Parts" that includes 418.

- Search for Section 418.104, which contains the requirements for hospice clinical records.

How might a hospice health information manager use this document?

2. Visit the Victoria Hospice Society's Web site at http://palliative.info/resource_material/PPSv2.pdf to view and read about the Palliative Performance Scale. What three purposes might the Palliative Performance Scale serve?

CASE STUDY

A 66-year-old woman and her two daughters present themselves at the hospice. The woman's attending physician suggests that she investigate hospice as a health care alternative. The woman has breast cancer with bilateral mastectomies and has recently been found to have metastases to the liver. Her physician has stated that she could have additional chemotherapy, but that her liver cancer may not respond. At this point, other than mild pain, she is able to get around relatively well. She is not sure she wants to have additional chemotherapy; it made her terribly ill the first time. Her daughters and their families (both have two children; all are under the age of 10) are her only close relatives. She has been divorced since her first mastectomy. One daughter lives 5 minutes away; the other daughter lives 40 minutes away. Upon further discussion with the daughters, you learn that the first daughter wants only what her mother wants and will support whatever decision she chooses; the second daughter wants her mother to have the additional chemotherapy no matter what and cannot understand why anyone would "just give up." You are the admission representative.

1. What would you tell this woman and her daughters about hospice?
2. What problems do you anticipate this family having?
3. How would you respond to the second daughter's comment that hospice is "just giving up"?
4. Is this patient appropriate for hospice?

REFERENCES AND SUGGESTED READINGS

Corr, C., and Corr, D. (1983). *Hospice Care Principles and Practice*. New York: Springer Publishing Company.

Hospice care, Conditions of Participation, *Code of Federal Regulations*, Title 42, pt. 418, 2008 ed.

Joint Commission. (2010). *Standards for Home Health, Personal Care and Support Services, and Hospice*. Chicago: Author.

National Hospice and Palliative Care Organization. (2006). *Standards of Practice for Hospice Programs*. Arlington, VA: Author.

KEY RESOURCES

Hospice Association of America
http://www.nahc.org/haa

The Joint Commission
http://www.jointcommission.org

National Hospice and Palliative Care Organization
http://www.nhpco.org

Center for Medicare & Medicaid Services
http://www.cms.gov

CHAPTER 14

Dental Care Settings

FRANCIS G. SERIO, DMD, MS, MBA

DENISE D. KRAUSE, PHD

CHERYL L. BERTHELSEN, PHD, RHIA

LEARNING OBJECTIVES

Upon successful completion of this chapter, you should be able to:

- Identify the different practitioners associated with dental care and describe their roles.

- Describe documentation requirements specific to the practice of dentistry.

- Explain benefits of electronic dental records.

- Discuss the potential impact of managed care on dental practices.

- Describe utilization management strategies used in dentistry.

- Identify specific risks associated with dentistry and strategies to manage the risks.

- List the information needs of the dental office.

- Identify the important components of electronic dental record and practice management systems.

- Describe potential career opportunities in the dental setting for HIM practitioners.

Setting	Description	Synonyms/Examples
Dental Office	A private practice facility where patients receive dental care.	
Dental Clinic	A department within a larger health organization where patients receive dental care	Within a community health center Within a VA medical center Within a prison Within a dental school Within a local government health department
Dental School	A school within a university where dentists and dental hygienists are educated and trained	School of Dentistry or Dental Medicine College of Dentistry or Dental Medicine

INTRODUCTION TO CARE SETTINGS

Dental practitioners may treat patients in a variety of settings. Whenever a patient receives a dental examination or treatment, a dental record is created or supplemented. Each setting poses unique conditions and challenges in the provision of dental care for patients, the type of documentation generated, and the management of dental records. Today, all new dental facilities use **electronic dental records (EDRs)** and digital imaging. Many older facilities are making analog to digital conversions as well.

Care Settings

Solo Dental Practice

A **solo dental practice** is owned and operated by one dentist. The dentist owns or leases the office building or suite and all the necessary equipment and furnishings to run what is in essence a small business. The solo-practice dentist usually employs several personnel consisting of at least a receptionist and a dental assistant, but may also employ an office manager to oversee the day-to-day business operations of the practice. Dentists may employ a full-time dental hygienist or contract with a hygienist to come to the office one or several days per week to provide either routine preventive care or definitive periodontal treatment. Some dentists elect to perform routine checkups and cleanings themselves.

Although the solo-practice dentist is responsible for his or her patients 24 hours a day, in reality a general dentist is not often called when the practice is closed. Occasionally, a patient may need a prescription for an antibiotic or pain medication, but the instances in which a dentist has to meet a patient at the office during off-hours are rare.

The solo-practice setting has been remarkably stable over the years, despite increasing competition. Figure 14-1 contains information about the practice setting of dentists in the United States in 2007 (American Dental Association, 2007). Solo-practice dentists sometimes rent space in their offices

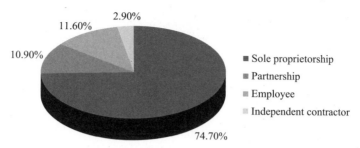

Practice Settings of Dentists

- Sole proprietorship
- Partnership
- Employee
- Independent contractor

2.90%
11.60%
10.90%
74.70%

FIGURE **14-1** Distribution of dentists in initial practice. Most dentists eventually are in solo practice.

to another practicing dentist to supplement office income or hire a newly licensed dentist to work as an associate. The associate dentist, possibly either an employee or independent contractor, receives only a portion of the fees collected for work performed, and the remainder of the fee reimburses the practice for use of office and equipment, with some profit for the owner dentist. The solo-practice dentist is responsible for maintaining dental records of all patients treated. Dental records for patients of tenant dentists who rent space on evenings and weekends are the responsibility of the tenant, not the dentist-owner of the practice. When the solo practitioner retires, he or she must store and maintain the dental records of patients as long as state statute dictates. If a dentist sells the practice, the dental records usually transfer to the dentist buying the practice, as these patient records constitute the majority of the value of the practice.

Group Dental Practice

A **group dental practice** is composed of two or more dentists practicing together. The group of dentists is usually incorporated as a legal entity, and the corporation, rather than the individual dentists, owns and operates the business. Ownership of the corporation may be shared equally among the owner-dentists, or there may be one or two majority owners, with the remaining dentists as minority owners. The amount of money each dentist earns from the business is usually based on how well the business does as a whole and the percentage of ownership in the corporation instead of individual productivity. There may, however, be bonuses based on individual productivity. A group practice may also be composed of two or more dentists who share office expenses and equipment but are not incorporated. They practice as a group to benefit from sharing the expenses of running the business but maintain separate financial records and are distinct business entities.

Group dental practices may be composed of dentists practicing in the same specialty (orthodontists) or different specialties (general dentists plus an endodontist, periodontist, and prosthodontist). Multiple specialties allow the dentists to refer patients needing specialty care to a dentist within the group rather than to an outside practice. Single specialty groups use the same type of equipment and instruments and can share them. Multispecialty groups need a wide variety of instruments specific to the specialties involved. Dentists within the group practice usually share on-call service for each other to deal with patient emergencies. Dental records of patients of group practices are also usually shared. The records are available to any dentist in the group seeing a patient during an emergency appointment. It is the corporation's responsibility to store and maintain the dental records over time.

Clinics in Academic Institutions

All universities that have a dental school to educate and train dentists have clinics for patients to receive dental treatment. Dental care is provided by dental students under close supervision of faculty, who are licensed dentists. Patients pay significantly reduced fees for dental care, but the treatment may take many more visits to complete than in a private dental office. Schools that educate and train dental hygienists may be associated with a dental school, four-year college, or a community college. The care provided to patients at a dental hygiene clinic is limited to procedures that a dental hygienist is allowed to perform by state licensure rules.

The dental records generated in academic settings serve purposes beyond the documentation of care provided. They are important evidence of the student's progress toward and preparation for graduation and licensure. Most schools require dental students and dental hygiene students to complete a certain number of specific dental treatments and procedures or successfully pass competency examinations before they are eligible to take state board licensing examinations or graduate. Dental records in academic settings are also important in research. Faculty members are involved in the discovery of new treatment modalities, diagnostic tests, restorative materials, prostheses and anesthetics, as well as the invention of new devices, instruments, and equipment. New methods of preventing dental decay and periodontal (gum) disease are being studied and proven at major dental schools throughout the world. Dental records within these institutions are important to that progress. Dental records in large institutions may also be used for public health research, such as tracking disease trends.

Third-Party Organizations

Dentists and patients may participate in a variety of third-party organizations (primarily insurance plans or managed care organizations) to assist patients in the payment for dental services. For more detail on these organizations, see the Reimbursement section of this chapter. In most instances of third-party payment, the care is provided in the dentist's private office, although there are separate dental clinics for some health plans in certain parts of the country.

Acute Care Hospital

Large academic health centers and acute care hospitals may have an associated dental clinic or dental emergency room. Patients served in this setting may be victims of trauma who have sustained an injury to face or teeth (alone or in addition to other types of injuries), or patients requiring general anesthesia for dental treatment. Patients may receive dental treatment in the emergency room, as an inpatient, or as an outpatient. Dental records of these treatments may be included in hospital records for an inpatient or maintained separately for emergency room patients or outpatients. Storage and maintenance of these dental records are the responsibility of the associated institution.

Many of these hospitals also provide outpatient dental care through a general dental residency program. Care is provided by graduate dentists who are receiving advanced training in general dentistry from a group of attending dentists. These dental records are maintained by the dental department or may be part of the hospital's general medical record.

Other Settings

There are many other settings where dental treatment may be provided and dental records created and maintained. Prisons usually have dental clinics to care for inmates. The Department of Veterans Affairs (VA) hospitals also have dental clinics to serve the dental needs of veterans. Active military bases usually have dental clinics associated with the base hospital or medical clinic. Some colleges and universities have dental clinics to care for the dental needs of students. Community health centers may also provide both routine and emergency dental care for patients. The storage and maintenance of dental records are the responsibility of the entity operating the clinic, not the dentists providing the care, as most dentists are employees in these settings.

Types of Patients

Children and Adolescents

Dentistry has changed for children in the twenty-first century. The use of fluoride has made a tremendous impact in the prevention of dental **caries** in children. The National Institute of Dental and Craniofacial Research (NIDCR) estimates that 58 percent of children aged 2 to 11 are caries-free in their primary dentition and that 41 percent of children aged 11 to 17 are caries-free in their permanent dentition (CDC, 2007).

Early childhood caries (ECC), also known as nursing caries or baby bottle tooth decay (BBTD), is a problem for infants and toddlers. Children who are allowed to go to bed at night with a bottle filled with liquid other than water develop caries in their **primary teeth** (baby teeth). A study of Head Start children across five southwestern states found that 24 percent of all children had ECC (Barnes et al., 1992). Unfortunately, the public has not been well educated about this problem. A study of midwestern college students found that only 39 percent of respondents had heard of BBTD and 32 percent of those thought it was a fictional health problem (Logan et al., 1996). A 1991 study on inappropriate infant bottle feeding for Healthy People 2000 found that 95 percent of children 6 months to 5 years old had used a bottle, and 20 percent of them were put to bed with a bottle with contents other than water (Kaste & Gift, 1995). More than 8 percent of children 2 to 5 years old still used a bottle, thus highlighting the need for widespread education on the risks of bottle feeding. Retention of primary teeth is important for function, aesthetics, childhood self-esteem, and to hold proper space for the eruption of permanent teeth.

Chipping, fracturing, and loss of primary and permanent teeth caused by falls and accidents are common. A child typically begins to lose primary teeth at ages 5 to 7. When development is delayed, dental intervention may be needed to ensure the eruption of healthy permanent teeth. The dentist may need to pull stubborn primary teeth that fail to come out on their own. Many American children and adolescents receive orthodontic treatment (braces to straighten teeth). Orthodontic and palatal deformities caused by thumb-sucking or persistent use of pacifiers are also problems requiring corrective orthodontic care and sometimes **orthognathic surgery** (corrective jaw surgery).

Adults

Adults generally have more dental disease that may require costly treatment than do children. Many children from 1950 to 1970 had teeth filled with a variety of materials to treat dental caries. Over time as these patients age, dental restorations may gradually fail, requiring replacement by larger and larger fillings, with the possible need for **root canal therapy** (RCT) and prosthetic **crowns**. The National Institute of Dental and Craniofacial Research (NIDCR) estimates that 57 percent of the elderly and 21 percent of the 18 to 64 age population have root caries. Adults also develop gingivitis and periodontal disease. If periodontal disease is left untreated, jawbone supporting the teeth is lost, teeth loosen, and teeth eventually fall out. A missing tooth, from trauma or decay, can cause problems. The empty space in the adult's mouth allows teeth to shift, changing the way the person bites and chews. Bony tissue in the mandible and maxilla can erode, making prosthetic restoration difficult. Adults also suffer chips, fractures, and loss of teeth from falls, accidents, and assaults. Some adults seek dental treatment for solely cosmetic reasons. Cosmetic dentistry includes dental implants for missing teeth, orthodontics to straighten teeth, and veneers to cover badly stained teeth or to improve smile aesthetics.

Pregnant Females

The dentist needs to be very careful about inadvertently exposing the developing fetus to radiation from **radiographs** (X-ray films). Female patients of childbearing age are routinely questioned about the possibility of being pregnant before radiological exams are performed. Use of digital radiographs significantly reduces a patient's exposure to radiation. Routine dental cleaning and checkups are very important for pregnant women. Although dental treatment can be safely performed on pregnant women into the second trimester, some choose to wait until after delivery to have teeth repaired. Gingival inflammation (gingivitis) may also occur in some pregnant women due to hormone fluctuations and poor oral hygiene.

The Elderly

As more individuals live longer lives, they are more likely to keep most, if not all, of their teeth. The number of adults over age 65 who had all of their natural teeth extracted dropped from 26.2 percent in 1999 to 18.5 percent in 2008 (National Center for Chronic Disease Prevention & Health Promotion, 2009).

This retention of teeth has changed the approach to treatment for the elderly, with an emphasis on prevention and maintenance of the natural dentition. While at one time the loss of teeth meant having to use removable complete dentures that were often unstable, significant progress in the use of dental implants has allowed people to have a stable dentition, either of crowns and bridges or of implant-stabilized and -retained dentures.

The living situations of the elderly can have a great effect on oral health and disease. Those who live independently are generally in good physical health and also enjoy good oral health. Those with chronic illnesses or in dependent living situations may have many oral health problems. One study of VA patients found that only 6 percent of healthy, independent-living patients were **edentulous** (without teeth), and those who had teeth were missing an average of 4.5 teeth. But 49 percent of the patients living in a VA nursing home or those hospitalized for illness were edentulous, and those who had teeth were missing an average of 12 teeth and had an average of 5 decayed teeth (Loesche et al., 1995).

The problem of lack of proper dental care and oral hygiene for nursing home residents is well documented. Increasing the percentage of long-term care facility residents receiving dental services was identified as a national goal in Healthy People 2010 and continued as an objective for Healthy People 2020 (DHHS, 2009). Figure 14-2 demonstrates the prevalence of dental health problems among nursing home residents in the state of Washington (Kiyak et al., 1993).

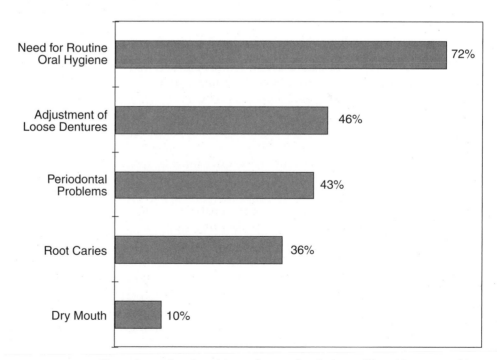

FIGURE **14-2** Dental needs of residents in nursing homes. (Graphic created by C. Berthelsen, based on data from Kiyak et al., 1993.)

Patients with Special Challenges

Patients who are physically or mentally developmentally challenged pose special problems when they need dental care. These patients may not cooperate with the dentist and may be unable to understand simple commands such as "open your mouth." More functional individuals may be able to cooperate for a short time but may be unable to sit still long enough for the needed treatment. Nevertheless, they still need preventive and restorative dentistry to maintain optimum health. Major restorative treatment for these patients is generally carried out under deep sedation or general anesthesia, which may preclude treatment at a typical dental office and require admission to an outpatient surgery facility or hospital.

Individuals with mental illness can be difficult for the dentist to treat. Patients suffering hallucinations and uncontrolled psychosis may be unable to cooperate with the dentist. They may be treated normally if well controlled on proper psychotropic medications. However, the dentist must be aware of what medications the patient takes to avoid interaction with anesthetic drugs used in dentistry. Psychotropic medications can cause drowsiness, drooling, extremely dry mouth, excessive salivation, nervousness, uncontrolled movements of the tongue, muscle rigidity, and nasal congestion requiring mouth breathing. These side effects may cause discomfort to the patient undergoing dental treatment and difficulties for the dentist.

Patients who are physically challenged may not be easy to treat. Deformities may make sitting in the dental chair very uncomfortable. Paralysis may impair the patient's ability to sit or balance in a normal dentist chair. A hearing-impaired patient may not be able to hear the dentist's commands. These patients should be treated in a setting that can adapt to their disability.

Patients with serious medical illnesses may also pose special problems to the dentist. A patient with severe heart disease may suffer angina or elevated blood pressure while at the dentist's office. Patients may be using portable oxygen tanks, feeding tubes, or a central line for intravenous fluids. Neurologic disease (Parkinsonism) may cause uncontrollable head shaking and tongue movements. Stroke survivors may be less able to control swallowing or have minimal gag reflex. Care must be taken when treating these patients. A thorough understanding of the patient's medical problems and associated symptoms is important. The patient's medical and dental history should always be available for the dentist to review when treating the patient.

Types of Providers

General Dentists

A **dentist** usually completes four years of college and four years of dental education before becoming licensed to practice. A dentist earns either a DDS or a DMD degree. A general dentistry practice focuses on a wide range of skills, including examination, diagnosis, and treatment of simple and complex conditions in patients from young to old. The general dentist is much like a family practice physician, taking care of the dental health of all members of the family, providing periodic checkups and cleanings, and monitoring the condition of teeth and gums. The general dentist is allowed to perform almost all dental procedures he or she is appropriately trained to perform according to state license, but many choose to refer patients to specialty dentists for more complex care. Many general dentists focus on prevention, basic restorative care (fillings, crowns, bridges, and dentures), and cosmetic procedures.

Dental Specialties

There are nine dental specialties recognized by the American Dental Association. They are dental public health, endodontics, oral and maxillofacial radiology, oral and maxillofacial surgery, oral pathology, orthodontics, pediatric dentistry, periodontics, and prosthodontics. While several of these specialties are recognizable to most people, public health dentists, oral pathologists, and oral and maxillofacial radiologists usually practice in institutional settings. Specialty training ranges from an additional two to six years after dental school.

An **orthodontist** is a dentist who specializes in straightening teeth. Many orthodontists complete two years of specialty education following the four years of dental school to prepare for their specialty. Orthodontic treatment may be medically necessary or cosmetic. Patients are usually referred to an orthodontist by a general dentist for a consultation, and treatment begins when appropriate. Orthodontists use radiographs, impressions of the patient's teeth and bite, and a variety of orthodontic appliances (braces, retainers, bands and brackets bonded to teeth, headgear) to accomplish the goal of straightening teeth. Patients undergoing treatment see their orthodontist regularly over a period of several years. The dental record is important to the orthodontist to monitor the progress of treatment and must be available for reference every time the patient is seen.

A **periodontist** is a dentist who specializes in treating the tissues surrounding and supporting the teeth. Periodontal disease begins as an inflammation of the **gingiva** (gum tissue) and can progress to abscesses around the teeth and infection of the jawbones. As the disease progresses, the victim develops **loss of attachment (LA)** of teeth, the loss of supporting structures of the teeth. The teeth become loose and are eventually lost. Although periodontal disease is preventable, it is still quite prevalent among Americans. Studies during 1988 to 1991 indicate that more than 90 percent of Americans over 12 years of age had experienced some clinical LA. The LA increases with age, with 15 percent of Americans showing moderate or severe LA, although recent data (CDC, 2007) show a decrease in the prevalence and severity of periodontal disease across all adult age groups. Periodontal disease is treated by removing the bacterial plaque (the causative agent of the disease) and the calcified calculus deposits on the teeth. Depending on the severity of the disease, surgery or the use of antibiotics may be necessary. The key is to prevent the buildup of plaque and the initiation of disease in the first place. Patients are usually referred to the periodontist by a general dentist, although they may self-refer if they suspect a problem developing. Periodontists also perform surgical procedures to improve smile aesthetics and place implants.

An **endodontist** is a dentist who specializes in treating the inside of the tooth, the nerve and pulp. An endodontist performs root canal therapy to remove the dying or dead tissue from the root canal system found within the tooth. The patient may complain of severe toothache or a tooth that is very sensitive to anything hot or cold—foods, liquids, or breathing cold air. The patient then goes back to the referring dentist or a prosthodontist for restoration of the tooth with a crown. An endodontist may never see the patient again or may treat the patient for problems with a different tooth in the future.

A **prosthodontist** is a dentist who specializes in replacing missing teeth with a prosthetic device. Full-mouth dentures are required for an edentulous person. Other **prostheses** include partial **denture**, **bridge** with **pontic**, and dental **implant**. Terms related to prostheses include the following:

Prosthesis – a fixed or removable appliance to replace missing teeth. Examples are bridges, dentures, and partials.

Denture – a removable prosthesis (false teeth) that replaces the teeth in either the upper or lower jaw.

Bridge – a fixed appliance (prosthesis) that replaces missing teeth. A bridge is a series of crowns (abutments and pontics)

Abutments – the teeth on either end of a bridge on which the bridge sits

Pontic – the part of a bridge that replaces the missing tooth; the false teeth between the two abutments

Implant – a post that is implanted in the bone; a crown, bridge, or denture is then attached to the implant

An **oral maxillofacial surgeon** is a dentist who specializes in surgery to the mouth and facial bones. A patient may be referred for oral surgery by a general dentist for removal of an unusual growth of the mouth or tongue. A patient with **impacted wisdom teeth** (wisdom teeth that will not erupt through the gum) is referred for surgical removal of the teeth. It is not uncommon for an orthodontist to refer a patient for extraction of teeth before applying braces. Oral maxillofacial surgeons may work with orthodontists on patients with complex orthodontic and skeletal problems. These surgeons also place implants.

Dental Hygienists

A dental hygienist usually completes two years of special training at a community college or university before becoming eligible to take state board examinations for licensure. (The student may earn an associate's or bachelor's degree, depending on the length of the education program.) Dental hygienists are licensed to perform some of the same procedures that dentists perform. However, most states do not allow the dental hygienist to establish an independent practice. The hygienist must be under the supervision of a licensed dentist when performing treatments. The hygienist typically performs oral and dental exams, cleans teeth by removing **plaque** and scraping off hardened **calculus**, polishes teeth, and applies fluoride and **sealants** to teeth. Depending on the state, the hygienist may inject anesthetic agents and make and interpret radiographs (X-ray films). The hygienist plays an important role in the prevention of dental disease and is usually responsible for educating the dental patient about good hygiene and dietary habits that promote good oral health. Instructions provided to the dental patient include proper brushing and flossing techniques and recommendations for diet and lifestyle changes. In many dental practices, the hygienist is the professional who collects the patient's medical and dental history, records initial vital signs, and documents important examination findings in the dental chart. Related terms include

Plaque – (also known as biofilm) the sticky film on teeth made up predominantly of bacteria
Calculus – plaque/biofilm that has hardened, also known as tartar
Sealants – Formed from a plastic liquid applied to the chewing surfaces of the teeth, sealants quickly harden and protect teeth from bacteria that cause tooth decay.

Mid-Level Providers

Mid-level providers are oral health care providers trained to perform certain clinical procedures, allowing the dentist to have more time to examine and diagnose patients or perform more complex procedures. These providers, known as dental health aide therapists (DHAT) in Alaska and Minnesota, may be able to address the dentist shortage in various parts of the country. While there is controversy about the use of such providers, at the time of this writing, several other states are considering licensing this type of provider.

Dental Assistants

A dental assistant may receive formal training at a technical college or may be personally trained by a dentist. Many states do not license dental assistants, although there is a national certifying agency. The dental assistant's primary role is to assist the dentist in the treatment of patients. The assistant anticipates what instruments will be needed, hands the instruments to the dentist, holds instruments in position in the patient's mouth, and prepares dental materials. The hands of the dental assistant act as the dentist's second pair of hands. The dental assistant may also help the dentist in charting dental exam findings and writing treatment notes. Most dental assistants have limited education and training. Most state laws limit a dental assistant to an assistive role rather than a treating role.

REGULATORY ISSUES

Professionals providing dental care in the United States are regulated by the individual states. Each state is responsible for licensing dentists and dental hygienists who will practice in their state. Although there is no national licensure or credentialing for dental care providers, many states will recognize the license of a dentist from another state through credentialing or reciprocity procedures.

State Licensure

Most states have a board of dentistry that issues licenses to practice. The applicant must provide evidence of adequate training and demonstrate treatment skills through state board examinations. In New York, among other states, a dental school graduate must complete a one-year residency *in lieu* of a licensing exam. The applicant's personal integrity, mental health, and moral behavior are all evaluated to determine whether the person can safely practice in the state. Licensure is the primary means of protecting the public from incompetent dental practitioners. Dentists may have their licenses suspended or revoked for gross negligence, behavior that endangers a patient, sexual abuse of a patient, dispensing narcotics inappropriately, abusing drugs or alcohol themselves, or mental unfitness. Dentists may also be required to carry adequate malpractice insurance to be licensed to practice.

Drug Enforcement Agency (DEA) Regulations

Dentists prescribe a variety of medications during treatment of patients. They must adhere to federal and state regulations whenever a controlled substance is involved. A dentist may prescribe narcotic pain relievers, and they are regulated by the same laws that physicians must follow. A dentist must have a valid Drug Enforcement Agency (DEA, a division of the U.S. Department of Justice) number for patients to fill prescriptions for narcotics and other controlled substances at a pharmacy. Many states also require a state prescription number. The DEA number may be revoked if a dentist violates DEA regulations in prescribing narcotics. Dentists must also now have a National Provider Identifier (NPI) number from the Federal government in order to write prescriptions and to be reimbursed by many insurance companies.

Reporting of Adverse Effects of Medications and Dental Materials

Dentists use a variety of substances and materials in their treatment of patients and must report adverse or untoward effects of medications to the manufacturer, just as physicians and hospitals do. They are also supposed to report adverse reactions that patients have to dental materials used in restorations, including allergic reactions to metals and composite resin materials.

Other Reporting Requirements

Many spousal batteries occur with blows to the victim's face and teeth. Loosened, broken teeth and facial fractures are often diagnosed and treated by dentists. The dentist is legally obligated to report suspected cases of abuse to law enforcement authorities just as physicians and other health care providers are. Dental records may be used as evidence of repeated trauma indicative of battery or abuse.

In some states, the clinician who first diagnoses a malignant neoplasm is required to report it to a state cancer registry. Dental practitioners routinely screen patients for oral cancer and when a dental professional diagnoses a malignant neoplasm, it may be his or her responsibility to report it.

DOCUMENTATION

Over the past decade, dental practices have shifted from analog/paper records to electronic dental records and digital radiographs. The typical dental record of a patient visiting a general dentist consists of patient demographic information, financial information (especially insurance coverage), the medical and dental history, dental examination and charting, periodontal exam, dental radiographs, and treatment notes. Specialists have additional exam information, dental radiographs, and treatment notes. At a minimum, most practices will use electronic scheduling, billing, and financial programs. Electronic filing of insurance claims usually speeds up the reimbursement process considerably.

Patient Information

The first time a person visits a dental practice, certain identifying information is routinely collected, including name, gender, date of birth, age, marital status, address, home and work phone numbers, and Social Security number. The patient is usually given a form to complete to provide this information or may use an electronic kiosk with digital forms. The patient is also asked to provide the name and phone number of his or her personal physician. It may be necessary for the dentist to contact the patient's physician regarding proposed treatment, medication allergies, or medical conditions that affect the patient's dental care. The patient information form typically includes a statement that the patient or parent is asked to sign authorizing and consenting to the dental exam and treatment. Additional information such as employer, insurance carrier, and spouse's name, address, phone, and Social Security number is usually obtained to assist the dentist in collecting fees and insurance benefits to pay for care provided. The form may also include an assignment of benefits that allows the dentist to bill the insurance carrier and authorizes the carrier to send payment directly to the dentist. This information is then entered into the electronic dental record (Figure 14-3).

Medical and Dental History

A medical history questionnaire is usually given to the patient to complete at the first visit, along with the personal information form. The questions are usually answered with *yes* or *no* and cover a wide range of medical symptoms and diseases. *Yes* answers may require additional details. Many medical conditions are important in dental disease and treatment, and it is crucial that the dentist be provided with complete and accurate information before caring for a patient. Patients are asked to identify prescription and over-the-counter medications they take regularly and the date of their last visit to a physician. The form also asks the patient about the use of recreational drugs, HIV (human immunodeficiency virus) status, and history of hepatitis. Allergies to drugs and substances must be identified. Increasing numbers of health care workers and patients have developed a sensitivity to latex, the material used to manufacture disposable gloves. It is estimated that 12 percent of dental and health care workers are hypersensitive to latex (Safadi et al., 1996). Dental professionals need to identify patients who are hypersensitive to latex so that latex gloves are not worn while treating these patients. Many practices and institutions are now latex-free. (See Figure 14-4 for an electronic medical history.)

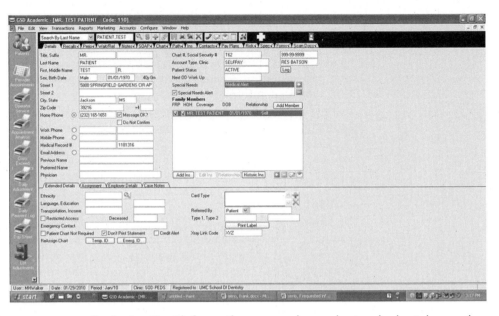

FIGURE **14-3** Typical patient information screen in an electronic dental record. (Courtesy of General Systems Design Group, Inc., Cedar Rapids, IA.)

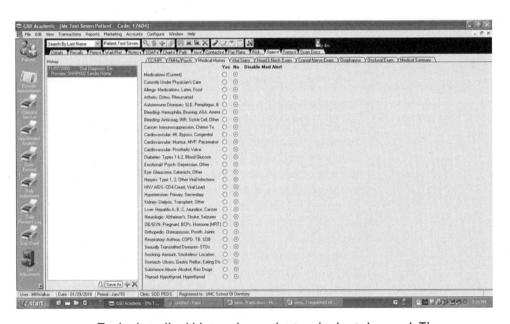

FIGURE **14-4** Typical medical history in an electronic dental record. The medical record may have different formats depending on the needs of the practice and individual preferences. (Courtesy of General Systems Design Group, Inc., Cedar Rapids, IA.)

A dental history, which is usually part of the medical history form, is also completed by the patient. The patient is asked about dental symptoms, previous dental treatments, and what prompted the visit to the dentist. The form may also contain questions about patients' dental routines at home, whether they are satisfied with the cosmetic look of their smile, and whether they are nervous or anxious about seeing the dentist.

The patient's medical and dental histories are reviewed by the dentist or dental hygienist with the patient. The professional asks further questions about items to which the patient answered *yes* to get a complete picture or clarification. Notes are made on the history form or elsewhere to document additional information provided in the interview.

Head, Neck, and Intraoral Examination

The first part of a routine dental exam evaluates the patient's general health. The dental care professional may take and chart an adult's blood pressure and other vital signs and make a note of the patient's general appearance. Next, the head and neck are examined for any abnormal findings such as enlarged lymph nodes, bruises or cuts on the face, or abnormal-looking growths. Positive findings are noted in the chart. The intraoral exam evaluates the appearance of the patient's mouth, lips, tongue, mucosa inside the cheek, tonsils, palate, and gums. Any abnormal or positive findings are documented in the chart. Growths that appear suspicious may prompt a referral to an oral surgeon. Patients with active cold sores and fever blisters (herpes simplex) should not receive treatment until the sores are healed to avoid the risk of spreading the herpes infection.

Dental Examination and Charting

The examination next focuses on the patient's teeth. The dentist documents information about each tooth in the patient's chart. This is commonly done using a graphic chart as in Figure 14-5. Every missing tooth and all existing restorations are charted. The chart indicates the surfaces involved, the size, and the material of each filling (e.g. **amalgam** or **composite**). Each tooth is visually examined and probed to ascertain whether decay is present or a restoration is cracked or failing. The dental charts of children note which permanent teeth have erupted, which primary teeth are still present, and the condition of the teeth.

Periodontal Examination

The health of the gingiva and supporting tissue of the patient's teeth is evaluated during the periodontal exam. The dentist or hygienist gently inserts a probe between the base of the tooth and the gingiva to measure the depth of pockets around the tooth. Periodontal disease is manifested by deepening pockets around the tooth, receding of the gingiva, and loss of attachment of the tooth. Each tooth is probed at six locations, three on the front surface and three on the tongue surface. Adults typically have a probing depth of 2 to 3 millimeters in each area around teeth, which is considered normal. If the gums bleed when probed, it may be a sign of early gingivitis. A depth of 4 to 6 millimeters is worrisome, and a depth of 9 millimeters or more means the tooth has very little attachment left and will likely be quite loose. Each probe measurement is recorded on a periodontal chart (Figure 14-6). The probing results are discussed

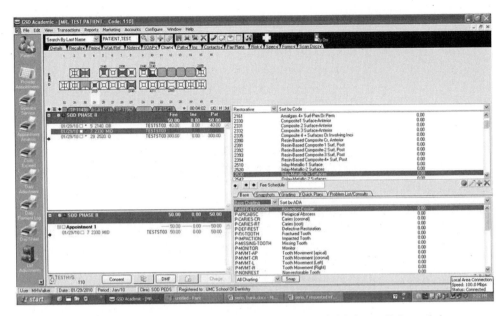

FIGURE **14-5** The dental charting screen shows the initial condition of the patient's teeth and restorations as well as the treatment plan and may be used to indicate completed procedures and initiate a fee charge. (Courtesy of General Systems Design Group, Inc., Cedar Rapids, IA.)

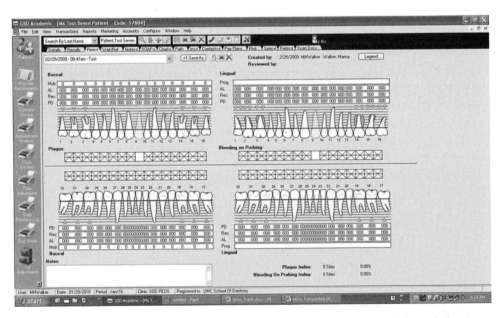

FIGURE **14-6** The condition of the patient's gums is recorded on the periodontal chart. Multiple charts may be compared over time to see if the patient's condition is improving or worsening. (Courtesy of General Systems Design Group, Inc., Cedar Rapids, IA.)

with the patient, and the dental caregiver points out specific teeth that should be flossed and brushed more carefully. A general description of the amount of calculus (hardened plaque) present is noted in the chart. Patients who have regular cleanings and checkups at recommended six-month intervals have a lot less calculus to be scraped off than do patients who have not seen a dentist in years.

Dental Radiography and Intraoral Photography

The dentist usually orders dental radiographs during the patient's first visit and at appropriate intervals thereafter. They may be full-mouth radiographs (multiple radiographs), a **panoramic radiograph** (all teeth shown on one film), or just **bitewing** radiographs (selected upper and lower teeth simultaneously). The radiographs become part of the patient's chart and are usually stored with the chart or electronically. Subsequent radiographs can be compared with previous radiographs to monitor progress of decay or periodontal disease or identify when a defect first appeared. Radiographs help the dentist confirm or discover the presence of dental disease. Insurance companies may ask the dentist to submit radiographs to verify the necessity of or completion of dental treatment. (See Figure 14-7 and Figure 14-8 for examples of dental radiography images.)

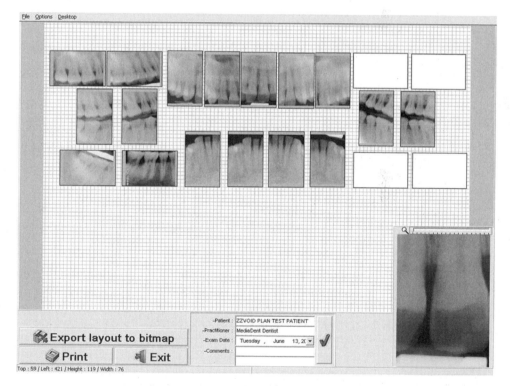

FIGURE **14-7** The full-mouth series (FMX) of radiographs shows the condition of the patient's teeth and bone that supports the teeth. Note the magnification of one image in the lower right box. Moving the cursor over a specific area of the FMX allows for a magnified view in the box. (Courtesy of Multi Media Dental Systems, Atlanta, GA.)

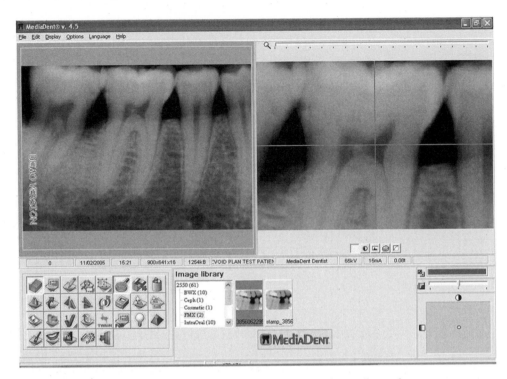

FIGURE **14-8** Another feature of the digital imaging software allows for greater magnification of the images. (Courtesy of Multi Media Dental Systems, Atlanta, GA.)

Abnormal lesions on the tongue or mucosa may be photographed using an intraoral camera. New computer imaging technologies now allow dentists to digitize the image of teeth and gums with a tiny video camera on a dental instrument inside the patient's mouth and display the image on a computer screen for the patient to see. The patient can be shown the problem the dentist sees and may then be more willing to have the problem fixed.

Treatment Plan

After the dental exam, periodontal exam, and radiographic exam, the dentist summarizes the diagnoses and outlines a properly sequenced treatment plan for the patient. The patient may just need **prophylaxis** (cleaning of teeth) and application of fluoride to prevent decay. Any decay, periodontal disease, or pathology found should be treated as soon as possible to minimize damage to the tooth. The dentist tells the patient what needs to be done, and the patient is encouraged to make a return appointment to get the work done. Unfortunately, not all patients are willing to have the work done, and some never return to receive the recommended treatment. Others may get minor restorations but refuse to have an expensive root canal or crown until an unbearable toothache develops.

Treatment Notes

All dental treatment is documented in the patient's dental chart. The dentist notes the type of anesthetic agent used, the type of nerve block and injection approach, the diagnosis or the location of decay on the tooth, and the type of material used to restore the tooth after removing the decay. This information is important for future dental care. The dentist may find that certain anesthetic agents do not numb the patient's tooth fast enough, long enough, or sufficiently. The dentist makes a note to choose a different agent for this patient the next time. Details about the restorative materials and techniques are important to track premature failures of restorations.

Legally, it is imperative that the dentist keeps complete treatment notes. If the dentist is called into any legal proceedings, the information in the chart may be critical for the dentist's defense. In a legal context, if something is not written down, it is assumed not to have happened. The surreptitious alteration of documents after the fact is illegal. Electronic dental records have safeguards against altering records after the fact. (See Figure 14-9 for an example of electronic treatment notes.)

Patient Education

Dentistry has made great strides in the prevention of dental caries and periodontal disease. This has been accomplished through education, the use of fluoride, changes in diet, and an improvement in personal oral hygiene. Most

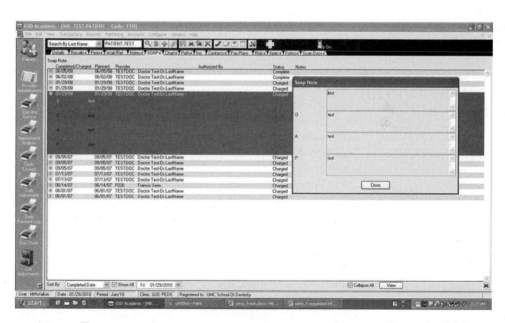

FIGURE **14-9** Treatment or progress note entries are mandatory to document both what has been done with the patient and any planned treatment. (Courtesy of General Systems Design Group, Inc., Cedar Rapids, IA.)

people now know that to maintain healthy teeth, they need to brush and floss their teeth daily to disrupt bacterial deposits now known as **biofilms,** cut down on consumption of sugary sweets, and use toothpaste and drinking water that has fluoride. Another aspect of patient education emphasizes the importance of periodic dental checkups and prophylaxis. Most dentists send patients a postcard or electronic message reminding them that it is time to come in for a checkup. These notices are important to the patient and to the financial viability of the dental practice.

The current generation of children has a lower prevalence of tooth decay and a higher probability of keeping their teeth for life. As Americans become more health conscious and take better care of their teeth, dentures may become a thing of the past.

Diet Evaluation

Some dental practices may perform an evaluation of the patient's dietary habits. Poor nutrition can contribute to dental disease. It is particularly important that adequate calcium is provided in the diet for the calcification of tooth enamel and maintenance of alveolar bone. Children, teenagers, and pregnant and menopausal women are most at risk for softening of the enamel and tooth decay caused by calcium deficiency. If a dietary evaluation is done, it is documented in the patient's chart along with recommendations provided to the patient.

REIMBURSEMENT

Dental patients often pay for their own dental care, but many have dental benefits through their employers. The most common form of third-party plan is traditional dental insurance. Under this form of reimbursement, the patient is covered for a percentage of the fee, based on the agreement negotiated between the employer and the third-party insurance carrier. The patient is responsible for any deductible and that part of the dentist's fee not covered by the insurance plan. Employers, patients, and dentists may also participate in managed care plans, capitation plans, preferred provider organizations (PPOs), and health maintenance organizations (HMOs). Under these arrangements, the dentist agrees to provide certain services for a set rate of reimbursement from the plan. A patient is responsible for the full fee for any necessary or elective services that are not specifically covered by the plan.

Dental Insurance

American employers have become more conscious of the dental needs of their employees and many now offer dental insurance in their benefit packages. About 61 percent of the U.S. population has private dental insurance coverage (NIDCR, 2001). Sometimes dental insurance is optional and the employee must pay a small premium for coverage. Sometimes it is totally free for the employee, with a small premium for the employee's spouse and family. A typical dental insurance policy covers checkups and preventive dentistry at 100 percent; filling-type restorations and extractions at 80 percent; and crowns, bridges, and other prosthetics at 50 percent of the plan's fee schedule for these services. Orthodontic treatment may be covered at 50 percent to a lifetime maximum of $1,000. Some policies may require the patient to pay a deductible on nonpreventive treatment each year before any treatment is covered, and most have a $1,000 to $2,000 limit of benefits per year.

Dentists generally appreciate treating patients with dental insurance. Collection of fees is simpler and easier for the patient, and many times the dentist can confirm insurance coverage and get the treatment plan approved before initiation of treatment. Dental insurance policies pay the percentages listed based on usual and customary fees for the geographic area. Occasionally, the amount the insurance company says it will pay for a certain treatment is lower than what the dentist charges. Either the patient must pay the difference or the dentist forgives it. Dental insurance payments are processed promptly if submitted correctly.

Dentists participating in a PPO agree to charge the patient only the amount allowed by the insurance company. Dentists agree to the reduced reimbursement because the plan also provides benefits for the dental practice. For example, there may be an increase in the number of patients because insured patients have incentives to receive care from a participating dentist. There may be discounts for PPO members on the cost of making crowns, bridges, and dentures from a central dental lab. Government plans such as Medicaid and CHIP (Children's Health Insurance Plan) cover dental care at a set reimbursement rate for children. Medicaid coverage for dental care is generally minimal and varies from state to state.

Self-Pay Patients

A significant number of patients must still pay cash directly for their dental checkups and treatments. Dental insurance is rarely available to retired people, and Medicare does not cover dental care for the elderly. The working poor, unemployed, disabled, and elderly have a difficult time paying for dental care. Most self-pay dental patients are those who recognize the importance of good dental health and can afford it or are willing to sacrifice to receive it.

HMO Plans

Many HMOs now include dental care in their plans. The plans vary in what is covered, amount of patient copayment, and availability. It is not uncommon for HMO plans to require patients to schedule routine checkups up to six months in advance for care and to provide limited availability for dental emergencies. This is part of the strategy for holding down costs.

Centers for Medicare & Medicaid Services

Medicare does not include benefits for dental care for the elderly. This segment of the population, with years of wear on their teeth or with no teeth left, is in great need of dental care to improve quality of life. The cost to taxpayers of adding dental coverage for the elderly would likely be prohibitive.

Medicaid and the Children's Health Insurance Program (CHIP) offer some dental benefits for children. Preventive checkups and necessary restorations for children are covered by Medicaid, but the number of dentists accepting Medicaid patients is quite limited. Medicaid coverage for adult recipients is an optional benefit by federal regulations, so many state Medicaid programs do not provide more than emergency coverage for adult dental care due to the expense.

TRICARE Dental Program

The TRICARE Dental Program (TDP) provides dental benefits for families of active-duty military personnel (Department of Defense, 2003). TDP coverage is generally good and is as acceptable to dentists as dental insurance. (TRICARE replaced the Civilian Health and Medical Program of the Uniformed Services [CHAMPUS], which used to be the source of dental coverage for families of military personnel.)

Veterans Affairs

Dental care is available to qualifying veterans at Department of Veterans Affairs medical centers. The patients pay little or no fees for treatment if obtained at the VA facility. There is no billing involved, but the facility must keep track of utilization to adequately staff and budget for the VA dental clinic. Veterans with private dental insurance policies generally obtain dental care through private dental practices rather than at a VA dental clinic.

INFORMATION MANAGEMENT

Information is crucial to the practice of dentistry, including information about individual patients, dental equipment and supplies, vendors, dental coverages of each insurance company, new medications and anesthetic agents, new treatment modalities, the epidemiology of dental disease, financial information about the practice, withholding and employment taxes, and more.

Treatment Coding and Classification

There are three main coding systems used in dentistry. The American Dental Association (ADA) has a coding system for diagnoses and procedures, the *Current Dental Terminology 2009–2010 (CDT)*. This coding system is typically used to file dental insurance claims for patients. It is also used by dental schools and dental hygiene training clinics to collect statistical information. Table 14-1 is a list of sample ADA codes.

Hospitals may occasionally bill a third-party payer for dental procedures. For example, although Medicare does not provide dental coverage, it will pay for dental services that are an integral part of a covered procedure (e.g., reconstruction of the jaw following accidental injury). Medicare will also pay for extractions done in preparation for radiation treatment of neoplastic jaw lesions. Diagnosis codes from the current clinical modification of the *International Classification of Diseases* are used by hospitals and medical centers for dental patients treated as inpatients, hospital outpatients, or emergency room patients. *ICD* dental procedure codes are used for inpatients. Codes from the Healthcare Common Procedure Coding System are used by

TABLE **14-1**

Common ADA Codes

Code	Description
0140	Limited oral evaluation
0150	Comprehensive oral evaluation
0210	Intraoral—complete series
1110	Prophylaxis—adult
1203	Topical fluoride—child

Source: American Dental Association. (2008). Survey Highlights. Online at https://www.ada.org/members/ada/prod/survey/08_sdpc_highlights.pdf.

the hospital to code dental procedures for hospital outpatients and emergency room patients or by dentists for procedures for which dental codes do not exist. Most hospitals do not bill dental insurance on a regular basis, but would follow the reporting and coding requirements of the dental insurance company when this occurs. A dentist in private practice performing a procedure covered under a dental plan in a hospital setting would submit his or her claim to the dental insurance company using *CDT* or other codes as appropriate and required by the payer. It is important to remember that dental coding and medical coding techniques are not compatible with each other and the requirements of the third-party payer for the given type of provider and setting must be followed.

Electronic Information Systems in Dentistry

Computers were originally used in dentistry primarily for practice management applications, which typically include accounting, patient billing, insurance claim tracking, appointment scheduling, payroll, and patient recall notices. In recent years, computers have been used increasingly for clinical applications as well. As systems and applications for dentistry continue to improve, the use of electronic information systems in the dental practice has steadily increased. To illustrate, in 1976, only 1 percent of dentists used computers in their practices, and less than 25 percent used commercial computing services. By 2000, 85.1 percent of dentists in the United States used a computer in the dental office, and 48.3 percent of these computers had Internet access (American Dental Association, 2001). Since that time, over 95 percent of dentists use a computer for some office functions. The American Dental Association (ADA) has done a side-by-side comparison of 40 practice management software packages, although there are many more on the market. The ADA Web site is a good resource for comparing dental software.

Practice Management Software

A computer software package to manage a dental practice may include the following modules.

Patient Registration   One of the primary functions of the software is the collection of patients' demographic information, including address, contact numbers, e-mail address, date of birth, insurance information, and possibly a digital photograph for the dental record.

Appointment Scheduling   The scheduling software should be flexible and fit the way the dental practice operates. It should provide for multiple dentists, multiple chairs, and double booking of patients if implemented in a group practice. The time slots must be variable according to individual practice patterns. One dentist may want to routinely allow an hour for a crown preparation, and another may want an hour and a half. Despite the routine time allowed for a procedure, there may be special patients or more complicated procedures that require more than the normal amount of time. The software must allow a standard allotment of time or a custom allotment of time for scheduling of appointments. (See Figure 14-10.)

The software must provide easy and flexible query capabilities. The receptionist may need to answer questions such as: What day is Jane Doe scheduled to come in? What is the next available one-hour slot for Dr. Brown? Which patient can be called to reschedule a later appointment so another patient with an emergency can be seen? Who is next to be scheduled on the waiting list?

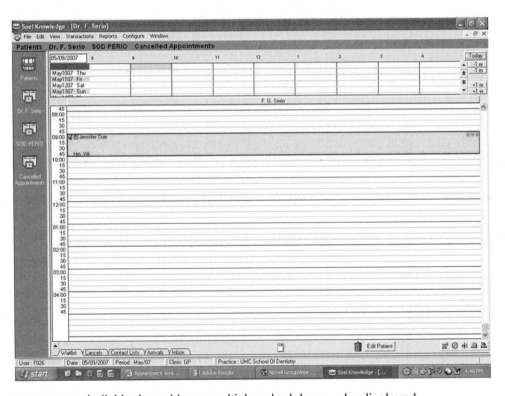

FIGURE **14-10** Individual provider or multiple schedules can be displayed simultaneously. (Courtesty of General Systems Design Group, Inc., Cedar Rapids, IA.)

Insurance Billing and Claims Tracking Insurance patients can compose a large portion of a dentist's practice. The cash flow of the practice will suffer severely if the process of billing and tracking claims is inefficient. The insurance claims module should be integrated with the patient accounts module and may be set up for electronic claims submission to third-party payers, thereby reducing paperwork, providing for greater accuracy, and permitting more rapid settlement of electronic claims. The software should be able to identify patients who have received treatment but for whom claims have not yet been submitted, patients who have preauthorization for treatment, claims that have not been paid 30 days after submission, and accounts that have received only a partial payment from the insurance company.

Another important function for dental practices serving large numbers of insurance patients is the ability to confirm benefit amounts and patient copayment amounts or deductibles. Most dentists prefer to collect copayment and deductible amounts at the time of service rather than to bill the patient after receiving partial payment from the insurance company. If the software identifies this amount at the time of checkout, the patient can be asked to pay the amount at that time.

Patient Accounting Information Although dentists would like to have all patients pay when treatment is rendered, it is not realistic to believe that this will always happen. Patient accounts software should keep track of total charges for the day, total charges for the family, amount paid and when, remaining balance, and age of balance, as well as the financially responsible party. The software should be able to print regular monthly billing statements for accounts with outstanding balances as well as an individual statement on demand and allow insertion of a special message to some or all recipients.

Software should follow accepted accounting principles and provide for closing the month, quarter, and fiscal year. Many dentists contract with an accountant to prepare tax returns and provide financial statements for the business. Accounting software must provide acceptable output and verification of financial matters for the dentist's accountant. Some dentists charge interest on outstanding balances but may request that a special account be exempt from interest charges. The software should be able to charge a specified interest rate on some accounts and none on others.

It is preferred to have patient accounts integrated with scheduling and patient recall. The system can then alert the receptionist when an appointment is being scheduled for a patient who has an unpaid balance from a previous visit. The system can also send a recall notice to a patient with an outstanding balance, with a message that the account needs to be brought up to date before scheduling another appointment.

Patient Recall Reminders Periodic checkups and teeth cleanings are important for dental heath. Dentists recognize that it is their professional responsibility to encourage patients to have this routine care and send reminders when it is time to be seen again. It is also important to the financial viability of the dental practice to see patients regularly. Practice management software should be able to identify patients who should receive a recall notice and patients who failed to respond to a previous recall notice. The software should be able to print envelopes and perform a mail merge to personalize the recall notices the patients receive. The system should keep track of when patient recalls are due and when they are sent. Some software programs can send recall notices as an e-mail message.

Patient Referral   Dentists, particularly specialists, like to know who is referring patients to their practice for care. Software should keep track of who referred each patient, prepare statistical reports based on the referring source and payment source, and compile a list of all patients referred by a specific dentist. The dentist may foster a social relationship with professionals who frequently refer patients. Referral letters can also be generated to send to the general dentist.

Practice Reporting   Reporting is an important function of practice management software for monitoring and effectively managing the business. Administrative and clinical reports providing data about patient account status, provider productivity, appointment utilization, and treatment plan procedures (completed or in progress) can be invaluable tools for running a successful dental practice.

Inventory Management   Some software includes the functionality to monitor inventory items, including supplies and equipment. This can make reordering more timely and efficient. The software application may even provide an interface for online ordering.

Electronic Dental Record

The electronic dental record is commonly being used in dental practices, especially among younger dentists or those renovating or establishing practices. Some software packages for the dental practice store the complete dental record, including digital radiographs, while others are more limited in functionality. The comprehensive electronic dental record stores medical and dental histories and the results of dental and periodontal examinations; provides alerts about medical conditions, allergies, and the need for antibiotic premedication; facilitates comparison between previous exams and current exams to aid in monitoring progression of disease; and manages treatment notes. The electronic record should interface seamlessly with digital radiography and imaging software, which provides compact and safe storage of dental radiographs and allows the dentist to share radiographs with a specialist or an insurance company via the Internet.

Computers in dental practice can be enhanced through the use of alternate methods of input such as voice recognition as well as touch-screen and pen-based computing. These features may facilitate ease of use by the dentist, hygienist, or dental assistant. Voice recognition may be a particularly promising feature, because it allows hands-free data entry. This type of input could also be useful in controlling the spread of infection in the dental office by removing the pen and paper, display, or keyboard as potential vectors for bacteria and viruses.

Computer Hardware and Networking

Most dental offices now have multiple computers. There may be a computer at each patient chair, in the radiology area, in private offices, as well as in the reception and business areas. Determining the layout and specifications of computers depends heavily on the practice management software being used and its specific requirements. Networking the computers allows them to communicate with one another, to share practice management and clinical software, to store and back up data in a single central location, and to share hardware resources such as printers, intraoral cameras, or digital signature pads.

Other Technological Devices

Digital cameras are becoming increasingly popular in the dental practice for taking photographs for the dental record, to help identify the patient or to show before-and-after treatment photos. Intraoral cameras capture images that can be helpful to educate the patient about treatment needs or to show progression of ongoing treatment. **Digital imaging** devices provide an alternative to traditional film X-rays. Digital radiographs can be integrated directly into the patient record and decrease the amount of radiation patients are exposed to.

Application Service Providers (ASPs)

For dental professionals who do not wish to maintain an office network, handle hardware and software upgrades, or be responsible for daily backups of data, an alternative may be to enlist the services of an application service provider (ASP). The dentist can contract with an ASP who, through an Internet connection, provides the practice management software. The ASP can store data for the practice, maintain network server equipment, upgrade software applications, and perform daily data backups. An unreliable or slow Internet connection, however, could be extremely detrimental to the well-being of the dental practice.

QUALITY IMPROVEMENT AND UTILIZATION MANAGEMENT

In small dental practices, a formal quality improvement program or plan is not the focus. However, a wise dentist will continuously try to improve the quality of the service provided. The Dental Society of the State of New York developed a peer-review program for quality assurance that stands as a model for other dental societies across the country (Benton & Shub, 1995). The American Dental Association (ADA) also promotes and supports peer-review programs for state dental associations (2009).

Clinical dental practice guidelines are well developed. For example, one model clinical guideline for general dentists for managing patients with adult periodontitis provides recommendations on the content of the medical, dental, social, and habit history; exam, diagnosis, and treatment documentation; and treatment guidelines (Workshop, 1994). Organizations that have published practice guidelines for dentistry are as follows:

- American Academy of Pediatric Dentistry
- American Academy of Periodontology

- American Association of Endodontists
- American Association of Oral and Maxillofacial Surgeons
- American Association of Orthodontists
- American College of Prosthodontists
- American Dental Association

To assist dental professionals with clinical decision making, the American Dental Association also provides a database of studies on dental topics, clinical recommendations, and resources at its Center for Evidence-Based Dentistry Web site: http://ebd.ada.org.

Large dental practices, particularly those associated with managed dental care and HMOs, are more interested in formally measuring quality and using quality indicators. Some suggested quality indicators for managed dental care are as follows:

- How long does it take to get an appointment for a routine checkup and cleaning?
- How long does it take to get an appointment for a new dental symptom?
- How many child and adolescent patients have sealants applied?
- How many third molar extractions are performed?
- How many enrollees received prophylaxis and checkups during the year?
- How many referrals were made to dental specialists?

Utilization of dental services is generally managed by dental insurance plans and HMOs providing dental benefits. The approaches to limiting expenses include the exclusion of benefits for preexisting dental conditions, requiring pretreatment authorization, and actively evaluating the necessity of treatment. Dentists may be required to submit copies of dental records and radiographs to justify the need for treatment. Patients self-manage utilization if large copayments and deductibles are instituted. Most dental plans, however, recognize the importance of preventive care in controlling costs, so they cover semiannual checkups and cleanings. Some plans impose an annual limit to benefits, exclude coverage for cosmetic dental procedures, and require the dentist to use the least expensive restorative method, for example, limiting the use of expensive gold crowns to molars only. Many dental plans do not cover treatment for temporomandibular joint (TMJ) syndrome, cosmetic orthodontics, and dental implants.

RISK MANAGEMENT AND LEGAL ISSUES

Injuries to Caregivers and Patients

An important area of risk management is injury to patients and practitioners. Potential for injury includes instrument traumas from needles, drills, and probes. Proper use of a "rubber dam," which isolates the operative field to the tooth undergoing treatment, can help prevent injury to the mouth and tongue. Burns from sterilization equipment and skin injuries from grinders are another area of risk. Proper training of personnel and consistent use of safety measures are important to prevent injuries. There is the potential for the patient or practitioner to suffer a foreign body or debris in the eye, which can be prevented if both the patient and dental practitioner wear safety goggles during dental treatment. Another potential risk is for the dental patient to accidentally swallow a foreign body during treatment. The natural gag reflex makes it easy for a patient to swallow a cotton roll, bite block, or small object accidentally dropped by the dentist. The rubber dam can be helpful in preventing this problem.

Musculoskeletal injuries to the neck and back from long hours of leaning over dental chairs are occupational hazards in dentistry. Repetitive motion injuries such as carpal tunnel syndrome and ulnar nerve compression are also common. To control risk, education of personnel on these issues is vital. All dental personnel should also protect themselves from contaminants by using standard barrier precautions. These precautions include safety glasses, a mask, disposable gloves, and possibly a full-length gown.

Malpractice and Negligence

It is universal practice for practitioners to routinely use disposable gloves and face masks while treating all patients. Practitioners should be very careful when they have open lesions on fingers and hands. Cuts and abrasions can be a source of bacteria transfer from patients to providers. Patients are at low risk of acquiring hepatitis, HIV, and other infections at the dental office. Infections acquired through dental treatment can be the result of negligent and improper procedures in the office.

Another area of potential problems is inappropriate or inadequate diagnosis or treatment of a patient's dental disease. Failure to treat early pulpitis can progress to dental abscess. A patient can suffer the loss of a permanent tooth because the dentist failed to diagnose or adequately treat a tooth early enough to save the tooth.

As in the medical field, adequate documentation is the best defense against malpractice and negligence suits. Dentists should document posttreatment instructions provided to patients, procedures performed, reactions to medications, and complaints of tooth pain and sensitivity. Dentists also need to know the limits of their expertise. Failure to refer a patient to a specialist for complicated conditions can result in malpractice.

Adverse Reactions to Medications and Dental Materials

Dentists should report dangerous and unusual medication reactions to the pharmaceutical company just as physicians do. It is particularly important to document the reaction in the patient's dental record, to avoid using the same agent again in the future with that patient. A variety of materials are used in dentistry and become a permanent part of a person's mouth. Adverse reactions to metal and other substances should be carefully evaluated and reported.

Dental Records for Identification of Individuals

Dental records are very useful in the identification of an individual, either dead or alive. Dental records are typically used by the coroner or medical examiner to identify a decedent. In mass disasters, such as airplane crashes and fires, dental records may be the only way to confirm the identity of a body. Occasionally, they can be useful in discovering the identity of a living patient who is unable to identify himself or herself due to some impairment.

ROLE OF THE HEALTH INFORMATION MANAGEMENT PROFESSIONAL

Health information management (HIM) professionals have a unique set of skills that can greatly benefit dental practitioners. Principles of documentation, confidentiality, and good information management are all relevant to the practice of dentistry. The growth of managed care and capitation requires education and planning for the financial survival of dental practitioners. There are many opportunities for the HIM professional to share skills with the dental profession.

With the advancement of technology, many dental practices are assessing their needs as they relate to information technology (IT) and IT infrastructures. What dental software package is the most appropriate for the practice? What other applications might be useful? How do the systems integrate for best business practices? What are the hardware requirements? Is a computer network necessary? If so, how should it be set up? How is electronic insurance filing done? How secure are the data? Many other questions may arise as technology is integrated into the dental practice. The HIM professional can be an invaluable consultant in these areas.

As more Americans receive dental care through managed care plans and insurance, there is a need for individuals with expertise in electronic billing, revenue cycle, and utilization review. The HIM professional who can manipulate and analyze electronic data may be invaluable in helping dental practices with business decisions such as estimating a capitation amount for a managed care plan or determining whether it would be advantageous to join a preferred provider organization. Expertise in quality improvement may be valuable for the compilation of quality indicators and the evaluation of patient satisfaction.

There are opportunities for HIM careers at dental clinics associated with academic institutions. The information management tasks are very much like those of a large ambulatory care clinic. In some environments that have yet to convert to electronic records, the management of checking charts in and out, getting paperwork completed, and releasing copies of charts and radiographs are also health information management functions. There are also statistics that must be collected and reported on patients seen in the clinic and what procedures each dental student has performed.

HIM professionals can also be involved in the design and selection of dental information systems, particularly as health care becomes more integrated. The goal of an electronic patient record with a comprehensive, lifetime history of each patient is a relatively new idea for dentistry. The dental profession may need help in understanding the technologies and approaches to integrating data. As dental records and systems become integrated with existing medical records and systems, the development of data dictionaries and combined master patient indexes will become issues. Also, as development of the national health information network moves forward, health information managers' knowledge of health information exchange and privacy and security regulations can be an asset to dental care providers desiring to participate in this endeavor.

TRENDS

Dental Services

The face of dentistry is changing in the twenty-first century. The dentist-to-population ratio is declining after having peaked in 1998. As there are fewer dentists in an increasing general population, and as older individuals continue to keep more of their natural teeth, the demand for dental services should remain strong for the foreseeable future. Many of these services will be elective in nature as more people ask for aesthetic dental procedures to improve their appearance. The demand for implant dentistry will also continue to increase as people demand stability for their prostheses and are in a position to afford this type of care.

Many health plans offer dental benefits as an enticement to subscribers. However, the capitation formulas used are sometimes inadequate. If all subscribers used the dental benefits offered, the plan would not be able to cover the costs of the care. To prevent financial disaster, some plans defer appointments for checkups by scheduling them up to six months in advance. Some limit the days and times that first-time patients can be seen. Another method of containing costs is postponing restorations until absolutely necessary. These types of cost-saving methods may not be in the best interests of the patient.

In a preferred provider organization (PPO), dentists provide services at a discount to members of the PPO. Because a PPO is a fee-for-service arrangement, the dentist is paid for each covered service rendered, but at a reduced rate. The dentist must determine whether the payments provided by the contract will be sufficient. Regardless of the type of arrangement, health plans should be carefully scrutinized on the financial viability of the dental benefits offered before dental practitioners join.

Dental Treatment

Dentistry is among the few health professions that have successfully discovered how to prevent disease and decrease its financial impact on society. The public has been well educated on the value of fluoridated water and toothpaste, the need to brush and floss regularly, and the value of frequent teeth cleaning and removal of calculus. The number of children and teens with dental caries has greatly decreased, and the number of elderly who still have their own teeth is increasing. The need for dentures is on the decline. New restorative materials, medications, and treatment procedures are being used. New methods of treating periodontal disease, the major cause of tooth loss, are being discovered. But, until individuals take greater responsibility for maintaining their oral health, the need for dental services will not diminish.

As the American lifestyle becomes more active, there is an increase in dental injuries. Most dental emergencies are the result of trauma, frequently involving the maxillary anterior teeth. Sports dentistry is a relatively new practice specialty. There continues to be great progress in the treatment of dental traumas. Teeth that have been knocked out can be reimplanted. Fractured teeth can be splinted and restored rather than extracted.

Dental implants have found their rightful place in mainstream dentistry. Cosmetic dentistry is very popular, although demand fluctuates with the health of the overall economy. Methods of treating discoloration of teeth from smoking and coffee are popular. Additionally, the number of adults undergoing orthodontic treatment has increased.

Another area of progress is in dental anesthesia. Some patients can comfortably undergo dental treatment without the use of anesthetic agents through the use of biofeedback, hypnosis, acupuncture, and other techniques. Painless dentistry enhances the acceptability of going to the dentist and thus increases the dental health of Americans.

Another new development in the practice of dentistry is the sale of oral devices. An antisnore device can be obtained from a dentist. It may be the solution to sleepless nights because of a loud, snoring partner. A splint called a nightguard, worn in the mouth at night to prevent bruxing or grinding of teeth, offers relief to many sufferers of temporomandibular joint (TMJ) syndrome. Dentists have even become involved in making mouth guards for sports. Although outside the realm of traditional dentistry, devices for the mouth available through dentists can improve the quality of life.

Technology in Dentistry

The next important trend is the increase in electronic information systems in dental practices. Virtually all new practices have electronic dental records, digital financial packages, and digital imaging. Electronic billing and benefit confirmation can be important for healthy cash flow. Efficient and convenient handling of appointment scheduling and recall notices provides great financial benefits. Technologies such as digital radiography, intraoral imaging, computer modeling of prostheses, and displaying after-treatment appearance stimulate the interest in electronic dental records.

Dental Informatics

The field of dental informatics is growing as dentists are beginning to realize the value of expert systems, automated clinical alerts and warnings, and digital information for clinical practice. Systems have been developed for digital imaging, digital radiology, digital charting, computer-assisted design and manufacture of dental restorations, and diagnostic aids.

SUMMARY

Although not a traditional setting of practice for health information management, increasing opportunities exist and future careers are possible in the area of dental care. The knowledge and skills of a health information manager can be applied to the management of dental records. The electronic health record is comprehensive and includes dental records. HIM professionals have the knowledge and skills needed to help dentists make the transition from paper to electronic records. As progress is made, information managers will need to understand both medical and dental records to manage integrated health information systems. Growth in managed dental care plans will demand better information systems for dentists to manage their dental practices, as well as knowledgeable individuals to manage the revenue cycle of the practice, thus providing opportunities for consulting and careers in managing dental information. Treatment and technological advances make dentistry an exciting and interesting field. The dental health care setting has great career potential.

KEY TERMS

amalgam   a silver-colored filling composed of several metals. Amalgams are usually placed on the back teeth (posterior teeth).

biofilm   an aggregate of microorganisms organized into a dynamic community and collecting on the teeth and under the gums

bitewing   a radiograph that shows the upper and lower teeth's biting surfaces on the same film. This radiograph shows the portion of the teeth above the gum line.

bridge   a fixed appliance (prosthesis) that replaces missing teeth. A bridge is a series of crowns (abutments and pontics).

calculus   plaque that has hardened. Also known as tartar.

caries   correct technical term for tooth decay.

composite filling   a tooth-colored filling.

crown   full-coverage restoration of a tooth when it cannot be restored by a filling.

dentist   a licensed health care professional specializing in the prevention and treatment of disorders of the oral cavity and associated body structures. A dentist possesses either a DDS or a DMD degree.

denture   a removable prosthesis (false teeth) that replaces all of the teeth in either the upper or lower jaw.

digital imaging   the use of computer-based technologies to make radiographic (X-ray) and other clinical images in order to diagnose dental diseases and conditions.

edentulous   having no teeth, toothless.

electronic dental record (EDR)   a computer-based dental record that stores the patient's pertinent demographic, diagnostic, treatment, and financial information.

endodontist   a dentist who specializes in treating diseases or injuries that affect the root tip or nerve of the tooth. The most common procedure is a root canal.

gingiva   the gums.

group dental practice   two or more dentists practicing together.

impaction   an unerupted or partially erupted tooth that will not fully erupt because it is obstructed by another tooth, bone, or soft tissue.

implant   a post that is implanted in the bone. A crown, bridge, or denture is then attached to the implant.

loss of attachment (LA)   the loss of the supporting structure of the teeth that causes the tooth to become loose and that may result in loss of the tooth.

oral maxillofacial surgeon   a dentist who specializes in surgery to the mouth and facial bones.

orthodontist   a dentist who specializes in straightening teeth.

orthognathic surgery   surgery to bring jaws into proper alignment.

panoramic radiograph   a radiograph taken outside of the mouth that shows all the teeth on one film. This may also be a digital image.

periodontist a dentist who specializes in the treatment of diseases of the gum or bone (supporting structure).

plaque also known as biofilm, the sticky film on teeth made up predominantly of bacteria. (See also *biofilm*.)

pontic the part of a bridge that replaces the missing tooth.

primary teeth the baby teeth, also known as the primary dentition; the baby teeth are replaced by adult teeth (permanent teeth).

prophylaxis the scaling, cleaning, and removal of calculus—preventive treatment.

prosthesis a fixed or removable appliance to replace missing teeth. Examples are bridges, dentures, and partials. Sometimes single crowns are considered prosthetics.

prosthodontist a dentist who specializes in replacing missing teeth with a prosthetic device.

radiograph a graphic image produced by the use of radiation.

root canal therapy (RCT) the nerve of the tooth is removed from the canal inside the root and replaced with a filling material.

sealant clear application of acrylic placed over the biting surface of the tooth to prevent decay.

solo dental practice a dental practice owned and operated by one dentist.

wisdom teeth the third molars; each of the four wisdom teeth is the eighth tooth from the center of the mouth to the back of the mouth. Wisdom teeth are often impacted (obstructed from erupting) and have to be extracted.

REVIEW QUESTIONS

Knowledge-Based Questions

1. Describe the roles of the dentist, the dental hygienist, and the dental assistant.
2. What are the typical percentages covered by dental insurance for various types of services?
3. What are the potential risks of injury to dentists or their employees?
4. List several important functional components of a dental practice management system.
5. Define the following terms: plaque, calculus, sealants

Critical Thinking Questions

1. Why does the dentist need to have a complete and accurate medical history for a patient?
2. Compare the frequency and purpose of patient visits to an orthodontist with those to an endodontist. What effect do these differences have on the management and content of dental records?
3. Computerization of which functions of a dental practice will have the most impact on the dentist's finances?
4. How could a dentist evaluate the quality of care he or she provides?
5. In general, how can the use of electronic systems in dentistry improve the quality of dental care?

WEB ACTIVITY

Visit the American Dental Association's (ADA) Web site at http://www.ada.org. Select "Public Resources," then "Oral Health Topics." Select a topic and write a brief report on the topic you selected and how this information might help the public or promote an understanding of the profession of dentistry.

CASE STUDY

Valley Dental Group is composed of three general practice dentists in the suburb of a large city. The group has a receptionist and an office manager. Most of the group's patients are from families with dental insurance. The benefits and coverages of the insurance policies are different. Some require preauthorization of all restorations, whereas others require only preauthorization for crowns, bridges, and dentures. Some policies have a family deductible for all dental care, whereas others have individual deductibles for nonpreventive care only. The usual and customary prices that the insurance companies allow for procedures are different, so the amount the patient must pay depends on the insurance policy.

The practice needs to organize the way the office handles the information flow to process insurance billing and track payments. Some of the tasks that need to be performed are:

- Verify the patient's insurance company and policy number.
- Keep track of deductible paid so far for family and/or family members.
- Submit insurance claim for services rendered.
- Determine the amount the patient's insurance policy will pay for the procedure.

- Collect the patient's copayment and deductible before the patient leaves the office.
- Follow up on insurance claims submitted that have not been paid.
- Handle claim rejections and bill patient for amount not covered.
- Collect statistics on the number of procedures done, the number of self-payments and insurance payments, the amount paid by insurance, and the number of claims rejected.
- Collect statistics that measure the productivity of each dentist in the group.

Design a system to accomplish these tasks. (Each student can be assigned a function in order to design a solution as a class project, or students can be assigned one or more parts to do individually.) Avoid duplication of effort and the storing of redundant data in your design. Write a report detailing a design that includes the following:

1. What information must be collected?
2. Describe the procedures to be used to accomplish tasks.

REFERENCES AND SUGGESTED READINGS

American Dental Association. (2008). Survey Highlights. [Online]. https://www.ada.org/members/ada/prod/survey/08_sdpc_highlights.pdf [2010, January 24].

American Dental Association. (2009). Peer Review & Quality Assessment. [Online]. http://www.ada.org/prof/prac/tools/peer_review.asp [2010, February 21].

Barnes, G. P., Parker, W. A., Lyon, T. C., Jr., Drum, M. A., & Coleman, G. C. (1992). Ethnicity, Location, Age, and Fluoridation Factors in Baby Bottle Tooth Decay and Caries Prevalence of Head Start Children [CD-ROM]. *Public Health Reports, 107*(2), 167–173. Abstract from SilverPlatter File: MedLine Item 92220922.

Benton, R. M., & Shub, J. L. (1995). Peer review. It's Good for Dentists and Patients [CD-ROM]. *New York State Dental Journal, 61*(6), 28–29. Abstract from SilverPlatter File: MedLine Item 95349891.

[CDC] Centers for Disease Control and Prevention. (2007, April). Trends in Oral Health Status: 1988–1994 and 1999–2004. U.S. Department of Health and Human Services. DHHS Publication Number (PHS) 2007-1698.

Department of Defense. (2003, June 16). *TRICARE Handbook*. [Online]. http://www.tricare.osd.mil/TricareHandbook/default.cfm [2003, July 25].

[DHHS] Department of Health and Human Services. (2009). *Developing Healthy People 2020*. [Online]. http://www.healthypeople.gov/ [2010, February 12].

Kaste, L. M., & Gift, H. C. (1995). Inappropriate infant bottle feeding. Status of the Healthy People 2000 objective [CD-ROM]. *Archives of Pediatric and Adolescent Medicine, 149*(7), 786–791. Abstract from SilverPlatter File: MedLine Item 95316126.

Kiyak, H. A., Grayston, M. N., & Crinean, C. L. (1993). Oral Health Problems and Needs of Nursing Home Residents [CD-ROM]. *Community Dentistry and Oral Epidemiology, 21*(1), 49–52. Abstract from SilverPlatter File: MedLine Item 93161712.

Loesche, W. J., Abrams, J., Terpenning, M. S., & Bretz, W. A. (1995). Dental Findings of Geriatric Populations with Diverse Medical Backgrounds [CD-ROM]. *Oral Surgery, Oral Medicine, Oral Pathology, Oral Radiology, and Endodontics, 80*(1), 43–54. Abstract from SilverPlatter File: MedLine Item 96012668.

Logan, H. L., Baron, R. S., Kanellis, M., Brennan, M., & Brunsman, B. A. (1996). Knowledge of Male and Female Midwestern College Students about Baby Bottle Tooth Decay [CD-ROM]. *Pediatric Dentistry, 18*(3), 219–223. Abstract from SilverPlatter File: MedLine Item 96379379.

[NIDCR] National Institute of Dental and Craniofacial Research. (2001). Distribution of U.S. Adult Population with Dental and/or Medical Insurance by Selected Demographic Characteristics, 1997 and 2001. [Online]. http://drc.hhs.gov/report/dqs_tables/pdf/10.pdf [2010, September 5].

National Center for Chronic Disease Prevention & Health Promotion. (2009). Behavioral Risk Factor Surveillance System (BRFSS). [Online]. http://apps.nccd.cdc.gov/BRFSS/ [2010, September 5].

Safadi, G. S., Safadi, T. J., Terezhalmy, G. T., & Taylor, J. S. (1996). Latex Hypersensitivity: Its Prevalence among Dental Professionals [CD-ROM]. *Journal of the American Dental Association, 127*(1), 83–88. Abstract from SilverPlatter File: MedLine Item 96166172.

Workshop on Quality Assurance in Dentistry (1994). Model Clinical Guidelines for Primary Dental Health Care Providers for Managing Patients with Adult Periodontitis. *Journal of Dental Education, 58*(8), 659–662.

KEY RESOURCES

American Dental Association
http://www.ada.org/

American Dental Hygienists Association
http://www.adha.org

Association of Managed Care Dentists
http://www.amcd.org

CHAPTER 15

Veterinary Settings

MARGARET L. NETERER, MM, RHIA

LEARNING OBJECTIVES

Upon successful completion of this chapter, you should be able to:

- List at least five similarities between veterinary and human health records.

- Explain why SNOMED CT® is preferred over *SNVDO* as a veterinary nomenclature and describe its importance to human and animal welfare in the twenty-first century.

- Explain the necessity of maintaining records for groups of animals rather than individual animals in particular veterinary care settings.

- Illustrate the similarities between veterinary and human medicine professionals.

- Describe the client's rights in information ownership and be able to identify the client in a given situation.

- Identify key organizations that provide the most current information relating to the practice of veterinary health information management.

Setting	Description	Synonyms/Examples
Veterinary Medical Center	A facility in which consultative, clinical, and hospital services are rendered and in which a large staff of basic and applied veterinary scientists perform significant research and conduct advanced professional educational programs.	Veterinary Teaching Hospital Animal Medical Center
Veterinary Hospital	A facility in which the practice conducted includes the confinement as well as the treatment of patients.	Animal Hospital
Veterinary Clinic	A facility in which the practice conducted is essentially on an outpatient basis.	
Veterinary Office	A facility where a limited or consultative practice is conducted that provides no facilities for the housing of patients.	
Veterinary Mobile Facility	A practice conducted from a vehicle with special medical or surgical facilities or from a vehicle suitable only for making house or farm calls. Regardless of mode of transportation, such practice has a permanent base of operations with a published address and telephone facilities for making appointments or responding to emergency situations.	
Veterinary Emergency Facility	A veterinary medical service whose primary function is the receiving, treatment, and monitoring of emergency patients during its specified hours of operation. A doctor is in attendance at all hours of operation, and sufficient staff is always available to provide timely and appropriate care. Doctors, support staff, instrumentation, medications, and supplies must be sufficient to provide an appropriate level of emergency care. This service may be an independent after-hours service, an independent 24-hour service, or part of a full-service hospital or large teaching institution.	
Veterinary On-Call Emergency Service	A veterinary medical service whose doctors and staff are not on premises during all hours of operation or whose doctors leave after a patient is treated.	

INTRODUCTION TO SETTING

The **veterinary** profession is practiced in a variety of care settings. The information presented for the learner in this chapter centers on the veterinary teaching hospital, the most probable employment setting.

Types of Patients

The term *patient* in this chapter refers to an **animal**. The animal's owner is the hospital's client.

According to James F. Wilson, DVM, JD, "Animals are usually classified according to species and distinguished as either domestic or wild. Problems occur with simple classifications like this, because certain species or individual animals do not fall neatly into either category. Others fit into both categories based on their use" (Wilson et al., 1988). For our purposes, this discussion distinguishes between domestic animals, including pets, and wild animals.

The domestic animals most commonly treated in veterinary teaching hospitals include small animals such as **canine** (dog), **feline** (cat), and other small animals (birds, parrots, snakes, lizards, hamsters, ferrets, etc.); food animals such as **bovine** (cow), **ovine** (sheep), **porcine** (swine), **caprine** (goat), llamas, and sometimes ratites (ostriches, emus, and rheas); and **equine** (horse).

Wild animals sometimes cared for in the veterinary teaching hospital setting include owls, eagles, hawks, songbirds such as sparrows and cardinals, deer, moose, and bears. These animals are usually cared for under the direction of the staff zoological veterinarian. Wolves or wolf-hybrid dogs are generally not treated in the veterinary teaching hospital, because they are unpredictable and could seriously injure a health care provider, the client, or other patients in the health care facility.

Types of Caregivers and Staff

Veterinary health care providers of the twenty-first century not only provide diagnostic and therapeutic services for animals of various species and uses, but are also engaged in protecting human health through the roles they play in environmental protection, food safety, and public health (*Veterinarians*, 2009).

The **veterinarian** has a professional degree from a college of veterinary medicine. Women now comprise nearly 68% of veterinarians in the 30 to 39 age group. In the group under the age of 30, more than 75% are female (Towner, 2009). The **American Veterinary Medical Association (AVMA)** has accredited 33 veterinary schools in the United States and Canada and 9 in foreign countries. A list of schools along with each school's contact information, accreditation status, and Web site link is available through the AVMA (http://www.avma.org/education/cvea/colleges_accredited/colleges_accredited.asp).

Similar to medical doctors (MDs) and doctors of osteopathic medicine (DOs), doctors of veterinary medicine (DVMs)—or veterinary medical doctors (VMDs)—may choose to pursue advanced training and take examinations in specialty boards. These include anesthesiology, critical care, dentistry, epidemiology, oncology, toxicology, laboratory animal medicine, **theriogenology** (animal reproduction), and many more. You can find the most up-to-date information on the recognized veterinary specialty organizations through the AVMA (Veterinary Specialty Organizations, 2010).

"A **veterinary technician** or **animal health technician** is a graduate of a two- or three-year AVMA-accredited program in veterinary technology. In most cases the graduate is granted an associate degree or certificate" (AVMA Policy on Veterinary Technology, 2004). A graduate of an AVMA-accredited four-year baccalaureate program in veterinary technology is known as a **veterinary technologist**. The veterinary technician performs under the direction, supervision, and responsibility of the veterinarian and is not allowed to diagnose, prescribe, or perform surgery unless permitted by state regulations. Information about individual programs is available through the AVMA (http://www.avma.org/education/cvea/vettech_programs/allprograms.asp).

The veterinary practice manager is responsible for the veterinary facility's business management, including human resource and financial management; organizational structure; marketing; and the areas of law, insurance, and ethics. A formal education in areas such as psychology, accounting, marketing, and business management is recommended. The practice manager is eligible for certification as a **certified veterinary practice manager (CVPM)** through the **Veterinary Hospital Managers Association (VHMA)**.

REGULATORY ISSUES

In many ways, the practice of health information management in the veterinary setting is less stressful than in human medicine settings that have multiple layers of government and third-party regulations to address. The obvious lack of detailed regulations often makes it easier to practice health information management because the HIM professional is freer to apply creative trends from human medicine that will work best for health care delivery for patients and procedures in the veterinary practice. On the other hand, stricter rules have the advantage of forcing compliance with good veterinary practice in situations in which a few veterinarians may be reluctant to relearn procedures or to expend money to make necessary advancements.

The practice of veterinary medicine is governed by individual state veterinary practice acts. The AVMA has established a model veterinary practice act, which is found at http://www.avma.org/issues/policy/mvpa.asp. (The purpose of a **model act** is to serve as a recommended pattern for state laws.) This AVMA model act provides definitions related to the practice of veterinary medicine (e.g., "animal," "licensed veterinarian," etc.). It also outlines licensing requirements and exceptions; establishes state boards of veterinary medicine; and outlines the processes of license application for the practice of veterinary medicine, license renewal, discipline of licensees, and appeal.

The veterinary practice act may fall under one of a variety of state codes (examples: Public Health Code [Michigan], Business and Professions Code [California], and Education Laws [New York]). A link to each state's veterinary medical association, practice act, board of veterinary medicine, and various rules affecting the veterinarian and his or her practice can be found at http://www.avma.org/advocacy/state/resources/default.asp, along with the name, address, and phone number of the state's board of veterinary medicine or executive officer of the board.

The AVMA establishes guidelines and policy statements for the practice of veterinary medicine through its executive board or House of Delegates. These guidelines are printed annually in the *AVMA Membership*

Directory and Resource Manual and are available at http://www.avma.org/issues/policy/default.asp.

The AVMA's Council on Education is the accrediting body for programs of study in veterinary medicine. Reference to the importance of medical record keeping is found in Standard 9.4, Clinical Resource: "Medical records must be comprehensive and maintained in an effective retrieval system to efficiently support the teaching, research, and service programs of the college" (AVMA, 2009).

The HIM service may provide the statistics necessary to document the number of patients available to the students in a typical year, to show that there are enough patients to provide quality clinical instruction. The survey forms (Figure 15-1, Figure 15-2, and Figure 15-3) request data on the **number of accessions** (the total number of times all patients were treated by the facility in a given time period), which include statistics on patient visits, hospitalizations, and field services.

Teaching Hospital

(Corresponds with AAVMC Survey 22)

Table A

Animal Species	Number of Patient Visits	Number Hospitalized	Number of Hospital Days
Bovine			
Canine			
Caprine			
Equine			
Feline			
Ovine			
Porcine			
Caged Pet Birds			
Caged Pet Mammals			
Avian Wildlife			
Other			

Number of Patient Visits – total number of times the patient visits the hospital (if Buffy visits the hospital 3 times this year, this would count as 3 visits).

Number Hospitalized – number of patients that were hospitalized.

Number of Hospital Days – cumulative days that the total number of patients were hospitalized.

FIGURE **15-1** AVMA Council on Accreditation, Clinical Resources of the Teaching Hospital, from http://www.avma.org/education/cvea/coe_self_study_teachhosp_tableA.pdf (Courtesy of AVMA. Used with permission.)

Ambulatory/Field Service Program

(Corresponds with AAVMC Survey 23)

Table B

Animal Species	# of Farm (site) Calls	# Animals Examined/Treated
Bovine		
Caprine		
Equine		
Ovine		
Porcine		
Other		

Number of Farm (site) Calls – total number of calls/visits made to farm/operations.

Number of Animals Examined/Treated – number of individual animals examined/treated.

FIGURE **15-2** AVMA Council on Accreditation, Clinical Resources of the Ambulatory/Field Service Program, from http://www.avma.org/education/cvea/coe_self_study_ambulatory_tableB.pdf (Courtesy of AVMA. Used with permission.)

Herd/Flock Health Program

(Corresponds with AAVMC Survey 24)

Table C

	Herd/flock health programs provided through institution/ state-owned animals		Herd/flock health programs provided through privately-owned animals	
	Please answer yes or no	# of sites	Please answer yes or no	# of sites
Dairy				
Beef Feedlots				
Cow-Calf				
Small Ruminants				
Swine				
Poultry				
Fish				
Equine				
Other				

FIGURE **15-3** AVMA Council on Accreditation, Clinical Resources of the Herd/Flock Health Program, from http://www.avma.org/education/cvea/coe_self_study_herd_tableC.pdf (Courtesy of AVMA. Used with permission.)

The data collected in these surveys correspond with data collected by the Association of American Veterinary Medical Colleges (AAVMC) that are used, along with other statistical data, in describing all aspects of academic veterinary medicine. The AAVMC also manages the Veterinary Medical College Application Service (VMCAS), which collects, processes, and distributes applications for admission to veterinary medical colleges.

Voluntary accreditation for companion animal hospitals is offered through the **American Animal Hospital Association (AAHA)**. AAHA, established in 1933, develops and circulates standards for traditional, general accreditation as well as for referral facility accreditation. The standards focus on the facility's patient-centered practice and assist the practice in setting future goals.

DOCUMENTATION

Current documentation elements will seem very familiar to the traditional HIM professional. They include the following:

1. Owner (client) identification: name, address, telephone numbers for home and office at a minimum; additional information may include names, addresses, and telephone numbers for alternate or co-owners of the animal.
2. Animal (patient) identification: name, identification number if applicable (i.e., tattoo or identification chip), species, breed, date of birth, sex, color, and/or markings
3. Vaccination history of the patient
4. Chief complaint: observations reported by the client
5. Medical history
6. Physical examination, including the current weight of the animal
7. Problem list
8. Diagnostic reports (e.g., laboratory, diagnostic imaging, etc.)
9. Patient-identifiable source data, including photographs, video recordings, audio recordings, diagnostic films, and electrocardiogram tracings
10. Consultation reports, including those of telephone consultations
11. Prognosis
12. Progress notes recording medical and surgical events should be made in chronological order; communications with the client should be documented, including waiver or deferral of recommended care.
13. Surgical and dental records, including the consent form signed by the client
14. Written discharge summary and instructions
15. Necropsy reports, when applicable. (A **necropsy** is a postmortem examination to determine the cause of death or the character and extent of changes produced by the disease.)
16. Financial records

Standards

The American Animal Hospital Association (AAHA) medical record service standards have much in common with accreditation standards for health information in human health care. For example, they address:

- Legibility
- Use of standard abbreviations
- Authentication of entries
- Documentation of communications between the health care providers and the client
- Security and confidentiality of paper and electronic records
- Use of standardized medical nomenclature for diagnosis and problem lists
- A recognized mechanism for standardized transmission and analysis of data

During the evaluation visit, the surveyor will ask for several medical records to be pulled for review. At the conclusion of the evaluation visit, the consultant will determine whether the practice has successfully passed each section of the accreditation standards, including the mandatory standards. The recommendation is sent to the Membership Audit and Control Committee for approval. The initial approval is for two years, with subsequent evaluation every three years.

The AVMA has produced several policy statements and guidelines that support the maintenance of veterinary health records. Those referenced below can be found in the current issue of the *AVMA Membership Directory and Resource Manual* as well as in the "Guidelines for Veterinary Prescription Drugs," initially approved in 1998 by the AVMA House of Delegates and updated regularly. The guidelines address record keeping as follows:

> Adequate treatment records must be maintained by the veterinarian for at least two years (or as otherwise mandated by law), for all animals treated, to show that the drugs were supplied to clients with whom a VCPR [veterinarian-client-patient relationship] has existed....
> Basic Information for Records (R) Prescriptions (P), and Labels (L)

- Name, address, and telephone number of veterinarians (RPL)
- Name (L), address, and telephone number of clients (RP)
- Identification of animal(s) treated, species and numbers of animals treated, when possible (RPL)
- Date of treatment, prescribing, or dispensing of drug (RPL)
- Name, active ingredient, and quantity of the drug (or drug preparation) to be prescribed or dispensed (RPL)
- Drug strength (if more than one strength available) (RPL)
- Dosage and duration
- Route of administration (RPL)
- Number of refills (RPL)
- Cautionary statements, as needed (RPL)
- Expiration date if applicable
- Slaughter withdrawal and/or milk withholding times, if applicable (RPL)
- Signature or equivalent (P)

(AVMA, Guidelines, 2010, Labeling and Record Keeping)

Format

The **problem-oriented medical record (POMR)** format or a combination of POMR and source-oriented format is most commonly used in the veterinary teaching hospital. The source-oriented health record is more common in non-teaching hospitals.

A variation of the family-oriented format is also quite common for **herd health** (sometimes referred to as **production medicine** or ambulatory care services) programs in teaching and nonteaching facilities. For instance, rather than generate a separate record on each of the one hundred cows examined or treated at Mr. MacDonald's farm on a particular day, the "MacDonald Farm" record would be maintained through the use of specialized forms or electronic formats that enable the health care provider to document treatments on a large number of animals at one time. Figure 15-4 displays a sample format for this "family" record for production medicine (PM) and equine (EQ) patients.

Forms of Documentation

The sophistication of record-keeping formats varies from paperless to hand-written 5-by-7-inch cards.

REIMBURSEMENT

Out of Pocket

Few owners have health insurance for their animals; therefore, they often make treatment decisions based on how much they can afford to pay out of pocket for an animal's care. For this reason, detailed and accurate written cost estimates, together with a signed informed consent, are essential elements in establishing the contractual relationship between the owner and the veterinarian, and become an important part of the veterinary health record. When generated through an electronic record-keeping system, the account can be flagged when the cost of care is reaching the estimated total agreed to by the owner. At that time, the health care provider attempts to reach the owner for authorization to continue beyond the original estimate. If the owner cannot be reached, the health care provider must make the decision of whether to continue testing and/or treating, and must document that decision in the health record.

Veterinary teaching hospital health records generally include the patient's final bill from each episode of care. As mentioned earlier, continuance of treatment sometimes takes into consideration how much the owner can afford to pay out of pocket. Along with an understanding of the patient's current medical condition, a review of expenditures made to date will help the owners make the correct decision for themselves and the animal.

Mortality Insurance

The economic value of some horses requires that the owner or owners secure mortality insurance on the animal. The insurance company's authorization to euthanize the animal may be more critical than the owner's when the insured animal is ill or injured and euthanasia is a strong option (Wilson et al., 1988).

MICHIGAN STATE
U N I V E R S I T Y

MSU Veterinary Teaching Hospital

Production Medicine
East Lansing, Michigan 48824-1314
Appointments: (517) 355-3500   Billing: (517) 353-4957

№ 05287

WHITE-CLIENT
YELLOW-MED. REC.
PINK-BUS. OFF.

CLIENT _____

CLINICIAN _____
DATE _____
REGFERRING _____
VETERINARIAN _____

TRIP FEE
____ 32011 CHUTE FEE   ____
____ 32110 REFERRAL   ____
____ 32109 REGULAR   ____

EMERGENCY FEE
____ 32211 6 A.M.-8P.M.   ____
____ 32212 8P.M.-6 A.M.   ____

EXAMINATION
____ 35219 A   ____
____ 35220 B   ____
____ 32020 PROF. SERV.   ____
____ _____   ____
____ _____   ____
____ _____   ____

TECHNIQUES

____ 32002 EPIDURAL   ____

____ 32107 TREATMENT   ____
____ _____   ____
____ _____   ____
____ _____   ____

REGULATORY
____ 32317 ANAPLASMOSIS   ____
____ 32319 BOVINE BTV   ____
____ 32321 BRUC. TEST-BOV ____
____ 32044 CALFHOOD VAC   ____
____ 32047 HEALTH PAPERS ____
____ 35065 PRV   ____
____ 35064 PRV + BRUC.   ____
____ 32048 SEROLOGY FORMS ____
____ 32049 TB INJ.   ____
____ 32050 TB READ   ____
____ _____   ____
____ _____   ____

SURGERY
____ 32058 CASLICKS
____ 32331 CASTRATE BOV (A)
____ 32332 CASTRATE BOV (B)
____ 32064 CASTRATE PROCINE
____ 32329 DEHORN BOVINE A
____ 32330 DEHORN BOVINE B
____ 35501 DEHORN ELEC C
____ 32031 LAMENESS-BOV. FOOT
____ 32035 LAME-WOOD BLOCK
____ 32075 LDA ROLL
____ 32074 LDA SURGERY
____ 32076 LDA TOGGLE
____ 32082 PROCINE HERNIA
____ 32307 TEAT
____ _____
____ _____
____ _____
____ _____

REPRODUCTION/OBSTETRICS
____ 32087 BSE-BULL
____ 35252 BSE-BULL PROGRAM
____ 32302 OB 15 MIN.
____ 32303 OB 30 MIN.
____ 32304 OB 45 MIN.
____ 32305 OB 60 MIN.
____ 35502 PELVIC MEASURE
____ 35214 RP
____ 32097 RECTALS-BOVINE
____ 32101 ULTRASOUND-BOV.
____ 32300 UTERINE INF.
____ 32105 VAGINAL EXAM-FA
____ _____
____ _____

CONSULTATION
____ 32310   0.5 HRS
____ 32311   1.0 HRS
____ 32311   1.5 HRS
____ 32318 FIELD INVESTIGATION
____ 32320 EQUIPMENT
____ _____

PHARMACY/SUPPLIES
____ 24083 BANAMINE/ML   ____
____ 24063 ASPIRIN 240GM   ____
____ 25303 BROWN GAUZE   ____
____ 24149 CAL GLUCONATE   ____
____ 24145 CAL MPK   ____
____ 25001 CATTLEMASTER-4-L5(5) ____
____ 24220 CYSTORELIN   ____
____ 24262 DEXYTROSE 50%   ____
____ 24469 LA-200 ML   ____
____ 24518 LUTALYSE 10ML/ML   ____
____ 24519 LUTALYSE 30ML/ML   ____
____ 24571 NAXCEL 1GM   ____
____ 24572 NAXCEL 4GM   ____
____ 24509 OTC 100MG/ML/ML   ____
____ 24620 OXYTOCIN 20U/ML/ML ____
____ 24629 PANMYCIN BOLUS/E   ____
____ 24638 PEN G 100ML/ML   ____
____ 25047 SOMUBAC 10 DS/VL   ____
____ 26666 TRIANGLE 9   ____
____ 35070 SIMPLEX   ____
____ 35221 MAGNET   ____
____ 24943 VENOSET IV SET   ____
____ 25163 VETRAP ROLL   ____
____ 35300 MISC. SUPPLIES   ____
____ __ _____   ____
____ __ _____   ____
____ __ _____   ____

OTHER SERVICES
____ 32010 BANDAGING   ____
____ 32030 LABS.-NON. CLINIC ____
____ 32051 SAMPLES HANDLING   ____
____ 32052 SAMPLES SHIPPING   ____
____ _____   ____
____ _____   ____

SUBTOTAL   ____
TEACHING DISCOUNT   ____

TOTAL   ____
NUMBER OF STUDENTS ____
SPECIES_____ NO_____ TREATED
_____ CONSULTED

COMMENTS _____
_____
_____
_____
_____

O-21781

FIGURE **15-4** Equine and production medicine records. (Courtesy Michigan State University, Veterinary Teaching Hospital.)

EQ 05080

MSU Veterinary Teaching Hospital
Equine Field Service
East Lansing, Michigan 48824-1314
Appointments: (517) 355-3500   Billing: (517) 353-4957

WHITE-CLIENT
YELLOW-MED. REC.
PINK-BUS. OFF.

CLIENT _____
CLINICIAN _____
DATE _____

TRIP FEE
__ 32208 EMERG. FEE 8AM-5PM   ___
__ 32210 EMERG. FEE 5PM-8AM   ___
__ 32109 REGULAR   ___
__ 32111 STABLE   ___

ANESTHESIA
__ 24004 ACEPROMZINE ML   ___
__ 32006 ADMIN. LOCAL   ___
__ 32007 ADMIN. NERVE BLOCK   ___
__ 34160 CARBOCAINE HCL/ML   ___
__ 25571 DORMOSEDAN ML   ___
__ 24735 ROMPUN 100MG/ML   ___
__ 24814 STADOL 2MG/ML   ___
__ 24913 TORBUGESIC ML   ___
__ 24944 VETALAR ML   ___
__ _____   ___

PHARMACY/SUPPLIES
__ 25305 ADAPTIC DRESSING   ___
__ 25441 AKTROL OPTH.   ___
__ 24048 ANTHELCIDE   ___
__ 24071 ATROPINE OINT   ___
__ 24074 AZIUM ML   ___
__ 24081 BANAMINE PASTE   ___
__ 24080 BANAMINE PK.   ___
__ 24083 BANAMINE INJ./ML   ___
__ 24094 BENZA-PEN INJ./ML   ___
__ 24097 BET. SCRUB OZ   ___
__ 25303 BROWN GAUZE   ___
__ 24141 BUTE 1GM. TAB   ___
__ 24138 BUTE INJ ML   ___
__ 25476 BUTE 4GM PASTE   ___
__ 24184 CHLORO OPTH   ___
__ 25174 COTTON SHEET   ___
__ 25667 DMSO SWEAT   ___
__ 24312 ELASTIKON 3″ ROLL   ___
__ 24326 EQVALAN   ___
__ 24322 EQUIMATE VL   ___
__ 24383 GENT 100MG/ML   ___
__ 24379 GENT. OPTH.   ___

SURGERY
__ 32014 DENT. FLOAT   ___
__ 32016 DENT. WOLF TOOTH   ___
__ 32059 CASLICKS   ___
__ 32342 CASTRATION (B)   ___
__ 32077 LACERATION (A)   ___
__ 32202 LACERATION (B)   ___
__ 32203 LACERATION (C)   ___
__ 32204 LACERATION (D)   ___
__ _____   ___
__ _____   ___

REPRODUCTION
__ 32086 AI-EQUINE   ___
__ 32024 DIAG. UTER. CULTURE   ___
__ 32098 RECTALS   ___
__ 32100 ULTRASOUND   ___
__ 32091 UTERINE BIOPSY   ___
__ 32337 UTERINE INF W/O MED   ___
__ _____   ___

PHARMACY/SUPPLIES
__ 24190 HCG VIAL   ___
__ 24519 LUTALYSE ML   ___
__ 24530 MAXITROL OPTH.   ___
__ 24549 MINERAL OIL OZ.   ___
__ 24591 NOL. OINT OZ.   ___
__ 24608 OPTHOCORT TUBE   ___
__ 24626 PANACUR PASTE   ___
__ 24638 PENICILLIN G ML   ___
__ 25216 PRD FLESH OINT OZ   ___
__ 25379 SMZ 480/TAB   ___
__ 25380 SMZ 960/TAB   ___
__ 24816 STATROL OPTH   ___
__ 24826 STRONGID PASTE   ___
__ 25163 VETRAP ROLL   ___
__ 24950 VETROPOLYCIN   ___
__ 25434 VETROPOLYCIN/HC   ___
__ 35300 MISC. SUPPLIES   ___
__ _____   ___
__ _____   ___
__ _____   ___
__ _____   ___

EXAMINATIONS
__ 32314 EXAM-/RECHECK   ___
__ 32315 EXAMINATION B   ___
__ 32316 EXAMINATION C   ___
__ 35210 EXAM-INSURANCE   ___
__ 32033 LAMENESS(UNITS)   ___
__ 32339 PREPURCHASE (B)   ___
__ 32045 REG.-HEALTH EXAM   ___
__ 32047 REG.-HEALTH PAPER   ___
__ _____   ___

VACCINATIONS
__ 32344 EQUINE FIVE WAY   ___
__ 32346 PNEUMABORT K   ___
__ 32347 POT. HORSE FEVER   ___
__ 32349 RHINOMUNE   ___
__ 32350 STRANGLES   ___
__ 32352 TETANUS TOXOID   ___
__ _____   ___
__ _____   ___

LAB
__ 32020 DIAG.-FOAL CITE TEST   ___
__ 32030 NON CLINIC LAB   ___
__ 32354 REG. COGGINS   ___
__ _____   ___

PROFESSIONAL
__ 32004 ADMINISTRATION   ___
__ 32010 BANDAGING   ___
__ 32040 PROFESSIONAL SVC.   ___
__ 32066 RADIOGRAPHS BASIC   ___
__ 32205 RADIOGRAPHS ADD.   ___
__ 32053 STOMACH TUBE   ___
__ _____   ___
__ _____

SUBTOTAL _____
CASH DISCOUNT _____
_____
TOTAL _____

NUMBER OF STUDENTS _____
SPECIES ___ NO __ TREATED
_____ (GROUP)

COMMENTS _____
_____
_____
_____
_____

O-20181

FIGURE **15-4** (*Continued*)

Euthanasia without the insurance company's authorization may lead to the company's refusal to pay the death benefit. Therefore, documentation of the name of the person(s) authorizing the euthanasia, along with their telephone number, the date, and the time of verbal authorization(s) in the health record, becomes vital for payment of the death benefit (Wilson et al., 1988).

Pet Health Insurance

As the availability of pet health insurance and veterinary medical and surgical insurance increases, so does the importance of complete, accurate veterinary health records. In the event that the insurance company finds the health record inadequate to justify the claim and refuses to pay for services rendered, the client may choose to take legal action against the veterinarian for the amount of the claim or seek the assistance of the state's insurance commissioner in resolving the issue (Wilson et al., 1988).

INFORMATION MANAGEMENT

Coding and Classification

The ability to easily retrieve information based on diagnoses or procedures is important in veterinary research as well as to track and study emerging or reemerging vector-borne or zoonotic infections. (A **zoonotic infection** is one that can be transmitted from animals to humans.) There are several systems used for this purpose in the veterinary setting. Coding and classification systems can meet this need, as can other methods such as the use of a controlled vocabulary, which is also described in this section.

SNVDO

The *Standard Nomenclature of Veterinary Diseases and Operations* (*SNVDO*) is based on the *Standard Nomenclature of Diseases and Operations*. The second abridged edition of *SNVDO* was published in 1976 by the Public Health Service. The nomenclature has only been maintained intermittently since that time but is still being used in a few North American veterinary teaching hospitals.

The diagnosis code in *SNVDO* consists of three parts: topography (four characters), etiology (four characters), and the structural or function code (one character). Unlike human medicine coding procedures, there is no emphasis placed on differentiation between principal and secondary diagnoses.

The procedure code in *SNVDO* consists of two parts: The first three characters are an abbreviated topography code and the last two characters depict the procedure performed in that topography.

Through the efforts of several members of the AVMA Committee on Standard Nomenclature and Coding, who were also board members of the Veterinary Medical Database (discussed further on in this chapter), it was decided in the early 1980s that the *Systematized Nomenclature of Medicine* (*SNOMED*) would, with the addition of unique veterinary terms, best meet the veterinary profession's information needs.

SNOMED CT®

SNOMED CT® (Systematized Nomenclature of Medicine Clinical Terms) was originally developed by the College of American Pathologists by combining SNOMED RT and the United Kingdom's Clinical Terms Version 3, or Read Codes Version 3, as it was formerly called. In April 2007, SNOMED CT® was acquired by the International Health Terminology Standards Development Organisation (IHTSDO). The terminology is available in U.S. English, UK English, Spanish, and Danish. Work continues on translations into French, Swedish, Lithuanian, and other languages. The following quote from the IHTSDO Web site explains the components of SNOMED CT®:

> From abscess to zygote, SNOMED CT includes more than 311,000 unique concepts. The concepts are organized in hierarchies, from the general to the specific. This allows very detailed ("granular") clinical data to be recorded and later accessed or aggregated at a more general level. "Concept descriptions" are the terms or names assigned to a SNOMED CT concept. There are almost 800,000 descriptions in SNOMED CT, including synonyms that can be used to refer to a concept.
>
> In addition, there are approximately 1,360,000 links or semantic relationships between the SNOMED CT concepts. These relationships provide formal definitions and other characteristics of the concept. One type of link is the "IS_A" relationship. This is used to define a concept's position within a hierarchy, e.g. Diabetes Mellitus IS_A disorder of glucose regulation (IHTSDO, n.d., para. 1-2).

SNOMED CT® is an electronic application that is accessed through a compatible browser. Figure 15-5 illustrates the SNOMED CT® CLUE browser interface, which was developed by David Markwell of the United Kingdom and is available from the Clinical Information Consultancy. The excerpt of information shown in Figure 15-5 displays the hierarchical nature of SNOMED CT®, which makes this system extremely powerful, rich, and intricate. It allows the user to enter and/or retrieve data as broadly or with as much granularity as necessary.

Kathleen Ellis, RHIT, RN, BS, and Roberta Schmidt, RHIA, health information management professionals for the colleges of veterinary medicine at the University of Illinois and Ohio State University, respectively, along with Jeff R. Wilcke, DVM, MS, DACVCP, Director of the AVMA's Secretariat to SNOMED International at the Virginia-Maryland Regional College of Veterinary Medicine, have been the leaders in adapting SNOMED CT® for use in the veterinary profession. The Secretariat has created a Web site (http://snomed.vetmed.vt.edu) offering user discussion forums for the purpose of developing standardized usage of the nomenclature in daily practice in the veterinary setting. (For the most current information on SNOMED CT®, refer to Internet link http://www.ihtsdo.org/snomed-ct/.)

Recognizing that "using standardized nomenclature improves communication from veterinarian to veterinarian and really improves patient care" (Sommars, 2009), the American Animal Hospital Association's Electronic Health Records Task Force chose SNOMED CT® as the platform for its list of standardized diagnostic terms that could be used by practitioners in small animal hospitals (Sommars).

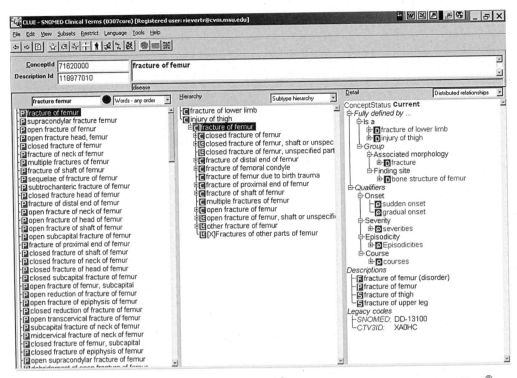

FIGURE **15-5** The rich detail of SNOMED CT® as viewed through the CliniClue® browser. (This material includes SNOMED Clinical Terms® [SNOMED CT®], which is used by permission of the College of American Pathologists. © 2002, 2003 College of American Pathologists. All rights reserved. SNOMED CT® has been created by combining SNOMED RT® and a computer-based nomenclature and classification known as Clinical Terms Version 3, formerly known as the Read Codes Version 3, Copyright. Since April 2007, SNOMED CT® has been owned by the International Health Terminology Standards Development Organisation [IHTSDO] based in Denmark. For more information on the CliniClue® browser, which is available from the Clinical Information Consultancy [CIC Ltd.], visit the Web site www.cliniclue.com)

Free Text

The Veterinary Medical Teaching Hospital of the University of California at Davis has developed its own in-house system whereby there is no coding of diagnoses or procedures. Health care providers enter their findings and recommendations into the information system in English and are then able to retrieve records the same way. A controlled vocabulary has evolved that standardizes the entries, but authors are able to bypass this vocabulary and enter their unique concept in their preferred terminology.

Data Sets
Veterinary Medical Database (VMDB)

The **Veterinary Medical Database (VMDB)** began in 1963 when a group of scientists from the National Cancer Institute (NCI) recognized a common interest in the prevalence of various forms of cancer in animals and met at Michigan State University in East Lansing to discuss how to best collect the data for study. They hypothesized that if data were collected on animal cancer, the study of that data would reveal information that is relevant to the study of cancer in humans. They recognized the necessity of abstracting data from the medical records of veterinary teaching hospitals and decided to modify the Standard Nomenclature of Diseases and Operations (SNDO) used for coding human medical records at that time. The resultant nomenclature, *SNVDO*, has been described previously. These data were gathered into a database at Michigan State University, supported by NCI until 1975, when the principal scientists were planning to retire. NCI representatives wanted to continue to purchase the data, and the participating veterinary schools wished to continue to participate because of the increased interest by faculty to also use the data in teaching and research. Therefore, the American Association of Veterinary Medical Data Program Participants, Inc. (AAVMDPP) was created.

At that time, the database was referred to as *VMDP*, the *Veterinary Medical Data Program*. The database was moved to Cornell University in 1975 because of the university's advances in computing capabilities. It remained at Cornell until 1987, when it was relocated to Purdue University and its name was officially changed to *Veterinary Medical Database (VMDB)* and became an umbrella organization to manage other veterinary databases such as the Canine Eye Registry Foundation (CERF), the Equine Eye Registration Foundation (EERF), and a DNA registry for progressive retinal atrophy (PRA).

Now residing in Urbana, Illinois, at the University of Illinois at Urbana-Champaign, the VMDB is mainly used by clinicians in veterinary teaching hospitals as a starting point for retrospective studies, teaching, and in scholarly publications. The database does not accommodate herd health or production medicine settings. Clinicians from participating university hospitals may search through their individual school's data or perform a nationwide or regional search for cases relevant to their topic, at no cost to the user. Outside agencies such as drug companies, pet food producers, and nonparticipating universities are charged for the searches they order.

Data Flow Data elements are abstracted from the patient's health record by the veterinary HIM professional in the teaching hospital. The abstract is then submitted electronically to the Veterinary Medical Database (VMDB), where it is stored for future retrieval by university faculty or administration, representatives of drug companies, breed clubs, pet food producers, and so on. The data may be useful in the process of making an application for a grant proposal, decision making about services to be offered by the health care facility, or marketing of a new product.

Maintenance of the Database Once the patient health record has been completed by the clinician, the diagnoses and procedures are coded by an HIM professional or, in some facilities, by the clinician. Additional data abstracted from the patient's record for submission include: medical record number, zip code of the animal's residence, attending clinician code, species, breed, date of birth, sex (including spayed, neutered, and so on), weight, color, admission date, discharge date, and discharge status (alive, died, euthanized, or discharged and referred). Data are submitted electronically.

The VMDB database administrator then runs the data through two edit programs. The *pre-edit* checks the internal consistency of the current abstract. Examples: Are the species and breed codes consistent? If the animal was spayed, does the abstract record the sex as "female-spay"? If the abstract fails the pre-edit checks, it is rejected and returned to the submitting institution for error correction and resubmission.

When an abstract passes the pre-edit, it moves into the next editing stage, the *edit-update*, which now compares the current abstract with the existing database, looking for a match in patient identification numbers for that institution. If there is a match with the identification number, several data elements are checked for consistency. For example, are the species, breed, and sex codes consistent with past submissions? If not, the record is rejected. Is the discharge status logical? If the identification number was abstracted as dead or euthanized in the past but is now alive with a subsequent discharge date, the record is rejected.

Rejected abstracts are reported to the participating institution for correction and resubmission. Once accepted by the VMDB for inclusion in the database, the record is available for reference by users.

OFA

The **Orthopedic Foundation for Animals (OFA)** was established in 1966 to provide registries for standardized evaluation for canine hip and elbow dysplasia. The organization's core objective of establishing control programs to lower the incidence of inherited disease has expanded to also include the following databases: patellar luxation, autoimmune thyroiditis, congenital heart disease, Legg-Calve-Perthes disease, sebaceous adenitis, congenital deafness, shoulder osteochondritis dessicans, and several DNA-based databases such as von Willebrand's Disease and progressive retinal atrophy (Orthopedic Foundation for Animals, n.d.).

Electronic Information Systems

The listing of vendors of veterinary hospital information systems changes frequently. Refer to Figure 15-6 for a listing of some current vendors. AVMA members continue to represent veterinary interests and concerns regarding standardized collection, storage, maintenance, and transmission of data by maintaining active membership in organizations such as **Health Level 7 (HL7)** (a standard for data exchange in health care) and **Logical Observations, Identifiers, Names, and Codes (LOINC®)** (a code system for laboratory and clinical observations).

Company Name	Location	Product Name
Advanced Technology Corp.	www.vetstar.com	VetStar
American Data Systems, Inc.	www.pawsnet.com	PAWS Veterinary Practice Management™
Animal Hospital Management System	www.bwci.com	BWCi Animal Hospital Management System
Animal Intelligence Software, Inc.	www.animalintelligence.com	
Butler Animal Health Supply	www.dvmmgr.com	DVM Manager
CCS, Inc.	www.completeclinic.com	Complete Clinic Software
ClienTrax	www.clientrax.com	ClienTrax
Doty Software	www.dotysoftware.com	VetMaster
e-Friends Software	www.efriendsus.com	e-Friends for DVMs
Eklin Medical Systems, Inc.	www.soundeklin.com	VIA® Practice Management Software
IDEXX Computer Systems	www.idexx.com/cornerstone	Cornerstone Practice Management System
ImproMed, Inc.	www.impromed.com	ImproMed Infinity
Informavet, Inc.	www.informavet.com	ALIS-VET
IntraVet	www.intravet.com	IntraVet
McAllister Software Systems	www.avimark.net	AVImark
Mobile Data Software	www.mdsvetinfo.com	VETinfo™
NuSoft Technologies	www.nusofttech.com	Preferred Veterinary Software
Ross Group	www.rossgroupinc.com	UVIS: Universal Veterinary Information System

Note: This list is not exhaustive and is not meant to be an endorsement by the author.

FIGURE **15-6** Veterinary practice information systems.

International Species Information System (ISIS)

The **International Species Information System (ISIS)** is an electronic, global zoological animal information system that began in 1973 and is now used by at least 825 zoos and aquariums in 76 countries on 6 continents. ISIS collects the age, sex, parentage, place of birth, circumstance of death, etc., on the specimen. It now has data on more than two million animals. The ISIS organization created the MedARKS (Medical Animal Records Keeping System) software package for each facility to assemble and report its own data. MedARKS includes anesthesia records, parasitology examination records; prescription records; and diagnostic test and sample storage records; clinical notes; pathology records; and inventory, history reports, and problem lists.

QUALITY IMPROVEMENT AND UTILIZATION MANAGEMENT

There are no formal requirements for quality assurance or utilization management processes in veterinary health care. Informally, however, quality of care is studied each time a veterinary teaching hospital health care provider uses health records for retrospective study in preparing for a lecture, writing a research grant proposal, or writing an article for a scholarly publication. The outcome of such a review is often discussed during faculty conferences, in meetings, or through publication. Changes to implement improvement are undertaken as appropriate.

RISK MANAGEMENT AND LEGAL ISSUES

Risk Management

With increasing public awareness of the value of animals in people's lives, litigation, attorney awareness of veterinary issues, the rising expectations of animal owners, and the increasing economic value of some animals, risk management is becoming more important in veterinary health care settings.

Michigan State University has developed an incident report form specifically for use in the veterinary teaching hospital. It is displayed in Figure 15-7. Once completed, it is forwarded to hospital administration and then to the university's risk management office. It is not kept in the patient's health record.

One area of tremendous risk in the veterinary health care setting is patient restraint. The AVMA's Professional Liability Insurance Trust quarterly report, *Professional Liability*, routinely provides synopses of claims received in the Trust office. The reports of human or patient injury sustained when owners attempt to restrain their ill or injured pets are numerous. When the owner is injured while attempting to restrain his or her own animal, the owner's insurance company often sues the veterinarian for recovery of medical costs associated with the incident.

Legal Issues

Determining Who the Client Is

This matter can sometimes be difficult. The legal system generally considers an animal to be a form of personal property. When someone calls to arrange an appointment for an animal or simply presents an animal for examination or treatment, ownership is implied, unless information to the contrary is given. In the large animal setting, the person who actually presents the animal for examination or treatment may be the owner, an agent for the owner, or simply a transporter. The owner(s) may not live in the same state where the animal resides or where the animal is being presented for examination or care. It is important, then, to carefully question the person who presents the animal, to accurately document the name(s) of the owner or owners, address, and phone number on the health record. If the presenter claims to be the agent, does this person have authorization from the owner to seek medical care for the patient and sign consents for treatment?

MICHIGAN STATE
UNIVERSITY

COLLEGE OF VETERINARY MEDICINE
Incident Report

PATIENT/CLIENT ID
(DO NOT FILE WITH MEDICAL RECORD)

TIME & PLACE	**DATE/TIME OF INCIDENT**	**LOCATION: (BE SPECIFIC)**

ANIMAL INFORMATION	**ANIMAL NAME:** **AGE/DOB:** **SPECIES:** **GENDER:** M ☐ F ☐ SPAYED/NEUTERED/GELDED ☐ UNKNOWN ☐ **DIAGNOSIS OR PRESENTING PROBLEM:**

CLIENT INFORMATION	**OWNER'S NAME** **TELEPHONE** **ADDRESS** **STREET** **CITY** **STATE** **ZIP CODE**

INCIDENT DESCRIPTION	**DESCRIBE WHAT HAPPENED:**

DESCRIPTION OF INJURY	**DESCRIBE INJURY, IF APPLICABLE: INCLUDE TYPE, SEVERITY, AND BODY PART INVOLVED AND ACTION TAKEN** **VETERINARIAN'S EXAMINATION/FINDINGS:**

WITNESSES GIVE THE FULL NAME & ADDRESS OF EACH WITNESS	**NAME**	**ADDRESS**	**PHONE#**

NAME/TITLE OF MSU EMPLOYEE COMPLETING REPORT: **PHONE:**

REVIEWED BY: **DATE :**

REFER TO NEXT PAGE FOR INSTRUCTIONS

M:\Inetpub\Internet\download\forms\RMI9.doc

FIGURE 15-7 Incident report. (Courtesy Michigan State University, Veterinary Teaching Hospital.)

Instructions for Completion of College of Veterinary Medicine Incident Report

1) Faculty or staff who become aware of the incident should initiate the form.
2) Document objectively with as much factual information as available. Avoid judgments, opinions or conclusions.
3) If incident is a result of equipment defect or failure, remove from service and preserve for examination.
4) Complete all sections of the form and forward to Risk Management & Insurance.
5) Refer all questions regarding claim or payment status to the Office of Risk Management and Insurance Office which has the responsibility for investigation and resolution of claims.

Complete this form for any unusual occurrence that is not consistent with desired service delivery.
Examples include but are not limited to:

Injury to animal
Medication error
Unpredicted response to treatment
Treatment complication
Complaint or dispute about fees
Any potential safety/risk concern

FORWARD COMPLETED FORM TO:

MICHIGAN STATE UNIVERSITY
RISK MANAGEMENT & INSURANCE
113 OLDS HALL
EAST LANSING, MI 48824-1047

FIGURE **15-7** (*Continued*)

The above reference to *owners* is another complicated issue. Some animals are owned by multiple people who are classified as co-owners. Some animals, especially horses, may be owned by a syndicate, which is an official association of persons. In these situations, it is wise to have one person identified as spokesperson for the group of owners, who is then contacted for consent to treatment. The information system must be able to document these various parties and their relationship to the patient.

Another confusing situation is the relationship between the breeder of the animal and the person who now has possession of the animal. The person with possession may be the "adopted" owner or simply a trainer. Again, careful questioning will produce records that are more accurate.

Dogs used in police canine units can also be registered incorrectly if the receptionist is not careful. The animal may actually live with its handler but is the property of the police department. The police department must be named as owner of the animal, with the officer listed as an alternate owner.

Litigation for Debt Collection

Debt collection accounts for almost all of the litigation encountered in the veterinary teaching hospital setting today. As discussed earlier, a signed estimate of charges and a signed informed consent are instrumental in collection of practice debts.

Prepurchase Examinations

Prepurchase exams are a particularly interesting part of the daily management of health information in the large animal veterinary teaching hospital. They are occasionally still referred to as breeding soundness examinations. They are common in equine medicine, but are also sometimes performed for cattle, swine, and dogs. The relationship between the examiner, the buyer, the seller, and agents for either the buyer or the seller is very complicated. State veterinary boards may address this issue in their regulations. This topic is thoroughly addressed in *Law and Ethics of the Veterinary Profession* (Wilson et al., 1988). In the best interests of the animal, the owner is responsible for authorizations and consents until the sale is final.

Wildlife Management

This venture is a cooperative one between the federal government and individual states. This is a very broad topic ranging from international law and international agreements to the issuance of permits for importation, exportation, transportation, inspection, and the use of animals in scientific research. Federal regulations also address wildlife rehabilitation facilities, pet stores, and wildlife auctions. For more information in a particular state, contact the Department of Fish and Game or the Department of Natural Resources.

Animal Cruelty

"Studies have shown a correlation between the incidence of animal abuse on the one hand, and child abuse, spousal abuse or mass murder on the other. . . . Animal abusers have a greater propensity of committing acts of violence against humans than those with no history of animal cruelty" (Lacroix, 1998).

With these startling facts in mind, veterinarians and animal health records are becoming vital resources in identifying, documenting, and reporting suspected abuse in order to prevent further injury to the animal, other animals, and humans.

Animal Welfare Advocates

These advocates impress on the veterinary health professional the importance of complete, accurate documentation of the course of the patient's illness and treatment during hospitalization or confinement in a research facility. Two types of patient records that the veterinary HIM professional pays particular attention to are those of the stray animal and the euthanized animal.

Stray Animals

These animals may be presented for treatment before being sent to the local humane society or animal control facility. It is very important to accurately document the date and time of arrival and departure or euthanasia of these animals, in addition to the treatment rendered while hospitalized, so that there is no question or doubt about what transpired during the animal's stay.

Euthanasia

This option is for the owner to consider when the quality of the animal's life is determined to be minimal and/or when the financial obligation outweighs the potential outcome of continued care. Documentation of the consent for euthanasia is best made in writing to verify the relationship of the signer to the animal. It is also important at the time of consent for euthanasia to determine whether the animal has bitten another animal or a human being, because of the potential for rabies exposure. During the discussion between the veterinary health care provider and the owner and subsequent signing of the consent for euthanasia, arrangements can be made for payment of the final bill. The actual procedure of euthanasia should then be documented with the time, date, product used, and signature of the veterinary health care provider performing the procedure. This documentation fully verifies that the owner's wishes were carried out and that the animal was not transferred to a new owner or a research project.

Change of Ownership

This situation occurs frequently in the veterinary field. It is important to document the change in the animal's health record by having the original owner sign a form verifying no further responsibility for the patient, the transfer of ownership to a new party, and identification on the form of the new owner. The new owner then has access to past health records of the patient for continued care.

Blood Donors

Animal blood donors are available to give blood for a transfusion to a patient. They sometimes reside at the hospital to be available on short notice and are often long-term residents whose health records become quite bulky. Detailed blood donation records are maintained, as well as health and vaccination updates.

Donation of Animals

Donations of animals are sometimes requested by owners who have an animal with a unique condition that, in their opinion, is not worth the financial commitment to treat. The owner may prefer to donate the animal as a teaching model rather than simply euthanize it. The client is asked to sign a form transferring ownership of the animal to a specific researcher and include the dollar value of the animal. This donation can often be used as a tax deduction.

ROLE OF THE HEALTH INFORMATION MANAGEMENT PROFESSIONAL

The veterinary HIM professional is responsible for establishing and maintaining information collection and retention systems that ensure accurate, complete, timely, and confidential health information for use in continued patient care, legal defense, education, and management decision making. Such records must also support the final bill.

Statistics are compiled and maintained for use by veterinary and human medicine professionals. For instance, each year the veterinary school is asked to submit statistics to the American Association of Veterinary Medical Colleges, which then develops a comparative data summary. Data elements collected include number of clients, number of patients, number of accessions, number hospitalized, and number of hospital days. Ambulatory care statistics are also collected on herd health or production medicine services. These statistics include number of farm calls made, number of animals involved, number of animals treated, and number of animals at risk.

Active participation in the **American Veterinary Health Information Management Association (AVHIMA)** helps the HIM professional develop a network for seeking new ideas and support. Unlike the human health care delivery setting where there may be another professional practicing just down the road, the AVHIMA membership is spread across the United States and Canada, usually with only one member in a given state. The use of a listserv keeps members connected and helps them to work through issues on a timely basis. It is very difficult to maintain continuity and momentum within AVHIMA with such distances between members. Active membership in the component state association of the American Health Information Management Association (AHIMA) may seem difficult because the patients are very different, but the use of technology and basic roles and functions are not changed, and it is important to maintain those liaisons for professional support and continuing education.

TRENDS

The electronic health record (EHR) is the major focus in many veterinary teaching hospital settings today.

The integration of SNOMED CT® into the veterinary teaching hospital setting, as well as those of private practices, runs parallel with the development of the EHR. The increased use of telemedicine influences the veterinary field and the EHR.

Lawsuits are increasing as public and attorney awareness of the practice and expectation of veterinary medicine increase. Additionally, demands are placed on the veterinary profession to answer to animal welfare advocates who wish to ensure the safety and wellness of all animals.

The increasing interest in and expanding use of animal health statistics as sentinels in human health necessitates common data elements that can be easily matched between the two areas of practice. Fewer family farms and more agribusiness ventures have necessitated more involved record keeping to meet state and federal government regulations.

Veterinary record systems are also used in the detection, tracking, and control of potential bioterrorism agents, many of which have been identified as zoonotic agents. Diseases that threaten human welfare and/or the safety of our food supply, such as the bovine spongiform encephalopathy (BSE) or "mad cow disease," anthrax, the West Nile virus, avian flu (H5N1), swine flu (H1N1), and bovine tuberculosis, are also under the purview of the veterinary HIM system.

Animals (canine, equine, marine mammals, etc.) are used by the Department of Defense and by local public safety departments in various capacities. They are trained at great expense in search and rescue or drug or explosives detection, for instance, to serve and safeguard the public, which makes efficient, accurate documentation of their health maintenance as important as the health record maintenance of their handlers.

SUMMARY

Many of the current roles and functions defined for the HIM professional in the traditional human health care delivery setting can be directly applied to the veterinary hospital. The additional information provided in this chapter can equip a health information manager with an interest in animal health to apply to a veterinary teaching hospital, local veterinary hospital, nearby zoo, veterinary information management software vendor, or research facility with an offer of expertise in establishing or maintaining an information system that will also protect the legal and financial interests of the veterinary professionals and the client.

There are at least three benefits the HIM professional can obtain by moving into this setting. Fewer government regulations related to maintenance of health records can be attractive. There is an opportunity to contribute to the field of veterinary science. The last, more subtle benefit is contact with animals, which is often a stress reliever.

KEY TERMS

American Animal Hospital Association (AAHA) promulgates standards for companion animal hospitals.

American Veterinary Health Information Management Association (AVHIMA) promotes quality patient care through the management of health information; is the nation's authoritative body on the management of veterinary health information; advances the competency of those working with veterinary health information; advocates for the profession on government, education, social, and business issues that affect the management of veterinary health information.

American Veterinary Medical Association (AVMA) The objective of the Association is to advance the science and art of veterinary medicine, including its relationship to public health, biological science, and agriculture. The association provides a forum for the discussion of issues of importance to the veterinary profession and for the development of official positions. The association is the authorized voice for the profession in presenting its views to government, academia, agriculture, pet owners, the media, and other concerned publics (AVMA Constitution, Article II).

animal any animal other than man, including fowl, birds, fish, and reptiles, wild or domestic, living or dead.

animal health technician (See *veterinary technician.*)

bovine cow or ox.

canine dog.

caprine goat.

certified veterinary practice manager (CVPM) an individual who, with at least three years' experience as a practice manager within the past seven years, at least 18 acceptable college or university credit hours pertinent to management, evidence of 48 hours of continuing education specifically devoted to management, and appropriate references, may apply to the Veterinary Hospital Manager's Association (VHMA) to take the written and oral examinations which, if successfully passed, designate the individual as a certified veterinary practice manager.

equine horse.

feline cat.

Health Level 7 (HL7) the application level, which is the highest level, of the International Standards Organization's (ISO) communications model for Open Systems Interconnection (OSI). HL7 is a standard for data exchange in health care.

herd health veterinary care provided to a group of animals at their residence rather than in a hospital setting.

International Species Information System (ISIS) a computer-based information system for wild animal species in captivity.

Logical Observations, Identifiers, Names and Codes (LOINC®) facilitates the exchange and pooling of results or vital signs for clinical care, outcomes management, and research; a code system for laboratory and clinical observations.

model act recommended legislation drafted by a national organization with the intent of promoting a degree of uniformity among state laws. State legislatures may or may not approve a model act in its entirety or at all.

necropsy a postmortem examination for determining the cause of death or the character and extent of changes produced by disease.

number of accessions the total number of times all patients were treated by the facility in a given time period. One patient may have multiple accessions.

Orthopedic Foundation for Animals (OFA) a collection of voluntary orthopedic and genetic disease databases of animals.

ovine sheep.

porcine swine.

problem-oriented medical record (POMR) a structured approach to patient care developed by Dr. Lawrence Weed in the late 1950s that has four major parts: database, problem list, initial plan, and progress notes/discharge summary.

production medicine the study and care of food animals that produce milk, meat, eggs, etc.

Standard Nomenclature of Veterinary Diseases and Operations (SNVDO) created in 1963 to standardize the collection of veterinary data in a national database, this coding system has been updated only intermittently since the 1970s.

Systematized Nomenclature of Medicine-Clinical Terms (SNOMED CT®) a multilingual health care clinical reference terminology providing a uniform nomenclature facilitating international sharing and analysis of both human and veterinary health data.

theriogenology the study of animal reproduction.

veterinarian one qualified and authorized to treat disease and injuries of animals.

veterinary of, relating to, or being the science and art of prevention, cure, or alleviation of disease and injury in animals, especially domestic animals.

Veterinary Hospital Managers Association (VHMA) provides individuals who are actively involved in veterinary practice management with a means of education, certification, and networking. Membership is comprised of animal hospital administrators, practice managers, office managers, veterinarians, and consultants.

Veterinary Medical Database (VMDB) a national collection system for data from veterinary teaching hospital patient records from the United States and Canada.

veterinary technician a member of the veterinary health care team knowledgeable in the care and handling of animals, in the basic principles of normal and abnormal life processes, and in routine laboratory and clinical procedures. The technician is primarily an assistant to veterinarians, biological research workers, and other scientists. A veterinary technician is a graduate of a two- or three-year AVMA-accredited program in veterinary science that generally awards an associate degree or certificate.

veterinary technologist   a graduate of a four-year AVMA-accredited program in veterinary technology or a person so recognized by the board in rules and regulations promulgated to regulate veterinary technologists.

zoonotic infection   an infection that can be transmitted from animals to humans. Zoonoses are of concern to both veterinary and human medicine.

REVIEW QUESTIONS

Knowledge-Based Questions

1. Which organization's accreditation program provides minimum standards for maintenance of veterinary health records in both general and referral facilities?
2. Why is a written cost estimate so important in veterinary practice?
3. Where would you find the most current advice on how to properly use SNOMED CT® in a veterinary setting?
4. Who authorizes release of information in a prepurchase situation?
5. Briefly explain the operation and uses of the VMDB.

Critical Thinking Questions

1. Provide an example of an instance in which a record would be maintained for a group of animals rather than an individual patient.
2. In the absence of a specific law or state regulation, what source should be consulted for advice in an uncomfortable legal situation related to a veterinary teaching hospital where you are employed?
3. Networking and continuing education activities are an important part of keeping up to date in a profession. However, the component state associations of the American Health Information Management Association do not offer programs specific to veterinary medicine. How would one keep current in veterinary health information management and still be able to maintain the credential as a registered health information technician or registered health information administrator?

WEB ACTIVITIES

1. Visit the VMDB Web site at http://www.vmdb.org and click on the hyperlink for health information managers. Select one of the topics or articles available for HIM professionals at this site and write a brief summary.

2. Search the Internet for information on pet insurance, visiting the Web sites of various pet insurance companies. Write a brief report on your findings.

CASE STUDY

Melanie Maloney has just taken a position as director of health information services at the Any State University College of Veterinary Medicine. The associate dean to whom she reports has informed her that the college is beginning work on the self-study report in preparation for an upcoming accreditation survey from the AVMA Council on Education (COE). In order to prepare for a discussion of the AVMA COE survey with the associate dean, Melanie decided to "do some homework" by visiting the

AVMA Web site to obtain insights into how she might participate in the accreditation process. She finds the COE manual at the AVMA Web site and locates information on the self-study report and a typical site visit schedule.

After reviewing the information from the COE manual at the AVMA Web site, answer the following questions:

1. Discuss the COE standards with which Melanie will need to be most familiar.
2. With which sections of the self-study might she assist?
3. How might she interact with the site visit team?
4. What issues might Melanie want to discuss with the associate dean to fully understand her role in the process?

REFERENCES AND SUGGESTED READINGS

American Veterinary Medical Association. AVMA Policy on Veterinary Technology. (2004, April). Retrieved October 11, 2009, from http://www.avma.org/issues/policy/veterinary_technology.asp.

American Veterinary Medical Association. Guidelines for veterinary Prescription drugs. (2010, November). Retrieved April 13, 2011, from http://www.avma.org/issues/policy/prescription_drugs.asp.

American Veterinary Medical Association. (2008–2009). *AVMA Membership Directory and Resource Manual* (57th ed.). Schaumburg, IL: AVMA.

American Veterinary Medical Association. (2009, April). Accreditation Policies and Procedures of the AVMA Council on Education (COE). Retrieved April 14, 2011, from http://www.avma.org/education/cvea/coe_standard.asp.

American Veterinary Medical Association. Career and School Information. Programs Accredited by the AVMA Committee on Veterinary Technician Education and Activities (CVTEA). Retrieved October 11, 2009, from http://www.avma.org/education/cvea/vettech_programs/allprograms.asp.

American Veterinary Medical Association. Career and School Information. Veterinary Colleges Accredited by the AVMA. Retrieved October 11, 2009, from http://www.avma.org/education/cvea/colleges_accredited/colleges_accredited.asp.

[IHTSDO] International Health Terminology Standards Development Organisation. (n.d.). *SNOMED CT Components*. Retrieved October 11, 2009, from http://www.ihtsdo.org/snomed-ct/snomed-ct0/snomed-ct-components/.

Lacroix, C. A. (1998, December). Animal Cruelty and the Role of Veterinarians. AVMLA Newsletter, IV(1), American Veterinary Medical Law Association publication.

Orthopedic Foundation for Animals. (n.d.). Retrieved October 11, 2009, from http://www.offa.org/history.html.

Sommars, J. (2009). Cracking the codes. *Trends Magazine, 25*(6), 59–63.

Towner, W. (2009, September 13). Women in Veterinary Medicine Growing. NewsandSentinel.com. Retrieved October 11, 2009, from http://newsandsentinel.com/page/content.detail/id/521626.html?nav=5054.

Veterinarians. (2009, February). Retrieved October 11, 2009, from http://www.avma.org/animal_health/brochures/veterinarian/veterinarian_brochure.asp.

Veterinary Specialty Organizations. (2010). Retrieved September 5, 2010, from http://www.avma.org/press/profession/specialties.asp.

Wilson, J. F., Garbe, J. L., & Rollin, B. E. (1988). *Law and Ethics of the Veterinary Profession*. Yardley, PA: Yardley Press, Ltd.

KEY RESOURCES

American Animal Hospital Association (AAHA)
http://www.aahanet.org

American Veterinary Health Information Management Association (AVHIMA)
http://www.avhima.org/

American Veterinary Medical Association (AVMA)
http://www.avma.org

American Veterinary Medical Association Professional Liability Insurance Trust
http://www.avmaplit.com

Animal Legal & Historical Web Center
  Michigan State University College of Law
  http://www.animallaw.info/index.htm

International Species Information System (ISIS)
  http://www.isis.org

Internet Resources on Veterinary Epidemiology
  http://www.vetschools.co.uk/EpiVetNet/

Netvet
  http://netvet.wustl.edu

Orthopedic Foundation for Animals
  http://www.offa.org

The One Health Initiative
  *http://www.onehealthinitiative.com/about.
  php*

Veterinary Hospital Managers Association, Inc.
  (VHMA)
  http://www.vhma.org

Veterinary Medical Database
  http://www.vmdb.org

Veterinary Practice Acts
  *http://www.avma.org/advocacy/state/
  resources/default.asp*

CHAPTER 16

Consulting

KAREN WRIGHT, MHA, RHIA, RHIT

SCOTT WRIGHT, MBA

LEARNING OBJECTIVES

Upon successful completion of this chapter, you should be able to:

- Identify the advantages and disadvantages of consulting.
- Assess personal strengths and weaknesses.
- Recognize the importance of positive leadership.
- Develop a business plan.
- Develop action plans.
- Evaluate government regulations, accreditation and information technology (IT) standards, and industry best practices.
- Develop compliance audits.

Examples of Settings	Examples of Possible Consultant Roles
Acute Care Hospital	Consults 8 to 40 hours per week until a project is complete; serves as project coordinator to help health care facilities understand information flow and reduce legal and regulatory risk and e-discovery review costs; serves as project coordinator of ICD-10-CM/PCS transition; researches Recovery Audit Contractor's (RAC) Web sites; reviews documentation necessary for determining medical necessity, present-on-admission indicators, and severity of illness; performs compliance audits (coding and security); serves as member of the charge master team; provides coding support; reviews bill holds and claims denied; provides education to administrators, the medical staff, and department supervisors and staff, in addition to health information department coders and staff
Veterinary Teaching Hospital	Consults 20 hours per month providing expertise regarding data collection for research purposes; storage and retrieval of records; and computerized databases utilized to collect health information of animals
Nursing Facility	Consults 8 to 16 hours per month; evaluates accreditation standards, government regulations, and industry best practices; serves as project coordinator for ICD-10-CM/PCS transition; researches RAC Web sites regarding audits; develops and conducts audits to ensure documentation compliance by various health care providers; substantiates health care services provided to Medicare and Medicaid residents; and prepares for state surveys and RAC audits
Home Health and Hospice	Consults 16 hours per month to review government regulations; develops and performs compliance audits to ensure information technology (IT) security and documentation to substantiate services provided in the patient's home via the supervision of a physician utilizing nurses, various therapies, and home health aids
Dialysis Center	Consults 8 to 16 hours per month; serves as project coordinator for the ICD-10-CM/PCS transition; provides support for compliance with government regulation, accreditation, IT transmission standards, and industry best practices; provides support and education of staff regarding privacy, security, and documentation compliance
Behavioral Medicine	Consults 25 hours per month; provides support for compliance with government and accreditation documentation regulations; provides education for staff regarding HIPAA, the American Recovery and Reinvestment Act (ARRA), and maintaining the security of protected health information; prepares and analyzes statistical reports related to documentation compliance, performance assessment, medical necessity, utilization review, and risk management; serves as project coordinator for the ICD-10-CM/PCS transition
Managed Care and Insurance Companies	Consults 8 to 40 hours per month to educate staff regarding compliance with HIPAA and ARRA, the maintenance and security of protected health information (PHI); provides support for the ICD-10-CM/PCS transition; develops and conducts compliance audits

Physician's Office or Group Practice	Consults 8 to 16 hours per month; oversees electronic health record (EHR) implementation and maintenance, educates and trains staff regarding HIPAA/ARRA and coding compliance; develops, writes, and revises policies; reviews denied claims, appeals, accounts receivable management, and review of remittance advice against charges listed on the patients' accounts; serves as project coordinator for the ICD-10-CM/PCS transition
Legal Practice	Consults 20 hours per month; evaluates government and Joint Commission documentation requirements; develops and performs audits to review health information documentation compliance or lack thereof
Health Information System Vendor	Consults 40 hours per month; provides expertise regarding information flow within health care facilities, e-discovery, HIPAA and ARRA privacy and security issues; develops information technology (IT) solutions that prevent breeches; as well as facilitates the accurate data capture, accessibility, and interoperability for health care facilities that meet all government, accreditation, certification, and electronic data transaction standards

INTRODUCTION TO SETTING

Health information management (HIM) consultants may work in any setting where health care is provided or for organizations that reimburse or bill for health services. Examples of organizations that can potentially benefit from the services of an HIM consultant include acute care hospitals, ambulatory surgery centers, veterinary teaching hospitals, nursing facility corporate offices and/or multiple facilities, hospice, dialysis centers, home health, behavioral medicine (mental health and substance abuse), rehabilitation facilities, third-party billing companies, large and small physician group practices, governmental agencies, and technology vendors. Although this chapter is geared toward the independent consultant, there are also many job opportunities for HIM professionals in consulting firms.

Who Consultants Work With

Although the HIM professional is usually hired to provide expertise related to documentation improvement and compliance issues, these functions cover many diverse tasks. However, the most challenging and rewarding part of a consultant's job is working as a team member with key decision makers such as health care executives; administrators, physicians, nurses, and clinical researchers; quality, utilization review, and risk management professionals; accountants, attorneys, and therapists (physical, occupational, and speech); as well as psychiatrists, psychologists, dietitians, social workers, and information technology professionals, to name just a few.

In preliminary meetings with potential clients, the consultant should first learn the organization's perception of its needs by interviewing various managers. This is a two-way interview process whereby both parties are attempting to clearly identify the tasks or projects for which the consultant will be hired. The consultant should have a professional presentation prepared and available on a CD or jump drive to showcase the skills necessary for the subject job and does not charge for the time spent on this task. As a follow-up, the consultant will prepare a summary statement as well as a thank you letter for the potential client (Wildi, 2010). The organization or the consultant may then decide whether or not to proceed.

Examples of Consulting Projects

The HIM consultant's knowledge of biomedical science; classification systems; electronic health records; data capture and computerized databases; privacy, security, and coding compliance issues; as well as retrieval, storage, and retention of health information in any medium makes him or her an asset to any health care facility.

A consultant may be hired by an acute care hospital to provide training on the Health Insurance Portability and Accountability Act (HIPAA) and American Recovery and Reinvestment Act (ARRA); review and revise policies and procedures; design a compliance plan, offer coding and classification system education; or assess physician documentation to ensure that it supports medical necessity, present on admission (POA), and the severity of illness as well as the accuracy of the diagnosis and procedure codes assigned. In this setting, the consultant could also serve as a member of the revenue cycle team that includes representatives from information technology (IT), clinical, patient financial services, utilization review, and HIM departments.

In nursing, behavioral medicine, and rehabilitation facilities, the consultant's focus may be quality improvement efforts designed to improve documentation and the collection of statistics. For example, the consultant may work in the corporate office for a nursing facility chain reviewing RAC Web sites regarding audit information, reviewing minimum data set (MDS) statistics reported to the state for each facility, or performing quality improvement activities. Specific reviews could include data related to significant changes such as percentage of residents who have decreased independence in their ability to perform two activities of daily living, percentage of residents with a new infection, percentage of residents with a moderate level of pain occurring every day, percentage of residents with one or more pressure sores, or percentage of residents whose lab values demonstrate inappropriate levels of anticoagulants. The consultant may be a member of a team that designs care paths aimed at improving treatment outcomes or an educator who provides in-service education regarding how to improve documentation, confidentiality, or security, or how to assure that only the HIM department releases personal health information (PHI). The consultant may also provide recommendations related to the retention of health information as well as develop, write, and revise polices.

A large or small physicians' group practice or individual physician who wishes to improve efficiency may seek an HIM consultant to provide coding and billing expertise as well as to select, implement, and manage an electronic health record (EHR) that streamlines the appointment, clinical data collection, and billing processes.

As noted in Chapter 15, some veterinary teaching hospitals are utilizing the Systematized Nomenclature of Medicine-Clinical Terms (SNOMED CT®) coding methodology for research purposes, and all require health information systems for animal records that are similar to those maintained by acute care hospitals for human records. An HIM consultant can provide expertise in several areas, including data collection for research purposes, storage and retrieval of records, electronic health record implementation, or electronic databases for collection of animal health information.

As the elderly population increases and health care facilities move toward an EHR, the demand for health care services and health information technologists and administrators will also increase. Today's fragmented health care system, the ICD-10-CM/PCS transition, the federal government's prospective inpatient and outpatient payment methodologies, the complexity of third-party payers' billing requirements, and the Centers for Medicare & Medicaid Services (CMS) Recovery Audit Contractor (RAC) program are providing numerous challenging employment or consulting opportunities for HIM professionals.

REGULATORY ISSUES

Federal health care regulations continue to increase in number and complexity. Examples include regulations to implement the Health Insurance Portability and Accountability Act (HIPAA), the American Recovery and Reinvestment Act (ARRA) of 2009, and the Patient Protection and Affordable Care Act (PPACA) signed into law in 2010. Incentives and penalties authorized by ARRA may mean that many providers need assistance in converting to an EHR, updating policies and procedures, complying with meaningful use standards, interacting with multiple vendors, and managing e-discovery. Regulations implementing ICD-10-CM/ PCS provide opportunities for consultants to assist with the transition. The Recovery Audit Contract (RAC) program is another federal initiative that can cause health care institutions to look to HIM professionals for expertise, in addition to the need to comply with CMS's Prospective Payment System regulations as well as a multitude of different insurance companies' requirements. These are just a few of the challenges health care facilities face; thus there is a high demand for the skills of HIM professionals. HIM consultants must stay abreast of the changes in the health care environment by networking with other consultants; reading professional trade journals; researching the *Federal Register* as well as licensing, accrediting, certification, and IT transaction standards; and pursuing additional education to keep up with technological change. To help the client organization accomplish its goals with regard to regulatory requirements, the consultant may need to facilitate the development of an action plan (see Figure 16-1).

- Determine all steps necessary to attain goal.
- Assign responsibility for each step.
- Set deadlines for each goal.

FIGURE **16-1** Steps to develop action plans.

DOCUMENTATION

If the client organization has contracted with the consultant to evaluate compliance with documentation standards, the consultant will need to research all appropriate regulations, accreditation guidelines, and best practices, as well as develop and perform a compliance **audit**. The key documentation points can be incorporated into an audit sheet, which the consultant can use to review a random sample of the client organization's records. The consultant then computes, analyzes, and presents a statistical summary of the results to the appropriate executives. Completion of the audit cycle may involve educating those who document in the records and then conducting a follow-up audit to determine improvement (see Figure 16-2).

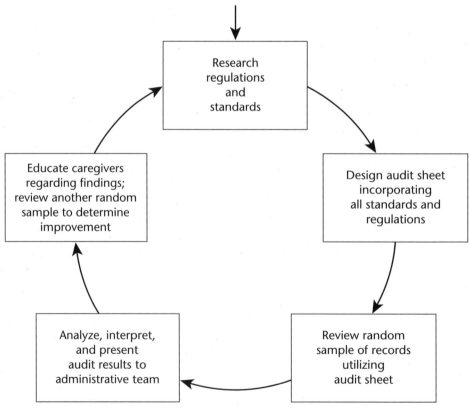

FIGURE **16-2** Documentation audit cycle.

REIMBURSEMENT AND COMPLIANCE

There are many consulting opportunities in the area of reimbursement and compliance. The issues of documentation, coding, and the revenue cycle are all areas where the consultant can provide expertise. If the client organization believes its code-based reimbursement is not what it should be, the organization may contact a coding consultant for assistance. Sometimes the consultant may find that the organization's coders are coding properly but that inadequate documentation is the true cause of missed revenue. At other times the consultant may find that both coding and documentation are in need of improvement. Whatever the finding, the consultant must be careful to be as objective as possible when auditing for reimbursement purposes. To guard against bias in findings, the consultant should not enter into a "contingency" contract with a client in which the consultant's fees are based on increasing reimbursement (e.g., the client pays the consultant a percentage of the increased revenue).

The initial CMS Recovery Audit Contractor (RAC) program identified incorrect coding and a failure to document medical necessity as major issues (Wilson, 2009). RAC audits identify improper payments for Medicare claims to recover funds for the Medicare program. When a pattern of improper payments indicates possible fraud, the RAC auditors are required to notify CMS, and the **Office of the Inspector General (OIG**, the agency charged with protecting the integrity of the Medicare and Medicaid programs) may investigate the providers involved. In some cases, a provider may enter into a **corporate integrity agreement (CIA)** as part of a settlement with the OIG to avoid defending itself against fraud or abuse charges. In this circumstance, the provider may contract with the consultant as an independent reviewer to meet the OIG's requirements for ongoing monitoring and training in appropriate coding.

Finally, all health care providers who receive payments under Medicare or Medicaid are expected to have compliance programs to guard against fraud and abuse. Guidance documents for the development of compliance programs for various types of providers have been available from the OIG since 1998. However, compliance programs were voluntary until mandated by the Patient Protection and Affordable Care Act in 2010. Although the details of the OIG's guidance varies somewhat for each type of provider, common components of compliance programs include internal monitoring and auditing, development of compliance standards or policies, designation of a compliance officer or contact, appropriate training and education of the workforce, an appropriate response or investigation when offenses are detected, as well as other elements (OIG, n.d.). A small provider may not have the resources to fully implement its own compliance program and may contract with a consultant for services to meet some of the requirements.

ROLE OF THE HEALTH INFORMATION MANAGEMENT PROFESSIONAL

Choosing to be an independent consultant is synonymous with starting a new business and being self-employed. A successful health information consulting practice requires an RHIT or RHIA credential, relevant work experience, and careful research and planning. One should start by performing a rigorous self-assessment of interpersonal communication skills. Individuals who possess these skills often already have a strong network of professional contacts in place, making it easier to market themselves. Research indicates that organizations use their contact networks to select consultants more than any other method. Many independent consultants start by consulting on a part-time basis. Health care facilities often seek consultants because they do not wish to hire a full-time credentialed HIM professional. They want an individual who can provide certain services for a few hours each month or for a specific project. Satisfied clients often provide referrals. It may take a while to build a client base that provides an income that permits giving up the benefits associated with a full-time job.

Expertise in a particular profession or skill is a small part of being a consultant—the larger issue is the ability to run a business. Although a health information consulting business may be launched with a minimum of capital expense, perhaps only a computer and a telephone, it is critical to formalize the business by developing certain key documents. The consultant should formally document a mission statement, marketing plan, and a list of services to be offered. It is also helpful to compile a list of strengths and weaknesses, measurable personal and business objectives that can serve as an annual plan. Other documentation should include an objective statement of the percentage by which the client base will increase yearly, a list of clients who need these services, the demographics of potential clients, a list of competitors, equipment and office space requirements, and the number of employees now and in the future. Finally, the consultant should develop both monthly and yearly revenue and expense budgets. Later, if the consultant needs to develop a **business plan** (a formal document summarizing the operational and financial objectives of a business), the basics are already in place. A business plan includes the details of how the objectives are to be attained, including budgets and other financial forecasts. Lenders and investors generally require a business plan as one of the documents they study when making a decision whether to lend to or invest in a business.

Formulating business plans (see Figure 16-3) as well as annual plans is a good idea. Because HIM consulting is a knowledge-based business, very few funds should have to be raised to get started. However, a business plan is necessary if the consultant seeks capital (e.g., a loan from a bank). Some consultants have found it helpful to utilize business plan software in developing their business plans. A quick search of the Internet yields numerous business planning programs to evaluate. In 2010, the following were examples of business planning Web sites:

- http://www.bplans.com
- http://www.planware.org/bizplan.htm
- http://www.sba.gov/smallbusinessplanner
- http://www.businesstown.com/planning/creating.asp
- http://www.soyouwanna.com/site/syws/bizplan/bizplan.html

> Executive Summary
>
> Description of the Business
>
> Marketing Strategies
>
> Competitor Analysis
>
> Financial Projections

FIGURE **16-3** Typical business plan format.

Leadership Ability

A consultant should have extensive previous experience, be an excellent communicator, possess leadership skills, have the appropriate credentials, and, above all, have a good reputation. Being of good repute means that others believe an individual is trustworthy, hardworking, and honest. Leadership has been defined as an influence process (Maxwell, 2007). Any time an individual attempts to persuade others toward accomplishment of a goal, he or she is practicing leadership. A key role of the consultant is to work with others to ensure organizational and departmental compliance with laws, regulations, standards, polices, and procedures. In addition, consultants must be able to write proposals, solve problems, train staff, perform research (qualitative and quantitative), deal well with complexity and chaos, and be self-confident, self-reliant, disciplined, resilient, and financially astute. A consultant must be able to read between the lines to assess potential clients' needs and to negotiate mutual expectations about the consultant's role in that process. He or she must be able to see the big picture and to communicate it clearly to others.

Leaders have high standards. When leaders lack character, they also lack integrity. Good leaders show no discrepancy between what they appear to be and who they are. They take responsibility and are credible, transparent, honest communicators with nothing to hide. Good leaders follow through to the final detail.

According to Harvard psychologist and professor Howard Gardner, who specializes in the theory of multiple intelligences, a high cognitive intelligence (IQ) does not ensure success. What is more important in the business world today than knowing one's own strengths and weaknesses is the ability to get others to think about their abilities positively and in a way that maximizes their potential. Gardner states that the difference between success and failure is not taking courses to sharpen technical skills, but figuring out how, given one's abilities, to adjust to a given situation. An astute businessperson has interpersonal intelligence, which is the ability to understand other people, what motivates them, how they work, and how to work cooperatively with them (Koch, 1996). It is very important for the consultant to take the time to focus, give undivided attention to the client, and really listen as they communicate their needs.

A consultant must continuously seek to strengthen his or her interpersonal and technical skills. Teaching a course at a local community college is a challenge that can aid in the maintenance of current knowledge in one's field. The HIM professional also must pursue additional education and training to stay current with the vast changes that are occurring in the field as well as to meet continuing education requirements necessary to maintain professional credentials. However, just as important as current knowledge of the rapidly changing health care environment is gauging the attitude and ability of self as well as others to accept such change. Be prepared to listen and allow the individuals most affected by a change to provide ample input regarding decisions that affect them. For example, physicians and nurses who currently use an EHR report that it can take up to three months to fully learn and adapt to using a computer to document clinical information but that a well-implemented system is worth the transition (Rollins, 2003; Wager et al., 1999). One of the keys to a successful EHR implementation is the involvement of the clinician users in the transition.

One leadership challenge that a consultant faces is that often the consultant's power is based on influence and expertise, not on organizationally mandated authority. The consultant makes recommendations to the client, and the client can choose to follow those recommendations or not. The consultant may have good ideas to help the client with many challenges, such as getting work done with imperfect people, setting clear goals and direction, training, development, and delegation. However, on occasion, the consultant may meet with resistance and conflict, intense competition, or rejection and criticism by others and find that as a result the client discards the consultant's ideas or terminates the consultant's contract. Learning to nurture, mentor, and encourage oneself can help the consultant handle failures and continue to be willing to take risks. Also, developing a supportive personal and professional network assists the consultant in maintaining a positive attitude when difficulties arise.

Being responsible for influencing others requires acting ethically. Consulting involves a personal struggle based on acting on self-interest versus acting for the benefit of others. The consultant may encounter individuals who are self-serving and arrogant; who withhold information; who seek power and recognition; who are poor listeners; who spend a great deal of time protecting their own status; and who are unable to accept criticism. In these circumstances, the consultant must demonstrate leadership and not be discouraged, serving as a constant positive force to each facility served. Recently, newspapers have reported numerous incidences of businesses' financial failures because of the illegal and unscrupulous acts of individuals in high-level management positions. In these situations, unbridled greed, the improper use of power, and a sense of entitlement replaced integrity. A consultant must guard against conflicts of interest and maintain high ethical standards.

What Fees Do HIM Consultants Charge?

The consultant must carefully assess future needs as well as current financial needs. The following questions raise factors to consider when determining what to charge: What will it cost the consultant to provide services?

The consultant must invest in clothes and office accoutrements that exemplify professionalism. For example, the consultant should purchase professional invoice software and have a place where professional phone calls may be made and received. It is not acceptable to try to talk to a client with a dog barking, children talking, and a video playing in the background. Whether or not travel is involved will also affect the costs of operating a consulting practice. Success depends upon generating enough revenue to cover all expenses. Often, the most financially successful consultants are those who can minimize expenses. Another question to consider: What will the market bear? Today, many are choosing to become self-employed consultants because of high unemployment; thus the consultant faces fierce competition. In setting fees, the consultant will need to consider what others charge for similar services. A third question is: What is the consultant's reputation based on the testimony and referrals of others? What an independent consultant charges is determined in part by the individual's abilities, prior experience, and previous success.

Managing any business requires meticulous record keeping and careful analysis of current as well as future expenses. It is helpful to prepare a personal income statement that includes all current revenue and expenses. An individual considering self-employment should have adequate cash reserves to cover expenses for a three-month period, given that consultants may have to wait for payment for periods longer than 90 days.

When an employer pays a salary, it often includes holidays, personal or vacation leave, medical leave, health insurance plans, and the employer portion of FICA tax. Benefits the employer provides are estimated at between 20 and 30 percent of the employee's gross salary. In addition, the employer provides office space, furniture, computer equipment, telephone, travel, and training. A person who is in the process of making a decision to give up the benefits of working for someone else in order to establish his or her own business should realize that business revenue must be high enough to cover more than just the consultant's salary.

As a case study, consider a consultant who desires to earn a salary of $75,000 per year. The consultant adds 38 percent to this gross salary figure for fringe benefits and $20,000 for operating expenses. This totals $123,500 that the consultant must bill per year to maintain the desired income level. Dividing this figure by 220 working days indicates that the consultant must charge around $561 per day or roughly $70 per hour at a minimum. Because it is common for an independent consultant to experience gaps in workload, it isn't realistic to expect to be engaged in billable consulting work 220 days per year. Therefore, to be able to pay oneself a salary of $75,000 may require charging a higher daily or hourly fee to allow time for seeking new clients and other activities for which no revenue is earned directly. If travel is involved, the consultant must cover those expenses as well and might charge a flat fee (for example, $1,000 per day) or may negotiate a contract in which the client agrees to pay travel expenses. Failure to plan and count the cost of being self-employed can lead to business collapse. Individuals who are interested in consulting should seek wise counsel and learn from others how they made the transition from being employees to being self-employed. Networking at professional meetings and conferences as well as in online forums can help the consultant in seeking advice. Many have been deceived and have failed because of the assumption that high hourly charges by consultants mean self-employment will be financially lucrative and provide more personal freedom. In addition, not considering the importance of a balanced lifestyle that provides adequate time with spouse, children, extended family, and friends can lead to great personal loss as well as financial failure. In establishing an independent consulting practice, it is advisable to proceed cautiously and conservatively.

Seeking Clients

Individuals whom the consultant knows professionally and personally are the best source of referrals. The consultant should keep in regular contact with these individuals. Membership in professional organizations, such as AHIMA, is also very valuable. Volunteer to speak at professional meetings and write blogs and articles for professional publications to build credibility. Send out e-mails and a quarterly newsletter to your clients as well as potential new clients. Join a business-oriented social networking site. Satisfied clients are an excellent source of referrals. Create a Web page to market services on the Internet, perhaps hiring another consultant to achieve the desired Internet image. Develop a logo and color scheme and use it consistently on stationery, business cards, and the Web page. Develop a professional one-page résumé as well as an academic résumé that lists publications and work experience. Perform public service activities to network with individuals in your community. Provide free seminars. Hold a block party and attend and support community events. To decide whether to advertise in a trade journal, assess how previous or current clients were obtained.

Working at Home

Consulting requires an ability to develop a container for oneself, stay focused, work unsupervised, and have healthy boundaries. A *container* refers to the place in which focused work is performed both physically and mentally. For consultants who work from home, a physical workspace container needs to be planned—a place recognized and respected as the office space of the new business.

This space can be a guest room planned in such a way that a sofa or futon in the room provides an extra bedroom when necessary yet serves most of the time as an attractive, efficient office. Explore the tax laws with an accountant if you plan to use this office space as a tax deduction. Plan a space that meets work needs. A countertop around the periphery of a room with shelves above it and file cabinets under it provides a lot of desktop and storage space inexpensively. It may be difficult to find furniture at a reasonable price that utilizes all current physical space perfectly.

The consultant should utilize ergonomic techniques that facilitate comfort and convenience. For example, an adjustable computer monitor should be purchased so that the top of the screen can be positioned at or slightly below eye level (OSHA, n.d.). An adjustable keyboard tray is needed for the keyboard so that the fingers, wrists, and elbows remain in a straight line to reduce the risk of cumulative trauma disorder. The chair should have adjustable arms, back, and seat. The seat should be capable of being lowered or raised so the knee and hipbone are in a straight line, with the feet placed firmly on the floor or on a footrest. A space for the computer that allows work materials to be placed on both sides so that everything needed for work is within arm's reach is a part of the office plan. The workspace and desktop should be free of glare and shiny objects. A window as the backdrop for a computer is not advised due to the glare. However, mini blinds to regulate outside light can be utilized. Paint, furnishings, and countertops that have a matte finish and are of soft colors create a space that facilitates calmness, clarity, and simplicity. Fabric and carpet can be utilized to reduce noise and create an ambiance of comfort and softness.

Computer software can be used to accomplish many tasks such as word processing, résumé and form design, and data analysis and computation as well as producing professional presentations.

Being focused mentally requires setting boundaries. Work at home is conducted in the same fashion as one would act as an HIM department director in a health care facility. The integrity of the home office must be respected. Let the answering machine handle personal calls or unwanted telephone marketing ploys. To minimize interruptions, educate friends and family about work hours and ask not to be disturbed. A parent working at home does not mean that a babysitter is no longer necessary. Being focused and productive means devoting full attention to the task at hand, with minimal interruptions. If small children are at home, hire a babysitter and set clear boundaries. Develop instructions regarding minimizing telephone and television use and noise levels; what activities children are permitted, where, and with whom; how to handle minor emergencies; any medications a child routinely takes and which neighborhood children are permitted in the house or yard; and caring for household pets. It is advisable to crate train all pets while they are still young so they can be willingly and quietly confined in the event it is necessary.

It is not unusual that family members find it difficult to accept and respect an individual's professional role at home. Generally, it is not known what an individual really does at work, and family might not recognize activities conducted in a home office as work. Relatives can present multiple disruptions and expect work to cease so that their personal needs are met. A consultant must set firm boundaries and limits with family members as well as with babysitters and friends.

In some instances, a consultant may find that a working environment away from home is the best solution. A thriving practice may warrant the employment of an administrative assistant to free time for networking, marketing, and seeking additional contracts.

Office Equipment

Consultants need to have certain equipment to efficiently conduct business. Following is a checklist of suggested items:

- Computer with high-speed Internet access
- Dedicated phone service (a cell phone and a land line)

- Answering system or voice mail
- Fax machine
- Copier, scanner, and printer

Computer

Computers have become an integral part of day-to-day business for consultants. To determine what type of computer setup is best for an individual's needs, a few questions need to be answered:

- Is access to the computer needed when traveling to clients?
- Are heavy graphics involved?
- What type of software will be used (e.g., word processing, database, spreadsheet, graphics, presentations, reporting, data mining)?
- What types of peripheral devices are needed?

Thinking these questions through will help in determining the type of computer that will best fit one's needs. In most cases, it is not necessary to purchase the very latest model with the fastest speed available. Current models available in any large electronics store can easily handle most consultant applications. It is generally not necessary and not prudent to procure the most advanced system in the store. Buying a model that has been on the market for six months will cost considerably less and be more than adequate. Regardless of the type of computer selected, it is important for the consultant to have a means of backing up critical data to protect important business assets in the event of a system failure. Software is available to schedule automatic backups to an external hard drive. Online backup services are also available and offer the advantage of storing backup data securely off-site.

The consultant will need to decide whether to invest in a laptop or desktop computer or both. The big advantage with a laptop is its portability. While in a hotel room, at a restaurant, or flying to an appointment, work can be readily accessed. Many laptop models are just as capable as their desktop counterparts. As useful as a laptop can be, however, there are still some features of the smaller version that are inferior to a desktop model. For one, the keyboard can be awkward and mouse control is usually relegated to a touchpad on which the user maneuvers his or her fingers to direct the cursor. However, a regular mouse can be connected to the laptop when space permits, and the laptop can also be connected to a regular keyboard and monitor for better ergonomics. The variety of portable computing devices continues to grow, with new options appearing on a regular basis. Again, the consultant should consider the type of device that is needed for the consultant's particular situation and weigh the costs and benefits before purchasing a mobile computing solution.

Internet access is a necessity in the consulting arena today. E-mail is a way of life in business. E-mail accounts can be set up at no cost on such sites as Yahoo.com and Gmail.com. For a fee, one can also obtain an e-mail domain name using the name of the consultant's business. Consultants should consider having their own Web page that describes their expertise and services available. Usually, a simple Web site can be built for a nominal fee. A consultant who uses the Internet extensively will need high-speed Internet access such as cable, DSL, or satellite.

Telephone and Wireless Services

Consultants definitely need at least one telephone and probably should have two. A new consultant may be surprised to learn that charges for a standard business line generally are higher than charges for a residential line. However, to attempt to share one line with family members, a fax machine, or the Internet could lead to busy signals and missed calls that would be detrimental to business. Consultants who visit various clients in different locations need a cell phone in order to be reached easily. Many consultants find that a smart phone offers numerous advantages, including the ability to send and receive e-mail messages and keep track of contacts and appointments while away from the office.

Answering System or Voice Mail

Consultants need to be able to receive voice messages at any time. An answering system or voice mail is critical. Answering devices need to have a very good sound quality. Remember, consultants always need to maintain a professional image, and a voice greeting that presents a garbled or muffled message does not make a good impression. Also, if the consultant will need to check messages while away from the office, an answering system that provides this feature should be selected. Voice mail is simply an automated answering service provided by the phone company or wireless communications provider. Voice mail messages generally can be checked from any telephone. Most providers charge a small monthly fee for voice mail services.

Fax Machines, Copiers, Scanners, and Multipurpose Devices

Documents often need to be sent back and forth between a consultant and a client. Fax machines allow for rapid transmission of printed documents that cannot or should not be e-mailed. Some consultants fax newsletters to their clients who request them, as a means of keeping in touch. Fax machines are affordable and easy to use. A consultant may also need to scan documents to email to clients, so a scanner may also be a desirable piece of equipment. However, the consultant should be aware that unencrypted email does not meet HIPAA security requirements; therefore, the consultant should not transmit documents containing protected health information to a client across different networks by regular email.

If copies need to be made on a regular basis, then a copy machine should be purchased or leased. Copiers range in price from hundreds to tens of thousands of dollars. If purchasing or leasing a copier, also consider the cost of toner and other supplies, which can add quite a bit to the operating costs of some machines. If copies are not made that often, using a local copying service may be more feasible.

An alternative to buying several different pieces of office equipment would be to purchase a multipurpose machine that acts as a printer, fax machine, scanner, and copier. Prices for these devices are very reasonable, and they can save substantial office space.

Negotiating Contracts

The HIM consultant should take an active role in designing a work contract, seeking the help of an attorney in producing a contract that clearly spells out the consultant's needs regarding pay, authority, responsibility, and so forth. A written contract may outline the number of hours to be worked in a specific health care facility and the fee charged per hour by the consultant. Some contracts may include reimbursement for mileage and other travel expenses. The contract outlines responsibilities on the part of both participants. It often states that the contract employee (consultant) is responsible for all payroll deductions such as taxes, health insurance, and retirement. If the consultant is going to charge for information provided to the facility via phone consultation or if some projects are going to be completed in the consultant's home office (such as preparing a policy and procedure manual or designing forms), clarify how this time will be billed. Most consulting contracts are for a one-year period, and a new contract is signed annually or is self-renewing. Most health care facilities want the contract to read that it can be voided at any time with 30 days' advance notice. Usually it is not possible to negotiate a termination clause. Clients often require the consultant to maintain professional liability insurance coverage. Figure 16-4 is only an outline of possible contract elements and should not be considered a model for contract development. A consultant should seek legal advice and ensure that any contract is HIPAA compliant and appropriate to the legal and business environment of the state and community.

The privacy standards of HIPAA and Title XIII of ARRA, known as the Health Information Technology for Economic and Clinical Health (HITECH) Act, have specific requirements regarding the business associates of a covered entity. (Recall from Chapter 1 that a covered entity may be a health plan, a health care clearinghouse, or a health care provider. In this discussion, we will use a health care provider as an example of a covered entity.) A **business associate** is a person who is not a member of the health care provider's workforce but performs work on behalf of the provider that involves the use or disclosure of protected health information (Definitions, 2002). Because a consultant is not considered to be a member of the health care provider's workforce, the HIPAA privacy rule dictates that the consultant have a written business associate agreement or contract with the facility. One example of the types of issues covered by the business associate agreement would be a provision for safeguards to prevent inappropriate use or disclosure of protected health information on the part of the consultant. The U.S. Department of Health and Human Services' Office for Civil Rights provides sample business associate contract provisions on its Web site that the HIM consultant may want to review (OCR, 2006). The HITECH Act has placed additional obligations for privacy and security on business associates and also extends the threat of civil and criminal penalties for violations of privacy and security standards to business associates.

CONSULTING AGREEMENT

This Agreement is made effective as of July 1, 20XX, by and between **Agency** and **Consultant**.

Consultant has a background in Health Information Systems Management and is willing to provide services to **Agency** based on this background.

Agency desires to have services provided by **Consultant**.

Therefore, the parties agree as follows:

1. DESCRIPTION OF SERVICES. Beginning on July 12, 20XX, **Consultant** will provide the following services (collectively the "Services"):
   a. Provide education for personnel regarding appropriate documentation for medical records.
   b. Provide information and other technical assistance for compliance with XXXX Department of Mental Health regulations.
   c. Provide technical assistance with quality assurance plans, activities, and reviews.
   d. Provide technical assistance to ensure compliance of Medical Records with XXXX Department of Mental Health regulations.
   e. Other duties within the scope of Health Information Systems Management expertise as requested by the Executive Director.

2. PERFORMANCE OF SERVICES. The manner in which the Services are to be performed and the specific hours to be worked shall be determined by **Consultant**. **Agency** will rely on **Consultant** to work as many hours as may be reasonably necessary to fulfill **Consultant's** obligations under this Agreement, not to exceed six and onehalf hours per month unless approved in advance by the board of directors of **Agency**.

3. PAYMENT. **Agency** will pay a fee to **Consultant** of $XX.00 per hour for the Services. This fee shall not be payable until receipt of third-party revenues.

4. LICENSURE/CERTIFICATION. **Consultant** shall at all times maintain all licensure and certifications required of a medical records technician and shall be responsible for any costs associated with such licensure and certification.

5. TERM/TERMINATION. Either party may terminate this Agreement upon giving 30 days, written notice to the other party. This Agreement shall terminate automatically on June 30, 20XX.

6. RELATIONSHIP OF PARTIES. It is understood by the parties that **Consultant** is an independent contractor with respect to **Agency** and not an employee of **Agency**. **Agency** is not responsible for withholding and shall not withhold FICA or taxes of any kind from payments made to **Consultant**. **Consultant** shall not be entitled

FIGURE **16-4** A sample contract (not to be used as a model).

to receive any benefits that employees of **Agency** may be entitled to receive, and shall not be entitled to workers' compensation, unemployment compensation, medical insurance, life insurance, paid vacations, paid holidays, pension or social security on account of her work under this Agreement.

7. EMPLOYEES. **Consultant's** employees, if any, who perform services for **Agency** under this Agreement shall also be bound by the provisions of this Agreement. At the request of **Agency, Consultant** shall provide adequate evidence that such persons are **Consultant's** employees.

8. INJURIES. **Consultant** acknowledges **Consultant's** obligation to obtain appropriate insurance coverage for the benefit of **Consultant** (and **Consultant's** employees, if any). **Consultant** waives any rights to recovery from **Agency** for any injuries that **Consultant** (and/or **Consultant's** employees) may sustain while performing services under this Agreement.

9. INDEMNIFICATION. **Consultant** agrees to indemnify and hold **Agency** harmless from all claims, losses, expenses, fees including attorney fees, costs and judgments that may be asserted against **Agency** that result from the acts or omission of **Consultant, Consultant's** employees, if any, and **Consultant's** agents. If professional liability insurance is available to cover her acts or failure to act as a health information manager, **Consultant** shall obtain such insurance, at her own expense.

10. CONFIDENTIALITY. **Consultant** recognizes that **Agency** has and will have the following information:

    — client information and other proprietary information (collectively, "Information") that are valuable, special and unique assets of **Agency. Consultant** agrees that **Consultant** will not at any time or in any manner, either directly or indirectly, use any Information for **Consultant's** own benefit, or divulge, disclose, or communicate in any manner any Information to any third party without the prior written consent of **Agency. Consultant** will protect the Information and treat it as strictly confidential. A violation of this paragraph shall be a material violation of this Agreement.

11. CONFIDENTIALITY AFTER TERMINATION. The confidentiality provisions of this Agreement shall remain in full force and effect after the termination of this Agreement.

12. RECORDS AND RETURN OF RECORDS. Upon termination of this Agreement, **Consultant** shall deliver all records, notes, data, memorandum, models and equipment of any nature that are in **Consultant's** possession or under **Consultant's** control and that are **Agency's** property or relate to **Agency's** business.

13. NOTICES. All notices required or permitted under this Agreement shall be in writing and shall be deemed delivered when delivered

FIGURE **16-4** (*Continued*)

in person or deposited in the United States mail, postage prepaid, addressed as follows:

Company: name/address

Consultant: name/address

Such address may be changed from time to time by either party by providing written notice to the other in the manner set forth above.

14. ENTIRE AGREEMENT. This Agreement contains the entire agreement of the parties and there are no other promises or conditions in any other agreement whether oral or written. This Agreement supersedes any prior written or oral agreements between the parties.

15. AMENDMENT. This Agreement may be modified or amended if the amendment is made in writing and is signed by both parties.

16. SEVERABILITY. If any provision of this Agreement shall be held to be invalid or unenforceable for any reason, the remaining provisions shall continue to be valid and enforceable. If a court finds that any provision of this Agreement is invalid or unenforceable, but that by limiting such provision it would become valid or enforceable, then such provision shall be deemed to be written, construed, and enforced as so limited.

17. WAIVER OF CONTRACTUAL RIGHT. The failure of either party to enforce any provision of this Agreement shall not be construed as a waiver or limitation of that party's right to subsequently enforce and compel strict compliance with every provision of this Agreement.

18. APPLICABLE LAW. This Agreement shall be governed by the laws of the State of (name of state).

Consultant

By:

Agency

By:

FIGURE **16-4** (*Continued*)

TRENDS

Consulting is projected to be the fastest growing industry in the United States (Bureau of Labor Statistics, 2010). Many professionals laid off due to a downward turn in the economy find employment as consultants. The Bureau of Labor Statistics projects that employment for HIM professionals will grow much faster than average, because the electronic health record broadens and alters job responsibilities. The overall increase in demand for HIM services should also increase the need for HIM consultants. Other factors contributing to the need for consultants are an increased emphasis on compliance activities, the complexity of regulations and managed care and their effect on various health care settings, and health care providers' need to operate effectively and efficiently in an ever-changing environment.

SUMMARY

Starting a new business as a consultant is challenging and requires careful research and planning. Once consulting contracts are obtained, success depends on the ability to gain administrative support and rapport and on the delivery of excellent service. It is important to develop long-range goals and money management skills. Obtaining the help of an attorney and an accountant can help to avoid legal difficulties and to ensure compliance with the tax code.

It is a good idea to seek and gain employment in various health care settings, volunteer, read professional journals, attend workshops and seminars, take college courses, and pursue additional credentials to promote personal marketability.

The ability to set healthy boundaries and provide a container where focused work can be performed both mentally and physically is necessary. The consultant may design a home office space that incorporates **ergonomic** techniques to facilitate comfort and convenience or rent office space away from home.

The HIM consultant should take an active role in negotiating a contract that meets the needs of the client as well as the consultant and that spells out clearly the fee charged, what is covered, what is not covered, and when payment is expected.

The first item on the agenda of a consultant is to seek a clear understanding of the client's needs. Consider the initial interview with the client a two-way interview to find out the needs and whether you clearly understand and can meet these needs. Prepare a written summary of the interview and write a thank you letter.

Then, after obtaining a new contract for a health care facility, review the client's needs and develop a plan to address them. For example, if the contract calls for assessment of facility documentation, review all the relevant regulations regarding documentation requirements, develop an assessment tool, conduct random audits, prepare reports that apprise the client of your findings, and seek the client's feedback. Copies of all audits and reports submitted to the client should be kept and maintained for future reference.

KEY TERMS

audit   retrospective review of selected health care records or data documents to evaluate the quality of care, services provided, documentation, or coding compared with predetermined standards.

business associate   under HIPAA, a person who is not a member of the covered entity's (e.g., the health care provider's) workforce but performs work on behalf of the covered entity that involves the use or disclosure of protected health information.

business plan   a formal written document summarizing the operational and financial objectives of a business. The business plan also includes the details of how the objectives are to be attained, including budgets and other financial forecasts. Lenders and investors generally require a business plan as one of the documents they study when making a decision whether to lend to or invest in a business.

corporate integrity agreement (CIA) an agreement that a health care provider or health plan reaches with the Department of Health and Human Services' Office of the Inspector General (OIG) as part of a settlement agreement when allegations of improper reimbursement have been made.

ergonomics designing workspaces and equipment to fit the human body to maximize comfort, convenience, and efficiency at work.

Office of the Inspector General (OIG) a subdivision of the U.S. Department of Health and Human Services. "The mission of the Office of Inspector General is to protect the integrity of Department of Health and Human Services (HHS) programs, as well as the health and welfare of the beneficiaries of those programs. . . . The OIG's duties are carried out through a nationwide network of audits, investigations, inspections and other mission-related functions performed by OIG components" (OIG, n.d.).

REVIEW QUESTIONS

Knowledge-Based Questions

1. Explain the concept of a corporate integrity agreement (CIA) and the role a consultant might play when such an agreement is in effect.
2. Explain what a documentation audit is and the documentation audit cycle.
3. Describe desirable characteristics of a consultant.
4. Explain the basis for the consultant's power in a consulting situation.
5. Explain the factors a consultant should consider in setting fees.
6. Describe the equipment that an independent consultant may need.
7. Explain the concept of a business associate under HIPAA.
8. Define leadership.
9. Describe why a consultant should not enter into a "contingency" contract with a client.
10. Summarize the privacy standards of HIPAA and ARRA/HITECH regarding business associates.
11. Describe the key elements of a business plan for an independent consultant.

Critical Thinking Questions

1. Explain the difference between cognitive intelligence and interpersonal intelligence.
2. A health information consultant charges $100 per hour and works the equivalent of 200 billable 8-hour days per year. Taxes, insurance, travel, and other expenses consume about 70 percent of the consultant's gross revenue.
   a. What is the consultant's gross annual revenue (i.e., the total amount she receives from her clients before taxes and other expenses)?
   b. What is the consultant's net annual income (i.e., her take-home pay after taxes and other expenses)?

WEB ACTIVITY

Find the Conditions of Participation or Conditions for Coverage for one of the settings discussed in any previous chapter. (One Web source for locating these documents is http://www.cms.gov/CFCsAndCoPs/ at the Centers for Medicare & Medicaid Services.)

Within the Conditions, locate the medical or clinical record standards for the selected setting. Develop an audit form that a consultant could use to audit the documentation in the selected setting, based on the record standards found in the Conditions.

CASE STUDY

Identify the problem areas for the facility described below and prepare a written recommendation addressing a plan of correction for each site.

You have been hired as a consultant for a behavioral health care facility that is comprised of 11 client service sites. They are Joint Commission accredited and are anticipating a survey soon. After initial visits to each site, your analysis of deficiencies includes:

Site 1—Residential Chemical Dependency Program for Adolescents

The medical records are well organized and in good order, but after closer inspection you find that the physician responsible for completing physical exams does not assess clients' motor skills, which is a requirement for adolescent admissions. You also find that though the history and physical is performed and dictated by the physician within 24 hours, the typed report does not appear in the chart for weeks.

Site 2—Residential Chemical Dependency Program for Adult Women

Joint Commission and state standards require that a master treatment plan be completed within 14 days of admission. A representative sample review of the facilities' charts reveals no treatment plans. Upon closer scrutiny you learn that none of the clients admitted in the past three months have treatment plans in their charts either.

Site 3—Outpatient Mental Health Clinic with 600 Active Clients

After conducting a study to determine the record retrievability rate, it is learned that 75 percent of the records are inaccessible. The day the study was completed, only 40 clients had been scheduled for appointments. This location only has two health information clerks, and one has been pulled frequently to answer the phone at the intake desk.

Site 4—Outpatient Chemical Dependency Site with 125 Active Clients

A quantitative analysis process has been set up and the record clerk trained. However, no quantitative analysis has occurred. Upon a return visit to analyze the situation, it is found that the records clerk is also the office manager with responsibilities to answer the phone, schedule appointments, conduct financial intakes, maintain time sheets for clinicians, and complete general correspondence.

Site 5—Outpatient Chemical Dependency Site with 40 Active Clients

Upon receiving a subpoena duces tecum and a court order, a clinical supervisor fails to notify the organization's clinical director, health information manager, or an administrator. Instead, she takes the records home and asks her husband, who is an attorney, for advice.

REFERENCES AND SUGGESTED READINGS

[AHIMA] American Health Information Management Association. Recovery Audit Contractor (RAC) Toolkit. Available online at www.ahima.org/infocenter/documents/RACToolkitFINAL.pdf.

Blanchard, K., & Hodges, P. (2003). *The Servant Leader.* Nashville, TN: Thomas Nelson, Inc.

Bureau of Labor Statistics, U.S. Department of Labor. (2010). *Career Guide to Industries (2010–2011 ed.).* Management, Scientific, and Technical Consulting Services. Available online at http://www.bls.gov/oco/cg/cgs037.htm [2010, April 7].

Cassidy, B. (2010). ARRA's Impact on HIM. *Journal of the American Health Information Management Association, 81,* 48–49.

[CMS] Centers for Medicare & Medicaid Services. Recovery Audit Contractor. Available online at www.cms.hhs.gov/RAC.

Coleman, D. (2006). *Social Intelligence.* New York: Bantam Dell.

Friedl, S. (2010). Steve Friedl's Unixwiz.net Tech Tips—So You Want to Be a Consultant? Retrieved February 6, 2010, from http://unixwiz.net.

Greenwald, R. (2010, February 8). How to Succeed in the Age of Going Solo. The Journal Report. *Wall Street Journal,* pp. R1 & R3.

Industrial Commission of Ohio, Division of Safety and Hygiene. (n.d.). Survival Guide to Computer Workstations. Available online at http://www.ehs.ohio-state.edu/index.asp?page=ohse.computer.

Koch, C. (1996, March 15). The bright stuff. *CIO Magazine*. [Online]. http://www.cio.com/.

Leonard, M. A. (2010). A RAC Primer for LTC Facilities. *Journal of the American Health Information Management Association, 81*, 56–58.

Levine, D. I., & Gilbert, A. (1999). Knowledge Transfer: Managerial Practices Underlying One Piece of the Learning Organization. Available online at www.irle.berkeley.edu/cohre/knowledge.html.

Maxwell, J. C. (1993). *Developing the Leader within You*. Nashville, TN: Thomas Nelson, Inc.

Maxwell, J. C. (2007). *The 21 Irrefutable Laws of Leadership*. Nashville, TN: Thomas Nelson, Inc.

Mitchell, S. (2003). Taking the Initiative with Nursing Home Quality. *Journal of the American Health Information Management Association, 74*(3), 56.

Nagel, S. (2003, February 10). HIM's Role in the Revenue Cycle. *For the Record*, pp. 31–33.

National Center for Health Statistics. ICD-9-CM Official Coding Guidelines for Coding and Reporting. Available online at http://www.cdc.gov/nchs/icd/icd9cm_addenda_guidelines.htm.

National Center for Health Statistics. ICD-10-CM Official Coding Guidelines for Coding and Reporting. Available online at http://www.cdc.gov/nchs/icd/icd10cm.htm.

Centers for Medicare & Medicaid Services. ICD-10-PCS Official Coding Guidelines. Available online at https://www.cms.gov/ICD10/.

[OSHA] Occupational Safety & Health Administration. (n.d.). Computer Workstations. [Online]. http://www.osha.gov/SLTC/etools/computerworkstations/components_monitors.html [2011, April 19].

[OCR] Office for Civil Rights. (2006). Sample Business Associate Contract Provisions. *Medical Privacy—National Standards to Protect the Privacy of Personal Health Information*. [Online]. http://www.hhs.gov/ocr/privacy/hipaa/understanding/coveredentities/contractprov.html [2010, April 6].

[OIG] Office of the Inspector General. (n.d.) Compliance Guidance. [Online]. http://oig.hhs.gov/fraud/complianceguidance.asp [2011, April 19].

Pyle, L. S. (2008, December 03). Home Based Business Reality Check. *Entrepreneur*. Retrieved March 9, 2010, from http://www.entrepreneur.com/homebasedbiz/homebasedbizcolumnistlestleyspencerpyle/article.

Siropolis, N. (1994). *Small Business Management: A Guide to Entrepreneurship*. Boston: Houghton Mifflin Company.

Squazzo, J. (2003). Doctors Not Ready for HIPAA. *Journal of the American Health Information Management Association, 74*(2), 10.

Torrance, K. (2010). Unveiling the invisible department. *Journal of the American Health Information Management Association, 81*(2), 50–51.

[USDHHS] U.S. Department of Health and Human Services Office of Inspector General. (2010, February). Recovery Audit Contractors' Fraud Referrals. OEI-03-09-00130. Retrieved March 30, 2010, from http://oig.hhs.gov/oei/reports/oei-03-09-00130.pdf

Wager, K. A., Lee, F. W., Glorioso, R., & Bergstrom, L. (1999). Working Smarter, Not Harder, in a Family Practice. *Journal of the American Health Information Management Association, 70*(6), 44–46.

Wildi, R. (2010, February 20). Consultant [personal communication].

KEY RESOURCES

American Health Information Management Association
http://www.ahima.org

Association of Management Consulting Firms
http://www.amcf.org

Electronic Discovery Reference Model
http://edrm.net

Information Management Reference Model
http://edrm.net/projects/imrm

Institute of Management Consultants USA
http://www.imcusa.org

Internal Revenue Service
http://www.irs.ustreas.gov

INDEX

AA. *See* Alcoholics Anonymous
AAAHC. *See* Accreditation Association for Ambulatory Health Care
AAHA. *See* American Animal Hospital Association
AAIDD. *See* American Association on Intellectual and Developmental Disabilities
ACA. *See* American Correctional Association
Academic institution dental clinics, 494
Accountable Care Organization (ACOs), 141, 142
Accreditation, 12, 20
  AAAHC and, 122–23
  ambulatory care, freestanding, 74–75
  CARF International and, 227–28, 274, 275, 302, 400, 401
  CHAP and, 439, 440, 466–67, 485
  hospice, 466–67
  hospital-based care and, 35
  intellectual disabilities facilities and, 314–15
  long-term care, 364
  managed care voluntary, 121–23
  NCQA and, 122
  URAC and, 123
Accreditation Association for Ambulatory Health Care (AAAHC), 122–23
Accreditation Commission for Health Care (ACHC), 439, 440–41, 458
  hospice and, 466–67
ACHSA. *See* American Correctional Health Services Association
ACOs. *See* Accountable Care Organization
ACS. *See* American College of Surgeons
Active treatment, 311, 343

Activities of daily living (ADL), 349, 384
  OTs and, 393
Acute inpatient care, 474, 475, 488
Acute rehabilitation units, 391, 430
Addiction Severity Index (ASI), 292, 302
ADL. *See* Activities of daily living
Administrative simplification, 8, 20
Adolescents
  CASSP and, 222, 256
  dental care and, 495–96, 511–12
  mental health services and, 222–25
  substance abuse treatment and, 269
  wrap-around services and, 224–25, 258
Adult
  dental care, 496
  mental health services, 216–22
AFO. *See* Ankle-foot orthosis
After-hours crisis services, 222
Agency for Healthcare Research and Quality (AHRQ), 136
Agreement, consulting, 571–73
AHRQ. *See* Agency for Healthcare Research and Quality
Aide, hospice, 472
Alcoholics Anonymous (AA), 263, 302
Amalgam, 505, 523
Ambulation aids, 397, 398–99, 430
Ambulatory care, freestanding, 107
  accreditation, 74–75
  ASC reimbursement system, 92–93, 106
  capitation and, 93
  caregiver types, 72–73
  coding and classification in, 94–95
  compliance and, 75–76, 107
  computer systems in, 98–101
  data and information flow in, 95–98
  data sets in, 101
  documentation and, 77–91
  documentation record formats, 87–89

  EHR and, 99–100
  encounter form, 79, 80, 107
  e-prescribing in, 100, 107
  EPSDT and, 93, 107
  fee-for-service and, 91–92
  HIM in, 104–6
  history and physical, 77, 79
  IM and, 94–101
  lab and X-ray reports, 79
  legal issues, 103–4
  licensure, 73
  Medicare certification, 73–74
  MPFS and, 92
  patient types, 72
  problem list, 79, 81–82, 109
  quality management and, 101–2
  record linkage to other sites, 98
  registration, 77, 78, 109
  regulatory issues, 73–76
  reimbursement and, 91–93
  risk management, 103–4
  settings, 70–72
  special documentation requirements, 82–87
  trends, 105–6
  UM in, 102–4
Ambulatory payment classifications (APCs), 64
  composite, 45, 47
  discounted and, 45
  hospital-based care, 45–48
  observation codes and, 47
  pass-through payments and, 47–48
  status indicators and, 45, 46, 65
Ambulatory surgery, 31, 64
Ambulatory surgery centers (ASCs), 70, 71, 106
  Medicare certification and, 74
  reimbursement and, 92–93, 106
  special documentation requirements, 82–83
American Animal Hospital Association (AAHA), 533, 550

American Association on Intellectual and Developmental Disabilities (AAIDD), 324, 325
American College of Surgeons (ACS), 2, 20
American Correctional Association (ACA), 193, 208
American Correctional Health Services Association (ACHSA), 205, 208
American Physical Therapy Association (APTA), 393
American Public Health Association (APHA), 193–94, 208
American Recovery and Reinvestment Act (ARRA), 6, 20
EHRs and, 53, 64
American Society of Addiction Medicine Patient Placement Criteria, second edition revised (ASAM PPC-2R)
inpatient/residential treatment and, 267
levels of care defined by, 265
outpatient/partial hospitalization treatments and, 266–67
outpatient treatment and, 265–67
American Spinal Injury Association, 421–22
American Veterinary Health Information Management Association (AVHIMA), 549, 550
American Veterinary Medical Association (AVMA), 529, 550
Amputation, 399
Animal, 528–29, 550. *See also* Veterinary care
AAHA and, 533, 550
cruelty, 547
euthanasia, 548
health technician, 529–30
OFA and, 542, 551
Ankle-foot orthosis (AFO), 398
Annual staffings, 318, 343
Answering system, 569
Anterior cord syndrome, 422
APCs. *See* Ambulatory payment classifications
APHA. *See* American Public Health Association
Application service providers (ASPs), 517
Appointment
block method of, 95, 106
dental care, 514
system, 98, 106
APTA. *See* American Physical Therapy Association
ARRA. *See* American Recovery and Reinvestment Act
ASAM PPC-2R. *See* American Society of Addiction Medicine Patient

Placement Criteria, second edition revised
ASC reimbursement system, 92–93, 106
ASCs. *See* Ambulatory surgery centers
ASI. *See* Addiction Severity Index
ASPs. *See* Application service providers
Assessment, 312, 343. *See also* Care area assessment; Outcome and Assessment Information Set-C
CAHPS, 136
clinical assessment record, 276–82, 302
CMAT, 239
comprehensive, 357–60, 385, 441, 443, 458
comprehensive resident assessment, 357–60, 385
dialysis, 153–59
HAVEN, 445, 459
hospice, 471–72
intellectual disabilities facilities, 326
IRF-PAI, 415, 417–19
long-term care, 357–60
mental health services, 228–29, 230–31
OBRA, 357, 385
QAPI, 56–57, 167–68, 174, 483–85
RAI, 357, 386
rehabilitation, 414, 424–25
self-care scales, 424–25
substance abuse treatment, 276–82
Audit
compliance, 560, 575
long-term care, 381–82
RAC and, 5, 24
Audited, 448, 458
AVHIMA. *See* American Veterinary Health Information Management Association
AVMA. *See* American Veterinary Medical Association

BA. *See* Business associate
Baby bottle tooth decay (BBTD), 495
Bereavement, 473, 488
Bipolar disorder, 217–18, 255
Birth centers, 70, 72, 82, 83, 106
Bitewing, 507, 523
Block appointment method, 95, 106
Blood donation, veterinary care and, 548
Bovine, 529, 550
Bridge, 500, 523
Brown-Sequard syndrome, 422
Bureau of Citizenship and Immigration Services (USCIS), 185, 208
Bureau of Immigration and Customs Enforcement (ICE), 184–86, 208
Business associate (BA), 9, 20, 570, 575
Business plan, 562–63, 575

CAA. *See* Care area assessment
CAHPS. *See* Consumer Assessment of Healthcare Providers and Systems
Calculus, 500–501, 523
Canine, 529, 550
CAPD. *See* Continuous ambulatory peritoneal dialysis
Capitation, 5, 20, 93, 107, 125, 142
Caprine, 529, 550
Care area assessment (CAA)
process, 357–60, 384
resources, 358, 384
summary, 358–59, 384
Care area triggers (CATs), 358, 384
Caregiver types
correctional facilities, 188, 191
dialysis, 150–51
freestanding ambulatory, 72–73
home health care, 437–38
hospice, 465–66
hospital-based care, 34
intellectual disabilities facilities, 312–14
long-term care, 350–54
managed care, 119–20
mental health services, 225–27
rehabilitation, 392–95
substance abuse treatment, 271–73
veterinary care, 529–30
Care plan, 358, 384, 443, 458, 471–72
CARF International (Commission on Accreditation of Rehabilitation Facilities), 302, 400, 401
mental health and, 227–28
substance abuse treatment and, 274, 275
Caries, 495, 523
Case management, 220
Case managers, 226, 272
Case-mix
reimbursement, 366–67, 384
variable, 161
Case Mix Assessment Tool (CMAT), 239
Case-mix groups (CMGs), 415, 430
CASSP. *See* Child and Adolescent Service System Program
CATs. *See* Care area triggers
Cauda equina syndrome, 422
CCHP. *See* Certified Correctional Health Professional Program
CCP. *See* Correctional Certification Program
CCPD. *See* Continuous cycling peritoneal dialysis
CDI. *See* Clinical documentation improvement
CDM. *See* Charge description master
CE. *See* Covered entity
Center for Mental Health Services (CMHS), 222, 255

Center for Substance Abuse Prevention (CSAP), 268, 302
Center for Substance Abuse Treatment (CSAT), 291, 302
Centers for Medicare & Medicaid Services (CMS), 3, 20, 120–21
dental care and, 511–12
home health care and, 439–40, 458
hospice and, 466–67
hospital-based care and, 234
long-term care and, 355, 356
patient database form and, 404–9
preadmission screening and, 403–9
rehabilitation and, 400, 401–9
60 percent rule and, 402–3
Central cord syndrome, 422
Certification period, 441, 458
Certified Correctional Health Professional (CCHP) Program, 205, 208
Certified medication technician (CMT), 352
Certified nurse midwives (CNMs), 72–73, 107
Certified veterinary practice manager (CVPM), 530, 550
Cervical orthoses, 398
Change of designated hospice, 469
CHAP. *See* Community Health Accreditation Program
Charge description master (CDM), 42, 64
Chargemaster, 42, 64
Chemical restraint, 234–35, 255
Child and Adolescent Service System Program (CASSP), 222, 256
Children
dental care and, 495–96, 511–12
mental health services and, 222–25, 235–36
restraint of, 235–36
wrap-around services and, 224–25, 258
Children's Health Insurance Program (CHIP), 4, 20
dental care and, 511–12
Chronic kidney disease (CKD), 148, 173
CIA. *See* Corporate integrity agreement
Civil money penalties, 355, 385
CKD. *See* Chronic kidney disease
Claims
data, 131
tracking, 515
Classification. *See also* Ambulatory payment classifications; ICD-10-CM; ICD-10-PCS
AAIDD and, 324
ambulatory care, freestanding, 94–95
correctional facilities, 200
dental care, 512–13
dialysis, 160, 161

home health care, 448–52
hospice, 480–81
ICPC and, 95, 108
intellectual disabilities facilities, 323–25
long-term care, 369–70
mental health services, 244, 246
of prisons, 181
rehabilitation, 421–25
substance abuse treatment, 288–89
TBI, 423–24
veterinary care, 538–40
CLIA. *See* Clinical Laboratory Improvement Amendments of 1988
Clinical assessment record, 276–82, 302
Clinical depression, 217, 256
Clinical documentation improvement (CDI), 5, 21
Clinical Laboratory Improvement Amendments of 1988 (CLIA), 121, 142
Clinical Performance Measures (CPM) Project, 168–70, 173
Clinic outpatient, 33, 64
Close of care documentation, 473
CMAT. *See* Case Mix Assessment Tool
CMGs. *See* Case-mix groups
CMHC. *See* Community mental health center
CMHS. *See* Center for Mental Health Services
CMS. *See* Centers for Medicare & Medicaid Services
CMT. *See* Certified medication technician
CNMs. *See* Certified nurse midwives
COB. *See* Coordination of benefits
Coding. *See also Healthcare Common Procedural Coding System*
ambulatory care, freestanding, 94–95
color, 97, 107
correctional facilities, 200
dental care, 512–13
dialysis, 160, 161
HCPCS, 51–52, 94–95, 107, 128–29, 451–52
home health care, 448–52
hospice, 480–81
ICD-10-PCS, 9, 22
intellectual disabilities facilities, 323–25
long-term care, 369–70
mental health services, 244, 246
rehabilitation, 420
substance abuse treatment, 288–89
veterinary care, 538–40
Coinsurance, 117, 142
Color coding, 97, 107
Commission on Accreditation of Rehabilitation Facilities. *See* CARF International

Common working file (CWF), 56, 64
Community Health Accreditation Program (CHAP), 485
home health care and, 439, 440
hospice and, 466–67
Community health centers, 70, 71, 107
Community mental health center (CMHC), 214–15, 256. *See also* Mental health services
Community Support Program (CSP), 219
Compliance
ambulatory care, freestanding, and, 75–76, 107
audit, 560, 575
consulting regarding, 561
officer, 60
plans, 75–76, 107
substantial, 355, 386
Composite, 505, 523
Composite APCs, 45, 47
Comprehensive assessment, 357–60, 385, 441, 443, 458
Comprehensive outpatient rehabilitation facility (CORF), 392
Comprehensive resident assessment, 357–60, 385
Computer systems, 53–55, 98–101
Concurrent review, 136, 142
Conditions of Participation (COP), 439, 459
Confidentiality
correctional facilities and, 196–97
HIPPA and, 9–12
intellectual disabilities facilities, 339–40
mental health services, 250–51
substance abuse treatment, 273, 292–93, 294, 302
Confidentiality of Drug and Alcohol Abuse Records. *See* 42 C.F.R. Part 2
Consolidated billing, 366, 384
Consolidated Renal Operations in a Web-enabled Network (CROWNWeb), 162, 173
Consulting
agreement, 571–73
answering system or voice mail for, 569
business plan, 562–63, 575
compliance and, 561
computer and, 568–69
documentation, 560
fees, 564–66
HIM and, 382–83, 561–73
leadership ability and, 563–64
long-term care and, 382–83
multipurpose office devices for, 569
negotiating contracts, 570–73
office equipment, 567–69
project examples, 558–59
regulatory issues, 559–60

Consulting *(Continued)*
  reimbursement, 561
  seeking clients, 566
  settings, 556–57
  telephone and wireless service for, 569
  trends, 573–74
  working at home, 566–67
Consumer Assessment of Healthcare
    Providers and Systems (CAHPS), 136
Consumer-directed health plans
  FSA, 118, 142
  HRA, 118–19, 142
  HSA, 119, 143
Continuity of care, 219, 256
Continuous ambulatory peritoneal
    dialysis (CAPD), 149, 150, 173
Continuous care, 474, 475, 488
Continuous cycling peritoneal dialysis
    (CCPD), 149–50, 173
Continuous quality improvement
    (CQI), 248–49, 256
Contract negotiation, 570–73
Conus medullaris syndrome, 422
Coordination of benefits (COB),
    126–28, 142
COP. *See* Conditions of Participation
Copayment, 124, 142, 199, 208
Core team summary sheet, 327–28,
    330–31
CORF. *See* Comprehensive outpatient
    rehabilitation facility
Corporate integrity agreement (CIA),
    561, 576
Correctional Certification Program
    (CCP), 206, 208
Correctional facilities
  ACA and, 193, 206
  ACHSA and, 205
  administrative information, 197–98
  ancillary/emergency services for, 191
  APHA and, 193–94, 208
  caregiver types, 188, 191
  CCHP Program and, 205, 208
  CCP and, 206, 208
  coding and classification and, 200
  confidentiality and, 196–97
  correctional health record, 194–97
  DOC and, 180–81, 208
  documentation, 194–98
  EHR and, 200
  health transfer summary form, 188,
    189–90
  HIM and, 194–97, 205–7
  HIPPA and, 200–202
  HSD and, 180, 208
  ICE and, 184–86, 209
  IM, 199–202
  inmate age and, 186–87
  inmate gender and, 187
  inmate offense and, 187
  jails, 179, 184–85, 208
  juvenile facilities, 184–85, 209
  legal issues, 204–5

  licensure regarding, 192
  nature of illness and, 188
  NCCHC and, 193, 209
  on-site *vs.* off-site services, 186
  overview, 178–80
  patient types, 186–88
  prisons, 179, 181–83, 209
  quality management and, 203
  regulatory issues, 192–94
  reimbursement and funding,
    198–99
  rights and, 179
  risk management, 204–5
  settings, 178–92
  specialty services, 191–92
  state, 180–81
  state *vs.* contracted firms, 181
  technology and, 206–7
  TJC and, 193
  transfer and, 196
  trends, 206
  UM and, 203–4
Correctional health record
  format, 194–95
  numbering and filing, 195
  overview, 194
  retention and destruction, 195
  transfer and, 196
Counselors, substance abuse treatment
    and, 272
Court-ordered substance abuse
    treatment, 293–94
Court ordered treatment, 251–52
Court-referred clients, 271
Coverage criteria, rehabilitation,
    411–13
Covered entity (CE), 8, 21
CPM. *See* Clinical Performance
    Measures Project
CPT. *See* Current Procedural
    Terminology
CQI. *See* Continuous quality
    improvement
Creating Home meetings, 383
Credentialing, 137–38
Credentials verification organization
    (CVO), 138, 142
Crowns, 496, 523
CROWNWeb. *See* Consolidated
    Renal Operations in a Web-enabled
    Network
CSAP. *See* Center for Substance Abuse
    Prevention
CSAT. *See* Center for Substance Abuse
    Treatment
CSP. *See* Community Support Program
Culture change movement, 383, 385
Curative therapy, 465, 488
Current Procedural Terminology
    (CPT), 95, 107, 370
  home health care and, 451–52
  hospice and, 481
  managed care and, 128–29

CVO. *See* Credentials verification
    organization
CVPM. *See* Certified veterinary
    practice manager
CWF. *See* Common working file

DASIS. *See* Drug and Alcohol Services
    Information System
Data and information flow
  in ambulatory care, freestanding,
    95–98
  claims, 131
  dialysis, 160–62
  external data reporting, 373
  HEDIS, 134, 143
  home health care, 452
  HOP QDRP, 6, 22
  hospice, 479–80
  intellectual disabilities facilities,
    318–20, 322–23
  long-term care, 370–73
  mental health services, 243–44,
    245–46
  patient, 161–62, 404–9, 482
  referral data, 131, 144
  State DIGs, 247–48
  substance abuse treatment,
    286–87
Databases
  rehabilitation, 421
  VMDB, 541–42, 551
Data sets
  ambulatory care, freestanding, 101
  dialysis, 163–66
  home health care, 453
  hospice, 482–83
  intellectual disabilities facilities,
    325–37
  long-term care, 357–60, 370–72,
    374–76
  MDS, 357–60, 370–72, 374–76
  mental health services, 247–48
  substance abuse treatment,
    289–90
  TEDS, 290, 304
  UACDS, 55, 65, 101
  UHDDS, 55, 65
  veterinary care, 541–42
*Data Standards for Mental Health
    Decision Support Systems*
    ("FN-10"), 241, 256
Day programming, 220–21
DEA. *See* Drug Enforcement Agency
Death Notification form, ESRD,
    163, 166
Debt collection litigation, 546
Decision-support systems,
    99–100, 107
Deductible, 117, 142
Deemed status, 12, 21
Delusions, 217, 256
Denial, 448, 459

Dental care
  academic institution clinics, 494
  adults, 496
  adverse reactions and, 519
  appointment scheduling, 514
  ASPs, 517
  assistants, 501
  BBTD, 495
  charting, 505, 506
  children and adolescents and,
    495–96, 511–12
  CMS and, 511–12
  coding and classification, 512–13
  DEA and, 502
  dental informatics and, 522
  dentists distribution in, 492–93
  diet evaluation, 510
  documentation, 503–10
  elderly and, 496–97
  electronic dental record, 516
  electronic information systems,
    513–17, 522
  endodontist, 500
  examination, 505–7
  general dentists and, 498–99
  group dental practice, 493–94, 523
  HIM and, 520–21
  HMOs and, 511
  hospital, acute care, and, 494–95
  hygienists, 500–501
  IM, 512–17
  imaging, 507–8
  injuries and, 518–19
  insurance, 510–11, 515
  insurance billing/claims tracking,
    515
  inventory management, 516
  legal issues, 518–20
  malpractice and negligence and, 519
  medical and dental history and,
    503–5
  mid-level providers, 501
  NFs and, 497
  oral maxillofacial surgeon, 500, 523
  orthodontist, 499
  other settings of, 495
  patient education, 509–10
  patient information, 503, 504
  patient types, 495–98
  periodontist, 499
  practice management software,
    513–14
  pregnant female, 496
  prosthodontist, 500, 524
  provider types, 498–501
  QI, 517–18
  recall reminders, 515–16
  records used for identification,
    519–20
  referrals, 516
  regulatory issues, 501–2
  reimbursement, 510–12
  reporting requirements, 502
  risk management, 518–20
  self-pay, 511, 515
  self-pay accounting information,
    515
  settings, 492–95
  solo dental practice, 492–93, 524
  special challenge patients, 498
  specialties, 499–500
  state licensure, 502
  TDP and, 512
  technological devices, 517
  third-party organizations, 494
  treatment notes, 509
  treatment plan, 508
  trends, 521–22
  UM, 518
  VA and, 512
Dentists
  distribution, 492–93
  general, 498–99
Denture, 500, 523
Department of corrections (DOC),
  180–81, 208
Dependents, 119, 142
Depression
  clinical, 217, 256
  manic, 217, 257
Detainee, 182
Developmental disability, 311, 343.
  See also Intellectual disabilities
  facilities
Diagnosis related group (DRG), 64.
  See also Medicare-Severity DRGs;
  Medicare severity long-term care
  diagnosis related groups
  hospital-based care and, 42–44
  managed care and, 130–31
  revenue generation and, 126, 142
*Diagnostic and Statistical Manual of
  Mental Disorders*, fourth edition,
  text revision (DSM-IV-TR), 244,
  246, 256
  intellectual disabilities facilities and,
    323–24
  mental health services and, 219
  substance abuse and, 262–63,
    288–89
Diagnostic evaluation and psychiatric
  medication management, 220
Dialysate, 149, 173
Dialysis, 173
  aggregate data, 162
  assessment and plan of care, 153–59
  CAPD, 149, 150, 173
  caregiver types, 150–51
  case-mix variable and, 161
  CCPD, 149–50, 173
  coding and classification, 160, 161
  CPM project, 168–70, 173
  data and information flow, 160–62
  data sets, 163–66
  documentation, 152–59
  EHR and, 162–63
  ESRD Death Notification form,
    163, 166
  ESRD medical evidence report, 163,
    164–65
  ESRD networks and, 148, 152, 153,
    174
  *ESRD Program Interpretive
    Guidance* document, 157, 158
  ethical issues, 171–72
  evaluation areas, 154
  facility, 148–49, 173
  federal regulations, 152
  government surveys and, 151–52
  HD, 149, 174
  HIM and, 172
  IM, 160–66
  KDOQI and, 170
  legal issues, 171–72
  medical record model and, 157–59
  patient care plan, 155–56
  patient data, individual, 161–62
  patient education/training, 157
  patient reassessment, 155
  patient types, 149–50
  PD, 149, 174
  performance improvement and, 167
  plan implementation, 156–57
  prescription, 154–55
  prevalence of modality types, 150
  QI, 167–70
  regulatory issues, 151–52
  reimbursement, 159–60
  risk management/ethical issues,
    171–72
  settings, 148–51
  transplantation referral tracking,
    157
  types of, 149
  UM, 170–71
Diet evaluation, dental care, 510
Dietitians, 354
Digital imaging, 517, 523
DIHS. *See* Division of Immigration
  Health Services
Direct care staff, 328–29, 343
Disability, 396, 430
Discharge planning, 136, 142
Discharge summary, 236
  rehabilitation, 413–14
Discharge *vs.* revocation, hospice, 476,
  479
Disciplines, 438, 459
Discounted, 45, 64
Division of Immigration Health
  Services (DIHS), 185, 208
DME. *See* Durable medical equipment
DOC. *See* Department of corrections
Documentation
  ambulatory care, 37, 38–39, 77–91
  birth centers, 82, 83
  CDI and, 5, 21
  close of care, 473
  consulting, 560

Documentation *(Continued)*
  correctional facilities, 194–98
  dental care, 503–10
  dialysis, 152–59
  EHR, 88–89
  emergency patients standard
    example, 37
  encounter form, 79, 80
  family numbering system and,
    91, 107
  filing methods, 90–91
  history and physical, 77, 79
  home health care, 441–45
  hospice, 471–73
  hospital and, 35–42
  immunization, 83–84
  IM standards and, 36
  industrial health centers, 84, 87
  inpatient, 472–73
  integrated format, 87–88
  intellectual disabilities facilities,
    315–21, 338–39
  lab and X-ray reports, 79
  long-term care, 357–64
  managed care, 123–24
  mental health services, 228–38
  patient, 35–42, 89–91, 472–73
  POMR, 87, 88, 109, 535, 551
  problem list, 79, 81–82
  record formats, 87–89
  registration and, 77, 78, 109
  rehabilitation, 410–14
  risk management and, 103–4
  service nature and, 35–36
  special requirements, 82–87
  substance abuse treatment,
    275–85
  surgery standard example, 36–37
  teaching physicians and residents
    and, 39–42
  TJC and, 36–39
  veterinary care, 533–35
  volunteer, 472
Downcodes, 447
DRG. *See* Diagnosis related group
Drug and Alcohol Services
  Information System (DASIS), 290,
  303
Drug Enforcement Agency (DEA),
  502
DSM-IV-TR. *See Diagnostic and
  Statistical Manual of Mental
  Disorders,* fourth edition, text
  revision
Dual diagnoses, 217, 218, 256,
  270–71, 303
Dual insurance coverage, 126–28
Durable medical equipment (DME)
  home health care and, 438, 459
  orthotics, 397–98, 431
  used in rehabilitation, 397–400
Duty to warn, 251, 256

EAPs. *See* Employee assistance
  programs
Early and Periodic Screening,
  Diagnostic, and Treatment (EPSDT),
  93, 107
Early childhood caries (ECC), 495
Economic credentialing, 138
ECUs. *See* Environmental control units
Edentulous, 497, 523
EHR. *See* Electronic health record
Elderly, dental care and, 496–97
Election
  of hospice benefit statement,
    475–76
  of hospice care, 468
Electronic health record (EHR), 8,
  15, 21
  ambulatory care, freestanding,
    using, 99–100
  ARRA and, 53, 64
  correctional facilities and, 200
  dialysis and, 162–63
  format, 88–89
  IM and, 53–55, 98–101
  managed care and, 133–34
  meaningful use and, 53–55
  mental health services and, 253
  veterinary care and, 549
  work flow using, 96–97
Electronic information systems
  dental care, 513–17, 522
  home health care, 452–53
  hospice, 481–82
  IM and, 132–34
  intellectual disabilities facilities, 325
  long-term care, 373–74
  rehabilitation, 421
  substance abuse treatment, 290
  veterinary care, 542–43
Eligibility, 132, 142
Emergency care, 31–32
  for correctional facilities, 191
  documentation, 37
  outpatient, 33, 64
Emergency Medical Treatment and
  Active Labor Act (EMTALA), 59,
  64
Employee assistance programs (EAPs),
  270, 303
EMTALA. *See* Emergency Medical
  Treatment and Active Labor Act
Encounter, 101, 107, 131, 142
Encounter form, 79, 80, 107
Endodontist, 500, 523
End-stage renal disease (ESRD), 148,
  173. *See also* Dialysis
  CPM project, 168–70, 173
  Death Notification form, 163, 166
  *ESRD Program Interpretive
    Guidance* document, 157, 158
  medical evidence report, 163,
    164–65

  networks, 148, 152, 153, 167, 174
Environmental control units (ECUs),
  397, 400, 430
E-prescribing, 100, 107
EPSDT. *See* Early and Periodic
  Screening, Diagnostic, and
  Treatment
Equine, 529, 551
Ergonomics, 574, 575
Erythropoietin stimulating agents
  (ESAs), 159, 174
ESRD. *See* End-stage renal disease
ESRD networks, 148, 152, 153, 167,
  174
ESRD Program Interpretive Guidance
  document, 157, 158
Estelle v. Gamble, 179
Euthanasia, animal, 548
External data reporting, 373
Extremity orthoses, 398

Family
  numbering system, 91, 107
  planning centers, 72, 107
Federal Bureau of Prisons (FBP), 182,
  208
Federally qualified health centers
  (FQHCs), 70, 71, 74, 107
Federal regulations, hospital-based
  care, 34–35
Federal survey, 357, 385
Fee-for-service, 21, 91–92, 107
Fees
  consulting, 564–66
  Medicare and, 40, 92, 108
  negotiated, 125
  percentage, 126
  RBRVS and, 125–26
Feline, 529, 551
FI. *See* Fiscal intermediary
Filing methods, 90–91
FIM®. *See* Functional Independence
  Measure instrument
*Final Rule, Hospital Conditions of
  Participation of Patients' Rights*
  (CMS), 234
Financial indicators, 135–36
Financial systems, 98–99, 107
Fiscal intermediary (FI), 42, 64
Fixed costs, 447, 459
Flexible Spending Account (FSA), 118,
  142
Flexner Report, 2, 21
"FN-10." *See Data Standards for
  Mental Health Decision Support
  Systems*
42 C.F.R. Part 2, Confidentiality of
  Drug and Alcohol Abuse Records,
  273, 302
485 (Home Health Certification and
  Plan of Care), 441, 442, 458

FQHCs. *See* Federally qualified health centers
Freestanding rehabilitation hospitals, 391, 430
Free text, 540
FSA. *See* Flexible Spending Account
F-tags, 377–78
Functional history, rehabilitation, 410
Functional Independence Measure (FIM®) instrument, 418, 424–25, 430
Funding
  correctional facilities, 198–99
  home health care, 445–48
  hospice, 474–79
  intellectual disabilities facilities, 321
  long-term care, 364–69
  mental health services, 239–40
  rehabilitation, 414–19
  substance abuse treatment, 285–86

Gatekeeper, 115, 142
General inpatient care, 474, 475, 488
Glasgow Coma Scale, 423
Group dental practice, 493–94, 523
Group model HMO, 116, 142
Growth and development charts, 83, 85–86, 107

Habilitation, 313, 343
Hallucinations, 217, 256
Handicap, 396, 430
HAVEN. *See* Home Assessment Validation and Entry
HCBS. *See* Home and Community Based Services Waiver
HCCs. *See* Hierarchical Condition Categories
HD. *See* Hemodialysis
Healthcare Common Procedural Coding System (HCPCS), 51–52, 94–95, 107
  home health care and, 451–52
  managed care and, 128–29
Healthcare Effectiveness Data and Information Set (HEDIS), 134, 143
Health information exchange (HIE), 16, 21
Health information manager (HIM). *See also specific subject*
  ACOs and, 141
  in ambulatory care, freestanding, 104–6
  AVHIMA and, 549, 550
  compliance officer, 60
  consulting and, 561–73
  correctional facilities and, 194–97, 205–7
  correctional health record and, 194–97

dental care and, 520–21
dialysis and, 172
enrollment management and, 139
external consultant *vs.* full-time employee, 382–83
health information services and, 59–60
home health care and, 457
hospice and, 485, 486–87
hospice quality monitoring and, 485
hospital-based care and, 59–62
IDS/Ns and, 140, 143
inmate confidentiality and, 196–97
intellectual disabilities facilities and, 341–42
long-term care and, 380–83
in managed care, 139–41
medical home and, 106, 108
mental health services and, 252–54
rehabilitation and, 427
revenue cycle and, 61
risk management and, 140
role of, 18–19, 59–62
substance abuse treatment and, 295, 300
veterinary care and, 548–50
Health information technology (HIT), 16, 21
Health Information Technology for Economic and Clinical Health Act (HITECH), 8–9, 21
Health Insurance Portability and Accountability Act of 1996 (HIPPA)
  administrative simplification provisions, 8–9, 21
  code set standards, 9
  correctional facilities and, 200–202
  intellectual disabilities facilities and, 339–40
  mental health services confidentiality and, 250–51
  privacy and, 9–12
Health Level 7 (HL7), 542, 551
Health maintenance organizations (HMOs), 143
  characteristics of, 115
  dental care and, 511
  group model, 116, 142
  IPA model, 116–17, 143
  long-term care and, 368
  MCOs and, 115–17
  mixed model, 117, 143
  network model, 116, 143
  staff model, 116, 123–24, 144
Health record banking, 17, 21
Health Reform. *See* Patient Protection and Affordable Care Act
Health Reimbursement Arrangement (HRA), 118–19, 142
Health Savings Account (HSA), 119, 143

Health services director (HSD), 180, 208
Health transfer summary form, 188, 189–90
HEDIS. *See* Healthcare Effectiveness Data and Information Set
Hemodialysis (HD), 149, 174
Herd health, 535, 551
HHPPS. *See* Home Health Prospective Payment System
HHRG. *See* Home Health Resource Group
HIE. *See* Health information exchange
HIE organization, 21–22
Hierarchical Condition Categories (HCCs), 129–30, 143
High-technology assistive devices, 397, 400
Hill-Burton Act, 2, 22
HIM. *See* Health information manager
HIPPA. *See* Health Insurance Portability and Accountability Act of 1996
HIT. *See* Health information technology
HITECH. *See* Health Information Technology for Economic and Clinical Health Act
HL7. *See* Health Level 7
HMOs. *See* Health maintenance organizations
Home and Community Based Services (HCBS) Waiver, 342, 343
Home Assessment Validation and Entry (HAVEN), 445, 459
Homebound, 437, 459
Home care visits, 437, 459
Home health aides, 438
Home health care, 459
  ACHC and, 439, 440–41
  caregiver types, 437–38
  CHAP and, 439, 440
  CMS and, 439–40, 458
  coding and classification, 448–52
  comprehensive assessment, 441, 443, 458
  CPT and, 451–52
  data and information flow, 452
  data sets, 453
  DME and, 438, 459
  documentation, 441–45
  electronic information systems, 452–53
  financial stability and, 447–48
  485 and, 441, 442, 458
  HAVEN and, 445, 459
  HCPCS and, 451–52
  HHPPS and, 446–47
  HIM and, 457
  home health aides and, 438
  ICD-10-CM and, 448–51, 452
  IM, 448–53

Home health care *(Continued)*
  integrated format and, 444
  legal issues, 456–57
  Medicaid and, 439–40, 445
  Medicare and, 439–40, 445–48
  NAHC and, 439
  NPP and, 441
  OASIS-C and, 444–45, 449–51, 452
  overview, 436–37
  patient types, 437
  payer mix, 447
  problem-oriented record, 443
  QI, 453–54
  regulatory issues, 439–41
  rehabilitation, 392
  reimbursement and funding, 445–48
  risk management, 455–56
  satisfaction committee/monitoring, 456
  settings, 436–38
  skilled nursing agencies and, 437
  source-oriented record and, 443, 460
  specialty services, 438
  TJC and, 439, 440, 459
  trends, 457–58
  UM, 454
Home Health Certification and Plan of Care. *See* 485
Home Health Prospective Payment System (HHPPS), 446–47
Home Health Resource Group (HHRG), 446
HOPPS. *See* Hospital Outpatient Prospective Payment System
HOP QDRP. *See* Hospital Outpatient Quality Data Reporting Program
Hospice, 488
  accreditation, 466–67
  aide and, 472
  assessment/plan of care and, 471–72
  benefit periods, 476–79
  bereavement and, 473, 488
  caregiver types, 465–66
  certification requirements, 471
  close of care documentation, 473
  CMS and, 466–67
  coding and classification, 480–81
  continuous care, 474, 475
  CPT and, 481
  data and information flow, 479–80
  data sets, 482–83
  discharge *vs.* revocation, 476, 479
  documentation, 471–73
  election of benefit statement, 475–76
  election of care, 468
  electronic information systems, 481–82
  general inpatient care, 474, 475
  HIM, 485, 486–87
  history, 464
  ICD-10-CM and, 480–81

IDT, 465–66
IM, 479–83
inpatient documentation, 472–73
inpatient unit, 472–73, 488
legal issues, 486
licensure, 466–67
Medicare and, 466–70, 474–79, 483–85
NAHC and, 439, 459
NHPCO and, 467
overview about, 464–65
Palliative Performance Scale and, 477–78
patient data, 482
patient types, 465
per diem, 475
primary caregivers, 466
QAPI, 483–85
quality measures, 484
quality monitoring and HIM, 485
regulatory issues, 466–70
reimbursement and funding, 474–79
resource data, 482–83
respite care and, 474–75
risk management, 486
routine home care and, 474
settings, 464–66
terminally ill and, 465, 467–68, 471
trends, 487–88
UM, 485
unit of care in, 465
volunteers, 470, 472
Hospice Medicare benefit and regulations
  certification, 467–68
  clinical records, 470
  election of hospice care, 468
  other facilities contracting, 469
  overview, 467
  plan of care, 469–70
  revocation, 468–69
  volunteers, 470
Hospital
  AAHA and, 533, 550
  dental clinic in, 494–95
  freestanding rehabilitation, 391, 430
  inpatients, 5–6, 22, 31, 33, 42–44, 64
  Latin derivation of, 464
  outpatients, 6, 22, 33, 45–48, 64, 65, 266–67, 303
  partial hospitalization treatments, 266–67, 303
  PATH and, 41–42
  payment issues and, 4–5
  twentieth-century health care and, 2
  UHDDS and, 55, 65
  VHMA and, 530, 551
Hospital-based care
  accreditation and, 35
  ambulatory care, 31–32
  APCs and, 45–48
  billing and, 50, 51

caregiver types, 34
CDM and, 42
CMS and, 234
documentation and, 35–42
DRG and, 42–44
federal regulations and, 34–35
HIM and, 59–62
IM, 51–56
inpatient short-term acute care, 31
issues, 34–35
legal issues, 58–59
licensure and, 34
LTAC, 32–34
LTCH PPS and, 48–49
Medicare and, 42–49
MS-DRGs and, 43–44
patient types, 32–34
PHP and, 32, 65
quality management, 56–57
reimbursement, 42–51
risk management, 58–59
settings, 30–32
trends, 62
UM and, 57
Hospital Inpatient Prospective Payment System (IPPS), 42–44, 64
Hospital Inpatient Quality Reporting (IQR), 5–6, 22
Hospitalist, 34, 64
Hospital Outpatient Prospective Payment System (HOPPS or OPPS), 45–48, 64
Hospital Outpatient Quality Data Reporting Program (HOP QDRP), 6, 22
HRA. *See* Health Reimbursement Arrangement
HSA. *See* Health Savings Account
HSD. *See* Health services director

ICAP. *See* Inventory for Client and Agency Planning
ICD-10-CM (*International Classification of Diseases*, 10th Revision, Clinical Modification), 9, 22, 94, 108, 128
  home health care and, 448–51, 452
  hospice and, 480–81
  intellectual disabilities facilities and, 323
  long-term care and, 369–70
ICD-10-PCS (*International Classification of Diseases*, 10th Revision, Procedural Coding System), 9, 22
ICE. *See* Bureau of Immigration and Customs Enforcement
ICF/MR. *See* Intermediate care facility for the mentally retarded
ICPC. *See* International Classification of Primary Care

IDS/Ns. *See* Integrated delivery systems/networks
IDT. *See* Interdisciplinary team
IM. *See* Information Management
Immunization, 83–84, 107
Impacted wisdom teeth, 500, 523
Impairment, 396, 430
Implant, 500, 523
Incentive-based program, 6
Incident reports, 104, 107
Incident to, 92, 108
Indemnity insurance, 117, 143
Independent practice association (IPA) model, 116–17, 143
Individualized treatment plan (ITP), 276, 283–85, 303
Individual program plan (IPP), 316–18, 327, 328, 329, 343
Industrial health centers, 70, 71, 84, 87, 108
Information Management (IM). *See also* Classification; Coding; Data and information flow; Data sets; Electronic information systems; Health information manager
  ambulatory care, freestanding, and, 94–101
  correctional facilities, 199–202
  dental care, 512–17
  dialysis, 160–66
  EHRs and computer systems, 53–55, 98–101
  electronic information systems, 132–34
  home health care, 448–53
  hospice, 479–83
  hospital-based care and, 51–56
  intellectual disabilities facilities, 322–37
  long-term care, 369–76
  managed care, 128–34
  mental health services, 240–48
  record linkage to other sites, 98
  rehabilitation, 420–25
  standards, 36
  substance abuse treatment, 286–90
  veterinary care, 538–43
Informed consent, 137
Injuries
  dental care and, 518–19
  requiring rehabilitation, 395–96
Inmate, 178, 199, 208
Inpatient psychiatric facility prospective payment system (IPF PPS), 239, 256
Inpatient rehabilitation facility (IRF), 426, 428
Inpatient Rehabilitation Facility Patient Assessment Instrument (IRF-PAI), 415
  discharge section, 419
  FIM® Instrument, 418

function modifiers, 418
  information sections of, 417
  quality indicators, 419
Inpatient Rehabilitation Validation and Entry (IRVEN), 421, 431
Inpatient short-term acute care, 31
Inpatient unit, hospice, 472–73, 488
Institute of Medicine, 22
Insurance. *See also* Health Insurance Portability and Accountability Act of 1996
  CHIP, 4, 20, 511–12
  coinsurance, 117, 142
  dental care and, 510–11, 515
  dual insurance coverage, 126–28
  indemnity, 117, 143
  long-term health care and, 367
  veterinary care and, 535, 538
Integrated delivery systems/networks (IDS/Ns), 140, 143
Integrated format, 87–88, 108, 444, 459
Intellectual disability, 311, 343, 498
Intellectual disabilities facilities
  AAIDD and, 325
  accreditation, 314–15
  administrative data, 326–27
  administrative staff, 313–14
  admissions/transfers/discharge at, 315
  annual staffings, 318
  assessment data, 326
  caregiver types, 312–14
  coding and classification, 323–25
  confidentiality, 339–40
  core team summary sheet, 327–28, 330–31
  data and information flow, 318–20, 322–23
  data sets and, 325–37
  deaths, 338
  direct care staff, 328–29
  documentation, 315–21, 338–39
  DSM-IV-TR and, 323–24
  electronic information systems, 325
  error correction, 338
  habilitative staff, 313
  health care staff, 312–13
  HIM and, 341–42
  HIPPA and, 339–40
  ICD-10-CM and, 323
  IM, 322–37
  incidents and accidents, 338
  individual data maintained at, 318–20
  individuals served, 311
  Intellectual Disability: Definition, Classification, and Systems of Supports and, 325
  IPP and, 316–18, 327, 328, 329
  legal issues, 339–41

Manual on Terminology and Classification in Mental Retardation and, 324
  MAR and, 336
  Medicaid and, 314–15, 321
  nursing data, 336–37
  physician standing orders, 329, 333–36
  QI, 337
  records protection/retention, 340–41
  regulatory issues, 314–15
  reimbursement and funding, 321
  risk management, 338–39
  settings, 310–14
  technology use, 339
  training objectives, 310–11
  trends, 342
  24-hour active treatment schedule, 328–29, 332
  types, 314
  UM, 337–38
  updating worksheet, 327
  written policies and procedures, 340
Intellectual Disability: Definition, Classification, and Systems of Supports, 11th edition (AAIDD), 325
Intensive outpatient or partial hospitalization treatments, 266–67, 303
Interdisciplinary team (IDT), 312, 344, 465–66, 488
Intermediate care facility for the mentally retarded (ICF/MR), 344
International Academy of Life Care Planners, 426–27
International Classification of Diseases, 10th Revision, Clinical Modification. *See* ICD-10-CM
International Classification of Diseases, 10th Revision, Procedural Coding System. *See* ICD-10-PCS
International Classification of Primary Care (ICPC), 95, 108
International Species Information System (ISIS), 543, 551
Inventory for Client and Agency Planning (ICAP), 321, 344
Inventory of Substance Abuse Treatment Services (I-SATS), 290, 303
Involuntary commitment, 216, 256, 294–95, 296–99, 303
IPA. *See* Independent practice association model
IPF PPS. *See* Inpatient psychiatric facility prospective payment system
IPP. *See* Individual program plan
IPPS. *See* Hospital Inpatient Prospective Payment System

IQR. *See* Hospital Inpatient Quality Reporting
IRF. *See* Inpatient rehabilitation facility
IRF-PAI. *See* Inpatient Rehabilitation Facility Patient Assessment Instrument
IRVEN. *See* Inpatient Rehabilitation Validation and Entry
I-SATS. *See* Inventory of Substance Abuse Treatment Services
ISIS. *See* International Species Information System
ITP. *See* Individualized treatment plan

Jails, 179, 184–85, 208
Jewett brace, 398
The Joint Commission (TJC)
    ambulatory care and, 37, 38–39, 74–75
    correctional facilities and, 193
    documentation and, 36–39
    emergency patients standard example, 37
    home health care and, 439, 440, 459
    hospice and, 466–67
    IM standards of, 36
    intellectual disabilities facilities and, 314–15
    long-term care and, 355–56, 364
    managed care and, 122
    mental health services and, 227–28
    rehabilitation and, 400–401
    substance abuse treatment and, 273–74, 275
    surgery standard example, 36–37
Juvenile detention facilities, 184–85, 209

Kidney Disease Outcomes Quality Initiative (KDOQI), 170
Kinesiotherapist, 395, 430

LA. *See* Loss of attachment
Laboratory
    ambulatory care, freestanding, 79
    CLIA and, 121, 142
    long-term care and, 353
LCDs. *See* Local Coverage Determinations
Leadership ability, 563–64
Legal issues
    ambulatory care, freestanding, 103–4
    correctional facilities, 204–5
    dental care, 518–20
    dialysis, 171–72
    home health care, 456–57
    hospice, 486

hospital-based care, 58–59
intellectual disabilities facilities, 339–41
long-term care, 380
managed care, 137–39
mental health services, 249–52
rehabilitation, 426–27
substance abuse treatment, 292–95
UM and, 58–59, 103–4
veterinary care, 544, 546–48
Length of stay, rehabilitation, 415, 416
Level of care evaluation, 372, 373
Licensure, 22
    ambulatory care, freestanding, 73
    correctional facilities, 192
    dental care, 502
    hospice, 466–67
    hospital, 34
    long-term care, 355, 363–64
    surveys, 355, 385
Life care plan, 426–27, 430
Local Coverage Determinations (LCDs), 93, 108
Locum tenens, 92, 108
Logical Observations, Identifiers, Names, and Codes (LOINC®), 542, 551
Longitudinal patient record, 15, 22
Long-term acute care (LTAC)
    hospital patients, 32–34
    rehabilitation and, 391
Long-term care
    accreditation, 364
    activities/therapeutic recreation in, 352–53
    auditing, 381–82
    caregiver types, 350–54
    civil money penalties and, 355
    CMS and, 355, 356
    CMTs, 352
    coding and classification, 369–70
    commercial insurance and, 367
    comprehensive resident assessment, 357–60, 385
    data and information flow, 370–73
    data sets, 374–76
    dietitians, 354
    discharge/transfer, 362
    documentation, 357–64
    electronic information systems, 373–74
    external consultant *vs.* full-time employee, 382–83
    external data reporting, 373
    federal requirements, 357–63
    F-tags, 377–78
    HIM and, 380–83
    HMOs and, 368
    IM, 369–76
    independent contractors, 353–54
    laboratory and radiology services, 353

legal issues, 380
level of care evaluation, 372, 373
licensed physicians, 350–51
managed care payers, 368
MDS data, 357–60, 370–72, 374–76
Medicaid and, 364–66, 367
Medicare and, 364–65, 366–67
MS-LTC-DRGs and, 48–49
nurses, 351
Nursing Home Compare Web site, 378–79
overview, 348
patient types, 349–50
permanent residents receiving nonskilled care, 349
permanent residents receiving skilled care, 349–50
pharmacists, 354
plan, 361–62
private pay for, 368–69
QI, 377–79
regulatory issues, 354–56
rehabilitation services, 353–54
reimbursement and funding, 364–69
resident rights, 362–63
respiratory therapists, 354
respite care, 350
risk management, 380
SCU residents, 349
settings, 348–54
short-term patients, 350
SNF benefit, 366–67
social services, 352
state licensure, 355, 363–64
supplies and services utilization, 372–73
surveys and, 355, 356
TJC and, 355–56, 364
trends, 383
UM, 379–80
Long-term care hospital prospective payment system (LTCH PPS), 48–49
Loss of attachment (LA), 499, 523
Low Utilization Payment Adjustment (LUPA), 446
LTAC. *See* Long-term acute care
LTCH PPS. *See* Long-term care hospital prospective payment system
LUPA. *See* Low Utilization Payment Adjustment

MACs. *See* Medicare Administrative Contractors
Malpractice, 519
Managed care
    AAAHC and, 122–23
    accreditation, voluntary, 121–23
    ACOs and, 141
    benefit levels and, 132

caregiver types, 119–20
claims data and, 131
COB and, 126–28
consumer-directed health plans, 118–19, 142, 143
CPT and, 128–29
credentialing and, 137–38
documentation, 123–24
DRG and, 130–31
economic credentialing and, 138
EHR and, 133–34
federal program changes and, 141
governmental regulation, 120–21
HEDIS and, 134, 143
HIM in, 139–41
IM, 128–34
informed consent and, 137
intellectual disabilities facilities and, 321
legal issues, 137–39
long-term care and, 368
MCOs, 115–18, 124, 143, 240, 300–301
NCQA and, 122
overview, 114–15
patient types, 119
provider reimbursement, 125–26
QI in, 134–36
referral data and, 131, 144
regulatory issues, 120–23
reimbursement method advantages/disadvantages, 127
revenue codes and, 131
revenue generation, 124–28, 142, 143
risk management, 137–39
settings and plans, 114–20
state regulation, 121
TJC and, 122
trends, 140–41
UM, 136–37
URAC and, 123
Managed care organizations (MCOs), 115, 143
HMOs, 115–17
mental health services and, 240
point-of-service plans, 118
PPOs, 117
revenue, 124
substance abuse treatment and, 300–301
types of, 115–18
Managed indemnity plans, 117–18, 143
Manic depression, 217, 257
Manual on Terminology and Classification in Mental Retardation (AAIDD), 324
MAR. *See* Medication administration record
MCOs. *See* Managed care organizations

MDS. *See* Minimum data set
Meal on Wheels, 438
Meaningful use, 6, 22
Medicaid, 3, 22. *See also* Centers for Medicare & Medicaid Services
dental care and, 511–12
EPSDT, 93
home health care and, 439–40, 445
intellectual disabilities facilities and, 314–15, 321
level of care per diem, 367
long-term care and, 364–66, 367
mental health services funding, 239
overall facility cost per diem, 366
rehabilitation and, 400, 401–9
reimbursement resources, 93
RUGs and, 367
substance abuse treatment and, 274, 285
Medicaid Integrity Program (MIP), 5, 22, 76, 108
Medical home, 18, 23, 106, 108
Medical indicators, 135
Medically managed intensive inpatient treatment, 267, 303
Medicare, 2–3, 23. *See also* Centers for Medicare & Medicaid Services
ambulatory care, freestanding, certification for, 73–74
APCs and, 45–48
carrier, 42, 64
certification, 12, 23
continuous hospice care and, 474, 475
dialysis reimbursement, 159–60
DRG and, 42–44
election of hospice benefit statement, 475–76
fee schedule payments and, 40, 92, 108
general inpatient care, 474, 475
HHPPS and, 446–47
home health care and, 439–40, 445–48
hospice benefit periods, 476–79
hospice care levels, 474–75
hospital-based care and, 42–49
long-term care and, 364–65, 366–67
LTCH PPS and, 48–49
mental health services funding, 239
OASIS-C and, 444–45
Palliative Performance Scale and, 477–78
Part A SNF benefit, 366–67
PATH and, 41–42
prospective payment systems, 7
rehabilitation and, 400, 401–9
reimbursement resources, 93
reimbursement to hospitals, 42–49
respite care and, 474–75
RHC certification and, 74

routine home care and, 474
RUGs and, 366
set-aside trust, 427
substance abuse treatment and, 285
teaching physicians and residents and, 39–42
Medicare Administrative Contractors (MACs), 42, 64
Medicare Advantage, 120–21, 143
Medicare Conditions of Participation
continuous hospice care and, 474, 475
general inpatient care and, 474, 475
hospice benefit periods and, 476–79
hospice care levels, 474–75
hospice QAPI and, 483–85
hospice UM and, 485
Palliative Performance Scale and, 477–78
respite care and, 474–75
routine home care and, 474
Medicare hospice benefit and regulations
certification, 467–68
clinical records, 470
election of hospice care, 468
other facilities contracting, 469
overview, 467
plan of care, 469–70
revocation, 468–69
volunteers, 470
Medicare Improvements for Patients and Providers Act of 2008 (MIPPA), 159, 168
Medicare Payment Advisory Commission (MedPAC), 428
Medicare Physician Fee Schedule (MPFS or PFS), 92, 108
Medicare Prescription Drug, Improvement, and Modernization Act of 2003 (MMA), 3, 23
Medicare-Severity DRGs (MS-DRGs), 43–44, 65
Medicare severity long-term care diagnosis related groups (MS-LTC-DRGs), 48–49
Medication administration record (MAR), 336
MedPAC. *See* Medicare Payment Advisory Commission
Members, 119, 143
Mental health services
accreditation, 227–28
adolescents and, 222–25
adults and, 216–22
aides/direct care workers, 226
assessment and, 228–29, 230–31
bipolar disorder and, 217–18
caregiver types, 225–27
case managers, 226
chemical restraint and, 234–35
children and, 222–25, 235–36

Mental health services *(Continued)*
client types, 216–25
clinical depression and, 217
CMHC, 214–15, 256
CMHS and, 222, 255
coding and classification, 244, 246
confidentiality, 250–51
court ordered treatment, 251–52
CQI, 248–49
data and information flow, 243–44, 245–46
data sets, 247–48
dental care and, 498
discharge summary and aftercare plans, 236
documentation, 228–38
DSM-IV-TR and, 219
dual diagnoses and, 217, 218, 256
EHR and, 253
"FN-10" and, 241
HIM and, 252–54
IM, 240–48
legal issues, 249–52
MCOs and, 240
medical personnel, 225
MHSIP and, 240–41, 257
MICA and, 218, 257
occupational therapists, 227
physical restraint and, 234
progress notes, 233
QI in, 249
recreation therapists, 226–27
regulatory issues, 227–28
reimbursement and funding, 239–40
restraint and, 234–36, 237–38
risk management, 249–52
SAMHSA, 222, 268
schizophrenia and, 217
settings, 214–24
SMI and, 217–18, 257
special procedures, 233–36
State DIGs, 247–48
support services, 220–22
telephone technologies, 254
temporary mental problems and, 216
therapists, 225, 226–27
training and, 235
treatment methods and, 219–20
treatment plan, 229, 231–33
trends, 253–54
UM, 249
Mental Health Statistics Improvement Program (MHSIP), 240–41, 257
Mental illness with chemical addiction (MICA), 218, 257
Mental retardation, 311, 312, 343, 344. *See also* Intellectual disabilities facilities
MHSIP. *See* Mental Health Statistics Improvement Program

MICA. *See* Mental illness with chemical addiction
Mid-level providers (MLPs), 72, 108
Milwaukee brace, 398
Minimum data set (MDS), 385
long-term care and, 357–60, 370–72, 374–76
RAVEN and, 374
MIP. *See* Medicaid Integrity Program
MIPPA. *See* Medicare Improvements for Patients and Providers Act of 2008
Mixed model HMO, 117, 143
MLPs. *See* Mid-level providers
MMA. *See* Medicare Prescription Drug, Improvement, and Modernization Act of 2003
Model act, 530, 551
Model Spinal Cord Injury System, 421
Monitoring, 456
Motor vehicle accidents, 128
MPFS. *See* Medicare Physician Fee Schedule
MS-DRGs. *See* Medicare-Severity DRGs
MS-LTC-DRGs. *See* Medicare severity long-term care diagnosis related groups

National Association for Home Care and Hospice (NAHC), 439, 459
National Commission on Correctional Health Care (NCCHC), 193, 209
National Committee for Quality Assurance (NCQA), 122, 143, 227–28
National Coverage Determinations (NCDs), 93, 108
National databases, rehabilitation, 421
National Guideline Clearinghouse (NGC), 136
National Hospice and Palliative Care Organization (NHPCO), 467
National Patient Safety Goals (NPSG), 23
National Quality Forum (NQF), 15, 23
National Quality Measures Clearinghouse (NQMC), 136
National Registry of Evidence-based Programs and Practices (NREPP), 291, 303
National Spinal Cord Injury Data Base, 421
National Survey of Substance Abuse Treatment Services (N-SSATS), 290, 303
Nationwide Health Information Network (NHIN), 16, 23
NCCHC. *See* National Commission on Correctional Health Care

NCDs. *See* National Coverage Determinations
NCQA. *See* National Committee for Quality Assurance
Negligence, 519
Negotiated fees, 125
Negotiating contracts, in consulting, 570–73
Network model HMO, 116, 143
NFs. *See* Nursing facilities
NGC. *See* National Guideline Clearinghouse
NHIN. *See* Nationwide Health Information Network
NHPCO. *See* National Hospice and Palliative Care Organization
Non-physician practitioner (NPP), 441, 459
NPs. *See* Nurse practitioners
NPSG. *See* National Patient Safety Goals
NQF. *See* National Quality Forum
NQMC. *See* National Quality Measures Clearinghouse
NREPP. *See* National Registry of Evidence-based Programs and Practices
N-SSATS. *See* National Survey of Substance Abuse Treatment Services
Number of accessions, 531–32, 551
Nurse. *See also* Skilled nursing facilities
CNMs, 72–73, 107
intellectual disabilities facilities and, 336–37
long-term care, 351
rehabilitation, 394–95, 431
skilled nursing agencies and, 437
Nurse practitioners (NPs), 72–73, 108, 272
Nursing facilities (NFs), 348, 385. *See also* Skilled nursing facilities
dental needs in, 497
Nursing Home Compare Web site, 378–79

OASIS-C. *See* Outcome and Assessment Information Set-C
OBQI. *See* Outcome-based quality improvement
OBQM. *See* Outcome-based quality management
OBRA. *See* Omnibus Budget Reconciliation Act
OBRA assessments, 357, 385
Observation codes, 47
Observation services, 32, 65
Occupational health centers, 70, 71, 108
special documentation requirements, 84, 87

Occupational therapist (OT), 227, 393, 430
Occurrence reports, 104, 108
OFA. *See* Orthopedic Foundation for Animals
Office equipment
  answering system or voice mail, 569
  computer, 568–69
  consulting, 567–69
  multipurpose devices, 569
  telephone and wireless service, 569
Office of the Inspector General (OIG), 75–76, 108, 561
Office of the National Coordinator for Health Information Technology (ONC), 16, 23
OIG. *See* Office of the Inspector General
Olmstead v. Lois Curtis and Elaine Wilson, 342
Omnibus Budget Reconciliation Act (OBRA), 357
ONC. *See* Office of the National Coordinator for Health Information Technology
Operational indicators, 135
OPPS. *See* Hospital Outpatient Prospective Payment System
Oral maxillofacial surgeon, 500, 523
Orthodontist, 499, 523
Orthognathic surgery, 496, 523
Orthopedic Foundation for Animals (OFA), 542, 551
Orthotic device, 397–98, 431
OT. *See* Occupational therapist
Outcome and Assessment Information Set-C (OASIS-C), 460
  described, 444
  diagnosis codes and, 449–51, 452
  Medicare and, 444–45
  OBQI/OBQM and, 453–54
Outcome-based quality improvement (OBQI), 453–54, 460
Outcome-based quality management (OBQM), 453–54, 460
Outcomes, 440, 460
Outliers, 447
Outpatient
  commitment, 214, 257
  treatment, 265–66, 303
Ovine, 529, 551

P4P. *See* Pay-for-performance
Pacemaker neurostimulation devices, 429
Palliative care, 465, 467, 488
Palliative Performance Scale, 477–78
Panel, 125, 143
Panoramic radiograph, 507, 523
Paraparesis, 422
Paraplegia, 422

Part A SNF benefit, 366–67
Partial Episode Payment (PEP), 446
Partial hospitalization program (PHP), 32, 65
PAs. *See* Physician assistants
Pass-through payments, 47–48
PATH. *See* Physicians at Teaching Hospitals
Patient
  acute inpatient care, 474, 475, 488
  ambulatory care, freestanding, 72
  ASAM PPC-2R and, 265–67
  clinic outpatient, 33, 64
  CORF and, 392
  correctional facilities, 186–88
  data and information flow, 161–62, 404–9, 482
  database form, 404–9
  dental care, 495–98, 503, 504, 509–10
  dialysis, 149–50, 155–57, 161–62
  documentation, 35–42, 89–91, 472–73
  emergency outpatient, 33, 64
  general inpatient care, 474, 475, 488
  home health care, 437
  hospice, 465, 472–73, 474, 475, 482, 488
  hospital-based care types of, 32–34
  identifier, 89–91, 108
  inpatient, hospital, 5–6, 22, 31, 33, 42–44, 64
  inpatient short-term acute care, 31
  IPF PPS and, 239, 256
  IRF, 426, 428
  IRF-PAI, 415, 417–19
  IRVEN and, 421, 431
  longitudinal patient record, 15, 22
  long-term care, 349–50
  managed care, 119
  MIPPA and, 159, 168
  NPSG and, 23
  outpatient, hospital, 6, 22, 33, 45–48, 64, 65, 266–67, 303
  PIP-DCG, 129, 144
  portals, 101, 108
  registration, 98, 109
  rehabilitation, 391–92, 395–97, 404–9, 415, 417–19, 426, 428
  rights, 234
  substance abuse treatment and, 265–67, 304
  types, 33–34
  veterinary care, 528–29
Patient-centered medical home model, 18, 23
Patient database form, rehabilitation
  CMS and, 404–9
  discharge planning section of, 409
  home description section of, 404, 408
  medical database section of, 406
  medical history section of, 406–8

status prior to admission section of, 404
Patient Protection and Affordable Care Act (PPACA), 15, 23–24
Patient safety organizations (PSOs), 15, 24
Payer mix, 447, 460
Pay-for-performance (P4P), 5–6, 24
Payment issues
  federal and federal-state programs and, 2–4
  fraud/abuse/waste, 5
  hospitals and, 4–5
  incentive-based program and, 6
  Medicare prospective payment systems, 7
  in other settings, 6–7
  P4P, 5–6
PCEs. *See* Potentially compensable events
PCP. *See* Primary care provider
PCPM. *See* Per contract per month
PD. *See* Peritoneal dialysis
PDAs. *See* Personal digital assistants
Pediatric preventive health services, 82, 83–84
Pediatric rehabilitation, 396
PEP. *See* Partial Episode Payment
Per contract per month (PCPM), 132
Per diem, 4, 24, 125, 143, 366, 367, 475
Periodontal examination, 505–7
Periodontist, 499, 524
Peritoneal dialysis (PD), 149, 174
Per member per month (PMPM), 132
Personal digital assistants (PDAs), 100
Personal health record (PHR), 16–17, 24
Personal injury cases, 128
Person-centered planning, 312, 344
PFS. *See* Medicare Physician Fee Schedule
Pharmacists, 354
PHI. *See* Protected health information
Philadelphia collar, 398
PHP. *See* Partial hospitalization program
PHR. *See* Personal health record
Physiatrist, 392–93, 431
Physical escort, 235–36
Physical restraint, 234, 257
Physical therapist (PT), 393–94, 431, 438
Physician
  PFS and, 92, 108
  private practices, 70–71, 109
  quality reporting system, 102, 109
  standing orders, 329, 333–36
  substance abuse treatment and, 271–72
  teaching, 39–42
Physician assistants (PAs), 72–73, 109, 272

Physician Quality Reporting Initiative (PQRI), 6, 24
Physicians at Teaching Hospitals (PATH), 41–42
Pioneer Network, 383
PIP-DCG. *See* Principle In-Patient Diagnostic Cost Group
Place of residence, 464–65, 488
Plaque, 500–501, 524
PMPM. *See* Per member per month
Point-of-service plans, 118
POMR. *See* Problem-oriented medical record
Pontic, 500, 524
Porcine, 529, 551
Potentially compensable events (PCEs), 58, 65
PPACA. *See* Patient Protection and Affordable Care Act
PPO. *See* Preferred provider organization
PPS. *See* Prospective payment system
PQRI. *See* Physician Quality Reporting Initiative
Practice management software, dental care, 513–14
Preadmission certification, 136, 144
Preadmission screening, 403–9
Preauthorization, 136, 144
Pre-commitment evaluation screening form, 296–99
Preferred provider organization (PPO), 117, 144
Pregnant female, dental care and, 496
Prepurchase examinations, 547
Preventive care, 82, 83–84, 114–15, 267–68, 302
Primary caregiver, 466, 489
Primary care provider (PCP)
  as gatekeeper, 115
  preventive care and, 114–15
Primary teeth, 495, 524
Principle In-Patient Diagnostic Cost Group (PIP-DCG), 129, 144
Prisons, 179, 209
  classification of, 181
  configurations of, 181–82
  FBP and, 182, 208
  health screenings and, 183
Problem list, 79, 81–82, 109
Problem-oriented medical record (POMR), 87, 88, 109, 535, 551
Problem-oriented record, 443, 460
Production medicine, 535, 551
Program manuals, 93, 109
Program transmittals, 93, 109
Progress notes, 233
Prophylaxis, 508, 524
Prospective payment system (PPS), 4, 7, 24
Prospective review/precertification, 102, 109
Prosthesis, 397, 399, 431, 500, 524

Prosthetic devices, 397, 399
Prosthodontist, 500, 524
Protected health information (PHI), 9–12, 24
Provider types, dental care, 498–501
PSOs. *See* Patient safety organizations
Psychologist, 394, 431
Psychosis, 214, 257
Psychosocial rehabilitation, 220, 257
Psychotropic medications, 214, 257
PT. *See* Physical therapist
Public health departments, 70, 71, 109

QAPI. *See* Quality Assessment/Performance Improvement
QI. *See* Quality improvement
QIO. *See* Quality improvement organization
QMRP. *See* Qualified mental retardation professional
QSOA. *See* Qualified service organization agreement
Quadriplegia, 422
Qualified mental retardation professional (QMRP), 312, 344
Qualified service organization agreement (QSOA), 293, 304
Quality Assessment/Performance Improvement (QAPI), 56–57, 167–68, 174, 483–85
Quality improvement (QI)
  AHRQ tools for, 136
  dental care, 517–18
  dialysis, 167–70
  home health care, 453–54
  indicators, 135–36
  intellectual disabilities facilities, 337
  long-term care, 377–79
  in managed care, 134–36
  mental health services, 249
  rehabilitation, 425–26
  substance abuse treatment, 291
  veterinary care, 544
Quality improvement organization (QIO), 5, 24
Quality management
  ambulatory care, freestanding, and, 101–2
  correctional facilities and, 203
  hospital-based care and, 56–57
  OBQM, 453–54, 460
  physician quality reporting system and, 102, 109
Quality of care, 357, 385
Quality of life, 357, 386

RAC. *See* Recovery Audit Contractor
Radiograph, 496, 524
  panoramic, 507, 523
Radiology
  ambulatory care, freestanding, and, 79

long-term care and, 353
RAI. *See* Resident assessment instrument
Rancho Los Amigos Levels of Cognitive Function Scale, 423–24
RAPs. *See* Resident assessment protocols
Rating systems, rehabilitation, 421–25
RAVEN software, 374
RBRVS. *See* Resource-based relative value scale
RCT. *See* Root canal therapy
Reason for visit, 77, 109
Recall reminders, 515–16
Recertification, 441, 460
Recovery Audit Contractor (RAC), 5, 24
Recreational therapists, 226–27, 273
RECs. *See* Regional Extension Centers
Referral, 131, 144
Referred hospital outpatient, 33, 65
Regional Extension Centers (RECs), 16, 24
Regional health information organization (RHIO), 16, 24
Registered health information administrators (RHIAs), 380
Registered health information technicians (RHITs), 380
Registration
  ambulatory care, freestanding, 77, 78, 109
  patient, 98, 109
Regulatory issues
  ambulatory care, freestanding, 73–76
  consulting, 559–60
  correctional facilities, 192–94
  dental care, 501–2
  dialysis, 151–52
  governmental regulation, 120–21
  government surveys, 151–52, 174
  home health care, 439–41
  hospice, 466–70
  intellectual disabilities facilities, 314–15
  long-term care, 354–56
  managed care, 120–23
  mental health services, 227–28
  rehabilitation, 400–409
  substance abuse treatment, 273–75
  veterinary care, 530–33
  voluntary accreditation, 121–23
Rehabilitation, 431
  acute units, 391, 430
  ambulation aids, 397, 398–99
  American Spinal Injury Association and, 421–22
  assessment, 414, 424–25
  caregiver types, 392–95
  CARF and, 227–28, 274, 275, 302, 400, 401

classification and rating systems used in, 421–25
CMGs and, 415
CMS and, 400, 401–9
coding, 420
CORF and, 392
coverage criteria, 411–13
databases, 421
discharge summary, 413–14
DME used in, 397–400
documentation, 410–14
electronic information systems, 421
FIM® instrument and, 418, 424–25
freestanding rehabilitation hospitals, 391, 430
functional history, 410
high-technology assistive devices, 397, 400
HIM and, 427
history and physical exam, 410–11
home health care, 392
IM, 420–25
independent living and, 428–29
information flow, 420
injuries requiring, 395–96
IRF and, 426, 428
IRF-PAI and, 415, 417–19
IRVEN and, 421, 431
kinesiotherapist, 395, 430
legal issues, 426–27
length of stay, 415, 416
life care plan and, 426–27
long-term care and, 353–54
LTAC facilities, 391
medical supervision and, 403
Medicare set-aside trust and, 427
nurse, 394–95, 431
orthotics, 397–98, 431
OT, 393, 430
other health care workers applying, 395
outpatient facilities for, 391–92, 428
patient database form, 404–9
patient types, 395–97
pediatric, 396
physiatrist, 392–93, 431
postacute care providers, 427–28
preadmission screening and, 403–9
prosthetic devices, 397, 399
psychologist, 394
psychosocial, 220, 257
PT, 393–94
QI, 425–26
regulatory issues, 400–409
reimbursement and funding, 414–19
risk management, 426–27
self-care assessment scales, 424–25
settings, 390–400
60 percent rule and, 402–3
SNFs providing, 391
social worker, 394, 431
speech-language pathologist, 394, 431

of spinal cord injury, 396
TBI and, 396, 423–24
team, 392, 431
technology and, 397, 400, 429
terminology surrounding, 396–97
TJC and, 400–401
trends, 427–29
UM, 426
wheelchairs, 399–400
Rehabilitation impairment categories (RICs), 415
Reimbursement
ambulatory care, freestanding, 91–93, 106
APCs and, 45–48
ASC, 92–93, 106
billing and, 50, 51
capitation and, 93
case-mix, 366–67, 384
CDM and, 42
consulting, 561
correctional facilities, 198–99
dental care, 510–12
dialysis, 159–60
DRG and, 42–44
EPSDT, 93
fee-for-service, 91–92
home health care, 445–48
hospice, 474–79
hospital-based care, 42–51
HRA, 118–19, 142
intellectual disabilities facilities, 321
long-term care, 364–69
LTCH PPS and, 48–49
managed care and, 125–26, 127
mental health services, 239–40
MPFS, 92
MS-DRGs and, 43–44
other payers, 51
rehabilitation, 414–19
resources, 93
substance abuse treatment, 285–86
veterinary care, 535, 537
Renal Management Information System (REMIS), 162, 174
Renal replacement therapy (RRT), 148, 174
Resident assessment instrument (RAI), 357, 386
Resident Assessment Instrument Manual, 357
Resident assessment protocols (RAPs), 357, 386
Residential/inpatient treatment, 267, 304
Residential living, 221–22
Residents, 65
documentation regarding, 39–42
PATH and, 41–42
Resource-based relative value scale (RBRVS), 92, 109, 125–26
Resource utilization groups (RUGs), 366, 367, 386

Respiratory therapists, 354
Respite care, 350, 474–75, 489
Restraint
chemical, 234–35
of children, 235–36
mental health services and, 234–36, 237–38
physical, 234
Retrospective review, 103, 109
Return-to-work physicals, 87, 109
Revenue codes, 52, 65, 131
Revenue cycle, 61
Revenue generation, managed health care
capitation, 125, 142
COB and, 126–28
discounted charges, 126
DRGs and, 126, 142
MCO, 124
negotiated fee schedule, 125
percentage fee schedule, 126
per diem, 125, 143
provider reimbursement, 125–26
RBRVS fee schedule, 125–26
salary, 125
Revocation, 468–69, 476, 479
RHCs. *See* Rural Health Clinics
RHIAs. *See* Registered health information administrators
RHIO. *See* Regional health information organization
RHITs. *See* Registered health information technicians
RICs. *See* Rehabilitation impairment categories
Rights, 179, 234, 362–63
Risk contracts, 368, 386
Risk management
ambulatory care, freestanding, 103–4
correctional facilities, 204–5
dental care, 518–20
dialysis, 171–72
documentation and, 103–4
HIM and, 140
home health care, 455–56
hospice, 486
hospital-based care, 58–59
intellectual disabilities facilities, 338–39
long-term care, 380
managed care, 137–39
mental health services, 249–52
rehabilitation, 426–27
substance abuse treatment, 292–95
UM and, 58–59, 103–4
veterinary care, 544, 545–46
Root canal therapy (RCT), 496, 524
Routine home care, 474, 489
RRT. *See* Renal replacement therapy
RUGs. *See* Resource utilization groups
Rural Health Clinics (RHCs), 70, 71, 74, 109

SAMHSA. *See* Substance Abuse and Mental Health Services Administration
Satisfaction committee, 456
Schizophrenia, 217, 257
Screening and evaluation, 222
SCU. *See* Special care units
Sealants, 500–501, 524
SED. *See* Serious emotional disturbances
Self-care assessment scales, 424–25
Self-help recovery groups, 268
Serious emotional disturbances (SED), 222, 257
Serious mental illness (SMI), 217–18, 257
Set-aside trust, Medicare, 427
Settings, health care, 13
  ambulatory care, 31–32, 70–72
  consulting, 556–57
  correctional facilities, 178–92
  dental care, 492–95
  for dialysis, 148–51
  home health care, 436–38
  hospice, 464–66
  hospital, 30–32
  inpatient short-term acute care, 31
  intellectual disabilities facilities, 310–14
  long-term acute care, 32
  long-term care, 348–54
  managed care, 114–20
  mental health services, 214–27
  rehabilitation, 390–400
  substance abuse treatment, 262–73
  types of, 30, 31
  veterinary care, 551
60 percent rule, 402–3
Skilled nursing agencies, 437
Skilled nursing facilities (SNFs), 348, 386
  long-term care and, 366–67
  postacute care and, 428
  rehabilitation provided in, 391
SMI. *See* Serious mental illness
SNFs. *See* Skilled nursing facilities
SNOMED CT® (Systematized Nomenclature of Medicine Clinical Terms), 539–40, 551
SNVDO. *See Standard Nomenclature of Veterinary Diseases and Operations*
Social Security Disability Income (SSDI), 219, 257
Social services, 352
Solo dental practice, 492–93, 524
SOMI-type brace (Sternal Occipital Mandibular Immobilizer), 398
Source-oriented record, 443, 460
Special care units (SCU), 349
Speech-language pathologist, 394, 431
Spinal cord injury
  data base, 421
  rehabilitation of, 396

SSDI. *See* Social Security Disability Income
SSI. *See* Supplemental Security Income
Staff model HMO, 116, 123–24, 144
Standard Nomenclature of Veterinary Diseases and Operations (SNVDO), 538, 551
Standards, 440, 460
Standard scheduling, 95, 109
Standard surveys, 355, 386
Standing orders, 329, 333–36
State agency, 12, 25
State DIGs. *See* State Mental Health Data Infrastructure Grants for Quality Improvement
State Mental Health Data Infrastructure Grants for Quality Improvement (State DIGs), 247–48
Status indicator, 45, 46, 65
Sternal Occipital Mandibular Immobilizer. *See* SOMI-type brace
Subacute care, 350, 386
Subscribers, 119, 144
Substance Abuse and Mental Health Services Administration (SAMHSA), 222, 268
Substance abuse treatment
  AA and, 263, 302
  adolescents and, 269
  caregiver types, 271–73
  CARF and, 274, 275
  case managers and, 272
  client types, 268–71
  clinical assessment record and, 276–82, 302
  clinical documentation, 276–85
  coding and classification, 288–89
  confidentiality and release of information, 273, 292–93, 294, 302
  counselors and, 272
  court-ordered, 293–94
  court-referred clients and, 271
  CSAP and, 268, 302
  CSAT and, 291, 302
  data and information flow, 286–87
  data sets, 289–90
  documentation, 275–85
  DSM-IV-TR and, 262–63, 288–89
  dually diagnosed and, 270–71
  EAPs and, 270
  educational/prevention/early intervention programs, 267–68
  electronic information systems, 290
  evolution of, 263, 265
  42 C.F.R. Part 2 and, 273
  HIM and, 295, 300
  IM, 286–90
  inpatient/residential, 267, 304
  intensive outpatient/partial hospitalization, 266–67
  involuntary commitments, 294–95, 296–99

I-SATS and, 290, 303
ITP and, 276, 283–85
legal/administrative documentation, 276
legal issues, 292–95
levels of care, 265
MCOs and, 300–301
Medicaid and, 274, 285
Medicare and, 285
outpatient, 265–66
PAs and NPs and, 272
physicians and, 271–72
QI in, 291
recreational therapists and, 273
regulatory issues, 273–75
reimbursement and funding, 285–86
risk management, 292–95
SAMHSA and, 222, 268
self-help recovery groups, 268
settings, 262–73
settings overview, 262, 265
TJC and, 273–74, 275
trends in, 300–301
UM, 291–92
women and, 270
Substandard quality of care, 355, 386
Substantial compliance, 355, 386
Superbill, 79, 80, 109
Supplemental Security Income (SSI), 219, 257
Supplies and services utilization, 372–73
Surgery. *See also* Ambulatory surgery centers
  ambulatory, 31, 64
  documentation, 36–37
  orthognathic, 496, 523
  telesurgery, 18, 25
Survey, validation, 151–52, 174
Systematized Nomenclature of Medicine Clinical Terms. *See* SNOMED CT®

TBI. *See* Traumatic brain injury
TDP. *See* TRICARE Dental Program
Teaching physicians
  documentation regarding, 39–42
  Medicare and, 39–42
  PATH and, 41–42
Technology
  advancements, 17–18
  changes, 15–17
  correctional facilities and, 206–7
  high-technology assistive devices, 397, 400
  HIT, 16, 21
  HITECH, 8–9, 21
  intellectual disabilities facilities and, 339
  ONC and, 16, 23
  rehabilitation and, 397, 400, 429
TEDS. *See* Treatment Episode Data Set

Telehealth, 18, 25, 207, 209
Telemedicine, 25, 207, 209
Tele-mental health, 254
Telepsychiatry, 254
Telesurgery, 18, 25
Temporary mental problems, 216
Terminal digit, 97, 109
Terminally ill, 465, 467–68, 471, 489
Tetraparesis, 422
Tetraplegia, 422
Therapists
    kinesiotherapist, 395, 430
    mental health services, 225, 226–27
    occupational, 227, 393, 430
    PT, 393–94, 431, 438
    recreation, 226–27, 273
    respiratory, 354
Theriogenology, 529, 551
Thoracolumbar orthoses, 398
TJC. *See* The Joint Commission
Training objectives, 310–11, 344
Transplantation referral tracking, 157
Traumatic brain injury (TBI), 396, 423–24
Treatment Episode Data Set (TEDS), 290, 304
Trends
    ambulatory care, freestanding, 105–6
    consulting, 573–74
    correctional facilities, 206
    dental care, 521–22
    home health care, 457–58
    hospice, 487–88
    hospital-based care, 62
    intellectual disabilities facilities, 342
    long-term care, 383
    managed care, 140–41
    mental health services, 253–54
    rehabilitation, 427–29
    substance abuse treatment, 300–301
    veterinary care, 549–50
TRICARE Dental Program (TDP), 512
24-hour active treatment schedule, 328–29, 332

UACDS. *See* Uniform Ambulatory Care Data Set
UHDDS. *See* Uniform Hospital Discharge Data Set
UM. *See* Utilization management
Uniform Ambulatory Care Data Set (UACDS), 55, 65, 101
Uniform Bill, 50, 51
Uniform Hospital Discharge Data Set (UHDDS), 55, 65
Uniform Reporting System (URS), 241, 258
United Network for Organ Sharing (UNOS), 163

University health centers, 70, 71–72, 109
UNOS. *See* United Network for Organ Sharing
Upcodes, 447
Updating worksheet, 327
URAC, 123, 144, 227–28
Urgent care centers, 70, 71, 109
URS. *See* Uniform Reporting System
USCIS. *See* Bureau of Citizenship and Immigration Services
Utilization guidelines, 357, 386
Utilization management (UM)
    in ambulatory care, freestanding, 102–4
    correctional facilities and, 203–4
    dental care, 518
    dialysis, 170–71
    home health care, 454
    hospice, 485
    in hospital-based care, 57
    intellectual disabilities facilities, 337–38
    legal issues and, 58–59
    long-term care, 379–80
    managed care, 136–37
    mental health services, 249
    prospective review/precertification, 102
    rehabilitation, 426
    retrospective review in, 103, 109
    risk management and, 58–59, 103–4
    substance abuse treatment, 291–92
    veterinary care, 544

VA. *See* Veterans Affairs
Validation survey, 151–52, 174
Variable costs, 447, 460
Veterans Affairs (VA), 512
Veterinary care, 551
    AAHA and, 533, 550
    animal cruelty, 547
    AVHIMA, 549, 550
    AVMA and, 529, 550
    blood donation and, 548
    caregiver types and staff, 529–30
    change of ownership and, 548
    client determination in, 544, 546
    coding and classification, 538–40
    CVPM, 530, 550
    data sets, 541–42
    debt collection litigation and, 546
    documentation, 533–35
    EHR and, 549
    electronic information systems, 542–43
    euthanasia and, 548
    free text and, 540
    HIM and, 548–50

IM, 538–43
ISIS, 543, 551
legal issues, 544, 546–48
model act and, 530, 551
mortality insurance and, 535, 538
number of accessions, 531–32
OFA, 542, 551
out of pocket pay, 535
patient types, 528–29
pet health insurance and, 538
prepurchase examinations, 547
QI and UM, 544
record formats, 535, 536–37
regulatory issues, 530–33
reimbursement, 535, 537
risk management, 544, 545–46
settings, 551
SNOMED CT® and, 539–40, 551
SNVDO and, 538, 551
standards, 534
technician, 529–30, 551
technologist, 529–30, 552
theriogenology, 529, 551
trends, 549–50
UM, 544
VHMA and, 530, 551
VMDB, 541–42, 551
wildlife management and, 547
Veterinary Hospital Managers Association (VHMA), 530, 551
Veterinary Medical Database (VMDB), 541–42, 551
VHMA. *See* Veterinary Hospital Managers Association
VMDB. *See* Veterinary Medical Database
Voice mail, 569
Volunteers, 466, 489
    documentation, 472
    hospice, 470, 472

Walk-ins, 96, 109
Wee FIM®, 425
Wheelchairs, 399–400
Wildlife management, 547
Wisdom teeth, impacted, 500, 523
Women
    dental care for pregnant, 496
    substance abuse treatment and, 270
Worker's Compensation, 128
Working at home, as consultant, 566–67
Wrap-around services, 224–25, 258

Zone Program Integrity Contractor (ZPIC), 5, 25
Zoonotic infection, 538, 552
ZPIC. *See* Zone Program Integrity Contractor